The Complete IS-IS Routing Protocol

Hannes Gredler and Walter Goralski

The Complete IS-IS Routing Protocol

Hannes Gredler, MA, Schwaz, Austria
Walter Goralski, Professor, Phoenix, AZ, USA

British Library Cataloguing in Publication Data
A catalogue record for this book is available from the British Library

Library of Congress Cataloging-in-Publication Data
Gredler, Hannes.
The complete IS-IS routing protocol / Hannes Gredler, Walter Goralski.
p. cm.
Includes bibliographical references and index.
ISBN 1-85233-822-9 (pbk. : alk. paper)
1. IS-IS (Computer network protocol) 2. Routers (Computer networks) I. Goralski, Walter. II. Title

TK5105.5675.G74 2004
004.6′2--dc22 2004049147

ISBN 1-85233-822-9 Springer-Verlag London Berlin Heidelberg
Springer Science+Business Media
springeronline.com

Typesetting: Gray Publishing, Tunbridge Wells, Kent, UK
Printed and bound in the United States of America
34/3830-543210 Printed on acid-free paper SPIN 10962268

To Caroline, for making sense of it all.

Walter J. Goralski is a Senior Member of Technical Staff with Juniper Networks Inc. and an Adjunct Professor of Computer Science at Pace University Graduate School in New York. He has spent more than 30 years in the data communications field, including 14 years with AT&T, and is the author of several books on DSL, the Internet, TCP/IP and SONET, as well as of articles on data communications and other technology issues.

Hannes Gredler is a Professional Services Consultant at Juniper Networks Inc., where he is deploying/advising for numerous carriers and ISPs running the IS-IS, BGP and MPLS suite of protocols in their core backbones. He has been in the telecom industry for 7 years and holds a Master's degree for Manufacturing and Automation from the Technical University of Graz (Austria). Hannes holds a CCIE certification (#2866) since 1997 as well as JNCIE (#22) certification since 2001. Besides his engagement at Juniper Networks, Inc., Hannes is actively involved in Open-Source Developments of networking decoders, where he contributed large parts of the Routing and Signaling Protocol Engines for tcpdump/libpcap http://www.tcpdump.org/ and Etherreal http://www.ethereal.com.

Hannes currently lives near Innsbruck, Austria. He is married and has three daughters.

Foreword

IS-IS has always been my favourite Interior Gateway Protocol. Its elegant simplicity, its well-structured data formats, its flexibility and easy extensibility are all appealing – IS-IS epitomizes link-state routing. Whether for this reason or others, IS-IS is the IGP of choice in some of the world's largest networks. Thus, if one is at all interested in routing, it is well worth the time and effort to learn IS-IS.

However, it is hazardous to call any routing protocol "simple". Every design decision, be it in architecture, implementation or deployment, has consequences, some unanticipated, some unknowable, some dire. Interactions between different implementations, the dynamic nature of routing, and new protocol features all contribute to making routing protocols complex to design, write and deploy effectively in networks. For example, IS-IS started as a link-state routing protocol for ISO networks. It has since evolved significantly: IS-IS has IPv4 and IPv6 (and IPX) addressing; IS-IS can carry information about multiple topologies; link attributes have expanded to include traffic engineering parameters; a new methodology for restarting IS-IS gracefully has been developed. IS-IS even has extensions for use in "non-packet networks", such as SONET and optical networks, as part of the Generalized Multi-Protocol Label Switching (G-MPLS) protocol suite.

Understanding all of what IS-IS offers and keeping abreast of the newer protocol features is a weighty endeavour, but one that is absolutely essential for all serious networking engineers, whether they are developing code or running networks. For a long time, there were excellent books on OSPF, but very little on IS-IS. This encyclopaedic work changes that. Now, at last, there is a book that does IS-IS justice, explaining the theoretical aspects of IS-IS, practical real-life situations, and quirks in existing implementations, and gives glimpses into some troubleshooting tools.

You couldn't ask for a better-matched pair of guides, either. Hannes: intense, passionate, expert; and Walter: calm, clear, expert. Between the two, they have produced a comprehensive, up-to-date text that can be used for in-depth protocol study, as a reference, or to catch up with the latest developments in IS-IS.

Happy reading!

Kireeti Kompella
Distinguished Engineer, Juniper Networks Inc.
Common Control and Measurement Plane (ccamp) IETF Working Group Chair

Credits and Thanks

The authors would specifically thank the following individuals for their direct or indirect support for this book:

Walter

First of all, thanks to Hannes for giving me the opportunity to be involved in this project. What I know about IS-IS, I have learned from the Master. Patrick Ames made this book a reality, and Aviva Garrett provided inspired leadership. My wife Camille provided support, comfort, and the caring that all writers need.

Hannes

My biggest personal thank-you goes to my beloved wife Caroline. While she did so many good things for me, most importantly she created the environment for me that allowed me to write. Without her ongoing, loving support this book would never have been written up and finally published.

Patrick Ames has left a profound footprint on that book. While he had possibly the hardest job on earth (chasing part-time authors for manuscripts beyond due dates) he always kept calm, professional and provided care and input on all stages of this book. Without him this book would not have made its way.

Next I want to thank probably the best review team on IS-IS in the industry: first, the Juniper Engineering Team, most notably Dave Katz, Ina Minai, Nischal Sheth, Kireeti Kompella and Pedro Marquez who always took time and answered my questions in great detail. Tony Przygienda kept an eye from the IETF perspective on content accuracy and gave numerous suggestions to improve the text. The Service Provider Reviewing Team (Dirk Steinberg, Markus Schumburg, Ruediger Volk/Deutsche Telekom) and Nicolas Dubois (France Telekom) gave a lot of design inputs from the operational perspective.

Finally, I want to thank my Home Base, the Juniper Customer Service Europe Team: Jan Vos who initially helped in advocating writing a book and generously donated Company Lab and Team Resources; Anton Bernal for teaching me a lot about ATM; Josef Buchsteiner supported my work everyday by several useful discussions and help with lab setups. Finally, my team mate, Peter Lundqvist, for sharing a lot of his vast knowledge with me and being always good for a good laugh.

Contents

1

Introduction, Motivation and Historical Background

The Intermediate System to Intermediate System (IS-IS) routing protocol is the de facto standard for large service provider network backbones. IS-IS is one of the few remnants of the Open System Interconnect (OSI) Reference Model that have made their way into mainstream routing. How IS-IS got there makes a colourful story, a story that was determined by a handful of routing protocol engineers. So in this very first chapter, it makes sense to explore the need for a book about IS-IS, cover some recent routing protocol history and give an overview about various IS-IS development stages. Finally, the chapter introduces a sample network and explains the style used in the figures throughout the book.

1.1 Motivation

One of the oddities of IS-IS is that there are hardly any materials available covering the *entire* protocol and how IS-IS is used for routing Internet Protocol (IP) packets. The base specification of the protocol was first published as ISO 10589 in 1987 and did not apply to IP packets at all. From then on, however, most of the work on the protocol has been done in the IS-IS working group of the Internet Engineering Task Force (IETF). The IETF was responsible for two major changes to the OSI vision of IS-IS. First, they extended the protocol by defining additional Type-Length-Values (TLVs) carrying new functionality. But then the IETF went much further and clarified many operational aspects of IS-IS. For example, adjacency management had not been exactly defined in RFC 1195, the first request for comment (RFC) to relate IS-IS to an IP environment. The lack of details caused implementers to code behaviours differently from what the basic specification required the protocol to do. As a result, there is a lot of good IS-IS literature available that covers the base IS-IS protocol and its extensions, but not the implementation details. However, discussing IS-IS purely on a theoretical basis is not enough. Throughout this chapter, you will find that a lot of the reasons why things are the way they are in IS-IS is dependent on implementation choices (often caused by router operating system (OS) constraints), not the fundamentals of the IS-IS specification. And that is the whole reason for this book.

Real-world IS-IS implementations are the main focus of this book. The two vendors shipping all but a tiny fraction of the IS-IS code used for IP routing on the Internet are Cisco Systems, Inc. and Juniper Networks, Inc. The routing OS suite of Juniper Networks

Inc. (JUNOS Internet software) and Cisco Systems (IOS) are subjected to close examination throughout this book. We will compare implementation details, and compare the overall implementation against the specification. Furthermore, both IOS and JUNOS carry scalability improvements for IS-IS, which will be highlighted as well.

The purpose of this book is to provide a good start for the self-education of both the novice and the seasoned network engineer in the IS-IS routing protocol. The consistent approach is to explain the theory and then show how things are implemented in major vendor routing OSs. That way, we hope to close the gap between barely specified specification and undocumented vendor-specific behaviour.

1.2 Routing Protocols History in the 1990s

IS-IS started off as a research project of Digital Equipment Corporation (DEC) in 1986. Radia Perlman, Mike Shand and Dave Oran had worked on a successor network architecture for Digital's proprietary minicomputer system family. The suite of protocols was named DECNET. By the time the product became DECNET phase IV, it was obvious that the architecture lacked support for large address spaces and displayed slow convergence times after re-routing events like link failures. Clearly, a new approach to these problems, which occurred in all networks and with all routing protocols at the time, was desperately needed.

1.2.1 *DECNET Phase V*

The new architecture called DECNET Phase V was based on an entirely new routing technology called *link-state* routing. All previous packet-based network technology at that time was based on variations of distance-vector routing (sometimes also referred to as Bellman-Ford routing) or the Spanning Tree Algorithm. The idea of routers disseminating and maintaining a topological database on which they all performed a Dijkstra (Shortest Path First, or SPF) calculation was a revolutionary approach to networking. This database processing demanded a certain amount of sophistication in router CPUs (central processing units) and not all routers had what it took. However, all of the urban legends revolving around the "CPU-intensive" and cycle-wasting properties of link-state algorithms mostly had their origin in subjective opinions about router power at that time. Certainly no modern router needs to worry about the CPU cycles needed for link-state algorithms.

The most interesting property about DECNET Phase V was that it was – and is – a very extensible protocol. It runs directly on top of the OSI Data Link Layer protocol. That makes the protocol inherently independent of any higher Network Layer Reachability Protocol. In 1987, the International Organization for Standardization (usually abbreviated as ISO) adopted the protocols used in DECNET Phase V as the basis for the OSI protocol suite. A whole array of networking protocols was standardized at the time. A brief list of the adopted protocols would include:

- Transport Layer (TP2, TP4)
- Network Layer Reachability (CLNP)
- Router to Host (ES-IS)

- Router to Router, Interdomain (IDRP)
- Router to Router, Intradomain (IS-IS)

Finally, the *Intermediate to Intermediate System Intradomain Routing Exchange Protocol* (to give IS-IS its official name) was published as ISO specification ISO 10589. First-time readers tend to get confused by the sometimes arcane "ISO-speak" used in the document. IS-IS itself, in contrast to its specification, is actually a fine, lean protocol. After learning which sections of ISO 10589 to avoid, readers find that IS-IS is a simple protocol with almost none of the complicated state transitions that make other interior gateway protocols (IGPs) so difficult to operate properly under heavy traffic loads today. Besides the ISO jargon in the specification, readers often get caught up in and confused by the distinctions between the routing protocol definitions (IS-IS itself) and the higher-level network reachability definitions (known as the connectionless network protocol, or CLNP) and this makes differentiating IS-IS and CLNP more difficult. Henk Smit, a well-respected implementer of the IS-IS protocol, once with Cisco Systems, noted on the NANOG Mailing List:

> IS-IS is defined in ISO document 10589. It defines the base structures of the protocol (adjacencies, flooding, etc). Unfortunately it also defines lots of CLNP specific TLVs. So it looks like IS-IS is a routing protocol for CLNP, and the IP thing is an add-on. That is partly true, but the ability to carry routing info for any layer 3 protocol is a well designed feature. I suspect IS-IS might be easier to understand if the CLNP specific part was separated from the base protocol.

So IS-IS can be used for routing IP packets just as well as the other major link-state protocol, the Open Shortest Path First (OSPF) protocol. But why bother having another link-state IGP for routing TCP/IP, especially if it is so similar to OSPF? At first sight, supporting both OSPF and IS-IS seems to be a double effort. Only by looking back can it be easily understood why IS-IS has its place in today's Internet.

1.2.2 *NSFNet Phase I*

In 1988, the NSFNet backbone of the Internet was commissioned and deployed. The NSFNet was the first nationwide network that routed TCP/IP traffic. The IGP of choice for the NSFNet was a lightweight knockoff version of IS-IS, which was later documented in RFC 1074 as "The NSFNET Backbone SPF based Interior Gateway Protocol". The implementer and author of the document is now a famous name in the history of internetworking history: Dr Yakov Rekhter, at this time working at IBM on networking protocols at the Thomas Watson Research Center. The main differences between the IS-IS as defined in ISO 10589 and that used on the NSFNet were encapsulation, addressing, media support and the number of IS-IS levels. The NSFNET backbone IGP ran on top of IP rather than directly on top of the OSI Link Layer, and IP Protocol Type 85 was used as a transporting envelope. ISO 10589 only specified a CLNP-related address space called the Network Service Access Point (NSAP). Rather than defining an extra TLV that carried IPv4 addresses and administrative domain information, both types of information are folded into a 9-byte NSAP string which is illustrated in Figure 1.1.

The next NSFNet compromise in total IS-IS functionality involved the support for only point-to-point (p2p) interfaces. This greatly simplified the program coding as the adjacency management code did not have to worry about things like Designated Routers

Field	Bytes
Administrative Domain	2
Reserved	2
IPv4 Address	4
Reserved	4

FIGURE 1.1. The early NSFNet protocol maps an IPv4 address in the NSAP field for IP routing

(DRs) and what IS-IS called "pseudonode" origination. Pseudonode origination and LAN "circuits" will be covered in greater detail in Chapter 7, "Pseudonodes and Designated Routers". At that time, this change was perceived as no big deal as the NSFNet was a pure WAN network consisting of a bunch of T1 (1.544 Mbps) lines.

The NSFNet link-state routing protocol gave NSFNet its first experience with the sometimes catastrophic dynamics of link-state protocols and resulted in network-wide meltdowns. We will cover the robustness issues and the lessons learned from the infancy of link-state routing protocols in Chapter 6, "Generating Flooding and Ageing LSPs". But early bad experiences ultimately provided a good education for the early implementers, and their knowledge of "how *not* to do things" helped to create better implementations the second time around.

1.2.3 *OSPF*

In 1988, the IETF began work on a replacement for the Routing Information Protocol (RIP), which was proving insufficient for large networks due to its "hop count" metric limitations. Also, the limited nature of the Bellman-Ford algorithm with regard to convergence time provided serious headaches in the larger networks at that time. It was clear that any replacement for RIP had to be based on link-state routing, just like IS-IS. The Open Shortest Path First Working Group was born. The OSPF-WG group closely watched the IS-IS developments and both standardization bodies, the IETF and ISO, effectively copied ideas from each other. This was no major surprise, as mostly the same individuals were working on both protocols.

The first implementation of OSPF Version 1 was shipped by router vendor Proteon. A short while later, both DECNET Phase V (which was effectively IS-IS) and OSPF were being deployed. Controversy and dispute raged within the IETF concerning whether to adopt IS-IS or OSPF as the officially endorsed IGP of the Internet. At that time, there was much fear expressed by some influential individuals about the perceived "OSI-fication" of the Internet. Those fears were fed by the belief on the part of the OSI camp that IPv4 was just a temporary, "non-standard" phenomenon that ultimately would go away, replaced by firm international standards like CLNP, CMIP and TP2, TP4. Most discussions about what was the best protocol were based on emotions rather than facts. At one IETF meeting there was bickering and shouting, and even a T-shirt distributed displaying the equation: *IS-IS* = 0

It is hard to believe today that there were ever any serious doubts about the future of IP. But things did not change until 1992. With the rise of the World Wide Web as the "killer application" for the new, global, public Internet, it was evident that the Network Layer protocol of choice was to be the Internet Protocol (IP) and not CNLP. The projected demise of CNLP nurtured the belief that the entire OSI suite of protocols would disappear soon.

The IETF reckoned that there should be native IP support for IS-IS and formed the IS-IS for IP Internets working group. In 1990, IS-IS had become "IP-aware" with the publication of RFC 1195, authored by Ross Callon, a distinguished protocol engineer now with Juniper Networks. RFC 1195 describes a set of IP TLVs for *Integrated* IS-IS which can transport both CLNP and IP routes. These early IP TLVs and their current successors are discussed in greater detail in Chapter 12, "IP Reachability Information" and Chapter 13, "IS-IS Extensions".

The IETF continued both IGP working groups (OSPF-WG, ISIS-WG) and wisely left the decision which protocol to adapt to the marketplace. The IETF declared both protocols as equal, which proved in fact not to be really true, since there was some soft, but persistent, pressure to give OSPF preference for Internet applications. Hence people often say, "IS-IS and OSPF are equal, but OSPF is *more equal*." Ultimately, Cisco Systems started to ship routers with support for both OSPF and CLNP-only IS-IS (useless for IP), but commenced work on Integrated IS-IS, which could be used with IP.

1.2.4 *NLSP*

In the 1980s, LAN software vendor Novell gained popularity and finally emerged as the primary vendor of PC-based server software. The Novell Packet Architecture was composed of both a Network Layer protocol they called the Internet Packet Exchange (IPX) protocol and a routing protocol to properly route packets between sub-nets. Novell's first generation routing protocol was based on RIP and used distance vector technology. Novell then decided to augment their network architecture with link-state routing. At that time, DEC was widely known for their link-state routing experience, and so Novell recruited Neil Castagnoli, who was one of the key scientists at DEC responsible for DECNET Phase V.

One of the prime goals of IS-IS from the very start was independence from Network Layer routing protocols. In other words, IS-IS just distributed route information, and did not particularly care which protocol was actually used to transport traffic. Novell came up with NLSP, which was effectively an IS-IS clone. Many of the original IS-IS mechanisms and protocol data unit (PDU) types were retained. For IPX-specific routing information and Novell-specific service location protocols (used to find which stations on the LANs were servers) the TLVs from 190 to 196 have been allocated for Novell-specific routing needs. Although NLSP looks largely the same as IS-IS, some of the mechanisms, particularly the "stickiness" of the DR election process, make NLSP incompatible with regular IS-IS routers.

Both the IP and the NSLP extensions demonstrate the flexibility built into IS-IS from the very start. Adding another protocol family, for example IPv6, is just a matter of adding a few hundred lines of code, rather than having to rewrite the entire code base. OSPF, on the other hand, needed to be re-engineered twice until it got to be both extensible *and* IPv6-ready. And OSPF is still not completely neutral towards Network Layer protocols other than IP.

Responding to increasing demand from customers, Cisco Systems began shipping NLSP in 1994. Because NLSP and IS-IS are so similar, Cisco's engineering department decided to do some internal code housekeeping and merged the base functions of the two protocols in one "tree". This rewriting work was the springboard for one of the most respected IGP routing protocol engineers in the world. Cisco Systems hired a software engineer named Dave Katz from Merit, the management company of the NSFNet backbone. Merit was, in the early 1990s, the place where many of the huge talents in Internet history got their routing expertise.

1.2.5 *Large-scale Deployments*

Cisco gained a lot of momentum in the early 1990. The company attracted all the key talent in routing protocol and IP expertise and finally got more than a 98 per cent market share in the service provider equipment space. When the first big router orders were placed and the routers deployed for the Web explosion, Internet service provider (ISP) customers started to ask their first questions about scalability. Service providers were interested in a solid, quickly converging protocol that could scale to a large topology containing hundreds or even thousands of routers. Cisco's proprietary, distance-vector EIGRP was not really a choice because the convergence times and stability problems of distance-vector-based protocols were well known from word-to-mouth in the service provider community. Ironically, it was Cisco's recent code rewrite that made IS-IS more stable than the implementations of OSPF available at the time. For a while, IS-IS was believed to be as dead as the OSI protocols. However, the 1980s mandate of the US government for supporting OSI protocols under the Government OSI Profile (GOSIP) specification (which was still in effect), plus recently gained stability, made IS-IS the logical choice for any service provider that needed an IGP for a large number of nodes.

From about 1995 to 1998 the popularity of IS-IS within the ISP niche continued to grow, and some service providers switched from OSPF. Even in large link-state areas, IS-IS proved to be a stable protocol. At the beginning of 1998, the European service providers switched from their trying EIGRP and OSPF experiences to IS-IS, most notably because of the better experiences that the US providers had with IS-IS. That trend continues today. All major European networks are running routing protocols based on IS-IS.

1.2.6 *IETF ISIS-WG*

From 1999, most of the IS-IS extensions for IP are done within the IETF and not within ITU-T or ISO committees. Most of the basic IS-IS protocol is maintained in ITU-T, but little of it has changed in the past decade. The IS-IS working group inside the IETF (http://www.ietf.org/html.charters/isis-charter.html) maintains the further development of IS-IS. Most IETF work is typically carried out in the form of mailing lists. There are further details about this split of responsibilities and the resulting issues in Chapter 17, "Future of IS-IS".

There is a small group of individuals from vendors and ISPs interested in the further development of IS-IS. Because the community is so small, consensus is reached very fast and the standardization process itself is often just a matter of documenting the existing behaviour that has already been deployed in the field.

All the most recent enhancements to IS-IS have initially been published as Internet drafts. At the end of the year, all the major extensions are either republished as an RFC or are placed in the RFC editors' queue for release. Activity on the IETF mailing list is nowadays moderate to low, as all of the most pressing problems and extension behaviours have already been solved. Chapter 17 deals with the future of the protocol and highlights some of the not-yet deployed extensions, which concern service discovery and aids to network operations.

1.3 Sample Topology, Figures and Style

In an effort to make the individual chapters more concise and to be consistent, we have applied a common style and topology to illustrations. In order to put the different scenarios that are explained throughout into perspective, we refer to a small service provider network as illustrated in Figure 1.2. We believe that a realistic reference topology is of

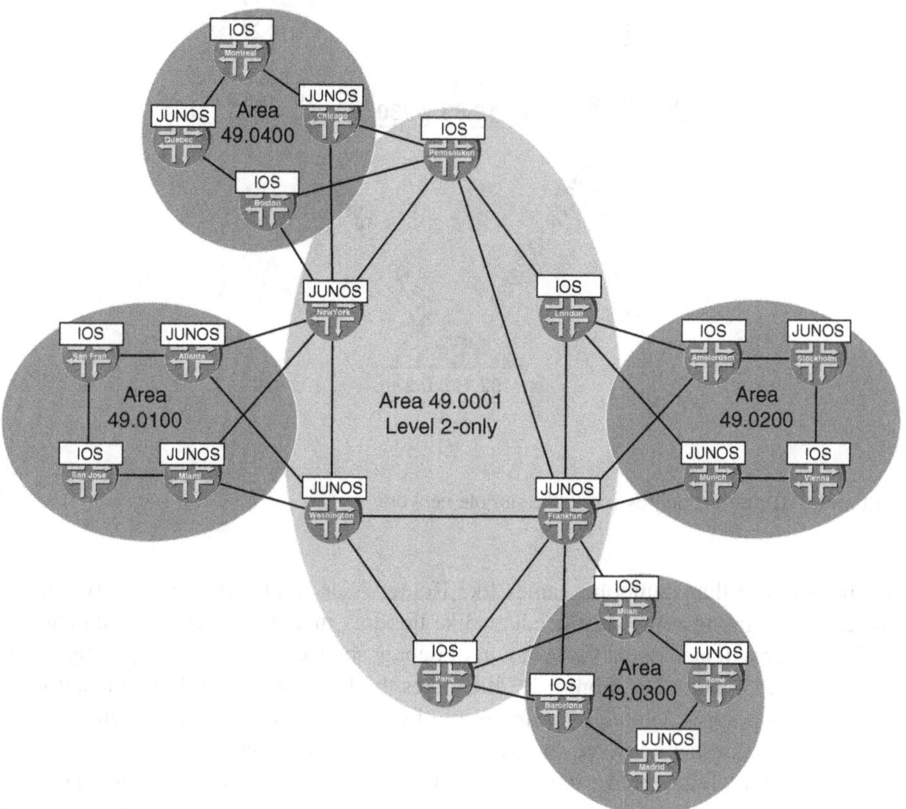

FIGURE 1.2. Throughout the book a consistent Multivendor Sample Network is used for better illustration

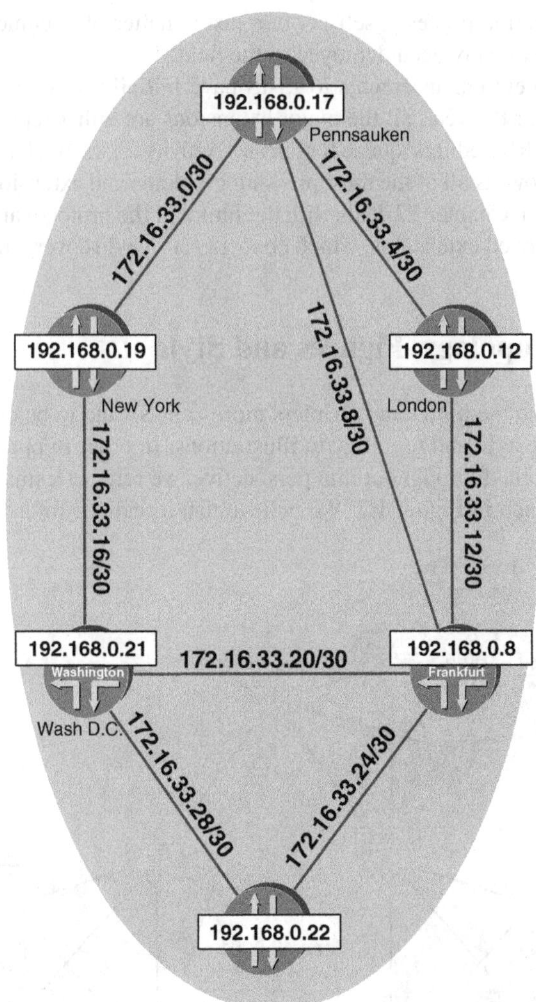

FIGURE 1.3. IP sub-net addressing in the sample network

much more use than symbolic names like Router A or Router B, particularly when it comes to explaining complex procedures like flooding in a distributed environment.

The reader will also find a vast amount of debug, show command and tcpdump output containing IPv4 addresses. Figure 1.3 illustrates the IPv4 sub-net address allocation for the sample topology. Although the majority of display output has been taken from live routers on the Internet, we have changed the addressing to a common scheme. Although in a real network one would never deploy addressing based on non-routable RFC 1918 addresses, this is done throughout the book in order to protect the integrity of public, routable address spaces. The 172.16.33/24 address range has been allocated to link addressing and the 192.168.0/27 pool is allocated for router loopback addresses.

This book should also serve as a reference for people learning about the encoding style of the IS-IS protocol. Too often the authors found the entire TLV and sub-TLV structure difficult to understand. Figure 1.4 illustrates the shading style used to colour all protocol-related illustrations. The darker the background colour, the lower the field is located in the OSI protocol stack. So the dark gray shading indicates link-layer encapsulation such as Ethernet or PPP or C-HDLC. Then gray tones are used for the IS-IS common header, IS-IS PDU specific headers, the TLVs and its sub-TLVs.

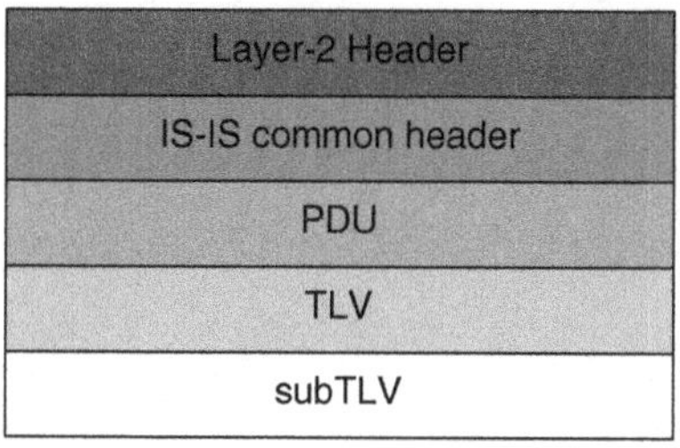

FIGURE 1.4. The shading of the fields in the illustrations indicates the layering in the OSI Reference Model

2

Router Architecture

Every networking professional knows the situation. You're at a party with relatives where people always seem to know somehow that you deal with the Internet (probably those relatives). If you have bad luck, at some stage the conversation at the table is about the Internet and how it might work. The trickiest task is then to explain to Grandma in five minutes how the Internet works. Not that Grandma bothers to try and understand. In fact, she still thinks that all those cables that disappear into the wall go all the way under the Atlantic and that's the way that it works.

But the truth is, explaining how the Internet works is surprisingly easy: the Internet consists of a vast collection of hosts and routers. Routers are the "glue" that holds these hosts together. The routers form a meshed network, very much like the road system where the routers can be compared to interchanges or junctions and the fibre optic cables in between the routers are the highways. The host computers are like houses placed on smaller roads (these side roads are smaller networks or sub-nets), each having a unique address.

Surprisingly, Internet hosts and routers are almost completely isolated from each other. Hosts do not generally exchange any signalling information with routers. All that hosts need to know (normally by static configuration) is the address of the router on their local sub-net. Hosts can forward any non-local traffic for hosts on other networks to this *default router* or *default gateway*. Almost everyone reading this book has probably configured this default on their local PC or workstation. In contrast to the hosts, which almost have no routing information at all besides the default route, the routers have all the routing information they need. However, the routers do not have any idea about the applications (such as a Web browser) or the transport protocols (such as HTML) that applications rely upon. It is the hosts that do indeed have to know about the state of the transport protocol and how applications access the network. This is the first instance where, for the sake of simplicity, a clever *partitioning* of the problem has occurred. This chapter presents more examples where you realize that there is more than one place in the overall Internet and router architecture where *partitioning* the original problem has helped to resolve the issue. *Partitioning* is the architectural tool that helps scale the IP universe further than at first appears possible.

In the last 20 years the Internet has scaled from just a bunch of hosts to a global mesh of hundreds of millions of computers. This chapter discusses the architecture of the global public Internet and the global routing paradigm. Next, it takes a close look at the building block of the Internet, which is the *router*. Common router architectures, and terms like *control plane* and *forwarding plane* and why partitioning a router into a control plane and forwarding plane makes sense, will all be explained. For further illustration, common routing platforms from both Cisco Systems and Juniper Networks will be discussed at the end of the chapter.

2.1 Architecture and the Global Routing Paradigm

The current routing and forwarding architecture follows a *datagram-based, End-System (host) controlled, unidirectional, destination-oriented, hop-by-hop routing* paradigm. Don't worry, all of these technical terms are explained piece-by-piece below.

1. *Datagram-based:* Routers only think in terms of datagrams, which are packets that flow independently from host to host without regard for sequence or content integrity. In this respect routers are unlike End Systems which *have* to track the state of connections, perform all kind of transport protocol (TCP) functions like making sure arriving packets are in sequence, asking for resends of missing packets, and so on. A router is completely oblivious to the *sessions* that it has to transport between hosts. Early routers had *knobs* (small, on/off configuration tags like "disable/enable") for packet lookup, filtering and accounting on a per-flow (session) basis. However, the impact of introducing a session or flow orientation to core routers and the resulting load of the system was just too big. Today, flow orientation, which demands session awareness in every router, and high-speed circuits are mutually exclusive. Flow orientation is only enabled on low-bandwidth circuits (2 Mbps or less), due to its high CPU impact. Core routers today are completely unaware of any sessions or flows. This *stateless* behaviour means that a route lookup for a packet at time $N + 1$ is totally independent of the packet lookup at time N. The router just tries to deliver the packet as fast as it can. If a packet cannot be delivered because the outbound interface is congested, then the packet will be queued. If the queues (some call them *buffers*) are saturated then the packet will be silently discarded. Silent discard is a technique that does not send explicit congestion messages to the sender. Suppressing explicit congestion messages does not further harm the networks' resources if the network is already saturated. Although core routers should not worry about individual flows they must not change reorder packets within a given flow. Typically, it is expected that the end systems receive packets in sequence. There might be situations, as in re-routing scenarios or badly implemented load-sharing mechanisms, where packets in a single flow are re-sequenced by the transit routers. The IP routing architecture completely offloads key functions like flow control, reliable transmission, and re-sequencing to the End Systems. This allows simpler router functions.
2. *End System controlled:* Sometimes the term *end-to-end principle* is used when discussing transport protocols like TCP. In the TCP architecture, all of the complexity of providing a reliable streaming service is on the shoulders of the end systems. Functions like flow control, reliable transmission and re-sequencing of messages (packet content) in a stream are the duties of the transport protocol. An End System opens a session, transmits data and eventually closes the session. For the transmission of data all it relies upon is the *unreliable* datagram relaying service that the routers offer to the End Systems. Figure 2.1 shows how an application like the *Simple Mail*

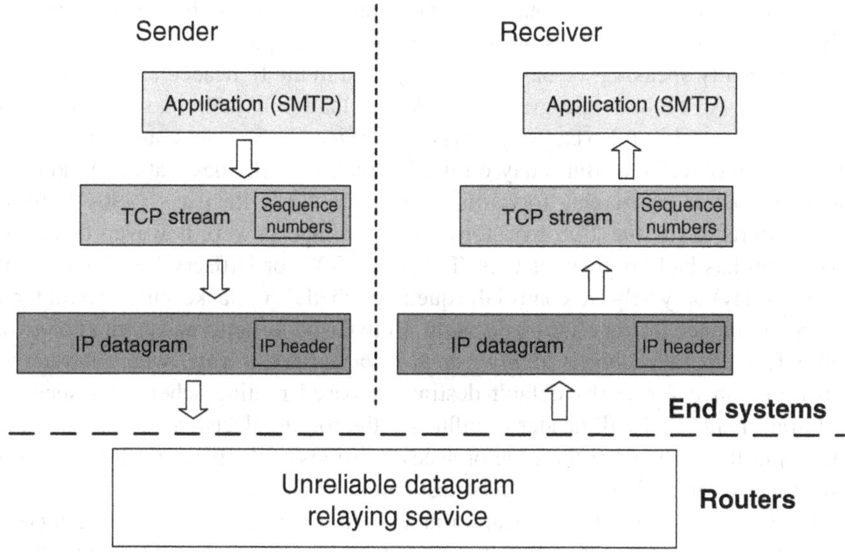

FIGURE 2.1. A basic networking stack, showing the different responsibilities for hosts and routers

Transfer Protocol (SMTP) augments the stream with transport protocol level information like sequence numbers. The augmented transport stream next is passed down the network protocol stack to the IP layer where each message segment is prepended with an IP header. The packet then leaves the End System and is either sent directly to the receiving end system (if it is on the same network) or passed to the default router. Then the transport protocol just hopes that the message segment eventually arrives at the receiving end system. All the transport protocols can do on both sides is *detect* a missing segment. By looking at the sequence numbers, the transport protocol detects a missing segment and requests retransmission if desired (some forms of real-time traffic, like voice and video, do not have the luxury of this option). Even more sophisticated actions are performed by the transport protocols. For example, if the pace of the receiving segments is varying, typically an indication of congestion, the receiver can signal back to the sender to back off and reduce the transmit rate. The only way of communicating congestion from the routers to the End Systems is increased delay or packet loss, which is just a case of *infinite delay*.

3. *Unidirectional:* Some communication architectures like ATM or Frame Relay have the implicit assumption that the circuit going from End System A to End System B is utilized for the opposite direction. This means that traffic from End System B to End System A follows exactly the same path (a *connection*) through the network. In the IP routing world, this is not necessarily the case. Routing information, which are pointers to traffic sources, are always *unidirectional*. For working communication a router needs to have *two* routes: one route pointing to the sender's network and one route pointing to the receiver's network. Popular networking troubleshooting tools like the ping program always check to see if there is bidirectional connectivity between a pair of hosts.

4. *Destination-oriented:* Each router along the transmission path between a pair of End Systems has to make a decision where to forward the packets. This decision could, hypothetically speaking, be based upon any field in the IP header, such as marked in Figure 2.2. All of the bright-gray fields like destination IP address, source IP address and precedence bits (also called the Type of Service (TOS) byte) could form the basis for a routing decision. But today on the Internet, only the destination IP address is used by routers for making forwarding decisions. Since the early 1990s there have been efforts to use the TOS byte for routing lookups as well; however, this routing paradigm has had no great success. Today the TOS (or Diffserv byte, as it is often called today) only helps to control the queuing schedule of packets inside a router, but cannot influence the forwarding decision. Both Cisco Systems and Juniper Networks offer features called *policy routing* or *filter based forwarding*, where the network operator can override the default destination-based routing scheme by specifying arbitrary fields in the IP header to influence the routing decision. But these features are typically deployed at the edge or access portions of the network. It is safe to say that the core of the Internet is purely destination-oriented.
5. *Hop-by-hop routing:* Communication architectures like ATM rely on a connection setup where the sender predetermines the route to the destination. Once a message is put on a previously established *Switched Virtual Connection* (SVC) the message will be relayed straight from the source to the destination without complex routing decisions in the intermediate systems (usually called *switches* in such connection-oriented architectures). The whole transmission path is pre-computed by the source. The ATM forwarding paradigm thereby follows a *source routing* model. The IP routing architecture is very different. Clearly there are common ideas, such as that the packet should use the shortest path from the source to the destination. But contrary to ATM switches, IP routers each compute *independently* what the *best* route is from A to B. Obviously, this must follow a common scheme that each router follows, otherwise forwarding loops could result from conflicting path selection algorithms. The common path selection algorithms are various forms of *least-cost* routing. Each routing protocol defines a set of metrics, and if there is more than one next hop with equal metrics, a tie-breaking scheme allows each router to determine the "best" route to a

				Bytes
Version	Header length	TOS	Total length	4
Identification		Flags	Fragment offset	4
Time to live		Protocol	Header checksum	4
Source address				4
Destination address				4

FIGURE 2.2. In the IP routing paradigm forwarding decisions are based on the destination IP inside the IP header

given destination, but only from the viewpoint of the local router. This concerted, but still independent, computing of forwarding tables in routers is called *hop-by-hop* routing.

Four of the above five points specify how routers should "think" in terms of forwarding traffic. In 1985, when the first commercial routers shipped, peak processing of packets at 1000 packets per second (pps) were feasible. With the explosion of Internet traffic, routers today must offer *sustained* packet processing rates of hundreds of millions pps. What has changed? While the original forwarding paradigms are still in place, router hardware and architectures have constantly improved a router built in 2004 can forward at a factor of 10,000 more traffic than a router made in 1992.

2.2 General Router Model

In the Internet model, smaller networks are connected to bigger networks through routers. Originally routers were implemented on general purpose workstations (typically UNIX-based platforms; PCs running DOS or Windows were much too slow). These early routers had a single CPU, which had to do two things:

- Routing
- Forwarding

Routing means discovering the network topology and disseminating information about directly connected sub-nets to other *neighbour* routers. *Forwarding* refers to the look-up and transfer of packets to the matching outbound next-hop for a given packet. Routing, as defined here, mainly concerns signalling information and forwarding mainly concerns user information.

As long as the general purpose processor has infinite processing power and memory, the union of both routing and forwarding functions in the same device does no harm. Practically speaking, processing power and memory are *always* finite resources and experience has shown that the two functions mutually influence each other in their competition for processing and storage resources. Unifying routing and forwarding may cause stability problems during transient conditions, for instance, when a large traffic trunk needs to be rerouted. Typically, during these transient situations, both the routing subsystem of the box as well as the forwarding subsystems are extraordinarily stressed.

The stress occurs because the routing subsystem has to calculate alternative paths for the broken traffic trunk and, at the same time, the forwarding process may be hit by a large wave of traffic being rerouted through this router by another router. And that is exactly the problem with the unified design combining routing and forwarding. It only works as long as just *one* subsystem is stressed, but not *both*.

For example, what happens when the central CPU is 100 per cent utilized? Not all traffic can be routed and packets have to be dropped. If the signalling or control traffic generated by the routing protocols is part of the dropped traffic, this may result in further topology changes and result in endless stress (churn) that propagates through the whole network.

Such meltdowns have occurred in every major ISP network throughout the last decade, and the result was a radical design change in how routers are built. The forwarding subsystem was separated from the general purpose platform, and migrated to custom hardware that can forward hundreds of millions of packets per second. Customized hardware development was necessary as the Internet growth outperformed any PC-based architecture based on, for example, PCI buses.

Figure 2.3 shows essentially how modern routers are structured. The router is partitioned into a dedicated control plane and a forwarding plane. The control plane holds the software that the router needs to interact with other routers and human operators. Routers typically employ a powerful command line interface (CLI), which is used for provisioning services, configuration management, router troubleshooting and debugging purposes. Operator actions are written down in a central *configuration file*. Changes of the configuration file are propagated to the routing processes that "speak" router-to-router protocols like OSPF or IS-IS or Border Gateway Protocol (BGP). If the same routing protocol is provisioned on both ends of a direct router-to-router link, then the routers start to discover each other in their network. Next, IP routing information is exchanged. The *remote* network information is entered in the *local* routing table of the *route processor*. Next, the forwarding table entries in the control plane and the packet forwarding plane have to be synchronized. Based on this routing table, the forwarding plane starts to program the router hardware, which consists of Application Specific Integrated Circuits (ASICs) or Field Programmable Gate Arrays (FPGAs), with a subset of the routing table, which is now called the *forwarding table*. The forwarding table is usually a concise version of the full routing table containing all IP networks. The forwarding table only needs to know routes useful for packet forwarding.

The fowarding plane consists of a number of "input interfaces" (IIF) and a number of "output interfaces" (OIF). The router itself thinks in terms of *logical* interfaces. The physical interface is the actual wire (or fibre) over which the packets flow. In order to actually use a physical interface for forwarding traffic, there needs to be at least one IP address assigned to the interface. The IP address combined with a physical interface is called a *logical interface*. There can be more than one logical interface per physical interface if the underlying physical media supports channel multiplexing like 801.1Q, Frame

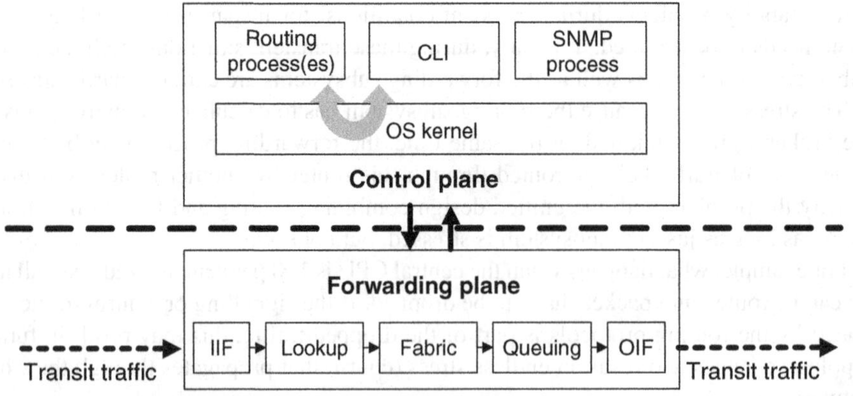

FIGURE 2.3. A blueprint of a modern router showing a clear separation of control plane and forwarding plane

Relay DLCIs or ATM VCs, since each can have an IP address associated with it. If there is no IP address assigned to a logical interface, then any traffic arriving on that interface will be discarded.

Once traffic arrives on the input interface there is typically a lookup engine that tries to determine the next-hop for a given IP address prefix (the prefix is the network portion of the IP address). The next-hop information consists of an outgoing interface plus Layer 2 data link framing information. Since the outgoing interface is not enough for multi-access networks like Ethernet LANs, the router needs to prepend the destination Media Access Control (MAC) address of the receiver as well.

Next, the packet is transported inside the router chassis by any form of switch *fabric*. Common switch fabric designs are crossbars, shared memory, shared bus and multistage networks. The last stage before final sending of a packet to the next-hop router is the queuing stage. This buffers packets if the interface is congested, schedules and deliver packets to an outgoing interface.

2.3 Routing and Forwarding Tables

Just what is the difference between a routing and a forwarding table? The short answer is *size* and amount of *origin information*. The routing table of a well-connected Internet core router today uses dozens of megabytes (MB) of memory to store complete information about all known Internet routes. Figure 2.4 shows why such a massive amount of memory is needed. A router needs to store all the routes that it receives from each neighbour. So for each neighbour an *Input Routing Information Base* (RIB-in) is kept. Due to path redundancy in network cores, a prefix will most likely be known by more than one

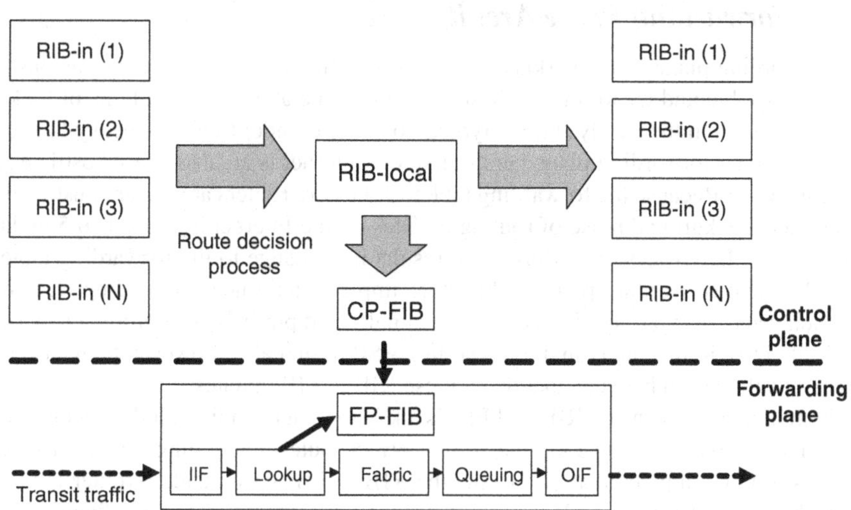

FIGURE 2.4. Internet core routers need to store what routes have been learned and advertised on a per neighbour basis

path. What the routing software does is to determine the "best" path for a given prefix, sometimes through a complicated tie-breaking process when metrics are the same. After this route selection process the routing software knows the outgoing interface for all of the prefixes it has learned from all of its neighbours. This processed table is called the *Local Routing Information Base* (RIB-local). The RIB-local table also stores a large amount of data associated with the prefix, information such as through which protocol was the route learned, which ISP originated the route information, if the route is subject to frequent failures (flapping), and so on. Modern routers store about 50–300 bytes of additional administrative information for each route, useful for troubleshooting routing problems, but adding to the resource requirements of the router.

A full-blown Internet routing table from a single upstream contains about 140,000 routes consumes about 20–30 MB of memory. This is still a massive amount of memory if it has to be implemented in an expensive semiconductor technology. For example, the ultra fast SRAMs typically used for CPU caches provide faster lookup speeds than DRAM memory chips, but at great cost, so DRAM is often used for this purpose. The benefit of DRAMs is smaller cost per bit of storage compared to SRAM chips. The router designer has to make a call between speed and size to keep the cost competitive and is always looking for tradeoffs like this.

Luckily, the forwarding plane does not need all of the administrative information in the routing table. All it needs to know is the IP address prefix and a list of next-hop interfaces. The route processor typically extracts the forwarding table out of the routing table. The route processor generates the Route Processor Forwarding Information Base (RP-FIB) and downloads a copy to the forwarding plane. The forwarding plane uses the matching Forwarding Information Base (FPFIB) for traffic lookups and sends packets to the corresponding interface.

2.3.1 *Forwarding Plane Architectures*

The forwarding plane is the workhorse of the router. It has to match prefixes against the forwarding table and try to find the best matching route at a rate of millions of lookups per second both in the steady state of typical loads, and under transient, heavy load conditions. From a forwarding plane perspective the Internet is an absolutely hostile environment. Why? Because the forwarding tables of the core routers are under constant flux. The typical background noise of routing updates on the Internet is about 1 to 5 updates *per second*. Many times this information results in a change to the forwarding table as well. An ideal forwarding plane architecture implements a new forwarding state with zero delay and has no traffic impact to other, unaffected prefixes. Therefore, a new next-hop is effective immediately in the forwarding ASICs. In reality, however, there are some pieces of software in between that delay these RIB to FIB updates.

The relationship between RIB and FIB is a key to understanding modern router operation. These tables must be coordinated for correct router functioning. The next section presents a naïve implementation of how the RIB to FIB state inside a router is propagated, but no real router implementation does it this way. Then some refinements are added to the basic procedure, which results in what is considered as the state-of-the-art forwarding plane implementation.

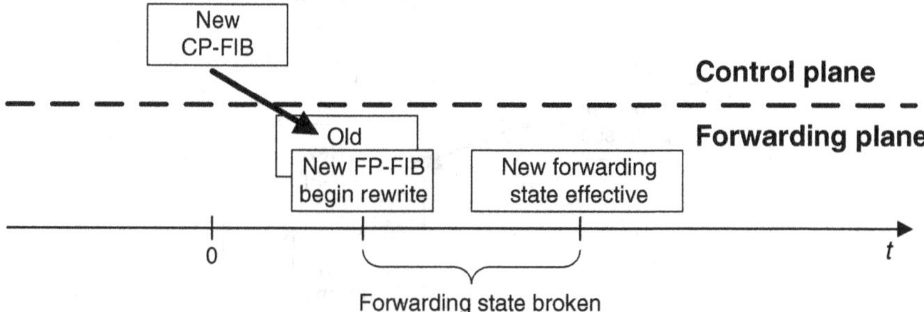

FIGURE 2.5. There are transient stages during the update of an entire FIB, which would cause a bogus forwarding table state

2.3.1.1 Naïve Implementation of RIB to FIB Propagation

Figure 2.5 shows the timing of events that occur once a better route to a destination IP prefix is found. First of all, the routing protocols perform a tie-break to find the new "best" route, then the reduction of the RIB-local table information has to be performed. The RIB-local table, which is about 20–30 MB, needs to get reduced to the 1–2 MB FIB table size. Next, the FIB needs to be downloaded to the forwarding plane, which then reprograms the forwarding tables of the ASICs. Because of this time lag, the overall convergence time on the network is impacted. Much worse, if the old FIB is being overwritten with the new FIB, the traffic typically does not stop flowing. So it might happen that the traffic is forwarded based on an outdated FIB. Now, the old FIB was consistent and the new FIB is also consistent – however, for the transient period when the old FIB is being overwritten, an incorrect bogus forwarding state may occur.

2.3.1.2 Improved Implementation of RIB to FIB Propagation

There are three ways to fix the incorrect transient FIB stages that may occur during rewrites of the FIB.

1. *Stopping (and buffering) the inbound interfaces.* If the router has dedicated lookup engines at the input side it may simply turn off the respective inbound interface or buffer inbound traffic for a short period of time. If there is no traffic to look up, there is also no incorrect transient stage that may harm forwarded traffic. The downside of this method is that other interfaces may be affected. In most router architectures several input interfaces share a route-lookup processor. Therefore all input interfaces that share a common route-lookup processor need to be turned off. If the update rate is high enough, for instance, from rerouting large trunks, which results in many prefixes pointing to new next-hop interfaces, this approach could easily paralyze the box.
2. *Paging between FIBs.* Paging is a quite effective way of avoiding any kind of transient stage. The idea is simple: double the amount of lookup memory and divide it into two halves, one called Page #1 and the other Page #2. Figure 2.6 shows the basic paging principle. The lookup processor uses Page #1 and Page #2 is used to hold the new FIB table. Once the FIB update is complete the lookup processor swaps pages, which is

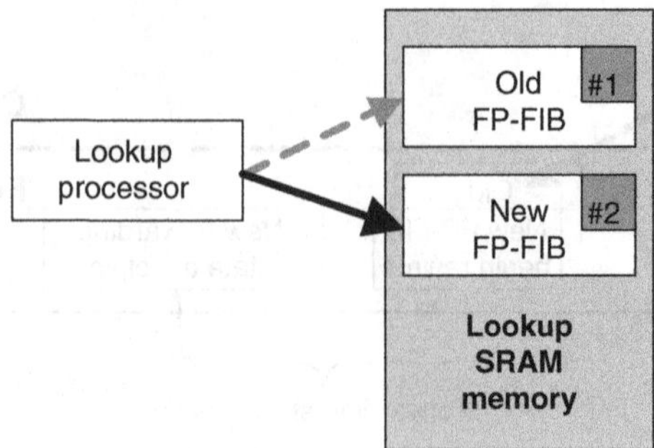

FIGURE 2.6. Page swapping is an old but still effective way of presenting always-consistent FIB structures to the lookup system

typically a single write operation, into a register on the lookup ASIC. While this fix completely avoids the transient problem it can be very expensive since it requires doubling the size of memory. And most implementations that use paging still suffer from the problem of FIB regeneration. Reducing approximately 30 MB of control information down to 1–2 MB of forwarding table up to 5 times per second has still a large impact on the CPU. The next approach completely avoids this huge processing load.

3. *Update-friendly FIB table structures:* One of the classic problems of computer science is the *speed vs. size* problem. For Internet routing tables there are known algorithms to compress the overall table size down to 150–200 KB of memory and thus optimizing the lookup operation. However, applying slight changes to those forwarding structures is an elaborate operation because in most cases the entire forwarding table needs to be rebuilt. Table space-reducing algorithms have long run-times and do not consider the time it takes to compute a newer generation of the table. It is nice that the full Internet routing table can be compressed down to 150 KB, however, if the actual calculation takes several seconds (a long time for the Internet) on Pentium 3 class microprocessors, another problem is introduced. The router might have to process every BGP update 200 milliseconds (ms), or 5 times per second. So if an algorithm (for example) has a run-time of 200 ms it is 100 per cent busy all the time. The *atomic FIB table* structure, introduced to address this situation, has an important property: it is neither designed for minimal size nor is it designed for optimal lookup speed. Atomic FIB table structures are optimized for a completely different property, which is called *update-friendliness*. *Atomic* is a term borrowed from the SQL database language and addresses the same issue in database structures. For example, in an SQL database, if a user is updating a price list, they are facing exactly the same problem: there could be several other processes accessing portions of the same database record that is trying to be updated. You can either put a lock on the database record (the counterpart of stopping the interfaces) or arrange your database structure in a way that a single write operation cannot corrupt your database. Each write process now leaves the database in a consistent state, and such behaviour is called an *atomic update*. The same technique can be applied to forwarding tables as well. If a FIB has to be updated, it can be done on-the-fly without disrupting or harming any transit traffic. Figure 2.7 shows

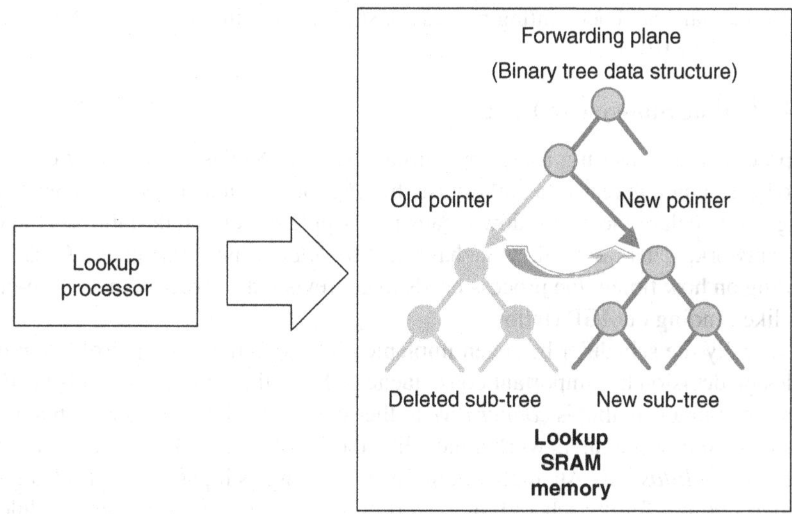

FIGURE 2.7. An atomic update of a routing table sub-tree does not harm any transit traffic

how an entire branch of new routing information is first stored in the lookup SRAM, and then a new sub-tree is built up. This operation does not harm any transit traffic lookups at all, because the new sub-tree is not yet linked to the old tree. A final write operation switches a single pointer between the old sub-tree and the new sub-tree.

Not all of these three approaches are mutually exclusive. In later examples of real routers, it will be shown that sometimes more than one of these techniques is used in order to speed up RIB to FIB convergence.

It is clear from this forwarding plane discussion that updating even simple data structures like forwarding tables on-the-fly, particularly on routers that have to carry full Internet routes, is not an easy task and requires careful system design. Similar diligence is necessary when writing software for the control plane, or routing engine, and the next section considers these architectures.

2.3.2 *Control Plane Architectures*

Control plane software suffers from similar problems first encountered on first-generation routers implemented on general purpose routing platforms. There are several sub-systems that compete for CPU and memory resources. In first-generation routers the forwarding sub-system always hogged CPU cycles. Partitioning the system into a forwarding plane and control plane avoided the packet processing stress placed on the routing protocols. However, a modern control plane has to do more than just run a single instance of a routing protocol. It usually also has to run a variety of software modules like:

- Several instances of the command line interface (CLI)
- Several instances of multiple routing protocols including OSPF, IS-IS and BGP
- Several instances of MPLS-related signalling protocols like RSVP and LDP

- Several instances of accounting processes, such as the Simple Network Management Protocol (SNMP) stack

2.3.2.1 Routing Sub-system Design

Each process that runs on a router operating system (OS) has *time-critical* events that need to be executed in real-time, otherwise the neighbour routers might miss one "Hello" message and declare the router down, causing a ripple effect that destabilizes the entire router network. Therefore, all OSs have a *scheduler* which dispatches CPU cycles depending on how timely the process needs to get revisited in order to meet time-critical events like sending out IGP Hellos.

Historically the scheduler has been implemented *inside* the routing protocol module. That design decision has important consequences. First, the routing protocols need to be implemented in a way that is *cooperative* to the scheduler. Figure 2.8 shows that routing software and their schedulers work almost like the old Windows 3.11, offering a form of *cooperative multitasking*. An application can run as long as it passes control back to the scheduler. In order for the scheduling to work it has to *cooperate* with the scheduler and try not to run too long. Often the routing protocols processes need to be *sliced* and run a piece at a time in order to meet timing constraints.

On busy boxes sometimes the individual sub-processes do not return control in time back to the scheduler, which causes the following well-known message logs. In the case of a sub-process not returning control in a timely manner to the scheduler, Cisco Systems routers would log a CPU-HOG message like the following:

IOS logging output

```
Aug 7 01:24:07.651: %SYS-3-CPUHOG: Task ran for 7688msec (126/40),
process = ISIS Router, PC = 32804A8.
```

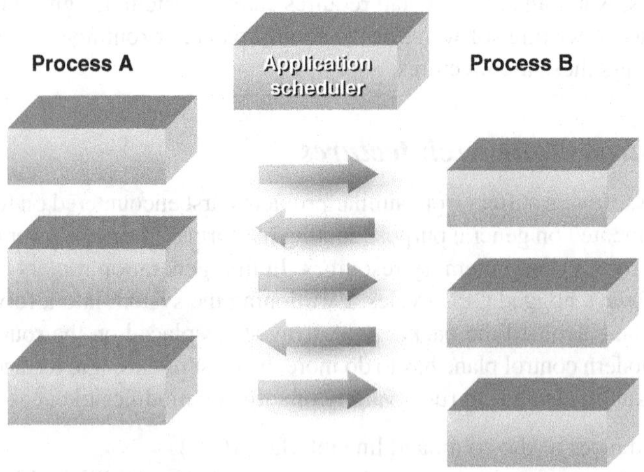

FIGURE 2.8. Per-application scheduling requires that the routing software is written in a cooperative way

A similar message type exists for Juniper Networks routers where the sub-processes cannot be revisited in time. The Routing Protocol Daemon (RPD) logs an `RPD-SCHEDULER-SLIP` message to its local logging facility:

JUNOS logging output

```
Aug 7 03:19:07 rpd[201]: task_monitor_slip: 4s scheduler slip
```

Special code adjustments need to be taken to avoid CPU-HOGS and scheduler slips. The routing code constantly needs to sanity check itself to make sure it is not using too many resources and so harming other sub-processes in the system that may be more critical, like sending OSPF or IS-IS Hellos. In the *carrier-class* routing code expected by large ISPs, a lot of the code base just deals with *timing* and avoiding all sorts of what are called *race conditions*, which adds a lot of complexity to the code.

Today the majority of operating systems like Windows NT/2000/XP, Linux, or FreeBSD do their scheduling in the *kernel* and not in the application. Writing application scheduler cooperative code turned out to be a daunting task which was not sustainable over time. Contrary to the application scheduler of the routing protocol subsystem, the kernel scheduler works as illustrated in Figure 2.9. Here the application (the routing protocol) does not need to be written in a cooperative way. The kernel scheduler interrupts (or *pre-empts*) running processes and makes sure that every process is receiving its fair share of CPU cycles.

Unfortunately, the hard pre-emption of kernel schedulers also has some dangers: IP routing protocols are very dependent on each other and need to share a large amount of data. IS-IS, for instance, needs to share its routing information with BGP so BGP can make optimal route decisions, RSVP path computation is dependent on the Traffic Engineering Database (TED), which is filled with IS-IS topology data, and so on. The most efficient way of sharing large amounts of data is with a shared memory design to share these data structures. The combination of shared data structures with pre-emptive kernel scheduling may result in transient data corruption. Figure 2.10 illustrates this. IS-IS changes a prefix in the routing table, during the write operation IS-IS gets pre-empted by the BGP process, which needs to package and send a BGP update. The BGP process

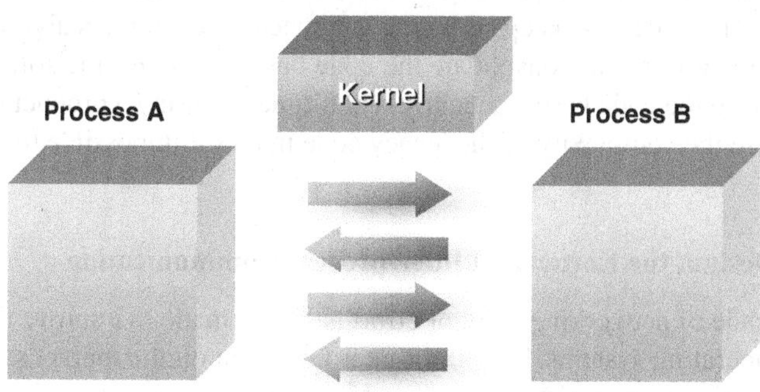

FIGURE 2.9. Kernel schedulers do not require the application to cooperate for scheduling

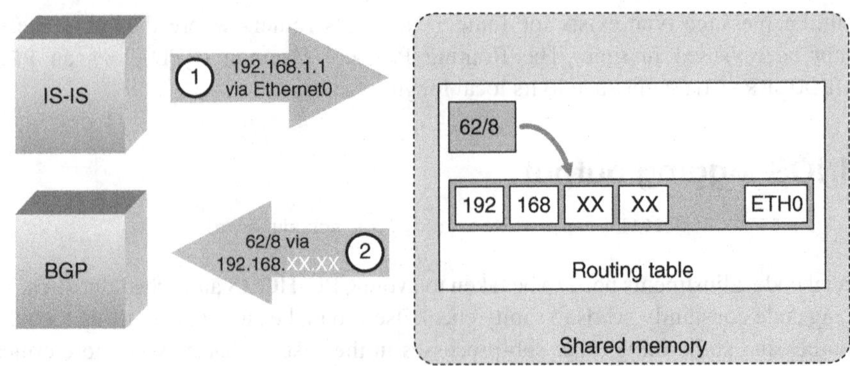

FIGURE 2.10. If a process gets pre-empted during a write operation data may get corrupted

reads the incomplete prefix and, given how the memory was initialized at that time, advertises bad information to other BGP routers. The scary thing for troubleshooting is that the data corruption only lasts for a couple of milliseconds. As soon as the scheduler passes control back to IS-IS, the full prefix will be written to the routing table. It would take complicated measures to ensure that the data gets locked during write operations to overcome these sort of issues, which are quite common.

Most routing software deployed on the Internet still runs based on cooperative schedulers. Why is such seeming anachronism still present? The clean-sheet design, of course, would be where a big "all protocols" routing process is partitioned into individual subprocesses. Each routing protocol instance would run in a dedicated process. Scheduling between the routing modules would be purely pre-emptive and there would also need to be a means of efficient data sharing, while still avoiding all sorts of data corruption through use of sophisticated locking schemes or the use of clever APIs.

To be fair to router vendors, at the time when the first implementations of routers were built there were almost no solid implementations of real-time kernels available on the open market. So the engineers simply had to be pragmatic and code a scheduler for themselves. But this history lesson has shown that *pragmatism* can easily turn into *legacy* if care is not taken, and legacy systems can be hard or almost impossible to change or fix. So most routing software still suffer from custom schedulers that run inside of the routing protocols. The code base keeps growing, and because customers always ask for new features, there is no time to consolidate the code base and revise the software architecture. Not revising the code base frequently will ultimately bring a product to the point of no return where the complexity of the legacy code makes it impossible to further extend functionality.

2.3.2.2 OS Design, the Kernel and Inter-process Communication

In the last decade of networking, a lot of effort has been made to improve the overall stability of the operating systems. The first router OSs seen on the market started out with CPUs that did not support *virtual memory*. Virtual memory is a technique that assigns each process a private chunk of the system's memory. With this approach, if Process #1 tries to access Process #2's memory, then Process #1 is immediately terminated. Why then is virtual memory today imperative? Virtual memory greatly enhances the overall system stability by limiting local damage.

No matter how much time and resources put into testing efforts, there will be always some bugs that are only unveiled in a production environment. So there is some residual risk that certain processes will crash. What virtual memory helps is to mitigate the *impact* that a crashed piece of software has to the overall system. In early router OSs, for example, a tiny bug in relatively unimportant parts of the system, like the CLI, could overwrite another process's BGP neighbor tables. The result would be incorrect advertisements and incorrect processing of incoming data that might cause not only the entire router to crash, but also affect other routers as incorrect information is propagated in turn and ripples through the network to crash other routers.

Modern control plane software typically consists of 1–2 millions line of code, which leaves plenty of room for lots of bugs. A software design technique called *graceful degradation* is becoming more important for distributed systems like router networks. The basic idea is that a big piece of software is broken down in small atomic modules. – To provide isolation each module gets its own process and virtual-memory. However, sometimes processes need to share data being held by another process. For example, listing a neighboring router's route advertisements requires the CLI to ask the BGP process what routes it received from neighbors. All the processes need to use a common exchange mechanism like a message-passing API in order to interact with each other. The message-passing API is one of the things that each modern kernel offers to its processes. The kernel itself is the root of the operating system. It starts and stops processes and passes messages along between processes.

Figure 2.11 shows an example of a message-passing atomic-module system. The kernel offers a generalized, uniform messaging system for interaction and thereby provides unmatched stability. Do not be misled: the kernel does not stop individual processes from *crashing*. But it does help limit the *impact* of the crashed piece of software on *other* processes in the same system. After a process dies, the kernels watchdog waits a couple of seconds and restarts the broken software again. It is common practice to write a log entry into the system's log that a process has been crashed and restarted, ultimately alerting the Network Operation Center (NOC) to the problem.

The advantage is clear: a single network incident like, for example, a bug in IGP Adjacency Managements crashes only one Adjacency and does not take out the entire router for 2–3 minutes to complete a reboot.

No of the two Vendors implementation discussed in this book encompasses the idea of atomic modules communicating through the kernel. The main argument of the proponents of monolithic software is that the amount of data sharing that is required for example in the routing subsystem will overload the inter-process communication system of the kernel. The traditional vehicle is to share memory between modules inside a process. The disadvantage here is full fate-sharing: If there is a single software problem in the process the entire process will crash and render the router control-plane unusable for minutes.

However it remains to be seen if the atomic modules and massive inter-process communication model can perform at a similar performance level than today's shared-memory

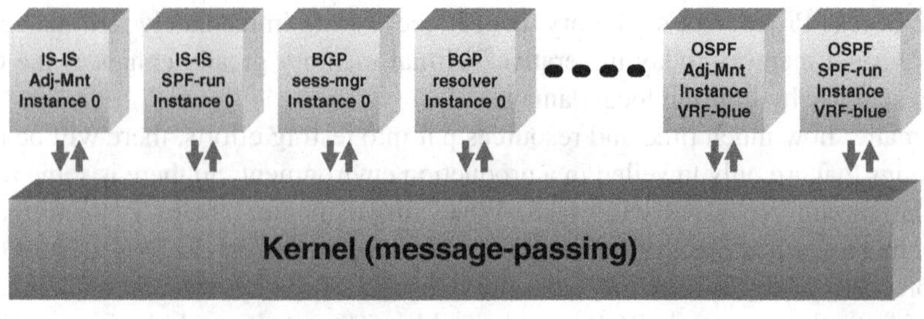

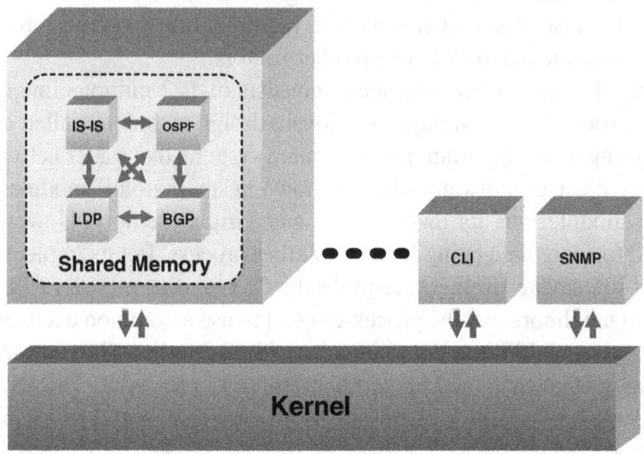

FIGURE 2.11. Modern OSs offer a message-passing API for processes to communicate to each other

model. If atomic-modules get close to par they are the next logical step to evolve router control plane software.

In summary, proper partitioning of the control plane software helps prevent local bugs from spreading to a system-wide crisis. Virtual memory shields the processes and their associated memory from each other. In order to exchange information between processes, the kernel offers a message-passing API. Once again, scaling by partitioning has helped to solve the problem of OS instability.

2.4 Router Technology Examples

Building routers is a complicated and daunting task. There are probably only a few dozen people in the industry that *really* know how to architect and design a modern router, because of the inherent complexity. A lot of the insight on how to build routers that scale was gathered by actually deploying premature implementations of software and using the feedback that the deployment experience provided into the design of next-generation routers. In the next few sections, popular router models and their design concepts will be outlined.

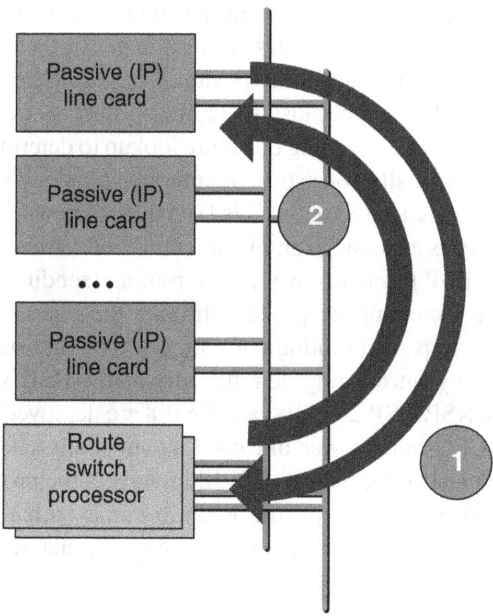

FIGURE 2.12. The first generation Interface Processor (IP) Cards did not embed route-lookup functionality. All the traffic has been passed via the Route Switch Processor (RSP).

2.4.1 *Cisco 7500 Series*

The Cisco 7500 series of router was the most successful router ever built for Internet core applications. Figure 2.12 shows the overall structure of the box. Basically, it is a redundant shared bus system with one element dual-homed to both buses. The shared buses have different speeds, depending on the revision level. Bus speeds range from the CxBus (533 Mbit/s half-duplex) to the CyBus (1.2 Gbit/s half-duplex) and finally the CzBus (2.5 Gbit/s half-duplex).

The Route Switch Processor (RSP) has to run both the routing software and also needs to switch packets. The first-generation interface cards are called *Interface Processors* and are from Network-Layer viewpoint purely passive devices. The IPs perform Layer-1 (Physical Layer) and Layer-2 (MAC Layer) related tasks like verifying CRC checksums, SONET messaging or ATM SAR functions. If a packet enters the box, an interrupt is signalled to the RSP. The RSP fetches the packet and does a route-lookup to find the corresponding outbound interface. All relevant modifications to the IP header, such as TTL decrementing and recalculating the IP header's checksum, are done by the RSP. Then the packet is copied to the outgoing interface where it ultimately leaves the chassis.

The RSP forwarding module needs to have efficient route-lookup structures in order to spend minimum lookup times before making forwarding decisions. The forwarding information base (FIB) is known to Cisco Systems as the Cisco Express Forwarding (CEF) Table. In Figure 2.13 there are two examples of how the lookup for IP address 4.6.2.1 traverses the CEF Table. The basic structure is a 256-way 4-level structure called an M-tree. The four levels are located at the /8, /16, /24 and /32 prefix boundaries. Each node contains 256 pointers to other nodes farther down the hierarchy. Each node also contains a flag that tells the lookup process to terminate. In the illustration, this flag is shown as a black dot. For example, for the IP address 192.158.253.244, the lookup stops after the third memory reference because there are no further specific routes available. Finally, the lookup process ends by doing one more lookup to determine the outgoing next-hop information, which typically consists of an interface plus Layer-2 encapsulation data such as MAC addresses. To Cisco Systems, this last table is known as the *Adjacency Table*.

The Cisco 7500 router is a classic example of a mid-1990s router that has a monolithic architecture where the RSP has to do two things: routing (sending and receiving routing updates) and switching (moving the packets through the chassis). In busy boxes, the switching load severely impacted routing convergence time and stability. Cisco Systems addressed the problem by introducing new flavours of the RSP, which had more CPU horsepower. Today the RSP, RSP-2, RSP-4 and RSP-8 are deployed in the field. However, just putting in more CPU horsepower did not fundamentally address the architectural problems – they were masked for the next 12–18 months in the product lifecycle.

The problem of high CPU load on the RSPs became increasingly severe as ISPs wanted to sell premium services like Class of Service (CoS)-enabled or security-tightened

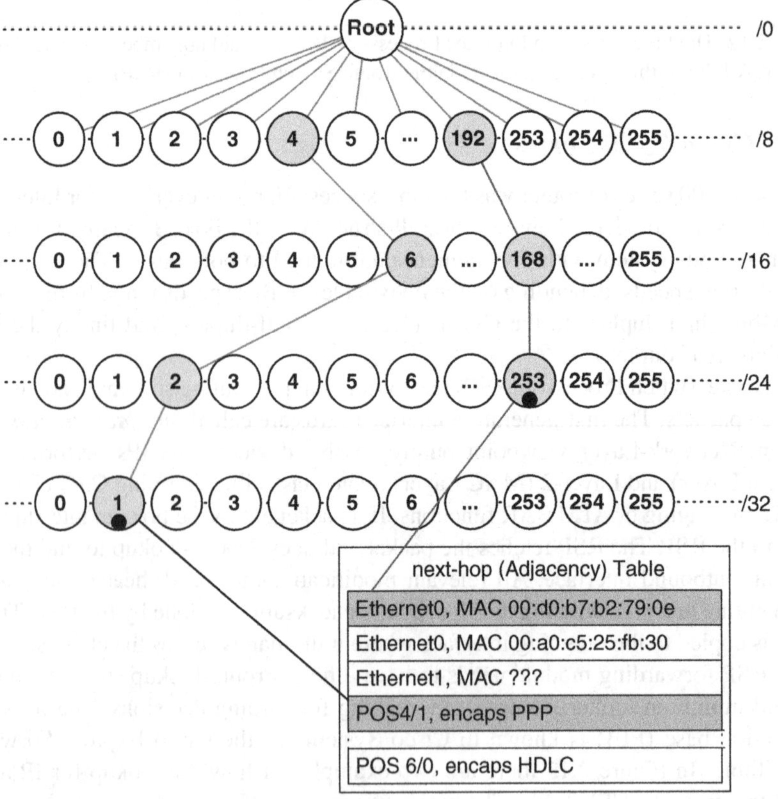

FIGURE 2.13. The Cisco Express Forwarding (CEF) Table ensures minimum route-lookup times by only four memory references

networks. Doing additional classification and firewalling work besides the plain-vanilla destination IP address route lookups resulted in decreased forwarding performance, in some cases down to several 10K pps. The 7500 architecture had to be extended to offload much of the switching decisions down to the interface level. With the next generation of Interface Ports, the *Versatile Interface Processor* (VIP) was born.

2.4.2 *Cisco 7500 Series + VIP Processors*

The VIP concept is an improvement to the passive line card architecture of the plain 7500 series. The slots of the routers are populated with VIP cards, which are essentially carrier cards that hold Port Adapters (PAs). The PAs perform similar low-level functions to the older IP line cards. The VIP adapter itself runs a custom, stripped down version of IOS that harbours mostly switching and classification functions in order to offload the RSP from switching the packets. The VIP architecture was a real step forward in improving switching performance and bus utilization. Using the old-style IP line cards, the bus was used twice, as shown in Figure 2.12: once for the IP to RSP transfer, and then for the RSP to IP transfer. Figure 2.14 shows that if the packet is transferred direct from one VIP to another, the bus is traversed only a single time.

The distributed VIP architecture revealed an interesting issue: how to replicate the FIB table to several line cards? As the route lookup was done in a distributed fashion, a piece of software needed to make sure that the local FIB gets replicated to all the VIP adapters in the system. Distributed CEF (dCEF) was developed to provide the proper care and feeding of VIP line cards. But deployment of dCEF in the field revealed a weakness in the way that FIB tables are built: the VIP card is a pure *switching* entity, and as such it

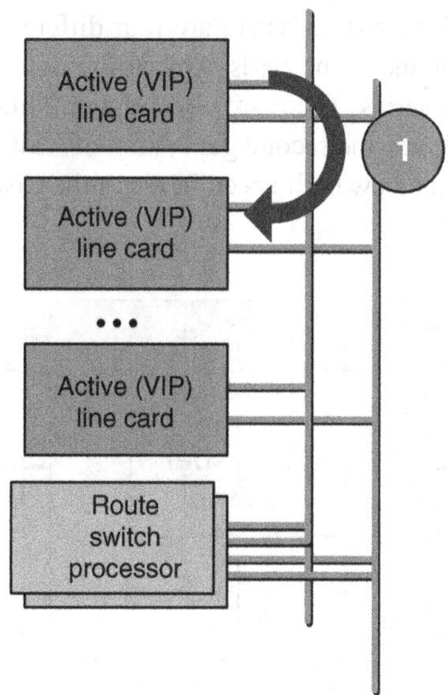

FIGURE 2.14. The Versatile Interface Processor transfers VIP to VIP traffic without Route Switch Processor intervention

also needs a piece of software that calculates the FIB based on the RIB. During transient conditions when, for example, a large part of Internet traffic is rerouted, FIB computation turns out to be a fairly expensive task. The VIP card does local switching and the RSP performs control plane functionality, *plus* building the FIBs on behalf of the VIP adapters. And that is exactly the weak point of the architecture, because the RSP still needs to do too much work that would be done better at the VIP card level. There is no true decoupling of forwarding and control functions here. For better stability, it probably would have been a better design choice to replicate the local RIB to the VIP cards and let them do the FIB generation.

Around the same time, it became apparent that the enormous growth of the Internet was outpacing advances in bus speeds. So the 7500s, which had once been the core routers, moved to the edge and began performing customer traffic and route aggregation functions. The concept of the shared bus had to be replaced by a true fabric enabling line card speeds beyond OC-12/STM-4 speeds of 622 Mbps, which is still the architectural limit of the 7500 + VIP series. It was clear that changing the heart of the router, which is the fabric, leads to a change of the line-cards, the VIPs and the PAs. Essentially a whole new router needed to be designed.

2.4.3 *Cisco GSR Series*

The Cisco 12000 Series, sometimes referred to as the Gigabit Switch Router (GSR), is basically a meshof high-speed VIPs that perform independent, local route and classification lookups. Figure 2.15 illustrates the concept in brief. The glue that holds these line cards together is a single-stage crossbar that provides up to 80 Gbit/s I/O bandwidth. The successor of the 12000 Series is the 12400, which offers an increased crossbar bandwidth of 320 Gbit/s. The route processor and the crossbar fabric are designed redundant. If one component breaks the other will take over. There are four different types of line cards for the GSR Series, starting with Engine-0 line cards, which offer only software processing like the VIP processors on the 7500 series. There are also Engine-2 line cards using custom ASIC hardware and Engine-3 cards are the second generation of ASIC hardware. Finally, Engine-4 line cards are targeted for the new high-speed fabric of the Cisco 12400 Series intended to

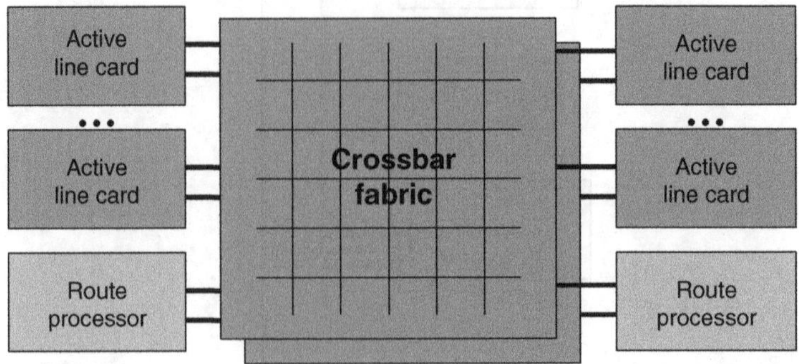

FIGURE 2.15. The GSR 12000 Series concept is a crossbar fabric surrounded by active line cards

accommodate ASIC-supported high-speed lookups on four port OC-48/STM-16 (about 2.4 Gbps) and single port OC-192/STM-64 (about 10 Gbps) line cards.

Although Cisco Systems has to support a variety of hardware platforms, they offer an easy-to-use uniform CLI across all platforms that enhance their popularity. The original plan was to have a single code-base across all platforms, known as the Internetworking Operating System (IOS).

2.4.4 *Cisco IOS Routing Software*

Unlike many other router operating systems, IOS is not based on any commercial real-time OS. IOS is a complete new development written by Greg Satz and Kirk Lougheed, early Cisco software engineers. There were some ideas inspired from TOPS-20, an ancient DEC operating system, but that was about it. The biggest issue with IOS today is its monolithic structure. IOS is not even a complete operating system in the sense of UNIX or Windows. IOS is more like a single program that runs on a dedicated piece of hardware. IOS does not include virtual memory protection, nor can new processes be added at runtime. The lack of virtual memory protection is the main reason why IOS crashes typically affect the entire machine and not just individual subsystems: there is just a *single program running* and no partitioning at all. There are no demarcation points, things like kernels, user processes and schedulers. IOS is just a single big program that is executed from startup to shutdown.

IOS is based on a 20-year-old concept, and its main weakness is this monolithic code structure. Until the runtime environment is changed, it will be hard if not impossible to re-engineer the system for future requirements, such as the carrier-class availability (known as "5 nines") that the public infrastructure needs and deserves. Because of the huge amount of code that needs to be carried from one product variation to the next, the best thing to do with IOS is probably to start from scratch.

This desire to change the monolithic router OS infrastructure and to develop a second-generation routing operating system was the genesis for newer companies like Juniper Networks. It will come as no surprise to learn that the initial engineers writing the JUNOS operating system were experienced engineers drafted from Cisco having the insight (gathered from direct experience) into which design pitfalls to avoid in order to build a stable, scalable router.

2.4.5 *Juniper Networks M-Series Routers*

Juniper Networks M-series routers were the first in the industry to offer a true decoupling of the forwarding plane and control plane. Figure 2.16 shows the Juniper Networks separation between Routing Engines (RE) and a Packet Forwarding Engine (PFE). The Routing Engine is an off-the-shelf Intel-based industry-standard PC platform with a very small form factor. The link between the RE and the PFE is a standard Fast Ethernet link that runs a proprietary protocol called the Trivial Network Protocol (TNP). TNP takes care of the proper care and feeding of the lookup and queuing ASICs, and also retrieves (for example) interface statistics from the chassis. TNP also provides a *tunnelled* mode where it carries packets sourced by the RE targeted for an interface (such as routing

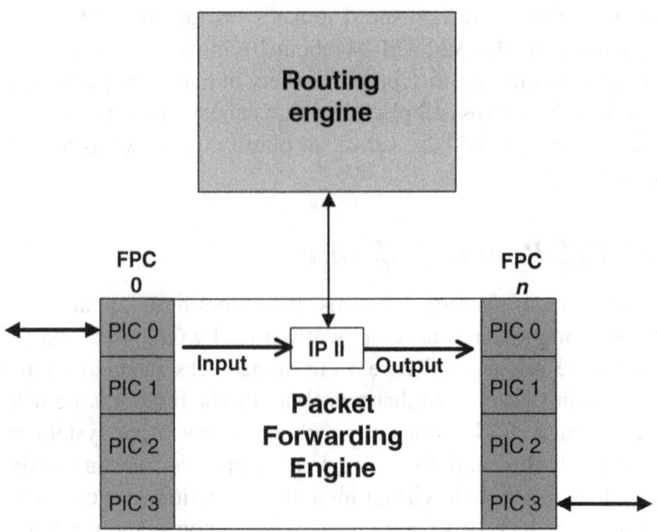

FIGURE 2.16. The M-Series encompasses a truly separated forwarding and control plane

protocol packets). The tunnel mode is necessary so that the RE can communicate with the outside world. It is worth noting that no matter what JUNOS feature is turned on, no transit traffic ever gets processed by the RE. The RE only needs to take care of control traffic. Additionally, all traffic from the PFE to the RE is rate-limited in order to protect the RE under all circumstances, even during denial-of-service attacks.

The PFE is a collection of custom ASICs interconnected by a distributed, shared memory fabric. The line cards follow a similar physical approach to the VIP adapters of Cisco. There are Flexible PIC Concentrators (FPCs), which are carrier cards for the Physical Interface Cards (PICs). The PIC itself can be compared to a PA in the VIP architecture. Essentially, these are simple devices that just take care of proper physical framing, CRC checksumming and alarm generation (SONET/SDH PICs). But in contrast to the VIP architecture, the FPCs do *not* perform any route-lookup. The FPCs' ASICs only process a packet at Layer-2, strip all Layer-2 framing and then pass the packet to a central route lookup chip, the Internet Processor 2 (IP2). The IP2 can only do route lookups and packet filter lookups. Once a next-hop matching any field in the IP header (typically, but not always, only the destination IP address) is found, the outbound FPC fetches, queues and finally transmits the packet to the PIC. The PIC again performs only Layer-1 related functions like checksumming and so on. The IP2 FIB table structure has been optimized for update friendliness. In fact, a change in next-hop under full load does not cause a single packet to drop! The FIB table size is 16 MB, providing room for about 1100K routes, many times more than the Internet could need for years to come.

Feature-rich lookup, classification hardware, and a clear architectural avoidance of transit traffic on the RE is the foundation for the elusive goal of true separation of the forwarding plane and the control plane.

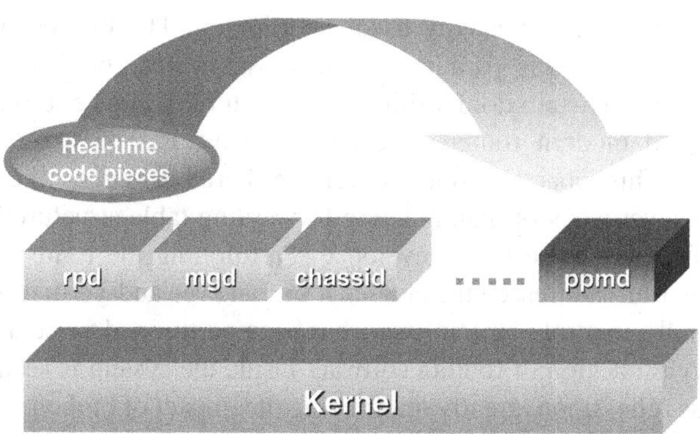

FIGURE 2.17. JUNOS software is partitioned across many user level processes

2.4.6 *JUNOS Routing Software*

The JUNOS operating system is built around a FreeBSD 4.2-STABLE UNIX operating system. The kernel is different to the usual FreeBSD kernel. Special care has been taken to ensure scalability and the kernel is modified to support multiple routing tables, millions of routes and thousands of interfaces. Because UNIX offers full virtual memory protection, the system is split up in many different user processes, as illustrated in Figure 2.17. The routing code is still bundled in a single process for all the routing protocols across all routing instances, so the issue of scheduling is still present. If a large wave of BGP updates hits the system, it is possible to miss sending IGP Hellos. But the UNIX-based package also provides a way around this issue. There is a dedicated daemon (server process) in JUNOS called the Periodic Packet Management Daemon (PPMD). The IGPs register with PPMD, which sends out the IGP Hellos on their behalf. PPMD completely offloads Hello processing from the RPD, and the RPD does not need to handle periodic Hellos at all. The RPD is notified by PPMD if an important event like an adjacency expiration occurs. PPMD runs with the highest scheduling priority in the system and may pre-empt any process to make sure that every IGP Hello is delivered in time.

In summary, JUNOS is a true example of a second-generation router operating System. Many lessons learned from deployment experience with Cisco IOS have been incorporated into the software. The software is modular in order to overcome the fate-sharing problems in monolithic designs. At the time of writing, the number of active processes in a functioning router was 37, an extraordinary number. Partitioning the code carefully ensures that each single subsystem becomes maintainable and protects the overall system from avalanche effects caused by local bugs.

2.5 Conclusion

The evolution of the Internet is so fast that it is difficult for core routers to keep up. Both forwarding user traffic and processing control traffic in a network that doubles in speed and size every nine months is a daunting task. To tackle the problem of scaling, one common technique is repeatedly used: partitioning. The first occurrence of partitioning is the Internet routing paradigm itself. Hosts need to perform more dissimilar functions than routers have to do. Partitioning is the tool of choice to scale router scalability problems. In modern routers, the control plane has been separated from the forwarding plane. This separation does not rely on shared resources like CPU cycles and memory. Next, clever ways of manipulating forwarding table structures while forwarding traffic at full speed have been developed. Partitioning the route lookup and table maintenance functions addressed the challenges of an ever-and-yet-never-quite converging Internet. Finally, control plane software has been partitioned twice. First, the interaction and memory protection of routing software inside the system is secured via a kernel that each process relies upon, greatly minimizing the impact of broken software. Second, the routing protocols are split up into a real-time component and a non-real-time component, further improving convergence time granularity as well as removing a lot of complexity from the routing code.

All in all, partitioning is the prevailing scaling method that helps to scale the Internet and its building block, the router.

3

Introduction to the IOS and JUNOS Command Line Interface

In the router world, ISPs and carriers got used to the fact that routers are configured and managed using an ASCII-based command line interface. Even if this seems scary the first time, especially when used to fancy graphical user interfaces (GUI), command line interfaces give unmatched control over the router and provide a powerful troubleshooting tool.

The Internet is a network that is constantly under flux – somebody somewhere is always changing something. Moreover, new protocol standards evolve, new releases of routing software are deployed, peering policy may change as a result of business constraints or acquisitions, and so on. All this makes for a challenging environment that, at least not up to now, could be modelled in the form of a GUI. In this chapter we will give a basic overview of how to interact with this kind of interface. You will learn in this chapter how to upload a new configuration, how to query IS-IS related status and finally how to troubleshoot and debug adjacency formation and link-state databases.

3.1 Common Properties of Command Line Interfaces (CLI)

When Cisco Systems shipped it first product called "ISH" back in 1986, no one imagined that the company would be redefining how operators interacted with routers for the next two decades. At first sight a command line interface might look primitive; however, there are important aspects and elements that helped the company achieve its breathtaking success. There are many theories about why Cisco Systems got to where they are in the industry today. From a technical viewpoint, two key properties helped people feel comfortable with the Cisco router's interface. The first is that after changing the router's configuration, everything was written into a single file that is kept in the Non-Volatile RAM (NVRAM) of the router. Virtually everything that the router does, for example running routing protocols, performing access control, or using static routes, is controlled by this single file. The second important aspect is that the router's configuration file was an ASCII file and is therefore human-readable. Unlike other router companies who stored their configuration file in binary form, the IOS configuration files could be read out on the fly and everybody understood exactly what the router was supposed to do.

There are two other main advantages of single ASCII configuration files. First, support gets easier. It is a matter of fact that a large fraction of support calls are configuration related. An ASCII configuration file enabled operators to simply copy and paste their router configuration into an email when requesting support. The Technical Assistance Centre (TAC) could then very quickly see if this was a configuration issue or if the software had a bug and further analysis of the problem was required. There are even those in the industry who argue that ASCII-based configuration files make the support organization scale more effectively and work most efficiently.

The second main advantage is that customers did not need to have a live router to generate configuration files. If the router's configuration was stored in binary form, there is no opportunity for a third-party application or a "quick-hack" script to generate a valid configuration file. Router configurations that could be generated by standard UNIX tools like SED, AWK and PERL were a first-generation way of eventually making a provisioning API available for configuration robot tools.

Perhaps Proteon (an ancient router vendor from the 1980s) had an interface that provides the best example of how *not* to do router configuration:

- Configuration was purely done using menus that never showed you where you were in the configuration statement hierarchy.
- Configuration and show commands had a totally different look and feel (for those who are familiar with this, just recall the jumping between T5 and T6 command shells).
- Everything was stored in a binary file.
- There was no possibility to employ external provisioning tools.

Cisco overtook Proteon in the market at the end of 1980s for various reasons. But one reason was definitely the odd command line interface of Proteon routers. Not that a sound CLI automatically paves the way for success in the router industry, but it clearly does help.

The two ASCII-based command line interfaces of IOS and JUNOS are similar to each other in some respects, and different in others. The following sections highlight these *common* elements. Then the differences between IOS and JUNOS (and also the intended improvements JUNOS made to IOS) will be discussed as well.

Routers are typically accessed in three ways:

- RS232 serial console
- In-band access via telnet or Secure Shell (SSH)
- Out-of-band access via telnet or SSH.

Once you have logged on the router, there are two general modes of talking to the router. The first one is called the *operational* mode. This mode is mainly used to explore what the router and its environment are doing, what routes are being installed in the system and if interfaces are carrying traffic. The other mode is the *configuration* mode. In the *configuration* mode the router's *behaviour* is controlled, for example, what IP address does it have, what routing protocols parameters are used, who can access the router or network, and so on.

3.1.1 *Operational Mode*

Once you log into a router you usually find yourself in operational mode. The trailing ">" sign indicates that you are working in operational mode. In JUNOS the prompt looks like this:

```
hannes@New-York>
```

And for IOS, the prompt would look like this:

```
London>
```

What you will always see is the *hostname* (the name of the router) followed by the ">" sign. In JUNOS you also see the username followed by the "@" sign before the hostname. Now you can issue commands to the router. The commands are organized in a hierarchical fashion as shown in Figure 3.1. The more arguments a command has, the more specific the command gets. For instance, a `show isis database London` just shows a single link-state database (LSDB) entry, while `show isis database` shows all LSDB entries.

```
hannes@Frankfurt> show isis database London
IS-IS level 2 link-state database:
LSP ID                      Sequence     Checksum     Lifetime     Attributes
London.00-00                0x1af        0xa977       25314        L1      L2
1 LSPs

hannes@Frankfurt> show isis database
IS-IS level 1 link-state database:

IS-IS level 2 link-state database:
LSP ID                      Sequence     Checksum     Lifetime     Attributes
London.00-00                0x1af        0xa977           25314 L1 L2
Amsterdam.00-00             0x1a7        0x3dd0           31088 L1 L2
New-York.00-00              0x1a2        0x16f5           46510 L1 L2
Penssauken.00-00            0x19a        0x3ec             5184 L1 L2
408 LSPs
```

The arguments for a command are separated by a simple blank. Sometimes the router has too few arguments and this forms an unambiguous command. Typically, routers complain about an ambiguous command with a prompt:

```
hannes@Frankfurt> show isis

syntax error, expecting <command>.
```

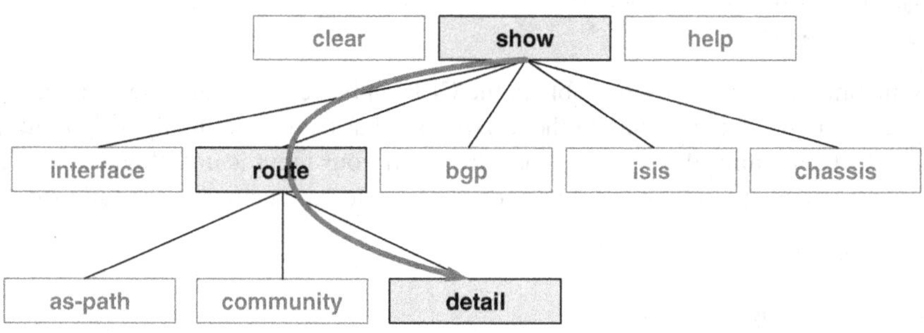

FIGURE 3.1. The command line space is organized in a hierarchical fashion

This is from a router running JUNOS and

```
Munich>show isis
% Incomplete command.
```

is from an IOS-based router. However, there is an easy way to discover what kinds of commands the router gives you: context-sensitive help.

3.1.1.1 Context-sensitive Help

At any time, you can enter a question mark (?) at the user prompt, which makes the CLI display all the options that are available at this point in the command-line hierarchy:

```
hannes@Frankfurt> show isis ?
Possible completions:
  adjacency          Show the IS-IS adjacency database
  database           Show the IS-IS link-state database
  hostname           Show IS-IS hostname database
  interface          Show IS-IS interface information
  route              Show the IS-IS routing table
  spf                Show information about IS-IS SPF calculations
  statistics         Show IS-IS performance statistics
```

You will see the keywords that are available, plus a brief descriptive text about what kind of information is displayed by the respective option.

If the question mark is keyed in the middle of an argument, the CLI shows you what valid completions are still left. Note above that there are two keywords after `show isis` starting with the letter "S". The keywords "spf" and "statistics" both start with the same letter. What you can do is issue a `show isis s` command and then type the question mark:

```
hannes@Frankfurt> show isis s?
Possible completions:
  spf                Show information about IS-IS SPF calculations
  statistics         Show IS-IS performance statistics
```

The router shows you the two possible completions. If there are no valid completions then the router simply responds with:

```
hannes@Frankfurt > show isis j?
No valid completions
```

Sometimes the keywords available in the CLI can be very long and the command line interfaces often offer shortcuts to the keywords. That is, it is not really a shortcut, it is more that the command line parser looks to see if your input is unambiguous and then accepts the keyword. So the commands do not have to be specified to the full extent:

```
London> sh is d
```

produces the same output as:

```
London> show isis database
```

3.1.1.2 Auto-complete

Sometimes these shortcuts are also known as *auto-complete* functionality. It is not quite the same thing, however. What auto-complete means is that you can press the <TAB> key every time you want to check if you have supplied enough characters for a keyword so the command is unambiguous. For example, if you enter:

```
London> show i<TAB>
```

then you get:

```
London> show i
```

In other words, nothing happens if the letters supplied are ambiguous. However, if you supply enough letters like:

```
London> show is<TAB>
```

then you get:

```
London> show isis
```

Auto-complete proved to be a powerful tool for experienced users quickly needing output, for instance, when troubleshooting a network problem.

The second major mode of router CLI operation is the configuration mode that controls the router's behaviour.

3.1.2 *Configuration Mode*

You can switch from the operational mode to the configuration mode by issuing commands like `configure` or `configure terminal`. On JUNOS routers you see that you are now in configuration mode because the prompt has been changed from ">" to "#"

```
hannes@New-York> configure
Entering configuration mode
[edit]
hannes@New-York#
```

You also can see that you are in the configuration mode because each time you press the <ENTER> key your prompt is prepended by [EDIT], which always indicates that you are in the configuration mode.

On IOS platforms you cannot get directly to configuration mode. You first get into what is called the privileged `enable` mode.

```
London>enable
Password: *******
London#conf terminal
Enter configuration commands, one per line. End with CNTL/Z.
London(config)#
```

Just as in JUNOS there is the # indication in the prompt that tells you that you are in configuration mode. You also see the `config` keyword in parentheses after the router's hostname and the prompt.

The configuration mode CLI also has a hierarchy, as described in the operational mode, for show commands. The prompt again indicates what part of the hierarchy the operator is configuring. For example, if you want to configure parameters that are related to the IS-IS subsystem, you specify simply `router isis` and then the system puts you in the router isis context.

```
London#conf t
Enter configuration commands, one per line. End with CNTL/Z.
London(config)#router isis
London(config-router)#
```

You see that you are working in a different context because the prompt changes. A similar thing happens to the prompt in JUNOS command line interfaces:

```
hannes@New-York> configure
Entering configuration mode
[edit]
hannes@New-York# edit protocols isis
[edit protocols isis]
hannes@New-York#
```

The information in the square brackets is called the editing context. A simple `[edit]` means that you are on the top-level of the configuration hierarchy. When you move around in the hierarchy using the `edit` command, the prompt changes accordingly.

3.1.3 *Emacs Style Keyboard Sequences*

There are people in the industry who believe that the UNIX Emacs editor is a *problem* itself; there are others who believe it is a *solution* to all kind of problems. While the authors generally like the highly customizable nature of what is probably the most powerful editor around, there are others who complain that it is hard to configure and make it do what you want . One thing about Emacs that is distinctive is the way that you move the cursor around on the screen. Emacs has certain key-combinations that can put the cursor at the beginning of a line or at the end of a line, and so on. Moving quickly around and editing a command really speeds up the way of talking to the router. Figure 3.2 shows the most commonly-used Emacs sequences. CTRL-A and CTRL-E for moving to the beginning or end of a line are the ones used most often. IOS and JUNOS both implement the Emacs keystroke sequences, and once you are used to it, it greatly speeds up administering the router.

3.1.4 *Debugging*

Modern routers give you a vast amount of debugging options where you can trace virtually everything that the router is doing. Both JUNOS and IOS have a rich tracing facility to show what the routing software is doing. Each protocol has its very own knobs that you can turn on. Similar to operational mode and configuration mode, there is also a hierarchy as to what kind of feature or protocols can be debugged. The purpose of turning on the debugging facility is to help you during the troubleshooting process. Unfortunately, the way that the debuggers are managed in each is very different and will be discussed in the IOS and JUNOS specific sections. The important point is that both platforms give you a powerful debugging facility for troubleshooting complex networking problems.

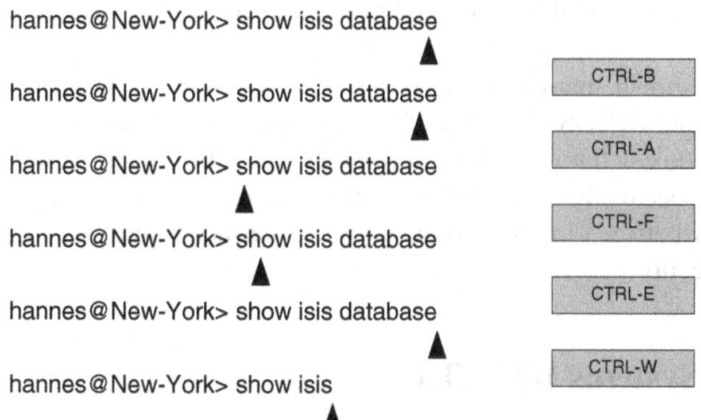

FIGURE 3.2. IOS encompasses Emacs style keystrokes for faster navigation of the cursor

3.1.5 *IP Troubleshooting Tools*

Router operation systems like IOS and JUNOS also have standard IP troubleshooting tools (like ping and traceroute) on board. The ping and traceroute utilities often have been enhanced for core-routing applications. One example of such enhancements is the ability to specify the routing table which the system should use to determine the outgoing interface. Other examples are the ability to manually specify the source IP address or to bypass a routing table. So both the ping and traceroute utilities are available, but have some enhancements far beyond the off-the-shelf ping and traceroute commands that are included with host operating systems. So when you first use them, make sure to use the online help function by keying the question mark to see what kind of additional options the system offers.

3.1.6 *Routing Policy*

Even if this is a book about IS-IS, there are many times when the IS-IS protocol needs to interact with other routing protocols, or even transfer prefix reachability information from one protocol to the other. Both JUNOS and IOS have a rich set of software features that control the flow of routing information between protocols. The software is very versatile and in the JUNOS case it even has a "language" all of its own that controls the metrics and properties of a routing advertisement depending on the administrative policy in the network. In the IOS and JUNOS specific sections you will see specifics of IOS and JUNOS routing policy implementations.

3.1.7 *Logging*

Sometimes during troubleshooting you are more interested in past events than current status. So it may be important to know when a BGP session last flapped or when a SONET/SDH link went down. Both IOS and JUNOS allow you to log events to three places:

- Console (if there is an emergency/urgent action) that every user should know
- Local log file
- Central Logging Hosts (Syslog)

The logging facility is highly configurable and allows you to classify all internal events and log to one of the three possible logging targets.

As has been shown, many elements of the command line interface are common to both the Cisco IOS and JUNOS CLI. Even if you are used to one system's CLI, our experience has been that you can figure out how to configure the other vendor's routers within a few days, given access to lab equipment or decent training. However, there are some important differences between the two command line interfaces, and these are highlighted in the next two sections.

3.2 Cisco Systems IOS CLI

Cisco IOS is the most popular CLI look and feel for talking to networking devices. Its enormous success has made it the de facto standard in the networking industry. Many vendors simply cloned it to avoid training new operational methods during the product introduction cycle. In the next section, IS-IS-related examples of how to use the Cisco CLI are presented. Then the differences in the JUNOS implementation are described.

3.2.1 *Logging into the System, Authentication, Privilege Level*

You can log into the Cisco system using a serial RS232 connection on the router's console or dial-in via telnet or the Secure Shell (SSH) Protocol. Cisco Systems routers do not have a designated Out-of-Band Management Port, so only the two options for accessing the router, direct and dial-in, are available. Once you have the physical or logical connections working properly (and Cisco serial cables for console connections use odd pin arrangements), you should see a message that prompts you for a password:

```
(11:29 hannes@unixbox:~) telnet Pennsauken
Trying 192.168.48.146 ...
Connected to Pennsauken.
Escape character is '^]'.
User Access Verification

Password: *******
Pennsauken>
```

On a system that has per-user authentication (not the default) you have to enter a username/password pair:

```
(11:31 hannes@unixbox:~) telnet London
Trying 192.168.17.1 ...
Connected to London.
Escape character is '^]'.

User Access Verification

Username: hannes
Password: *******
London>
```

IOS assigns every terminal session a privilege level between 1 and 15. You can display the privilege level anytime using the command `show privilege`:

```
London>show privilege
Current privilege level is 1
```

You cannot really cause any harm to the system or modify its configuration and disrupt traffic using a privilege level of 1. It is a privilege level dedicated to monitoring purposes only. If you want to modify the system's configuration or turn on debugging for in-depth troubleshooting then you have to change this low privilege level. You can ask your network administrator to change the privilege level either for your user-id or for the specific terminal line used to configure the router.

If you know the *enable* password you can jump immediately to privilege level 15, which lets you do everything within the router, for example, changing the configuration, rebooting the box, resetting line cards, and so on:

```
London>enable
Password:
```

Then this will verify the enable privilege level:

```
London#show privilege
Current privilege level is 15
London#
```

Now you are in enable mode, which means that you have the full set of show and configuration commands available, as discussed in the next section.

3.2.2 *IS-IS-related Show Commands*

At the end of the 1980s, IS-IS was being used as the routing protocol in a purely CLNP protocol environment. This was also the time when Cisco because successful in the enterprise marketplace with its multiprotocol router products. No one initially had in mind to use the IS-IS routing protocol for routing IP, not even the engineers at Cisco. Because of that, there is still some non-IP legacy in the user interface left. Moreover, Cisco always wanted to keep the router configurations portable from IOS release to IOS release, and this desire had by that time caused configuration statements to become scattered over several different places in the user interface. In IOS, IS-IS support for CLNP came first, and support for IP, and the necessary troubleshooting tools, came later. So a lot of IS-IS-related commands are found under the `show clns` command and not at the `show isis` branch which would be more obvious from today's perspective.

Do not be confused about the CLNP/CLNS abbreviations. CLNP is the Network Layer Protocol of the OSI suite. CLNS is the name of the entire suite of protocols. If one wants to compare this with the IP protocols then CLNP would be equivalent to IP and CLNS to TCP/IP which is also the name of the entire family of protocols and not limited to only the IP and TCP protocol.

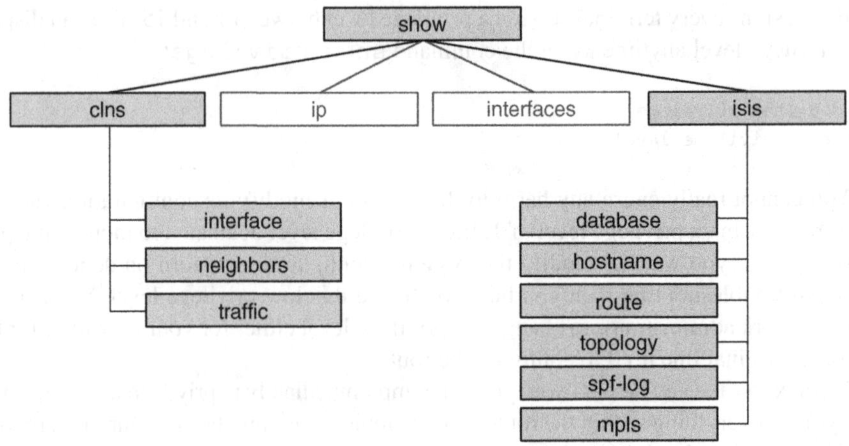

FIGURE 3.3. The IOS CLI tree for IS-IS-related operational commands

Figure 3.3 lists the most important IS-IS-related show commands in a tree-style representation. Almost everything that is important is thankfully under the `show isis` branch of the tree. The only major exceptions are the `show clns neighbor` command that shows IS-IS adjacencies and `show clns traffic` which gives a good overview as to what kind of IS-IS packets the router is sending and receiving. The use of the commands will be documented and detailed in the subsequent chapters. But first, a look at the different ways to alter the Cisco router's configuration is in order.

3.2.3 *Interface Name-space*

In the configuration file you need to configure properties of the router. In an IOS environment, in many cases the routing-related parameters are *properties* of the physical interface. The interfaces can be referenced using *configuration mode* or *operational mode*. In this section, the naming conventions used for the interfaces inside a Cisco router will be highlighted.

In IOS, there are physical and virtual interfaces. The list of physical interfaces covers all modern network interface technologies, such as:

- Asynchronous Transfer Mode (ATM)
- Ethernet
- Fast Ethernet
- Gigabit Ethernet
- Packet over SONET/SDH (POS)
- Serial

There are also two types of virtual interfaces:

- Loopback
- Null

Virtual interfaces, in contrast to physical interfaces, have the nice feature that they *never* go down. Because of this property, the loopback interface especially is used for terminating TCP-oriented routing and signalling protocols like BGP or MSDP. Because the loopback interface never goes down (as long as the router is functional), the routing protocol packets are able to enter the router over any physical interface. After all, the function of the IGP (OSPF, IS-IS) is to route around those interfaces that have gone down. This approach is much better than to terminate router 2 router sessions on interface addresses.

The second virtual interface is the *null* interface. It also never goes down, but is used for different purposes. There are two applications for the null interface:

- Trashing traffic
- Announcing aggregate routes

Generally, a router should forward packet traffic. However, there are times when a router should route traffic to the "bit bucket". A good example for this is traffic targeted to the RFC1918 private address spaces, which should never appear in packet headers on the global public Internet. These addresses are intended for local use, and packets with this source or destination address must not be forwarded to the Internet. It is common practice to install static routes for the private network addresses that point to a NULL interface on each border router inside your Autonomous System (AS):

```
London# show running-configuration
[ … ]
ip route 10.0.0.0 255.0.0.0 Null0
ip route 172.16.0.0 255.240.0.0 Null0
ip route 192.168.0.0 255.255.0.0 Null0
```

In an IP environment, it is one of the duties of the routing protocols to report that a certain sub-net is unreachable. The routing protocols propagate this change and all routers along the path recompute their IP routing tables. From an Internet perspective, this behaviour is a real issue. In Chapter 10, there will be more details regarding why a re-computation of routes can be an expensive (in technical, not commercial terms) process. Typically, the Internet is not interested in an update that a /24 prefix from the other side of the planet is unavailable, because it keeps so many routers busy updating their new forwarding state. So the more common practice is to announce *aggregate routes* and to *suppress* all the *specific routes* that may be internal to a network, as shown in Figure 3.4. But in order to exist at all, routes, aggregate or not, need to refer to a next-hop interface, which leads to the next router to forward traffic to. The null interface serves this next-hop purpose for aggregates: it is always up. And you get another feature for free – the null interface trashes all traffic to destinations that do not have more specific routes. If sub-net (for example) 192.168.33/24 is not known internally (that is, no more specific routes are known), and there is a port-scanning source from the Internet, then the null interface trashes all that traffic. However, the main purpose of this feature is to suppress announcements of specific routes as shown in Figure 3.4, which shows the flapping of 192.168.44/24 towards the Internet.

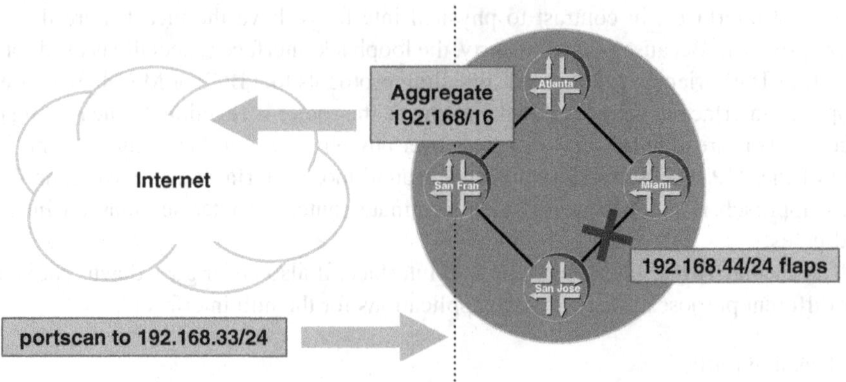

FIGURE 3.4. Aggregate routes are typically advertised by AS border routers

Returning to physical interfaces, all of the high-end Cisco router models (7500 and 12000 Series) have several slots that can hold up to 16 line cards depending on the exact router model. On the line card there may be one or more ports. The number of ports varies with the line speed of the ports. The lower the line speed, the higher the port density.

The physical ports are referred to in a slot-number/port-number fashion. The following are examples of complete interface names in the IOS name-space:

- GigabitEthernet3/0
- POS5/1
- ATM0/0
- Serial 1/0

The numbering of the slots and ports starts at 0. So the first slot position in the router chassis is referred to as 0. In the digital world counting typically starts at zero.

The simplest way to access the properties and current state of an interface is to use the `show interface <interface-name>` command:

```
London# show Interface POS3/0
POS3/0 is up, line protocol is up
  Hardware is Packet over SONET
  Description: "Interface to Amsterdam POS4/1"
  Internet address is 172.16.25.1/30
  MTU 4470 bytes, BW 155000 Kbit, DLY 100 usec, rely 255/255, load 1/255
  Encapsulation HDLC, crc 16, loopback not set
  Keepalive set (10 sec)
  Scramble enabled
  Last input 00:00:00, output 00:00:07, output hang never
  Last clearing of "show interface" counters never
  Queueing strategy: fifo
  Output queue 0/40, 0 drops; input queue 0/75, 0 drops
  5 minute input rate 120457000 bits/sec, 28800 packets/sec
  5 minute output rate 130429920 bits/sec, 26107 packets/sec
```

```
412058846 packets input, 4066852672395 bytes, 0 no buffer
Received 0 broadcasts, 0 runts, 0 giants, 0 throttles
         0 parity
1 input errors, 1 CRC, 0 frame, 0 overrun, 0 ignored, 0 abort
627685025 packets output, 4025356699702 bytes, 0 underruns
0 output errors, 0 applique, 4 interface resets
0 output buffer failures, 0 output buffers swapped out
3 carrier transitions
```

The output contains information about the Layer-2 encapsulation, maximum transmission unit (MTU), the current forwarding rate (expressed in packets and bytes), plus counters for the aggregate number of bytes and packets that have been processed through this interface.

For IS-IS-related purposes, you will often see the interface names, for example, in commands like `show clns neighbor`:

```
London# show clns neighbor
System Id     Interface     SNPA       State    Holdtime     Type      Protocol
Frankfurt     PO3/0         *PPP*      Up       22           L2        IS-IS
Munich        PO4/1         *PPP*      Up       20           L2        IS-IS
```

3.2.4 *Changing Router Configuration*

In IOS you tell the router to take configuration input and to transfer it to the central configuration file using the `configure` command. The standalone `configure` command will prompt you to enter the way that you want to input the configuration file:

```
London#configure
Configuring from terminal, memory, or network [terminal]?
Enter configuration commands, one per line. End with CNTL/Z.
London(config)#
```

The memory option lets you source the configuration file from a memory storage device inside the router, such as flash-disks or the NVRAM. But a more typical way is from the network or from the terminal. From the network means that you have to specify a trivial FTP (TFTP) server and a filename, and the router will then attempt to pull down the file using the TFTP protocol.

```
London#conf network
Address or name of remote host [255.255.255.255]? 192.168.1.1
Source filename [London-confg]?
Configure using tftp://192.168.1.1/London-confg? [confirm]
```

The most common way is to put the router into configuration mode and then enter the configuration statements manually from the terminal. This is the most likely way of interacting with the router in day-to-day operation:

```
London#configure terminal
Enter configuration commands, one per line. End with CNTL/Z.
London(config)#
```

Now you are in configuration mode at the top (global) level of the configuration. Notice the `(config)` phrase between the # sign and the hostname. This shows that you are now in configuration mode at the top level. In IOS, the configuration file is structured into a few hierarchy levels. You can configure the top level, but this is further divided into interface configuration modes and router configuration mode. IOS provides only this two-level configuration scheme. You either configure something at the top level (for example, user and access information) or configure something under the interface or router hierarchy. You can jump between the levels by just typing in the new context. For example, if you are in global configuration mode and you want to configure an IS-IS property for an interface, then you can change the context by just typing in the interface name:

```
London(config)#
London(config)#interface pos5/3
London(config-if)
```

You are now in interface configuration mode, and this is verified by the prompt, which has changed from `(config)` to `(config-if)`.

You can jump back to the top-level hierarchy by simply typing `exit`. Note that you are just exiting the context and not the configuration mode itself. If you want to exit the configuration mode then you type `exit` at the top level:

```
London(config)#router isis
London(config-router)#exit
London(config)#interface pos5/3
London(config-if)#exit
London(config)#exit
```

Alternatively you can enter CTRL-Z in any context to immediately terminate the configuration mode and get back into operation mode:

```
London(config)#interface pos5/3
London(config-if)# ^Z
London#
```

This *flat hierarchy* approach has the advantage that the location of certain parameters is usually intuitive. However, the big disadvantage is that as the configuration file gets bigger and bigger, and the router must perform many different functions (as, for example, an edge router would), the configuration file may look unstructured, messy and confusing.

In any case, once in the correct *context*, just type in the configuration command, which is typically structured in a *keyword N * [optional-parameter] parameter* format. For instance, the following command would set the IS-IS hello timer on a given interface to 20 seconds. The function of this timer is not important for now, Chapter 5 details all of the specifics and consequences of the IS-IS hello timer parameter.

```
London(config)#interface pos5/3
London(config-if)#isis hello-interval 20<ENTER>
```

Once you press the <ENTER> key the command is parsed and then executed immediately. So whatever you do, *think* beforehand and make sure that whatever you change does not cut you off from router access (this happens more often than you might expect).

There are configuration changes that require an entire set of commands to be entered on a router. And if you enter them in the wrong order, then your in-band terminal (telnet) session might be cut off. A good example of this is authentication of routing updates. Typically, you have to specify a *shared secret* password that is stored locally on the router. The second configuration step is a reference to the password, which makes the router send authenticated information, but also makes the router *expect* authenticated routing information with the shared secret. Imagine what happens if you mix up the order: first you tell the router that everything has to be authenticated, and so is also expected to *arrive* authenticated. What happens is that you will receive a few Hello messages and then your router drops the adjacency because nothing has been actually authenticated because there is no password yet! If you are relying on the network for configuration access, hope that there is someone local you can reach to correct the problem through a direct console connection.

The authentication example is basically a two-step configuration *transaction*. The term *transaction* was borrowed from SQL database environments, which faced the problem everyday that structured, multi-field data are not entered and stored all at once. Because of transient conditions like two users modifying the same database records at the same time, corrupted data was often the result. All modern databases offer *transactional integrity*, which locks the database until the entire transaction is finished. In the router world, this would mean that you can finish all the commands that belong together for a desired functionality and the session would never be disrupted. Unfortunately, the IOS user interface does *not* give you transactional integrity, which means that you cannot configure a set of commands in any order without risk of disrupting your in-band telnet session. For a configuration transaction that involves more than one configuration step, finding out the proper order of the commands is a daunting task and sometimes not even possible! This is especially true if machines like provisioning systems or configuration robots are doing the configuration of the router more or less unsupervised, then the provisioning software gets infinitely complex.

What can be done about this IOS immediate-change feature? The best current practice is that the provisioning systems overwrite not the active configuration, but the Cisco *startup-configuration* file and reboot the router at 3:00 am in the morning. Modifying the startup-configuration file has the advantage that the configuration does not get effective immediately. As the name implies, it only becomes active the next time the router is rebooted. The following command loads a file named "London-startup-config" and overwrites the startup configuration file of the router:

```
London#copy tftp://192.168.1.1/London-startup-config startup-config
```

What you have to do for this new configuration to become active is to reboot the router (either automated or manually). This of course implies that you have designed enough redundancy into the network so that you do not cause any major outages by the router going out of service for the approximately 3 to 4 minutes it takes for the reboot, which is a common time for large core routers like the GSR 12000 series:

```
London#reload
Proceed with reload? [confirm]
Connection closed by foreign host.
```

The router asks for confirmation and finally reboots with the new startup configuration file. It should be noted here that sometimes it is not that easy to reboot the router right away. Network redundancy is relatively easy to implement just by doubling the number of routers in the core. However, when it comes down to the edge, especially for customer access routers, what you need is a *system* redundancy, where you can do a full-chassis reboot of a box without causing disruption. Unfortunately, routers are not as advanced in terms of redundancy and resiliency as (for instance) public voice network switches, so there is always some risk. So the missing *transactional* configuration feature for provisioning IOS is still a major concern for large ISPs and carriers.

3.2.5 *IS-IS-related Configuration Commands*

As in the operational modes, IOS also has a structure for the configuration tree. All IS-IS-related configuration is stored under the `router isis` and under the `interface <N>` branch. Figure 3.5 gives a tree representation of commands and options that can be configured in IOS platforms. This tree is based on IOS 12.0(23)ST, a very common software release that many ISPs and carriers use.

3.2.6 *Troubleshooting Tools*

Cisco routers include a number of tools for use in troubleshooting router problems. The two most helpful tools are the Cisco Discovery Protocol (CDP) and the debug command.

3.2.6.1 Cisco Discovery Protocol (CDP)

When you configure routers, first make sure that the packet-carrying circuits are up and have a properly configured IP address on both sides of the link. You need an IP address to properly test two-way connectivity using the `ping` command. However, there are several cases, especially in troubleshooting, when you just want to verify that the data link (OSI RM Layer-2) is up and is capable of transporting packets. Unfortunately, there is no standard "ping-like" tool available that operates on OSI RM Layer-2 without an IP (Layer-3) address. But Cisco has developed a clever tool called the Cisco Discovery Protocol (CDP) to address that problem. CDP is encapsulated in a sub-network access protocol (SNAP) frame. Encapsulating CDP in a SNAP frame has the advantage that it can be run on virtually all media, including Ethernet, Frame-Relay, ATM, PPP and Cisco-HDLC. It is enabled by default on all Cisco routers. You can verify if you have Layer-2 connectivity, even on interfaces without assigned IP addresses, using the `show cdp neighbors` command.

```
London#show cdp neighbors
Capability Codes: R - Router, T - Trans Bridge, B - Source Route Bridge
                  S - Switch, H - Host, I - IGMP, r - Repeater

Device ID        Local Intrfce     Holdtme    Capability     Platform    Port ID
Munich           POS1/0            171        R              12416       POS6/0
Pennsauken       POS5/3            132        R              12416       POS12/0
```

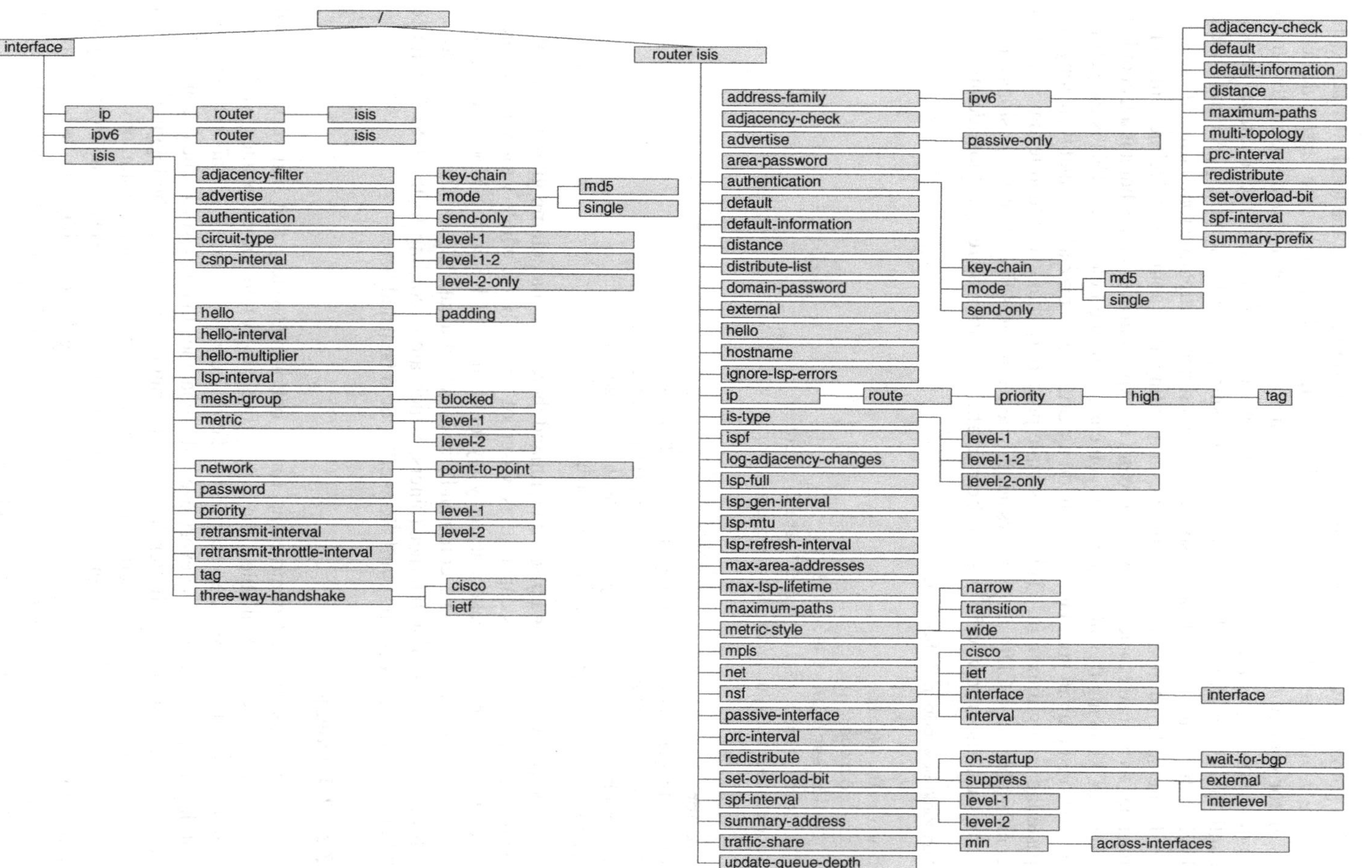
/
interface
ip
router
isis
ipv6
router
isis
isis
adjacency-filter
advertise
authentication
key-chain
mode
md5
single
send-only
circuit-type
level-1
level-1-2
level-2-only
csnp-interval
hello
padding
hello-interval
hello-multiplier
lsp-interval
mesh-group
blocked
metric
level-1
level-2
network
point-to-point
password
priority
level-1
level-2
retransmit-interval
retransmit-throttle-interval
tag
three-way-handshake
cisco
ietf
router isis
address-family
ipv6
adjacency-check
default
default-information
distance
maximum-paths
multi-topology
prc-interval
redistribute
set-overload-bit
spf-interval
summary-prefix
adjacency-check
advertise
passive-only
area-password
authentication
key-chain
mode
md5
single
send-only
default
default-information
distance
distribute-list
domain-password
external
hello
hostname
ignore-lsp-errors
ip
route
priority
high
tag
is-type
level-1
level-1-2
level-2-only
ispf
log-adjacency-changes
lsp-full
lsp-gen-interval
lsp-mtu
lsp-refresh-interval
max-area-addresses
max-lsp-lifetime
maximum-paths
metric-style
narrow
transition
wide
mpls
net
nsf
cisco
ietf
interface
interface
interval
passive-interface
prc-interval
redistribute
set-overload-bit
on-startup
wait-for-bgp
suppress
external
interlevel
spf-interval
level-1
level-2
summary-address
traffic-share
min
across-interfaces
update-queue-depth

The output shows you the hostname of the neighbouring device, the local interface to the remote device, the "platform name" of the router, and the port that the remote device is using for your connection. The port is particularly interesting if you are doing low-level troubleshooting with field personnel at the remote end. You can direct them to the port configuration or even submit a configuration snippet that the remote personnel should load on the router. Often field personnel are not used to configuring routers, and if asked to configure an IP address or a certain line card setting, they sometimes decline. This is not intended as an insult to field teams, who can't be experts in everything, but it is a fact of life. However, knowing the interface name, you can say to the field team "This is the configuration. Just plug in your laptop, login, do a `configure terminal` and then copy and paste the configuration in." This is a simple procedure that every field technician feels comfortable with. CDP also conveys additional parameters like software versions and IP addresses. The `show cdp neighbor detail` command reveals those details:

```
London#show cdp neighbor detail
------------
Device ID: Munich
Entry address(es):
  IP address: 192.168.48.151
Platform: cisco 12416, Capabilities: Router
Interface: POS1/0, Port ID (outgoing port): POS6/0
Holdtime : 161 sec

Version :
Cisco Internetwork Operating System Software
IOS (tm) GS Software (GSR-P-M), Version 12.0(17)ST6
Copyright (c) 1986-2002 by cisco Systems, Inc.
Compiled Tue 07-May-02 00:49 by dchih
```

In the `show cdp neighbor` command there is also a column giving some information about the router's capabilities. Cisco of course has a whole variety of products available that process packets at many layers of the OSI Reference Model. The `show cdp neighbor detail` command shows you in a capabilities line at which layers the device operates. For Internet routers, which are according to the OSI Reference Model *Layer-3* devices, the word "Router" should be listed here.

3.2.6.2 Debugging

Cisco IOS was the first commercial router operating system that had very powerful debugging messages available. The debugging sub-system of the router works very simply. You enter a structured command like `debug <keyword>`. This sets an internal flag in the software to log every event that matches that keyword. The output is then written to a local logging buffer. The administrator can read out the logging buffer in real-time on his vty (virtual terminal, just another term for telnet) session or on the console. Additionally, all logs can be stored on an external syslog server and logged by the router to this particular server with the syslog protocol. The debugging flags are structured in a tree-like fashion, just like the operational and configuration commands. The structure of *debug-tree* is shown in Figure 3.6.

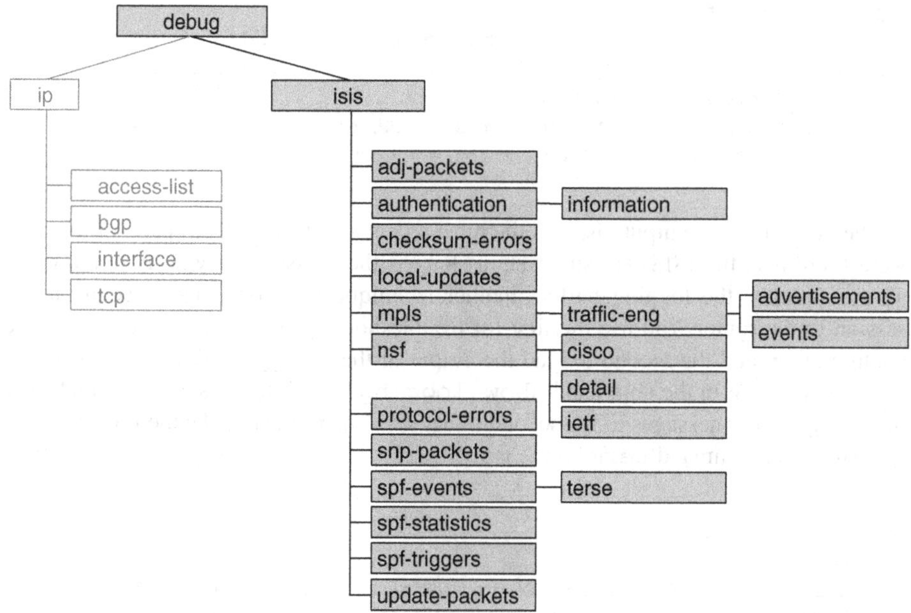

FIGURE 3.6. IOS CLI for IS-IS-related debug commands

For example, if you do not know if your router is sending and receiving Hello packets, you could set a debug flag to record all output in a logging buffer. Make sure that you are in privileged (enable) mode before setting any debug flag, otherwise the system would refuse to do so. This is a kind of safety check to avoid abuse and service degradation by excessive logging, which places an additional load on the router. The assumption is if you are given the enable password then you should know what you are doing. The setting of certain debug flags can even make the router freeze because it is so busy writing log messages to the logging buffer. Here is an IS-IS example of debug use:

```
London#debug isis adj-packets
IS-IS Adjacency related packets debugging is on
London#
```

Initially, nothing seems to be happening because you do not see any output on the screen. However, the system is logging sent or received Hello packets, which are the packets that bring up IS-IS adjacencies. You can examine the contents of the logging buffer by issuing a `show logging` command:

```
London#show logging
Syslog logging: enabled (2 messages dropped, 0 messages rate-limited,
 0 flushes, 0 overruns)
  Console logging: level debugging, 1894 messages logged
  Monitor logging: level debugging, 143 messages logged
  Buffer logging: level debugging, 1894 messages logged
  Logging Exception size (4096 bytes)
  Trap logging: level informational, 1810 message lines logged
```

```
Log Buffer (16384 bytes):
*Jul 12 21:38:27.216 UTC: ISIS-Adj: Sending serial IIH on Serial3/0, length 4469
*Jul 12 21:38:29.056 UTC: ISIS-Adj: Rec serial IIH from *HDLC* (Serial3/0),
 cir type L2, cir id 01, length 58
*Jul 12 21:38:29.056 UTC: ISIS-Adj: rcvd state UP, old state UP, new state UP
*Jul 12 21:38:29.056 UTC: ISIS-Adj: Action = ACCEPT
```

The bottom of the output displays the most recent events and which parts of the software (here it is the ISIS-Adj sub-system) logged the message. If you do not want to always monitor the logging buffer, another technique is to open up a second telnet session to the router. You use the first for troubleshooting the router and changing the configuration, and the second to read the output of the debugger. Additionally, because repeatedly typing in the command `show logging` is a bit tedious, you can make the router log all the messages to the second telnet session. You can make the router do this by issuing the command `terminal monitor`:

```
London#terminal monitor
London#
*Jul 12 21:51:20.072 UTC: ISIS-Adj: Sending serial IIH on Serial3/0, length 4469
*Jul 12 21:51:21.228 UTC: ISIS-Adj: Rec serial IIH from *HDLC* (Serial3/0),
 cir type L2, cir id 01, length 58
*Jul 12 21:51:21.228 UTC: ISIS-Adj: rcvd state UP, old state UP, new state UP
*Jul 12 21:51:21.228 UTC: ISIS-Adj: Action = ACCEPT
```

If you now issue a show logging command, you see your most recent logs as well as an indication that the system is writing the logging buffer to a virtual terminal (telnet session):

```
London#show logging
Syslog logging: enabled (2 messages dropped, 0 messages rate-limited,
 0 flushes, 0 overruns)
  Console logging: level debugging, 1856 messages logged
  Monitor logging: level debugging, 109 messages logged Logging to: vty2(91)
  Buffer logging: level debugging, 1856 messages logged
  Logging Exception size (4096 bytes)
  Trap logging: level informational, 1808 message lines logged
```

Additionally, it may sometimes be interesting to see what kind of debug flags the router has set. The `show debugging` command displays you all debug flags currently catching events, which are logged to the logging buffer:

```
London#show debugging
CLNS:
  IS-IS Adjacency related packets debugging is on
London#
```

Once you have finished your troubleshooting session, make sure that you turn off debugging! Excessive debugging may degrade performance of the control plane and hence seriously harm the system. The quickest command to turn off all debug flags is the `undebug all` command.

```
London#undebug all
All possible debugging has been turned off
London#
```

3.2.7 *Routing Policy and Filtering of Routes*

A router running all different kinds of routing protocols is still not enough for today's marketplace. Modern routing OSs have a strong support for controlling what kinds of routes are accepted and advertised in turn to neighbours. What sounds so easy to do at first is actually one of the most complex parts of a vendor's routing code. Handling routing policy often requires a dedicated language to specify every detail of what type of routing policy you need in your routing domain.

Looking at the IOS command line style and hierarchy, you can see that there is no single place where routing policies are configured. That's no big surprise – with IOS, because of its multiprotocol nature, each routing protocol implements its own routing policy processing as part of the protocol's specific routing code. So one policy module is there for RIP, one for IS-IS, and another one for BGP. This design choice is actually very convenient as long as your routing policy stays simple. However, for more complex policies, this approach quickly becomes difficult to maintain, given the different styles sometimes used in the protocol's redistribution policy. With the rise of BGP as an interdomain protocol and *the* protocol for policy processing, it was clear that a new, common way of configuring routing policies had to be implemented in IOS. That common routing paradigm in IOS is called *route-maps*. We will discuss only IS-IS-specific routing policies and route-maps, and only briefly. But this is fine. Due to the way IS-IS is used by service provider's routing policies, which is as a pure topology discovery protocol, there are not many IP routes in the IS-IS routing protocol to worry about distributing, because BGP does that job much better. We do not need policy processing in IS-IS as much as we would need it in a book about BGP. Typically, in an ISP's IS-IS network, there is only one place where policy processing takes place: when passing down routes from IS-IS Level 2 to Level 1. But let's keep that aside for a while – there is more about IS-IS hierarchical routing levels in Chapters 4 and 12.

A good example of an IS-IS protocol-specific policy is the `redistribute isis ip level-2 into level-1 distribute-list 101 metric-style wide` command. This seems like a very complex statement, but it is really quite simple. It just tells the router to send (redistribute) any IS-IS Level-2 IP routing information to the Level-1 routers (`isis ip level-2 into level-1`) and use a larger metric field than originally specified (`metric-style wide`). The details of the redistribute command are covered in Chapter 12. For now, the important part of the command is the `distribute-list 101` statement. The distribute-list refers to an *extended-access-list*, which is a list of IP prefixes. In IOS, many sometimes complex policy operations can be done with a single command plus an extended-access-list. In the following example, the *extended-access-list* referred to by the `distribute-list 101` command is shown:

```
London# show running-config
[ ... ]
access-list 101 permit ip 192.168.1.0 0.0.0.255 any
access-list 101 permit ip 192.168.3.0 0.0.0.255 any
[ ... ]
```

Confusingly, IOS can also use route-maps, which are the more flexible IOS routing policy language. The `route-map` command introduces a multi-line sequence of match/action pairs ordered by a sequence number. The most important clauses are the `match` and `set` statements. These allow you to match on arbitrary prefix properties, such as the interface it was learned (received) from, associated BGP community lists, or even reference other access lists. The `permit` and `deny` keyword control the action if and when a prefix is matched. The `permit` keyword means that the prefix generally is accepted by the router and can only be modified by means of the `set` command. The `deny` keyword means that a prefix is dropped upon match. An example route-map looks like this:

```
London# show running-config
[ ... ]
route-map hannes permit 10
 match community 2
 set metric 20
route-map hannes deny 20
 match community 13
[ ... ]
```

3.2.8 *Further Documentation*

There is a huge set of IOS-related material around. Probably the best starting site is Cisco's online manuals, which can be accessed at http://www.cisco.com/univercd/cc/td/doc/product/software/index.htm.

3.3 Juniper Networks JUNOS CLI

The IOS-style CLI is the standard in the industry and many vendors copied it for their own products. When Juniper Networks released the first version of its routing software named JUNOS Internet software, many industry observers believed that it would be a clone of the IOS CLI as well. However, the engineers at Juniper Networks who were in charge of the user interface did not want to create just another clone of the IOS CLI. Being mostly ex-Cisco employees, they had developed a good understanding of the limitations (especially the provisioning aspect) of the IOS software. For them it was crystal clear that they wanted to create something new. So they replaced parts of the user interface that did not work well and kept the properties that made IOS so successful.

3.3.1 *Logging into the System and Authentication*

When you first log into a router running JUNOS, the first difference you see from IOS is that the system prompts you in a UNIX fashion for a username and a password:

```
(20:45 hannes@unixbox:~) telnet frankfurt
Trying 192.168.77.12...
Connected to frankfurt.
Escape character is '^]'.

Frankfurt (ttyp0)

login: hannes
Password: *********

--- JUNOS 5.3R2.4 built 2002-06-03 18:59:57 UTC

hannes@Frankfurt>
```

This is because the underlying base OS for JUNOS is a heavily modified FreeBSD. FreeBSD is a free UNIX clone just like the more popular Linux UNIX. Your can get further information about FreeBSD at http://www.freebsd.org/.

But make no mistake: JUNOS and the original FreeBSD are different OSs, and large parts of the networking-related kernel routines have been changed. FreeBSD is targeted for a host operating system environment, much like a networked PC. Typically, host operating systems have:

- A single routing table
- 1–3 network interfaces
- Tens of routes to handle

An operating system targeted for both edge and core routing functions has to handle many more of each. Specifically, these needs are:

- Hundreds of routing tables
- Thousands of interfaces
- 100,000s of routes

However, there are still lots of things that remained in JUNOS, such as all the networking tools (telnet, SSH, ping and traceroute utilities) or, as in the previous example, the login procedure.

Once you are logged in with your username, you have a set of privileges that are associated with your username, similar to IOS. You can display those privileges by issuing a `show cli authorization` command.

```
hannes@Frankfurt> show cli authorization
Current user: 'hannes' class 'super-user'
Permissions:
   admin              -- Can view user accounts
   admin-control      -- Can modify user accounts
   clear              -- Can clear learned network information
```

```
  configure              -- Can enter configuration mode
  control                -- Can modify any configuration
  edit                   -- Can edit full files
  field                  -- Special for field (debug) support
  floppy                 -- Can read and write from the floppy
  interface              -- Can view interface configuration
  interface-control      -- Can modify interface configuration
[ … ]
  security               -- Can view security configuration
  security-control       -- Can modify security configuration
```

This is one of the improvements that JUNOS offers. Instead of having a privilege level of 1–15 assigned to the user-profile with each IOS command mapped to a *minimum privilege-level*, each user profile in JUNOS is now associated with a set of *flags* that control which parts of the system the user can access or even modify. The system is so flexible that you can even break down which user can control what configuration lines of the router's configuration file. Using this, you could implement authorization schemes, such as Operator A can only modify BGP, and Operator B can only configure IS-IS. However, explaining the full extent of the authorization sub-system is beyond the scope of this book. The only time you need to check that the network administrator has assigned the necessary privileges is when a certain IS-IS-related keyword does not show up where it should. In JUNOS there is the concept of user interface *views*. If you do not have sufficient privileges then you do not even *see* the commands and keyword in the user interface – they simply do not exist for that user – and neither auto-complete nor entering a question mark reveals those missing commands because they are not part of this user's access profile. Consider the following example. User *hannes* has been given superuser privileges. As a superuser, he can access the `request system reboot` command, which will shut down all server processes and then reboot the router. If the user *frank* logs in and is associated with the *read-only* profile and wants to issue the same request, the command does not exist:

```
frank@Frankfurt> request ?
Possible completions:
  message        Send a text message to other users
```

For the user *frank* only the request message command exists, which would send a message to all the connected users terminal session. Auto complete (pressing the TAB key) does not produce any other completions beside the `message` keyword. Even if you try to manually enter the `request system reboot` command the system acts as if it does not know the command.

```
frank@Frankfurt> request system reboot
                                 ^
syntax error, expecting <command>.
frank@Frankfurt>
```

Please keep this concept in mind when exploring the IS-IS commands shown in the rest of this book on a functioning router. If a certain command does not show up as expected, it could be that the network administrator has not granted you the access level required to reveal one of the commands you might be looking for.

3.3.2 *IS-IS-related Show Commands*

Once you are logged into the JUNOS system, you are first placed into operational mode, as in IOS. You know that you are in operational mode by looking at the prompt. If the prompt is terminated using a ">" character then you are in operational mode, just as in IOS:

```
hannes@Frankfurt>
```

Figure 3.7 shows the commands that are available in operational mode.

Unlike the Cisco implementation of the IS-IS Protocol, the JUNOS version was written only to transport IP and not CLNP reachability information. Therefore all operational commands are accommodated under the `show isis` branch of the CLI tree. Almost

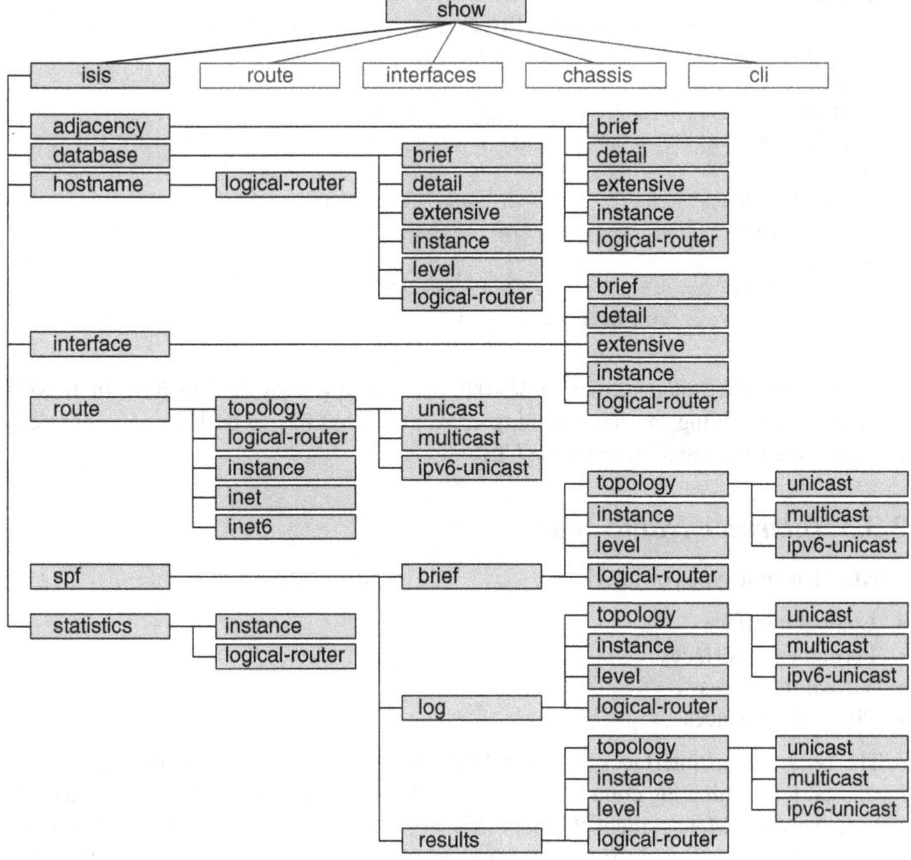

FIGURE 3.7. The JUNOS CLI tree for IS-IS-related operational commands

every command in the hierarchy has a *command-modifier* as the last argument. Command modifiers control the level of output that the command provides to the user. For example, if you issue a `show isis interface brief` command, then the output shows you all interfaces that have IS-IS configured. The keyword `brief` at the end of the command tells the router that you only wish to see-*minimal* information available for the interface:

```
hannes@Frankfurt> show isis interface brief
IS-IS interface database:
Interface L CirID Level 1 DR          Level 2 DR              L1/L2 Metric
so-2/1/0.0 2 0x2 Disabled             Point to Point          10/3500
so-3/0/0.0 2 0x1 Disabled             Point to Point          10/240
[ … ]
```

The *extensive* command modifier tells the router that you wish to see *all* information that the router maintains for a given interface including timers and much more:

```
hannes@Frankfurt> show isis interface extensive
IS-IS interface database:
so-2/1/0.0
  Index: 16, State: 0x6, Circuit id: 0x1, Circuit type: 2
  LSP interval: 100ms, CSNP interval: disabled
  Level 2
    Adjacencies: 1, Priority: 64, Metric: 3500
    Hello Interval: 9 s, Hold Time: 27 s
so-3/0/0.0
  Index: 14, State: 0x6, Circuit id: 0x1, Circuit type: 2
  LSP interval: 100ms, CSNP interval: disabled
  Level 2
    Adjacencies: 1, Priority: 64, Metric: 240
    Hello Interval: 9s, Hold Time: 27s
[ … ]
```

JUNOS interface names, like so-3/0/0.0, are also different than in IOS. In JUNOS there is an underlying interface naming convention that has to be learned to correctly configure the router and interpret the CLI output.

3.3.3 *Interface Name-space*

JUNOS has four types of interfaces:

- Logical interfaces
- Permanent interfaces
- Virtual interfaces
- Physical interfaces

The only *logical* interfaces inside JUNOS are instances of the loopback (lo0) interface, used for terminating control traffic like BGP, MSDP, management protocols like the Simple Network Management Protocol (SNMP), Telnet and Secure Shell (SSH). There is no NULL interface as in IOS that can be used to trash traffic. Instead, JUNOS has a special next-hop type for trashing traffic. JUNOS also has a special *aggregate* facility for the announcement of aggregate routes. However, a detailed explanation of these is beyond the scope of this book.

The two *permanent* interfaces are the fxp0 and the fxp1 interfaces. Juniper Networks Routing Engines (REs) are off-the-shelf, industry-standard PCs that take care of the care and feeding of the Packet Forwarding Engine (PFE). The REs have two Fast-Ethernet Interfaces, one of them exposed to the outside world and one of them connected to the packet-forwarding complex. Those Fast Ethernet Interfaces are based on Intel chipsets and, in good FreeBSD tradition, those interfaces are referred to using the name *fxp*.

You can configure the fxp0 interface (the one exposed to the outside world) only. Don't attempt to configure the fxp1 interfaces: your configuration change might very well interfere with internal RE to PFE communication. The typical application of the fxp0 interface is to use it for out-of-band (OOB) management access. This interface can be used to send out all kinds of routing and signalling information, however, it cannot be used to carry transit traffic. Figure 3.8 shows why JUNOS does not allow this. Traffic entering the router would have to be squeezed through the fxp1 interface (the internal Fast Ethernet Segment), which is dedicated to carrying control traffic only. Whenever the PFE realizes that a route should use the fxp1 port as a next-hop for transit traffic, then the fabric generates an ICMP unreachable packet back to the sender. Because of this design choice, you get a modest amount of security for your management segment, which now cannot be accessed from the Internet.

JUNOS makes a clear distinction between physical interfaces and logical interfaces. On the physical interface level you can control properties of OSI Reference Model Layer 1 and 2. Examples of such properties are:

- Link MTU size
- Encapsulation method
- Frame checksum computation
- Layer 1 framing format
- Full/Half duplex operation

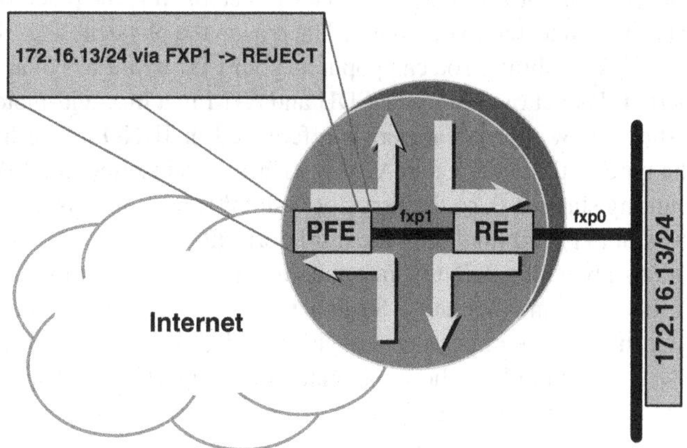

FIGURE 3.8. Sub-nets connected to the fxp0 management port are not reachable from the Internet

TABLE 3.1. JUNOS uses two-letter names for its different interface media types.

JUNOS interface abbreviation	Interface media/type
at	ATM over SONET/SDH ports
e1	E1 ports
e3	E3 ports
fe	Fast Ethernet ports
so	SONET/SDH ports
t1	T1 ports
t3	DS-3 ports
ge	Gigabit Ethernet ports
t3	Aggregated Ethernet ports

Logical interfaces typically have properties from OSI Reference Model Layer 3. Examples of such properties are:

- IP addresses/Prefix lengths
- ISO NETs
- Filters
- ICMP behaviour (redirect suppression)
- And many more…

First, consider the interface naming for the physical interfaces. (The logical interfaces are a superset of the physical interfaces, so we start with the *simple* things first). JUNOS has a structure similar to IOS as far as the interface naming is concerned: the first two letters always describe what media type the interface is. Table 3.1 shows the two-letter abbreviations and the corresponding fully specified interface media types. What follows (after a dash) are three numbers separated by slashes. The three numbers represent the FPC Slot, the PIC slot and the port number. If you are not familiar with Juniper Networks hardware don't worry: the FPC card is a carrier card like the VIP card for the Cisco 7500 Series. The FPC mostly contains buffering memory as well as classification and queuing hardware. The PIC card is then mounted on top of the FPC card. This is how the FPC got its name of *Flexible PIC Concentrator.*

PIC is an abbreviation for *Physical Interface Connector*. It is the place where the fibre and copper lines are connected to the router. The reason the physical lines do not directly connect to the FPC is flexibility. You can populate your FPC with PICs of arbitrary media-types like Ethernet, Packet over SONET/SDH and ATM in a mix-and-match fashion.

Figure 3.9 shows how a physical port is referenced in JUNOS. The first part is the interface media type: "at" stands for an ATM interface. It is inserted into FPC chassis slot Number 3 (counting starts at 0, so the first slot is slot #0 and slot #3 is the *fourth* slot) on the second PIC slot (#1) and finally on the third port (#2).

The good news about the JUNOS interface-naming scheme is that it is consistent throughout all the platforms (M- and T-Series). On every platform from the little M5 up to the T640, the interface naming stays consistent: FPC, then PIC, and finally the port number. Below is an example of how the status of an interface is displayed using the `show interface <interface-name>` command:

```
hannes@Pennsauken> show interfaces so-0/0/0
Physical interface: so-0/0/0, Enabled, Physical link is Up
```

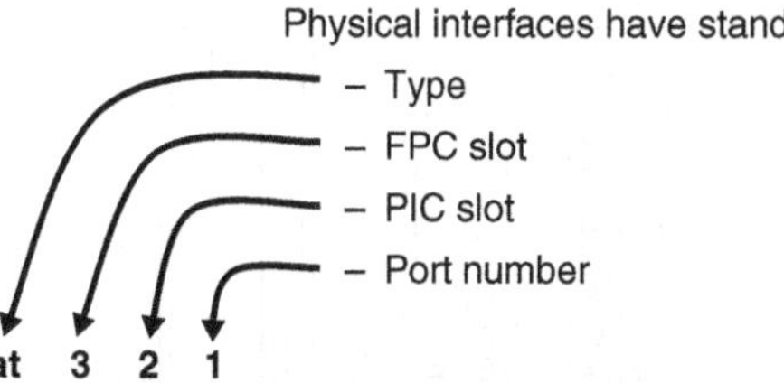
Physical interfaces have standard names
– Type
– FPC slot
– PIC slot
– Port number
at 3 2 1

FIGURE 3.9. JUNOS interface names are notated in interface-type/FPC slot/PIC slot/port number order

```
Interface index: 11, SNMP ifIndex: 14
Description: to-New-York-so-7/0/1
Link-level type: Cisco-HDLC, MTU: 4474, Clocking: Internal, SDH mode,
 Speed: OC3, FCS: 16,
Payload scrambler: Disabled
Device flags    :   Present Running
Interface flags:    Point-To-Point SNMP-Traps
Link flags      :   Keepalives
Keepalive settings: Interval 10 seconds, Up-count 1, Down-count 3
Keepalive: Input: 507921 (00:00:06 ago), Output: 510818 (00:00:05 ago)
Last flapped    : 2002-08-07 13:58:35 CEST (2d 08:58 ago)
Input rate      : 42783824 bps (21297 pps)
Output rate     : 58047120 bps (15777 pps)
SONET alarms    : None
SONET defects   : None
```

3.3.4 *IS-IS-related Configuration Commands*

Like IOS, JUNOS has a configuration mode. You need to get into configuration mode first (if you have the related privileges to do so) to modify the router's central configuration file.

You can get into configuration mode by issuing the `configure` command:

```
hannes@Frankfurt>] configure
Entering configuration mode
[edit]
hannes@Frankfurt#
```

You know you are in configuration mode in two ways – first the prompt terminates with the hash (#) sign, and second the line before the prompt displays the configuration level (or *context*) you are in. In JUNOS there is a multi-level hierarchy of configuration commands. This is unlike Cisco IOS where the configuration file is only structured into two levels. Figure 3.10 shows a full overview of the IS-IS-related configuration options available in JUNOS configuration mode.

All options are under the `protocols isis {}` branch. When you want to configure the `protocols isis {}` context you have to change to that context first using the `edit` command.

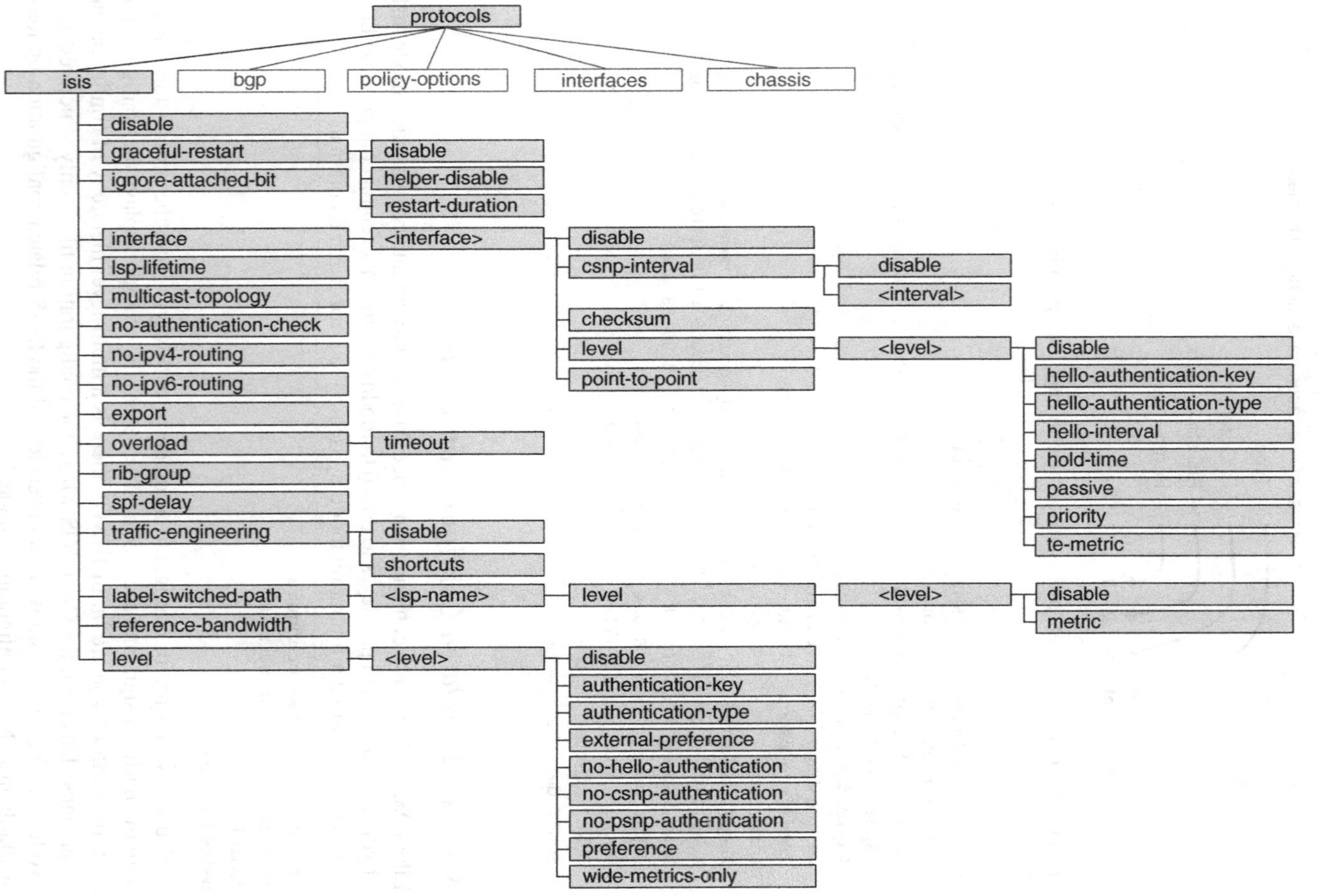

FIGURE 3.10. The JUNOS CLI tree for IS-IS-related configuration commands

```
[edit]
hannes@Frankfurt# edit protocols isis
[edit protocols isis]
hannes@Frankfurt#
```

The context displayed between the brackets changes to the `protocols isis` context. Imagine the configuration hierarchy as a file system, and the different contexts are the directories. The `edit` command behaves like the UNIX `cd` command, which is used for changing directories.

If you want to go from there and edit the IS-IS Level-2 configuration then you simply enter the following command:

```
[edit protocols isis]
hannes@Frankfurt# edit level 2
[edit protocols isis level 2]
hannes@Frankfurt#
```

You can go back to the top level using the `top` command. The `top` command compares best to the UNIX `cd /` command which puts you at the root of a UNIX file system tree:

```
[edit protocols isis level 2]
hannes@Frankfurt# top
[edit]
hannes@Frankfurt#
```

If you want to exit the configuration mode, type at any level `exit configuration-mode`, which puts you back in operation mode. The prompt then changes back to ">".

```
[edit protocols isis level 2]
hannes@Frankfurt# exit configuration-mode
Exiting configuration mode
hannes@Frankfurt>
```

Using the `edit` and `top` command, you can move around in the configuration hierarchy without altering any configuration elements.

3.3.5 *Changing the Configuration*

The file system analogy explains the JUNOS configuration concept most clearly. The `cd` command is used to move around in the file system hierarchy but it does not change any of the files. In a UNIX file system, you create new files (for example) by using text editors like Emacs or Vi. But you do not need to learn the often cryptic Emacs and Vi keyboard sequences to configure a JUNOS router. This is just an analogy. The text editor equivalents in JUNOS are the `set` and `delete` commands. With the `set` command you do actually set a flag in the configuration hierarchy.

Reconsider Figure 3.10. If you want to configure an interface to perform checksumming, in the `protocols isis {}` context you would type:

```
[edit protocols isis]
hannes@Frankfurt# set interface so-3/0/0.0 checksum
```

```
[edit protocols isis]
hannes@Frankfurt#
```

Going back to the file-system analogy, this command simply sets the checksum flag in the `protocols isis interface so-3/0/0.0` folder.

One of the most interesting concepts in JUNOS is that you can display the configuration any time you are in configuration mode by using the `show` command. In IOS, this is not possible, and you would have to exit configuration mode and type a `show running-configuration` command to verify that your command has been properly accepted and is part of the configuration file. Most network administrators compensate by having two IOS terminal sessions open for each Cisco router. On the first you put yourself into configuration mode, and on the second you stay in operational mode and issue the `show running-configuration` commands to check your configuration changes.

But in JUNOS, the `show` command displays the configuration file at this context level and all levels below:

```
[edit protocols isis]
hannes@Frankfurt# show
interface so-3/0/0.0 {
  checksum;
}
[edit protocols isis]
```

Don't get scared by the curly braces. They are just another representation of the folder-like structure, and are very familiar to C-language programmers. They just help to visualize the configuration hierarchy, as their use in programs helps to visualize coding levels. For instance, if we change the editing context back to the top-level, then we would see the folder structure (plus more curly braces) from the top-level perspective:

```
[edit protocols isis]
hannes@Frankfurt# top
[edit]
hannes@Frankfurt# show
[ … ]
protocols {
  isis {
    interface so-3/0/0.0 {
      checksum;
    }
  }
}
[ … ]
[edit]
hannes@Frankfurt#
```

The counterpart of `set` is the `delete` command. As the name implies, it is used to delete a certain flag from the configuration. For instance, to remove the checksumming flag from interface so-3/0/0.0, then the command would be `delete interface so-3/0/0.0 checksum`:

```
[edit protocols isis]
hannes@Frankfurt# delete interface so-3/0/0.0 checksum
[edit protocols isis]
hannes@Frankfurt# show

[edit protocols isis]
hannes@Frankfurt#
```

A very convenient use of the `delete` command is that you can specify both individual elements and even entire branches (folders) for deletion. For instance, if you have a rich set of parameters configured under the `protocols isis level 2 {}` branch, and you do not want to delete the elements one by one, you can delete the entire level 2 configuration by issuing a `delete level 2` command.

```
[edit protocols isis]
hannes@Frankfurt# show
[ … ]
level 2 {
  authentication-key "$9$f5z69CuIEy36cl"; # SECRET-DATA
  authentication-type md5; # SECRET-DATA
  no-hello-authentication;
  wide-metrics-only;
  preference 100;
}
[ … ]
[edit protocols isis]
hannes@Frankfurt# delete level 2
[edit protocols isis]
hannes@Frankfurt# show

[edit protocols isis]
hannes@Frankfurt#
```

As with file systems in the UNIX world, you can access a configuration from *any context* – all you have to do is specifying the full *path* in the configuration hierarchy. Therefore, you can turn on checksumming from the `protocols isis {}` hierarchy level:

```
[edit protocols isis]
hannes@Frankfurt# set interface so-3/0/0.0 checksum
[edit protocols isis]
hannes@Frankfurt#
```

But this can also be done from the top-level hierarchy (note the longer path in the command):

```
[edit]
hannes@Frankfurt# set protocols isis interface so-3/0/0.0 checksum
[edit]
hannes@Frankfurt#
```

Unlike IOS, when you enter the `set` and `delete` commands your JUNOS configuration does not become *active* immediately. You can modify the configuration file as much and as often as you like, even deleting it fully and starting from scratch (not often a good idea, but possible). Even complete deletion will not do any harm or disrupt your connectivity to the router – yet.

3.3.6 *Activating a Configuration*

JUNOS changes its configuration on a transactional model. You really have two configurations in the system:

- The active configuration
- A candidate configuration

The *active configuration* is the one that the router currently executes. The candidate configuration is originally a *copy* of the active configuration created when you enter configuration mode, and it is the candidate configuration which is modified. Think of it like a document that you open and modify – nothing changes until you do a SAVE on your wordprocessor. The analogy of the wordprocessor's SAVE in JUNOS is the `commit` command. The `commit` command does a syntax and sanity check of the *candidate configuration* and, if satisfied, copies the *candidate configuration* to the *active configuration.*

```
[edit protocols isis]
hannes@Frankfurt# commit
commit complete
[edit protocols isis]
hannes@Frankfurt#
```

Do not forget to commit your changes when you start working with JUNOS. You might wonder why the changes did not take effect. If you are used to an IOS environment, forgetting to do a `commit` is a frequent mistake.

In wordprocessors there is the UNDO function if you made a change and you want get back to a previous version of your document. JUNOS has a similar mechanism, which is executed using the `rollback` command. You can go back to up to nine versions of the configuration history by specifying a number after the `rollback` command.

```
[edit]
hannes@Frankfurt# rollback 3
[edit]
hannes@Frankfurt#
```

Note that the rollback command loads a *historical* configuration as just another *candidate* configuration. It is only re-activated using the `commit` command again.

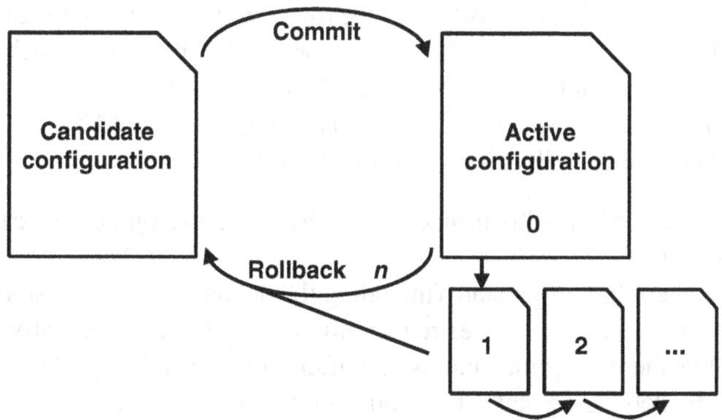

FIGURE 3.11. JUNOS has a transactional system for changing, activating and rolling back configurations

Figure 3.11 presents an overview of how the commit and rollback commands synchronize between the *active, candidate* and *historical* configuration files.

When you first go into the configuration mode, it means that up to now *there has been no* candidate configuration, and the candidate configuration is copied unchanged from the active configuration. If a change to the candidate configuration is made and committed, then the candidate configuration replaces the active configuration. The old active configuration is moved into the "archives". Historical configurations in the archive are numbered like the log rotation tools you may know from UNIX operating systems. Up to fifty instances of the file are kept. During a commit operation, historical file #49 is rolled out and deleted. The remaining other nine configuration files are renamed. Config #1 becomes Config #2, Config #2 becomes Config #3. And finally the previous active configuration becomes historical Config #1.

The JUNOS configuration editor is a very comfortable piece of software that you should enjoy using, especially those familiar with programming. Even more important are the troubleshooting facilities, which you need to know in order to debug customers' problems of all kinds.

3.3.7 *Troubleshooting Tools*

In the Cisco IOS, debugging routing protocol traffic is done using the `debug` command once you are in privileged (enable) operational command mode. JUNOS is very transaction-oriented and a transition from one configuration state to another has to be explicitly executed using the `commit` command. And in JUNOS, debugging is done in the configuration mode, not operation mode. Why?

Recall that turning on the debugging facility is a potentially dangerous thing and can put the router out of commission very quickly. Just imagine what might happen if you receive 140,000 routes from an Internet route reflector and you have turned on detailed debugging for each and every BGP packet. Most likely the router will be busier writing the debug output to the local hard disk than doing something more useful, like routing packets. Therefore, many network administrators are very cautious about permitting operators to use debug.

So one of the JUNOS design choices was that debugging should be part of the configuration file. There are actually several reasons for this:

- You can at least track who turned on a certain debug output, in case the router becomes unstable.
- A router's full configuration state (including the debugging state) is stored in one file. For certain events, it may be desired to monitor the events constantly, like protocol errors. In IOS the debugging state is lost after a reboot and so you need to manually turn on all the debugging states that you want to monitor after a router reboot.
- Because it is part of the configuration file, you can take advantage of the `commit confirmed` command. The `commit confirmed` command performs an automatic rollback of the router to a safer state after a certain amount of time if the router becomes unstable or unreachable. (This rollback is indeed automatic: you have to make the change explicitly permanent to countermand this action.)

Each configuration branch in the JUNOS command line hierarchy like `interfaces`, `protocols isis`, `protocols bgp` has a dedicated `traceoptions` branch where you can configure all the events you want to debug. But first you have to specify a file where all the debugging output is written. In JUNOS, you can't just tell the router to (for instance) put out all debug output directly to the console. You have to first write the entire debug output into a file. However, you can make the CLI display all the new lines in the file and display those on the console in real-time. The configuration snippet below shows a typical configuration for tracing (debugging) the IS-IS routing process:

```
[edit]
hannes@Frankfurt# show
[ … ]
protocols {
  isis {
    traceoptions {
      file isis-trace size 10m;
      flag error;
      flag state;
      flag normal;
      flag lsp;
    }
  [ … ]
  }
}
```

The `traceoptions` configuration branch always consists of two mandatory statements. The `file` statement specifies the filename plus arbitrary properties like protection, maximum file size until it is rolled over and so on. The `flag` statement describes

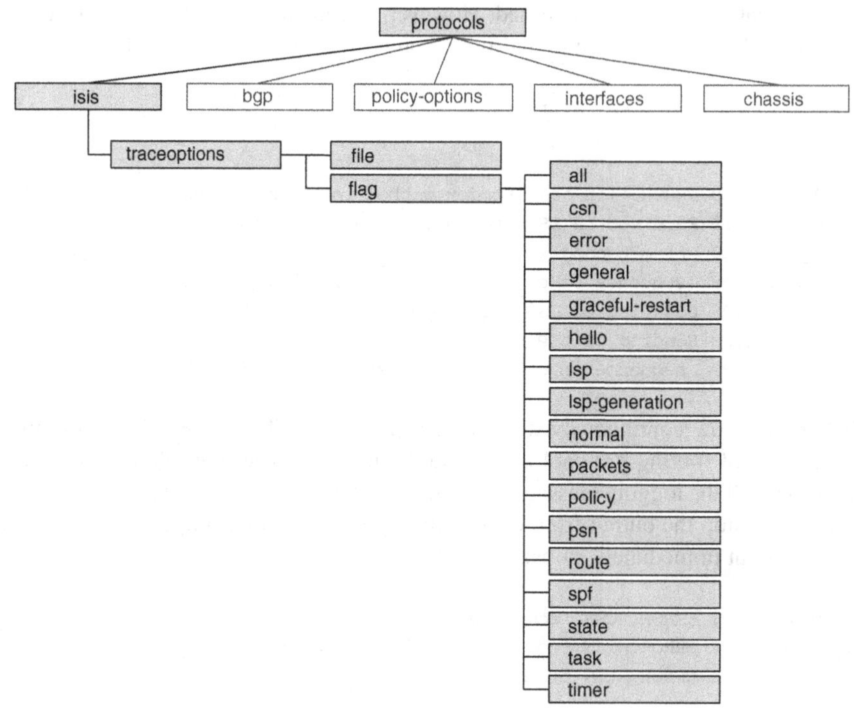

FIGURE 3.12. The IS-IS traceoption flags control the verbosity of the logfile

feature-specific event triggers that make the router log a line in the specified file. Each routing protocol has different flags: BGP has different `traceoption` flags to IS-IS, and so on, since routing protocols can work in fundamentally different ways. Figure 3.12 list the current layout of the traceoptions for the `protocols isis {}` branch.

You can examine the entries in the log file using the `show log <logfile-name>` command:

```
hannes@Frankfurt> show log isis-trace
Aug 9 23:06:25 trace_on: Tracing to "/var/log/isis-trace" started
Aug 9 23:06:26 Received L2 CSN, source London, interface so- 2/1/0.0
Aug 9 23:06:26     LSP range Penssauken.00-01 to ffff.ffff.ffff.ff-ff
Aug 9 23:06:26     packet length 179
Aug 9 23:06:26 ERROR: CSN from London without authentication
Aug 9 23:06:26 Sending L2 CSN on interface so-3/0/0.0
Aug 9 23:06:26     LSP range 0000.0000.0000.00-00 to Stockholm.00-00
Aug 9 23:06:26     packet length 1478
```

The `show log` command starts displaying the file from the beginning, but it does not display any additions to the end of the file made in real-time as the display scrolls. You know the log file is displayed from the beginning because the first line contains the statement that tracing has just started. However, if you want to display the most recent additions to the end of the file in real-time, you need to start a *monitor* job.

```
hannes@Frankfurt> monitor start isis-trace
hannes@Frankfurt>
*** isis-trace ***
Aug 10 00:14:29 ERROR: IIH from London without authentication
Aug 10 00:14:29 Received L2 LSP Stockholm.00-00, interface so-3/0/0.0
Aug 10 00:14:29  from London
Aug 10 00:14:29  sequence 0x7c2, checksum 0x55bf, lifetime 65522
Aug 10 00:14:29 Updating L2 LSP Stockholm.00-00 in TED
Aug 10 00:14:29 Sending L2 LSP Stockholm.00-00 on interface fe-2/1/0.0
Aug 10 00:14:29  sequence 0x7c2, checksum 0x55bf, lifetime 65522
```

The router now continuously displays any new traces that are written to the file. If there is a lot of routing protocol activity in the network, your console might get overwhelmed by all the logging messages and you won't even be able to type anything to stop the flood. To stop the output from overwhelming your console, simply type ESC Q and then the output immediately stops;

```
Aug 10 00:22:01 ERROR: CSN from London without authentication
Aug 10 00:22:01 ERROR: CSN from London without authentication
Aug 10 00:22:01 ERROR: CSN from London without authentication

*** monitor and syslog output disabled, press ESC-Q to enable ***
```

The output is now suspended, and resumes when the ESC Q toggle is used again. But even with console output suspended, the monitoring job is still active, as shown by issuing the `monitor list` command:

```
hannes@Frankfurt> monitor list
monitor start "isis-trace" (Last changed Aug 00:23:37 20)
hannes@Frankfurt>
```

Finally, to stop the output to the console, issue a `monitor stop isis-trace` command. Don't forget to unsuspend the output by pressing ESC Q again, otherwise you may wonder when you issue your next `monitor start` command why there is no output appearing on the screen:

```
hannes@Frankfurt> monitor stop isis-trace
hannes@Frankfurt>
*** monitor and syslog output enabled, press ESC-Q to disable ***
```

The traceoptions tell you about system internal events as seen by the routing software. Sometimes the routing protocol messages seen from an interface perspective (as opposed to the router perspective) may be critical for troubleshooting purposes. JUNOS has built-in protocol analyzer software, which is basically an enhanced version of the UNIX tcpdump utility. It is invoked using the `monitor traffic interface <interface-name>` command. There are a lot of additional options for the monitor traffic command. The most important is the `size` option, as the tcpdump default only captures 68 bytes of a packet, typically enough to display the headers of an IP packet, but not always enough for a complete analysis of problems. If you need to troubleshoot routing protocols you should specify at least the maximum size of the packet, because all of the information is critical – not just the headers. For IS-IS this maximum size is 1492 bytes:

Tcpdump output

```
hannes@frankfurt> monitor traffic interface fe-0/0/1 size 1492
Listening on fe-0/0/1
00:37:30.219626 OSI, IS-IS, length: 77
  L2 Lan IIH, hlen: 27, v: 1, pdu-v: 1, sys-id-len: 6 (0), max-area: 3 (0)
  source-id: 1921.6807.7003, holding time: 120s, Flags: [Level 1, Level 2]
  lan-id: 1921.6807.7003.02, Priority: 70, PDU length: 77
    IS Neighbor(s) TLV #6, length: 6
      SNPA: 00d0.b7b2.71cc
    Protocols supported TLV #129, length: 2
      NLPID(s): IPv4 (0xcc), IPv6 (0x8e)
    IPv4 Interface address(es) TLV #132, length: 4
      IPv4 interface address: 172.17.33.1
    IPv6 Interface address(es) TLV #232, length: 16
      IPv6 interface address: fe80::7777:69ff:fea0:8001
    Area address(es) TLV #1, length: 4
      Area address (length: 3): 49.0001
    Restart Signaling TLV #211, length: 3
      Flags [none], Remaining holding time 0s
    Checksum TLV #12, length: 2
      checksum: 0x5dfd (correct)
```

The `monitor traffic` command is very useful for diagnosing low-level protocol errors. Because it provides very detailed output (as shown in the previous example), it is also a good tool for learning about the IS-IS protocol.

3.3.8 *Routing Policy*

JUNOS probably has the most powerful language for controlling routing information flow between routers. Because subsequent chapters modify the default behaviour as to how IS-IS passes on routes to other routers, some familiarity with the JUNOS Routing Policy Language (RPL) is required.

In JUNOS virtually every flow of routing information, even the flow of prefixes internal to the routing protocol (like the transfer of routes on an OSPF Area Border Router (ABR) from one area to another) is subject to policy processing. Policies are present simply *everywhere* in the routing sub-system.

In order not to reinvent the semantics of policy processing a new for each protocol, Juniper Networks' engineers took a different approach. Policies are stored in a *protocol-neutral* way

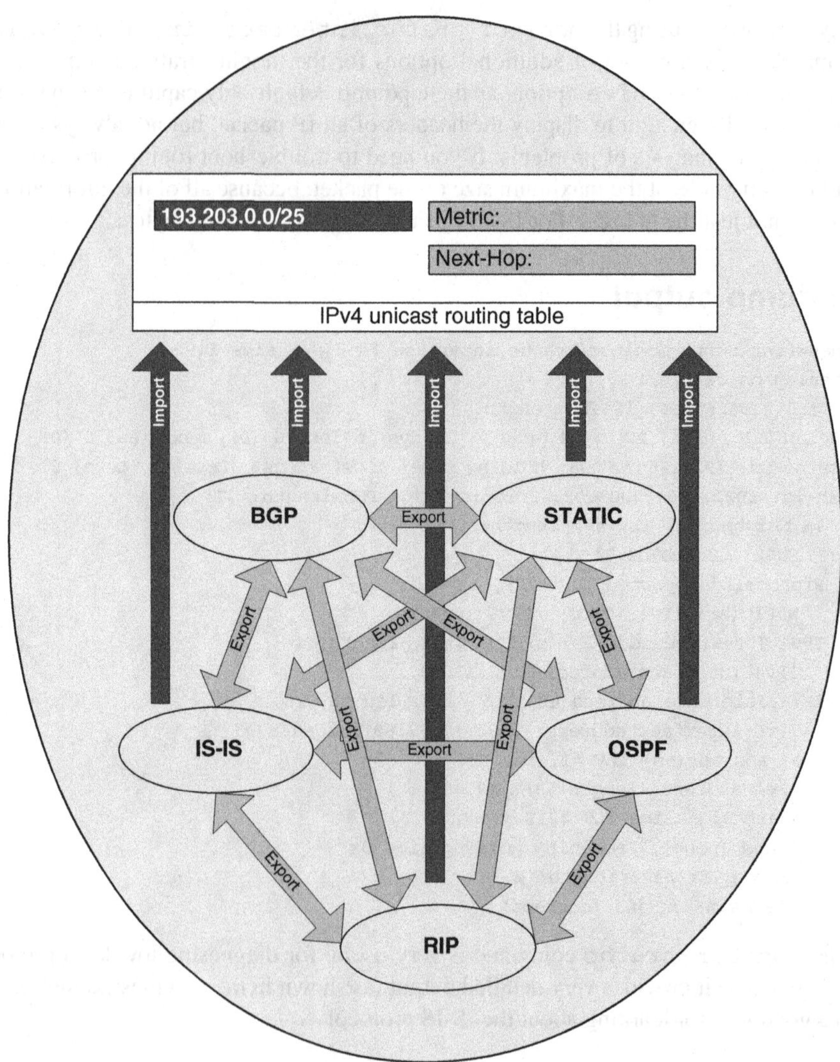

FIGURE 3.13. In IOS the protocols own all the transactions for route redistribution

in the system and may be used by any protocol. Figure 3.13 illustrates the differences between the policy processing model on IOS platforms and JUNOS.

In the IOS model, the flow of routes occurs *between* the various protocols. If, for example, you want to configure redistribution from RIP to OSPF, the RIP process tells the OSPF process that it has routes that may be included for redistribution. In JUNOS, there is not that much interaction in between the protocols – there is a defined "choke point" where all protocols install their routing information, which is the main unicast routing table inet.0. So for each protocol one or more routing policies can be called. The

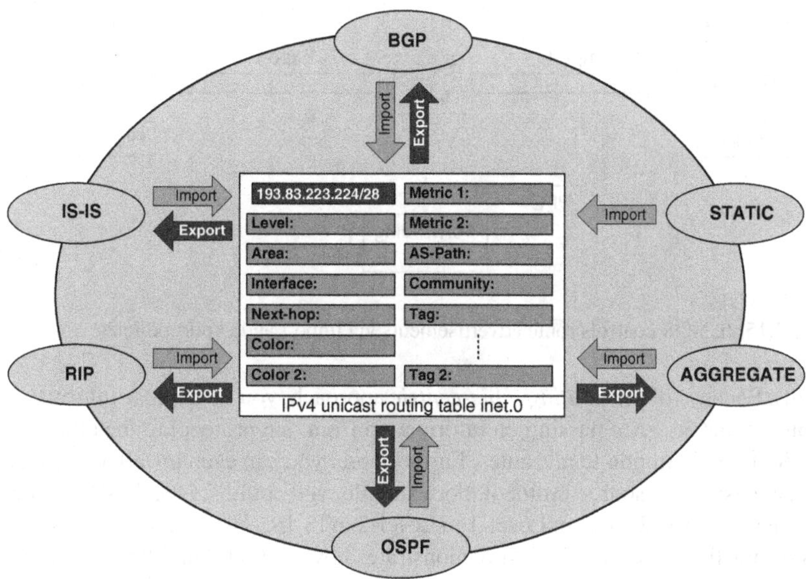

FIGURE 3.14. In JUNOS the main routing table holds up meta-attribute information from all possible routing protocols

JUNOS model is shown in Figure 3.14, where the routing entry in the central routing table holds "metainformation" about all routing protocol attributes.

Let's compare how IOS and JUNOS work when it comes to routing information redistribution. Consider a Cisco IOS configuration example where we redistribute RIP routes to OSPF:

```
London#show running-config
[ ... ]
router ospf 1
  redistribute rip subnets
```

The configuration makes the router take all RIP routes and redistribute them to OSPF with a default metric of 1. The interesting thing here is that we *lose* the metric information of the original RIP routes. Maybe it would be important to the OSPF part of the network what metric (in RIP it is called the *hop count*) the prefixes originally had, but that is not possible.

In JUNOS things work differently: each route carries all the attributes that the different routing protocols generate. Each route has fields for storing BGP attributes like the community or AS-Path attributes, as well as OSPF and IS-IS information like the OSPF area or IS-IS level. Each protocol fills in the fields that are relevant to the respective protocol when a route is installed in inet.0. For example, BGP fills in fields called Metric-1 and Metric-2 for BGP local preference and multi-exit discriminator (MED), and retains the BGP community and AS-Path as well. In contrast, a route learned through OSPF would only fill in the Metric and Tag fields (if it is an external route and the OSPF Tag is

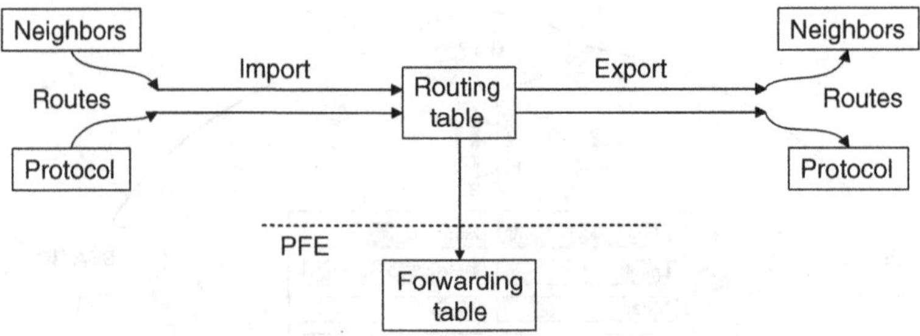

FIGURE 3.15. JUNOS controls route advertisements via import and export policies

present). Because of this *routing table-centric* approach, you do not lose information like the routing metric when passing on information from one protocol to the other, because some fields are common to all routes. Furthermore, you can even install an attribute that does not exist in the source protocol. For example, you could set the AS-Path when certain routes are passed on from Level-1 to Level-2 in IS-IS. (Not that this particular example is of practical relevance, it just demonstrates how powerful and flexible the JUNOS policy language is.)

JUNOS policies work fairly directly: all they can do is either reject or modify incoming routing updates, or alter or suppress outgoing routing updates. Policies can therefore be applied on the inbound and on the outbound side of a routing protocol. In JUNOS an inbound policy is called an *import* policy and an outbound policy is called an *export* policy. Figure 3.15 shows where import and export policies take effect.

The import policy controls which routes get installed in the unicast routing table. An export policy controls which routes are advertised to neighbouring routers. Note that only routes that are installed in the routing table inet.0 are exportable to other routers. A route that is known to JUNOS but not installed in inet.0 is called a *hidden route* in JUNOS. Many issues arise when routes can plainly be seen arriving at the router, but are never advertised because for one reason or another they have become hidden routes and seem to have been swallowed up by the router in question.

In JUNOS, there is no interaction directly between the protocols. There is just interaction between an individual routing protocol and the routing table as shown in Figure 3.15. Each routing protocol may call one or more import and export policies. The interesting thing is that there is a common syntax for routing policies irrespective which routing protocol calls the policy. For illustration, create a simple policy that selects the entire set of static routes present on a router. Routing policies consist of a *match* clause and an *action* clause. The JUNOS keyword for the match clause is *from*, and the action clause is introduced by the keyword *then*:

```
policy-options {
  policy-statement all-statics {
    from protocol static;
    then accept;
  }
}
```

The above example shows a very simple policy. It creates a policy named *all-statics* under the policy-options branch of the configuration hierarchy. Next, it defines the match and action clauses. If the route's originating protocol is "from" static, then accept that prefix. Note that in the "then" part no detailed action is actually specified for the prefix. This is largely dependent on which routing protocol has called the policy, and where the policy is applied.

For example, if the policy is applied as an export policy within OSPF:

```
protocols {
  ospf {
    export all-statics;
  }
}
```

This means that all prefixes that are installed in the inet.0 routing table *and* are static routes (these alone match the policy `all-statics`) will be redistributed into OSPF and announced to all OSPF neighbours.

But if the same policy is applied as an export policy within BGP:

```
protocols {
  bgp {
    group internal {
      export all-statics;
      neighbor 172.26.250.2;
      neighbor 172.26.244.11;
      [ ... ]
    }
  }
}
```

This means that all the static routes present in the inet.0 table are not announced to all OSPF neighbors as in the previous example, but only to the BGP peers present in the peer-group internal. So the ultimate result depends on where the policy is applied.

Policy processing is typically deployed for filtering BGP routes. Generally, IS-IS policies are simple, one-to-three term policies, which are easily readable. To learn more about the JUNOS routing policy language and policy processing in general, the Juniper Networks Book Initiative (JNBI) lists pointers to good books with more detailed elaboration on about policy processing.

3.3.9 *Further Documentation*

The entire documentation about Juniper Networks Routers is available on the Juniper Networks public website at http://www.juniper.net/techpubs/. Further documentation and books about JUNOS routing technology is posted at http://www.juniper.net/company/jnbi/.

3.4 Conclusion

Both JUNOS and IOS offer the network operator powerful user interfaces to provision, troubleshoot and change the network and router configurations. Interestingly, although both IOS and JUNOS) user interfaces are different, there are plenty of common elements, such as plain-text ASCII configuration files, two working modes (operational mode and configuration mode), auto-completion of commands, Emacs-style keyboard sequences, and a rich debugging facility. Experience from training NOC teams has shown that because of these common elements, an engineer that is used to one router OS can, after a short learning and introduction phase, pick up the necessary skills to adapt to a new environment quickly and easily.

4

IS-IS Basics

The main challenge for people wanting to learn about IS-IS is that the specifications are scattered across multiple standardization bodies. There is no single place to look at and get a quick overview about IS-IS and how it routes the IP protocols. Meanwhile, all the extensions to the base IS-IS protocol are documented in more than 25 documents, which makes it difficult for novice users to get a quick overview.

This chapter provides a quick overview of IS-IS. A lot of the topics introduced in this chapter will be explained in more detail in subsequent chapters. If you just want to get a quick overview of how IS-IS works all you have to do is read this chapter.

Readers of the basic specification of IS-IS (ISO 10589) will most likely be surprised by the constant use of OSI jargon that tries to invent an OSI counterpart for every term and acronym used in IP and the Internet. So reading this often arcane language for understanding can be very difficult. Also, there is a lot of extra information contained in the base specification unrelated to the protocol itself, like implementation details and even advice on how to code. However, most of this advice is completely outdated and it has become common to ignore most of the specification text. Once you have developed an understanding about the jargon and what paragraphs *not* to read and consider, you will find that IS-IS is a lean but powerful protocol, easy to use and even simpler to understand.

However, jargon cannot be completely avoided in IS-IS. This chapter also assumes that readers are familiar with the basic concepts of the OSPF routing protocol and the terms used in the IP protocol family. At first, there will be translation of OSI jargon to IP terminology, but later in the book we use the OSI terms, which should become familiar as the book progresses.

4.1 IS-IS and the OSI Reference Model

IS-IS is very different than other network routing protocols because it runs natively on Layer 2 of the OSI Reference Model. What does that mean? Unlike the IP routing protocols like RIP, OSPF and BGP, IS-IS does not need valid interface addressing information to transmit a message. Of course IS-IS needs some information to properly transmit routing messages, but compared to other IP routing protocols, the IS-IS configuration file is far smaller.

Running natively on Layer 2 of the OSI Reference Model has another important aspect, which is suitability for routing multiple protocols. In fact IS-IS is totally agnostic about what kind of prefixes it transports in its message. Figure 4.1 shows the position of IS-IS in the networking stack. Here, IS-IS messages are directly encapsulated for an

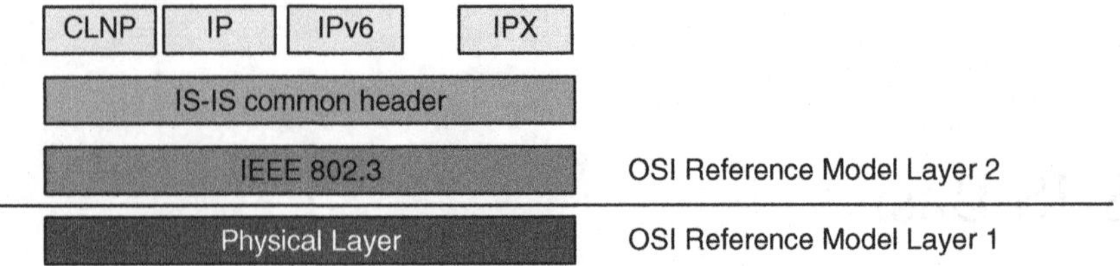

FIGURE 4.1. IS-IS is a true multiprotocol IGP as it runs native on Layer-2

802.3 Ethernet. And in the message is reachability information from the various network layer protocols such as IPv4, IPv6 and even IPX. Netware uses a clone of IS-IS called *Netware Link State Routing Protocol* (NLSRP), which shares most of the message types with IS-IS, and it is used for conveying Netware's IPX reachability information. Figure 4.1 also shows, somewhat surprisingly for those used to IP, that ISO's Layer 3 protocol, CLNP, is dependent on IS-IS and not the other way around as it would be with IP and OSPF.

This misconception is common, as we have learned over and over again when giving IS-IS training classes. Most students think that running CLNP is the prerequisite for running IS-IS. This belief is reinforced if the students first learn about IS-IS on Cisco's IOS. For code legacy reasons, you have to enable CLNS routing first before you can run IS-IS on IOS platforms. Even for the majority of IOS `show` commands there is still only the `show clns` ... syntax instead of `show isis` .... Therefore most people think that IS-IS runs over CLNP, even though the *contrary* is the case. IS-IS is an *independent* protocol and CLNP is just one of the many protocol address families it can transport.

IS-IS only understands two interface types: broadcast and point-to-point (p2p) media. The most common example of broadcast media is of course the family of Ethernet speeds (10, 100, 1000, 10,000 Mbps). But there are also older technologies like Token Ring, and FDDI. In recent years there has been increased demand for *Resilient Packet Ring* (RPR) technology, which is mostly an FDDI knockoff, but augmented with SONET/SDH headers, which makes the frames transportable using SONET/SDH Time Division Multiplexing (TDM) equipment. Resilient Packet Rings appear to IS-IS as broadcast media using the usual LAN 48-bit IEEE MAC addresses. Of all these media types, Ethernet is the most commonplace by far and is also the only broadcast media type that will be referenced throughout the book. Figure 4.2 shows how a native IS-IS message is encapsulated in Ethernet frames. All IS-IS messages are sent to one of the two well-known multicast MAC addresses 0180:c200:0014 or 0180:c200:0014. On broadcast media such as Ethernet there are no IS-IS unicast messages. IS-IS wants to make sure that *every* router connected to the LAN hears *all* of its messages. The source MAC address is typically the burned-in-address (BIA) of the sending Ethernet port. Next is the length field, which tells the receiver how long the entire Ethernet frame will be. The next two bytes indicate the destination service attachment point (DSAP) and source service attachment point (SSAP). Each major networking protocol has an SAP code point assigned. The two SAPs indicate which parts of the system talk to each other. A DSAP of 0xFE and a SSAP of 0xFE means that an OSI protocol on the sender side wants to talk to an OSI protocol on the receiver side (oddly, the DSAP and SSAP don't have to match, but most protocols

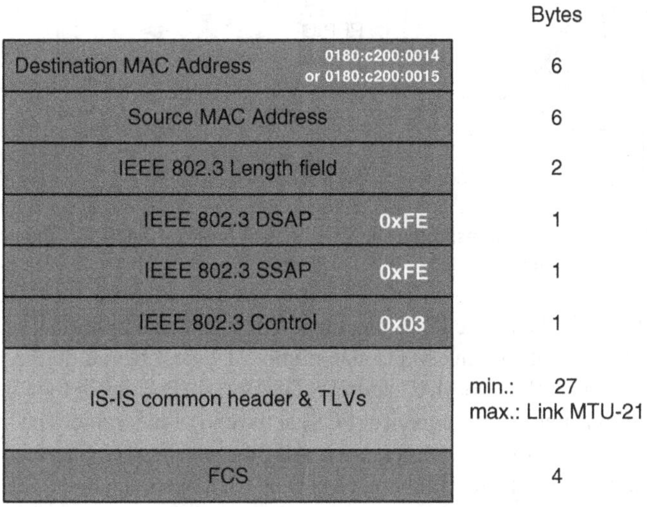

	Bytes
Destination MAC Address 0180:c200:0014 or 0180:c200:0015	6
Source MAC Address	6
IEEE 802.3 Length field	2
IEEE 802.3 DSAP 0xFE	1
IEEE 802.3 SSAP 0xFE	1
IEEE 802.3 Control 0x03	1
IS-IS common header & TLVs	min.: 27 max.: Link MTU-21
FCS	4

FIGURE 4.2. IS-IS messages are transported over Ethernet using IEEE 820.3 (802.2 LLC) encapsulation only

only understand other versions of themselves). The last byte before the common IS-IS header is the control byte which tells the receiver if the sender desires flow-control at the Ethernet level. IS-IS does not do flow-control at the MAC level, and turns it off using the code point value of 3.

For Ethernet there are in general three different methods of encapsulating higher layer information (packets) inside Ethernet frames. The encapsulation method shown in Figure 4.2 is called 802.3 or, in Cisco Systems-IOS-speak, *SAP* encapsulation. There is also the Ethernet II encapsulation also known as DIX or ARPA encapsulation, which replaces the length field of the 802.3 encapsulation format with a 16-bit type code. Assigning all type codes with values greater than 1500 (the limit for the length field) avoids collisions between code points and valid frame lengths, which must be less than 1518 bytes altogether. The final encapsulation method is called sub-network access protocol (SNAP), and is an extension of the IEEE 802.3 encapsulation. The DSAP and SSAP are set to 0xAA (the "SNAP SAP") and this indicates that another 5-byte header follows, which gives the protocols inside more room for type information and eases the allocation of code points for vendor-proprietary protocols. This is achieved by prepending the 3-byte organizational unit identifier (OUI) that each Ethernet vendor has been assigned before the 2-byte protocol code point (which is actually the DIX Ethernet type field that the length field replaced!).

Interestingly, IS-IS *never* used any other encapsulation than 802.3. So although there are OSI code points for the two other encapsulation methods (Ethernet II and SNAP) they have *never* been widely used for IS-IS. Most IS-IS implementations did not even accept IS-IS messages with a non-IEEE 802.3 encapsulation style. Today, IEEE 802.3 encapsulation is the only possible Ethernet encapsulation for IS-IS and the two others are considered to be "illegal".

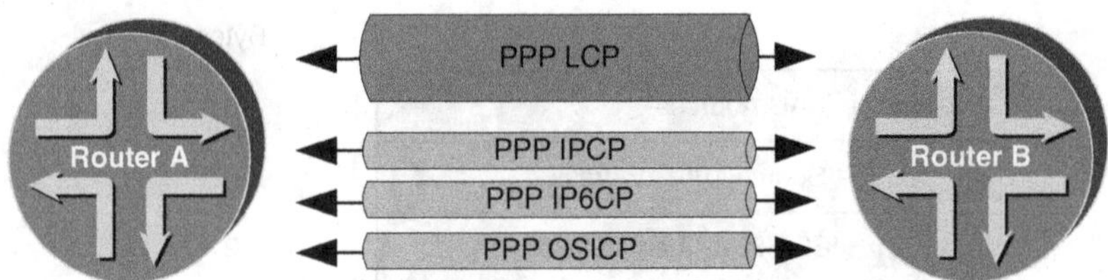

FIGURE 4.3. Before traffic is transported the OSI control protocol and PPP line control protocol have to get into *opened* state

Inside the frame is the native IS-IS message, which can be a minimum of 27 bytes and at maximum the size of the link MTU size minus 21 bytes. If you do the mathematics, 21 bytes is the sum of the two MAC address, DSAP, SSAP, Control byte fields, plus the 4 bytes of trailing frame check sequence (FCS) at the end of the frame. The link MTU size varies with the type of Ethernet chipset in use. All Ethernet network interface cards (NICs) must support at least the standard Ethernet MTU of 1518 bytes (including FCS). However, there are chipsets around which can generate *jumbo frames* which generate Ethernet frames up to 9000 bytes in length. That's the reason the maximum IS-IS packet length is dependent on the actual link MTU size and is not a simple number. The maximum amount of IS-IS information that can be stored in a standard Ethernet Frame is 1518 minus 21, or 1497 bytes. IS-IS must ensure that it does not transmit frames any larger than that even if it has to fragment the IS-IS message and scatter pieces across several Ethernet frames (there is no support for fragmentation on the Ethernet level). There is more about fragmentation and how IS-IS deals with larger than link-MTU-sized packets in Chapter 9.

For point-to-point media there are a variety of encapsulations like PPP, Cisco-HDLC, Frame Relay and ATM RFC1483/2684 encapsulation. However, the most common encapsulation is the Point-to-Point-Protocol (PPP), which will be the only one that is used throughout the book. PPP has been designed to carry multiple network layer protocols. Figure 4.3 shows the PPP model of multiplexing several protocols over a single link. First, a protocol called the PPP line control protocol (LCP) opens up the circuit and first negotiates parameters concerning the link. Examples of LCP duties are negotiation of authentication, compression, three-way handshake etc.

Next, for each network protocol like IP, IPX, IPv6 and OSI, there is a dedicated control protocol (CP). For instance, the IP Control Protocol (IPCP) assigns an IP address when dialling in to a service provider's access server. So the control protocol negotiates per-network-protocol properties. For encapsulation of IS-IS messages over the point-to-point circuit, first, the OSICP has to come up successfully. OSICP is a very lightweight protocol, sometimes not even considered a protocol, more like something along the lines of a capability announcement like "Hey! I can speak OSI, so you can send me OSI frames if you want." Once the control protocol is done, the payload frames are transported using a pre-protocol assigned code point. Figure 4.4 shows the structure of an IS-IS frame that has been encapsulated in PPP. The frame simply gets prepended using the OSI code point 0x0023. Minimum frame size (assuming the smallest possible IS-IS message of 27 bytes) is 27 plus 4 (PPP overhead), or 31 bytes. The biggest frame once again depends on the link MTU size of the underlying circuit. Typically, SONET/SDH circuits have a maximum

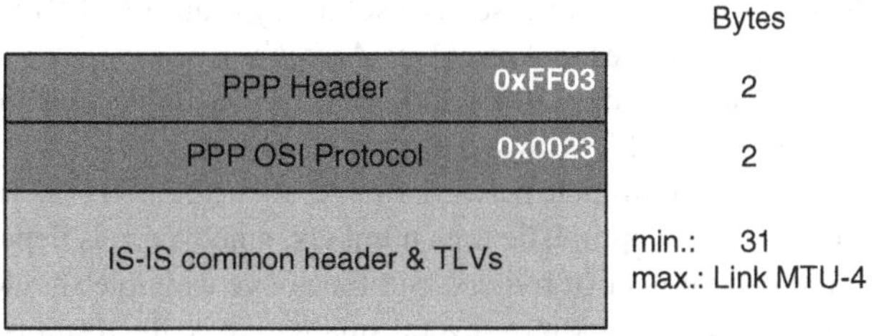

FIGURE 4.4. IS-IS over PPP

transmission unit of 4474 bytes. By subtracting the PPP overhead (4 bytes) from the 4474 bytes, this results in 4470 being the maximum MTU size on most point-to-point circuits.

IS-IS skipped all the hassle of complicated varieties of encapsulation and interface models by specifying very clearly in the specification how the format of the final frame looks. This clearly helped interoperable implementations to exist right from the beginning.

4.2 Areas

OSI structures its network topology in a distinctive way. IS-IS is much more flexible when it comes down to migrating parts of the network to another routing protocol or grooming existing ones. The tool to make that happen is called an *area.*

In the infancy of link-state protocols, the whole network consisted of a single set of routers that all shared a common database to compute the best paths through the network. At this time almost everybody working in standardization bodies seemed to be concerned about the nature of the SPF algorithm and doubted the scaling abilities of link-state routing protocols in general. In light of the exponential nature of the SPF algorithm, where the CPU demand seemed to grow infinite, the IS-IS protocol developers made an interesting move.

The idea was to structure a large network in smaller parts called areas. The topological horizon of the IS-IS routers becomes smaller to keep the CPU less busy during the route calculation process. But if a bigger network is split into smaller networks, then a set of disjoint sub-networks results. In order to connect these islands there need to be routers that route traffic *between* the areas. Even if the topological horizon and hence the computational complexity of the SPF run has been reduced, the network still has to retain all available reachability information and the routers at the area borders inject that reachability information into each other's areas. Figure 4.5 shows how this is done. The Big IS-IS network 4711 is split into two areas: Area 47 and Area 11. The computational complexity has been halved; however, in order to ensure full connectivity the router between Area 47 and Area 11, Router A, summarizes and injects all the reachable prefixes from Area 47 to Area 11, and Router B does the reverse. The IP prefixes in this example assume the reader is familiar with IP addressing and style. However, the transported prefixes are not restricted to just IP, they could be from any address family. Router A and Router B summarize their local prefixes and advertise them into the other areas. Router A sends a summary route 172.16/16 representing the local 172.16.X/24 prefixes (including its own) towards Area 11 and Router B sends a summary route 172.17/16, resulting from all the local 172.17.X/24 prefixes in Area 11, to Area 47.

The effect is remarkable – today, 1000–2000 routers in a single area are said to represent the upper boundary of IS-IS. With support of areas the network can grow to arbitrary size – today the biggest multi-area networks have about 12,000–15,000 routers. The authors do not endorse these optimistic area numbers, since a lot, is dependent on other factors than just the raw number of routers. But the above example should make it clear that by splitting up a large network into several smaller areas, the result is a network that is much more scalable than with a single-area approach.

Note that in Figure 4.5 Router A and Router B are members of their assigned areas and are not part of both areas. To those familiar with OSPF, this may seem odd at first, but IS-IS makes a distinction between area boundaries and the routing hierarchy levels that result. Decoupling area boundaries from routing hierarchy levels allows greater flexibility for migrating, joining, or splitting areas. The tool in IS-IS for creating routing hierarchies is called a *level.*

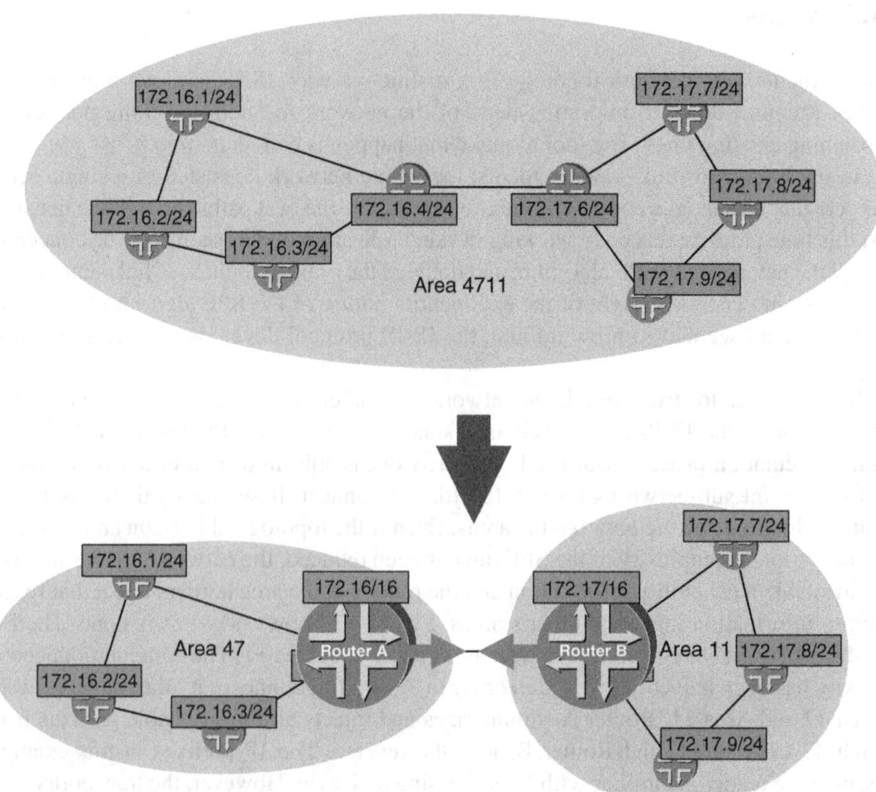

FIGURE 4.5. For a working hierarchical routing, the border routers need to summarize the reachability information of their areas and inject it to the other areas

4.3 Levels

To understand why the introduction of an *area* leads to the idea of a level scheme to denote routing hierarchies, compare the OSPF routing hierarchy with IS-IS. Figure 4.6 shows the differences between OSPF areas and IS-IS areas. In OSPF, the area border router (ABR) has two interfaces in each area: one interface in Area 51 and another interface in Area 0. One could say the demarcation line between the two areas is through the "middle" of the ABR. In IS-IS, it is the other way around: there is not a special ABR that sits between two areas. Routers stay in their assigned areas. One could say here that the demarcation line is through the middle on the link between the routers in two areas.

How can two routers ever exchange routing information if they are in two entirely separate areas? In OSPF, the Area-ID of the routers at each end of the link has to match, otherwise no *adjacency* will form between the two routers. An adjacency is a kind of *promise* that a pair of routers can mutually exchange traffic. More about adjacencies and how they are formed is found in Chapter 5.

In IS-IS, the Area-ID does not necessarily have to match for an adjacency to come up. The reason is that for every link that runs IS-IS, there is a little tag indicating the kind of *topology level* to which the link should belong. Each router in an IS-IS network builds two different topologies: the Level-1 topology and the Level-2 topology. Figure 4.7 shows this. Each link carries one of three possible tags: L1, L2 or L1L2, which tells the router in which topology level the link wishes to participate: Level-1, Level-2, or both.

Based on the level tags shown in Figure 4.7, the resulting topology is illustrated in Figure 4.8. There are links in the figure that have non-matching Area-IDs on both ends of the links (like the L2-only links between Areas 47, 11 and 12). However, Level-2 adjacencies are a bit kludgy by nature. All routers participating in the Level-1 topology *do* have to share their Area-IDs; otherwise no adjacencies will form up, just as in OSPF. But when a link is configured for Level-2, a matching Area-ID is not important as far as adjacency formation is concerned. An adjacency will form no matter if the Area-IDs match or not. For the IS-IS Level-2 backbone, the only constraint is that the Level-2 topology must be continguous, and no Level-2 routers are isolated from any others.

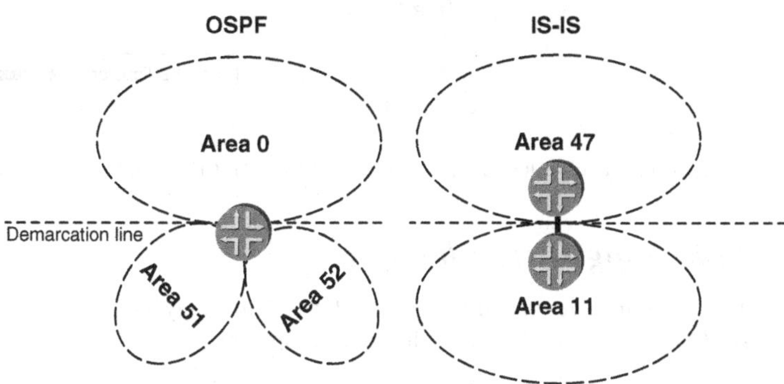

FIGURE 4.6. OSPF vs. IS-IS topological boundaries

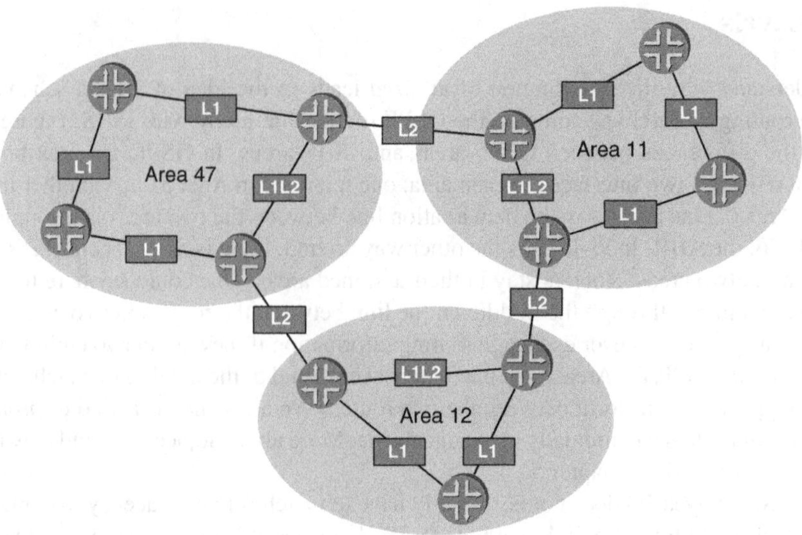

FIGURE 4.7. The level information is configured on a per interface basis; three tags are possible per circuit – L1, L2 and L1L2

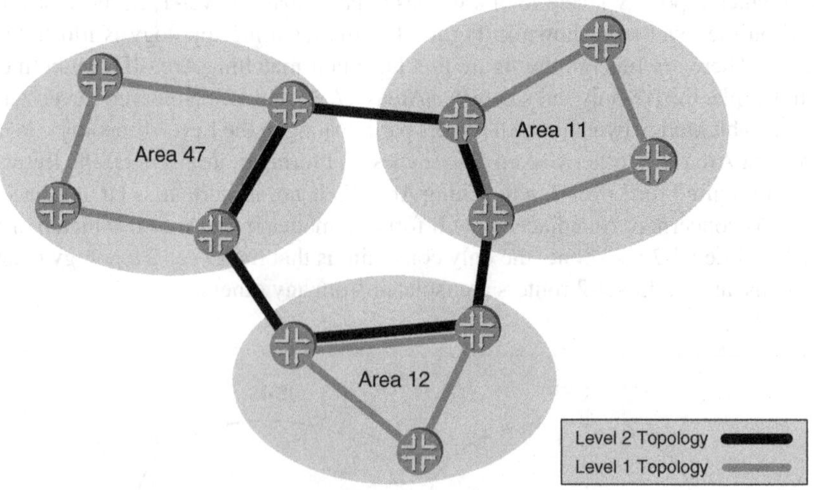

FIGURE 4.8. The resulting Level-1 and Level-2 topology based on Figure 4.7

4.3.1 *IS-IS Routing Hierarchy Rule*

Routers that share the same *Area-IDs* determine the Level-1 topology, and Routers that share a *continguous set of Level-2 circuits* determine the Level-2 topology

The interesting thing here is that a link can participate in both (Level-1 and Level-2) topologies. And having a (logical) extra link handy is useful and helps to avoid

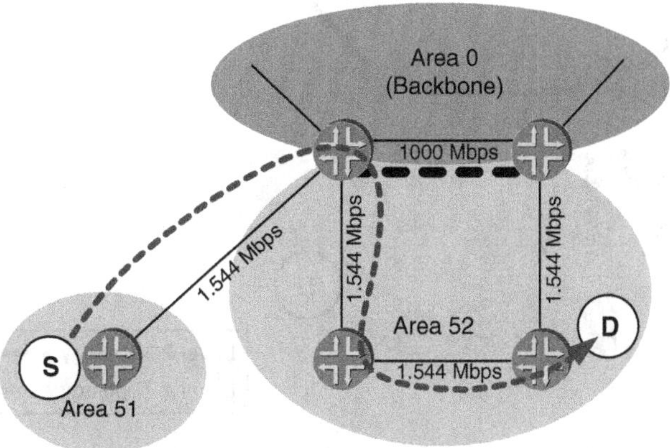

FIGURE 4.9. The OSPF constraint that one interface can only be in one area can cause sub-optimal routing

sub-optimal routing. Figure 4.9 shows how OSPF routes *inter*-area versus *intra*-area traffic. Consider traffic flowing between the two leaf-sites S (source) and D (destination). Traffic arrives at the ABR and OSPF has two routes available to route that traffic – one direct route (the intra-area) over two low-speed T1 circuits, and another route that leads over the backbone (the inter-area route), which has one T1 segment less and plenty of bandwidth available, as there is a Gigabit Ethernet segment in the path. But just like any other hierarchical routing protocol, OSPF prefers to get inter-area backbone traffic to intra-area routes as soon as possible. So ultimately the traffic takes the path indicated by the gray arrow.

Common practice to fix that problem in OSPF is to spend money to put another link between the two Area Border Routers as indicated by the thick black dotted line. This link is configured to run in Area 52 and produces a lot of new, low-cost paths to avoid the slower T1 hopping of traffic. In IS-IS the problem is solved similarly, except that you do not have to expense *two* Gigabit Ethernet router ports! Figure 4.10 shows how IS-IS avoids this expense by the level between the routers that were OSPF Area Border Routers IS-IS L1L2 capable. Now, over the same physical circuit (the Gigabit Ethernet Segment), IS-IS forms adjacencies on a *per-level* basis, and both Level-1 and Level-2 adjacencies form on the same link. Therefore, the Gigabit Ethernet link is an integral part of Area 52 and preferred when traffic travels from S to D.

4.3.2 *Route Leaking Between Levels*

Every routing protocol passes a certain amount of routing information up the routing hierarchy, and other routing information is passed down the routing hierarchy. There is a *bi-directional* flow of routing information known as *route leaking*. To better understand how IS-IS leaks routes between levels, first look at how OSPF passes routing information up and down. Figure 4.11 shows how OSPF leaks information between levels. For simplicity reasons, this example uses the *default* behaviour of how OSPF leaks routes. Of

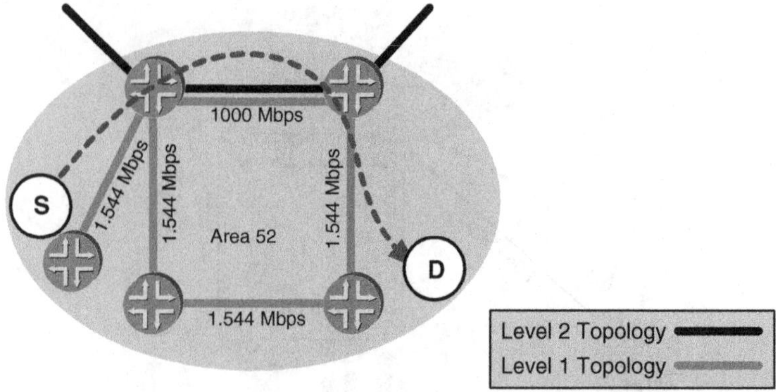

FIGURE 4.10. IS-IS can share a link between Level-1 and Level-2 topologies – this fixes the sub-optimal routing problem in a cost-effective way

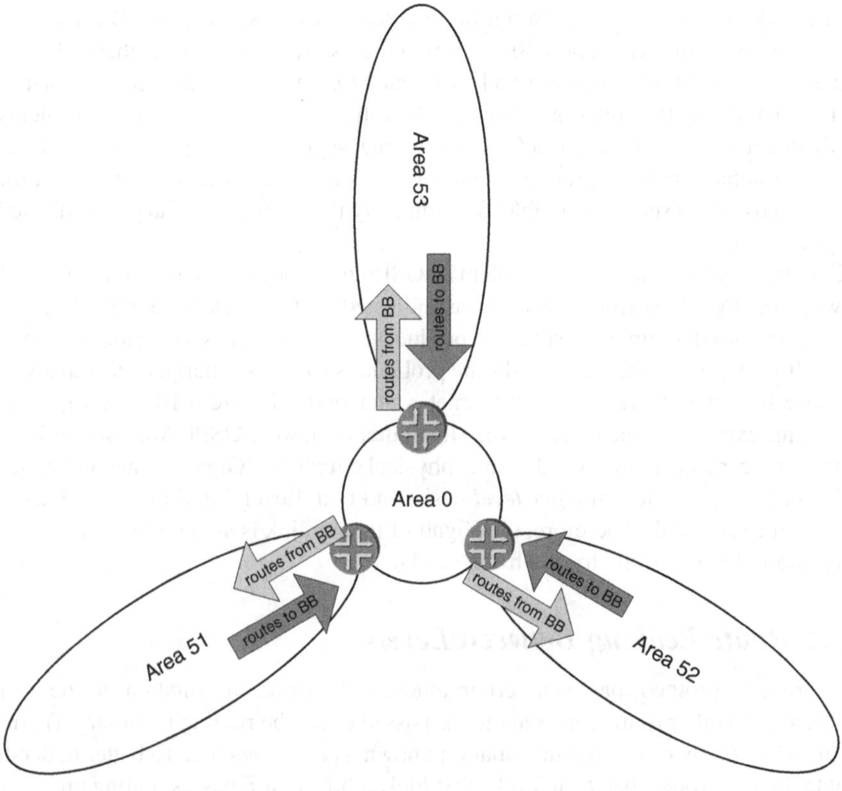

FIGURE 4.11. OSPF short-circuits reachability information between all areas, which can be a scaling harm

course, there are lots of other ways to leak OSPF routes between areas, such as *Totally-Stubby-Areas*, *Stub-Areas* and *Not-So-Stubby-Areas* (NSSA), but this is just an example. In our example network, there are three areas interconnected by three OSPF Area Border Routers, and the backbone is OSPF Area 0. In OSPF, each ABR takes the routes it calculated from the non-zero areas and redistributes it automatically to the backbone. The gray arrow indicates this step. The backbone in turn redistributes all the routes it has learned from all of the areas and feeds back that information to each as well. Ultimately, each router gets all the routing information. This is one of the scaling issues of OSPF: the fact that each area sees all the routes. This has resulted in all the add-on OSPF concepts (Totally-Stubby-Areas, NSSA) to fix that behaviour.

IS-IS is very different in this respect. Similarly to OSPF, it leaks information from Level-1 to Level-2. However, IS-IS does *not* leak down any information from Level-2 to Level-1. Figure 4.12 shows how IS-IS deals with route distribution in a hierarchical routing environment. IS-IS sets a bit in its routing messages for the respective areas. This particular bit is called the Attach bit or, for short, the ATT bit. Any router that is part of the Level-2 topology (that is, the router has at least one adjacency on a Level-2 circuit in the "Up" state) must set the ATT bit on messages. The routers in the areas simply calculate their shortest

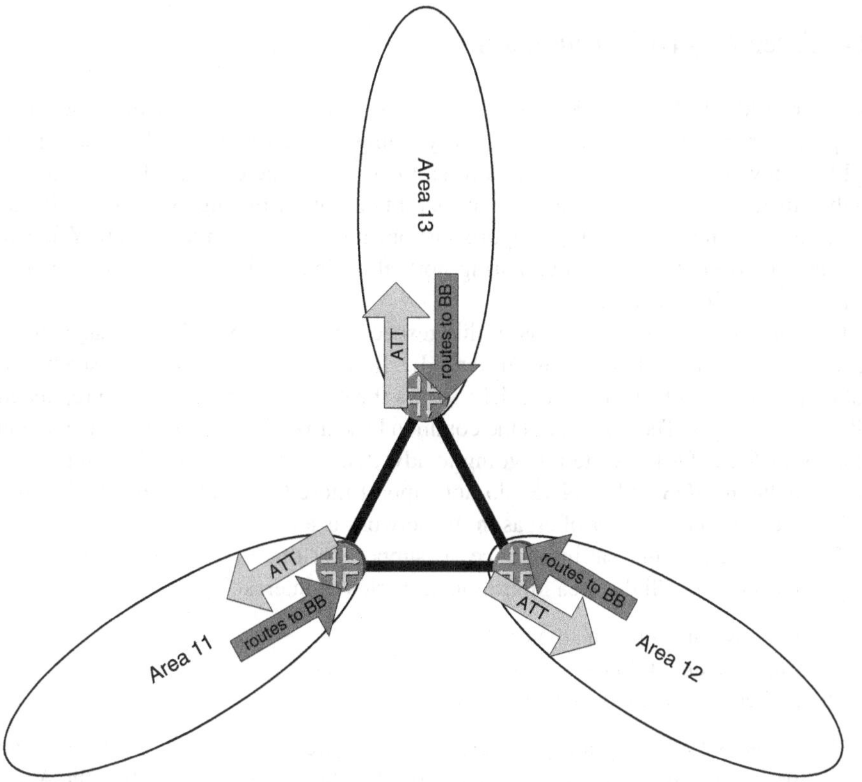

FIGURE 4.12. IS-IS does not distribute all reachability information down to the Level-2. Routes just flow up and never down the hierarchy, which is a good scaling property

path to the closest router that has sent messages with the ATT bit set and installs a default 0/0 route in its routing/forwarding table pointing to the closest L1L2 router. This is *exactly* the behaviour of Totally-Stubby-Areas in OSPF, and no wonder, since both address the same issue. However, in IS-IS you can do a few things that cannot be achieved using Totally-Stubby-Areas in OSPF, like injecting external routing information into the cloud. Luckily, OSPF NSSAs fix that problem. So to quickly explain to those familiar with OSPF the way that IS-IS leaks its routing information, it is safe to say "Almost like NSSA!". There will be more details on how exactly route leakage works in IS-IS, using a lot of examples and router configurations, in Chapter 12 "IP Reachability Information".

Assigning links arbitrarily to the two topologies proved to be a very flexible design tool that today no network designer would be without. It would seem, then, that addressing and address allocation is not an important aspect of an IS-IS network design, but do not be misled. A careful area design is what prepares an IS-IS network for all kinds of migration and expansion. A clear understanding of the differences between area addressing and the routing hierarchy is at first a bit difficult to understand in IS-IS. However, there is also a lot of operational flexibility that results from this differentiation, particularly when it comes to *migrating* areas.

4.4 Area Migration Scenarios

In contrast to OSPF, an IS-IS router can be in *multiple* areas at the same time. Having support for more than one area is mandatory to migrate area addresses. If a routing protocol has only support for one area at a time, then the change of area addresses becomes highly disruptive. Just think about the disruptive nature of migrating an OSPF area, which is a routing protocol that supports just one area address per adjacency. You cannot migrate an OSPF network's area during normal business hours: you need to allocate a maintenance window for it.

IS-IS is friendlier to migrations in this respect. In the IS-IS Hello messages there is room enough to support more than one Area-ID. In each IS-IS message, the first 8 bytes are called the *common header*. Figure 4.13 shows the common header that is prepended to all IS-IS messages. The last byte in the common header is a pre-indicator of the maximum amount of Area-IDs the system is going to advertise. However, most IS-IS implementations (including IOS and JUNOS) do not support more than 3 areas in these messages (of course, the total number of areas in the network is another matter).

This is no real limitation in practice, as support for three areas for one router at the same time supports all the area migration scenarios of interest, which are:

- Merging two areas into a single area
- Splitting one area into two areas
- Renumbering two areas to a new area

How does IS-IS treat a pair of routers that have different Area-IDs? And how is adjacency formation affected by different Area-IDs? IS-IS does not require that the Area-ID matches before a Level-1 adjacency comes up – support for multiple Area-IDs has been mentioned already. So there is no *single* Area-ID that has to match. But first IS-IS collects

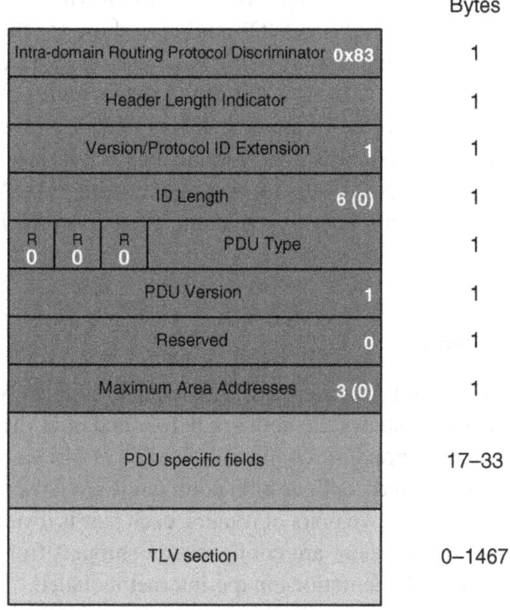

FIGURE 4.13. The IS-IS common header consists of 8 bytes that are contained in every IS-IS message. The last byte consists of the number of areas that the router supports

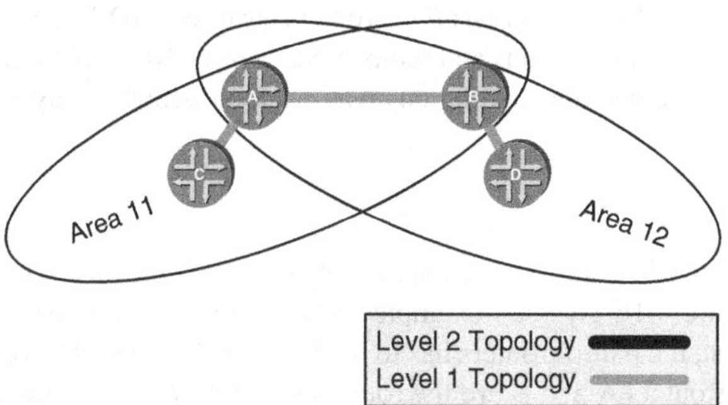

FIGURE 4.14. In an IS-IS Level-1 network there can even be multiple area addresses as long there is at least a pair of routers present in both areas

the *advertised* Area-IDs from both sides of the link. Then IS-IS looks to see if there is an Area-ID in common. If there is *at least one* matching area address then the Level-1 adjacency goes into the Up state. Figure 4.14 shows four routers (A, B, C, D), and not all of them are in the same area. No problem! As long as there is at least a single pair of routers that is present in both areas (Router A and B), the adjacency between A and B goes into the Up state and the routes of all four routers get distributed and finally received by all the routers in the Level-1 network.

Before going into the details of the migration scenarios, it will be helpful to show some configuration snippets from JUNOS and IOS and also show for the first time the ISO Network Entity Titles (NETs), which may be new. All you really need to know is that the first few bytes of the NET specify the Area-ID, but the exact number of bytes varies. The reason why there is no fixed mapping of the Area-ID into the NET is because the NETs are variable in size and, depending on the address format, the Area-ID size also varies. There is a more detailed presentation of NETs later in this chapter, in the "OSI Addressing" section.

The most common migration scenarios will demonstrate how flexible IS-IS interprets the term *area*.

4.4.1 *Merging Areas*

Figure 4.15 shows two disjoint Areas 11 and 12, which are ultimately to be joined into a common Area 11. The figure shows the network before and after the migration. Next to the router there is the corresponding configuration snippet – a snippet far from being complete – just the IS-IS-related configuration commands are presented. This migration is rather simple. First, there are two pairs of routers, each pair is disjoint to the other pair. As this is a *multivendor* book, there are configuration snippets from the two dominant (IOS and JUNOS) IS-IS implementations in the Internet included.

The migration does not happen atomically (in a single step). Several transient configurations have to be followed for a smooth transition. To be non-disruptive, first an additional NET is configured on Router A. For a short period of time Router A is configured with two NETs: 11.aaaa.aaaa.aaaa.00 and 12.aaaa.aaaa.aaaa.00. In the next step, add the common Areas NETs to Router C as well. Now all the routers have Area-ID 12 configured. Now we can clean up existing configurations and remove the Area 11 NET off Routers A and C. So the areas have been merged into a common area in a non-disruptive way.

4.4.2 *Splitting Areas*

Splitting areas is done in a similar fashion to merging areas, just (in a sense) in the opposite direction. Figure 4.16 gives an example of how to break an existing area into two smaller areas. First, the pair of routers has to be determined that will have both Area-IDs. In this example, Routers A and B are the routers which have both Area-IDs configured. The migration "style" here is again from the centre to the edge. So, first, the Area 11 NETs are configured on the Routers B, A, and D. Finally, Area 12 is removed from Router C. Again, the whole area can be configured in a non-disruptive fashion as long as the configuration order is maintained.

4.4.3 *Renumbering Areas*

Renumbering areas means that one or more areas get a new Area-ID. This example change of Area-IDs does not just affect some routers in the network, but all routers in the network. Nevertheless, if the correct order is followed, even this complex migration can be accomplished in a simple and non-disruptive fashion.

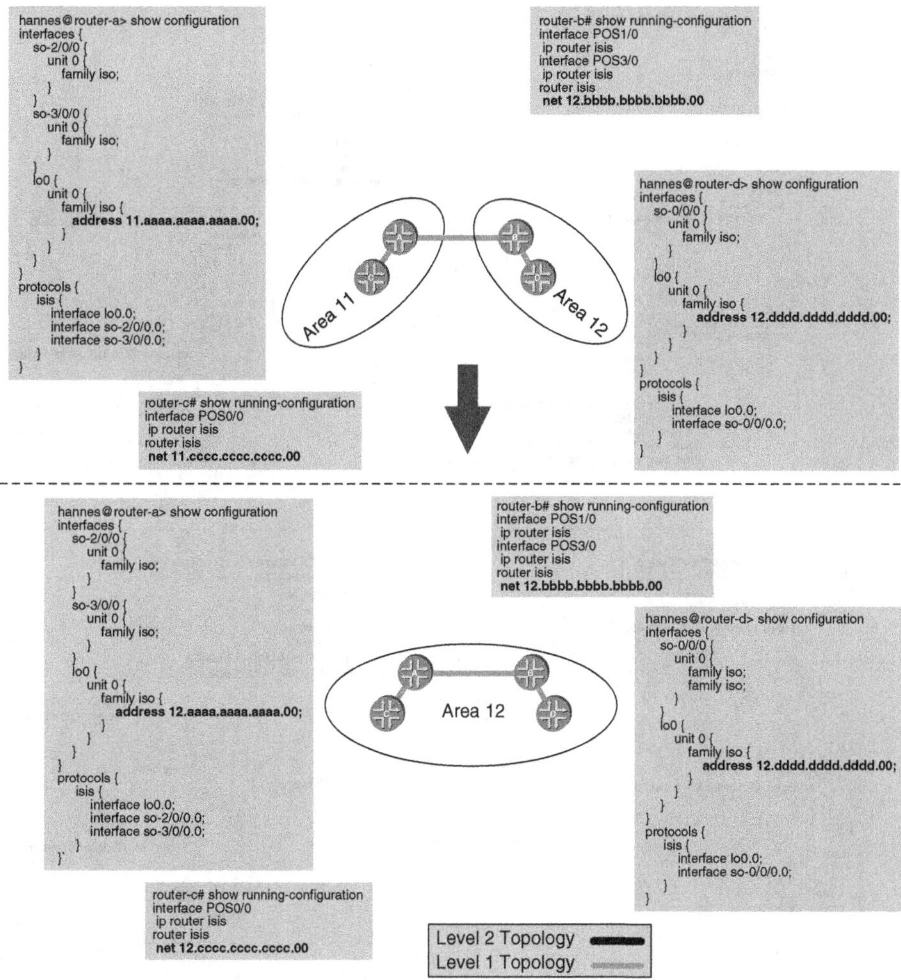

FIGURE 4.15. IS-IS area merging example

Figure 4.17 shows that, first, the new area that all routers should migrate to is configured on all the routers. This can be done without regard for any specific order. Next, both Area 11 and Area 12 are removed by deleting the NETs from the respective routers. That simple! Recall that the maximum number of NETs supported on a single router is three. So having the freedom of assigning three different Router IDs to a single router enables you to accomplish any arbitrarily complex area migration scenario, since more than three Area-IDs are never required.

Levels are a handy tool that allows the routing hierarchy to be independent of the area addressing. The next section contains a short overview on how IS-IS stores its route information and calculates routes throughout the network.

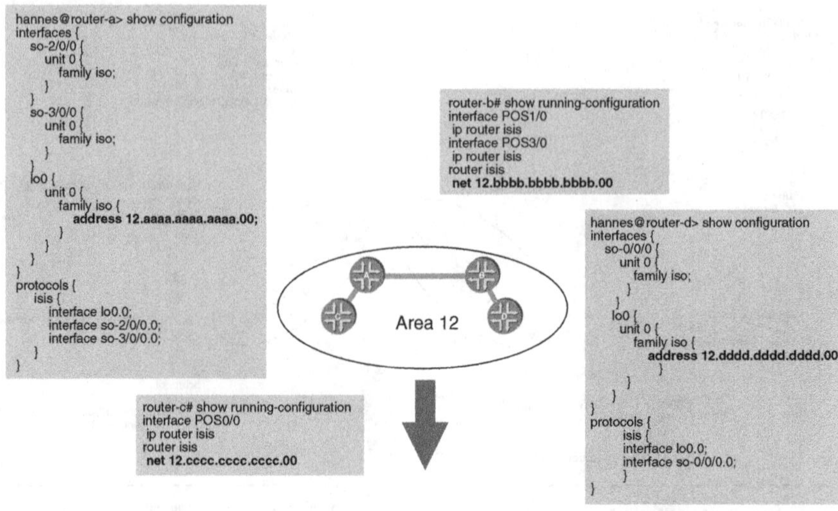

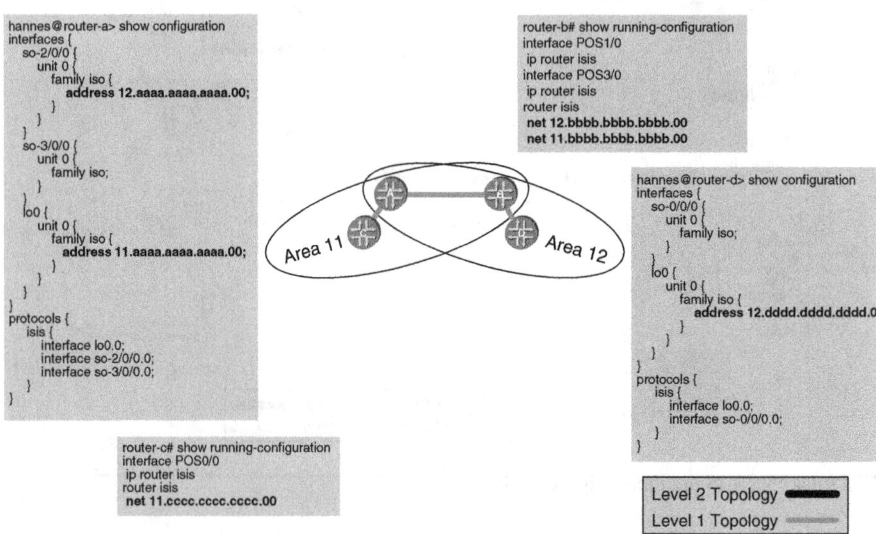

FIGURE 4.16. Area splitting example

4.5 Local SPF Computation

IS-IS follows a simple principle called *distributed databases* and *local computation*. Distributed databases means that all routers agree how many routers are in the network and how they are connected with each other. Local computation means that each router receivers the same topological information and prefixes unaltered. So, for example, no router is allowed to *change* the originator's information.

IS-IS stores all information about other routers and links in the link-state database (LSDB). There is a dedicated LSDB per Level: one for the Level-1 and one for the Level-2.

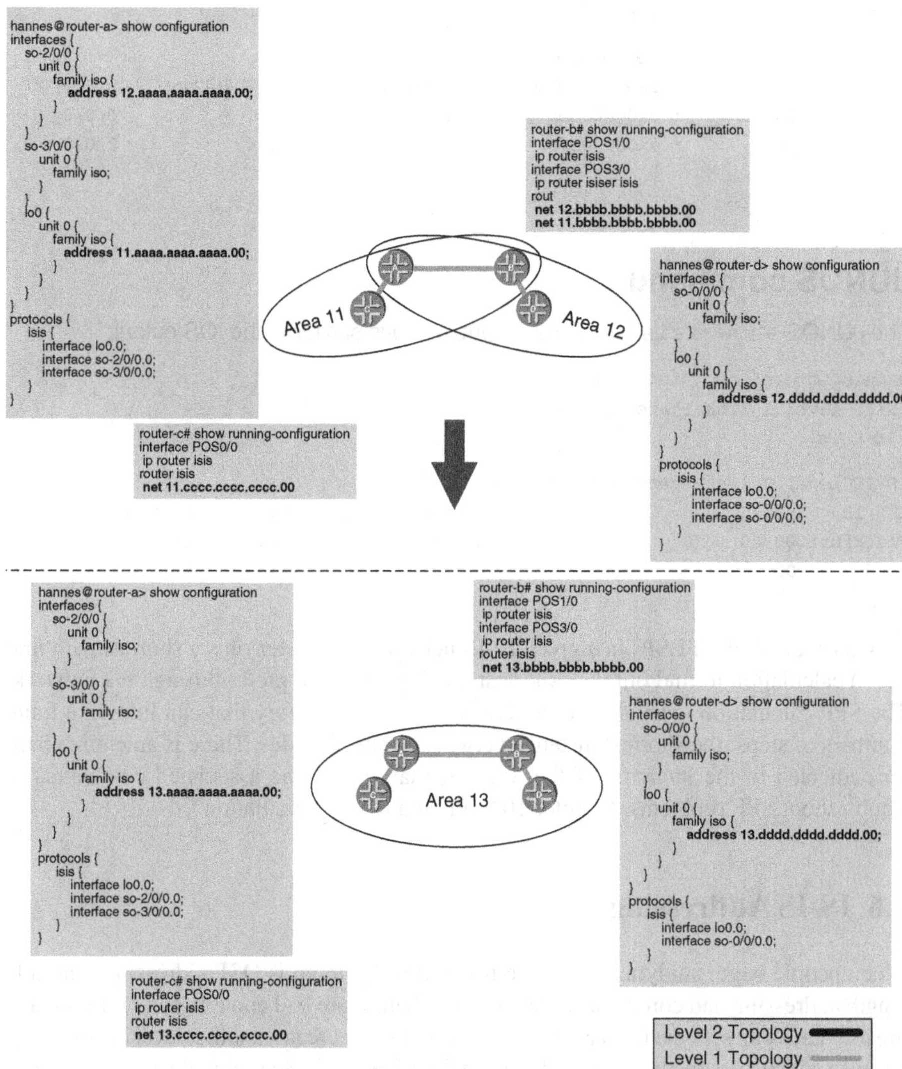

FIGURE 4.17. Area renumbering example – during configuration the worst case is that 3 areas are necessary, which is the reason that 3 areas is the default that every vendor does support

You can display the contents of the database using the `show isis database` command on both IOS and JUNOS.

IOS command

The `show isis database` command shows first the Level-1 and next the Level-2 database.

```
Frankfurt#show isis database

IS-IS Level-2 Link State Database
LSPID                 LSP Seq Num    LSP Checksum    LSP Holdtime     ATT/P/OL
Frankfurt.00-00     * 0x000003db     0x4BA7          692              0/0/0
London.00-00        * 0x00000570     0xCD17          42134            0/0/0
[...]
```

JUNOS command

The JUNOS `show isis database` output looks similar to the IOS output:

```
hannes@London> show isis database
IS-IS level 1 link-state database:
  0 LSPs

IS-IS level 2 link-state database:
LSP ID                Sequence     Checksum      Lifetime      Attributes
Frankfurt.00-00          0x3db       0x4ba7         62094      L1    L2
London.00-00             0x570       0xcd17         63349      L1    L2
[...]
```

After receipt of all LSPs in a given IS-IS network, the router runs a shortest path first (SPF) calculation to find out the "shortest path" for a given prefix through the network. The SPF calculation is an algorithm derived from graph theory that can find, in a finite numbers of steps, the shortest distance between a pair of nodes. There is an entire chapter dedicated to the internals of the SPF calculation and the associated commands to troubleshoot SPF problems, Chapter 10 "SPF and Route Calculation".

4.6 IS-IS Addressing

When people begin studying IS-IS, the first pitfall for them is OSI addressing. Variable length addressing and complicated delegation schemes are bad enough. But IS-IS inheriting its addressing scheme from the CLNP address family creates another level of confusion because sometimes the boundaries between CLNP and IS-IS are not clear to the novice.

IS-IS addressing follows a different semantic style and paradigm than IP addresses do. However, it is surprisingly simple compared to IP addressing. In this chapter, the OSI addressing paradigm will be discussed in comparison to IP. At the end, several examples of addressing schemes, plus guidelines for assigning and delegating OSI addresses in a network, will be presented.

4.6.1 *IP Addressing*

Before introducing OSI addressing, consider the basics of IPv4 addressing. (This book does not consider IPv6 addressing, but IS-IS works just as well with IPv6 as IPv4, another advantage compared with the extensive re-writes needed for OSPFv6.) The IPv4, address is a fixed, 32-bit entity. It has a different meaning for routers and for hosts like PCs or workstations. Please note that the term "hosts" in this context has nothing to do with mainframe technology. It is simply a term borrowed from ancient IP terminology meaning a computer or workstation that runs IP. For a host, the address consists of two parts: The network part and the host part. The boundary between the network and host part is defined using the *network mask*. The network mask is typically a continguous sequence of bits usually written down in decimal notation. For instance, a 24-bit "netmask" could be written as 24 consecutive bits, or in more readable decimal representation as 255.255.255.0. Since the introduction of classless interdomain routing (CIDR) in the Internet, as described in RFC 1518, it has become common not to write up the entire netmask, but just the *prefix-length*. The prefix-length is the decimal representation of the "bit border" between the network and the host part of the IP address. The shorter the prefix-length, the larger the host count beyond. Table 4.1 shows the relationship between a few selected prefix lengths (netmasks) and the potential host count.

Why is the netmask or prefix-length important? Because routers and hosts figure out, based on the prefix-length or netmask, if a destination address is on the local sub-net or not. If the prefixes of the source and destination match, then the stations are on the same sub-net (or at least they *should* be for IP to work properly).

Consider the example in Figure 4.18, which shows IP address 192.168.218.133/24. The trailing /24 indicates a network/hosts border at 24 bits. The router (and other hosts) applies the netmask to find out if a given source/destination address pair in a packet is on the same sub-net. If this example, host 192.168.218.133 wants to communicate with host 192.168.218.22. Each IP device knows that the destination host is local. How? The two IP addresses are compared, but just to the network boundary: in this case only the first 24 bits are compared. The first 24 bits match (192.168.218 = 192.168.218), so the destination host must be on the same sub-net. Therefore the packet is sent directly to the destination host. What if the destination IP address is not on the local network (the prefixes do not match)? Then the packet needs to be forwarded to a *default-router* which is always

TABLE 4.1. Host count by prefix length

Prefix length	Netmask	Host count
/8	255.0.0.0	16777216
/12	255.240.0.0	1048576
/16	255.255.0.0	65536
/20	255.255.240.0	4096
/21	255.255.248.0	2048
/22	255.255.252.0	1024
/23	255.255.254.0	512
/24	255.255.255.0	256
/25	255.255.255.128	128
/26	255.255.255.192	64
/27	255.255.255.224	32
/28	255.255.255.240	16
/29	255.255.255.248	8
/30	255.255.255.252	4
/31	255.255.255.254	2
/32	255.255.255.255	1

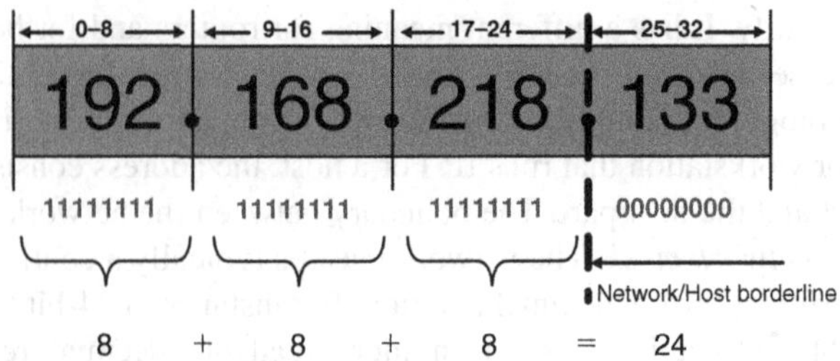

FIGURE 4.18. The border between network and host parts of the IP address

present on every LAN connected to another IP sub-net (the Internet is the collection of *all* public IP sub-nets). The default router on the LAN runs a routing protocol like IS-IS and interdomain routing protocols like BGP to learn where the destination prefix is located (actually, the router only cares about the *next-hop* closer to the destination). Based on that information, the router builds up its routing table, extracts a forwarding state from that, and populates the forwarding ASICs. When traffic arrives, the router tries to find out the *best match* prefix for a given IP packet destination address and forwards the traffic one hop closer to its destination. A lot of the information in this book covers how IS-IS learns and distributes IP prefixes.

Before considering the OSI addressing scheme, the IP *addressing model* needs to be detailed first. Each protocol address family differs in terms of things like: Where are addresses applied? At the interface-level or at the box-level, do addresses have to be unique? What is the scope of addresses? How easy is renumbering? These kinds of questions and the resulting answers is what we refer to as the *addressing model*. In the following sections, the IP addressing model is examined and answers provided for the above questions. Along the way, we discuss the differences between *numbered* and *unnumbered* interfaces and how all of this relates to the OSI way of addressing.

4.6.2 *IP Addressing Model*

In the IP world, each address on a router needs to be assigned to a sub-net, and the IP address it uses to attach that sub-net must be unique. In illustration, Figure 4.19 shows an IP router with five physical and one logical interfaces. The router holds two Gigabit Ethernet interfaces and three Packet-over-SONET/SDH (POS) interfaces. Each of the two physical interfaces holds an address. In the figure, both Gigabit Ethernet circuits are configured using /24 addresses, which is a very typical prefix length for POP LANs. The POS interfaces are true point-to-point interfaces and therefore do not need more than two IP addresses (one for each end of the link). A /31 address would be the prefix of choice for point-to-point interfaces. Unfortunately, /31 interface routes have long been treated like a pariah among IP prefixes. When assigning IP prefixes, two special addresses in the prefix-range are reserved and must not be used, the first and the last address of the prefix range. The first address typically represents the sub-net itself and the last address is used as a broadcast address for subnet-wide broadcasts. However, a /31 address has only room for

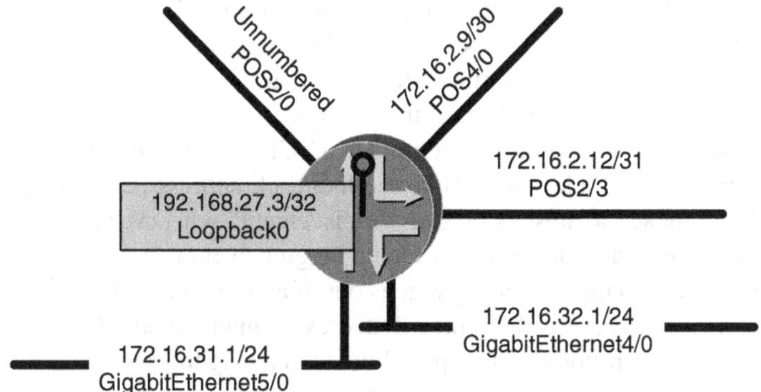

FIGURE 4.19. An IP router typically has an IP address configured on all interfaces

2 addresses (the one host bit). If the first one and the last one of these two addresses must not be used to satisfy the IP conventions, there is actually nothing left to be assigned to devices. Therefore /31 routes have never been used in the past. However, for point-to-point interfaces, no one needs a sub-net descriptor and a broadcast address because in a point-to-point environment there is just one neighbour, which hardly requires a broadcast to reach. RFC 3021 revises the common practice of assigning the first and the last address to sub-net and broadcast addresses for /31 prefixes and makes them usable again. Although modern routers all support /31 prefixes per RFC 3021, the management software of the most common OSS management suites lack this support and often display error messages like "Illegal Network Mask" when they scan the router's interface tables and do see a /31 allocation. So, before introducing /31 addresses in your network, check with your Network Management System vendor and see if the software supports /31 netmasks. We find /30 addresses for point-to-point interfaces to prevail in most networks.

Before discussing the unnumbered interface POS2/0 in the figure, the *Virtual Loopback0* interface is discussed first. Why would anyone need a *virtual* interface? Virtual interfaces have the advantage of not being tied to hardware, which can fail, and therefore never go *down*. In the TCP/IP family, any session between a pair of computers is tied to IP addresses, which in most cases are tied to hardware. Therefore, we want to tie our sessions to the most reliable interface. Designers of early routing software introduced the loopback interface for that purpose. Most session-oriented routing protocols source their BGP updates from a loopback interface. This has the advantage that if the underlying physical hardware fails, the BGP session can be rerouted as well, resulting in overall better resiliency behaviour for the router's control plane. The loopback interface is also the interface that is used when Network Operation Centre (NOC) teams want to access the router. Theoretically, any IP address that has been assigned to any of the interfaces can be used to access the router. However, if the interface is currently down, this will not work. If the router's loopback address is used in management sessions, there is always at least one interface in the "up" state, as long as the router is functioning at all. When IP engineering teams prepare routers for the live network, typically the first address that is configured on the router is the loopback interface.

The unnumbered interface is an interface that does not carry IP addresses, and this practice is intended to save IP addresses. Additionally, many people see the advantages of unnumbered interfaces as less administration and housekeeping of IP addresses, which are typically of importance at the edge of the network. Many IP protocols rely on the existence of IP addresses, for instance, to terminate a TCP session. How are sessions terminated using unnumbered addresses? Here the loopback address performs an interesting function. The loopback address is used as "replacement" whenever a packet leaves the router. For instance, if a router wants to send a logging event that a link has gone down, and the shortest path to the logging host goes out of an unnumbered interface, the router uses its loopback IP address as the source IP address. Unnumbered interfaces do have the disadvantage of fewer troubleshooting possibilities. If a neighbouring router *does* have an IP address, a simple ping will find out if it is capable of responding. However, with unnumbered interfaces, no ping to the neighbouring router helps, because there is no IP address assigned to the interface. What *can* be pinged is the neighbouring router's loopback address. However, this assumes a proper routing of the loopback IP address, and this requires a routing protocol like IS-IS. If the problem is that routing protocol does not work or does not come up, then troubleshooting gets difficult. Most networks use numbered links in the core and unnumbered interfaces some place at the edge, if at all. In most cases, unnumbered interfaces are not used anywhere in the network.

Why are loopback and unnumbered interfaces that important? In the OSI addressing section, it will be shown that the IP addressing style and the OSI addressing style can be compared (and also easily explained) using the loopback and unnumbered interface addressing model.

4.6.3 *OSI Addressing*

IS-IS inherited its addressing structure from the OSI suite of networking protocols, as many other protocols (such as ATM) did. Before the structure of OSI addresses is explored, the addressing model of an OSI router should be discussed. Figure 4.20 shows the way that OSI addressing is accomplished. First of all, there is just one OSI address per router, which is typically assigned to the central routing process like in Cisco Systems' IOS, or to a virtual loopback interface as in Juniper Networks JUNOS. There can be more than one OSI address assigned per router for address migration purposes, however, the scope of an assigned address is router-wide. There are no other interface addresses assigned to an OSI router. End Systems (hosts in IP) discover and register their addresses with the IS-IS router using a protocol called ES–IS (End-System to Intermediate System), a protocol that exists in parallel with IS-IS and is at the same level in the networking stack. As far as IP routing is concerned, ES–IS does not play a role here, because the IP End Systems use a static-allocation method to "discover" their router. The term "unnumbered" is used deliberately in Figure 4.20 because that best describes OSI routing works: at least one NET per router needs to be configured and then the router sources all routing messages with the configured NET. Compared to the IP model, OSI behaves exactly as if a user configured just a single address for the loopback interfaces and configured all the other interfaces in the chassis as unnumbered.

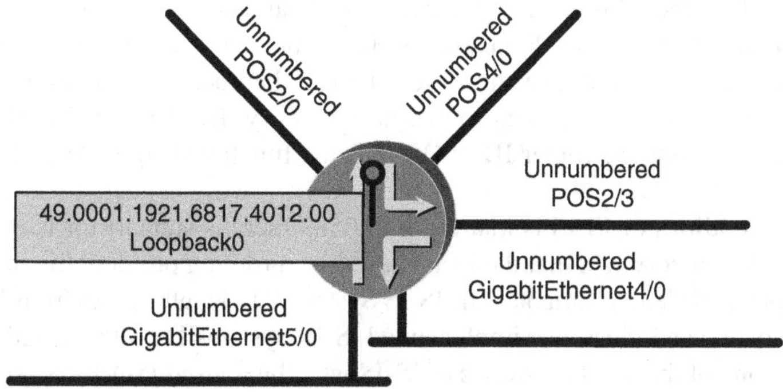

FIGURE 4.20. IS-IS only needs one address per router

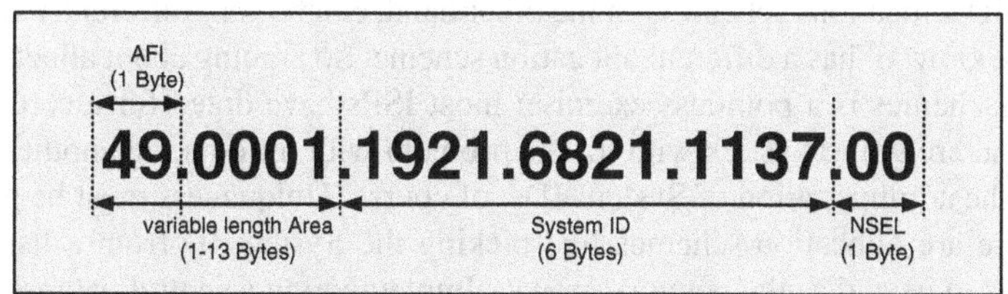

FIGURE 4.21. The Network Entity Title (NET)

This discussion has been using the terms *OSI address* and *NET* interchangeable, which is correct. The NET is technically a *subset* of a full OSI address structured as illustrated in Figure 4.21. The NET consists of three parts:

- The Area-ID
- The System-ID
- The NET Selector (NSEL)

The NET is easier to understand when read from right to left and not from left to right as an IP address.

4.6.3.1 NSEL

The last byte of the NET is called the *selector* or NSEL byte. For IS-IS, without exception, this byte must be zero. If it is not zero, then no adjacencies form. Compared to the IP world, the NSEL is like the protocol field in the IP header, and can further multiplex several sub-systems on a given NET. For IS-IS routers, the NSEL is always set to zero to mean "this system".

4.6.3.2 System-ID

Any link-state routing protocol must ensure that each node in the network can be identified uniquely. If a node cannot be identified uniquely then all subsequent functions of the protocol will fail, including LSP origination, SPF calculation and so on. Having non-unique System-IDs in a network has one of the nastiest failure patterns troubleshooters will ever encounter. Often it takes hours to establish that there *is* an ambiguity problem, and then it takes many more hours to uniquely identify the "bad guy" in the network. When contrasting then the router ID in OSPF is the functional equivalent of System-ID in IS-IS.

One of the oddities of IS-IS is that in ISO 10589 there is support for *variable length* System-IDs. The theory was that the ideal way to be a routing protocol for anybody is to make the System-ID length variable. The IS-IS System-ID's length ranges from 1 to 8 bytes, but thankfully no vendor has ever implemented IS-IS System-IDs with a length other than 6 bytes. It is one of the great mysteries of IS-IS why the revised ISO 10589 specification still supports System-IDs of other than 6 bytes in length. The length of the System-ID is included in the IS-IS common header (see Figure 4.13). Today, virtually all router implementations do updates from IS-IS speakers with a System-ID length other than 6 bytes.

System-ID allocations schemes, on the other hand, can be very different. Almost every network we know of has a different allocation scheme. So arguing about allocation and/or delegation schemes is a pointless exercise: most ISPs have opted for a certain scheme long ago and are going to stick with it. The problem with introducing another allocation scheme is the administration of System-IDs, of course. Uniqueness must be guaranteed, and so there are allocation schemes like picking the System-ID from a list (this very quickly gets to its end as the network grows). Implementing a central database to generate unique System-IDs for a network is better, but usually means additional implementation costs. The best current practices we have seen so far are based on translation schemes that translate the IP loopback address into an IS-IS System-ID. The IP address should be unique already, although it is a bit smaller than the System-ID (32-bit IP address vs. 48-bit System-ID). But a translation scheme that translates to a *bigger* numbering space does not *lose* information, so the property of uniqueness is retained. Calculating the System-ID based on the IP address actually avoids all kinds of extra System-ID management work, because the System-ID is simply inherited from the IP address, and most service providers already have tools and systems in place to administer IP address allocation. Figure 4.22 shows the most common IP address conversion schemes for the IS-IS System-ID, and these are discussed below.

1. **BCD encoding**. The first method is known as binary coded decimal (BCD) encoding. The idea is very simple. Write up an IP address in decimal notation. Make sure that every number is a 3-digit number by filling in with leading zeros. Figure 4.22 shows the IP address 192.168.2.117 becoming the string 192168002117. Finally, just change the position of the dots. After each 4 digits, put a dot, so the System-ID becomes 1921.6800.2117. BCD encoding is by far the most common translation scheme.
2. **Direct translation**. In the second method, make a copy of the hex notation of the IP address directly into the byte positions 3, 4, 5 and 6 of the System-ID. This approach is not very friendly to human operators, except for living hex calculators (how many readers knew instantly that 117 decimal is 0x75?). The only advantage here is that machines (probes or robots) can convert the IP addresses a bit easier, but it is not worth the effort. There is no real advantage over the first approach, so this scheme is rarely used.

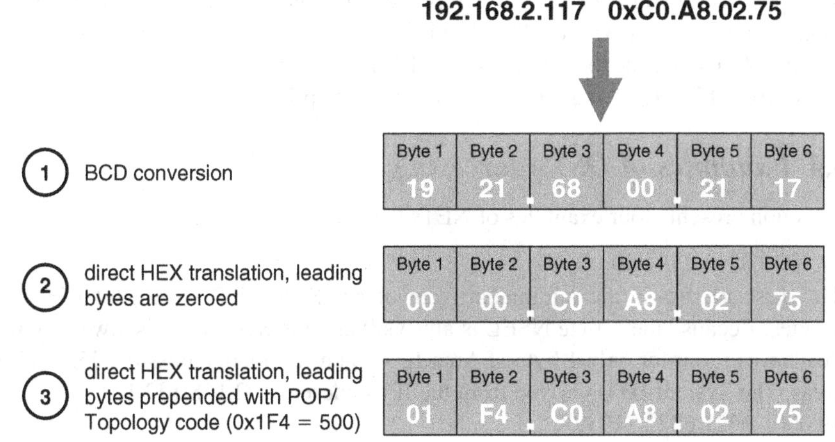

FIGURE 4.22. The three most common conversion schemes to calculate the System-ID based on the loopback IP address

3. **Direct translation and prepending with POP/Topology codes**. The third scheme is mostly used to guarantee unique topologies if a system runs multiple IS-IS routing process instances. Similarly to the second scheme, the hex-encoded IP address is copied down to the byte positions 3, 4, 5 and 6 of the System-ID. But then the first two bytes are filled with some sort of topology or POP code. The idea here is to guarantee uniqueness, even among the instances of the routing process. If IS-IS is run as the routing protocol between VPN customers, and even this customer should have a unique System-ID, this method makes a lot of sense. The System-ID space is big enough to afford the luxury of making multiple instances of NETs unique, even inside a router. This scheme is mostly used in very large deployments of the IS-IS protocol.

4.6.3.3 Area-ID

The Area-ID is the variable part of the NET and can range from 1 byte to 13 bytes in length. In most deployments, Area-ID sizes of 1, 3 or 5 bytes are used. The content of the first byte tells how to interpret the rest of the Area-ID. This first byte is called the *Address Family Identifier* (AFI).

The following well-known AFIs are defined:

39 DCC (data country code)
45 E.164
46 ICD (International code designator)
49 private-addressing

E.164, DCC, or the ICD addressing schemes are not covered in this chapter because they describe pure delegation schemes either according to a phone-numbering plan (E.164), per country (DCC), or per international organization (ICD). For more about AFIs, see the ATM Forum Addressing User Guide version 1.0.

Because selecting an Area-ID is a purely local AS matter, any of the preceding three methods can be used, or AFI 49. This AFI has been especially created for purely private addressing. AFI 49 can be thought of as the RFC 1918 of OSI addressing. RFC 1918 delegates the 10/8, 172.16/12 and 192.168/16 prefixes for private use.

4.6.4 *Examples of OSI Addressing*

This section presents four examples of NETs that can be used in a network.

- 01.1921.6813.2134.00
  This first address is the minimalist form of an IS-IS NET, with a total length of 8 bytes. Because the 1-byte NSEL is always 0 and the System-ID is always 6 bytes, this leaves room for only 1 byte of Area-ID, which results in a possible 255 different areas. The System-ID is derived from the IPv4 address 192.168.132.134.
- 49.0001.1921.6822.2193.00
  This second address is the most commonly deployed format of an ISO NET. It uses the "private" AFI 49 along with a 2-byte area number, which even gives large IS-IS clouds plenty of room to grow. The System-ID is derived from the IPv4 address 192.168.222.193.
- 49.0CF8.0001.1930.8322.3228.00
  If two service providers merge, there might be Level-1 Area-ID collisions. The second example can be enhanced to make the Area-ID unique by extending the Area-ID to 4 bytes and prepending a 2 byte routing domain (ISO talk for the OSPF AS number, or ASN) in the form of the 2-byte area number. Note that 0x0cf8 is the hex encoding for ASN 3320. The System-ID is derived from the IPv4 address 193.83.223.228.
- 47.0005.0000.0000.0000.20ff.0001.0100.8806.3201.00
  This last 20-byte NET is the extreme case of IS-IS addressing. RFC 1237 contains further details about how the space between byte #2 and byte #9 is structured, and what the leading 0x0005 represents. Prepended to the System-ID is the 2 byte routing domain, along with the 2-byte area number. Note that 0x20ff is the hex encoding for ASN 8447. The System-ID is derived from the IPv4 address 10.88.63.201.

4.6.5 *Configuring NETs*

You can configure any of the above NET formats. But where they are configured is different depending on router NOS: in JUNOS the NET is configured under the `interfaces lo0` branch, and in IOS the NET is configured using the keyword `net` under the `router isis` section.

IOS configuration

```
New-York# show running-configuration
[ … ]
router isis
  net 49.0cf8.0001.1930.8322.3228.00
[ … ]
```

JUNOS configuration

```
hannes@London> show configuration
[...]
interfaces {
  lo0 {
    unit 0 {
      family inet {
        address 172.31.208.1/32;
      }
      family iso {
        address 49.0cf8.0001.1930.8322.3228.00;
      }
    }
  }
}
[...]
```

You can configure any of these formats on JUNOS, by setting the address under the `family iso` statement on *any* interface. Normally, the virtual loopback `interface lo0` is used, just for consistency.

4.7 Names, System-, LAN- and LSP-IDs

Even if it is simple to derive System-IDs from IP addresses, in a modestly large network there might be several different types of conversion schemes. Troubleshooting such a network is not an easy task, as you always need to remember what conversion scheme a node's System-ID has been based on. Troubleshooting a large set of adjacencies also poses a problem, because looking at a long listing of System-IDs (which have little to do with the IP addresses on the routers), it is not always easy to find out what router corresponds to the Down adjacency.

JUNOS configuration

```
hannes@London> show isis adjacency
[ ... ]
show isis adjacency
Interface          System               L  State        Hold (secs) SNPA
so-4/2/0.0         1921.6800.1014       2  Up                    26
so-5/2/0.0         1921.6800.1018       2  Up                    27
so-5/3/0.0         1921.6800.1011       3  Up                    25
so-6/2/0.0         1921.6800.1012       3  Up                    28
so-6/3/0.0         1921.6800.1012       3  Up                    27
[ ... ]
```

However, exactly the same problem is also known to OSPF deployments: it is sometimes very awkward to troubleshoot adjacencies from just a big list of IP addresses. The human brain is simply not built for doing pattern matches on IP addresses (evolution

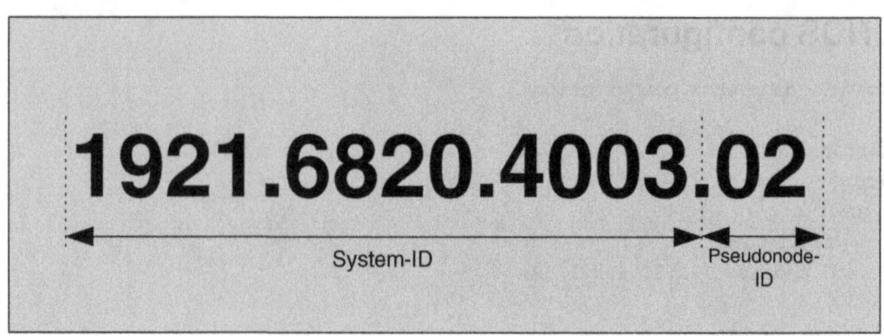

FIGURE 4.23. The LAN ID occurs in many IS-IS messages – the first 6 bytes represent a System-ID and therefore the CLI renders the output using the Hostname-to-System-ID database

might eventually change this). In OSPF, the problem has been fixed by utilizing the Domain Name System (DNS) resolution service for translating IP addresses on an adjacency back to the name of a peer. This makes debugging much more convenient.

Utilizing the DNS for name resolution has two major problems as far as IS-IS is concerned:

- The DNS does not understand 48-bit System-IDs
- Relying on the DNS for convenient troubleshooting when the network may be in trouble creates a chicken-before-the-egg problem. Most troubleshooters really hate it when the System-ID lookup finds out that the DNS is not reachable, and this only by looking at their OSPF peers, and the output takes 15 seconds per DNS lookup-timeout period unless all the adjacencies are displayed. Also, statically defining the System-ID to name mappings can be a painful experience as someone has to synchronize the System-ID to name mappings manually across all routers in the network. One mismatched entry and people often get absolutely lost during the troubleshooting process.

IS-IS is much smarter in this respect. It has the name resolution service for IS-IS built into the protocol. When first displaying an IS-IS adjacency, operators are pleased to find that all systems are listed using their hostname. The mechanisms behind this unique translation service are discussed in Chapter 13 "IS-IS Extensions".

Then why discuss name resolutions in the introduction chapter? Just because IS-IS uses the System-ID in various places. The two commonest cases are in the LAN-ID and the LSP-ID, used for giving a routing update a unique ID. Figure 4.23 and Figure 4.24 show various IDs in the IS-IS protocol that use the System-ID as their first 6 bytes.

The name resolution scheme affects these IDs as well, so output is displayed in the form Washington.00-00 or Frankfurt.04 or London.00-00. The router is just trying to make the output as convenient as possible!

```
hannes@London> show isis adjacency
[...]
IS-IS level 1 link-state database:

London.00-00 Sequence: 0x175, Checksum: 0x2306, Lifetime: 3763 secs
  IS neighbour:                Frankfurt.04              Metric:        63
  IS neighbour:                Pensauken.00              Metric:        63
```

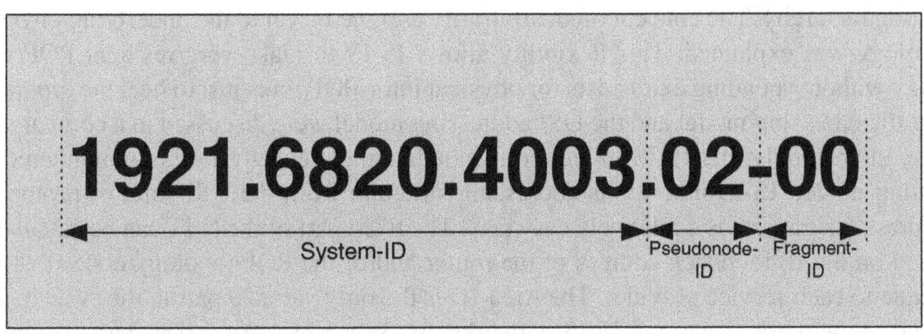

FIGURE 4.24. The LSP-ID uniquely identifies an IS-IS router announcement – the first 6 bytes represent the System-ID of the sender therefore the CLI renders the output using the Hostname-to-System-ID database

The System-ID field of the LSP-ID is displayed as a name. However, the origin router's System-ID is displayed with the `show isis hostname` command (the same in IOS and JUNOS), which displays the hostname cache on the local router.

IOS command

IOS marks the local node with an asterisk (*):

```
Frankfurt#show isis hostname

Level System ID              Dynamic Hostname
      1921.6800.1013         London
    * 1921.6800.1014         Frankfurt
      1921.6800.1018         Washington
[...]
```

JUNOS command

JUNOS displays in addition if the entry has been learned via other routers, or if it has been locally configured. The local node is always marked "Static".

```
hannes@London> show isis hostname
IS-IS hostname database:
System ID           Hostname                                   Type
1921.6800.1013      London                                     Static
1921.6800.1014      Frankfurt                                  Dynamic
1921.6800.1018      Washington                                 Dynamic
[...]
```

4.8 Summary

This chapter explored the foundations of IS-IS. The independence of area addressing and routing hierarchy was contrasted to the OSPF model where Area 0 implicitly makes up a routing hierarchy. The concept of an arbitrarily assigned level to the underlying physical topology was explained. This flexibility allows IS-IS to make very resilient POP topology without spending extra costs for physical intra-POP links just to heal the topology. The IP addressing model and the OSI addressing model were discussed in a comparative way; interestingly, the IS-IS model corresponds almost exactly to the unnumbered IP routing model. IS-IS inherits its addressing structure from the OSI suite of protocols. Address assignment is a relatively easy task. The fixed part of the NET can be calculated based on the IP loopback address of the router and/or the POP/topology codes that are unique to each service provider. The Area-ID is the only variable part in the system, and based on network size, most IS-IS networks use 3 or 5 byte Area-IDs. Most Area-IDs start with 49 because the 49/8 prefix has been allocated for private use – it is the RFC 1918 of the OSI suite. Finally, this chapter presented the IS-IS built-in name resolution service and several commands to display those ID formats which benefit from the address resolution service as well.

5

Neighbour Discovery and Handshaking

Virtually all routing (and signalling) protocols include a method of automatic *neighbour discovery* that enables a router to determine if there are any other adjacent routers running the same routing protocol. Once you enable IS-IS on an interface, the routing protocol will automatically find out if there are other routers out there speaking the same protocol and version and immediately start to interact with these remote routers. Additionally the routing protocol needs to verify if the link is two-way capable (that is, equally able to pass protocol traffic in both directions) before it can announce a Reachability Information TLV in a link-state PDU (LSP) and flood it throughout the topology. This verification of link capabilities and bi-directional checks is done using a process known as *handshaking*. This chapter examines how IS-IS routers perform neighbour discovery and handshaking on LAN and WAN circuits. Additionally, different properties of handshaking methods, such as the simple 2-way handshake and the inherent problems of using this 2-way handshaking method are discussed.

You will also learn the details of adjacency *finite state machine* changes and network stability improvement techniques like adjacency hold downs. Finally, requirements of highly resilient neighbour "liveness" checking will be presented and popular solutions will be explored including technologies like bi-directional fault detection. Everything will include configuration snippets, show command and debug output, plus tcpdump output for a better understanding of the IS-IS protocol.

5.1 Hello Message Encoding

Each routing protocol uses Hello messages for neighbour discovery and to perform handshaking. In IS-IS, just like in any other routing protocol, this function is performed through the use of what IS-IS calls *Intermediate System to Intermediate System Hello* (IIH) messages. IS-IS uses dedicated IIH messages for the two types of topologies a router can be configured to be a member of: there is one Hello type for the Level 1 adjacencies and one Hello type for the Level 2 adjacencies. There are more details about the IS-IS hierarchical Level 1/Level 2 routing paradigm in Chapter 4 "IS-IS Basics".

IS-IS supports two different circuit types: point-to-point (p2p) and broadcast LAN circuits. There is a dedicated type of Hello Message for point-to-point circuits and another one for broadcast circuits. So in theory there should be two Hello messages for each circuit type (point-to-point or broadcast) and two Hello message types for each Level, L1 or L2. This should total four distinct Hello message types.

In ISO 10589, however, there was some concern that running two Hellos (one per level) on point-to-point links would consume too much bandwidth on narrow-band links. So IS-IS is *optimized* for point-to-point circuits and only uses one PDU type for both levels. Figure 5.1 shows the structure of the IS-IS common header, which starts every IS-IS message. The 8-bit PDU type field indicates the type of message that is carried inside the IS-IS message. On the right of the figure there is a list of the nine distinct PDU types for IS-IS. Three out of the nine PDU types are reserved for Hello messages. The point-to-point circuit types share one PDU type (17) for both levels, so there are not really four different Hello messages but only three.

What do the Hello messages look like *on the wire?* Each IS-IS message type is prepended with an 8-byte common header that tells the receiver about the IS-IS protocol version being used, the header length, the maximum number of concurrent areas supported, as well as other IS-IS global parameters, such as the length of the System-ID field. Figure 5.1 shows the structure of the common header that is prepended to all IS-IS related messages. In the figure, you can see that some of the fields are already filled in with number values. We have chosen not only to show the frame structure, but also to show how the frames are populated with number values. These numbers represent constants and fill in the common header with typical values. It is interesting to note that some header fields, such as the number of supported areas and the length of the System-ID field, are set to zero. Zero has a special meaning in IS-IS. Using the zero value is equivalent to telling routers to use the *default* value for a field, which is not typically zero.

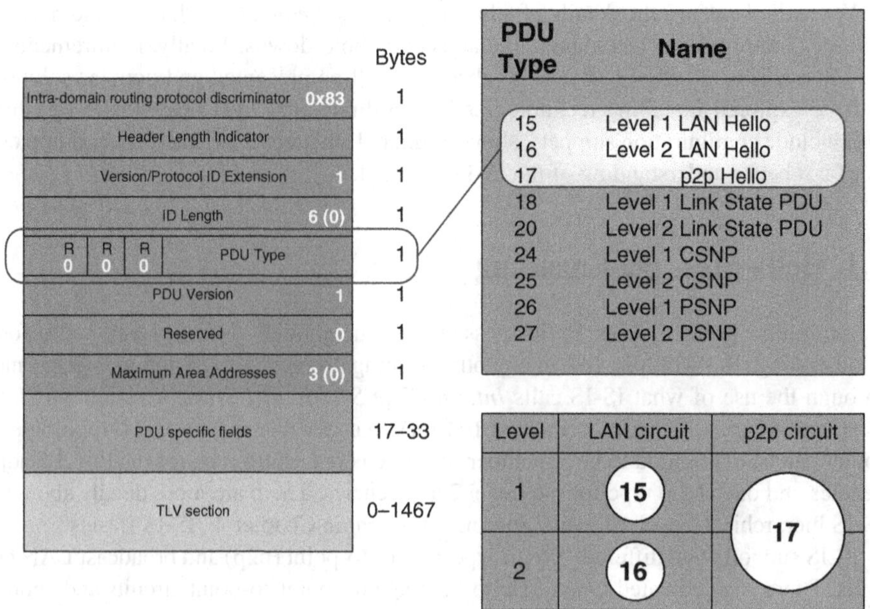

FIGURE 5.1. Three out of the nine IS-IS PDU types are allocated for Hello messages on p2p and broadcast circuits

Oddly, because the *default* value is not explicitly set out in detail in IS-IS, each implementation has to *intuitively* know the default values. The default value for System-ID-Length is 6 bytes and the default value for Maximum Area Addresses is 3, but these are really *de facto* defaults and not set out as hard limitations.

You should now have a basic understanding of IS-IS Hello messages. The following sections discuss LAN Hello messages and point-to-point messages in greater detail.

5.1.1 *LAN Hello Messages*

Figure 5.2 shows the structure of an IS-IS Hello message as it is used on LAN (IS-IS broadcast) circuits. First there is the IS-IS common header. The header length of LAN Hello messages is always set to 27 bytes – this represents the aggregate length of the common header (8 bytes) and the LAN Hello header (19 bytes). The PDU type is either 15 or 16 depending on whether or not this is a Hello message targeted for Level 1 routers or Level 2 routers respectively.

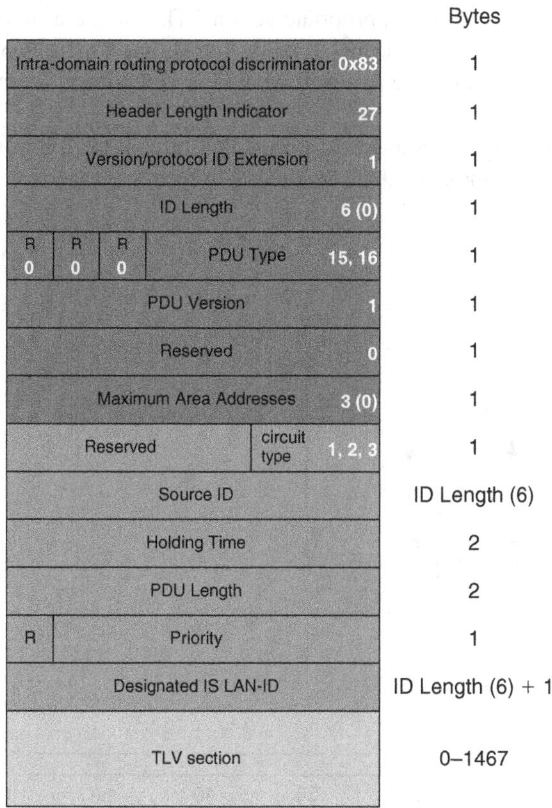

FIGURE 5.2. Structure of the L1, L2 LAN Hello PDU

The IS-IS LAN Hello message header starts with a field indicating which levels have been configured on this circuit (the LAN). For the two lower order bits (the six other high order bits are reserved and should be set to zero) there are three valid values:

- 0x1 Level 1 only
- 0x2 Level 2 only
- 0x3 Level 1 and Level 2

If the Circuit Type field is set to zero (both bits are zero, or "cleared" as code developers say) this represents an illegal value and the router will silently discard the Hello message, assuming that there is something broken.

The Source-ID field contains the System-ID (the default length is 6 bytes) of the sender.

Holding Time represents the time after which the neighbour wants to be declared dead. This sounds strange, but unlike humans, routers can specify their maximum session lifetime. Typically, default holding time values are between 27 and 30 seconds depending on the routing code implementation (IOS = 30 seconds and JUNOS = 27 seconds). Setting the holding time (for example) to 30 seconds is interpreted by the receivers of the Hello message as follows: "If the neighbour router with the reported System-ID does not send a Hello message for a period of 30 seconds, we'll declare the neighbour router dead and take appropriate action." This action usually involves telling the other neighbours that the adjacency relationship between these two routers has been terminated. Each Hello message received resets the countdown number for this *drop-dead* timer.

Figure 5.3 illustrates the sequence of events that refresh the hold timer. At t[0s], the router receives a Hello message that sets the hold timer to 30 seconds. So the receiving

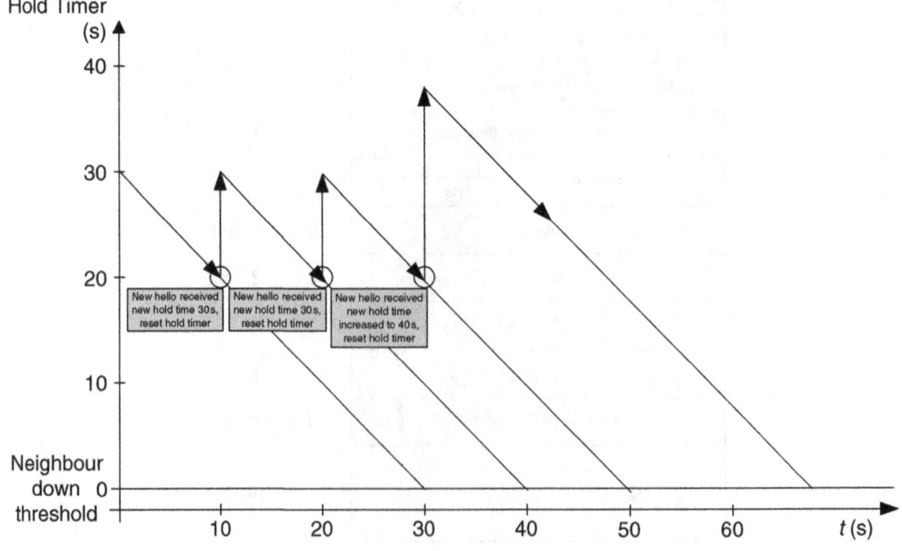

FIGURE 5.3. Each Hello message resets the hold timer

router initializes a countdown timer, starting at 30 seconds. Next, the neighbouring router will refresh the adjacency. To calculate the frequency for those refreshes there is a constant called the *Hello multiplier* which is by default set to the value 3. The neighbouring routers refreshes the Hello each (hold-timer divided by the Hello multiplier time) period. Using the default values of 30/3, the adjacency should get a refresh every 10 seconds. If a router wants to lower the Hello frequency, no problem, as long as the neighbouring router makes sure that the adjacency gets properly refreshed within the hold-time period. The Hello message is resent every 10 seconds (or t[10s,20s], as represented in Figure 5.3) resulting in a saw-tooth shaped figure over time. A router can also decide to change its hold-timer anytime – for example, at t[30s] a Hello message with the hold time set to 40 seconds is received. This resets the countdown timer, as might be expected, to 40 seconds. This is a unique capability among IP routing protocols: each IS-IS router can set its hold-timer independently from every other router on the network.

This feature is quite different from OSPF networks where the Hello and the dead timer have to match throughout entire sub-net, otherwise the routers will not form neighbour adjacencies. On OSPF LANs, changing timers on the fly is disruptive and lacks the flexibility that IS-IS gives you, unless you somehow manage to change all the Hello and dead timers at the same point in time using a configuration script/robot. IS-IS is much more operationally friendly in that respect, because IS-IS does not rely on any other routers to match its timers like OSPF does. In OSPF, all the timers have to be aligned with the designated router (DR).

In IS-IS such a change does not require any coordination/scripting effort. If you want to change your own timers, you simply do it in a step-by-step fashion with no service disruption at all.

The PDU Length field contains the length of the entire packet including the common header and the LAN Hello header.

The Priority and DIS LAN-ID fields are related to the election procedure of the Designated Intermediate System (DIS). Chapter 7, "Pseudonodes and Designated Routers", contains a detailed description of why a DIS is needed and how the DIS is elected on a LAN. The IS-IS DIS has much the same duties and functions as the OSPF DR.

Multiple adjacencies on a circuit are displayed differently in the command line interfaces of Cisco and Juniper Networks. Cisco IOS displays multi-level LAN adjacencies in *one* line, while JUNOS displays multi-level LAN adjacencies in *two* lines.

IOS command output

In IOS a Level 1 and Level 2 adjacency on a LAN circuit is displayed as *L1L2* in the `show isis Adjacency` output.

```
London#show clns neighbors
System Id    Interface   SNPA              State  Holdtime  Type  Protocol
Amsterdam    GigE8/0     00a0.a512.3318    Up     21        L1L2  IS-IS
Pennsauken   GigE4/0     00a0.a512.28d7    Up     18        L2    IS-IS
Frankfurt    FastE5/0    0090.6900.fe27    Up     24        L2    IS-IS
```

JUNOS command output

In JUNOS a Level 1 and Level 2 adjacency on a point-to-point circuit is displayed as two separate adjacencies in the `show isis Adjacency` output.

```
hannes@Munich> show isis Adjacency
Interface        System       L State       Hold (secs)      SNPA
ge-0/1/0.0       Vienna       2 Up               17          0:90:69:2b:e:7
ge-0/1/0.0       Vienna       1 Up               22          0:90:69:2b:e:7
ge-0/2/0.0       Munich-2     1 Up               21          0:90:69:2b:e:7
```

On point-to-point circuits there is a dedicated Hello type for adjacency management: the point-to-point IIH PDU (17), which will be highlighted in the next section.

5.1.2 *Point-to-point Hello Messages*

Figure 5.4 shows the basic structure of a Hello message used on point-to-point circuits. The point-to-point Hello message is a little shorter than its LAN counterpart, but essentially it contains the same set of information that the LAN Hello message does.

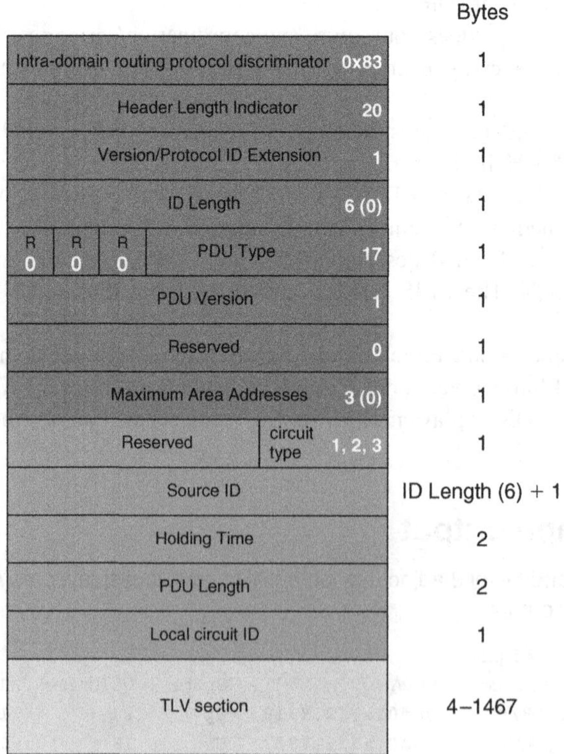

FIGURE 5.4. Structure of the point-to-point Hello PDU

For instance, the point-to-point Hello contains:

- Circuit Type
- Source ID
- Holding Time
- PDU Length

All of these fields have the same meaning and function as in the LAN Hello. Note that the Designated Router and Priority fields are missing. That's because on point-to-point circuits there is no election of a designated router, and so the point-to-point Hello message does not need to carry the Priority and DIS LAN-ID fields.

Additionally, there is the Local Circuit-ID field that carries the link's circuit number The IS-IS specification leaves it quite open as to what value should be inserted for the Local Circuit-ID. For example, in the IOS implementation, the Interface Index of the sender's interface is taken as the Local Circuit-ID. The JUNOS implementation always sets this value to 0x1. The JUNOS implementers of this "constant" Local Circuit-ID argue that the Circuit-ID is not needed anywhere for processing, such as in SPF calculations, timer countdowns, or anything else. The Local Circuit-ID is there for purely link-local *informational* purposes. And if something has just informational purposes, then no harm can be done by *not* setting it to anything other than a constant.

How can IS-IS build both Level 1 and Level 2 adjacencies on a point-to-point link with just one message type? Figure 5.2 showed that LAN Hellos have *two* PDU types, one for each level, whereas point-to-point Hellos share one PDU type for both levels. The difference in processing the point-to-point Hello compared to the LAN Hello is that receipt of a point-to-point Hello resets the hold timers for *all* levels, as indicated in the Circuit Type field. For example, if the Circuit Type field indicates that this is just a Level 1 adjacency, then just the hold timer of Level 1 is reset. The same logic goes for Level 2 and Level 1/Level 2 capable circuits – whatever level is indicated in the Circuit Type, those corresponding hold timers get reset.

In contrast to point-to-point Hellos, receipt of a LAN Hello just resets the hold timer according to the PDU type. A received Hello containing PDU Type 15 just resets the Level 1 hold timer, while a PDU Type 16 resets the Level 2 hold timer only.

Command line interfaces of routers have different ways of displaying a joint Level 1/Level 2 adjacency. For example, JUNOS displays an L1L2 adjacency on a point-to-point circuit as Level 3. Of course there is (yet) no Level 3, but the reason for this is simple: if you take the bit patterns of a Level 2 circuit (10b) plus the bit pattern of a Level 1 circuit (01b) the sum equals to (11b), which is the binary value for 3.

JUNOS command output

In JUNOS a Level 1 and Level 2 adjacency on a point-to-point circuit is displayed as *Level 3* in the `show isis Adjacency` output.

```
hannes@Frankfurt> show isis Adjacency
Interface        System      L State     Hold (secs) SNPA
so-0/0/0.0       Munich      3 Up             28
so-0/1/0.0       London      2 Up             27
so-0/2/0.0       Milan       2 Up             25
so-1/0/0.0       paris       2 Up             24
```

IOS command output

In IOS a Level 1 and Level 2 adjacency on a point-to-point circuit is displayed as *L1L2* in the `show clns neighbors` output.

```
London#show clns neighbors
System Id      Interface      SNPA      State    Holdtime    Type     Protocol
Amsterdam      PO4/0          *PPP*     Up       19          L1L2     IS-IS
Pennsauken     PO4/1          *PPP*     Up       18          L2       IS-IS
Frankfurt      PO4/1          *PPP*     Up       24          L2       IS-IS
```

To summarize, Hello messages are the method used for discovering neighbours. IS-IS routers send Hellos according to their configured link types, and wait for responses that are a match. Receipt of a matching Hello message means another router on the link is at least configured to run IS-IS. This is a good start, but not the whole story of establishing and maintaining a full IS-IS router adjacency.

The next step is to check if the underlying circuit to the neighbour router is *two-way capable*. Two-way capable means a pair of routers can transmit and receive their peer's Hello messages. A router needs to be sure that "I can see you and you can see me", before advertising an adjacency in its LSP. In order to verify two-way circuit capability the router needs to perform a *handshaking* function. There are several different handshake algorithms available and, unfortunately, some cannot even guarantee that the underlying link is two-way capable, due to a mistake in the ISO 10589 specification.

Even if the router is fooled by a broken handshake mechanism, nothing *breaks* on the network if (for example) the circuit is just one-way capable and the router announces the one-way reachability (I can see you, but you cannot see me) in its router LSP. During the SPF calculation there is a verification called the *two-way check* that makes sure no transit path is calculated through a one-way circuit. The two-way check will be described in more detail in Chapter 10 "SPF and Route Calculation".

Before IS-IS starts to verify two-way connectivity over a link it actually probes the link first to find out if it supports large packets for data exchange at a later stage.

5.2 MTU Check

In IS-IS the largest packet (which is typically the LSP) may become 1492 bytes (MAC layer excluded). IS-IS tests the link by artificially bloating its Hello size up to 1492 bytes. There is a dedicated Message Element in the Hello PDU called a Padding TLV that is used for this purpose. Figure 5.5 shows the structure of the Padding TLV #8. The content of the Padding TLV is filled up with random data. The information that it does contain does not matter – what matters is that it makes the PDU artificially big up to *maxLSPsize* (=1492 bytes). The tcpdump output below shows such a *padded* Hello.

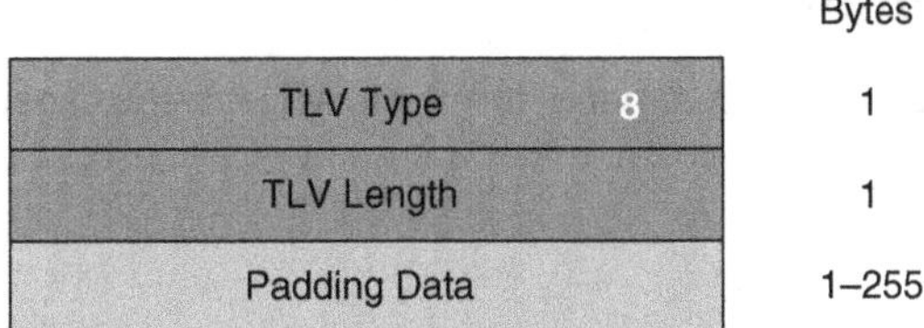

FIGURE 5.5. The Padding TLV #8 is used to bloat IIHs up to at least 1492 bytes

Tcpdump output

```
20:16:37.411690 OSI, IS-IS, length: 1492
  L1 Lan IIH, hlen: 27, v: 1, pdu-v: 1, sys-id-len: 6 (0), max-area: 3 (0)
    source-id: 1921.6800.1008, holding time: 120s, Flags: [L1, L2]
    lan-id: 1921.6800.1008.02, Priority: 64, PDU length: 1492
      IS Neighbor(s) TLV #6, length: 6
        SNPA: 0090.692b.0e52
      Protocols supported TLV #129, length: 1
        NLPID(s): IPv4 (0xcc)
      IPv4 Interface address(es) TLV #132, length: 4
        IPv4 interface address: 193.83.223.236
      Area address(es) TLV #1, length: 4
        Area address (length: 3): 49.0001
      Restart Signaling TLV #211, length: 3
        Flags [none], Remaining holding time 0s
      Padding TLV #8, length: 255
      Padding TLV #8, length: 255
      Padding TLV #8, length: 255
      Padding TLV #8, length: 255
      Padding TLV #8, length: 255
      Padding TLV #8, length: 150
```

If a router exchanges these bloated Hello PDUs in both directions then it can be sure that the underlying media sufficiently supports the maximum packet sizes necessary for IS-IS.

IOS and JUNOS do have different styles of how and when they do implement adjacency checks. IOS pads each and every Hello that it transmits on the wire. On large WAN Hub Routers that terminate a lot of circuits – for example on a Router running Frame relay or ATM circuits – periodic emission of large packets can be a burden to the control plane processor. If you know that your underlying link supports at least 1492 bytes sized packets then you can turn off the artificial bloating of Hello PDUs using the `no hello padding` router configuration command.

IOS configuration

The `no hello padding` command turns off MTU check against the underlying media.

```
!
router isis
  no hello padding
  [ ... ]
!
```

JUNOS encompasses a technique called *smart padding*, where the router transmits padded Hellos only at the beginning of the Adjacency Bring up. After both ends of a router have completed the handshake procedure JUNOS automatically omits the Padding TLVs in the Hello message. That behaviour is a nice compromise between strict MTU checking and making sure that the IS-IS router does not consume excess bandwidth in tight WAN environments. The brief Tcpdump output shows the JUNOS specific variation in packet sizes during an IS-IS Adjacency bring up.

Tcpdump output

```
20:16:37.411690 OSI, IS-IS, L1 Lan IIH, src-id 1921.6800.1002,
                lan-id 1921.6800.1002.02, prio 64, length 1492
20:16:37.412312 OSI, IS-IS, L2 Lan IIH, src-id 1921.6800.1002,
                lan-id 1921.6800.1002.02, prio 90, length 1492
20:16:37.414060 OSI, IS-IS, L1 Lan IIH, src-id 1921.6800.1003,
                lan-id 1921.6800.1003.02, prio 70, length 1492
20:16:37.414466 OSI, IS-IS, L2 Lan IIH, src-id 1921.6800.1003,
                lan-id 1921.6800.1003.02, prio 64, length 1492
20:16:37.418232 OSI, IS-IS, L1 Lan IIH, src-id 1921.6800.1002,
                lan-id 1921.6800.1003.02, prio 64, length 65
20:16:37.418742 OSI, IS-IS, L2 Lan IIH, src-id 1921.6800.1002,
                lan-id 1921.6800.1002.02, prio 90, length 65
20:16:37.420914 OSI, IS-IS, L1 Lan IIH, src-id 1921.6800.1003,
                lan-id 1921.6800.1003.02, prio 70, length 90
20:16:37.421055 OSI, IS-IS, L2 Lan IIH, src-id 1921.6800.1003,
                lan-id 1921.6800.1002.02, prio 64, length 90
20:16:37.423429 OSI, IS-IS, L1 Lan IIH, src-id 1921.6800.1002,
                lan-id 1921.6800.1003.02, prio 64, length 65
20:16:37.423909 OSI, IS-IS, L2 Lan IIH, src-id 1921.6800.1002,
                lan-id 1921.6800.1002.02, prio 90, length 65
```

The next few sections show how the IS-IS Protocol verifies two-way connectivity over a link. From now on, the term *handshaking* is used as a replacement for "verifying two-way connectivity". That is really all that handshaking means.

5.3 Handshaking

In the IS-IS specification there are two general ways of handshaking:

- 2-way handshake
- 3-way handshake

Figure 5.6 illustrates what occurs during a 2-way handshake. IS-IS is started on Router A. A Hello message is sent to Router B. As soon as Router B responds with a Hello Message of its own, Router A will declare the Adjacency with Router B up. The important aspect here is that Router A does not know if the Hello message from Router B is in *response* to the Hello message that Router A sent or if it is just *any* Hello message that Router B has generated (perhaps Router A's Hello message has been lost on the link). There is no state that is kept. That insight is significant later when we explore a failure conditions resulting from a pure 2-way handshake check. Of course the same procedure is executed from Router B's perspective as well. The Router B perspective is not shown in Figure 5.6, because the picture would have been too crowded and harder to understand. But Router B of course also sends a Hello message and as soon as Router B receives *any* Hello message from Router A, Router B will declare the adjacency up. Only two messages are necessary in the 2-way handshake. The 3-way handshake works differently.

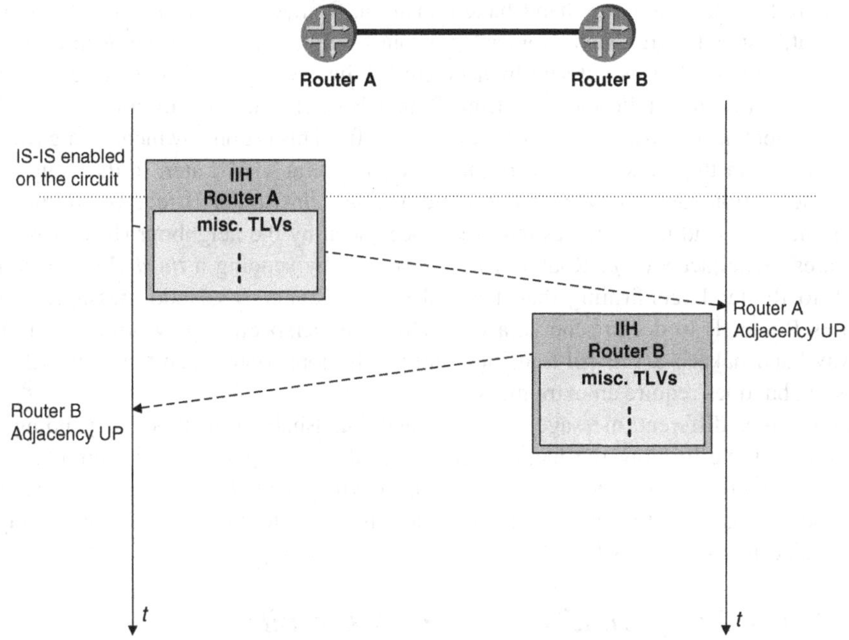

FIGURE 5.6. For 2-way handshakes only two messages are required to declare a circuit up

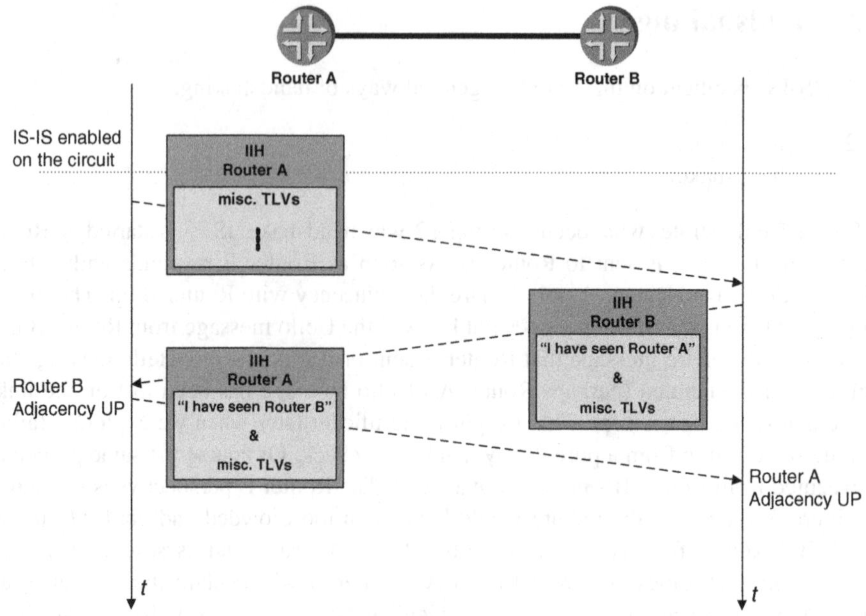

FIGURE 5.7. The 3-way handshake is a stateful transition

Figure 5.7 shows a 3-way handshake transition. Router A first sends the Hello message out, just as before. Next, Router B responds with a Hello message. Router A will know that this Hello was not sent by accident (in the 2-way case Router A never *really* knows) because the Hello message from Router B carries an indication that this Hello has been sent in *response* to Router A's original Hello. This is done by mentioning Router A explicitly in the message body, by means of a special TLV. Later, in the finite state machine section such an event is described as *Seenself.* Router B receives Router A's Hello message and now realizes that it has been seen by the neighbour (Router A) and declares the adjacency *up*. Router A now responds by sending a *third* Hello message back to Router B confirming that it has also seen Router B's Hello message, which causes Router B to declare the adjacency (from its perspective) now *up* as well. The 3-way handshake is a *stateful* transition and much more robust than the simple 2-way version, but does require an extra message.

IS-IS uses different message elements and handshaking methods depending on whether it is performing the handshaking on LAN or on point-to-point circuits. The following section shows where and in which environment the different handshaking methods are used, and what TLVs are encoded in the Hello messages to convey neighbour adjacency state in IS-IS.

5.3.1 *The 3-way Handshake on LAN Circuits*

On LANs, IS-IS uses a 3-way handshake. Figure 5.8 shows the state changes on the LAN from Router A's perspective. Please note that for better visibility again, only the state

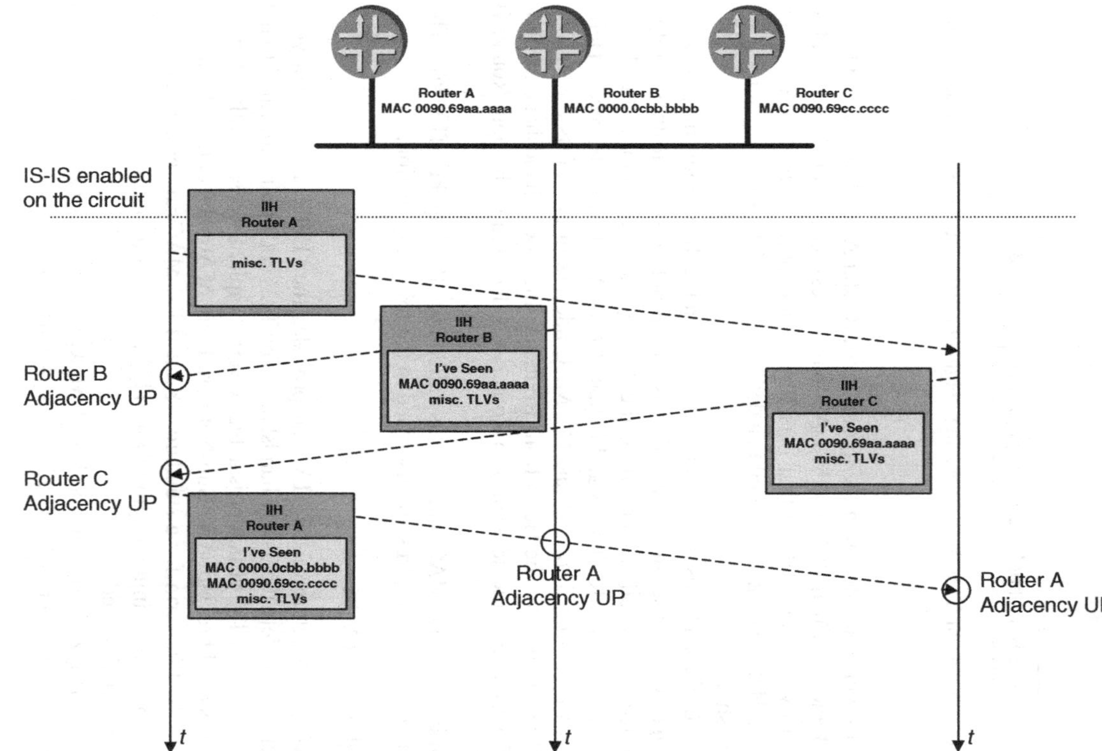

FIGURE 5.8. On LANs the routers need to send a list of visible neighbours to complete the 3-way handshake

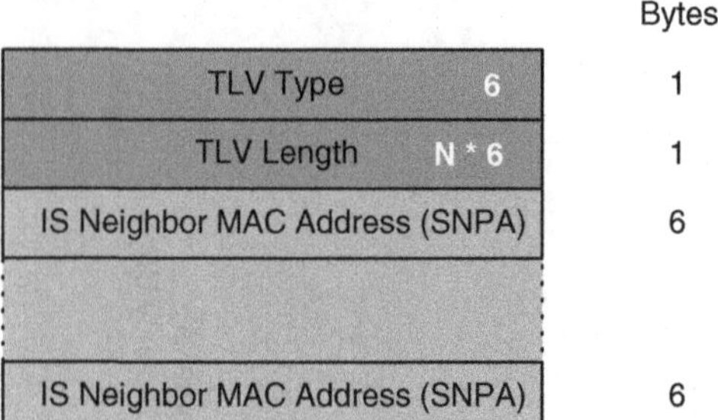

FIGURE 5.9. The IS Neighbour TLV #6 conveys the neighbour state for the 3-way handshaking procedure

transactions for Router A are shown in the figure. First, Router A sends a Hello onto the LAN. Routers B and C, which both get the LAN-based message of course, respond to Router A's Hello by sending a Hello that lists Router A's source MAC address from Router A's original Hello message encoded in a dedicated TLV. The structure of the TLV will be discussed shortly.

Router A receives these Hellos from Routers B and C and realizes "Hey, they both got my Hello message! Otherwise, my MAC address would not be listed in their Hello." Thus, Router A declares the adjacencies to Router B and C *up*. To complete the 3-way handshake, Router A notifies Routers B and C that Router A has seen the recent Hello from both of them by listing Router B and C's MAC address in one of its own TLVs. Once Routers B and C receive the Hello from Router A, the 3-way handshake is completed (due to *Seenself*) and the adjacency to Router A is declared up by both Router B and C.

The TLV that conveys the MAC addresses is called the "IS Neighbor TLV #6". The structure and encoding rules for this are discussed in the following section.

5.3.1.1 IS Neighbour TLV #6

Figure 5.9 shows the structure of the TLV that provides the "Hello, I have seen you" function in order to complete the 3-way handshake. The TLV code point allocated to the IS neighbour's TLV is #6. The structure is actually very simple. It is essentially an array of SNPAs. SNPA is an abbreviation for Sub-Network Point of Attachment. On broadcast LANs a SNPA is the ISO term for a standard, 48-bit IEEE MAC address. The 48-bits equals six bytes, so the maximum length of this TLV is always a multiple of six. If it is not, then the TLV is malformed.

On the network analyzer's output, the list of MAC addresses is listed under the IS Neighbour stanza. The number of MAC addresses (4 entries) matches the TLV length of 4 bytes ($4 \times 6 = 24$).

Tcpdump output

The IS Neighbour TLV #6 contains a list of MAC addresses of the routers that are visible from the sending router's perspective:

```
09:38:23.996041 OSI, IS-IS, length: 74
  L1 Lan IIH, hlen: 27, v: 1, pdu-v: 1, sys-id-len: 6 (0), max-area: 3 (0)
    source-id: 1921.6800.1012, holding time: 27s, Flags: [L1, L2]
      lan-id:  1921.6800.1012.02, Priority: 64, PDU length: 75
      IS Neighbor(s) TLV #6, length: 24
        SNPA: 0090.69b2.71ca
        SNPA: 0090.69b2.41cc
        SNPA: 0000.0c54.fadd
        SNPA: 0000.0c11.cc1e
      Protocols supported TLV #129, length: 2
        NLPID(s): IPv4, IPv6
      IPv4 Interface address(es) TLV #132, length: 4
        IPv4 interface address: 172.16.33.1
      Area address(es) TLV #1, length: 4
        Area address (length: 3): 49.0001
      Restart Signaling TLV #211, length: 3
        Flags: [none], Remaining holding time 0s
```

On LAN circuits there is only a single handshaking method available: the 3-way handshake using the IS-Neighbour TLV #6. On point-to-point circuits there is an implementation choice between 2-way and 3-way handshakes. The next section shows how handshaking on point-to-point circuits works, what flaws have been revealed in the original specifications, and how the handshake methods finally evolved.

5.3.2 *The 2-way Handshake on Point-to-point Circuits*

The original ISO 10589 specification proposed just a 2-way handshake on point-to-point circuits. Through implementation and deployment experience, several scenarios are known today where the use of 2-way handshakes causes IS-IS to get *blind spotted* and in the worst case, to completely black hole traffic.

Most of these failure scenarios are related to routers connected by *unidirectional* links, which is quite frequently the result of a failure to network equipment. In networking environments, unidirectional links can occur quite easily. Typically, a fibre path between a pair of routers is composed of two fibres: one for transmitting and one for receiving. If one of the two fibres breaks, the routers are reduced to *one-way* connectivity. In most cases this is not a big problem if there is just a simple fibre run between a pair of routers and the transmit fibre on one side breaks. The receiver on the other end of a fibre link will detect a loss of signal and the entire circuit is declared down. The trouble really starts if there is an active network element between the two routers, such as a LAN switch, so that the light is not missing on one side and the circuit always stays up.

Figure 5.10 shows Router A and Router B connected through an ATM switch. Please note that this problem is not just specific to the ATM technology. The ATM switch here serves just as an example: it could be any Layer 2 technology like an active Ethernet device or a Frame Relay switch and so on.

In total, there are four fibres in this small network. There is a pair of fibres between Router A and the ATM switch, and another pair of fibres between Router B and the ATM switch. Now imagine that the transmit link between Router B and the ATM switch

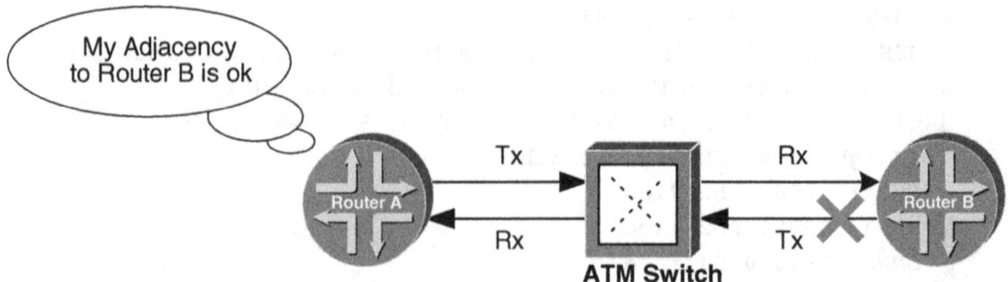

FIGURE 5.10. Active elements between routers do not propagate downstream loss of signal errors

breaks. Router A is still receiving a signal from the ATM switch, because the local link is still fine. But because "the light does not go out" at the Router A end, both sides (Router A and the ATM switch) think that everything is fine and the link is up and running to Router B.

Please note that in practice there are Layer-2 management protocols like LMI, PPP LCP or ATM OAM cells that would help to detect that there is an end-to-end connectivity problem. However, these protocols take time to detect error conditions and in the meantime IS-IS could have announced bogus information and flood it through the network.

This example of the conditions that result in unidirectional links will be the basis for most of the issues with the 2-way handshake in IS-IS. The next two sections describe very common failure scenarios that all start with one-way connectivity as the root cause of the problem.

5.3.2.1 Failure Scenario 1: SONET/SDH APS

In most carrier environments, an underlying SONET/SDH network is used to provision broadband links between routers. SONET/SDH networks are complex networks on their own and offer a variety of functions at the OSI-RM Layer 1, the Physical Layer. One of these functions is Automatic Protection Switching (APS), where "extra" bandwidth and ports in the network are provisioned to support redundancy of the SONET/SDH circuits.

There are rumblings in the networking industry that this additional layer of networking intelligence will be made obsolete in the near future and that IP routers will soon be connected just by raw Dense Wavelength Division Multiplexing (DWDM) pipes. This might come true for very high speed (OC-48/STM-16 and beyond) links in the core, but at the edges of the network and in regional access networks, SONET/SDH networks will be present for a long time to come. And DWDM has been stalled somewhat by expensive equipment, so a discussion of SONET/SDH APS and IS-IS is still important and will be so for the foreseeable future.

In any case, DWDM core or not, look at the edge of the network and assume the network uses transport capacity from a regional city or metropolitan area carrier. Typically the customer has the choice of an unprotected circuit or a protected circuit. In the protected circuit, the regional carrier pre-provisions bandwidth and ports in order to recover from failed or broken equipment in any part of the network. Assume this is the protected flavour of the circuit, which is always a good idea if the budget allows. What follows

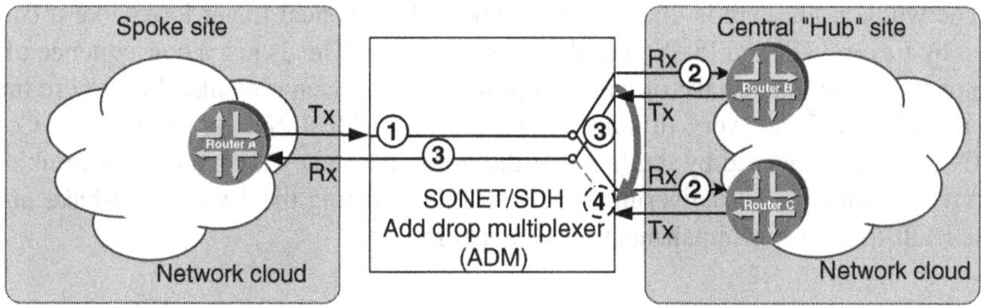

FIGURE 5.11. The protected SONET circuit is creating a unidirectional link in the backup case

does not require any detailed familiarity with SONET/SDH. All terms and equipment roles are fully explained as needed.

Figure 5.11 shows a failure scenario where Router A and Router B are connected by a SONET/SDH pipe. Router A is located at the *spoke* site and Router B is located at the central *hub* site. Additionally, a second redundant SONET/SDH port has been pre-provisioned in case a link to one of the routers or even the router itself at the central site fails. The SONET/SDH Add–Drop Multiplexer (ADM), the network element that links the routers at both customer sites, needs to make sure its ports are still up. In SONET/SDH networks, the ends of a SONET/SDH link (in this case, the routers) can send *heartbeat* signalling messages in the overhead bytes of the SONET/SDH transmission frame header for redundancy purposes. Routers A and B send *heartbeat* signals in order to inform the ADMs that everything is okay. If the ADM does not receive a heartbeat signal from the routers for a period of 50 milliseconds (ms), then the ADM will automatically switch over to the backup circuit (Router C).

Note that both Router B and Router C listen on the wire for APS signalling messages because the ADM connects both routers, *receive* fibres. However, Router C's *transmit* fibre is not ordinarily active (it is not needed). This fibre only gets activated in failure mode when Router B or one of its links goes down. Realize that this is a purposeful, one-way connection for SONET/SDH APS. It is exactly this one-way connection that will cause trouble in IS-IS environments. Consider the following scenario:

1. Router A sends a Hello message
2. Both Routers B and C receive the Hello message
3. Router B responds with a Hello message and declares the adjacency to Router A up
4. Router C also responds with a Hello message. But the Hello response does *not* get through to the spoke site (no active transmit). However, Router C thinks it has successfully delivered the Hello and declares the adjacency up. So Router A knows it has an adjacency with Router B and vice versa, which is fine. The problem is that Router C also thinks it has an adjacency with Router A and therefore will forward traffic down the "broken" (inactive) link, which is only to be used for APS purposes. This is a serious issue because the traffic from Router C to Router A will get black holed because the transmit fibre is not connected all the way through the ADM.

The whole point here is that a backup link at the Physical Layer looks like it can be used by Layer 3 (IP and IS-IS), but this is not the case. This is just a consequence of the use of the 2-way handshake on point-to-point circuits. Scenarios like this, where traffic gets black holed, are very difficult to troubleshoot. Most Network Operation Centre (NOC) teams are fooled by the fact that the router adjacency is up and their thinking is that the circuit *must* be delivering injected traffic. Trusting the 2-way handshake in this case leads to a serious impairment of the network.

5.3.2.2 Failure Scenario 2: Parallel Links

The previous failure scenario does not do any damage, because all the IS-IS routers in the network would soon realize during the SPF calculation that Router C believes it has an adjacency with Router A, but Router A does not report an adjacency to Router C. The SPF algorithm, which is used to calculate paths through the network, has an additional stability rule built in. If two routers do not indicate to each other that they have an adjacency, then the SPF algorithm disregards the adjacency between the two routers, which means that no transit traffic is sent over the unidirectional link. However, based on the previous failure condition, it is relatively easy to construct a *four* router scenario (two routers on each side of the link) where both sides report a *stale* adjacency that ultimately passes the 2-way check during the SPF calculation. This example simply uses a three router scenario for a clearer explanation of the underlying problem. So far, we have not mentioned the details of the SPF calculation, but there will be much more about that topic in Chapter 10 "SPF and Router Calculation".

This section shows one other example of failure. In this example even the SPF-2-way check will be spoofed, which serves as a last resort protection from black holing traffic.

Consider the scenario in Figure 5.12. Here there are two routers interconnected by two circuits composed of two fibres in each direction. Now, assume there are *two* fibre breaks. The transmit fibre from Router A to Router B on circuit #1 has failed and, in addition, the transmit fibre from Router B to Router A on circuit #2 is broken. Here is the sequence of events that happens:

1. Router A sends a Hello message on circuit #2
2. Router B responds to the Hello message on circuit #2 and declares the adjacency up
3. Router B sends a Hello message on circuit #1
4. Router A responds to the Hello message on circuit #1 and declares the adjacency up
5. Both Routers A and B tell other routers in the network that they can see each other, when in fact they can't because of the fibre failures mentioned earlier. This failure scenario passes even the check during the SPF calculation. This makes both Router A and B attract transit traffic which will be black holed by both sides.

So 2-way handshaking on point-to-point links in IS-IS suffers from robustness problems in practice. Therefore the basic IS-IS protocol needs to be extended so that the more reliable 3-way handshakes are made on point-to-point circuits. Using the error-prone 2-way handshake procedure results in the set of problems generated by unidirectional links due to APS or multiple fibre breaks. The 3-way handshake on point-to-point circuits is discussed in the following section.

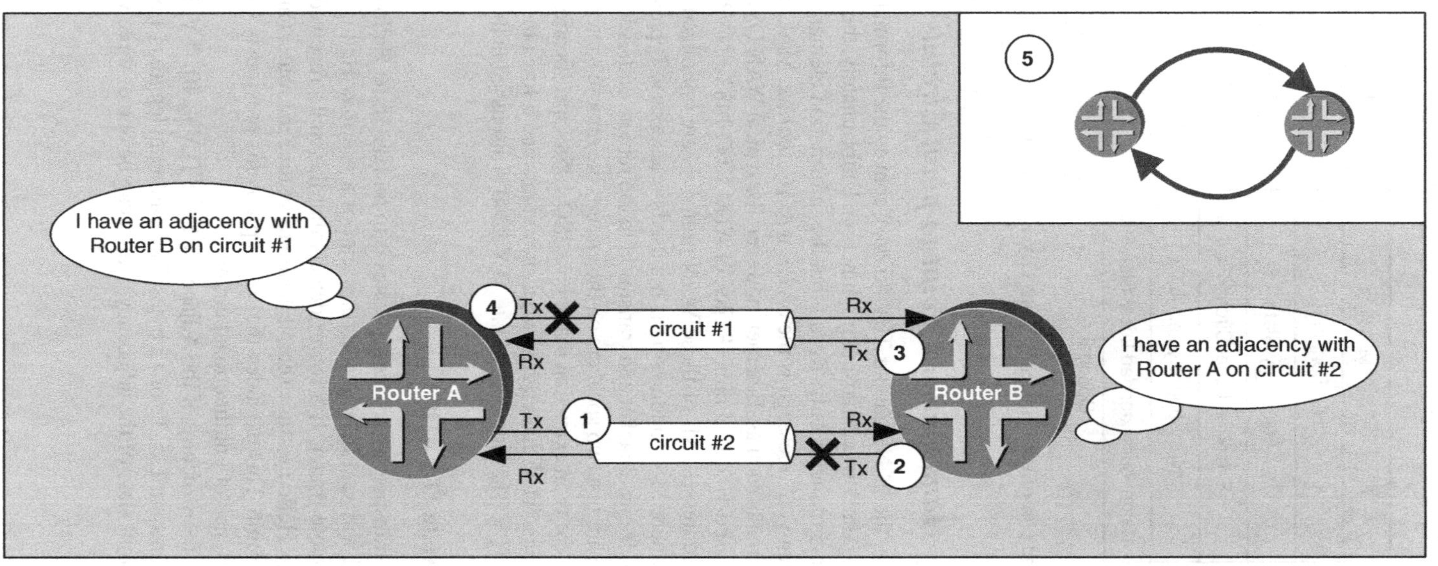

FIGURE 5.12. Two reported unidirectional LSP advertisements make other routers think that there is a single bi-directional advertisement

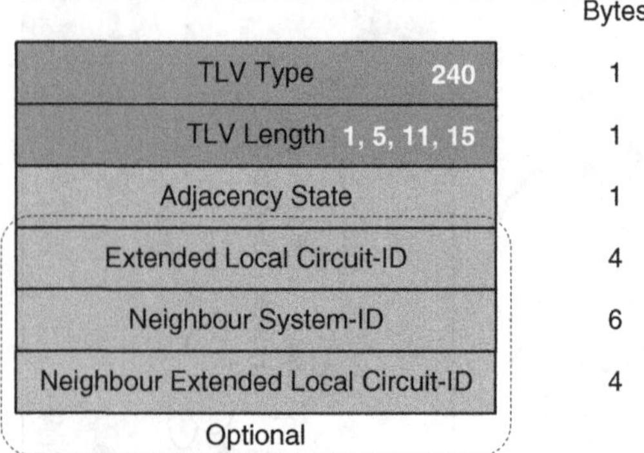

FIGURE 5.13. The second part of the Adjacency State TLV is optional

5.3.3 *The 3-way Handshake on Point-to-point Circuits*

In LAN environments, the IS Neighbour TLV #6 *does* convey the information elements needed for performing the 3-way handshaking function. Unfortunately, this specific TLV is tailored to LAN environments only. Recall that the information elements to transport the "Hello, I have seen you" message is the *SNPA*, a *MAC address*. MAC addresses are typical to broadcast circuits such as, Ethernet, however, the typical WAN OSI-RM Layer 2 protocols like PPP, Cisco-HDLC, Frame-Relay, or ATM RFC 1483-SNAP, do not have the notion of MAC addresses. All of those WAN protocols are optimized for point-to-point environments where MAC addressing is not used or necessary. Typically the WAN protocols just need to frame a packet and transmit it to the remote end. Addressing is not needed because there are just two speakers on the circuit: the remote router and the local router. Fortunately, there is an extension to the base ISO 10589 specification, RFC 3373, that specifies an optional TLV that carries *adjacency states* and a few other information elements in a special TLV. The Adjacency State TLV #240 is discussed in the next section.

5.3.3.1 Adjacency State TLV #240

The main purpose of transporting adjacency states is to find out if the Hello message that a router has received was sent *in response* to receipt of a *previous* Hello, or is just any Hello sent by the remote router. If a router detects that the Hello received was sent in response to a previous Hello message sent, it is safe to assume the routers are on a working, bi-directional circuit. This excludes the set of problems previously discussed that resulted from the presence of unidirectional circuits.

Figure 5.13 shows the structure of the Adjacency State TLV #240 TLV. The TLV is a variable length and can span 1, 5, 11 or 15 bytes. The minimum length is 1 byte. The first byte conveys the current state of the adjacency, which can be one of three values:

- 0x2 Down
- 0x1 Initializing
- 0x0 Up

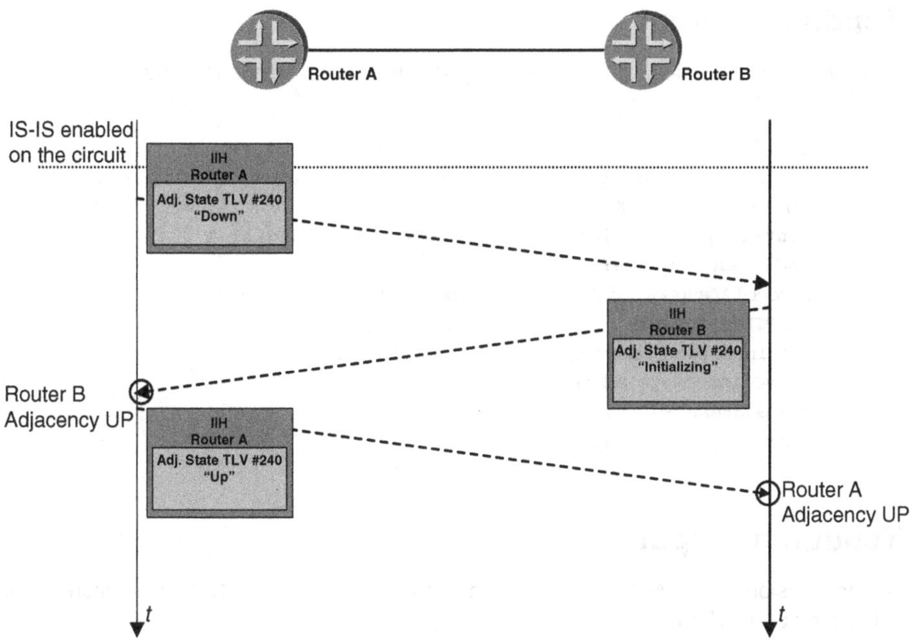

FIGURE 5.14. JUNOS always sends the 15-byte version of TLV #240, IOS per default sends the 1-byte version and optionally the 15-byte version

Figure 5.14 shows how the TLV content is changed during a 3-way handshake. Here is how the TLV works in the 3-way handshake:

1. Router A send a Hello reporting the adjacency as *Down*
2. Router B replies to Router A's Hello. Router B tells Router A that this particular Hello message was generated in response to Router A's previous Hello message by setting the Adjacency State to *Initializing*. Router A now knows that the circuit is truly bi-directional and declares the adjacency *Up*.
3. Router A sends a Hello back to Router B setting the Adjacency State to *Up* which causes Router B to declare the adjacency up on the Router B side as well.

There are two different flavours of the Adjacency TLV deployed in the field. The first one is derived from one of the first Internet drafts before the document was extended and finally went to RFC state. The early version is a crippled version which just carries a single byte adjacency state. The more recent flavour implements the full 15 bytes of RFC 3373. From the router's debug logs and show commands you cannot tell if you receive the single or 15-byte version. Tcpdump is used to reveal the version received.

Tcpdump output

Older versions of JUNOS and IOS only support the 1-byte Adjacency state TLV #240:

```
00:29:47.706711 OSI, IS-IS, length: 38
  p2p IIH, hlen: 20, v: 1, pdu-v: 1, sys-id-len: 6 (0), max-area: 3(0)
    source-id: 1921.6809.0034, holding time: 27s, Flags: [Level 2 only]
    circuit-id: 0x01, PDU length: 38
      Point-to-point Adjacency State TLV #240, length: 1
        Adjacency State: Up
      Protocols supported TLV #129, length: 1
        NLPID(s): IPv4
      IPv4 Interface address(es) TLV #132, length: 4
        IPv4 interface address: 172.16.5.156
      Area address(es) TLV #1, length: 4
        Area address (length: 3): 49.0001
```

Tcpdump output

Recent versions of JUNOS and IOS support the fully fledged, 15-byte version of the Adjacency State TLV #240:

```
11:35:23.248504 OSI, IS-IS, length: 50
  p2p IIH, hlen: 20, v: 1, pdu-v: 1, sys-id-len: 6 (0), max-area: 3 (0)
    source-id: 1921.6809.0034, holding time: 27s, Flags: [Level 2 only]
    circuit-id: 0x01, PDU length: 50
      Point-to-point Adjacency State TLV #240, length: 15
        Adjacency State: Up
        Extended Local circuit ID: 0x0000001a
        Neighbor SystemID: 2092.1113.4007
        Neighbor Extended Local circuit ID: 0x0000005f
      Protocols supported TLV #129, length: 1
        NLPID(s): IPv4
      IPv4 Interface address(es) TLV #132, length: 4
        IPv4 interface address: 172.16.5.156
      Area address(es) TLV #1, length: 4
        Area address (length: 3): 49.0001
```

Wrapping just the Adjacency State (1 byte) inside the TLV and not adding the optional 14 bytes information only addresses the unidirectional link problem to *some* degree. One issue is still open: A router can never be 100% sure if a change in the adjacency state is *targeted* to the receiver itself. A broken or flapping (rapidly up and down) link in a SONET/SDH environment, which frequently terminates at two different routers, can make IS-IS *blind spotted* and causes the same problems that have been observed with the plain 2-way checks.

This issue might seem very far-fetched or esoteric. But the IETF is known for delivering pragmatic protocols that solve *real* problems. The fact that the Adjacency State TLV was revised in a later version of the draft that finally went into RFC 3373 to include the Neighbours System-ID so that the neighbour can be sure that a change of adjacency state was generated by *receipt* of the neighbour's recent Hello message indicates that this was a real concern. If there was a state change by a neighbour and the Source-ID is not listed in the *Neighbor Extended Local Circuit-ID* field, then it was certainly not the receipt of the router's Hello change that triggered the state change.

Additionally, there was concern about the size (8 bits) of the Local Circuit-ID field in the point-to-point Hello message. Modern routers can be configured with literally thousands of interfaces (usually logical interfaces, but still interfaces) and so that field needed to be extended. TLV #240 transports 32-bit Local Circuit IDs, which should give any router plenty of Circuit-IDs for the time being. Normally routers insert the local interface index or SNMP index into this field.

Contemporary JUNOS releases support the 15-byte version of TLV #240 only. In IOS you can control the emission of the 1-byte or 15-byte version using the `isis three-way-handshake` interface configuration option.

IOS configuration

The `ietf` option to the `isis three-way-handshake` configuration command emits the 15-byte version of TLV #240. The default parameter is the `cisco` option which generates the one-byte TLV payload.

```
interface POS4/1
  [ ... ]
  isis three-way-handshake ietf
  encapsulation ppp
  [ ... ]
!
```

If an implementation follows ISO 10589 by the letter, then the expectation would be that after a completed 2-way or 3-way check, an adjacency goes into the *Up* state. However, this may not be the case. Most implementations perform additional checks before an adjacency is declared *Up*.

5.4 Sub-net Checking

IS-IS is often *expected* to be a true multi-protocol IGP. Because adjacency formation, database synchronization and topology calculation (through SPF) is based on Layer-2 information, one would expect that it is entirely decoupled from any network layer dependencies. That assumption does not match the deployed reality. IS-IS routers indeed *do* verify that the next-hop the router is announcing is valid. The receiving router checks all occurrences of the Interface Address TLV #132 and also checks it against the list of local IP addresses configured on that circuit. Figure 5.15 shows the structure of the IP Interface Address TLV #132 which is a simple list of IP addresses that contains a router's primary and secondary IP addresses.

Both IOS and JUNOS verify that there is a common IP sub-net. If there is no common IP sub-net there is also no viable next-hop that can be entered in a routing table, and therefore the adjacency is considered invalid and stays in the Down / Initializing state.

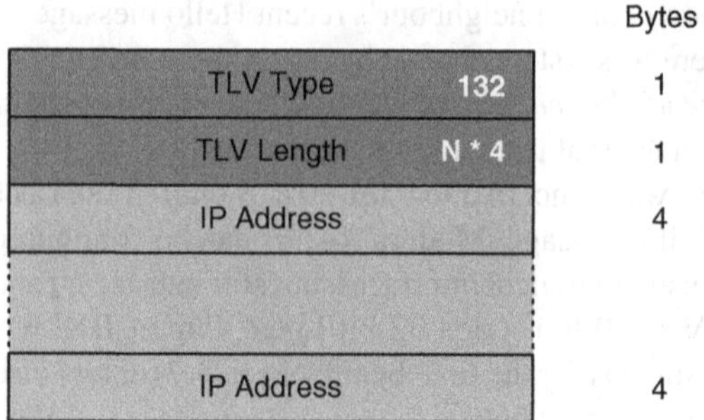

FIGURE 5.15. The contents of the Interface Address TLV #132 are matched against the local IP address to check if there is a matching sub-net

There is unfortunately no show command in the router CLI that reports a sub-net mismatch. You need to turn on debugging in IOS and tracing in JUNOS to get any indication there is something wrong in this regard.

In IOS, a sub-net mismatch can be detected once the `isis adj-packets` debug is turned on. In JUNOS, the trace option flag list needs to include the `error` flag.

IOS debug output

For IOS to detect sub-net mismatches the `debug isis adj-packets` needs to be turned on. Additionally you need to run `terminal monitor` to display the logging output on the vty.

```
London#debug isis adj-packets
IS-IS Adjacency related packets debugging is on
London#terminal monitor
Oct 26 22:33:11: ISIS-Adj: Sending serial IIH on POS4/1, length 4469
Oct 26 22:33:19: ISIS-Adj: Rec serial IIH from *PPP* (POS4/0),
    cir type L1L2, cir id 01, length 1492
Oct 26 22:33:19: ISIS-Adj: No usable IP interface addresses in serial IIH
    from POS4/0
```

JUNOS debug output

For JUNOS to detect sub-net mismatches the flag `error` under the proto-cols `isis traceoptions {}` stanza needs to be configured. The logging messages will then be written into the specified IS-IS logfile (`isis.log`)

```
hannes@Frankfurt> show log isis.log
Oct 26 22:16:13 trace_on: Tracing to "/var/log/isis.log" started
[ … ]
Oct 26 22:33:43 ISIS L3 periodic xmit to interface so-0/2/2.0
Oct 26 22:33:45 ISIS L3 hello from 1921.6800.1068 interface so-0/2/2.0
    absorbed
Oct 26 22:33:45 ISIS ERROR: IIH from 1921.6800.1068 without matching
    address, interface so-0/2/2.0
```

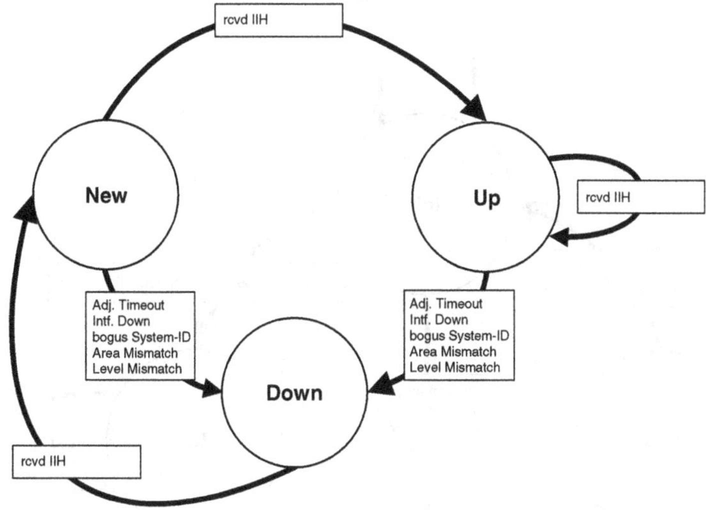

FIGURE 5.16. The finite state machine for a 2-way adjacency (deprecated)

After the sub-net check is positive, and there are no other configuration mismatches, such as misaligned authentication strings or circuit types and levels, the adjacency should go to the *Up* state.

The transition from *Down* to *Up* does not occur *immediately* after receipt of a valid IIH message. There are some intermediate states in between, and there is also some damping logic involved, which makes sure that the network is not overwhelmed because of a flappy link. The next section is about the adjacency finite state machine and hold down logic of adjacencies.

5.5 Finite State Machine

Most routing protocols maintain a finite state machine (FSM) for neighbour management. The FSM is a graph that describes steady states and the events that enable transitions from one state to another. In Figure 5.16 there is a FSM for a 2-way handshake.

The three states are:

- Down
- New
- Up

A receipt of a valid (level, area and authentication needs to match) IIH transitions from Down to New and finally to Up. A mismatch of level, area and authentication, or a timeout of interface down events immediately transitions the adjacency from Up to Down.

Two-way adjacencies and hence 2-way state machines are an anachronism (as demonstrated by the previous examples) and are deprecated today. Figure 5.17 shows the FSM for the 3-way handshake.

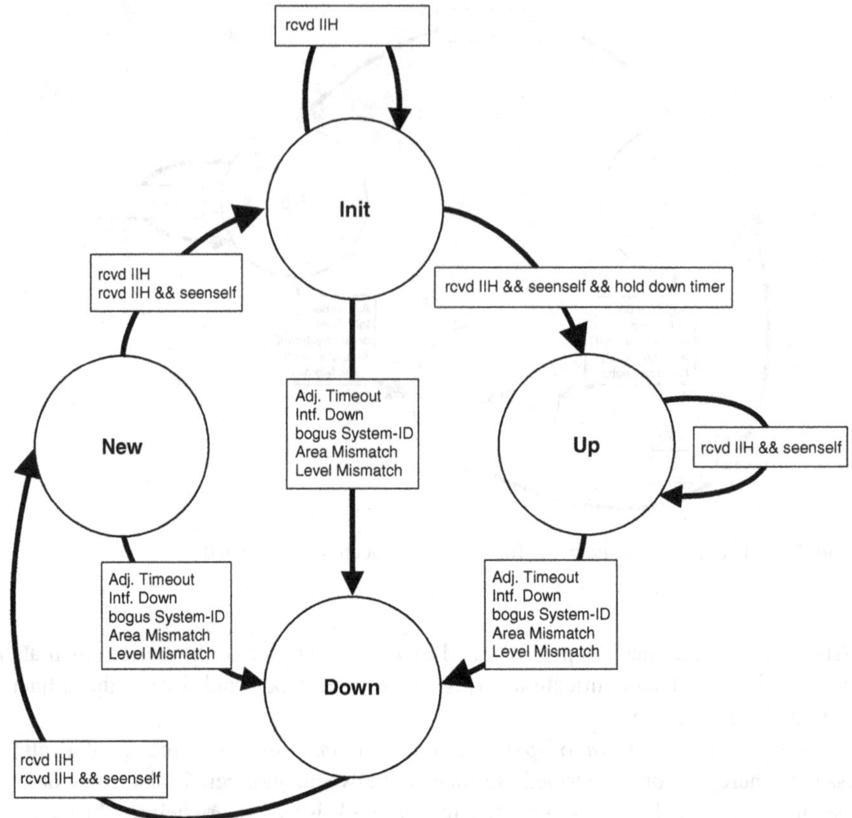

FIGURE 5.17. The Finite State Machine for a 3-way adjacency

The 3-way handshake encompasses four states:

- Down
- New
- Init
- Up

The additional *Init* state has been created for 3-way handshake functionality. Upon receipt of a valid IIH, the adjacency is moved to the *Init* state. From there a *Seenself* event is necessary to proceed to an *Up* state. The Seenself event can be an Adjacency State of 1 (Init) as part of the Adjacency State TLV #240, or the router's own SNPA listed in the IS Neighbour TLV #6.

As soon as an adjacency is declared Up the router needs to originate a LSP packet reporting the new adjacency to other routers in the network. A good IS-IS implementation tries to protect other routers from locally flapping adjacencies. That means if the local circuit is flapping at a high frequency, there is a risk that the entire network will be overwhelmed with LSPs. Both IOS and JUNOS use timers that artificially *hold down* an adjacency that is about to enter the *Up* state for a limited amount of time. Typically those timers are in the range of 1–60 seconds depending on factors such as:

- Flapping history
- Amount of LSP traffic
- Number of adjacencies per interface

If an adjacency has flapped frequently in the past then it is highly likely that it will flap in the future too. It is safe to hold down adjacencies longer if they have a higher amount of transitions over time. JUNOS does, for example, measure the amount of LSPs that are transmitted through local interfaces. If the amount of LSPs is higher than one LSP per second then probably the network is shaky and it is not safe to contribute to further churn by announcing an additional LSP. Finally, a common action is to treat point-to-point or single adjacency LAN circuits better than LAN circuits with multiple adjacencies. The idea behind that is if there are some adjacencies already in the Up state then we are probably in the middle of taking up a big LAN segment and there will be more changes to come. Waiting a little extra time here does not do a lot of harm but highly reduces the churn if a big LAN goes down.

For high-resiliency routing, it is imperative how fast the router detects that an adjacency is Down. In the FSM there are two events for Down transitioning: the *adjacency timeout* and *interface down* event. In the next section there is a short overview about IS-IS neighbour liveliness detection and how that impacts high-resiliency routing.

5.6 Neighbour Liveliness Detection

The Internet has evolved from an academic playground to a business-critical infrastructure. Customers and their Internet service providers are keen to tune the convergence speed in case a backup circuit has to be engaged. The most dominant element for convergence behaviour is *neighbour liveliness* detection. Today there are several options to detect if a circuit to an adjacent router is still able to deliver packets:

- IGP Hellos
- Interface Tracking
- LMI Protocol

The two major IS-IS implementations treat all three sources of information equally.

5.6.1 *IGP Hellos*

The historical way of detecting that a neighbour is down is by tracking receipt of a neighbour's Hello packets. That method has two disadvantages. First, on a busy router with many adjacencies the generation and receipt of hundreds of IIH messages may overwhelm the routing process. Second, many routing protocols do not support sub-second timers. Consider Figure 5.4, which displays a point-to-point IIH header. The Hold Time field is a discrete 16-bit field which supports timer values from 1–65535 seconds, but no sub-second timers. The same problem applies to the OSPF routing protocol: The Hello and Dead timer there needs to be conveyed in the protocol. The lowest unit are once again seconds. One of the nice things about IS-IS has been that the Hello timer does not need to get encoded on the Hello message. The Hello timer is a purely local matter. The timer that gets transported using the IS-IS protocol is the hold timer which can go down to 1 second. The Hello timer is therefore a fraction of the hold timer.

In IOS and JUNOS sub-second Hello timers are configured differently: IOS needs the keyword `isis hello-interval minimal` in its interface configuration. Depending on the `isis-hello-multiplier` value, IOS dispatches Hellos in fractions of this value.

IOS configuration

```
interface POS4/1
  [ … ]
  ip router isis
  encapsulation ppp
  [ … ]
  isis hello-multiplier 5 level-1
  isis hello-interval minimal level-1
!
```

Unfortunately, IS-IS has no show command to display its sub-second timers. The following Tcpdump output monitors the arrival times of the point-to-point IIH messages. Note that they are all spaced within 200 ms – a random jitter.

Tcpdump output

```
19:15:15.246711 In OSI IS-IS, p2p IIH, length: 4469
19:15:15.440708 In OSI IS-IS, p2p IIH, length: 4469
19:15:15.700683 In OSI IS-IS, p2p IIH, length: 4469
19:15:15.896695 In OSI IS-IS, p2p IIH, length: 4469
19:15:15.1082736 In OSI IS-IS, p2p IIH, length: 4469
```

In JUNOS, all you can configure is the hold timer. Set it to 1 second and the system dispatches Hellos at the hold-timer/3 frequency. Note that on point-to-point media you need to configure the hold-time to the same value on both IS-IS levels otherwise the system will use the default hold-time values of 27 seconds. The reason for this behaviour is the sharing of the Hello message between both levels.

JUNOS configuration

```
protocols {
    isis {
        [ … ]
        interface so-0/1/2.0 {
            level 1 hold-time 1;
            level 2 hold-time 1;
```

```
        }
        interface lo0.0;
    }
}
```

JUNOS displays the Hello timers in millisecond resolution using the `show isis interface detail` operational level command.

JUNOS command output

```
hannes@Frankfurt> show isis interface detail
IS-IS interface database:
so-0/1/2.0
  Index: 67, State: 0x6, Circuit id: 0x1, Circuit type: 3
  LSP interval: 100 ms, CSNP interval: 5 s
  Level  Adjacencies  Priority  Metric  Hello (s)  Hold (s)  Designated
                                                             Router
    1              1        64      10    0.333          1
    2              1        64      10    0.333          1
```

The JUNOS interface multiplier is hard coded (meaning it cannot be changed) to a value of 3. A hold-timer of 1 second therefore results in a Hello interval of 333 ms, which is the lowest Hello interval possible on JUNOS.

Relying on Hellos puts an upper boundary of 1 second to the detection time following a link-failure on the routing protocols. But by tracking an interface state, routers can detect the liveliness state much more quickly.

5.6.2 *Interface Tracking*

The chipsets that drive modern router interfaces report link errors, such as a loss of signal, to the routing sub-system within a few milliseconds. For high-speed detection, therefore, optical interfaces are the best choice. However, there are still similar problems, as illustrated in Figure 5.10. If there are active elements in the middle of the transmission chain, then local errors are not propagated downstream and the receiving router does not detect that the light went out.

SONET/SDH offers a true advantage over other physical media like Ethernet, which do not propagate local errors to downstream Network Elements.

Many Protocols like Frame Relay and ATM also include their own Local Management Interface (LMI) protocol which performs link-layer keep-alive checking, and so on. Unfortunately there is still no LMI-like protocol for Ethernet. Bi-directional fault detection attempts make a *neutral* liveliness-checking protocol available.

5.6.3 *Bi-directional Fault Detection (BFD)*

BFD is defined in draft-katz-ward-bfd-01, and its encoding rules are documented in draft-katz-ward-bfd-v4v6-1hop-00. BFD is an answer to the following problems:

- Link-Layer neutral high frequency keep-alive protocol
- Offload high frequency keep-alive processing from the IGP Layer

- Support sub-second timers on behalf of protocols that cannot
- Negotiate timers dynamically

The BFD protocol, unlike many other protocols, includes no auto-neighbour discovery. It has client software instead, typical of the IP routing protocols, and based on the detected IGP neighbours. The IGP asks the BFD module to set up a BFD session to the Link IP addresses of the provided neighbours.

BFD is (at time of writing this book) only available for JUNOS. The first release with support for BFD is JUNOS 6.1 onwards. The configuration of BFD is a property of the `interface {}` stanza inside the `protocols isis {}` branch.

JUNOS configuration

Under the `bfd-liveness-detection` stanza you can configure the minimum transmit interval plus the `detection-time` multiplier.

```
protocols {
    isis {
        interface so-1/2/0.0 {
            bfd-liveness-detection {
                minimum-interval 100;
                multiplier 5;
            }
        }
        [ … ]
        interface lo0.0;
    }
}
```

In this example the router emits Hello packets at a rate of once every 100 ms. If the neighbour does not receive BFD control packets for 500 ms, this router can declare the origniator dead and move to an interface down state in the FSM.

BFD runs on top of IP UDP port 3784 and 3785. Port 3784 is used for control packets and 3785 is used for Echo Mode traffic. The JUNOS implementation just supports control packets for liveliness detection. Echo Mode is envisioned for the future: the plan is that forwarding plane software can generate that traffic and the control plane is only needed for parameter setup.

The following Tcpdump output shows the parameters that are conveyed using the 24-bytes fixed length packet.

Tcpdump output

The BFD protocol runs on top of UDP port 3784 and 3785. It is meant as a high frequency keep-alive mechanism which augments routing protocols that do not have sub-second timer support.

```
09:32:30.884968 IP 172.16.223.236.3784 > 172.16.223.235.3784: BFDv0,
 length: 24
        Control, Flags: [I Hear You], Diagnostic: Control Detection
         Time Expired (0x01)
        Detection Timer Multiplier: 5 (500 ms Detection time),
         BFD Length: 24
        My Discriminator: 0x00000001, Your Discriminator: 0x00000002
          Desired min Tx Interval:  100 ms
          Required min Rx Interval: 200 ms
          Required min Echo Interval: 0 ms
```

Session state transactions are provided using the `Flag` contents. The Desired/Required Timer Fields are used for negotiating a common timer that both peers can accept. The pair of discriminators is necessary to multiplex several sessions between a pair of hosts.

After BFD has been enabled on both sides, one can verify if a BFD-capable neighbour has been found on the other end and if the BFD session is Up. The `show bfd session command` displays the session state.

JUNOS command output

Using the `show bfd session` command you can display the current state and details of the active BFD sessions.

```
hannes@Frankfurt> show bfd session extensive
                                                              Transmit
Address              State   Interface      Detect Time       Interval     Multiplier
172.16.223.236       Up      so-0/1/2.0            1.000         0.100          5
   Client ISIS L1, TX interval 0.100, RX interval 0.100, multiplier 5
   Client ISIS L2, TX interval 0.100, RX interval 0.100, multiplier 5
  Session up time 12:34:22, previous down time 00:00:06
  Local diagnostic CtlExpire, remote diagnostic None
  Remote heard, hears us
  Min async interval 0.100, min slow interval 1.000
  Adaptive async tx interval 0.100, rx interval 0.200
  Local min tx interval 0.100, min rx interval 0.100, multiplier 5
  Remote min tx interval 0.100, min rx interval 0.100, multiplier 5
  Local discriminator 1, remote discriminator 2
  Echo mode disabled/inactive

1 sessions, 2 clients
Cumulative transmit rate 10.0 pps, cumulative receive rate 5.0 pps
```

BFD is likely to become the dominant keep-alive protocol due its open implementation. It is expected to even be the protocol of choice between routers and servers. For server applications like voice-over IP or financial applications there are open-source BFD implementations for hosts available.

5.7 Summary

IS-IS adjacency processing has changed over the years. It started out with simple 2-way finite state machines and, due to the underlying problems of not detecting half-broken links, it quickly evolved to a 3-way FSM. It is remarkable that the defects of the underlying protocol have been solved with just the addition of an optional Adjacency State TLV. Reliably detecting that a neighbour is Up or Down is not enough for today's service provider environments. On the one hand the implementation has to be *slow* enough to protect the network from flapping adjacencies that are propagated through the network – on the other hand there is a need for quick keep-alive detection mechanisms. Due to the rise of Ethernet as popular core-facing interface technology, an LMI-like protocol like Bi-directional Fault Detection (BFD) had to be designed. The application of BFD to serve as an IGP detection protocol is just the start. It is expected that BFD will be used for other network protocols or other environments like application keep-alive detection for mission-critical servers.

6

Generating, Flooding and Ageing LSPs

Unlike distance vector protocols, such as RIP, link-state routing protocols, such as OSPF and IS-IS, don't tell only their neighbours about the *topology* of the network. Link-state protocols distribute both their *IP reachability* and topological view far beyond their adjacent neighbours, ultimately flooding this information to all routers in an area.

To keep the reachability information in the network current, link-state protocols need to have a basic set of functions available that can be used to *originate*, *distribute* and finally *revoke*, or *time-out* topology information. In IS-IS-speak, that piece of topology information is encoded in a link-state protocol data unit (LSP). This chapter covers these functions and the surrounding network events th at cause the IS-IS protocol to *generate*, *flood* and finally *age* LSPs.

Link-state routing protocols such as IS-IS follow a paradigm that can best be described as *distributed databases with local computation*, which is quite different to the way other common routing protocols like RIP and BGP work. Distributed databases are discussed in more detail in the following section.

6.1 Distributed Databases

Before explaining how a distributed database works, first consider what a *localized* database looks like and how routing protocols use it. *Localized* databases mean that every router has its own local view of the network and does not know the exact topology of the network as a whole. This is like a tourist in a foreign city having no clue about what the overall topology of the city (the street layout) looks like. All the tourist has is a local view of the places and streets that are next to the tourist's immediate location. This makes it very difficult to find the best path to a landmark or museum, and in the worst case situation, the tourist has to try out several paths, being careful not to circle around the same locations. Localized databases work the same way. In contrast, a *distributed* database approach works differently: here all of the routers share common information about what the network looks like. If the tourist in the example has got lost, a distributed database map would give them a more complete map of the best way to get to a particular destination in the city (or in this case, the network).

How does IS-IS compute the map of the network? If each router just contributes its local view to its neighbours, and if that information can be shared among all the routers in a network, then each will ultimately have a global map of the network. Link-state routing protocols, such as IS-IS, work like a jigsaw puzzle, as shown in Figure 6.1. Each router in the figure represents one piece of the puzzle, and if all of the puzzle pieces are present, then each router can start to put the puzzle together to acquire an understanding

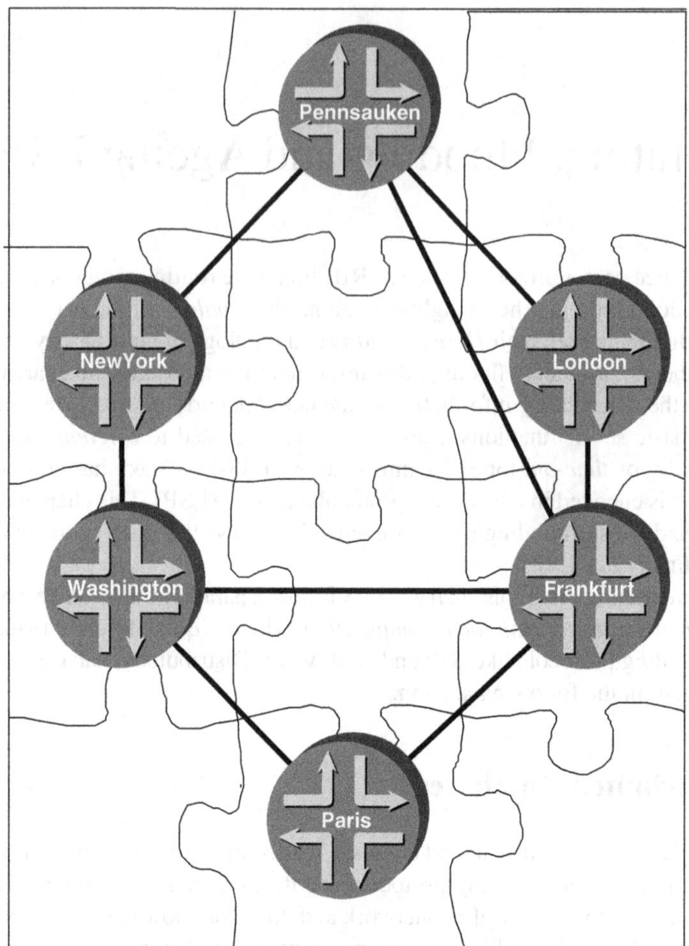

FIGURE 6.1. A distributed link-state database is like a jigsaw puzzle

of what the big picture looks like. The collection of puzzle pieces is called the *link-state database.* IS-IS has a number of techniques called *flooding* and *synchronizing* to get a complete map of the network. In this chapter, you will learn about the individual puzzle pieces, which are called *link-state protocol data units* (LSPs), and how IS-IS distributes the information they contain.

IS-IS, by default, tries to acquire two maps from its neighbours and therefore maintains two databases to store topology-related information. Information for the first map, which typically represents the topology inside the close collection of routers, called a point-of-presence (POP), is stored in the Level 1 (L1) database. Sticking with the lost tourist example, think of this as just a local map that guides you around the next few streets. The second map, which typically represents the backbone structure of the network, is stored in the Level 2 (L2) database. This would best compare to a nationwide map where all the freeways and highways are shown. You can take a quick look into both of these link-state databases to find out exactly *which* puzzle pieces the database holds by issuing a `show isis database` command on both the IOS and JUNOS software platforms.

IOS command output

The contents of the IS-IS link-state database can be displayed using the `show isis database` command:

```
Amsterdam# show isis database
[ … ]
IS-IS Level-1 Link State Database:
LSPID              LSP Seq Num    LSP Checksum    LSP Holdtime    ATT/P/OL
New-York.00-00     0x00002fac     0xC24F          60128           1/0/0
[ … ]
IS-IS Level-2 Link State Database:
LSPID              LSP Seq Num    LSP Checksum    LSP Holdtime    ATT/P/OL
LINX-gw.00-00      0x00000128     0xB8EF          36163           0/0/1
LINX-gw.01-00      0x00000128     0x455A          42001           0/0/0
VIX-gw.00-00       0x00000123     0xEFC1           5023           0/0/0
[ … ]
```

The output shows you one "puzzle piece" of information in each line. Each LSP is uniquely identified by its LSP-ID. The exact format of the LSP-ID will be discussed later in this chapter. All that is important for now is that it says something about the router that originated that LSP. The sequence number is a kind of version field that tells receivers which information is more recent. The checksum enables to check at the receiver if the LSP has been corrupted during its long way through the network. Finally, hold-time and the ATT/P/OL gives some information about the validity of that information and how long it will be valid, and just like a passport it has an expiration date.

JUNOS command output

In the JUNOS software, you can display the IS-IS database using the `show isis database` command. Watch for an inconsistency between the LSPs being sent and received, as this is a problem indication:

```
hannes@New-York> show isis database
IS-IS level 1 link-state database:
LSP ID                        Sequence    Checksum    Lifetime Attributes
New-York.00-00                  0x2fac      0xc24f       62063 L1 Attached
[ … ]
  4 LSPs

IS-IS level 2 link-state database:
LSP ID                        Sequence    Checksum    Lifetime Attributes
LINX-gw.00-00                    0x128      0xb8ef       36063 L1 L2 Overload
```

```
LINX-gw.01-00                    0x128     0x455a       41901  L1 L2
VIX-gw.00-00                     0x123     0xefc1        4922  L1 L2
[ … ]
  12 LSPs
```

The JUNOS software output contains similar information to the IOS software output. The only difference is the little bit more detailed breakdown of the so-called *attribute typeblock*, which will be discussed later in this chapter. As far as the attribute typeblock is concerned, the JUNOS output is more verbose than the IOS equivalent.

Based on the information in the two link-state databases for L1 and L2, each router in an IS-IS network computes the topology of the network *independently* of every other router. This principle of independent router operation is called *local computation*. This is the topic of the next discussion.

6.2 Local Computation

Routing protocols, such as RIP or BGP, compute the best path through a network in a *distributed* fashion. That is, no single RIP or BGP router knows what the other routers know about the route, and this is a real limitation. For instance, each time a RIP router passes on a route to its neighbour, the route gets a worse value. This "worseness" is indicted in a *metric* field, which represents the hop-count (number of routers) that a router is away from the router attached to the source sub-net. In Figure 6.2 the sub-net 192.168.1/24 is directly connected to RIP Router #1. Router #1 reports the sub-net to its neighbours with a hop count of 1. Router #2 learns the sub-net with a metric of 1 and reports it further to the right side of the figure after incrementing the metric field by one. The routing update therefore arrives at Router #3 with a metric of 2. But Router #1 has no idea what value this route has on Router #3. RIP routing illustrates how a distributed computation scheme works.

IS-IS utilizes a totally different way of calculating routing information. Before the route calculation takes place, all IS-IS routers distribute the information about the local views of the routers to each other. Intermediate routers along the way must not change these views (represented in the LSPs). After this distribution (flooding), a common route-calculation scheme, which in IS-IS is called the *shortest path first* (SPF) algorithm, is applied. Note that each router computes the routes independently from every other router.

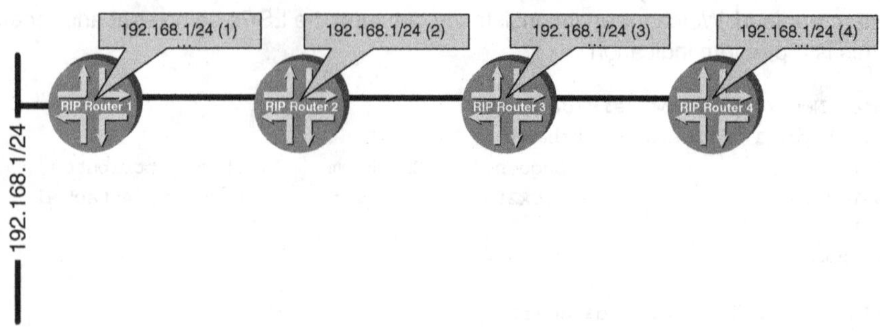

FIGURE 6.2. RIP calculates the metric in a distributed fashion

You can watch the result of the SPF calculation by issuing a `show ip route isis` command on IOS platforms and a `show isis route` command on Juniper Network routers.

In IOS, you cannot see the entire results of the SPF calculation – all you can see are the results that make it into the main routing table. That excludes redundant routers that happen to be in both IS-IS levels. The IS-IS learned routes that are active in the routing table can be displayed using the `show ip route isis` command.

IOS command output

```
Amsterdam#show ip route isis
[ ... ]
i L1   192.168.0.55 [115/10] via 172.16.144.2, POS3/0
i L1   192.168.0.57 [115/10] via 172.16.144.2, POS4/0
i L2   192.168.1.122 [115/10] via 172.16.177.18, GigabitEthernet3/0
[ ... ]
```

The output tells us basically what routes (second column) did get installed in the local routing and forwarding tables. Each line contains information about a single route. The first column shows the level. The numbers in the brackets after the route give information about the *weight* or, as it is called in Cisco IOS speak, the *administrative distance* of the routing protocol that inserted this route into the routing table (in this case, IS-IS). After the "via" statement the IP address of a locally connected router appears (the next-hop). Finally the end of each line gives the physical interface through which the next-hop can be reached and this is how packets to this destination will leave the router.

In the JUNOS software, you can display both the immediate results from the SPF calculation as well as the routes installed in the routing table. The SPF results are displayed using the `show isis route` command. The IS-IS learned routes that are active in the main routing table can be displayed using the `show route protocol isis` command.

JUNOS software command output

```
hannes@Pennsauken> show isis route
  IS-IS routing table    Current version:L1: 0 L2: 485
Prefix                  L     Version    Metric Type   Interface        Via
172.16.44.248/30        2         485     61770 int    so-3/0/0.0       London
192.168.49.5/32         2         485     67850 int    so-3/0/0.0       London
192.168.49.67/32        2         485     67860 int    so-3/0/0.0       London
192.168.52.177/32       2         485    127850 int    so-3/0/0.0       Frankfurt
192.168.54.164/32       2         485    128510 int    so-3/0/0.0       Frankfurt
172.16.176.0/24         2         485    121770 int    so-3/0/0.0       Frankfurt
172.16.176.32/30        2         485    127830 int    so-3/0/0.0       New-York
172.16.176.60/30        2         485    123790 int    so-3/0/0.0       New-York
[ ... ]
```

The format of the output is one route entry per line. The first column contains the route and the second column contains information about the level where this route did result from. The version field is just an internal number that tells you how the SPF run number based upon this route was calculated. The version field is typically not interesting in troubleshooting networks. The metric tells the distance relative to the local router of the prefix. Next is an indication whether the route is internal or external. Typically all the routes are internal unless routes have been injected from other routing protocols into the IS-IS database. Finally, the interface where the traffic leaves the router is displayed, plus the forwarding router's name.

JUNOS software command output

```
hannes@Pennsauken> show route protocol isis

inet.0: 118243 destinations, 246129 routes (118243 active,
0 holddown, 0 hidden)
+ = Active Route, - = Last Active, * = Both

172.16.44.248/30        *[IS-IS/18] 4d 12:57:11, metric 41550, tag 2
                          > to 172.16.5.93 via so-3/2/0.0
192.168.49.5/32         *[IS-IS/18] 2d 07:26:54, metric 67850, tag 2
                          > to 172.16.5.93 via so-2/3/0.0
192.168.49.67/32        *[IS-IS/18] 1d 20:01:28, metric 67860, tag 2
                          > to 172.16.5.93 via so-7/0/0.0
[ … ]
```

In the `show route protocol isis` output we can see a subset of routes that got displayed in `show isis` routes. Those are the routes that competed for installation in the routing table with other routing protocols that may have had similar information; however, the routes in this table are the ones that have won. In JUNOS the level of routes is displayed in the tag field – a tag 2 means that this is a Level 2 route. The number in the brackets is a similar value to the *administrative distance* for IOS platforms, called simply the *route preference*. The *to* and *via* keywords indicate the next-hop and the outgoing interface.

The universal transport vehicle to build the IS-IS database map is called a link-state protocol data unit or LSP for short, which is another OSI-speak word for link-state packet. In the following sections, you will see what information an LSP contains, how the LSP gets distributed, and how LSPs get throttled when the network is busy.

6.3 LSPs and Revision Control

The information element that transports IS-IS-related information to populate all the routers' link-state databases is called the *link-state PDU* or LSP. Each router in an IS-IS network generates at least one LSP that describes, as the name implies, the current *state of the links* to other routers. Actually, an LSP conveys more than *just* the state of the links or circuits on the router. Routers use LSPs as a kind of envelope to get different types of information elements such as IP routes, checksums and even router names across to other routers. LSPs need to be accurate and up-to-date. If, for example, a link between a pair of routers goes down, both routers must *immediately* tell the other routers in the network that the link is down. The other routers then update their link-state databases, schedule an SPF calculation, and remove that broken link from any transit paths in the network that might use the failed link.

Now, assume that a remote router gets two conflicting messages at the same time. That is, messages arrive almost at the same time claiming that a link is up *and* down. Consider Figure 6.3. There are three routers connected by point-to-point links. Unfortunately, the link between Router B and Router C is constantly going down, then up, and a short time later, it goes down again. In network-speak this a *flapping* link. Next, assume that Router B is a busy router with its CPU being loaded close to the ceiling. Therefore, Router B is slower in processing the link-down/link-up events. In addition, the subsequent regeneration of its LSPs that report the link as down or up to other routers is slower.

Figure 6.4 shows the LSP messages from Router A's perspective. Both Router B and Router C find out first that there is a link-up event. However, Router C processes that event far faster than the overloaded Router B. The trouble occurs as the link flaps again, this time transitioning from the *Up* to the *Down* state. Router B still did not send the previous LSP out because it was too busy. Router B's LSP is now outdated information because the link is now in the *Down* state. So both LSPs (Router B's old Up one and Router C's accurate Down one) arrive at the *same time* at Router A. Now Router A needs to decide which is the most *accurate* report – the Up or Down state message. The LSP to use should be the most recent one, but in the example the *most recent* rule would fail because the propagation delay from Router B to Router A made that inaccurate LSP arrive after Router C's up-to-date LSP. The conclusion here is that LSPs need to carry some sort of version information to *explicitly* tell the receiving router what is current and what is outdated LSP information.

6.3.1 *Sequence Numbers*

Link-state routing protocols carry version information through a *Sequence Numbers* field. IS-IS has a linear sequence number space starting from one and counting up. That means that the first LSP that is announced by a router has the sequence number 0x1. Each time the router issues a new view of the local environment to its neighbours, the router will package that information in an LSP, increment the sequence number by one, and send the LSP to all of its neighbours. The neighbours compare the incoming LSP with the LSP in the local database. If the received LSP is new to them (that is, the

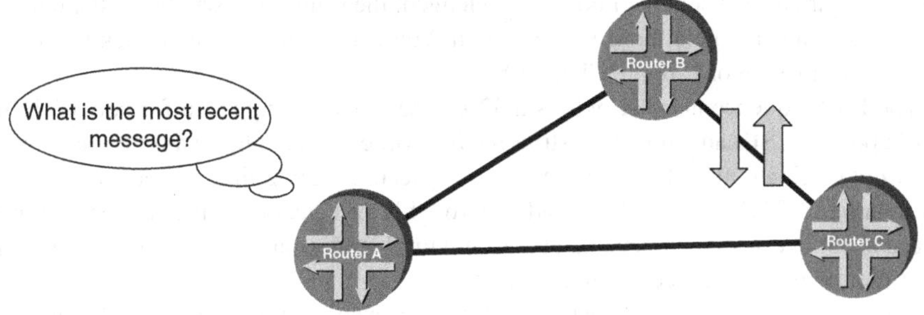

FIGURE 6.3. The routers have to find out what is the most recent event

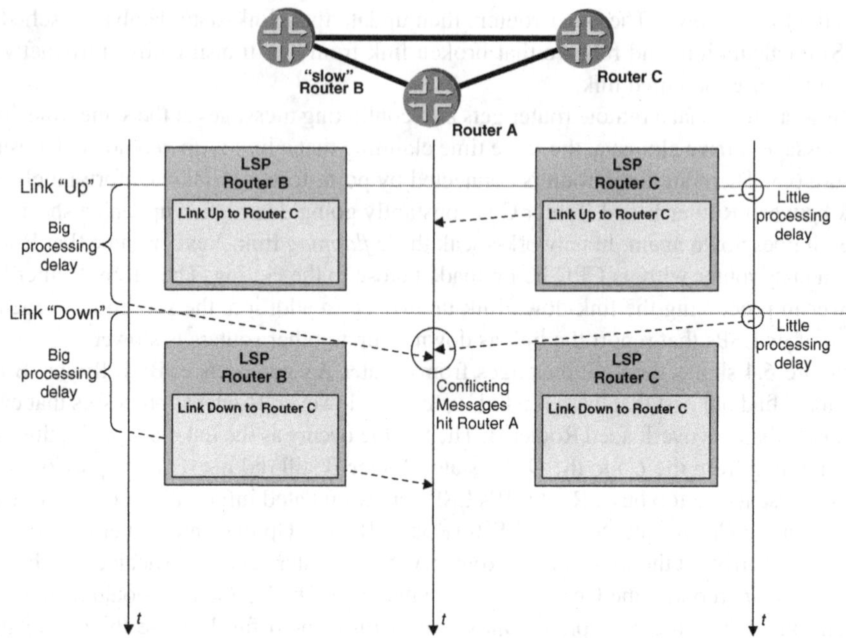

FIGURE 6.4. In distributed environments Router A can get confused if the Link-Up or Link-Down is the most recent event

received LSP is not in the local database at all), then they unconditionally install the LSP into their local link-state database. If the LSP is already installed in the database, the receiving router needs to check if the sequence number is higher than the sequence number of the LSP that is already installed in the link-state database. If the LSP is *newer*, then the router will flush (or discard) the existing LSP and update the LSP with the more recent one. If it turns out (like in the previous example) that the most recent arriving LSP is *older* (has a lower LSP sequence number) then the one installed in the link-state database and therefore carries outdated information, the received LSP is silently discarded. As IS-IS is a *reliable* protocol, the router will of course acknowledge receipt of that LSP to the neighbour that sent it. If not acknowledged, the router will see the LSP again after 5 seconds, once the neighbour retransmits it. You can learn more about acknowledging and retransmission of LSPs in Chapter 8.

The LSP sequence number field is a 32-bit identifier, giving room for about 4 billion LSP updates. LSPs are subject to strict *pacing*, which means, for example, that a router *must not* originate more than one LSP every 5 seconds. 2^32 times 5 seconds results in an interval of 21,474,836,480 seconds, or roughly 681 years. So the sequence number space is not likely to get to its end, at least not until readers are retired, which is typically the timeframe that engineers care about.

Seriously, it is just *assumed* that the LSP sequence space will not run out. Assumptions always cause a lot of trouble for engineers. The root-cause of the Y2K scare went back to assumptions about events that should not be a problem but ultimately were. The bottom line is the Y2K problem cost corporate customers a lot of money to sanity check their applications and to spot software problems before the millennium turnover. But IS-IS is well prepared in that respect, since there actually is something that can be done if the LSP sequence number space is ever maxed out. So what does a router do if it wants to originate a new LSP and *does* hit the ceiling of the LSP sequence space? Now, the assumption is that this ceiling will *never* be reached. But even if it finally is, there is a well-defined procedure to handle that event: the router must simply wait for a period of *max-age* seconds. This sounds odd at first: why does waiting solve anything? And how long does *max-age* last? As it turns out, it lasts a Lifetime – an LSP's Lifetime.

6.3.2 *LSP Lifetimes*

In addition to the revision information (the LSP sequence numbers), link-state protocols include in their LSPs a field called the *Lifetime*, which helps to control the maximum validity span of LSPs. A router announcing an LSP does not mean that the LSP will be valid forever, only for the number of seconds indicated in the Lifetime field of an LSP. Adding a Lifetime field to the protocol helps to protect against stale (and potentially wrong) entries in the link-state database. Consider a scenario where a router is taken out of the network by being powered down. The LSP(s) of that powered-down router is or are still installed in the link-state database of all the routers in the network. If the originating router did not *revoke* or *purge* them (you will see shortly how this works), the LSPs would stay in the link-state database forever. The Lifetime field in the LSP is a 16-bit entity, which means that the Lifetime field can be set as high as 2^16-1 or in decimal notation 65,535 seconds, or a little over 18 hours.

The Lifetime field provides an answer to the unlikely event of IS-IS LSP sequence number space exhaustion. Before an IS-IS router can generate a new LSP with a sequence number of 1, the router must wait until the Lifetimes of all previous LSPs it has generated has expired and the LSPs have disappeared from all other routers' link-state databases. At most, this wait (max-age) will be 18 hours. This sounds very high, but waiting 18 hours every 681 years should not be much of a problem for a network. And in practice, IS-IS implementations only use the maximum 18-hour Lifetime when extreme background flooding silence is needed. Most of the time, IS-IS uses the default Lifetime value of 1200 seconds (20 minutes). This value can be changed in most IS-IS implementations, and often it is changed. But what stops every LSP from disappearing from the network every 20 minutes? A periodic LSP refresh.

6.3.3 *Periodic Refreshes*

LSPs with maximum Lifetimes have the consequence that LSPs need to get *refreshed*. Refreshing means that a router has to re-originate its LSPs periodically. The re-origination interval has, of course, to be less than the LSP's Lifetime. For example, if the LSP is valid for 1200 seconds (the default value), the router needs to refresh the LSP in less than 1200 seconds in order to avoid removal of the LSP from the link-state database by other routers. The recommended *max-LSP-origination-interval* is the Lifetime minus 300 seconds. So in a default environment this would be 900 seconds.

Figure 6.5 shows in a timing diagram how and when a router refreshes its LSPs. Every 900 seconds an LSP with the *same* information content is created. Here, Router A always reports that the router has links in the Up state to Router B and C. Please note that for each refresh, the Sequence Number is incremented by one (bumped). Each time that LSP is refreshed, the Lifetime gets prolonged for another *N* seconds, as described in the Lifetime field (the default value is 1200 seconds).

Both Cisco IOS and JUNOS software do originate all LSPs with a default Lifetime of 1200 seconds, as suggested in the ISO 10589 specification. However, you can change this to higher values to reduce the amount of refreshes in the network (the refresh timer is seldom made a lower value). Often theses periodic LSP refreshes are called *refresh noise,* and network administrators want to reduce this noise close to zero. Both Cisco IOS and JUNOS software offer configuration knobs to change the maximum Lifetime of their LSPs and at the same time the re-origination interval derived from this value. IOS lets you define the Lifetime and refresh intervals independently from each other. All you have to make sure of is that the `max-lsp-lifetime` be a few hundred seconds higher than the `lsp-refresh-interval`. If you modify the `max-lsp-lifetime` do *not* forget to set the `lsp-refresh-interval` accordingly (a few hundred seconds lower than `max-lsp-lifetime`). If you forget to set the refresh interval, then the LSPs will get refreshed according to the default timer, which is 900 seconds. This will not break anything but it also does not help to reduce the refresh noise. The outcome might be an LSP originated with the maximum Lifetime of 65,535 seconds which will still be refreshed each 900 seconds.

In IOS you can set the LSPs Lifetime and refresh interval independently from each other, as shown in the following (note the bolded sections in this code listing).

IOS configuration

In IOS the `max-lsp-lifetime` and `lsp-refresh-interval` parameters need to be at least 300 s apart.

```
Amsterdam# show running-config
[ … ]
router isis
  max-lsp-lifetime 65535
  lsp-refresh-interval 65000
[ … ]
```

The JUNOS software only exposes the `lsp-lifetime` knob to the user interface. The developers at Juniper Networks feared that inconsistent setting of Lifetime and refresh interval might mess things up seriously. As an example, think about what might happen if the Lifetime is set to be *smaller* than the refresh interval. The refresh interval is calculated automatically. The refresh interval in a Juniper Networks router is the LSP Lifetime minus 317 seconds.

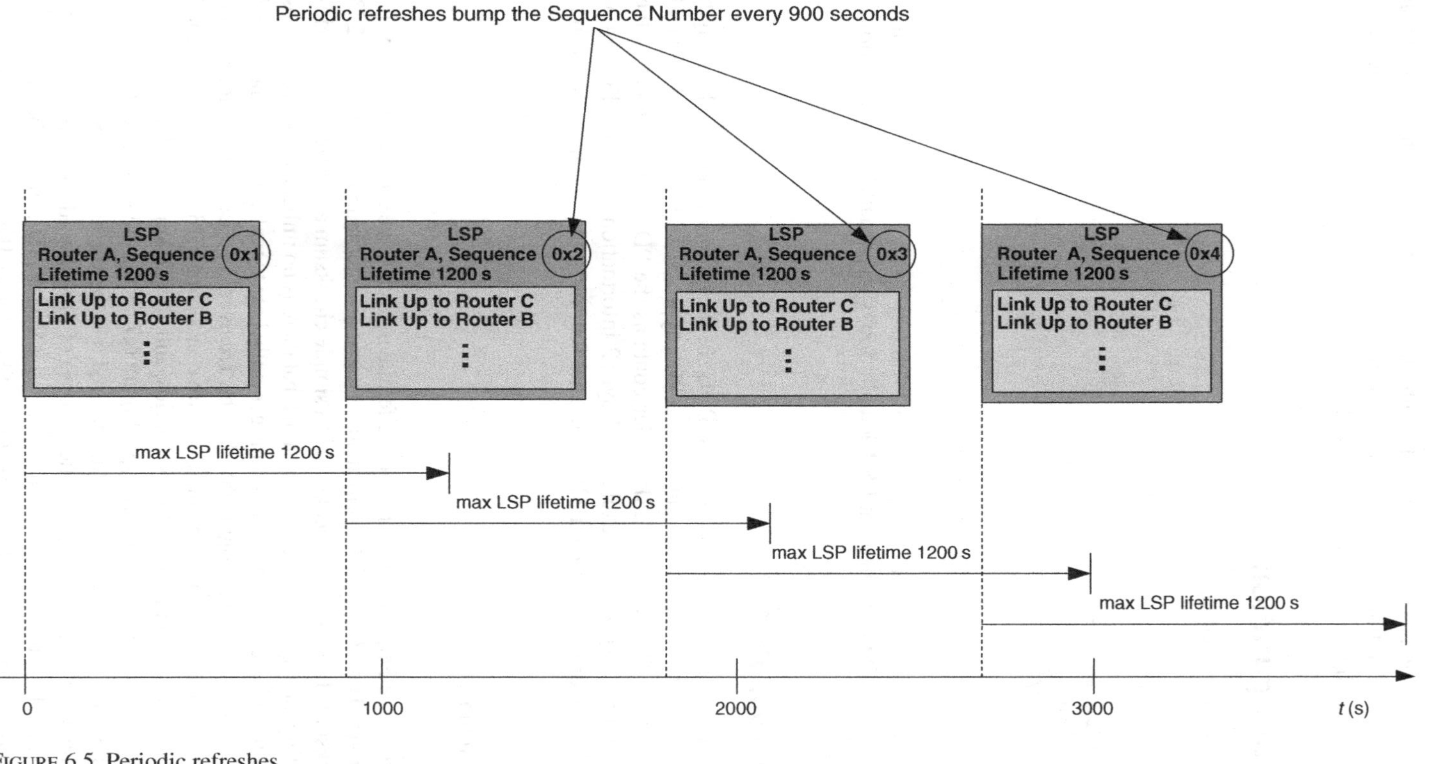
Periodic refreshes bump the Sequence Number every 900 seconds
LSP
Router A, Sequence 0x1
Lifetime 1200 s
Link Up to Router C
Link Up to Router B
LSP
Router A, Sequence 0x2
Lifetime 1200 s
Link Up to Router C
Link Up to Router B
LSP
Router A, Sequence 0x3
Lifetime 1200 s
Link Up to Router C
Link Up to Router B
LSP
Router A, Sequence 0x4
Lifetime 1200 s
Link Up to Router C
Link Up to Router B
max LSP lifetime 1200 s
max LSP lifetime 1200 s
max LSP lifetime 1200 s
max LSP lifetime 1200 s
0
1000
2000
3000
t (s)

FIGURE 6.5. Periodic refreshes

In the JUNOS software, the refresh interval is automatically calculated as the LSP refresh interval equal to the Lifetime minus 317 seconds. In the following listing, the relevant JUNOS software configuration is marked in bold:

JUNOS configuration

```
hannes@New-York> show configuration
[ … ]
protocols {
  isis {
    lsp-lifetime 65535;
    interface lo0.0;
    interface so-0/0/0;
  }
}
[ … ]
```

As we can control how long an individual LSP will last (given that there is no change in the network) we will unveil how an LSP actually looks and what particular information it contains.

6.3.4 *Link-state PDUs*

Figure 6.6 shows the structure of a link-state PDU. In the common header, the Length field is fixed to 27 bytes. The code points for the PDU type are 18 for Level 1 LSPs and 20 for Level 2 LSPs. The common LSP header contains the PDU length, which is the aggregate length of the IS-IS PDU excluding Layer 2 information (such as PPP, Cisco-HDLC, and MAC addresses). In the LSP header, the four most important elements are:

- Lifetime
- LSP-ID
- Sequence Number
- Checksum

The purpose of the Sequence Number and Lifetime fields was already discussed in the previous sections. The 16-bit Checksum field contains an international standard X.233 Fletcher Checksum. The Fletcher Checksum is a simple checksum algorithm that, in addition to protecting the payload of the LSP, ensures that there is no imbalance between zeros and ones in the resulting checksum. Checksums generally help to make bit errors introduced by WAN transmission more recognizable by the receiver. You can learn more about checksums and what particular problems they solve in Chapter 13, which gives a good overview of IS-IS checksumming, failure scenarios, and checksumming related defects.

The LSP-ID field determines the LSP type. Figure 6.7 shows the structure of the LSP-ID field. The LSP-ID is a fixed 8-byte field. The first 6 bytes are set to the System-ID of the LSP Originator. The System-ID has the purpose of uniquely identifying a router in the IS-IS network. If you are familiar with OSPF, the System-ID can best be compared with the *Router-ID*. The only difference is that OSPF Router IDs are 32-bits (4 bytes)

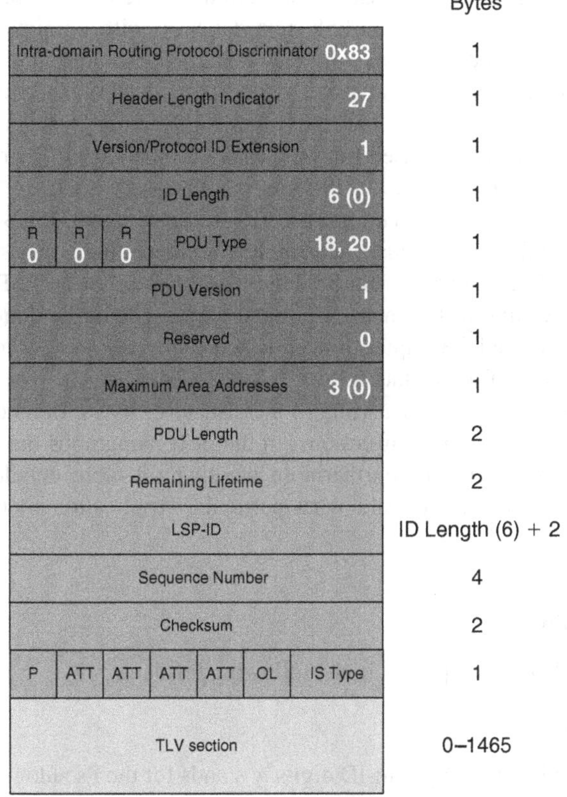

FIGURE 6.6. The format of a link-state PDU

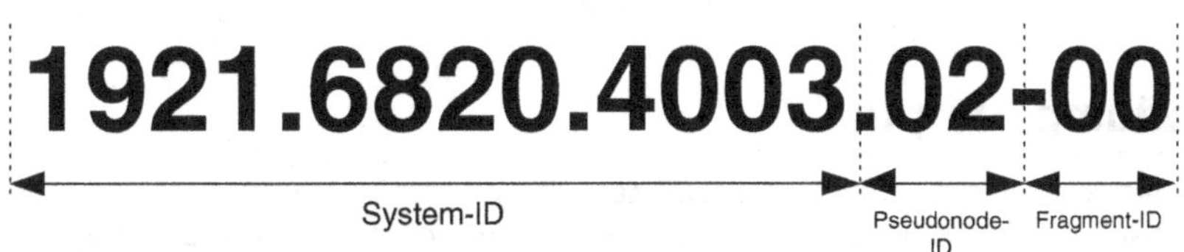

FIGURE 6.7. The elements of a LSP-ID

and IS-IS System-IDs are 48-bits wide. The only required property is that the System-ID has to be *unique*. Assignment of System-IDs, conversion schemes from OSPF-based IP Router-ID to IS-IS System-IDs, and further information about IS-IS addressing can be found in Chapter 4. The next byte in the LSP-ID field is called the *Pseudonode-ID*. The principle of pseudonodes are not easy to explain in a paragraph – that is why it takes an entire chapter to explain them. As a quick explanation, to an IS-IS router, a LAN consists of real routers (nodes) and one router that represents the whole LAN but does not really exist – the pseudonode. If the pseudonode byte is set to zero, we can be sure that this is a *real router*. If the pseudonode byte is non-zero then it represents the whole LAN . In IS-IS LANs are represented in the link-state database with a unique identifier. More information about pseudonodes and why they make sense is presented in Chapter 7.

The last byte in the LSP-ID field is called the Fragment ID. IS-IS runs directly on top of OSI-RM Layer 2, which does not have a built-in fragmentation function for larger-than-MTU-sized packets. IP-based routing protocols, such as OSPF, rely on IP to provide this fragmentation service, but IS-IS is not IP-based. So IS-IS needs to support fragmentation through the a*pplication* itself: IS-IS. Once again, IS-IS fragmentation is worth a chapter on its own, because there are lots of interesting issues surrounding IS-IS fragmentation such as "What should be done if a fragment of an LSP is missing", "Is there a special meaning to fragment *zero*", and "What should be done if the fragment space itself is exhausted?" Chapter 9 is dedicated to giving answers to these and other questions surrounding fragmentation.

LSP-IDs are not displayed as a string of 8 consecutive bytes. In modern routing software LSP-IDs follow certain conventions. In the next paragraphs the notation of LSP-IDs will briefly be discussed. Furthermore we spot on more detailed what bits the Attribute Type Block contains and what particular Application of the *Overload Bit* may be.

6.3.4.1 LSP Notation

Typically the LSP-ID is displayed in the following format:

```
xxxx.xxxx.xxxx.yy-zz
```

Here, an x stands for the System-ID digits, y stands for the Pseudonode-ID, and z represents the fragment number. Let's have a look at a tcpdump showing an LSP header and its contents. The following shows a real-world LSP. Look especially at the notation used for the LSP. The fields of the LSP header are shown in bold:

Tcpdump output

```
11:36:45.587565 OSI, IS-IS, length: 405
  L2 LSP, hlen: 27, v: 1, pdu-v: 1, sys-id-len: 6 (0), max-area: 3 (0)
    lsp-id: 1921.6800.0012.00-00, seq: 0x000002fd, lifetime: 1198s
    chksum: 0xe984 (correct), PDU length: 405, Flags: [ L1L2 IS ]
      Authentication TLV #10, length: 7
        simple text password: !$xyz00
      Area address(es) TLV #1, length: 4
        Area address (3): 49.0001
      Protocols supported TLV #129, length: 1
        NLPID(s): IPv4 (0xcc)
      Hostname TLV #137, length: 6
        Hostname: London
      IPv4 Interface address(es) TLV #132, length: 4
        IPv4 interface address: 172.16.1.33
```

```
IPv4 Internal Reachability TLV #128, length: 84
  IPv4 prefix:  10.254.47.8/30, Distribution: up, Metric: 5, Internal
  IPv4 prefix:  10.252.1.0/30, Distribution: up, Metric: 5, Internal
  IPv4 prefix:  10.254.1.48/30, Distribution: up, Metric:  1, Internal
  IPv4 prefix:  10.254.1.20/30, Distribution: up, Metric:  5, Internal
  IPv4 prefix:  10.254.3.4/30, Distribution: up, Metric: 25, Internal
  IPv4 prefix:  10.254.1.72/30, Distribution: up, Metric:  2, Internal
  IPv4 prefix:  10.254.1.28/30, Distribution: up, Metric:  5, Internal
Extended IS Reachability TLV #22, length: 75
  IS Neighbor: 1921.6800.1001.00, Metric: 5, sub-TLVs present (64)
    IPv4 interface address subTLV #6, length: 4, 10.154.1.6
    IPv4 neighbor address subTLV #8, length: 4, 10.154.1.5
    Unreserved bandwidth subTLV #11, length: 32
```

The first output of the second line shows us an LSP-ID. We recognize that this is an LSP-ID because it follows the xxxx.xxxx.xxx.yy-zz style. Only LSP-IDs follow that style. The last bold argument in the tcpdump output shows the so-called Attribute Type Block, which has in the example two bits set.

6.3.4.2 Attribute Block

What are the Flags [L1L2 IS] following the checksum? What are they used for? The last byte in the LSP header is often referred to as the attribute block. These 8 bits tell the receiver crucial information about the nature of the LSP. These 8 bits are:

- Bit 8 – P (Partition Repair) Bit
- Bit 7 – ATT-Error Bit
- Bit 6 – ATT-Expense Bit
- Bit 5 – ATT-Delay Bit
- Bit 4 – ATT-Default Bit
- Bit 3 – OL (Overload) Bit
- Bit 2 and 1 – IS Type Bits

The P (Partition Repair) Bit is what is known as a *capability indicator* that shows if the issuing router supports the partition repair functionality (that is, this bit indicates that capability). Partition repair means that a broken *Level 1* area can be healed through the *Level 2* IS-IS routers. It is not possible to be very specific here because Partition Repair is barely deployed and sometimes even not supported in certain IS-IS implementations such as JUNOS. Partition repair is left as an option to the implementer of the protocol, so this is not a major issue. Typically, if a specification says that something is optional, and if it is complicated to implement or does not solve a specific problem, this is enough justification to ignore that function entirely. So if you take the time and crawl through protocol specification, such as RFCs and Internet drafts or – even worse – ISO papers and documents, then you almost always can replace the word "should" with "can-be-ignored" in your mind.

The next four bits in the Attribute block, Bits 7 to 4, determine if the issuing Intermediate System is attached to another area or not. Only L1L2 routers may set this bit in their Level-1 LSPs. But why are there 4 bits denoted to this functionality, and not just one? Because at the time when ISO 10589 was specified (in the late 1980s) many people believed that routing protocols should support multiple topology databases, each set up for a particular purpose. The original idea was that IS-IS should calculate one topology database that would have the lowest bit error rate, one topology database for the least expensive paths in the network, one that reflects the lowest delay topology, and finally one that would be used if the sender of the packet were undecided which of the topologies to pick. This is an early form of Class-of-Service (CoS) enabled routing, which ultimately did not get deployed because network engineers felt uncomfortable (rightly so at the time) about supporting such multidimensional networks. Bits 5, 6 and 7 therefore got deprecated (not quite obsolete, but not promoted at all) over time. Today, as far as IP routing is concerned both JUNOS and IOS only support the default-metric, and hence just the bit 4 default topology, which only demands a single instance of SPF calculation. There are more places in the IS-IS specification where this CoS-based routing legacy pops up; however, in modern routing it has been entirely deprecated.

The Overload Bit is used (not surprisingly) to indicate that a router is in an overloaded condition. Initially, this was envisioned to serve as an indicator that a router had run out of memory. Running out of memory in a router is never good, but the impact of memory shortage is especially dramatic for link-state protocols: if a router cannot store all LSPs in its link-state database the router will not be able to calculate loop-free paths through the network. The idea behind the Overload Bit is that once the router notices that it is running short of memory, the router will simply refuse to play SPF with neighbours and pull itself out of the game. A router holding half of the information needed for proper SPF calculations, and disturbing the other routers by advertising this half-knowledge does more harm than a router that reliably takes itself off the network topology. The effect of a router originating its LSPs with the Overload Bit set is that during the SPF calculation, the router will be disregarded for delivery of *transit* traffic. The nice thing here is that the local sub-nets that the router still advertises in its LSPs are still reachable. You can read more about the advertisement of IP sub-nets in IS-IS in Chapter 12. So although the router is pruned from the network topology, the router is still reachable by non-transit packets. Figure 6.8 shows you the network impact of a router that has the Overload Bit set. New York has the Overload Bit set in its most recent LSP. Therefore, the routers in the network re-calculate their paths and re-route around New York. For instance, Washington to Pennsauken traffic is moved through the Frankfurt path. However, the local prefixes (and the loopback) IP address of the New York router are still reachable. Local traffic therefore still goes directly to New York.

The remaining two bits are the IS bits which indicate the topologies that the sender is in. Each router is always in a Level-1 topology even if the router software lets turn you off the Level-1 entirely off a Router. This is admitted a bit odd. So Bit 1 must always be set. However, Bit 2 is variable. If it is set the router is also present in the Level 2 topology.

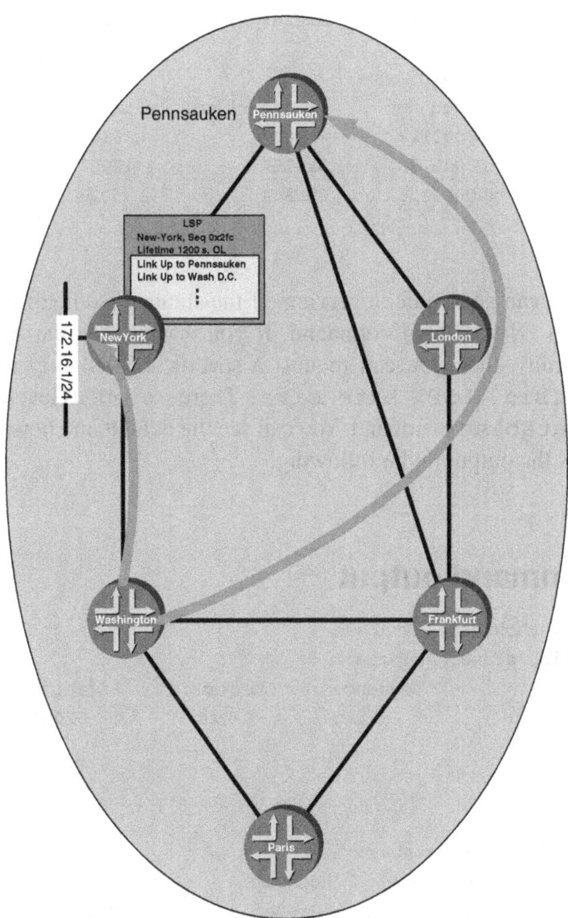

FIGURE 6.8. The overloaded routers' local prefixes are still reachable while transit-traffic is kept away

You can examine the contents of the Attribute block by issuing a `show isis database`. This command is supported on both IOS and JUNOS routers, as shown in the following:

IOS command output

```
Amsterdam# show isis database
[ … ]
IS-IS Level-1 Link State Database:
LSPID                LSP Seq Num     LSP Checksum     LSP Holdtime     ATT/P/OL
```

```
New-York.00-00       0x00002fac       0xC24F           60128            1/0/0
[ … ]
IS-IS Level-2 Link State Database:
LSPID                LSP Seq Num      LSP Checksum     LSP Holdtime     ATT/P/OL
LINX-gw.00-00        0x00000128       0xB8EF           36163            0/0/1
LINX-gw.01-00        0x00000128       0x455A           42001            0/0/0
VIX-gw.00-00         0x00000123       0xEFC1            5023            0/0/0
[ … ]
```

In JUNOS, you can get a quick overview of the status of some of the bits by issuing the `show isis database` command. If you want to see the Attribute block for one LSP specifically, then you can request a specific LSP's `extensive` output by issuing a `show isis <LSP> extensive`. There are various levels of output for the `show isis database` command. You can see the default and how the `extensive` modifier changes the output in the following:

JUNOS command output

```
hannes@New-York> show isis database
IS-IS level 1 link-state database:
LSP ID                     Sequence     Checksum      Lifetime     Attributes
New-York.00-00               0x2fac       0xc24f         62063     L1 Attached
[ … ]
  4 LSPs

IS-IS level 2 link-state database:
LSP ID              Sequence      Checksum      Lifetime     Attributes
LINX-gw.00-00          0x128        0xb8ef         36063     L1 L2  Overload
LINX-gw.01-00          0x128        0x455a         41901     L1 L2
VIX-gw.00-00           0x123        0xefc1          4922     L1 L2
[ … ]
  12 LSPs

hannes@New-York> show isis database LINX-gw extensive
LINX-gw.00-00      Sequence:    0x128,   Checksum:      0xb8ef,     Lifetime:
                                                                    36063 secs
   IS neighbor:      London.01 Metric:               2000
   IP prefix:   2.168.9.225/32 Metric:                  0 Internal
   IP prefix:     172.16.6.0/28 Metric:            2000  Internal
[ … ]
  Packet: LSP id: Vienna-ts1.00-00, Length: 98 bytes, Lifetime:
  36063 secs
    Checksum: 0xb8ef, Sequence: 0x128, Attributes: 0x7 <L1 L2 Overload>
    NLPID: 0x83, Fixed length: 27 bytes, Version: 1, Sysid length: 0 bytes
    Packet type: 20, Packet version: 1, Max area: 0
```

The use of the Overload Bit is one of the more interesting stories of IS-IS. The reason why and when this bit is set has changed dramatically over the years. At first, the use was straightforward: there were many router memory constraints. Memory in the late 1980s compared to today was expensive, and the chips had little capacity. In the late 1980s, most routers were running with 512 KB of memory. So memory was definitely a constraint, and the Overload Bit was used as intended.

But what about today? Memory isn't really an issue for IS-IS now. All modern Internet core routers have at least 256 MB of memory, and in many cases, they have even more memory. For example, the Juniper Networks T640 router has a route-processor that has a massive 2 GB for storing routing information. And IS-IS is not a particularly memory-intensive protocol. Massive amounts of memory are typically needed for storing BGP routes and paths. Even in the largest networks in the world, IS-IS does not consume more than 1.5 to 2.0 MB of memory. To give an idea how big these modern IS-IS networks are, think of an L1L2 router that is on the IS-IS Level 2 backbone with 1200 or more other routers. In addition, consider 200 or more routers at IS-IS Level 1. Thus, the link-state database is quite large. True enough, and yet it still does not consume more than between 0.1% and 1% of a modern route processor's memory. So what is it that drives the setting of the Overload Bit today? The answer to this is addressed in the next section.

6.3.4.3 Applications of the Overload Bit

In an Internet core router there are always two routing protocols running. One is for gathering *topological* knowledge and one carries a bulk amount of *reachability* information. The Interior Gateway Protocol (IGP) discovers the topological knowledge of the internal core network of an ISP. IS-IS is a member of the large family of IGPs. For the reachability information about bulk routes (Internet routes and customer routes), there is the Border Gateway Protocol (BGP), the interdomain routing protocol of the Internet. Each protocol does what it can do best. IS-IS quickly discovers, and then re-routes the internal network. Unfortunately, IS-IS is not very good in transporting a bulk amount of routing information across the internal network. IS-IS is in good company in being unsuited for this task with the rest of the IGPs (RIP, OSPF, EIGRP etc.).

All of the IGPs suffer from the same protocol defect, in that all of the IGPs do not have any *flow-control* mechanisms built into the protocol. This is the reason that they fail when a large number of routes have to be carried across the internal network. As long as the IGP routers are loaded moderately, there is not much of a problem. However, as with human beings, everything is different under stress. Once the network is exposed to protocol-related stress (a large amount of re-routing, heavy LSP processing, many flapping links, and so on), plus a large amount of BGP reachability information, the network starts to *churn*. Churning IGPs was the typical reason in the 1990s when people like the NOC-team managers and the Chief Technology Officer got paged out of bed in the middle of the night.

These lessons were learned and the implementations of the routing protocols did get better. There has also been more experience gained in network design. The pragmatic design rule today is that there *must not* be any other IP reachability information in the

IGP other than /30, /31 (point-to-point link IP sub-nets) and /32 routes (loopback addresses). No *customer routes*, no *server farm routes*, nothing except the IP sub-nets needed to run the internal infrastructure is put into the IGP's database. Common practice is that all of the IP reachability information is injected into BGP, which, because BGP runs on top of TCP, is very good in terms of flow-control. So if a BGP peer wants to throttle down a neighbouring speaker that is too fast, the router simply delays the TCP acknowledgements. Delayed TCP ACKs *emulate* a small bandwidth link. The fast speaker will back off and reduce the pacing of the route transmission.

But if BGP is so good, then why do we need IGPs like IS-IS? To answer this, you have to understand that there is some mutual dependency between the IGP and BGP. First of all, BGP runs on top of TCP, and in order for TCP to work, you need valid internal routes to get your BGP session up and running. Furthermore BGP needs some information about how *far* a BGP speaker is away to determine the *best* route – it is the IGP that supplies that information. On the downside BGP converges (produces consistent information in all BGP routers) very slowly particularly because it is not very good in detecting that a neighbour is down as it has very slow paced keep-alive timers. Once the BGP neighbour is determined to be down in the worst case, it can take up to 2 minutes for a BGP router to declare a neighbour down. IS-IS is much quicker (orders of 10–30 seconds) to detect absent peers. It is the *slowness* of BGP, more precisely the *slowness of iBGP* (BGP distributing information to the internal network), that mandates the use the Overload Bit today.

Consider the scenario shown in Figure 6.9. It shows a transit provider providing service to the customer ASs 2 and 3. The iBGP connections as they should be in the converged state are represented in the diagram as dotted curves. However, the internal BGP sessions to Core Router #2 are down because we had to reboot Core Router #2 (the reason for this reboot is unimportant, but happens occasionally). The router reboots, starts its routing processes (IS-IS and BGP), and tries to get the iBGP sessions up, but it can't! This is because IS-IS has not yet learned about the internal topology to acquire the necessary routing information in order to get the internal BGP sessions, which rely on TCP, up. IS-IS starts to discover its directly connected neighbours (Core Router #1, #3, Border Router A, B) and starts to *synchronize* its link-state databases. Database synchronization is discussed in more detail in Chapter 8.

After database synchronization, the IS-IS routing process schedules an SPF calculation and feeds the routing information resulting from that calculation into its local routing table. This is the beginning of the *black hole* state where packets flowing into a router have no place to go. Border Routers A and B immediately send Core Router #2 traffic targeted to local AS 2 and 3. The problem is that Core Router #2 does not yet have the transit BGP routes to know where to forward that traffic, as the iBGP sessions are not established yet. After a while, the sessions to the iBGP speakers are established (this can last up to several minutes) and Core Router #2 will have built up accurate forwarding states to pass on the traffic and so as not to black hole the packets any longer.

What can be done in IS-IS to help avoid entering a black-hole scenario? Consider what would happen if Core Router #2 sets the Overload Bit when sending its first LSP. During the subsequent SPF calculation, the Border Routers A and B will detect the Overload Bit

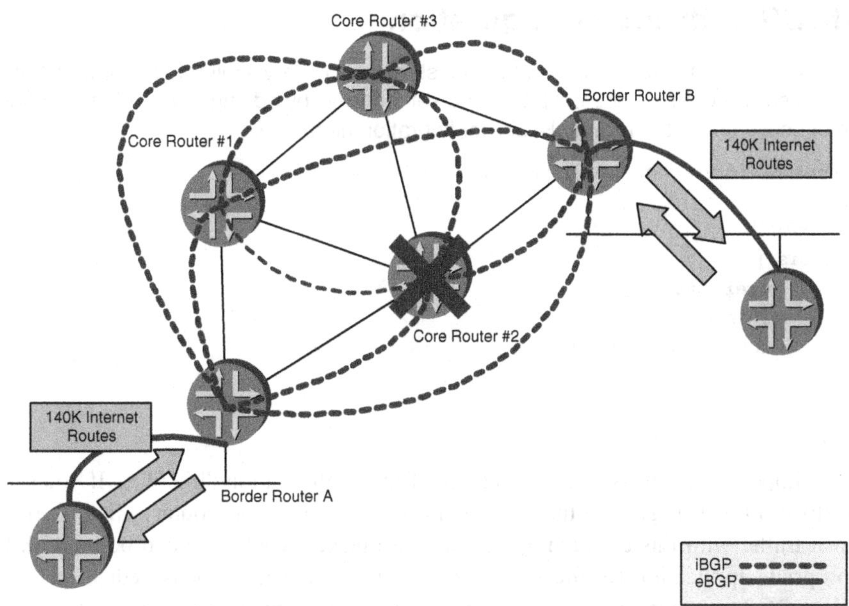

FIGURE 6.9. IS-IS and BGP routing is mutually dependent on each other; if both do not converge at the same time, traffic is black holed

during processing Core Router #2's LSP and will therefore eliminate Core Router #2 as a possible way to send transit traffic. The transit traffic will be routed around Core Router #2 over Core Routers #1 and #3. The good news is that Core Router #2's local sub-nets will still be reachable even if the router sets the Overload Bit, so the iBGP sessions to all the internal routers can be established successfully during the overload condition.

Most IS-IS implementations, including IOS and JUNOS software, support *static* setting of the Overload Bit. The following configuration statements show how to set the Overload Bit *statically*. The `set-overload-bit` command sets the Overload Bit for both levels of the IS-IS instance, as shown in the following:

IOS configuration

The IOS `set-overload-bit` command sets the Overload Bit persistent static and does not remove it after some time.

```
Amsterdam# show running-config
[ ... ]
router isis
 set-overload-bit
[ ... ]
```

JUNOS software configuration

In the JUNOS software, the configurations statement is very similar to the IOS one. In the JUNOS software the `Overload` Bit can be set statically by adding the overload configuration directive under the protocols isis configuration hierarchy.

```
hannes@New-York> show configuration
[ ... ]
protocols {
    isis {
        overload;
        interface lo0.0;
        interface so-0/0/0;
    }
}
[ ... ]
```

It is important to stress the *static* nature of the configuration directives. If you set the Overload Bit by using any of the two commands described, your router will not carry *any* transit traffic with this configuration. There are places where this can be helpful. One appropriate application for the static setting for the Overload Bit is dedicated devices such as BGP route reflectors, which are *intentionally* not meant to carry any transit traffic. Thus, do not start to panic if you see the Overload Bit set in your network – it is most likely set by the BGP route reflectors, which you do not want to carry any transit traffic. The static setting of the Overload Bit is also useful when doing hardware/software maintenance work on a router. Set the Overload Bit to get rid of all the transit traffic for the time being. Finish the maintenance work and clear the Overload Bit to carry on forwarding transit traffic. Manual clearing of the Overload Bit is not always possible; what is needed is an automated way of clearing the Overload Bit after some amount of time. There are two strategies for the timed clearing of the Overload Bit:

- *Unconditional.* Clear the Overload Bit after some (configurable) amount of time
- *Conditional.* Clear the Overload Bit once *all* of the iBGP sessions are in the *Up* state

The Unconditional option just requires that you know your network and how long it takes to collect BGP routes and populate the router with the correct forwarding state. The network administrator has to estimate a realistic value here. The Conditional option simply waits until all the internal BGP connections are in the *Up* state. Architecturally, this approach lacks some robustness in practice: just ask yourself what will happen if one or more of the iBGP sessions do *not* come up. The Overload Bit is never cleared at all. It is relatively easy to come up with scenarios where the Overload Bit will never clear if one of the iBGP peers is under constant up-down-up flux. So most networks do not use the conditional approach and use an unconditional fixed time value of 300 seconds. This five-minute value is a good balance allowing time to bring up even large internal iBGP meshes, while still relatively quick to clear the Overload Bit.

This dynamic setting and clearance of the Overload Bit is supported in both IOS and JUNOS software. IOS supports clearance of the Overload Bit according to both strategies (conditional wait-for-iBGP and the unconditional timer) during router startup.

The Overload Bit can be dynamically set and cleared during startup using the `set-overload-bit on-startup [<timeout> | wait-for-bgp]` configuration command in router-configuration mode, as shown in the following:

IOS configuration

```
Amsterdam# show running-config
[ … ]
router isis
 set-overload-bit on-startup 300
[ … ]
London# show running-config
[ … ]
router isis
 set-overload-bit on-startup wait-for-bgp
[ … ]
```

Juniper Networks engineers were a bit cautious about the dependency on both another protocol and on the all-or-nothing approach of waiting for *all* iBGP connections to come up. JUNOS, therefore, just supports unconditional clearance of the Overload Bit (Timer method).

JUNOS software configuration

In the JUNOS software, arbitrary timers between 60 and 1800 seconds can be specified that the router will wait until clearing the Overload Bit. Set the `overload timeout <timeout>` configuration directive under the protocols isis configuration hierarchy, as shown in the following:

```
hannes@New-York> show configuration
[ … ]
protocols {
    isis {
      overload timeout 300;
      interface lo0.0;
      interface so-0/0/0;
    }
}
[ … ]
```

Setting the Overload Bit during startup and dynamically clearing it with a timer is a useful tool to avoid black hole scenarios during transient network conditions. It is highly recommended that you configure the Overload timer on all the transit core routers.

A lot has been said about the individual bits in the LSP header and the scenarios in which they are used. Next, the way that LSPs are distributed through the network will be examined in more detail. The mechanism used in IS-IS to distribute LSPs is called *flooding*.

6.4 Flooding

Once a router has acquired its directly connected neighbours and built up adjacencies, it will tell other routers about its *local* adjacencies. To get the information across the whole network as quickly as possible, this information is *flooded*. But just what does flooding mean?

First of all, the flooding algorithm is slightly different depending on if a router *originates* the information or if the router just *receives* the information and *relays* it further. Figure 6.10 and Figure 6.11 show the differences between the two approaches.

In Figure 6.11, you can see that the router is originating an LSP. The router then simply sends this LSP out on *all* interfaces that have an adjacency in the Up state. If a router is receiving an LSP that the router has not originated, as shown in Figure 6.11, the router will simply send the LSP out on all interfaces *except* the one where the router got the LSP. The name *flooding* is derived from the fact that a received LSP will be sent out almost unconditionally on *all* other interfaces.

The basic flooding algorithm needs to be refined a little bit. One thing to make sure of is that the flooding stops at a certain point. If flooding does not stop, we would have an

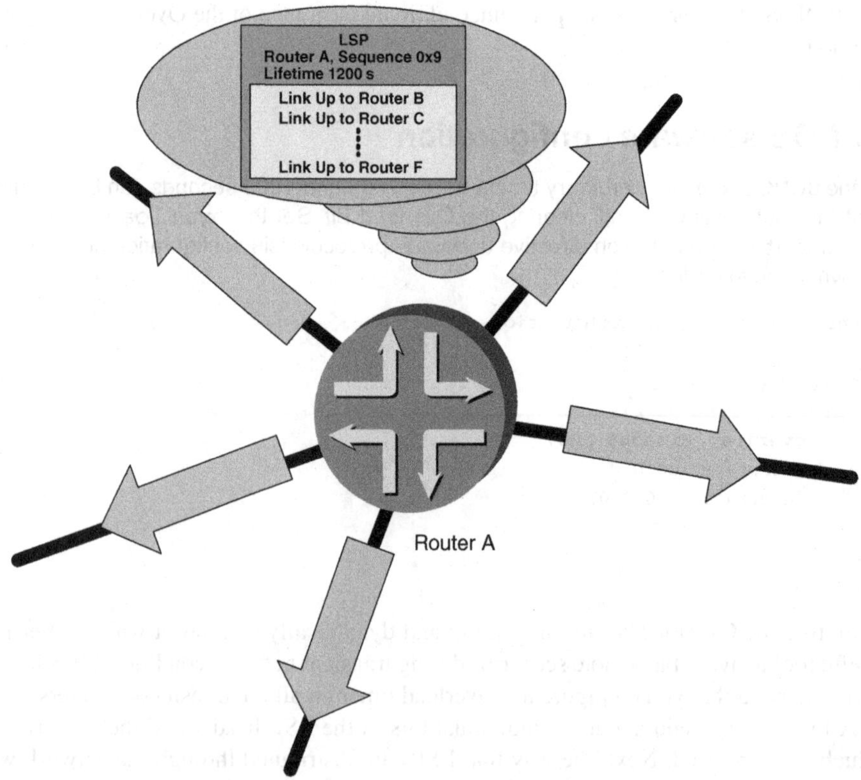

FIGURE 6.10. Self-originated LSPs are flooded on links with an adjacency in the Up state

endless, raging "LSP storm" circulating through the network. For example, consider a ring-like topology, as shown in Figure 6.12. Each router in the sample topology would just send the LSP farther on all interfaces, except on the one where the router received the LSP. So what controls the flooding and helps to prevent LSP distribution from exploding? Once again, it is the Sequence Number that controls the flooding. So let's refine the flooding algorithm to use the Sequence Number to prevent endless flooding.

First, a router must verify if a received LSP is newer (has a higher Sequence Number) than the one installed in the local database. If it is newer, then install the LSP in the database and send it out on all interfaces where there is an adjacency in the Up state. If the Sequence Number is less than or equal to the LSP in the database, then the router should simply discard the LSP. Going back to our example in Figure 6.12, where the update was circling endlessly, the difference can be seen. Once the update process is completed (after Step 6), then the flooding stops at Frankfurt because this router already knows about the LSP with Sequence Number 0x12.

6.4.1 *Is Flooding Harmful?*

The refined basic flooding algorithm is a quite robust information distribution scheme. It is robust because the algorithm relies very little on other routers and thereby makes sure

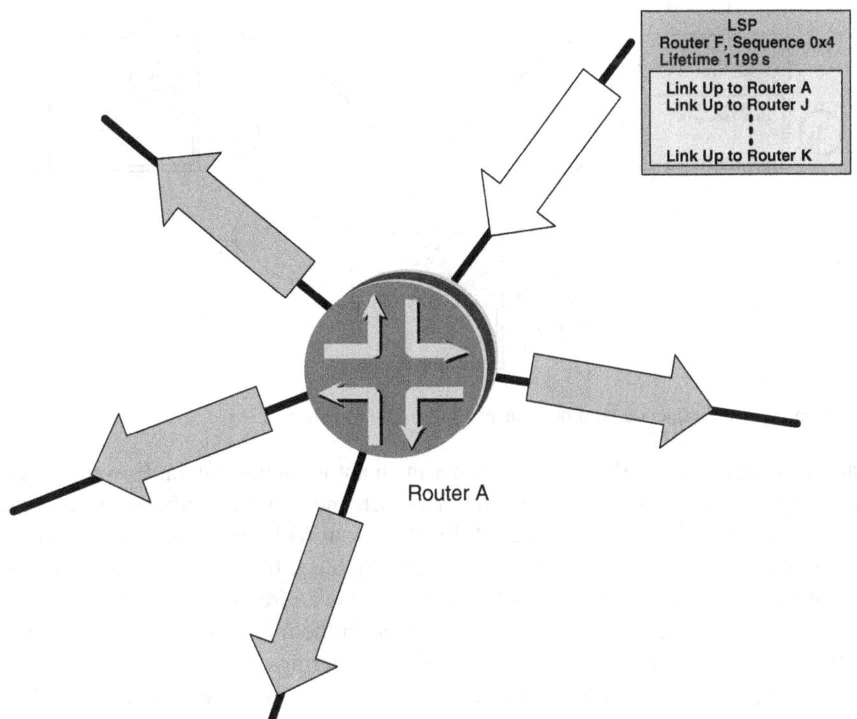

FIGURE 6.11. Relayed LSPs are flooded on links with an adjacency in the Up state, except on the one that originated the link

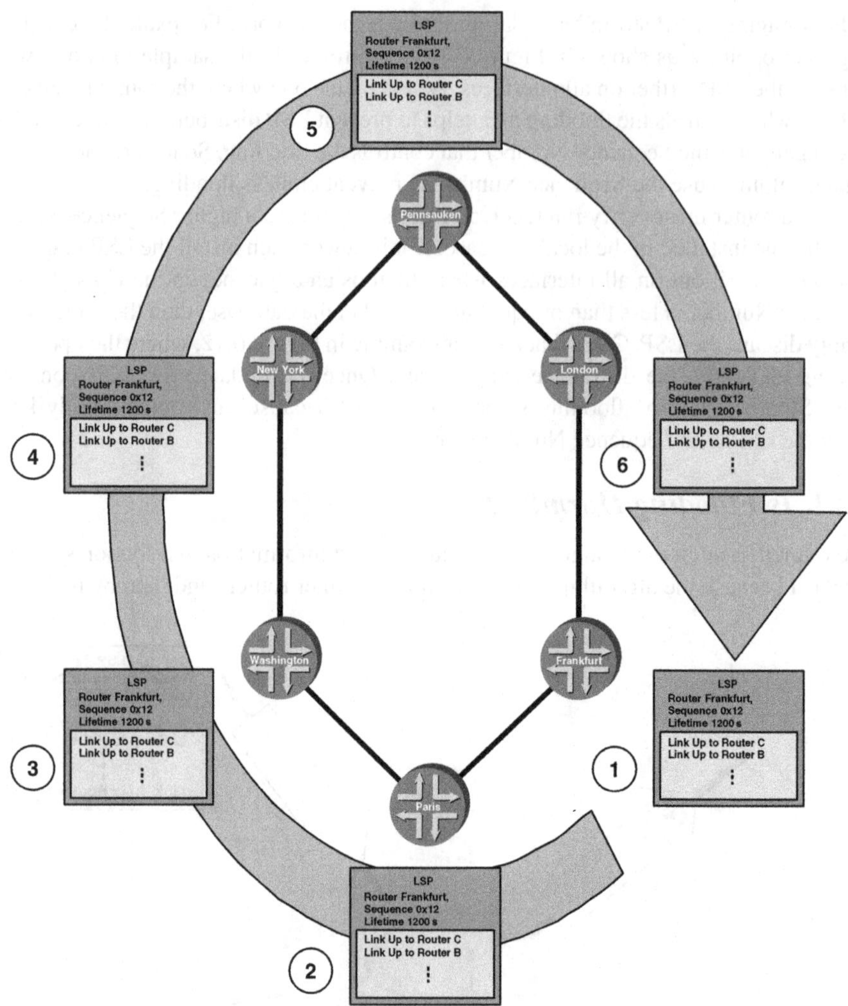

FIGURE 6.12. The Sequence Number causes the flooding to stop

that the message gets to the very last corner in an autonomous system. However, there is also a dark side to this robust scheme. This scheme is very inefficient in a densely meshed environment. Consider Figure 6.13. Here, four ATM switches interconnect a collection of routers. The physical connections are the black lines. The gray lines represent the connections at the logical level. Each gray line is a virtual circuit (VC) at the ATM level. This kind of networking setup was popular in the mid-1990s for various reasons, such as ATM interface speed, the absent traffic engineering capabilities of IP routers, and the limited processing power of software-based routers (ATM switches were hardware-based). You can learn more about these historical networking setups and why they are deployed in Chapter 14. For now, it is enough to note that ATM switches once connected IP routers, and sometimes they still do.

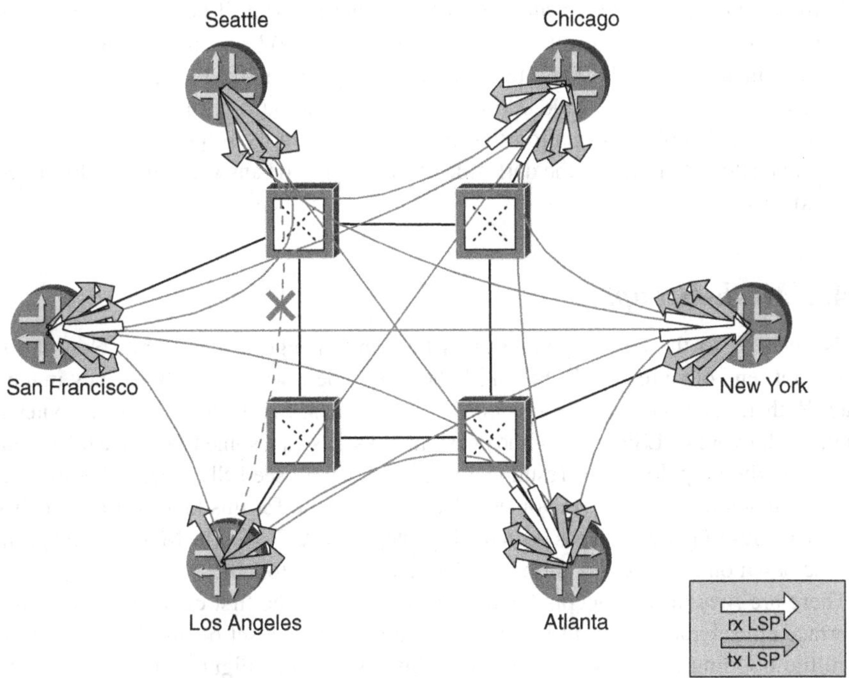

FIGURE 6.13. ATM overlay networks and flooding stress

Each router in the Figure 6.13 setup forms an adjacency with the other routers, effectively forming a *full-mesh*. So far, so good. Now, consider the following scenario: the ATM virtual circuit between Seattle and Los Angeles breaks for some reason, as indicated by the dotted gray line. Both Seattle and LA notice the break and therefore generate a new LSP (incrementing the Sequence Number and removing the adjacency between Seattle and LA). The new LSP is sent according to the flooding rule on all interfaces where there are adjacencies in the Up state. Thus, both Seattle and LA send four copies (gray arrows) of their new LSPs into the network. Next, the four other routers will receive the two LSPs (white arrows). Here is where the trouble starts: because the flooding algorithm is so simple, the algorithm does not yet know that all the other routers already been have updated and know that the adjacency between Seattle and LA is down. What follows is a multiplication of LSPs due to the simplicity of the flooding algorithm. All of the routers receive the two new LSPs and re-send the LSP to all the logical interfaces except on the ones on which they got the LSP (gray arrows). What results is that 32 LSPs are sent for a single broken ATM VC. This does not sound too stressful for a modern router's control plane; however, just think if there are not six routers, but 100 routers in the network. The problem is that the number of LSPs grows by the square of the number of routers, or in mathematical speak $O(N^2)$. Thus, a single failing VC in the network may generate up to 10,000 LSP updates, all flying around in a relatively short amount of time. This is an awful lot of stress for the control plane of a router, no matter how powerful.

Things get even worse with another failure scenario: what if not a single VC, but an entire router is going down (due to a reboot, for example)? The amount of LSPs grows by $O(N^3)$. In a network of 100 routers spanning a full-mesh, this means that a single failing router generates up to 1,000,000 LSPs in a short amount of time. Ironically, 99 per cent of the LSPs hold information that is already known by some other neighbour. So what can be done to mitigate the dark side of flooding? The answer to this is discussed in the next section.

6.4.2 *Mesh-Groups*

Let's go back to the basic flooding algorithm and change it a little bit. Now the rule is: Do not send out a received LSP on *all* the links where we have an adjacency in the Up state. Rather, send out the LSP on *some* of these links. Figure 6.14 shows a router that is not sending out an LSP on all of the possible links. Instead, some links have been *pruned* off the flooding topology. The result is that all routers still see LSP updates, but the excessive multiplication of LSPs is avoided. The official name for this kind of functionality is known as Mesh-Groups and has been documented in RFC 2973. The Mesh-Group pruning is done based on the topology of the network and is not automatic.

There are *two* basic concepts behind Mesh-Groups. The first concept is blocking an interface entirely, as shown in Figure 6.14. Here, one or a set of interfaces is removed from the flooding list. It is also very straightforward to configure on IOS and JUNOS software, as shown in the following two configuration snippets. Both vendors share the same spirit in their implementation of the Mesh-Group functionality. The LSP flooding in both vendors' implementations is an interface property. In IOS, you configure everything at the physical/logical interfaces prepended by the keyword `isis`. In JUNOS software, all the logical interfaces can be referenced directly under the `protocols isis interface` configuration branch, which is very practical, as the relevant information is then at one place.

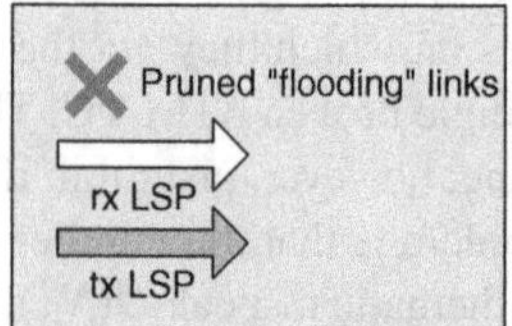

FIGURE 6.14. Mesh-Group blocks remove certain links from the flooding topology

IOS configuration

In IOS, LSP flooding can be reduced using the `isis mesh-group blocked` configuration command in interface-configuration mode, as shown in the following:

```
London# show running-config
[ ... ]
interface atm 1/2.1
 ip router isis
 isis mesh-group blocked
[ ... ]
```

In JUNOS the configurations statement is very similar. The first flavour of Mesh-Groups can be enabled by use of the `mesh-group blocked` config-uration directive under the `protocols isis interface <interface-name>` configuration hierarchy, as shown in the following:

JUNOS software configuration

```
hannes@Frankfurt> show configuration
[ ... ]
protocols {
     isis {
        interface at-4/0/0.200 {
              mesh-group blocked;
        }
     }
}
[ ... ]
```

You may ask why the word *Group* is contained in Mesh-Group. So far we have not configured a Group number. What is the Group number related to? This number is related to the refined version of Mesh-Groups where the flooding is not turned off *entirely* for an interface. Some LSPs are still sent. How is this second flavour of Mesh-Groups configured? First, all the logical interfaces on an IS-IS router have to be organized in groups of interfaces. In Figure 6.15 you can see that the first three interfaces have been grouped together in Mesh-Group #11 and the second three interfaces have been grouped together in Mesh-Group #47. Once an LSP is received over a logical interface (white arrow), the IS-IS router first determines the Mesh-Group number that the receiving interface belongs to. In our example the receiving interface belongs to Mesh-Group #11. When this LSP is now flooded to all neighbours, the router does flood the LSP on interfaces belonging to that specific group (Mesh-Group #11 with the gray arrows). This solves the multiplicative effect of basic flooding.

The second flavour of Mesh-Groups that has just been described can be configured in a similar way on IOS and in the JUNOS software. The only difference here is that a Mesh-Group Number replaces the keyword `blocked.` Similar to the `mesh-group blocked` command, this is configured under interface configuration mode.

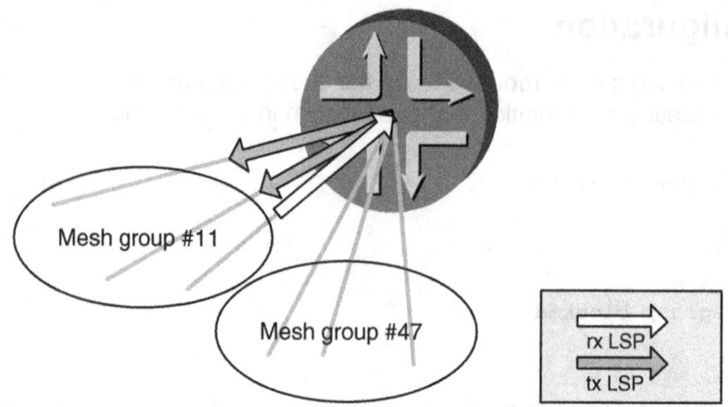

FIGURE 6.15. Mesh-Groups relay an LSP only to interfaces inside the same Mesh-Group

In IOS, LSP flooding can be reduced according to the second flavour of Mesh-groups using the `isis mesh-group <group-number>` configuration command in interface-configuration mode, as shown in the following:

IOS configuration

```
London# show running-config
[ … ]
interface atm 1/2.1
 ip router isis
 isis mesh-group 11
interface atm 1/2.2
 ip router isis
 isis mesh-group 11
interface atm 1/2.3
 ip router isis
 isis mesh-group 11
[ … ]
```

In JUNOS, the Mesh-Group Number replaces the `blocked` statement. The second flavour of Mesh-Groups can be enabled by use of the `mesh-group <group-number>` configuration directive under the `protocols isis interface <interface-name>` configuration hierarchy, as shown in the following:

JUNOS software configuration

```
hannes@Frankfurt> show configuration
[ … ]
protocols {
    isis {
        interface at-4/0/0.100 {
            mesh-group 11;
        }
```

```
            interface at-4/0/0.101 {
                mesh-group 11;
            }
            interface at-4/0/0.102 {
                mesh-group 11;
            }
        }
    }
    [ ... ]
```

Mesh-Groups help to reduce the flooding explosion in densely meshed environments. However, keep in mind that flooding is a necessity to get information across the internal network. In a sense, it is "too-much" flooding that causes harm. However, a "too-little" flooding strategy can cause harm in a different way. Thus, be very careful when setting up Mesh-Groups. Mesh-Groups cannot be so "tight" that they result in desynchronized link-state databases. In Chapter 8 you will learn about the impact of desynchronized link-state databases and what can be done to avoid them. At the end of the chapter, a refinement of ISO 10589 is presented to make sure that routers that have been accidentally pruned off the flooding topology (due to a wrong Mesh-Group configuration, for example) still receive good information for synchronization.

Although Mesh-Groups must be hand-configured by a network administrator, it is easy to determine if Mesh-Groups are needed by looking at the statistics that IOS and the JUNOS software can provide. For example, the relevant IS-IS statistics can be displayed using the `show clns traffic` command, as shown in the following:

IOS command output

```
Amsterdam# show clns traffic
[ ... ]
IS-IS: Time since last clear: never
IS-IS: Level-1 Hellos (sent/rcvd): 115/19
IS-IS: Level-2 Hellos (sent/rcvd): 120/14
IS-IS: PTP Hellos     (sent/rcvd): 0/0
IS-IS: Level-1 LSPs sourced (new/refresh): 10/0
IS-IS: Level-2 LSPs sourced (new/refresh): 14/0
IS-IS: Level-1 LSPs flooded (sent/rcvd): 2/2
IS-IS: Level-2 LSPs flooded (sent/rcvd): 3/2
IS-IS: LSP Retransmissions: 0
IS-IS: Level-1 CSNPs (sent/rcvd): 0/2
IS-IS: Level-2 CSNPs (sent/rcvd): 3/0
IS-IS: Level-1 PSNPs (sent/rcvd): 0/0
IS-IS: Level-2 PSNPs (sent/rcvd): 0/0
IS-IS: Level-1 DR Elections: 3
IS-IS: Level-2 DR Elections: 2
IS-IS: Level-1 SPF Calculations: 7
IS-IS: Level-2 SPF Calculations: 7
```

```
IS-IS: Level-1 Partial Route Calculations: 0
IS-IS: Level-2 Partial Route Calculations: 0
IS-IS: LSP checksum errors received: 0
IS-IS: Update process queue depth: 0/200
IS-IS: Update process packets dropped: 0
[ … ]
```

In every case, a big disparity between the LSPs being sent and the LSPs being received is an indication that there is excess flooding in the network that needs to be controlled via Mesh-Groups.

In the JUNOS software, you can display the global IS-IS statistics using the `show isis statistics` command. Watch for a disparity between LSPs being sent and received:

JUNOS software command output

```
hannes@Frankfurt> show isis statistics
IS-IS statistics for Frankfurt:
PDU type        Received    Processed    Drops       Sent    Rexmit
LSP               220201       220201        0     152846       381
IIH              5640823      5640823        0    3762071         0
CSNP             5486953      5486953        0    9893412         0
PSNP               32766        32766        0     192857         0
Unknown                0            0        0          0         0
Totals          11380743     11380743        0   14001186       381

Total packets received: 11380743 Sent: 14001567

SNP queue length: 0 Drops: 0
LSP queue length: 0 Drops: 0
SPF runs: 121371
Fragments rebuilt: 336
LSP regenerations: 151
Purges initiated: 0
```

Mesh-Groups solved a big problem in ATM or Frame-Relay overlay networks of the mid-1990s. However, today Mesh-Groups are of limited use because ATM and FR transport networks connecting routers have gone away for the most part. Today, routers are typically interconnected by packet-over-SONET/SDH links in a sparse-meshed fashion. A typical core router these days has on average no more than four or five interfaces facing other core routers. In these environments, Mesh-Groups are a nice tuning capability, but not the necessity they were only a few years ago when networks were melting down in the absence of a sound LSP flooding scheme.

6.5 Network-wide Purging of LSPs

The flooding of LSP updates the network with the most accurate state information. The link-state database is therefore continually increasing as new or updated information is added to it. If a link is down, issue a new LSP. When it comes back up, issue another new LSP. So far there have been no *negative* LSPs that make the database shrink in size. But what if IS-IS wants to *remove* a router from the distributed link-state database in all of the other routers in the network? There is always the option to wait until the LSP ages out, but that can take up to 65,535 seconds (18 hours, 12 minutes). For certain events, such as router removal, IS-IS needs to have the capability to issue a negative LSP update. This negative LSP, or *purge* LSP, exists and is a "crippled" version of the original LSP. All the purge LSP contains is the LSP header without any further information. The Header and the Checksum fields of the purge LSP header are set to zero to indicate that this is a purge. This *negative* LSP update, which is called a *network-wide purge*, is used for a variety of events. One of these events is DIS election.

6.5.1 *DIS Election*

On IS-IS broadcast links there is at least one router performing a special function. This IS-IS router is called the Designated Intermediate System (DIS). The role of the DIS was first discussed in Chapter 5. Each DIS borrows an ID that is unique across the network from the LAN on which it is the DIS. The DIS floods that LAN-ID throughout the network to tell other routers that there is connectivity to the LAN. Now, if the DIS is changed (re-elected) due to changes, such as a higher DIS election priority or the time-out of the old DIS, then the new DIS must generate a new LAN-ID and flood this throughout the network. The has-been DIS needs to remove the old LAN-ID from the network in order to ensure that it does not lead to corrupt network information. Figure 6.16 shows the chain of LSPs that are generated to accomplish this. In order to remove the stale LSP from the former DIS, the old DIS generates an LSP with the sequence number incremented by one, but with the Checksum and Lifetime set to zero. Each router that receives this purge LSP will remove the referenced LSP-ID from its link-state database.

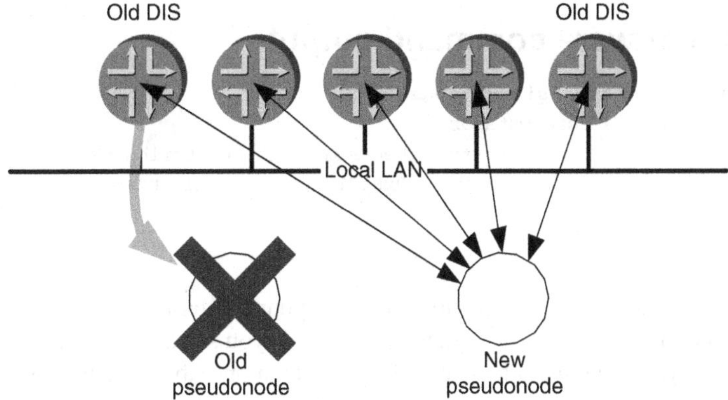

FIGURE 6.16. At DIS re-election the old pseudo node LSP gets purged

6.5.2 *Expiration of LSPs*

Whenever a router ages-out an LSP whose Lifetime has become zero, it needs to tell the other routers that the LSP has been aged out. Recall that each router has an internal clock and those clocks are subject to clock drifts. At the same time, all the routers in a given IS-IS level fundamentally rely on the fact that its link-state database is synchronized with all others. So for further robustness in the face of clock drift, the first router that detects that an LSP's Lifetime has gone to zero, initiates a network-wide purge of that expired LSP. Lifetime expiration of LSPs is common for routers that have been removed from the network for one reason or another. Recall that under normal conditions, each LSP gets refreshed by the Originator *before* it expires and therefore should *never* countdown the Lifetime field to zero. This should only happen during the purge of an LSP.

If a router purges an LSP from the link-state database, the LSP is not removed immediately. Instead, the LSP is retained for a ZeroAgeLifetime of 60 seconds. Keeping the purged LSP for 60 seconds ensures that an LSP is not re-learned (for instance) through an adjacency that has been Down and is now transitioning to Up again.

You can recognize a purged LSP that is still in the database if its Lifetime value is in brackets. This is similar to the accounting world, where red numbers are in brackets as well. And this is exactly what the User Interfaces do as well: they essentially show you a *zombie* – an LSP that is already dead but we keep it alive for visibility, helping us in the troubleshooting case.

IOS command output

```
Amsterdam# show isis database
[ … ]
IS-IS Level-1 Link State Database:
LSPID              LSP Seq Num    LSP Checksum    LSP Holdtime    ATT/P/OL
New-York.02-00     0x00002fb1     0x6f71          (23)            1/0/0
[ … ]
```

JUNOS software command output

```
hannes@New-York> show isis database
IS-IS level 1 link-state database:
LSP ID                       Sequence Checksum Lifetime Attributes
New-York.02-00                 0x2fb1   0x6f71   (48)     L1 Attached
[ … ]
  4 LSPs
```

Typically you do not see much purged LSPs in your database as this is a very rare case (DIS routers do not change very often). However, if you see a lot of bracketed LPSs or one LSP always containing a bracketed Lifetime then probably a malicious event like a flood-purge storm is raging because of duplicate System-IDs.

6.5.3 *Duplicate System-IDs*

Whenever a router receives an LSP that contains its own System-ID as Originator, and the router is sure that it did not generate this LSP, the router must assume that there is another router on the network that is configured with a duplicate System-ID. All the receiving router can do is to log this event and generate a purge LSP. The other router will most likely try to re-originate this LSP with a higher Sequence Number. Of course, this purge process needs to be carefully paced. Otherwise a flood-purge-storm will start to rage as the two routers continually try to update and purge each other's wrong LSP. You will see in the next section how these storms can be prevented. Actually, the LSP will be purged because duplicate System-IDs are also an obstacle for a clean SPF calculation. This ensures that the network itself stays clean.

6.6 Flow Control and Throttling of LSPs

In link-state routing protocols, the implementer needs to make an effort not to overwhelm neighbours with excessive LSP updates. Excessive LSPs might churn the network. In typical transport protocols such as TCP there is a built-in feedback mechanism that makes the sender slow down if the receiver feels overwhelmed. This is called *flow control.* However, virtually all IGPs (including IS-IS) have no way to tell a neighbour that the IS-IS router is busy and make the other neighbouring routers throttle down LSP transmissions. It is beyond the scope of this book as to *why* the protocol designers did not address flow control in the IS-IS specification. But this lack of flow control means that an IS-IS router has to carefully *pace* (spread out in time) LSPs toward a neighbour. In good IS-IS implementations there are a lot of built-in throttles that make the IS-IS router well behaved, even when the network is in a transient stage and several LSP updates are flying around. Additionally, there are also limits for how frequently a router can originate LSP updates. A router not only has to take care that it does not overwhelm its directly connected neighbours, but the router needs to take care that it does not overwhelm all the routers that are beyond the immediately adjacent neighbouring routers. Recall that all routers in a given IS-IS level need to dedicate some resources (such as CPU cycles, bandwidth and so on) to process and relay LSPs farther across the network. So let's be nice to these routers and not overload them, as we need them to distribute reachability information of all types.

Most modern implementations of the IS-IS protocol support a variety of control *knobs* that makes an IS-IS router *slower* instead of faster. Realize that going slower when there are transient conditions or LSP storms is the only option that a router has left if the router is to continue running. There are a couple of big "Must-Not's" that an implementation of IS-IS should never do.

We must not trash our neighbours. IS-IS Hellos must always be sent. If a router does not send IS-IS Hellos in time, the adjacency times out. Losing an adjacency in transient situations will additionally contribute more LSPs to a network that is already shaky to begin with.

We must not forget to acknowledge LSPs of a neighbour. Even when a router is under pressure in the form of extreme packet loads, not acknowledging an LSP update means that after five seconds the LSP will be retransmitted. So it is much better to acknowledge the LSP the first time before the LSP gets retransmitted. A retransmission consumes the resources of the neighbouring router as well as the receiving router because an LSP has to be retransmitted by the neighbour and re-processed on the receiving side as well.

So if making things *slower* is the only thing a router can do, exactly what kind of events need to be made slower or *throttled*? The important events to throttle are in the areas of:

- The LSPs on an interface
- Frequency of originating (generating) LSPs per router
- Retransmissions on a interface

Each of these is discussed in the following sections.

6.6.1 *LSP-transmit-interval*

The LSP *transmit interval* is one form of pacing that was originally mentioned in ISO 10589. The specification says that an implementation of IS-IS should make sure not to send more than 30 LSPs per second on a given broadcast link. Both IOS and JUNOS software extended this requirement that LSPs are paced on *every* IS-IS interface type (broadcast and point-to-point). You can tweak that throttling timer in both JUNOS software and IOS.

In IOS, LSP throttling can be enabled using the `isis lsp-interval <time>` configuration command in interface-configuration mode. The time is a constant expressed in milliseconds (ms). The default value is 33 ms. This example sets the LSP pacing so as not to exceed 20 LSPs per second (pacing of 50 ms means 20 LSPs per second).

IOS configuration

```
London# show running-config
[ … ]
interface atm 1/2.1
 ip router isis
 isis lsp-interval 50
[ … ]
```

In JUNOS software, the throttling of LSPs can be enabled by use of the `isis lsp-interval <time>` configuration directive under the `protocols isis interface <interface-name>` configuration hierarchy. The default value is 20 ms and generates 50 LSPs per second, which means that JUNOS software is contrary to the original 20 LSP-per-second specification, but this limit is fairly old in that respect. Modern routers should easily handle 50 LSPs per second. This example sets the JUNOS software value to the specification limit of 50 ms (20 LSPs per second).

JUNOS software configuration

```
hannes@Frankfurt> show configuration
[ ... ]
protocols {
    isis {
        interface at-4/0/0.100 {
          lsp-interval 50;
        }
    }
}
[ ... ]
```

LSP throttling by use of the `lsp-interval` command is a powerful mechanism to control the flooding pace to neighbouring routers in order to not overload them. There is another issue that has not yet been discussed: control traffic (LSP and related packets) may "push back" the user traffic (information packets) because control traffic always has precedence in terms of scheduling on the router interface cards. Unfortunately, the control traffic transmission rate does not get lower on low-bandwidth interfaces such as DS0 or fractional T1/E1 line – control traffic stays the same. You can easily imagine that on a low-bandwidth circuit transmitting 30 full-MTU sized packets does not leave much room for other types of packets. So it would be nice if there were a way to tell the router just to utilize a certain percentage of the interface bandwidth for control traffic. In IOS, you can configure the `bandwidth <bw>` statement on a (sub)-interface so that the router makes sure that there is not more than 50 per cent (for instance) of the interface bandwidth utilized for LSP transmission. This is the recommended option to use for low-bandwidth circuits.

IOS configuration

In IOS, LSP throttling is calculated automatically by setting the `bandwidth` parameter in interface configuration mode – this makes sure that not more than 50 per cent (for example) of the configured interface Bandwidth is dedicated to the routing protocol. This example sets the total bandwidth available for IS-IS traffic to 256 Kbps, which might be only a fraction of the total bandwidth available on the link (perhaps 2 Mbps):

```
London# show running-config
[ ... ]
interface Serial1/2
 ip router isisu
 bandwidth 256
[ ... ]
```

JUNOS software does not support automated calculation of LSP throttling because the lowest-speed interface cards on a Juniper Networks router starts at T1/E1 speeds (1.5 and 2 Mbps) and it is assumed that even with an LSP pacing of 20 ms this will not consume more than 50 per cent of the interface bandwidth. However, there may be fractional

T1/E1 circuits (less than the full bandwidth) configured as well, where LSP pacing might have to be adjusted.

However, the JUNOS software `lsp-interval` knob really helps to solve *two* problems: regulating the control-traffic-to-user-traffic ratio, and protecting neighbours during transient situations. So the lack of direct bandwidth control is not really an issue: the same knob can be used to solve both problems.

Note that the traffic subject to this pacing was *non-self-originated* traffic, which is traffic that has been originated by other routers, not the local router. In the next section, you learn about pacing of self-originated LSPs that come from the local router.

6.6.2 *LSP-generation-interval*

Routers need to limit how fast they announce changes to the network. A router does not just send an LSP and move on. Sending an LSP to the network essentially requests a replication service from the network to flood the LSP. So any LSP sent consumes tremendous resources from the network. The LSP sent may be replicated by hundreds of routers over thousands of links. By inserting pacing rules on the individual routers, you can make sure that the network does not melt down once more than one router has to say something. The ISO 10589 specification describes an architectural constant called *minimumLSPGenerationInterval* that serves this purpose. In vendor's documentation this is sometimes referred to as LSP *holddown*. The IS-IS specification recommends setting this value to 30 seconds. *Higher* intervals may lead to routers that are not responsive to changes in the network, whereas *lower* values may generate too much churn in the network.

For a long time, IOS has implemented a 5 second holddown interval to keep a good balance between the two extremes. Today, the frequency of LSP origination can be controlled using the `lsp-gen-interval <holddown> [<initial-wait> <minimum-holddown>]` configuration command. The first argument specifies the time between LSP builds. This is the timer that ISO 10589 mentions and is discussed previously. The interesting thing about LSP build holddown is that this is not enforced statically today. Modern implementations have a dynamic approach and try to strike a balance between responsiveness and stability. So there are two LSP holddown timers: a *fast* holddown and a *slow* holddown timer. Depending on how busy the network is, a router switches from fast behaviour to slow behaviour. The first couple of LSP builds are scheduled very quickly without LSP build holddown consideration. However, if more LSP builds are requested, then the router is probably in trouble and the router backs off to the normal *slow* LSP origination behaviour. The `initial-wait` timer specifies how fast the router fires off an LSP after first building it. In transient situations a router probably needs to update its LSP a few times and this `initial-wait` timer helps by accumulating a few builds. `Minimum-wait` controls the LSP build holddown in the fast phase.

How many LSPs need to be built until IOS switches from *fast* to *slow* behaviour? IOS uses a technique called *exponential back off* to toggle gradually between the two modes. Consider the IOS configuration snippet shown here. In IOS, there are three timers to control LSP holddown. The first timer specifies the LSP holddown in the slow phase expressed in units of seconds. The second timer specifies how many milliseconds to wait before sending the LSP. The third timer specifies the LSP holddown in the fast phase expressed in milliseconds.

IOS configuration

```
London# show running-config
[ ... ]
router isis
 lsp-gen-interval 5 200 1000
[ ... ]
```

Figure 6.17 shows the timing behaviour of the exponential back off algorithm. After the first LSP is built it is delayed for 200 ms (second value given) until it gets sent. Next, the holddown timer kicks in, therefore the *second* LSP originated will be delayed for at least 1000 ms (a full second) as specified in the third argument of the `lsp-gen-interval` configuration command. All subsequent LSP builds will be delayed by twice the previous holddown time: 2 seconds for the third LSP, 4 seconds for the fourth, and so on. The holddown time is limited to the first argument (5 seconds) of the `lsp-gen-interval` command as a precaution that the interval does not grow to an infinite value. So for every fast-build the LSP-Origination-Interval gets larger until it hits the ceiling of 5 seconds. After a particular router has stopped issuing LSPs for 20 seconds, the LSP holddown will be reset. This means that from here on any further LSP originations will receive fast holddowns again, but only for the first couple of LSPs.

The JUNOS software scheme has a two-step rate limit. First, there is a global LSP throttling similar to the one specified in ISO 10589. All the LSPs are paced using a 20 ms timer. Additionally, there is additional logic that damps adjacency and makes sure that the adjacency is reliably up for some time before advertising the adjacency. The global LSP gating is hard-coded; there is no user interface knob to change the value. The *slow* LSP holddown value is a base value 10 seconds with 25 per cent jitter (timing variation) applied. That means that subsequent LSP builds will be randomly delayed between 7.5 and 10 seconds. Jittering a timer makes the Event always happening earlier but never later than the original base value. This variation is useful to avoid global synchronization and the associated LSP storms and router churn. Recall that a new LSP makes all routers do several things at the same time (flooding, SPF calculation, and more), which in turn synchronizes the CPU peaks in a network. Smearing the CPU peaks across routers by adding some timer jitter helps to avoid churn across all routers.

In JUNOS software, there are also a number of fast builds, which are currently hard-coded to three fast builds of LSPs. The initial wait timer is hard-coded to 20 ms before the LSP is sent. The reason why there are no configuration knobs is the JUNOS software has adjacency holddown logic to make sure that the root cause of dynamic LSP changes (adjacency changes), will be damped (suppressed). Exactly how does this adjacency holddown logic work? After a successful three-way handshake, the router does not declare the adjacency Up immediately. The router will wait to see if it can sustain the LSP stress generated from the new adjacency. Each new adjacency can generate a lot of LSPs. Just think of a partitioned network that starts to heal. The healing router brings up

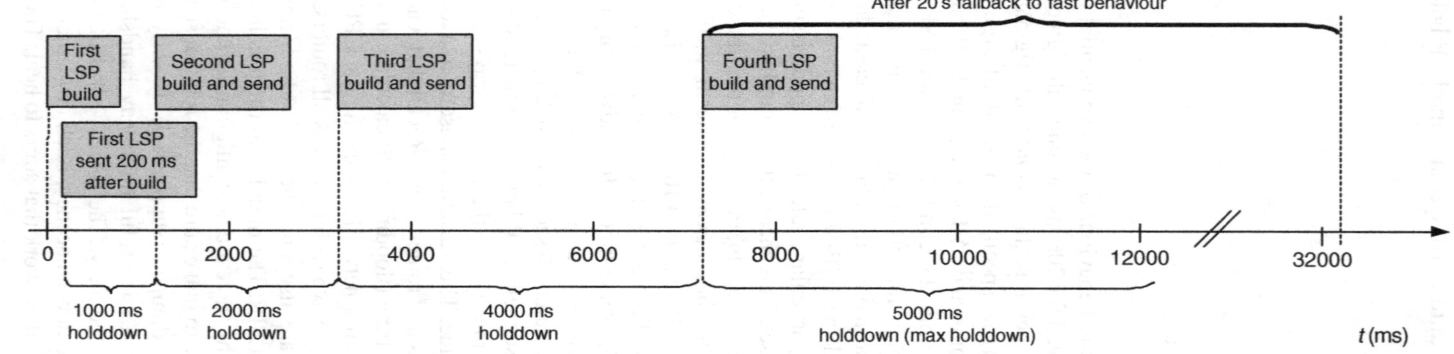

FIGURE 6.17. Exponential holddown gradually supresses LSPs, generation

the adjacency and is exposed to a massive amount of *new* LSPs sent to it from the new peer. In Chapter 8 you will acquire more insight as to just how IS-IS exchanges LSPs and the mechanisms that synchronize link-state databases.

Can the router sustain the stress generated from all the new LSPs hammering at it? The router does not know yet. Does it make sense to advertise a new LSP if the network is in flux? Probably not – so the router delays its own LSPs until the network is quieter. Just to be safe, the JUNOS software waits at least 20 seconds after an adjacency is declared Up before doing anything further with the to-be-generated LSP. Next, the router starts to measure the arrival rate of LSPs to see if things have become more stabilized. JUNOS software *still* holds the adjacency down until the LSP reception rate has gone down to 5 LSPs/per 5 seconds. After the maximum holddown period of 60 seconds, which begins after the IS-IS 3-way handshake, the adjacency will finally be advertised in the LSP.

That two-level approach (LSP gating plus adjacency holddowns) has proven to be a good mechanism that works in a variety of networking environements. The Juniper Networks development engineers felt that it was not necessary to expose a knob to change this behaviour to the user. (Knobs are good – but the knobs that I do not need are even better.)

6.6.3 *Retransmission Interval*

According to ISO 10589, each IS-IS router has to acknowledge LSPs within a five-second window or else the neighbouring router will re-transmit that new LSP. A router that is in trouble may not be able to respond within the five seconds. Therefore it makes sense to increase that retransmission timer to higher values for lower-powered, CPU-based routers. In JUNOS software, the five-second retransmission interval is hard coded and cannot be changed. In Cisco IOS the retransmission interval is configurable and can be controlled on a per-interface basis.

IOS configuration

In IOS, the retransmission timer is configurable. Setting the `isis retransmit-interval <interval>` command in interface configuration mode controls this timer, as shown in the following:

```
London# show running-config
[ ... ]
router isis
 isis retransmit-interval 5
[ ... ]
```

In Cisco IOS, you can also control how fast LSPs are sent once a router is in the retransmission window. This is another mechanism that helps a busy neighbour and makes sure that a sender does not overwhelm the receiving router with LSPs once the sender starts retransmitting LSPs. Here the router takes a non-acknowledgement of an LSP previously sent as a sign of trouble and therefore throttles down the LSP transmission rate. Recall that the default LSP transmission rate in Cisco IOS is 33 ms between LSPs. The default retransmission-throttling interval increases that value by a factor of 3, up to 100 ms. That should be sufficient to back off a troubled router. It is not recommended to go beyond 333 ms because the LSP pacing gets so slow that the network becomes unresponsive in terms of reaction to changes.

In IOS, the retransmission-throttling timer is configurable. Setting the `isis retransmit-throttle-interval <interval>` command in interface configuration mode controls this timer.

IOS configuration

```
London# show running-config
[ ... ]
router isis
 isis isis retransmit-throttle-interval 200
[ ... ]
```

6.7 Conclusion

The way in which an IS-IS implementation handles LSP dynamics separates amateur enthusiast code from professional developer's routing code. LSP dynamics is perhaps the most important feature to focus on when evaluating IS-IS vendors. Interestingly, there is almost nothing in the ISO 10589 specification that tells you how to implement IS-IS in a scalable and robust manner. For many router startups, the lack of experience in how to do this right has been a barrier to entrance in the high-end router market and it probably still is. Ironically, in the world of open specifications, there are still barely a dozen routing protocol software engineers who have the necessary experience to get the IS-IS code right the first time. Do not be misled. I am not asserting that no other engineers but these few can ever get IS-IS right. With enough time, and with customers willing to take the pain to obtain that operational experience with regard to what works and what does not, sooner or later every implementation of IS-IS can get to a level of what is called *Carrier-Class-Code*. There are a number of interesting routing software approaches used by other vendors, but these are not discussed in this book. Time and operational experience will tell what implementation of IS-IS will finally prevail in the Internet.

7

Pseudonodes and Designated Routers

Historically routers were used to network local sub-nets to each other. Routing protocols are optimized to run in a wide area network (WAN) environment which are typically point-to-point links like Serial Lines, Frame Relay or ATM. Due to the popularity of Ethernet since the mid-1980s routing protocols are required to operate and *scale* on broadcast circuits like Ethernet.

Broadcast networks allow multiple devices to see each other. For link-state routing protocols like IS-IS *multipoint* capability means additional forms of stress in the domains of Hello processing, database storage size dynamics like link-state database churn.

In this chapter you will learn how LAN circuits are different from p2p circuits, and what scaling challenges there are on p2p circuits. You will learn about the pseudonode concept, its nodal representation in the IS-IS link-state database and implications in the SPF algorithm. Finally the purpose of a *Designated Intermediate System* (DIS) and its election, pre-emption and timing details will be highlighted.

7.1 Scaling Adjacencies on Large LANs

Whenever there is a large number of routers on a LAN, lots of care must be taken. There are several aspects of the protocol to worry about: first, if there is a large number of speakers on the LAN there is a lot amount of Hellos to process. Just imagine a LAN with 100 IS-IS speakers generating in total 300 Hellos per second. If those 300 Hellos are evenly spread at one Hello each 3 milliseconds, as illustrated in Figure 7.1, no problem – this won't stress the internal scheduling of the Router OS too much.

However, the environment, especially once it comes down to routing protocols is *not* nice and far from being ideal. Therefore we may *never* assume ideal working conditions.

7.1.1 *The Self-synchronization Problem*

Murphy's Law dictates "If things *can* go wrong they *will* go wrong". The worst case scenario is that 99 Hellos hit the control plane of the receiving router at *once* as shown in Figure 7.2. Although the *average* CPU stress remains moderate if all the Hellos are evenly spread, there could be a short time shortage of resources (buffer memory and CPU) if a large number of Hellos arrives at once. The last line of defence in a peak load situation is to drop incoming Hellos. Arguably the buffers should be made *big enough* to absorb any peak load condition. So how *big* is *big enough*? One needs to make a trade-off here as well. Due to stability reasons a router should not buffer an almost *infinite* queue of incoming protocol packets. Processing very large queues may keep the router busy with

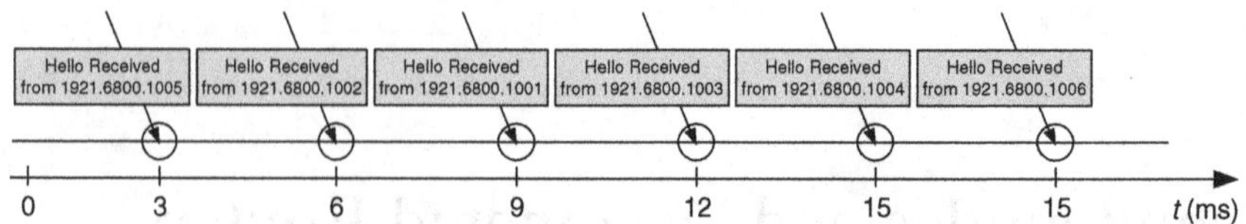

FIGURE 7.1. Even spread Hello arrival times are an ideal, desired environment

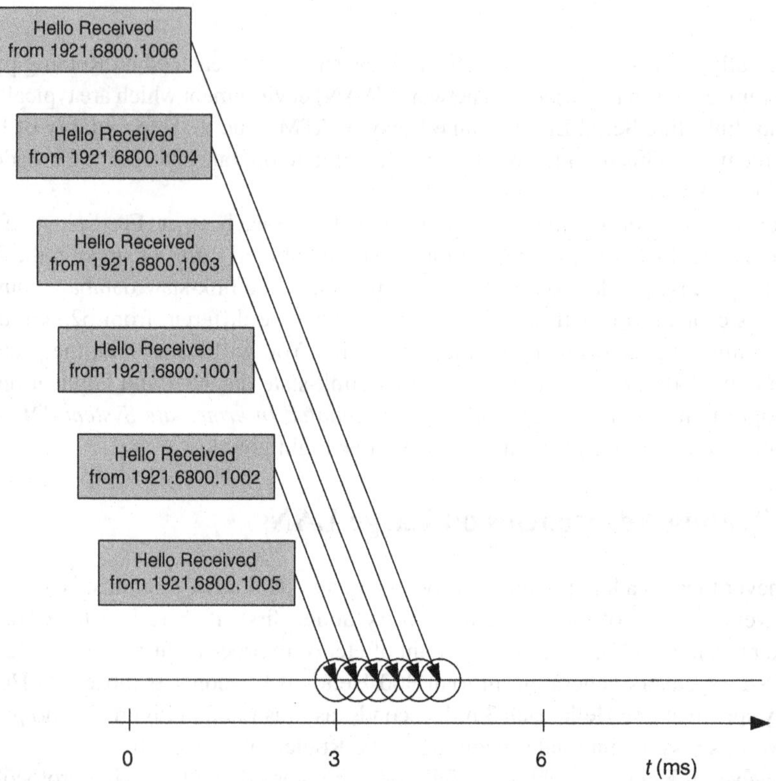

FIGURE 7.2. A lot of Hellos hitting the control plane CPU at the same time may exhaust resources

updates that are a few packets later withdrawn. On the other side there should be some *minimum* buffer to absorb short time bursts.

The worst case was previously described as "one Router hit by all Hellos of 99 Routers at once" and on first sight this might seem as unrealistic, artificial scenario. The reality is that without precautions in the routing code generates Hellos there will be a resulting effect called *self-synchronization*. Self-synchronization means that a router is immediately answering with a Hello to network events like adjacency changes and new neighbours. This behaviour tends to add up by all the speakers on the LAN and as a side-effect all the Hellos are scheduled at the same point, which is artificially generating an unwanted form of *peak-stress* followed by seconds of silence, as illustrated in Figure 7.2.

7.1.2 *Scheduling Hellos*

How is the Hello scheduled? This depends on the Hold timer which controls adjacency expiration. In order to *avoid* adjacency expiration each neighbouring router sends Hellos to reset the Hold timer before it expires. In every implementation of IS-IS there is an *internal* constant called the *Hello-Multiplier.* The Hello Interval is calculated by dividing the Hold timer by the Hello-Multiplier. The Hold timer reset by receipt of an Hello is illustrated in Figure 5.3 in Chapter 5 “Neighbour Discovery and Handshaking”.

For example, a Hold timer of 30 s and a Hello-Multiplier of 3 results in a Hello Interval of 10 s. If the system dispatches *exactly* each 10 s a Hello then there may be risk that the system is starting to self-synchronize and after some local network events all routers on the LAN will generate their Hellos at the same point in time.

To avoid the effect of self-synchronization ISO 10589 mandates to *jitter* timers for scheduling Hellos.

7.1.3 *Applying Jitter to Timers*

What does applying a *jitter* to timers mean and how does it attempt to solve the self-synchronization problem?

Applying a jitter means scheduling a Hello *before* it must be sent. The trick is that each router on a LAN deducts a *random time* off the original Hello timer. Because each router computes its own independent random number it is made sure that routers never send Hellos at the same point in time.

ISO 10589 mandates to apply a 25 per cent jitter on Hellos. The 25 per cent mean that a random number between the 0 and 25 per cent mark of the original timer is computed. The random number should be truly random in the sense that the numbers the random-generator produces have a uniform distribution over the entire space that it covers. For example, a 25 per cent jitter of an underlying 10 s Hello timer would result in a random time between 0 and 2.5 seconds. Finally the jitter is subtracted from the original timer. In Figure 7.3 the jitter calculation is illustrated.

Both IOS and JUNOS do apply a 25 per cent jitter to their Hello timer before scheduling the Hello for transmission. In the following tcpdump output you can see that the Timestamps are not spaced in discrete 10 s intervals – it is always varying a little less than 10 s.

Tcpdump output

```
00:11:39.391338 OSI, IS-IS, L1 Lan IIH, src-id 0000.0000.0002,
                  lan-id 0000.0000.0001.02, prio 65, length 74
00:11:48.951503 OSI, IS-IS, L1 Lan IIH, src-id 0000.0000.0002,
                  lan-id 0000.0000.0001.02, prio 65, length 74
00:11:57.061652 OSI, IS-IS, L1 Lan IIH, src-id 0000.0000.0002,
                  lan-id 0000.0000.0001.02, prio 65, length 74
00:12:05.451811 OSI, IS-IS, L1 Lan IIH, src-id 0000.0000.0002,
                  lan-id 0000.0000.0001.02, prio 65, length 74
00:12:14.671953 OSI, IS-IS, L1 Lan IIH, src-id 0000.0000.0002,
                  lan-id 0000.0000.0001.02, prio 65, length 74
```

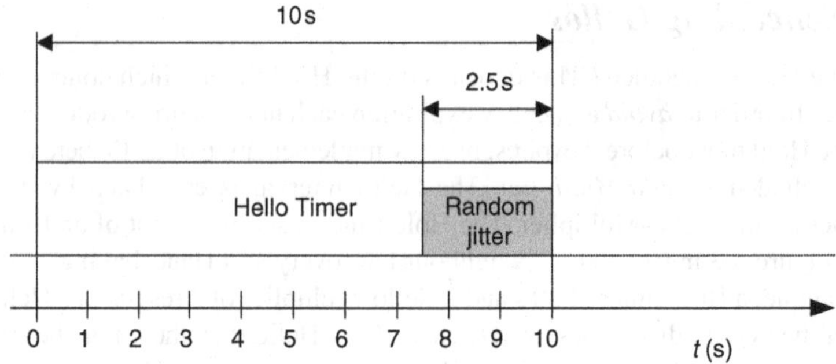

FIGURE 7.3. A 25 per cent jitter on the basis of a 10 s timer results in a random Hello between 7.5 and 10 s

Applying a jitter on the timers offers a good distribution of the scheduled Hellos among the LAN routers over time. It is used in many other places as well. IOS and JUNOS go much further as required by ISO 10589. For almost every one-time and periodic event the system applies jitter. Virtually all IS-IS packet dispatching routines apply between 5 per cent and 25 per cent jitter for Hellos (IIHs), Sequence Number PDUs (SNPs) and link-state PDUs (LSPs).

As soon as the router maintains a high number of adjacencies on the LAN circuit it needs to advertise them in its link-state PDU. A large number of LAN adjacencies raises the question of how to *represent* all the router-to-router relationships in the link-state database.

7.2 Pseudonodes

See Figure 7.4 for an illustration of six routers that are located on the same LAN. The LAN is *transitive*; this means that all the routers can see each other. Each of the routers generates an LSP and tells the world that it has five neighbours on the LAN by explicitly listing them inside the IS Reachability TLV #2 or #22.

Any-to-any connectivity lets grow the *size* of the link-state database by an order of $O(N^2)$. This is often referred to as the N^2 problem.

7.2.1 *The* N² *Problem*

Figure 7.5 illustrates the relationship between the size of IS-reach information in the link-state database and the number of routers on a LAN. Arguably the absolute size of the link-state database is a moderate problem compared to the dynamic effects of a full-mesh advertisement. Every time a new router N gets on the LAN, all the other routers $(N - 1)$ that have been on the LAN previously need to update their LSPs to list the adjacency to the new router. This results in a massive LSP update storm because *all* the routers on the LAN need to tell the network that there has been a change in adjacencies. The same update storm happens if a router is disconnected from the LAN.

The dynamic component (routers joining or leaving the sub-net) is a more important problem than database storage size.

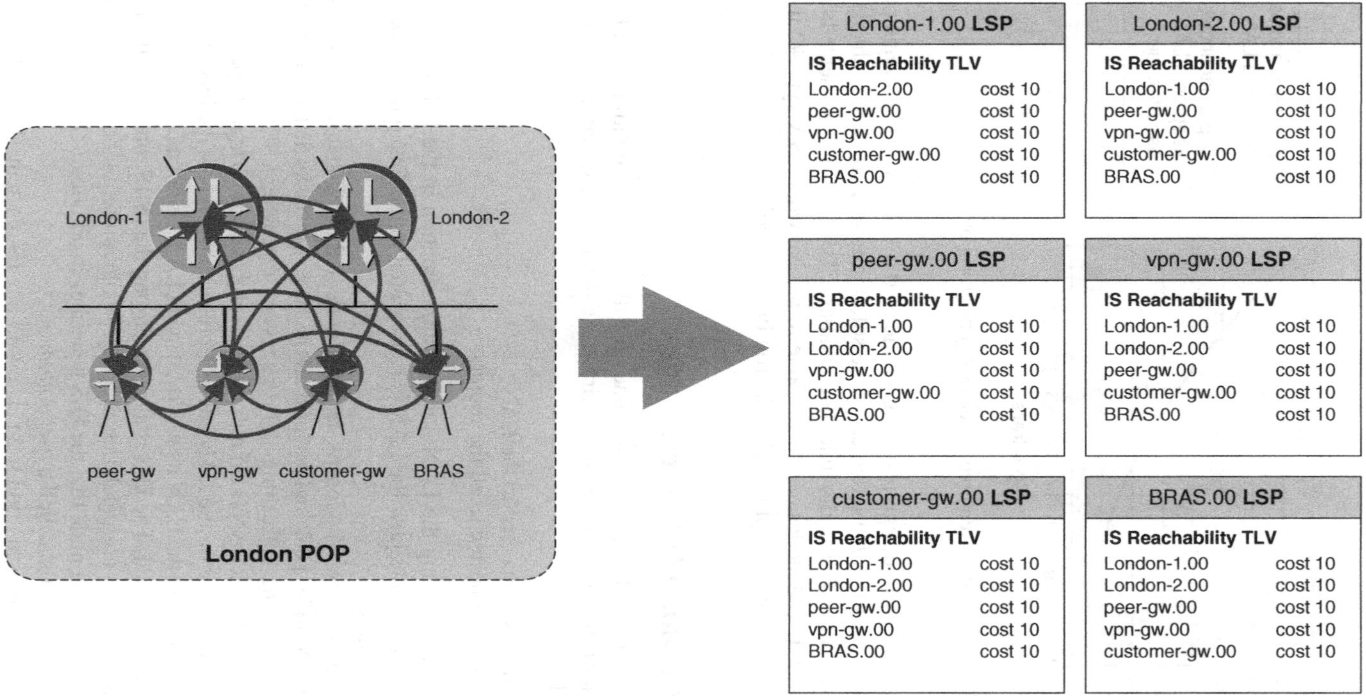

FIGURE 7.4. Five routers on the LAN require $O(N^2)$ storage space to accommodate all adjacencies

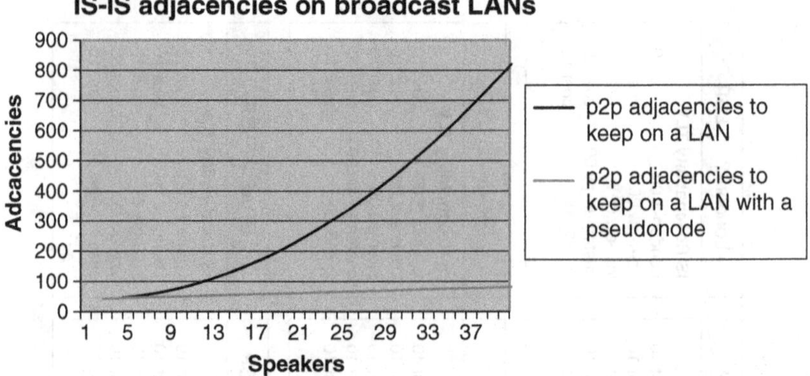

FIGURE 7.5. The number of required IS relationships grows by N^2

The IS-IS protocol design team was challenged *to turn this* N^2 *problem into a linear* problem in order to *scale* more nicely. The solution to this problem is changing the representation of the LAN in the link-state database. The LAN is represented by so-called *pseudonodes*. Pseudonodes are comparable to the Network LSA Type #2 in OSPF and are a very common concept in link-state routing protocols.

7.2.2 *Pseudonode Representation*

The solution the IS-IS design team came up with is quite straightforward: the router-to-router relationship is modelled in the link-state database just like the real *physical* connection relationship:

- Each router is connected to the LAN
- The LAN is connected to all the routers

So the idea of giving the LAN a nodal representation in the link-state database was born. Figure 7.6 shows how the LAN is represented in the link-state database as a node similar to a router.

The question is now who inserts the LAN node in the link-state database? How can we make the LAN node speak and perform all the necessary tasks that a real IS-IS router has to do, like generating, refreshing and if necessary removing LSPs?

One thing is clear: a LAN is a dumb piece of wire and has no logic to perform said tasks. Therefore *some* router on the LAN has to represent the LAN in the link-state database. It is almost like *lending* the LAN its *voice*. On each LAN circuit a *Designated Intermediate System* (DIS) is elected. The DIS is a router among the IS-IS routers on the LAN, which has, additionally to its normal duties, the purpose of representing the LAN in the link-state database. Because the node that the DIS generates in addition to its very own node is not a *real* routing node it is called a *pseudonode*.

Changing the representation from an any-to-any IS-reach mesh to a star topology with the pseudonode in the middle, greatly reduces the amount of adjacencies that routers on

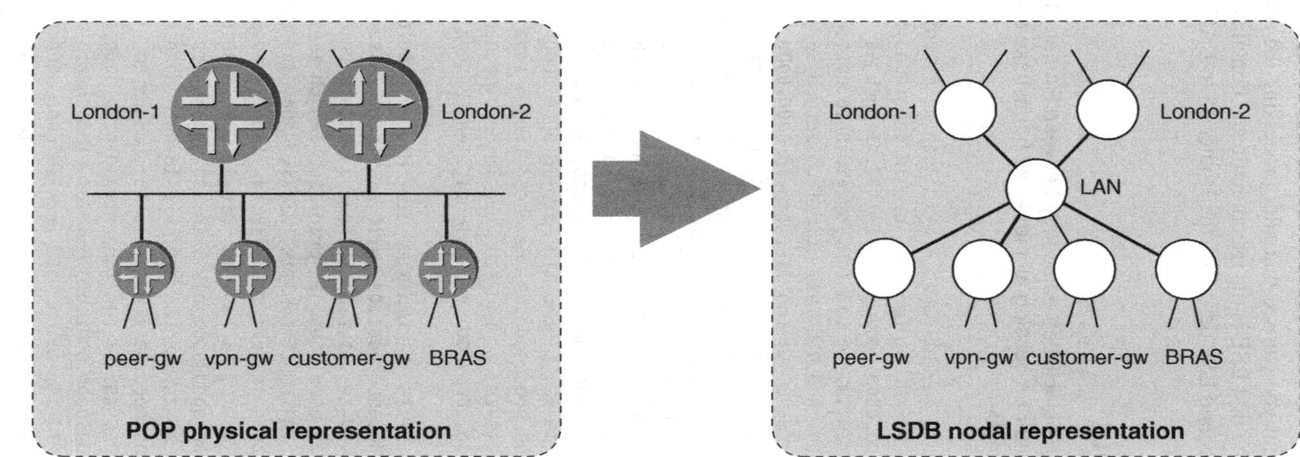

FIGURE 7.6. In the nodal representation of the link-state database the LAN becomes a node similar to a router

the LAN have to report. The original $O(N^2)$ scaling property turns into a $O(N)$ scaling behaviour. The LSP dynamics are improved as well. Once a new router comes online and declares the adjacency with the DIS up only *two* new LSPs will be generated.

In the tcpdump output you can see that after processing the adjacency only two new LSPs are generated. The first LSP is the pseudonode and contains the LAN to Router #3 IS Reachability. The second LSP describes the Router #3 to LAN Reachability.

Tcpdump output

On this LAN there is an established adjacency between Router #1 and #2. Next, Router #3 comes online and after processing all the 3-way handshake and padding procedures two new LSPs are generated.

```
17:37:45.769638 OSI, IS-IS, L1 CSNP, src-id 0000.0000.0001, length 99
17:37:45.799403 OSI, IS-IS, L1 Lan IIH, src-id 0000.0000.0001, lan-id
                    0000.0000.0001.02, prio 120, length 56
17:37:48.619494 OSI, IS-IS, L1 Lan IIH, src-id 0000.0000.0001, lan-id
                    0000.0000.0001.02, prio 120, length 56
17:37:50.204522 OSI, IS-IS, L1 Lan IIH, src-id 0000.0000.0002, lan-id
                    0000.0000.0001.02, prio 65, length 74
17:37:51.089607 OSI, IS-IS, L1 Lan IIH, src-id 0000.0000.0001, lan-id
                    0000.0000.0001.02, prio 120, length 56
17:37:51.273316 OSI, IS-IS, L1 Lan IIH, src-id 0000.0000.0003, lan-id
                    0000.0000.0003.02, prio 64, length 78
17:37:51.276579 OSI, IS-IS, L1 Lan IIH, src-id 0000.0000.0001, lan-id
                    0000.0000.0001.02, prio 120, length 1492
17:37:51.278286 OSI, IS-IS, L1 Lan IIH, src-id 0000.0000.0002, lan-id
                    0000.0000.0001.02, prio 65, length 1492
17:37:51.282142 OSI, IS-IS, L1 Lan IIH, src-id 0000.0000.0003, lan-id
                    0000.0000.0003.02, prio 64, length 1492
[ … ]
17:37:51.364655 OSI, IS-IS, L1 Lan IIH, src-id 0000.0000.0002, lan-id
                    0000.0000.0001.02, prio 65, length 1492
17:37:51.365221 OSI, IS-IS, L1 Lan IIH, src-id 0000.0000.0001, lan-id
                    0000.0000.0001.02, prio 120, length 1492
17:37:51.367212 OSI, IS-IS, L1 Lan IIH, src-id 0000.0000.0003, lan-id
                    0000.0000.0001.02, prio 64, length 1492
17:37:51.370734 OSI, IS-IS, L1 Lan IIH, src-id 0000.0000.0001, lan-id
                    0000.0000.0001.02, prio 120, length 62
17:37:51.374205 OSI, IS-IS, L1 Lan IIH, src-id 0000.0000.0002, lan-id
                    0000.0000.0001.02, prio 65, length 80
17:37:51.374484 OSI, IS-IS, L1 Lan IIH, src-id 0000.0000.0003, lan-id
                    0000.0000.0001.02, prio 64, length 92
17:37:51.376143 OSI, IS-IS, L1 Lan IIH, src-id 0000.0000.0001, lan-id
                    0000.0000.0001.02, prio 120, length 62
17:37:51.379266 OSI, IS-IS, L1 Lan IIH, src-id 0000.0000.0002, lan-id
                    0000.0000.0001.02, prio 65, length 80
```

```
17:37:51.390010 OSI, IS-IS, L1 LSP, lsp-id 0000.0000.0001.02-00,
                    seq 0x00000065, lifetime 65533s, length 62
17:37:51.455648 OSI, IS-IS, L1 LSP, lsp-id 0000.0000.0003.00-00,
                    seq 0x0000000c, lifetime 65533s, length 205
17:37:53.789837 OSI, IS-IS, L1 CSNP, src-id 0000.0000.0001, length 99
```

Using pseudonodes a single adjacency change triggers only two new LSPs which greatly reduces LSP churn. Also the original N^2 problem has been reduced to a linear problem. In the next section you will learn how the DIS allocates a unique Node-ID in order to represent the LAN in the link-state database.

7.2.3 *Pseudonode ID Selection*

Based upon Figure 7.4 we will explore how the pseudonode gets its Node-ID. Figure 7.4 shows a small LAN in the POP which connects six routers: two core facing routers (London-1 and London-2) and four customer facing access routers. Assume the London-1 core router is already the elected DIS. We will shortly explore how the DIS is elected: assume for now that London-1 is the DIS.

Each of the six routers gets its 6-byte System-ID from the NET that was configured on all the six routers. Figure 7.7 shows the structure of a link-state PDU ID (LSP-ID). Each LSP in the network carries an LSP-ID in its packet header. The first 6 bytes are set to the System-ID of the originating node. The last byte is used for Fragmentation. Fragmentation and the notion of the Fragment-ID will be explained in Chapter 9 "Fragmentation". The seventh byte is called the Pseudonode-ID and it is used for Pseudonode incarnations of the originating system. The first seven bytes is often referred to as the Node-ID.

The Pseudonode-ID number 0 has a special meaning. A zero indicates that this is the *real* instance of the router. A non-zero value represents a pseudonode. Figure 7.8 shows the nodal representation of the POP routers in the link-state database. Each square box represents an LSP. In the header you can see the Node-ID of the originating router in *two* representations. The upper line show the more *convenient* representation where the 6-byte System-ID gets replaced with a name. The lower line of the header also shows the Node-ID in digit representation. The System-ID name translation service will not be discussed further because it is described in Chapter 13 "IS-IS Extensions".

Note that all routing nodes have their pseudonode byte (7th) set to zero. Except the London-1 (1921.6804.4001.02) Node-ID carries a non-zero pseudonode byte. This

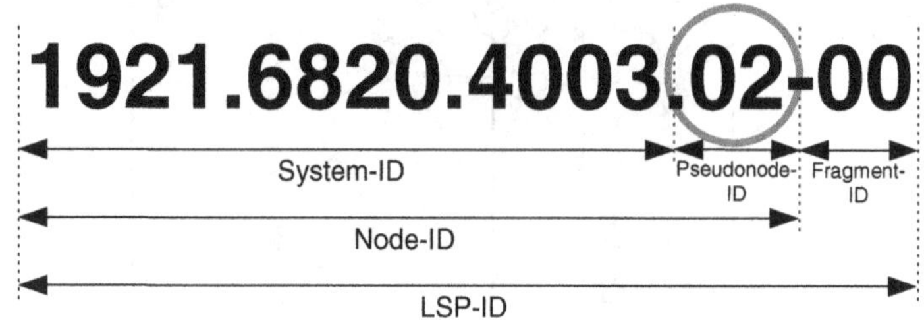

FIGURE 7.7. The LSP-ID dedicates one byte for pseudonode incarnations

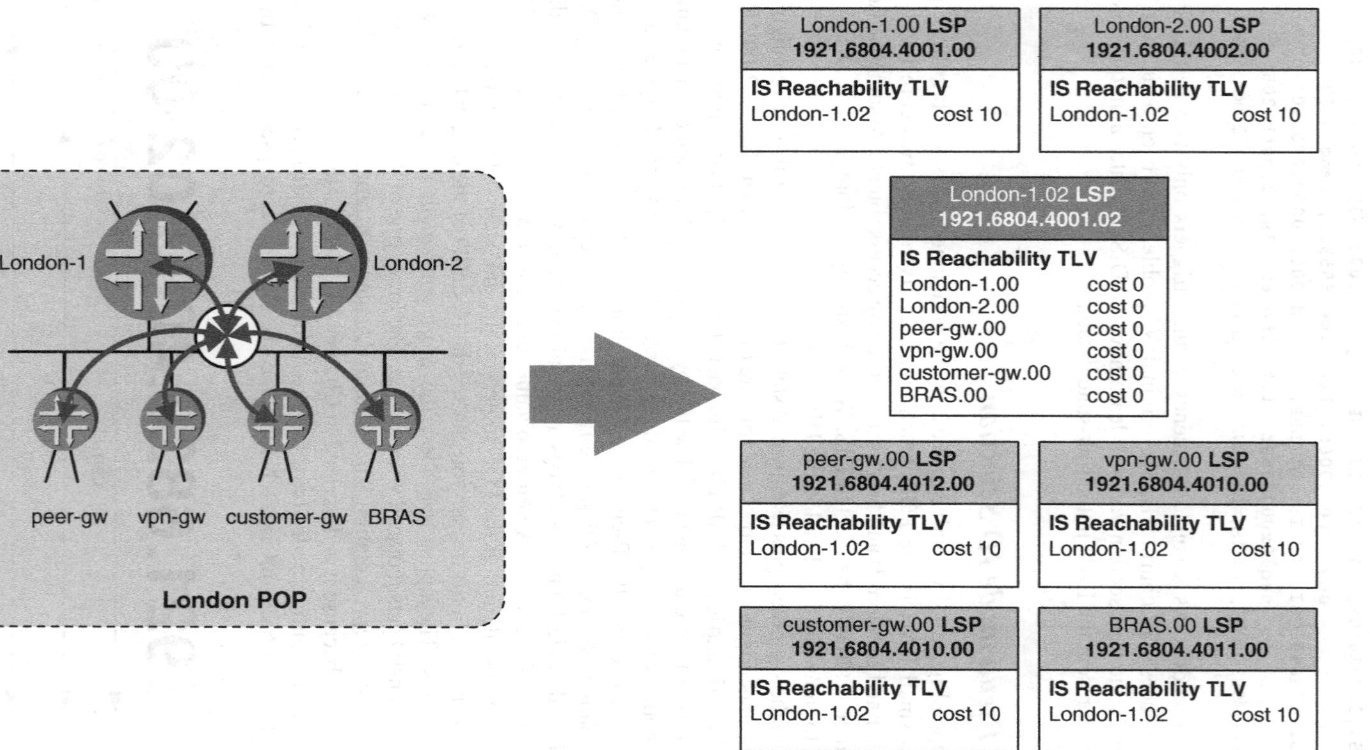
London-1
London-2
peer-gw
vpn-gw
customer-gw
BRAS
London POP
London-1.00 LSP
1921.6804.4001.00
IS Reachability TLV
London-1.02 cost 10
London-2.00 LSP
1921.6804.4002.00
IS Reachability TLV
London-1.02 cost 10
London-1.02 LSP
1921.6804.4001.02
IS Reachability TLV
London-1.00 cost 0
London-2.00 cost 0
peer-gw.00 cost 0
vpn-gw.00 cost 0
customer-gw.00 cost 0
BRAS.00 cost 0
peer-gw.00 LSP
1921.6804.4012.00
IS Reachability TLV
London-1.02 cost 10
vpn-gw.00 LSP
1921.6804.4010.00
IS Reachability TLV
London-1.02 cost 10
customer-gw.00 LSP
1921.6804.4010.00
IS Reachability TLV
London-1.02 cost 10
BRAS.00 LSP
1921.6804.4011.00
IS Reachability TLV
London-1.02 cost 10

FIGURE 7.8. The pseudonode *borrows* the System-ID from the DIS

Node-ID represents the pseudonode for the LAN. The pseudonode borrows the System-ID from the DIS on that LAN. London-1 is the DIS in our example and therefore the Pseudonode-ID is composed using the DIS System-ID plus an extra byte that makes it distinguishable from the DIS itself. There is no problem if several LSPs with the same System-ID are floating around as long the pseudonode byte makes the incarnation (DIS non DIS) clear.

The 8-bit wide Pseudonode field supports theoretically 255 pseudonodes. For most IS-IS implementations this is also the upper boundary of supported broad circuits. Most IS-IS implementations do allocate a Pseudonode-ID per broadcast circuit. Arguably the system would only need to allocate a unique Pseudonode-ID once it becomes the DIS on a LAN – however, there is yet no clear procedure how the system should behave when it runs out of Pseudonode-IDs. The most likely behaviour would be to set the LAN priority to 0 thereby indicating that the system does not wish to participate in the DIS election.

7.2.4 *Link-state Database Modelling*

Each adjacency on a LAN has a certain *cost*. Once a DIS generates pseudonodes it must make sure that the overall cost of the path through the LAN is not fudged. IS-IS does this by assigning asymmetrical cost to the pseudonode. Asymmetrical cost means that the cost from a router to reach the pseudonode is different than the cost from the pseudonode to reach a router. Figure 7.9 shows, for example, how a LAN cost of 10 is represented in the link-state database. Note that the cost to reach the pseudonode is the local configured IS-IS metric. In Figure 7.9 all IS-IS metrics are set to 10. The reverse direction from the pseudonode to the router has always a cost of zero. For real nodes an adjacency cost of 0

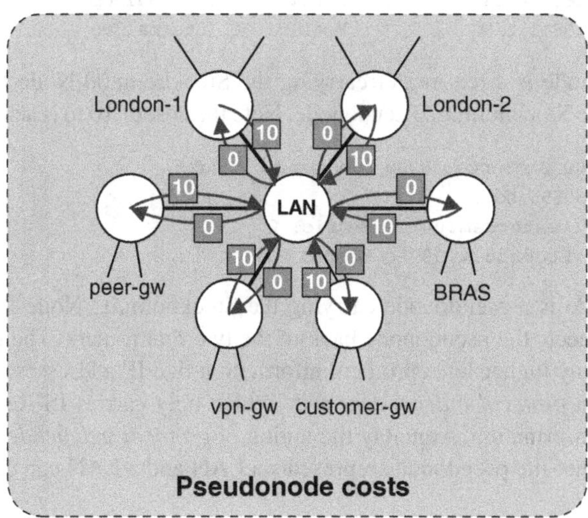

FIGURE 7.9. The cost to reach the pseudonode equals the link cost – the cost from the pseudonode to the real node is always zero

is an illegal value, accept for pseudonodes. You will see later in Chapter 10 "SPF and Route Calculation" that the pseudonode needs a special treatment during the SPF calculation because of those zero cost adjacencies.

The cost of adjacencies can be checked on the router's command line interface. You can check the cost between the Nodes using the `show isis database detail` command:

JUNOS command output

The JUNOS `show isis database detail` command displays how the routers are linked to the pseudonodes. The IOS command `show isis database detail` provides a similar output.

```
hannes@Stockholm> show isis database detail
IS-IS level 1 link-state database:

Amsterdam.00-00 Sequence: 0x187, Checksum: 0xbda7,
    Lifetime: 59556 secs
IS neighbor: Stockholm.02          Metric: 10
IP prefix: 172.16.1.0/24           Metric:  0 Internal Up
IP prefix: 192.168.1.1/32          Metric:  0 Internal Up
```

The first node is a real router carrying the Amsterdam.00 Node-ID. The router is linked to a Pseudonode Stockholm.02. Note the cost of 10 to reach the pseudonode.

```
Stockholm.00-00 Sequence: 0x2e, Checksum: 0x7157,
    Lifetime: 59554 secs
IS neighbor: Stockholm.02           Metric: 10
IP prefix: 172.16.0.4/24            Metric:  0 Internal Up
IP prefix: 192.168.1.2/32           Metric:  0 Internal Up
```

The second node is a real router carrying the Stockholm.00 Node-ID. The router is also linked to the Stockholm.02 Pseudonode. Note the cost of 10 to reach the pseudonode.

```
Stockholm.02-00 Sequence: 0x69, Checksum: 0x2d26,
    Lifetime: 59556 secs
  IS neighbor: Amsterdam.00      Metric: 0
  IS neighbor: Stockholm.00      Metric: 0
```

The third node is a pseudonode carrying the Stockholm.02 Node-ID. Note the zero cost which connects the pseudonode back to the two real routers. The pseudonode also does *not* carry any higher-level protocol information like IP addresses. The pseudonode can be seen as a *protocol independent* node which only carries IS-Reach and optional authentication information. Arguably the notion of *protocol independence* matches also the physical setup: the pseudonode represents a LAN and a LAN can carry *any* Layer-3 protocol.

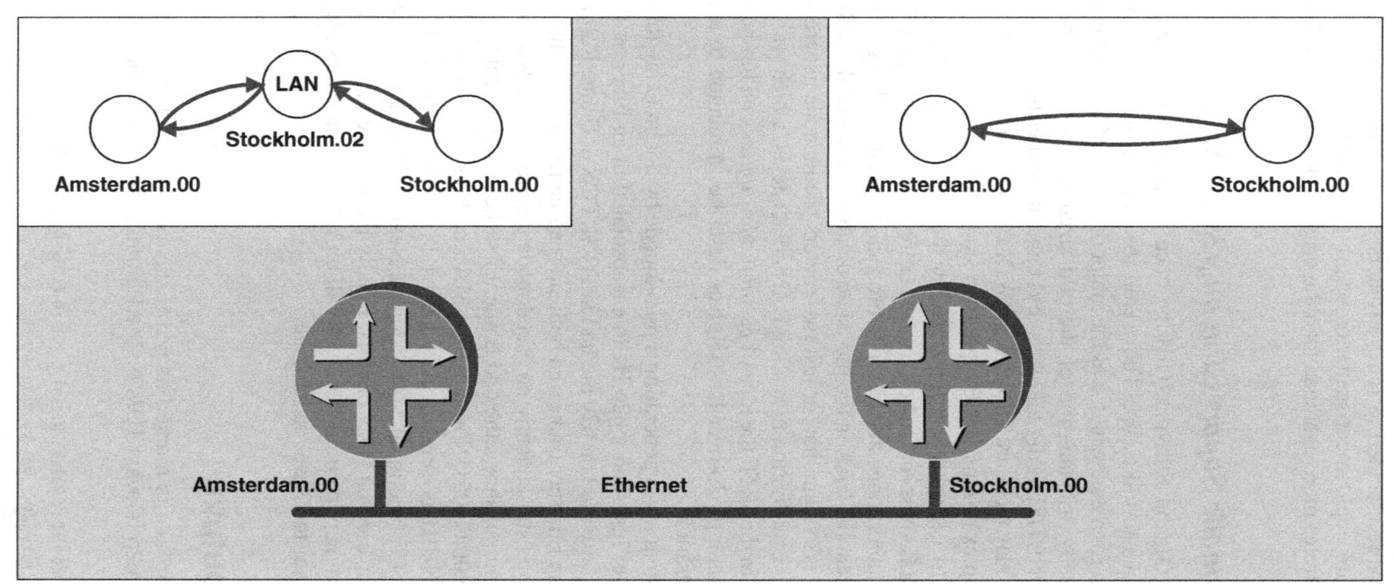

FIGURE 7.10. Two routers connected by an Ethernet link can be represented in two ways in the IS-IS link stake database

Pseudonodes were intended to relieve routers from additional processing overhead. However, there are deployment scenarios where the generation and maintenance of a pseudonode generates more overhead than the original point-to-point behaviour.

7.2.5 *Pseudonode Suppression on p2p LANs*

With the rise of Gigabit Ethernet (GE) the once for-access-only media has become a cheap and fast router-to-router pipe. The overall cost of transmission for a Gigabit Ethernet pipe is lower than for a pipe which was the major driver that GE is being deployed in p2p fashion. Historically, transmission of the odd sized (in the sense that it does not fit exactly in the SONET/SDH digital hierarchy) Gigabit Frames turned out to be an expensive operation. Today there are affordable DWDM systems available that allow a service provider to multiplex dozens of GE pipes on a single fibre.

The mandate to generate a pseudonode on the LAN circuit even if there are just two speakers on a LAN seems to be a useless exercise. Consider Figure 7.10 which illustrates how two routers connected by a p2p broadcast circuit need to generate a third node in order to represent the LAN in the link-state database. The nodal graph is shown in the top left corner. It is evident that for just two routers pseudonode generation is more than a overhead than a contribution to scaling LAN adjacencies, which was the original goal of pseudonodes. In the IETF the idea of *pseudonode suppression* has been born. Internet draft draft-ietf-isis-igp-p2p-over-lan-03 gives describes a method to avoid sending the pseudonode generation.

How can a system avoid generating a pseudonode by not breaking things? The idea of the draft is simple: Just send a p2p Hello encapsulated in an Ethernet frame. Recall the p2p PDU type is only used on p2p media like ATM, POS or Frame Relay. If a p2p-IIH is encapsulated in an Ethernet frame and both sides agree to suppress the pseudonode then no DIS election and subsequently no pseudonode generation needs to be executed.

The tcpdump output shows the odd frame. First the frame is sent to the MAC address All-IS (09.00:2b:00:00:05). Normally this MAC address is never used as the L1-LAN-IIH and L2-LAN-IIH is sent to the ALL-L1-IS (01:80:C2:00:00:14) and All-L2-IS (01:80:C2:00:00:15) functional MAC address. Next the PDU type is the p2p IIH which is otherwise never used on LAN circuits. Finally there is the p2p Adjacency State TLV which is also sent on p2p circuits only. Recall on LAN media the IS Neighbour TLV #6 is typically used for the 3-way handshake.

Tcpdump output

If an `isis interface` is marked as `point-to-point` then the router will pack a p2p Hello containing p2p relevant TLVs on the Ethernet frame and ship it to the All-IS LAN multicast Address.

```
23:41:19.490748 00:90:69:b2:58:2d > 09:00:2b:00:00:05, OSI, IS-IS, length: 58
    p2p IIH, hlen: 20, v: 1, pdu-v: 1, sys-id-len: 6 (0), max-area: 3 (0)
    source-id: 0000.0000.0002, holding time: 27s, Flags: [Level 1, Level 2]
    circuit-id: 0x01, PDU length: 58
```

```
    Point-to-point Adjacency State TLV #240, length: 15
      Adjacency State: Up (0)
      Extended Local circuit-ID: 0x00000041
      Neighbor System-ID: 0000.0000.0003
      Neighbor Extended Local circuit-ID: 0x0000005e
      Protocols supported TLV #129, length: 2
      NLPID(s): IPv4 (0xcc), IPv6 (0x8e)
    IPv4 Interface address(es) TLV #132, length: 4
      IPv4 interface address: 172.16.0.5
    Area address(es) TLV #1, length: 4
      Area address (length: 3): 49.0001
    Restart Signaling TLV #211, length: 3
      Flags [none], Remaining holding time 0s
```

Both IOS and JUNOS support pseudonode suppression. In JUNOS you need to configure the `point-to-point` keyword inside the `protocol isis interface` { } stanza.

JUNOS configuration

In JUNOS pseudonode suppression is activated by adding the `point-to-point` keyword inside the `protocols isis interface` {} stanza.

```
hannes@Stockholm> show configuration
[ … ]
protocols {
  isis {
    [ … ]
    interface ge-2/2/0.0 {
      point-to-point;
    }
    interface lo0.0;
  }
}
```

You can verify if the circuit was assigned to be a p2p media using the `show isis interface` command.

JUNOS command output

Once a broadcast circuit is configured for pseudonode suppression the `Point to Point` flag is listed instead of the DIS.

```
hannes@Stockholm> show isis interface
IS-IS interface database:
Interface      L CirID Level 1 DR           Level 2 DR          L1/L2 Metric
[ … ]
ge-2/2/0.0     3 0x1 Point to Point         Point to Point      10000/10000
lo0.0          0 0x1 Passive                Passive 0/0
```

The IOS configuration is similar to JUNOS. Pseudonode suppression is once again an interface property and can be configured using the `isis network point-to-point` configuration statement.

IOS configuration

The IOS configuration requires the `isis network point-to-point` statement to suppress pseudonodes.

```
Amsterdam# show running-config
[ … ]
!
interface GigabitEthernet0/0
  ip address 172.16.26.170 255.255.255.0
  ip router isis
  [ … ]
  isis network point-to-point
!
```

Unfortunately there is no explicit hint in IOS to display if the interface is actually running in p2p mode. The only difference to a regular broadcast interface is that the `DR ID` line is missing in the output.

IOS command output

On a point-to-point network configuration the output of the `show clns interface` command does omit the DR IDs.

```
Amsterdam#show clns interface GigabitEthernet0/0
GigabitEthernet0/0 is up, line protocol is up
  Checksums enabled, MTU 1497, Encapsulation SAP
  ERPDUs enabled, min. interval 10 msec.
  CLNS fast switching disabled
  CLNS SSE switching disabled
  DEC compatibility mode OFF for this interface
  Next ESH/ISH in 30 seconds
  Routing Protocol: IS-IS
    Circuit Type: level-1-2
    Interface number 0x6, local circuit ID 0x2
    Neighbor System-ID: Stockholm
    Level-1 Metric: 10, Priority: 64, Circuit ID: Amsterdam.02
    Number of active level-1 adjacencies: 1
    Neighbor System-ID: Stockholm
    Level-2 Metric: 10, Priority: 64, Circuit ID: Amsterdam.02
    Number of active level-2 adjacencies: 1
    Next IS-IS LAN Level-1 Hello in 2 seconds
    Next IS-IS LAN Level-2 Hello in 1 seconds
```

Another possibility is actually looking at the link-state database if one of the two routers on the LAN generates a pseudonode.

IOS command output

The database output shows that there is no pseudonode generated by either the Stockholm or Amsterdam router in the database. Additional evidence is that the two routers did link their adjacencies directly (targeting the .00 incarnation) to each other.

```
Amsterdam#show isis database detail
IS-IS Level-1 Link State Database
LSPID               LSP Seq Num     LSP Checksum    LSP Holdtime    ATT/P/OL
Amsterdam.00-00     * 0x0000019A    0xF613          818             0/0/0
  Area Address: 49.0001
  NLPID: 0xCC
  Router ID: 192.168.1.17
  IP Address: 192.168.1.17
  Hostname: Amsterdam
  Metric: 10          IS-Extended Stockholm.00
  Metric: 10          IP 172.16.1.0/24
  Metric: 0           IP 192.168.1.17/32
Stockholm.00-00       0x0000c1E9          0xE448        414       0/0/0
  Area Address: 49.0001
  NLPID: 0xCC
  Hostname: Stockholm
  Router ID: 192.168.1.8
  IP Address: 192.168.1.8
  Metric: 10          IS-Extended Amsterdam.00
  Metric: 10          IP 172.16.1.0/24
  Metric: 0           IP 192.168.1.8/32
```

The output reveals that no pseudonode is in the database and two routers are linked directly to each other as shown in the top right corner of Figure 7.10.

If we allow pseudonode generation then we have silently assumed so far that there is a DIS on the LAN that generates the pseudonode on behalf of the LAN. Before that happens a DIS needs to get elected. The following paragraph describes DIS election procedures and timing.

7.3 DIS and DIS Election Procedure

The good news is that the DIS election procedure is a very simple process. Due to its stateless nature a receiving router can immediately determine the DIS on the LAN. For DIS elections there are two fields in the LAN IIH header (see Figure 5.2) that are relevant:

- Priority field in the LAN-IIH
- The Source SNPA (=MAC address) of the sender

The Priority field is 7-bits wide and therefore Priority values between 0 and 127 can be configured. A Priority value of zero means that this system does not wish to become a DIS at all. In case there are many routers with the same Priority competing for the DIS then the Source SNPA (= the MAC address) tie breaks. The system with the numerically highest source MAC address then wins the beauty contest.

Each router computes the DIS locally after receipt of IIH messages by comparing it against its current DIS Priority and SNPA. For debugging purposes there is also a field in the LAN-IIH where each router on a LAN writes its current DIS *belief.*

7.3.1 *Pre-emption*

The DIS is pre-emptive. That means, if a router with a higher Priority comes online it immediately resigns from DIS ownership. To document that it has resigned it puts the winning router's Node-ID in its LAN-ID field. The following tcpdump output shows an example of how a router changes its LAN Priority and commences DIS ownership.

Tcpdump output

```
21:51:17.716553 OSI, IS-IS, L1 Lan IIH, src-id 0000.0000.0002, lan-id
                   0000.0000.0002.02, prio 65, length 74
21:51:19.813231 OSI, IS-IS, L1 Lan IIH, src-id 0000.0000.0001, lan-id
                   0000.0000.0002.02, prio 64, length 56
21:51:20.583435 OSI, IS-IS, L1 Lan IIH, src-id 0000.0000.0002, lan-id
                   0000.0000.0002.02, prio 65, length 74
21:51:22.557163 OSI, IS-IS, L1 CSNP, src-id 0000.0000.0002, length 83
21:51:23.516664 OSI, IS-IS, L1 Lan IIH, src-id 0000.0000.0002, lan-id
                   0000.0000.0002.02, prio 65, length 74
21:51:24.193870 OSI, IS-IS, L1 Lan IIH, src-id 0000.0000.0001, lan-id
                   0000.0000.0001.02, prio 120, length 56
```

Router #1 changes the LAN priority from 64 to 120, and becomes the highest Priority router on the LAN

```
21:51:24.196787 OSI, IS-IS, L1 Lan IIH, src-id 0000.0000.0002, lan-id
                   0000.0000.0001.02, prio 65, length 74
21:51:24.197468 OSI, IS-IS, L1 LSP, lsp-id 0000.0000.0002.02-00, seq
                   0x00000017, lifetime 0s, length 43
```

Router #2 resigns and purges the old pseudonode

```
21:51:24.220793 OSI, IS-IS, L1 LSP, lsp-id 0000.0000.0002.00-00, seq
                   0x0000001b, lifetime 1199s, length 158
21:51:24.444682 OSI, IS-IS, L1 LSP, lsp-id 0000.0000.0001.00-00, seq
                   0x00000120, lifetime 1198s, length 210
21:51:24.473860 OSI, IS-IS, L1 LSP, lsp-id 0000.0000.0001.02-00, seq
                   0x00000004, lifetime 1198s, length 76
```

Router #1 & #2 re-link their LSPs to the new pseudonode

```
21:51:24.484541 OSI, IS-IS, L1 Lan IIH, src-id 0000.0000.0001, lan-id
                   0000.0000.0001.02, prio 120, length 56
21:51:26.773307 OSI, IS-IS, L1 Lan IIH, src-id 0000.0000.0001, lan-id
                   0000.0000.0001.02, prio 120, length 56
```

```
21:51:29.373384 OSI, IS-IS, L1 Lan IIH, src-id 0000.0000.0001, lan-id
                  0000.0000.0001.02, prio 120, length 56
21:51:30.963776 OSI, IS-IS, L1 Lan IIH, src-id 0000.0000.0002, lan-id
                  0000.0000.0001.02, prio 65, length 74
21:51:31.773442 OSI, IS-IS, L1 Lan IIH, src-id 0000.0000.0001, lan-id
                  0000.0000.0001.02, prio 120, length 56
21:51:32.893696 OSI, IS-IS, L1 CSNP, src-id 0000.0000.0001, length 83
```

The new DIS (Router #1) sends a full CSNP report

7.3.2 *Purging*

After Router #2 resigns from ownership it purges its pseudonode. Purging means removing from the database. A new DIS has been elected and therefore the DIS wants to clean up its remnants.

A purged LSP contains nothing but the LSP header (and optionally authentication information if configured). Both the Lifetime and Checksum fields are set to zero. Both are illegal values. The Fletcher Checksumming Algorithm and the Lifetime can never become zero for a regular LSP packet.

Tcpdump output

A purged pseudonode LSP contains nothing but the LSP header and the Checksum and Lifetime fields are set to zero.

```
01:34:01.544481 OSI, IS-IS, length: 43
   L1 LSP, hlen: 27, v: 1, pdu-v: 1, sys-id-len: 6 (0), max-area: 3 (0)
    lsp-id: 0000.0000.0002.02-00, seq: 0x00000001, lifetime: 0s
    chksum: 0x0000 (purged), PDU length: 27, L1L2 IS
```

Purging is described in more detail in Chapter 6 "Generating, Flooding and Ageing LSPs".

The DIS ID can be easily spotted on JUNOS routers using the `show isis interface detail` command.

JUNOS command output

The last column of the `show isis interface detail` output lists the designated routers for each level on that LAN circuit.

```
hannes@Stockholm> show isis interface detail
IS-IS interface database:
ge-2/2/0.0
  Index: 64, State: 0x6, Circuit id: 0x2, Circuit type: 3
  LSP interval: 100 ms, CSNP interval: 10 s
```

```
 Level Adjacencies Priority Metric Hello (s) Hold (s) Designated Router
     1  2    120    10    3.000     9  Stockholm.02 (us)
     2  2     64    10    9.000    27  Amsterdam.02 (not us)
[ … ]
```

On IOS the DIS is revealed using the `show clns interface` command.

IOS command output

If the interface is not configured in p2p mode then for each active broadcast circuit a DIS is listed in the `DR ID` line.

```
Amsterdam#show clns interface GigabitEthernet0/0
GigabitEthernet0/0 is up, line protocol is up
  Checksums enabled, MTU 1497, Encapsulation SAP
  ERPDUs enabled, min. interval 10 msec.
  CLNS fast switching disabled
  CLNS SSE switching disabled
  DEC compatibility mode OFF for this interface
  Next ESH/ISH in 30 seconds
  Routing Protocol: IS-IS
    Circuit Type: level-1-2
    Interface number 0x6, local circuit ID 0x2
    Neighbor System-ID: Stockholm
    Level-1 Metric: 10, Priority: 64, Circuit ID: Amsterdam.02
    DR ID: Stockholm.02
    Number of active level-1 adjacencies: 1
    Neighbor System-ID: Stockholm
    Level-2 Metric: 10, Priority: 64, Circuit ID: Amsterdam.02
    DR ID: Amsterdam.02
    Number of active level-2 adjacencies: 1
    Next IS-IS LAN Level-1 Hello in 2 seconds
    Next IS-IS LAN Level-2 Hello in 1 seconds
```

Unlike OSPF there is just one DIS per LAN. This is often perceived as a disadvantage. However, the IS-IS protocol allows some clever trickery to become at the end more resilient than a OSPF Designated Router (DR) / Backup Designated Router (BDR) pair.

7.3.3 *DIS Redundancy*

In IS-IS there is no DIS redundancy. If the Adjacency to the DIS times out then a new DIS needs to be elected. The re-election can be done immediately as zero state is involved. So the upper bound is detection that the DIS went down. A JUNOS router does a nice trick once it becomes the DIS: it reduces its hold time by a factor of three. The default Hold timer in JUNOS is 27 s. Once the router commences as DIS the hold-time becomes 9 s.

Because of the hard-coded Hello-Multiplier of 3 the Hellos are scheduled at 3-second intervals. There is no similar function in the IOS Implementation of IS-IS.

Tcpdump output

The DIS (0000.0000.0001.02) sends its Hellos three times as fast as the other router.

```
02:40:10.009492 OSI, IS-IS, L1 Lan IIH, src-id 0000.0000.0001,
                  lan-id 0000.0000.0001.02, prio 120, length 62
02:40:12.879672 OSI, IS-IS, L1 Lan IIH, src-id 0000.0000.0001,
                  lan-id 0000.0000.0001.02, prio 120, length 62
02:40:15.509631 OSI, IS-IS, L1 Lan IIH, src-id 0000.0000.0001,
                  lan-id 0000.0000.0001.02, prio 120, length 62
02:40:16.227864 OSI, IS-IS, L1 Lan IIH, src-id 0000.0000.0002,
                  lan-id 0000.0000.0001.02, prio 65, length 80
02:40:17.789689 OSI, IS-IS, L1 Lan IIH, src-id 0000.0000.0001,
                  lan-id 0000.0000.0001.02, prio 120, length 62
02:40:20.239755 OSI, IS-IS, L1 Lan IIH, src-id 0000.0000.0001,
                  lan-id 0000.0000.0001.02, prio 120, length 62
02:40:22.619829 OSI, IS-IS, L1 Lan IIH, src-id 0000.0000.0001,
                  lan-id 0000.0000.0001.02, prio 120, length 62
02:40:23.847965 OSI, IS-IS, L1 Lan IIH, src-id 0000.0000.0002,
                  lan-id 0000.0000.0001.02, prio 65, length 80
02:40:24.889888 OSI, IS-IS, L1 Lan IIH, src-id 0000.0000.0001,
                  lan-id 0000.0000.0001.02, prio 120, length 62
02:40:27.429931 OSI, IS-IS, L1 Lan IIH, src-id 0000.0000.0001,
                  lan-id 0000.0000.0001.02, prio 120, length 62
02:40:29.690077 OSI, IS-IS, L1 Lan IIH, src-id 0000.0000.0001,
                  lan-id 0000.0000.0001.02, prio 120, length 62
02:40:31.828099 OSI, IS-IS, L1 Lan IIH, src-id 0000.0000.0002,
                  lan-id 0000.0000.0001.02, prio 65, length 80
```

The DIS is tuning *itself* to provide faster resiliency. With 9 seconds of detecting that the DIS is broken and no state for the re-election IS-IS is far more superior than OSPF even without a Backup Designated Router. The DIS convergence is only dependend of the dead interval (hold-timer) of the old DIS. Unlike IS-IS, OSPF cannot set its dead-interval to an arbitrary value because all those values need to match on a given LAN. Arguably one could tune down all the OSPF Hello and Dead timers but that would increase the stress on the LAN by a factor of three to get comparable results.

7.4 Summary

Broadcast interfaces like Ethernet are becoming increasingly popular as router-to-router link technology. Both multipoint and point-to-point setups have unique requirements to the IS-IS protocol. In a multipoint environment careful Hello scheduling and applying of jitter needs to be performed to avoid peak-stress through self-synchronization. Because of storage requirements and LSP churn avoidance the LAN needs to get nodal representation as a pseudonode. The pseudonode is deterministically elected and generates the pseudonode on behalf the LAN circuit which cannot speak for itself.

In multipoint setups the pseudonode functionality generates more overhead than gain and is often required to be turned off. A recent Internet draft describes how to build point-to-point adjacency on a 2-party LAN circuit without pseudonode generation.

8

Synchronizing Databases

Link-state protocols rely fundamentally on the fact that each router in a given area has the same view of the topology. Sharing the same view is the foundation for computing *converged* routes. Convergence means that each router computes routes in a way that moves packets one hop closer to the destination. If routes are not convergent, packets can take extra hops in the network to reach the final destination. The worst case for misaligned routes is a *forwarding loop* where packets are bounced back and forth between a pair of routers. In a changing network it is therefore paramount to get to a *synchronized* view of the topology as quickly as possible. New routers connected to the network need to query their neighbour's link-state databases to get on the same page as quickly as possible. This chapter discusses the IS-IS mechanisms to initially synchronize link-state databases between routers and periodically update the databases.

This chapter starts with a detailed discussion of the consequences of link-state database misalignments. It continues with a detailed explanation of database synchronization on point-to-point and broadcast links. Finally, refinements to ISO 10589 for increasing the robustness of the link-state database synchronization process are presented.

8.1 Why Synchronize Link-state Databases?

Unlike distance vector or path vector protocols, such as RIP or BGP, which compute their routes *by travelling through the network*, link-state protocols make a local computation based on shared and identical topological information. To contrast this difference better, let's consider the following example: Figure 8.1 shows how RIP calculates the distance to a network. Router A is locally connected to the sub-net 192.168.1/24. The router is distributing its reachability information to the prefix 192.168.1/24 by sending a RIP update to all of its neighbours (Router B and Router C) with a metric of 1. Routers B and C distribute the information further to other neighbouring routers by incrementing the metric field by one. Routers D and E, which receive the update, install the prefix 192.168.1/24 with a metric of 2 in their routing and forwarding tables. Observe that the actual calculation of the metric happens in a distributed fashion: Routers D and E do not know where the prefix originated. All they know is that it is two routers away and that Routers B and C have received the prefix. So Routers D and E do not have any topological visibility with regard to the prefix. Each router modifies the original advertisement by incrementing the metric field.

Link-state protocols, like IS-IS, work differently. Each IS-IS router in a given routing domain has to generate its own view of the local network to its neighbours. Next, all these

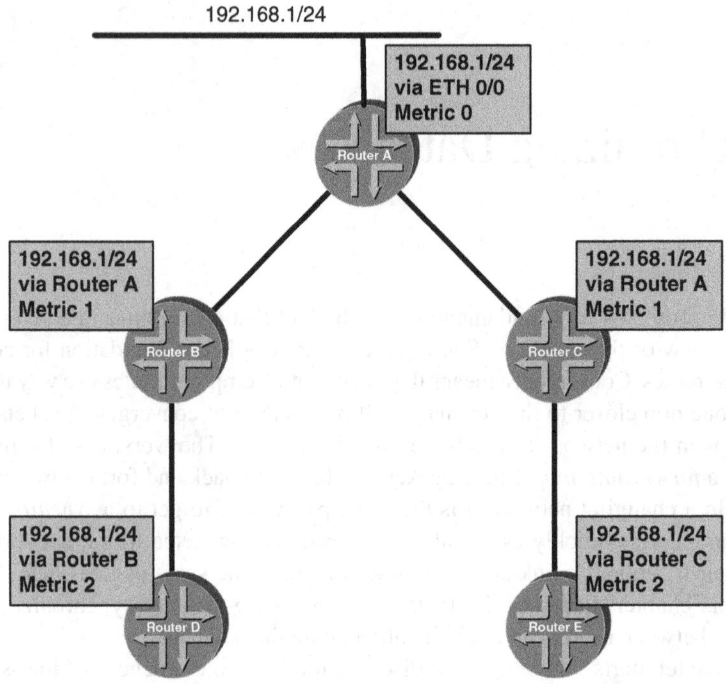

FIGURE 8.1. RIP sends out information about local networks plus remote networks by incrementing the metric field

individual, local views are passed on to the other routers. No router is allowed to change the original information. Ultimately, each router has the view of all other routers' neighbours. Based on *all* topological information that is available, the router can now independently construct a network topology graph and extract IP reachability information.

If the link-state databases are not synchronized, routers do not calculate routes that bring packets to their ultimate destination. Figure 8.2 shows the effect of desynchronized link-state databases.

The link between Washington and Frankfurt is broken. The Washington router knows immediately that the link is broken because it is directly connected and therefore senses a link loss in the following three ways:

- Missing IIHs
- Missing Layer-2 keep-alive packets
- Loss of carrier or loss of framing (on SONET/SDH circuits only)

In the first case, routers exchange IIHs to verify at the Network Layer that the exchange of control traffic works. The neighbour router is declared down after the *hold time* period. The hold time period is not a fixed value and may vary. An adjacent router will indicate the hold time period inside IIH packets.

The second indicator concerns the fact that routers periodically exchange Layer 2 (Data Link Layer) keep-alive messages to verify the integrity of the link. Virtually all

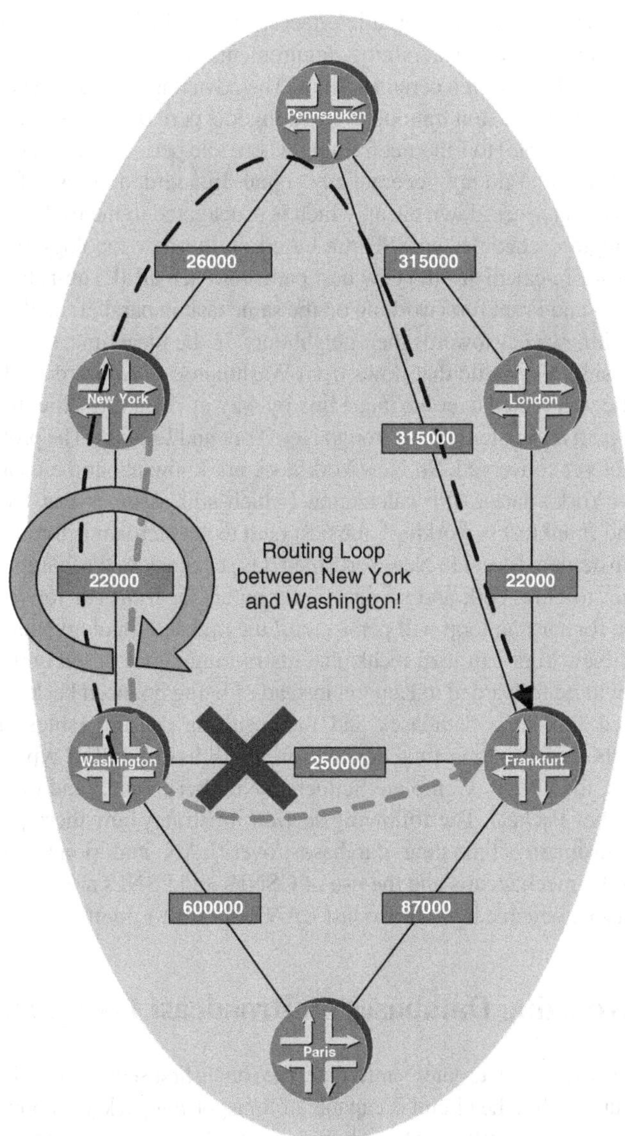

FIGURE 8.2. The link-state database of New York is not in sync, which causes a forwarding loop

(but Ethernet) OSI RM Layer 2 Protocols have embedded live-ness protocols that exchange keep-alive messages). If there is no response from the remote end for a certain amount of time (typically less than 30 seconds), then the link is declared down because of the inability to maintain a valid two-way connection. Loss of Layer 2 keep-alives triggers a so-called interface-down event that is propagated to the routing protocol stack.

Finally, modern routers often have optical interfaces. Here the carrier is the light. If you pull the optical fibre out of a router, then a loss-of-light (LOL) error is generated, which triggers an interface-down event. Serial interfaces, such as T1/E1, E3/T3, and Packet-over-SONET (POS) links, have strict framing requirements where even idle link data (no live packets) have to be framed in a certain format. The advantage is that a receiver can detect problems with the transmission framing even during idle periods without packet traffic. This is in contrast (for example) to Ethernet framing where idle periods (that is, where there is no transmission of packets) do not generate any signal. In addition, a loss-of-framing (LOF) error generates an interface-down event, which is propagated to the routing protocol stack.

Next, Washington schedules an SPF run based on the new topology information. The Washington router re-calculates the new best paths to reach all IP sub-nets in the network. Both Washington and Frankfurt (working on the same task in parallel) on the other side will disseminate their new *view* towards their neighbours. In the meantime, strange things begin to happen. Consider the traffic that flows from Washington to Amsterdam. Before the link break, the traffic was routed over the intact link by way of Frankfurt. After the SPF recalculation, the best path to Amsterdam is through New York and London. The problem is that the network has not yet converged. So New York does not know about the changed topology. Based on New York's latest SPF calculation (which still assumes that the link between Washington and Frankfurt is working), the best path to Amsterdam is through Washington. So traffic to Amsterdam is sent to New York, then it is sent back to Washington, then the traffic is sent again to New York and so on – a temporary or *transient* forwarding loop has formed and the forwarding loop will persist until the updated topology view has arrived at New York and New York can then recalculate its routing table. Based on the new routing table, packets will be forwarded to London instead of being bounced back to Washington.

Synchronized link-state databases and the resulting routing tables are crucial for bringing packets closer to their final destination. IS-IS has two PDU types for synchronizing databases: the CSNP (Complete Sequence Number Packet) and the PSNP (Partial Sequence Number Packet). The following section illustrates how these packet types are used for synchronizing link-state databases over LAN and point-to-point circuits. Unfortunately the mechanisms and the use of CSNPs and PSNPs are different depending on the media-type, which can be broadcast LAN or point-to-point.

8.2 Synchronizing Databases on Broadcast LAN Circuits

When IS-IS is activated on a router's interface, the router first sends some IIHs to its neighbours to find out whether the circuit is capable of transporting packets in both directions. In each of its IIHs the router embeds what it believes to be the *Designated Intermediate System* (DIS). In Figure 8.3 you can see the structure of a LAN IIH and the DIS field at the end.

The DIS has a special role on an IS-IS broadcast circuit. Besides the modelling of the LAN as a topology graph (as you saw in Chapter 7 "Pseudonodes and Designated Routers", the DIS has another function relevant to proper synchronization of link-state databases on LANs. Periodically (typically every 10 seconds), the DIS has to send a directory of its link-state database, which is received by all the routers on a LAN. Figure 8.4 shows the structure of a CSNP PDU.

The CSNP Interval is not a hard coded value and can be changed accordingly. Both IOS and JUNOS permit to set the `csnp-interval` to an arbitrary value between

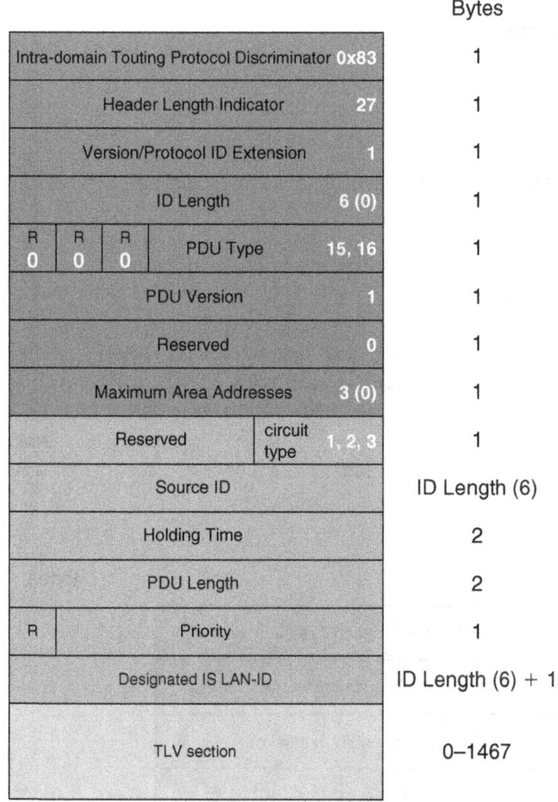

FIGURE 8.3. Each IS-IS router sends what it believes is the Designated Intermediate System at a given time

1–65535 seconds. Low values indicate a high load of generating and receiving CSNPs. The general recommendation on both platforms is to stick with the default values or increase the `csnp-interval` if there are lots of broadcast circuits on the router which need to be supplied with fresh CSNPs. Note that in IOS you can set the `csnp-interval` per level while JUNOS does not permit you to do that.

IOS configuration

```
interface GigabitEthernet0/2
  isis csnp-interval 30 level-1
  isis csnp-interval 40 level-2
!
```

JUNOS configuration

```
protocols {
  isis {
```

```
    interface ge-2/0/0.0 {
      csnp-interval 30;

    interface lo0.0;
  }
}
```

You can verify the settings by issuing a `show isis interface <ifname> detail` command on JUNOS.

```
hannes@London> show isis interface ge-0/2/0.0 detail
IS-IS interface database:
ge-0/2/0.0
  Index: 1, State: 0x6, Circuit id: 0x2, Circuit type: 3
  LSP interval: 100 ms, CSNP interval: 10 s
  Level Adjacencies Priority Metric Hello (s) Hold (s) Designated Router
  1     2           64       1200   9.000     40       Amsterdam.02 (not us)
  2     1           64       22000  3.000     40       London.02 (us)
```

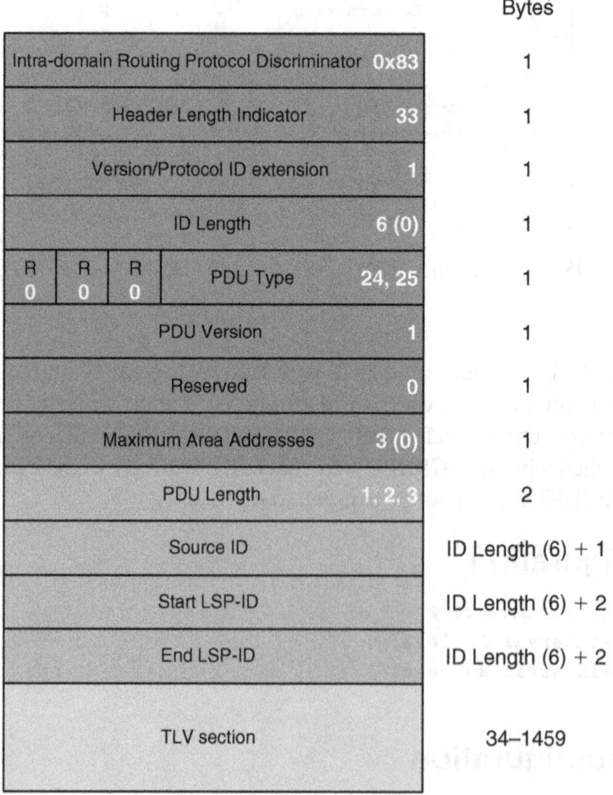

FIGURE 8.4. CSNP PDUs are used for conveying the headlines of the link-state database

You cannot verify the `csnp-interval` settings on an IOS router because the `csnp-interval` is not displayed under the `show clns interface <ifname>` command.

The CSNP on LAN circuits is sent using the well-known functional address *AllL1ISs* (0180:c200:0014) or to the well-known functional address *AllL2ISs* (0180:c200:0015) depending on the IS-IS level. The IS-IS common header that provides the receiver with the following information starts the CSNP PDU:

- Header length (this is always 33 bytes for the CSNP header)
- IS-IS protocol version that is used (always 1)
- Length of the System-ID (0 means the standard 6 bytes)
- Level (L1 CSNPs use PDU type 24, L2 PSNPs use PDU type 25)
- CSNP protocol version that is used (always 1)
- Number of area addresses that this IS supports (0 means support for 3 addresses)

The CSNP header holds the following information:

- PDU length (this is the length of the entire PDU including the common header, the CSNP header, and the payload)
- Source-ID (the System-ID plus a trailing zero byte)
- The Start LSP-ID plus the End LSP-ID (The LSP-ID describe Elements in the link-state database of the router)

After the CSNP header the rest of the PDU is filled using TLVs. You can learn more about TLVs in Chapter 11. In CSNP PDUs only two TLVs are used. The LSP-ID TLV #9 is used for link-state database synchronization and the Authentication TLV #10 are used for integrity checking.

If the entire LSP database fits into a single CSNP PDU, meaning there are no more than 90 LSP-IDs in the CSNP PDU, then the Start LSP-ID is set to 0000.0000.0000.00-00 and the End-LSP-ID is set to FFFF.FFFF.FFFF.FF-FF (the entire range possible). This is how the sender tells the receiver that this CSNP contains the full range of LSP-IDs that are present in the sender's database. Where does the maximum number of 90 LSP-IDs per CSNP PDU come from? Recall that 15 LSP-entries fill an LSP-entry TLV with 240 bytes. Add 2 bytes for TLV overhead to come up with 242 bytes. The LSP-entry TLV can repeat up to 6 times until the packet is completely full. Now, $6 * 242 = 1452$ bytes plus 33 bytes of header length = 1485 bytes. Therefore, 6 LSP-entry TLVs per packet $*$ 15 LSP-IDs per LSP-entry TLV, comes out to 90 LSP-IDs per packet:

$$6\frac{\text{LSP-Entry TLVs}}{\text{packet}} * 15\frac{\text{LSP-IDs}}{\text{LSP-Entry TLV}} = 90\frac{\text{LSP-IDs}}{\text{packet}}$$

Link-state databases that contain more than 90 entries send more than one CSNP PDU. The *first* CSNP PDU, Start LSP-ID, is set to 0000.0000.0000.00-00 and the End LSP-ID of the *last* CSNP PDU is set to FFFF.FFFF.FFFF.FF-FF. This all ones ending tells the receiver that this CSNP is the last one to describe the link-state database, and the transmission of LSP-IDs is completed. Between the first PDU and the last, other CSNP-PDUs insert the LSP-ID of the first and the last LSP-ID reported using the LSP-entry-TLV #9 in the CSNP header in the Start LSP-ID and End LSP-ID fields. It is assumed that the LSP-IDs are ordered by LSP-ID and they arrive in sequence.

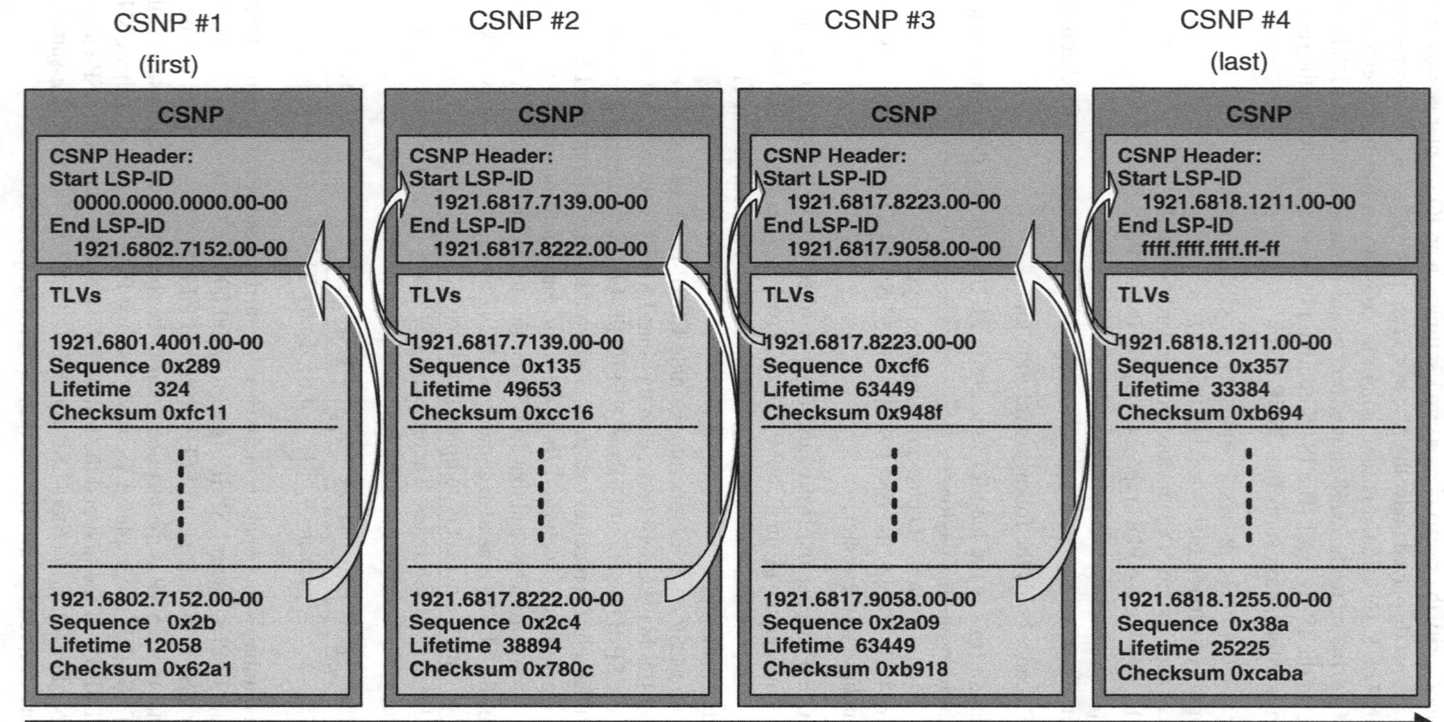

FIGURE 8.5. Link-state databases bigger than 90 LSPs need multiple CSNP PDUs for a full report

Figure 8.5 shows an example of a multi-packet CSNP, which is sent as a sequence of four frames. The first CSNP has the Start LSP-ID set to all zeros. The End LSP-ID is set to the last LSP-ID that is reported in the first CSNP (1921.6802.7152.00-00). The intermediate CSNPs set their Start and LSP-ID fields according to the first and last LSP-ID that is reported in the PDU. Finally, the last CSNP of the full update sets the End-LSP ID to all ones (FFFF.FFFF.FFFF.FF-FF) indicating that the full-report of all LSP-IDs is now completed.

The payload section of the CSNP PDU is filled with an information element called the LSP Entry. The LSP Entry is placed in the CSNP PDU by use of TLV encoding. You can find more information about TLV encoding in Chapter 11 "TLVs and sub-TLVs". Figure 8.6 shows the structure of the LSP Entry TLV. The TLV header consists of two bytes – the Type and the Length value. The Type value is #9 and the Length value is always a multiple of 16. The LSP Entry is a structure of 16 bytes that can be repeated up to 15 times in a TLV. The LSP Entry holds the header information of an LSP in the link-state database. This information is:

- LSP-ID (6 byte System-IDs plus 1 byte node-ID plus 1 byte fragment number)
- Sequence number (4 bytes)
- Remaining lifetime (2 bytes)
- Checksum of the corresponding LSP (2 bytes, standard Fletcher checksum)

By using these four parameters, an LSP can uniquely be identified in a link-state database. Additionally, for each LSP, two informative flags are kept for each circuit in order to control flooding, re-flooding, and acknowledging LSP updates. These two flags are called

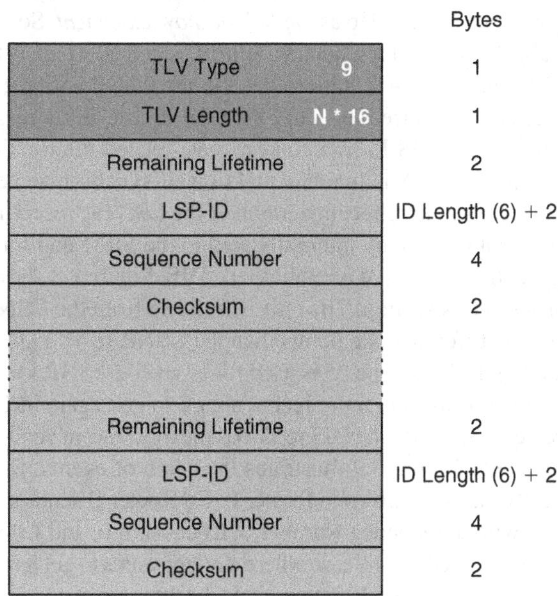

FIGURE 8.6. The LSP Entry TLV is a container for LSP headline figures like Sequence Number, Lifetime and Checksum

the SRM (Send Routing Message) and the SSN (Send Sequence Numbers) flag and are defined in ISO 10589. If the SRM is set on a link, this means that the corresponding LSP has to be sent out on that link. If the SSN flag is set, the corresponding LSP should be included in the next PSNP PDU. Note that these two flags are kept strictly internal to the router. They do not show up in any PDU that the router generates. However, what the flags do is influence the link on which LSPs and PSNPs are being sent.

Getting back to the header fields proper, the DIS extracts this header information from its link-state database and packages up to 15 LSP-IDs in a single TLV. Given an IS-IS MTU of 1497 bytes over Ethernet LANs, a DIS can package up to 6 times an LSP Entry TLV #9, resulting in up to 90 LSP-IDs in a single CSNP. So even in the largest networks in the world there are just a few CSNP packets going over the wire every 10 seconds. Next, each router on the LAN compares its own link-state database to the CSNP received from the DIS. If the DIS reports the same sequence number for an LSP-ID, then everything is fine. If not, then there are three basic mismatch conditions that can occur:

- The CSNP reporting an older version of a LSP
- The CSNP reporting a more recent version of a LSP
- The CSNP reporting an unknown LSP

If the CSNP received is an older version, then the action is simple. Because it appears that the DIS is not up to date, just tell the DIS about the new version of the LSP by re-flooding the most recent version of the LSP onto the LAN. Figure 8.7 illustrates the chain of events. Router B notices that Router A is still carrying an older version of the LSP RouterX.00-00 in its link-state database. So Router B floods the LSP RouterX.00-00 with the most recent sequence number (0x7a). Note, however, that no receiver acknowledges the re-flooded LSP. This principle is sometimes referred to as *implicit acknowledgement*. So how can the update be made more reliable? Just wait for a maximum of 10 seconds, which is the regular CSNP interval. If the LSP RouterX.00-00 is mentioned in the CSNP with the sequence number (0x7a) and the checksum is correct as well, then the update is successful. IS-IS is very unique in that respect, in that IS-IS tries to keep state-related information very low. The periodic transmission of CSNPs is fundamental to well-synchronized databases.

If the CSNP reported is a more recent version of the LSP, the receiving router needs to tell the DIS that it is out of sync by internally setting the SRM flag for this LSP. Setting the SRM flag triggers the sending of a PSNP to the DIS. Figure 8.8 shows the basic structure discussed earlier in this section. The only difference from the CSNP PDU is that the PSNP PDUs are using different code points than the CSNP. IS-IS PDU type 24 indicates a Level-1 PSNP and IS-IS PDU type 25 is used for a Level-2 PSNP. Once the PSNP PDU is formed, all the LSP-IDs that are more recent are packaged again in TLV #9s. Once the PSNP PDU is received at the DIS, the DIS re-floods the most recent version of the requested LSP back onto the LAN. Figure 8.9 illustrates the chain of events. Router A reports an LSP (RouterX-00.00) that is unknown to Router B. So Router B sends a PSNP mentioning RouterX-00.00, but with a Sequence Number 0, Checksum 0, and Lifetime 0. Sequence Number 0 is specially reserved for the case where a router wants to get its database synchronized. By setting Sequence Number, Lifetime, and Checksum to zero, a router on a LAN is indicating that it wants to get a copy of that LSP. Therefore Router A re-floods the latest copy of the LSP RouterX.00-00 onto the LAN. Once again, this re-flooding is done using

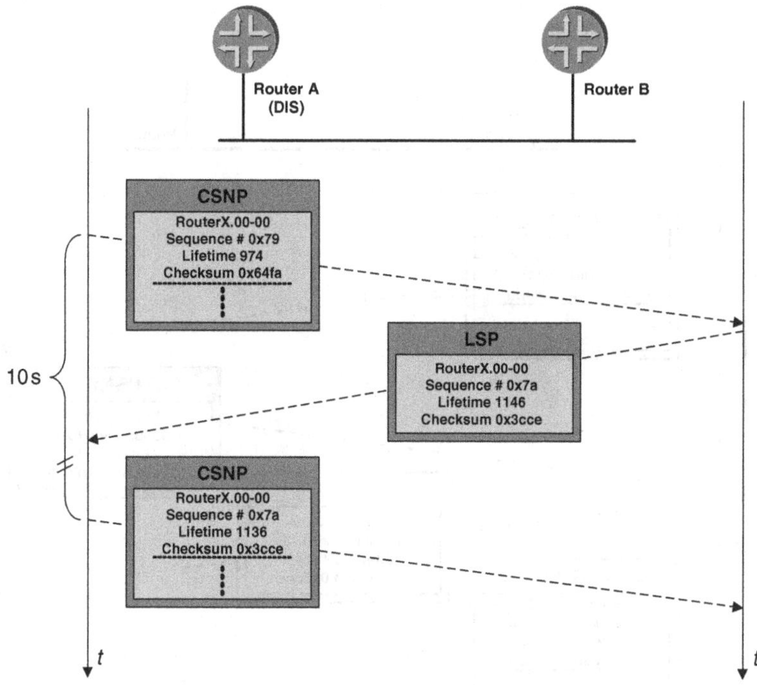

FIGURE 8.7. Router A reports an outdated LSP in its CSNP, which causes a re-flood of Router B and finally Router A reports that it is in sync again by reporting the latest sequence number

Field	Value	Bytes
Intra-domain Routing Protocol Discriminator	0x83	1
Header Length Indicator	17	1
Version/Protocol ID Extension	1	1
ID length	6 (0)	1
R 0 | R 0 | R 0 | PDU Type	26,27	1
PDU Version	1	1
Reserved	0	1
Maximum Area Addresses	3 (0)	1
PDU Length		2
Source ID		ID Length (6) + 1
TLV section		18–1475

FIGURE 8.8. The PSNP PDU reports just a subset of the LSP in the link-state database

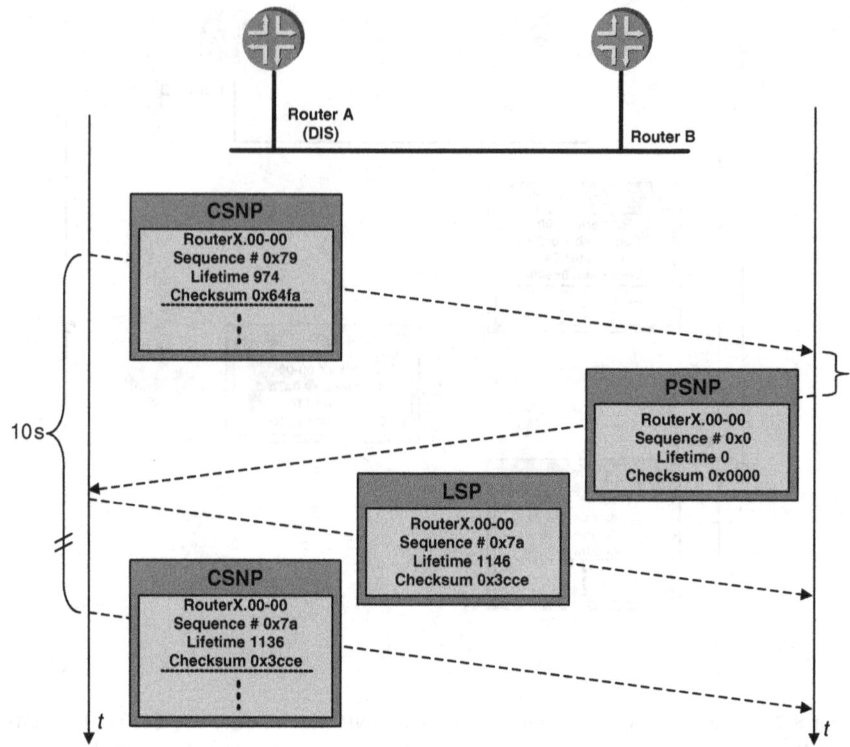

FIGURE 8.9. Router B requests a re-flood of new or unknown LSPs by sending a PSNP with Sequence Number and Checksum set to zero

"implicit acknowledgments". What might happen is that the LSP does not arrive at Router B, but this is not a problem: Router B would simply resend the PSNP after 5 seconds.

If the DIS reports a *new or unknown* LSP-ID in its CSNP PDU, then the router that detects the mismatch sends a PSNP requesting the missing LSP-ID by setting the three fields of Sequence Number, Lifetime and Checksum to zero, indicating to the receiver that the sender does not know anything specific about this LSP. The DIS will again re-flood the missing LSP. This procedure is typically executed when a new router becomes online.

Synchronization of LSPs on LAN segments is both simple and lean. Contrary to OSPF, which needs to keep a lot of state information for synchronizing link-state databases, IS-IS uses only two flags for each link: the SRM and the SSN flag.

Next, IS-IS synchronization on point-to-point circuits is discussed. Point-to-point links make different use of PSNPs and CSNPs than broadcast links, such as LANs.

8.3 Synchronizing Databases on p2p Links

All link-state routing protocols start their first synchronization after one common event: once an adjacency is declared up. Once an adjacency is up on a point-to-point link, the router

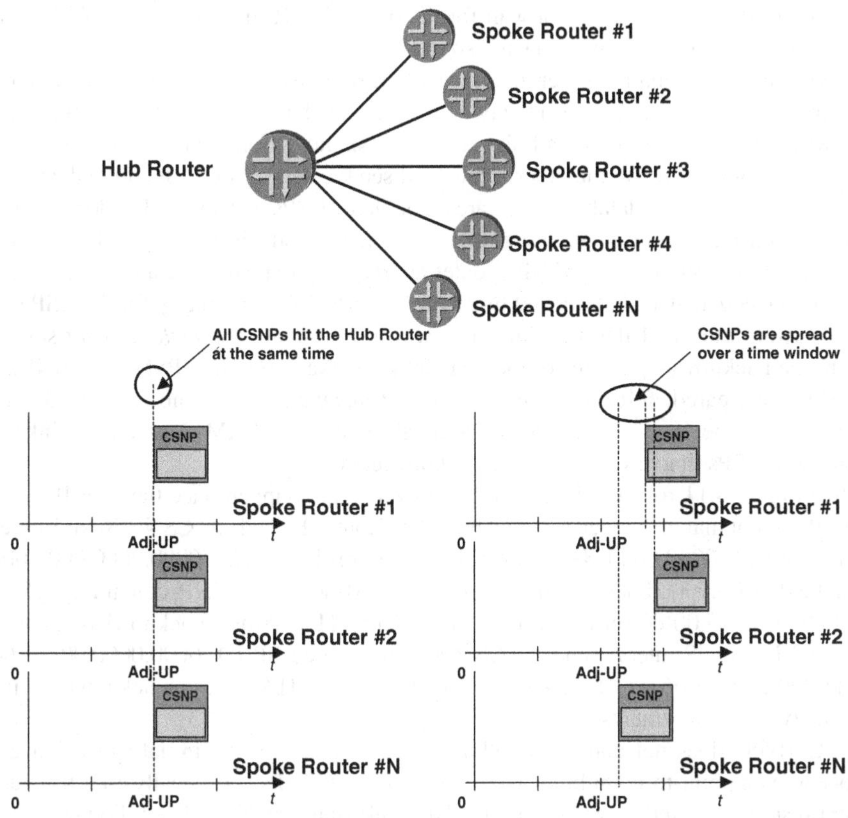

FIGURE 8.10. Jittering timers helps to spread the processing load over a broader time window

will jitter a 5-second timer by 25 per cent before sending a CSNP from its own database. Jittering by 25 per cent means that the router computes a random number between 75–100 per cent of the underlying timer; 75 per cent of 5 seconds equals 3.75 seconds. The result is a random timer between 3.75 and 5 seconds. The other router does the same thing. Jittering timers decouple any kind of synchronization effects causing traffic spikes between the two routers. See Figure 8.10 with a hub router and many spoke routers for an illustration of how *immediate* dispatch of PDUs might harm IS-IS peak load performance. If all spoke routers immediately generate a CSNP after the adjacency is up, then the hub router has to process a large number of CSNPs in a relatively short timeframe. This leads to a short-term peak-load on the hub router. Also, sending all this control traffic at once might harm other user traffic that runs on the physical link. Just imagine if the spoke links were not physical links but logical Frame Relay circuits (DLCIs) all on one physical link. This result might be short-term congestion or an abrupt increase in delay for user traffic. However, if routers jitter the timer before the CSNP is sent after the adjacency-up event, this reduces the short-term congestion and peak CPU utilization. After routers have sent the CSNP it will hang around for a few seconds until routers get the CSNP from the other neighbour. If the router does not wait for the other CSNP, then another CSNP is scheduled after 5 seconds (minus jitter) and so on.

However, if the sending router does receive the remote end's CSNP, then the router can compute the differences between the two link-state databases. For any LSPs that are missing with respect to the sender's link-state database, no action is taken. Just sending the CSNP is enough because the other router will see the sender's CSNP and realize that in the sender's link-state database there are a couple of LSPs missing. What does the other router do once detecting a database mismatch? – It re-floods the missing LSPs, of course.

On point-to-point links, the LSP updates are required to be reliable and therefore must be acknowledged. This is achieved by setting the SRM flag internally for the LSP being sent. Setting the SRM flag translates into a *waiting for an acknowledgement* state. As soon as an acknowledgement for the LSP arrives (by a listing in a PSNP or CSNP), the SRM flag is cleared, or it is *removed from the retransmission list*. If no acknowledgement arrives, then the IS-IS router will periodically check the SRM flags on all links and retransmit LSPs that have not yet been acknowledged.

See Figure 8.11 for the detailed chain of events that happen once the LSP-IDs in the CSNPs do not match. Router A sends its CSNP. Router B sends its CSNP. Next, Router A re-floods LSP 0000.0000.0005.00-00. Router B re-floods LSP 0000.0000.0006.00-00 and LSP 0000.0000.0006.00-01. Then, Router B sends a PSNP containing LSP-ID 0000.0000.0005.00-00 formatted in the LSP Entry TLV #9 as an acknowledgement for the LSP. Finally, Router A sends a PSNP containing the LSP-IDs 0000.0000.0006.00-00 and 0000.0000.0006.00-01 packaged in the LSP Entry TLV #9 as an acknowledgement for the two LSP fragments.

ISO 10589 does not mandate sending CSNPs except for the initial synchronization procedure on point-to-point links. However, sending CSNPs periodically after the startup event results in better synchronization of the link-state database. The following section explains how IS-IS link-state database synchronization is improved by sending periodic CSNPs.

8.4 Periodic Synchronization on p2p Circuits

In the IS-IS world of ISO 10589, there is an assumption that each link that can carry IS-IS Hellos can also carry IS-IS LSPs. At first sight, the previous sentence might sound odd and you may think, "Sure, why should a link that can carry a certain IS-IS packet type, not carry *arbitrary* IS-IS packet types?" But as demonstrated in Chapter 6 "Generating, Flooding and Ageing LSPs", there can be situations where the IS-IS flooding topology may get pruned. *Mesh-groups* are a good example of this situation. Certain redundant links are removed from the flooding topology in mesh-groups. As a result, there might be situations where parts of the network may get de-synchronized because the LSPs do not get through. In this environment especially, it might be a good idea to send some additional CSNPs to make sure that the neighbours are well synchronized. Of the two implementations of IS-IS from Cisco Systems and Juniper Networks that are the subject of this book, only Juniper Networks implements a more robust synchronization scheme.

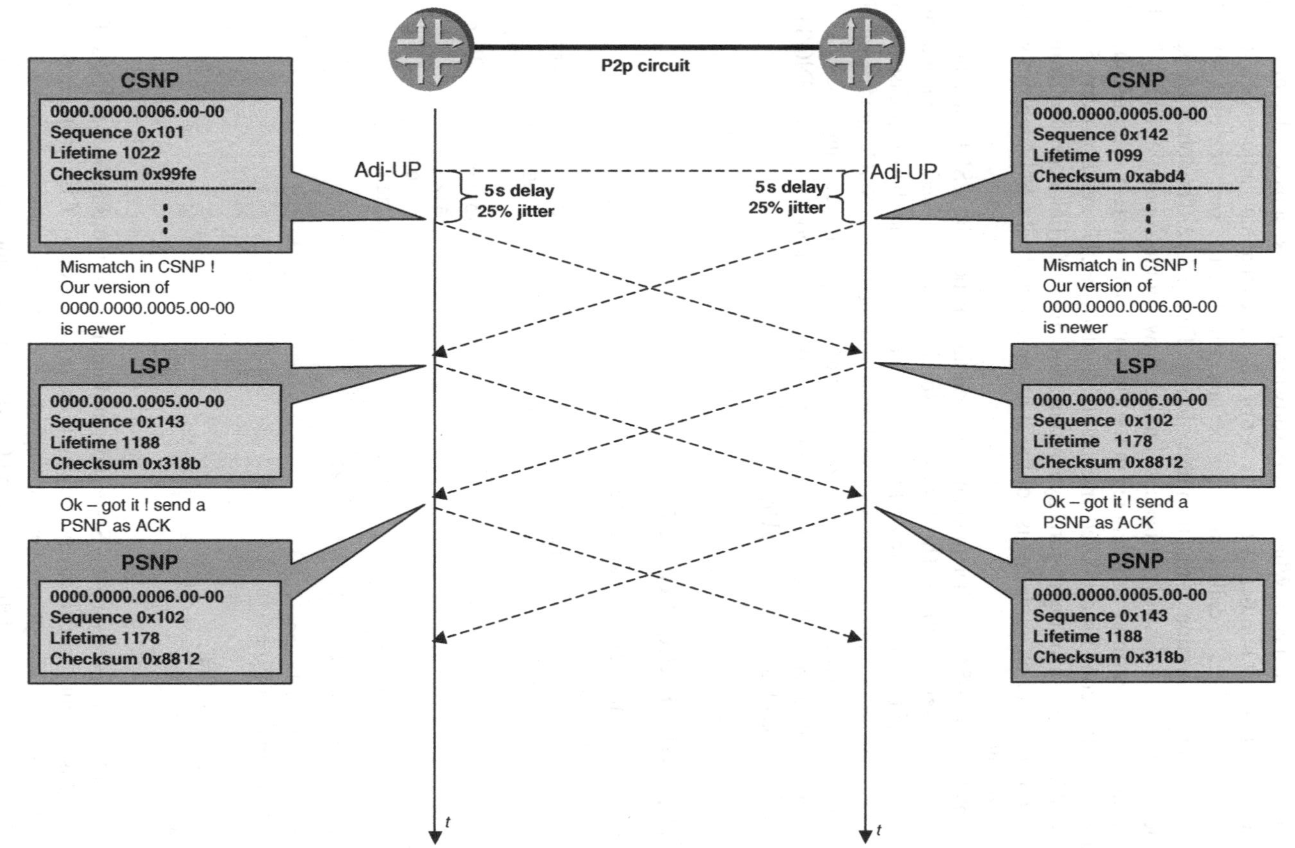

FIGURE 8.11. After the 3-way handshake each router sends a CSNP. If the two routers' LSDBs are de-synced both routers will LSP-re-flood the missing LSPs and send subsequent PSNPs for acknowledging those

JUNOS software periodically transmits CSNPs at both IS-IS levels on all (including p2p) circuits. The time base is not fixed, that is, the JUNOS software does not transmit its CSNP at a hard-coded rate. What JUNOS software does is take a base value of 5 seconds and multiplies that number by the number of interfaces that have adjacencies in the *Up* state. This technique is called *smearing* because one timer is *smeared* over several interfaces. For an illustration of this technique, look at Figure 8.12. The router has seven adjacencies, four interfaces (two broadcast links and two point-to-point circuits). Each interface carries one or more adjacencies in the Up state. Therefore, 5 seconds times 4 interfaces = a 20-second timer started on each of the interfaces. On average, every 5 seconds, a CSNP is sent, resulting in good synchronization. Even if a link is pruned from the flooding topology, for example by use of mesh-groups, periodical CSNPs ensure good synchronization.

Fortunately ISO 10589 neither mandates the sending of periodic CSNPs nor does it strictly discourage sending them. This hole in the specification is utilized by the smearing hack described previously. There are no known interoperability issues between Cisco IOS and JUNOS software. Except for the support calls that are generated by NOC teams that find the amount of CSNPs being generated *suspiciously high*, there are no relevant issues.

A typical `show isis statistics` output resulting from hooking up a JUNOS to an IOS router looks like this on the JUNOS side.

JUNOS command output

```
juniper@London> show isis statistics
IS-IS statistics for London:
PDU type        Received       Processed         Drops          Sent       Rexmit
LSP                41034           41034             0            95            0
IIH                   36              36             0            34            0
CSNP                   1               1             0        420859            0
PSNP                  87              87             0          5125            0
Unknown                0               0             0             0            0
Totals             41159           41159             0        426113            0

Total packets received: 41158 Sent: 426079

SNP queue length: 0 Drops: 0
LSP queue length: 0 Drops: 0
SPF runs: 10772
Fragments rebuilt: 104
LSP regenerations: 27
Purges initiated: 0
```

London only received a single CSNP and sent hundreds of thousands of CSNPs. By looking at this output you can easily see that there must be lots of Cisco routers on the other end, which typically just generate a single CSNP, once an adjacency comes up.

Finally, it should be noted that generating CSNPs comes at almost no cost because they are not difficult to build. CSNPs can be constructed by traversing internal tables in a single pass, and require no complex multi-field operations like checksum calculations. In addition,

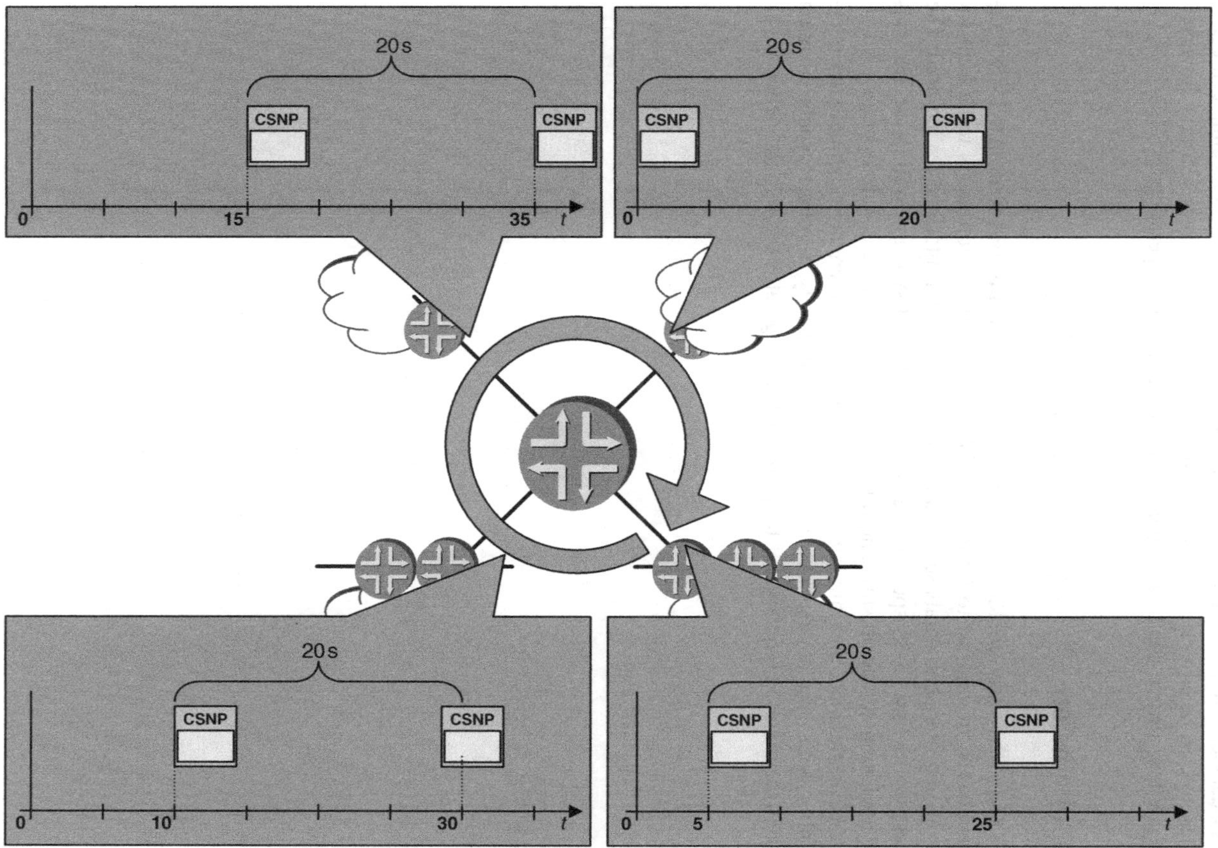

FIGURE 8.12. JUNOS sends a periodical CSNP each 5 s per routing process and distributes the load across all active interfaces

the content of the CSNP does not change frequently. Therefore the CSNP frame can be pre-computed and when the CSNP timer fires, the pre-computed frames are just transmitted over the wire. The pre-computed PDU needs only to change if there is an update in the link-state database. To be completely honest, CSNP construction is not *that* simple: the LSP lifetimes need to be adjusted as well, because all the LSPs age every second – however, once again inserting of lifetimes values is just a simple copy operation.

8.5 Conclusion

CSNPs and PSNPs are very simple and powerful mechanisms to synchronize IS-IS link-state databases. In contrast to OSPF, almost no state information needs to be kept for synchronizing link-state databases. Just two bits per LSP/per interface are required. The openness of the base IS-IS spec ensures that more robust synchronization mechanisms can be implemented and all surrounding routers can cooperate and interoperate.

Because of the inherent simplicity of the IS-IS protocol there are practically no interoperability issues for database synchronization. Ultimately, a robust synchronization scheme is the main prerequisite for loop-free forwarding paths through the network.

9

Fragmentation

Modern communication relies on packet networks. On each layer in the OSI reference model a message from higher layers needs to get packetized by lower layers. The underlying packet switching hardware that finally transports the frames across the Internet has most certain packet size constraints. Ethernet is a good example for these constraints, by not allowing individual packets to be bigger than 1518 bytes. Each layer in the OSI Reference Model needs to deal with the fundamental question: how will messages that do not fit the transport circuit packet be transported? In this chapter you will see some examples how IP and the IS-IS routing protocol solves the underlying problem by chopping messages into pieces and reassembling them at the receiver. Additionally the side effects of such chopping and reassembly techniques, which have been observed in big operational networks, will be highlighted.

9.1 Fragmentation and the OSI Reference Model

The OSI Reference Model relies on a layering technique. The purpose of the layering architecture is to hide the actual packet transport infrastructure from the driving application. The result is that the application does not need to care what packet-switching hardware, even what network protocol is used to convey the applications message as long as the receiver on the other end can de-multiplex the layering of message. The Transmission Control Protocol (TCP) is a good example for this. Figure 9.1 shows an example application like the Simple Mail Transfer Protocol (SMTP). SMTP relies on TCP for doing end-to-end flow control, re-sequencing and retransmission. TCP is dependent on a networking protocol like IPv4 or IPv6 to get packets finally relayed from Client A to Server B. During its journey from Client A to Client B the packet will be transported using various layers of Layer-2 transport networks such as (but not limited to) Ethernet, SONET/SDH, Frame Relay, ATM.

If you take a look how the original message (the email) is packaged into finally Ethernet, or SONET/SDH frames, you will notice that the message first is *split* by the transport protocol. Splitting the original application stream is necessary to get packets from streams which finally get packaged and repackaged several times. Think of it like putting a letter in an envelope, which is then put in a larger envelope, which is put in a larger envelope until the packet finally gets delivered. The envelope analogy works also when it comes down to frame *sizes*. When you want to put a message in an envelope then the envelope has to be larger for the message to fit into.

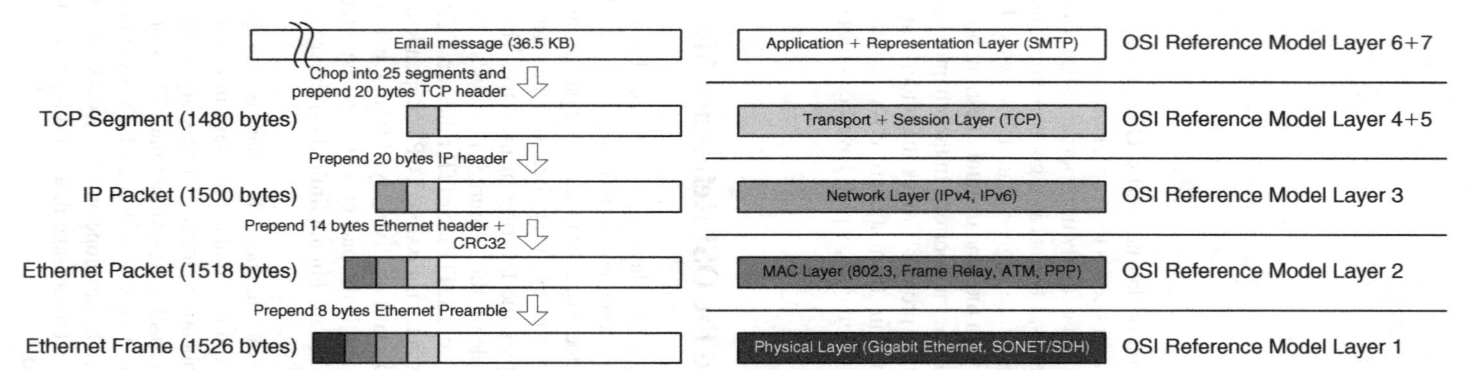

FIGURE 9.1. An SMTP character stream of data gets prepended by header information at all layers to properly transport it across the IP infrastructure. For proper chopping the transport protocol needs to know the MTU of the underlying packet transport infrastructure

In the example the original 36.5 KB stream is first split into 25 application segments that are 1460 bytes in size. Next the TCP header that holds the applications port numbers and other information is prepended which adds 20 bytes resulting in a frame that is called a *TCP segment*, which is 1480 bytes in size. The TCP segment gets prepended by an IP header, which gets prepended again by the Ethernet 802.3 headers. Ultimately the Ethernet preamble and the CRC32 checksum gets added to the frame resulting in 1526 byte physical frame that is ready for transmission.

How does the TCP stack know that it has to split the original email stream into chops of 1460 bytes?

Each layer in the OSI Reference Model has a constant called the maximum transmission unit (MTU). There is an MTU for TCP, there is one for IP and there is of course one for Ethernet, as well as for any other physical circuit. What most networking stacks do is backtracking of the MTU from the underlying circuit. Going back to the example, the first MTU that is determined is the one of the Ethernet circuit. The MTU here is defined as per the Ethernet specifications and is set to 1518 bytes. Meanwhile most Ethernet chipsets have support for frames larger than 1518 bytes up to 9 KB. 1518 bytes represents the lowest common denominator that each Ethernet device has to understand. The higher layer MTUs are derived from the Layer-2 MTU. They do vary dependend on the encoding size of the Layer-2 protocol. The IP MTU is the Ethernet MTU minus 18 bytes. The 18 bytes are necessary to store 6 bytes of source and destination MAC address, and 2 bytes for the Ethernet type field plus 4 bytes for the CRC32 checksum that gets appended to the end of the frame. The TCP MTU is the Ethernet MTU minus 18 minus 20. The typical IP header (without IP options that would make it longer) is 20 bytes in size. The story goes on by deducting 20 bytes of the TCP header size to figure out what the application segment size is. 1518 – 18 – 20 – 20 = 1460. For each interface, host operating systems calculate the MTU values to find out what is the maximum frame size that can be sent over a specific circuit. The operating system tries to *avoid* breaking an already packaged frame into pieces by looking at the MTU of the delivering circuit.

You can display the MTU size of a router by issuing the `show interface <interface-name>` command at the command line interface (CLI). This command is both available in IOS and JUNOS; however, on IOS it does not show you IS-IS-related information. For IOS a more detailed output can be obtained issuing the `show clns interface <interface-name>` command.

JUNOS command output

```
hannes@Amsterdam> show interfaces so-7/0/0
Physical interface: so-7/0/0, Enabled, Physical link is Up
  Interface index: 20, SNMP ifIndex: 19
  Description: STM-64 uplink -> Amsterdam-NewYork
  Link-level type: PPP, MTU: 4474, Clocking: Internal, SDH mode, FCS: 32,
   Payload scrambler: Enabled
  Device flags     : Present Running
  Interface flags  : Point-To-Point SNMP-Traps
  Link flags       : Keepalives
  Keepalive settings: Interval 10 seconds, Up-count 1, Down-count 3
```

```
Keepalive: Input: 96933 (00:00:04 ago), Output: 97571 (00:00:04 ago)
LCP state: Opened
NCP state: inet: Opened, inet6: Not-configured, iso: Opened, mpls: Not-
  configured
Input rate    :  268007728 bps (84371 pps)
Output rate   :  376305576 bps (86296 pps)
SONET alarms  :  None
SONET defects:   None

Logical interface so-7/0/0.0 (Index 14) (SNMP ifIndex 28)
  Flags: Point-To-Point SNMP-Traps Encapsulation: PPP
  Protocol inet, MTU: 4470, Flags: None
    Addresses, Flags: Is-Preferred Is-Primary
      Destination: 192.168.5.144/30, Local: 192.168.5.146
  Protocol iso, MTU: 4470, Flags: None
```

You can see in the JUNOS output that there is a clear separation between the physical interface and the logical interfaces and what kinds of protocols are spoken on the interfaces. The *physical* interface so-3/0/0.0 has got a Link-MTU of 4474 bytes. The logical interface so-7/0/0.0 (not the trailing additional trailing zero) has two protocols configured – ISO for running the complex of ISO protocols (but limited to IS-IS and ISHs in JUNOS) and IPv4. The Protocol MTU is 4 bytes less (4470) the Link MTU due to the PPP overhead.

In IOS you can display the IS-IS MTU for a given interface using the `show clns interface` command. Because the default encapsulation 802.3 LLC, which is in Cisco's terminology also called the `SAP`, is used, the MTU is being set to 1497 bytes.

IOS command output

```
London>show clns interface
Ethernet0 is up, line protocol is up
  Checksums enabled, MTU 1497, Encapsulation SAP
  ERPDUs enabled, min. interval 10 msec.
  CLNS fast switching enabled
  CLNS SSE switching disabled
  DEC compatibility mode OFF for this interface
  Next ESH/ISH in 32 seconds
  Routing Protocol: IS-IS
    Circuit Type: level-2
    Interface number 0x2, local circuit ID 0x3
    Level-2 Metric: 10, Priority: 64, Circuit ID: London.03
    Number of active level-2 adjacencies: 3
    Next IS-IS LAN Level-2 Hello in 79 milliseconds
[ … ]
```

As you have seen, JUNOS calculates the MTU on a per protocol basis as well. Generally speaking, it is important to understand that the MTU is a property of both physical interfaces and protocols related interfaces – there is no single MTU value per router interface. Whenever you hear somebody talking just about an MTU then you have to ask straight "what MTU are you talking about?" Ethernet, PPP, IP, MPLS, IPv6 MTU? An individual circuit can hold up to five different MTU values – true multiprotocol enterprise routers like the Cisco 7500 series calculate probably even more than five MTUs per circuit. There is one MTU for each *protocol* for each *physical interface*.

9.2 The Too-small MTU Problem for IP

The sender of the email message in the example tries to package the frame in order to fit perfectly to the maximum frame sizes of the underlying physical interface. What will happen if the sender is located on a physical circuit with a big physical MTU and one of the transit routers does not support that big-sized MTU? Consider Figure 9.2. The sender is located at a network segment that can transmit to a maximum packet size of 9172 packets. Typical examples for such a circuit would be Gigabit Ethernet "Jumbograms" or an ATM circuit. According to Figure 9.1 the operating system calculates the Maximum Segment Size (MSS) that TCP can accept in order to avoid sending oversized frames. The MSS is calculated by deducting the ATM overhead (SNAP frame size) and the IP plus TCP overhead resulting in a 9127 byte original application segment. Finally the sender dispatches the frame and it arrives at Router A. Next Router A determines the outgoing interface by doing an IP lookup. Before Router A starts to transmit the frame it first checks if the outgoing interface supports the frame size of the frame to be forwarded. The Interlink between Router AS and Router B is a SONET/SDH link, which has an MTU of 4474 bytes. From the IP perspective, the frame is 9167 bytes, does not fit on the outgoing circuit and cannot be transmitted.

There are three general ways of solving the varying-MTU problem:

1. Assume a minimum MTU that every circuit has to support
2. Design the carrying protocol to support fragmentation
3. Run an MTU discovery protocol

The TCP/IP family of protocols makes use of all three techniques. First of all it guarantees that each IP circuit can have at least an IP MTU of 576 bytes. If an application does not want to probe the path for maximum MTU or avoid any complex fragmentation and reassembly schemes then it simply does not send IP frames longer than 576 bytes over the wire. All the networking media that IP runs on has to have a mandatory support of 576 bytes otherwise the physical media would not be standardized by IP standardization committees like the IETF. That is the simplest but also most effective way of fragmentation avoidance. The drawback here is that there may be a lot of overhead: 45 bytes of transport overhead (TCP, IP and ATM SNAP header) compared to a total frame size of 9172 bytes means an overhead of 0.5 per cent. However, 45 bytes of transport overhead compared to a "coward" MTU of 576 means an overhead of 7.8 per cent. Quite a difference if you

FIGURE 9.2. How does the sender know the MTUs of all the intermediate network segments?

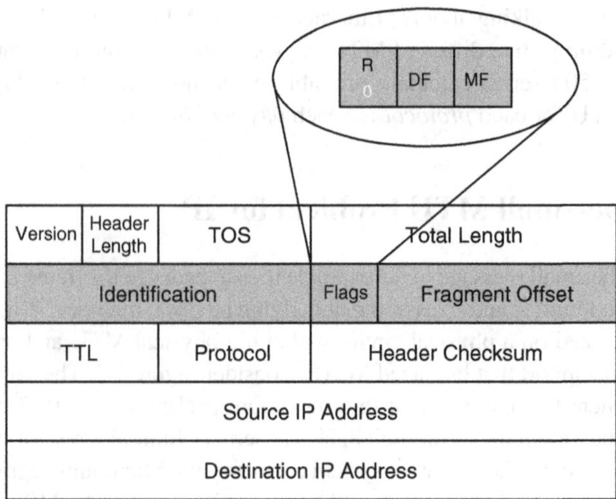

FIGURE 9.3. The gray-shaded fields are used for fragmentation-related purposes

consider for instance file-sharing applications (such as Gnutella, Kazaa and Morpheus), which are so common these days on the Internet.

The second way of dealing with too-small MTUs is that the underlying network protocol supports fragmentation methods that can be executed by intermediate routers. Fragmentation means that even an Intermediate System in the transmission path like a router may further chop the IP packet to transmit it over smaller MTU circuits. During the fragmentation process the router figures out how many fragments it needs and then it has to figure out the position of the fragment relative to the original packet. The IP protocol was designed from day one to have the capability of fragmentation. In the IP protocol there are several fields dedicated to fragmentation. See Figure 9.3 for an overview of the IP header and which fields are dedicated to fragmentation.

The first field is the *Fragment ID*. Each frame that is fragmented gets a unique 16-bit ID so that the receiver can correctly reassemble it. That is necessary, for instance, if you have two flows between a pair of hosts and both flows get fragmented. This ID identifies the two flows and helps the receiver to separate the fragments of the two flows. In hardware-based routers this is typically a simple counter that is simply incremented. Is this a perfect scheme? No – there may still be collisions – imagine a massive amount of flows that need to get fragmented and by accident the first flow and the 65,536th flow (this is when the 16-bit ID space overlaps) belongs to the same host. However, operational experience has proven that even such a simple scheme proved to be *good enough.* The rightmost 13 bits is called the Fragment-offset field. The Fragment-offset field is encoded in units of 8 bytes. Using 3 bits, 2^13 = 8192 unique offsets can be represented. Each offset is multiplied by 8 bytes which results in 65,536 bytes – the maximum size of an IP packet. The Flags field consists of 3 bits. The MSB must be set to 0. The DF (Don't Fragment) bit is used to indicate if the sender of the packet does not want to have it fragmented. If one of the circuits has too small an MTU and the DF bit is set then the router will respond using an Internet Control Message Protocol (ICMP) to indicate that there has been a problem. The More Fragment (MF) bit is an indicator for the receiver to wait with reassembling the frame. Typically all fragments except the last fragment do have this bit being set.

For a better understanding of the fragmentation related fields in the IP header, go back to the example shown in Figure 9.2.

If the 9167 bytes size frame needs to get fragmented the router first has to figure out how many fragments it will need. The PPP overhead of the link between Router A and Router B is 4 bytes, therefore the IP MTU on a SONET/SDH PPP Link is 4474 – 4 = 4470 bytes. Chopping up 9167 bytes requires three fragments as 9167/2 is 4584 and this would not fit. The router tries to figure out what the next 8-octet boundary is to chop the frame. Recall in the IP header fragmentation in 8 byte chunks is allowed due to the encoding scheme and encoding space of only 13 bits. The fragment offset is expressed in 8-byte units. The first fragment will be 4464 bytes as the next 8-octet boundary below 4470 is 4464. Fragment #2 will also be sized at 4464 bytes. The last frame has the MF bit cleared (as opposed to the first two fragments) and is sized to 239 bytes. The Fragment ID will be identical in all three fragments. The Fragment offset will be 0 in the first fragment, 558 (558 * 8 = 4464) in the second fragment and 1116 (2 * 558 * 8) in the last fragment. That is enough information for the receiver to reassemble the original packet. In the IP world the reassembly is not done by routers, the hosts implement it – therefore each operating system's IP stack must support reassembly of fragments.

Even if these mechanisms sound convenient at first sight, the idea that fragmentation is generally a thing to avoid only came after years of operating large networks. The TCP stack does not think in terms of fragments, it only thinks in terms of TCP segments – so if a fragment that has been generated by the IP Layer is lost, the entire frame is re-transmitted (and fragmented again by intermediate routers). In congested networks the "goodput" of fragmentation approaches zero depending on the overload level.

The third way is the most sophisticated. *Before* transmitting the message stream the path to the receiver is *probed* for the maximum MTU. This is possible by using fields in the IP header in a special way. The first packet that the application sends is sent using the full MTU size. However, the sender also sets the DF bit in the IP header. This does mean that, referencing our first example, Router A would send an ICMP back to the sender telling it that a fragmentation attempt was refused due to a set DF bit in the header. There is a dedicated ICMP message for this purpose which is defined in RFC 792.

Now the application tries to send the first segment using a lower MTU. If it gets an ICMP message back it tries again with a lower MTU unless it does not get back an ICMP error message. The exact algorithms for how the transport protocols estimate the MTU for the next try are out of the scope of this book. If you are interested in these probing techniques, RFC 1191 is a good place to start to learn about path MTU discovery. All modern transport stacks make use of path MTU discovery.

You have seen in this section how the IP protocol deals with frames that are in certain segments in a network too big to deliver. IP proved to be a quite flexible protocol as there are three different ways of dealing with the too-small-MTU problem that are: *avoid*, *fragment* or *probe*. In the next section you will learn about the messages in the IS-IS protocol that can get larger than the MTU and how IS-IS deals with it. For better illustration we will reference back to the three ways of how the IP protocol fixed the too-small-MTU problem.

9.3 The Too-small MTU Problem for IS-IS

IS-IS may generate frames that are larger than a single-link MTU. Just think of a large router that is injecting hundreds of IP prefixes. The space in (for example) an Ethernet packet may not be sufficient to store that vast amount of data. How is IS-IS dealing with link MTUs that are too small to convey a large amount of reachability information? Reconsider the three ways that the IP family of protocols solved the small-MTU problem:

- *Probing the path* and finding out what the largest MTU is – this is by concept impossible as IS-IS uses flooding for distributing its information. Flooding has no session orientation. Session orientation is needed for probing a path. Flooding basically means *all paths*. So path MTU discovery is not the tool of choice for finding out what the *smallest* MTU in the network is.
- *Fragmenting at the Network Layer* – unlike the IP routing protocols (OSPF, BGP) IS-IS runs directly on Layer-2 according to the OSI Reference Model. In the basic Ethernet protocol there is no support for fragmenting Ethernet frames. There is no support built into the Ethernet protocol that allows fragmenting packets like IP did, using fields like Fragment ID, Fragment Offset and the DF, MF bits. So fragmentation at the Ethernet level is not a choice either. What IS-IS implements is support to extend large messages over several packets. Arguably such a thing could best be described as *Fragmentation built into the* ***application*** *IS-IS*. The packet types and fields that IS-IS uses for multi-packet messages will be described shortly.
- *Assuming a minimum MTU* – IS-IS assumes a minimum MTU of 1492 bytes that every segment in the network must support. If there is a link MTU smaller than 1492 bytes then IS-IS simply refuses to build adjacencies. IS-IS checks the MTU during the handshake phase once new adjacencies are brought up. Why 1492 bytes? The recommendation to use 1492 bytes was due to the Ethernet MTU of 1518 bytes. How are 1518 bytes and 1492 related? Reconsider the structure of the IS-IS standard encapsulation in 802.3 LLC format in Figure 9.4. Subtract the following fields from the 1518 bytes maximum Ethernet Frame size:
  - 4 bytes FCS
  - 6 bytes source MAC address
  - 6 bytes destination MAC address
  - 2 bytes 802.3 Length field
  - 3 bytes DSAP, SSAP and Control byte

The result is 1518 – 21 = 1497 bytes. So why then restrict all IS-IS frames to 1492 bytes? Recall that the IS-IS designers had to accommodate the possibility that someone may encapsulate the IS-IS messages using *SNAP* encapsulation, which is also shown in Figure 9.4.

At the beginning of the 1980s the Ethernet designers were scared about the small code-point space that LLC encapsulation had to offer. The Sub-network Access Protocol (SNAP) was thought of as an extension for LLC Ethernet encapsulation to accommodate a bigger code-point space. The first application of the bigger code-point space was support for *vendor-specific* protocols. Using SNAP there is room for a 3-byte Organizational Unit Identifier (OID) followed by a 2-byte Protocol ID. Think of a SNAP header as a 5-byte extension to the 3-byte LLC header. Such extension schemes are often used in the communications

802.3 LLC Encapsulation

Field	Value	Bytes
Destination MAC Address	0180:c200:0014 or 0180:c200:0015	6
Source MAC Address		6
IEEE 802.3 Length field		2
IEEE 802.3 DSAP	0xFE	1
IEEE 802.3 SSAP	0xFE	1
IEEE 802.3 Control	0x03	1
IS-IS common header & TLVs		min.: 27 max.: Link MTU-21
FCS		4

802.3 SNAP Encapsulation

Field	Value	Bytes
Destination MAC Address	0180:c200:0014 or 0180:c200:0015	6
Source MAC Address		6
IEEE 802.3 Length field		2
IEEE 802.3 DSAP	0xAA	1
IEEE 802.3 SSAP	0xAA	1
IEEE 802.3 Control	0x03	1
SNAP header OUI	0	3
SNAP header PID	0x80FE	2
IS-IS common header & TLVs		min.: 27 max.: Link MTU-21
FCS		4

FIGURE 9.4. IS-IS formally specified encapsulation over 802.3 LLC and 802.3 SNAP Layer-2 encapsulation; however, all implementations today use 802.3 LLC encapsulation

industry. Most protocols have a special code-point reserved for further extension. In the LLC protocol, it is 0xAA that indicates that there is a 5-byte SNAP header to parse.

This is where the 5-byte difference between 1497 and 1492 comes from. The ironic thing here is that although absolutely no vendor ever implemented IS-IS over SNAP encapsulation, all implementations honour the 1492 bytes size of this "would-be-SNAP-encapsulated" boundary. Virtually all IS-IS implementations support just the LLC encapsulation, which leaves room for 1497 bytes for an IS-IS frame over standard Ethernet technology.

Figure 9.5 shows the output of a real-word IS-IS frame decoded by Ethereal, a public-domain protocol analyzer (http://www.ethereal.com).

Frequently students in classes notice that a router sends out the first set of Hellos up to the maximum size of an Ethernet frame to detect the MTU of the link, that the length of the IS-IS frame is 1497 bytes. You can check that out using the following debug and monitoring commands.

Tcpdump/JUNOS command output

```
hannes@London> monitor traffic Interface fe-0/0/0
00:01:36.850702 OSI, IS-IS, length: 1497
  L1 Lan IIH, hlen: 27, v: 1, pdu-v: 1, sys-id-len: 6 (0), max-area: 3 (0)
    source-id: 0000.0000.0002, holding time: 13s, Flags: [Level 1, Level 2]
    lan-id: 0000.0000.0002.02, Priority: 64, PDU length: 1497
      IS Neighbor(s) TLV #6, length: 6
        IS Neighbor: 0002.b32b.0e52
      Protocols supported TLV #129, length: 1
        NLPID(s): IPv4
      IPv4 Interface address(es) TLV #132, length: 4
        IPv4 interface address: 193.83.223.236
      Area address(es) TLV #1, length: 4
        Area address (3): 49.0001
    Padding TLV #8, length: 255
    Padding TLV #8, length: 255
    Padding TLV #8, length: 255
    Padding TLV #8, length: 255
    Padding TLV #8, length: 255
    Padding TLV #8, length: 160
```

On a router running IOS you can find out how big the packets that the router sends out are by using the `debug isis adj-packets` command.

IOS command output

```
London#debug isis adj-packets
IS-IS Adjacency related packets debugging is on
Jun 9 20:25:14.319 UTC: ISIS-Adj: Sending L2 LAN IIH on Ethernet0, length 1497
Jun 9 20:25:14.575 UTC: ISIS-Adj: Rec L2 IIH from 00d0.ba58.7e4b (Ethernet0), cir
 type L2, cir id 0010.0100.1005.03, length 1497
```

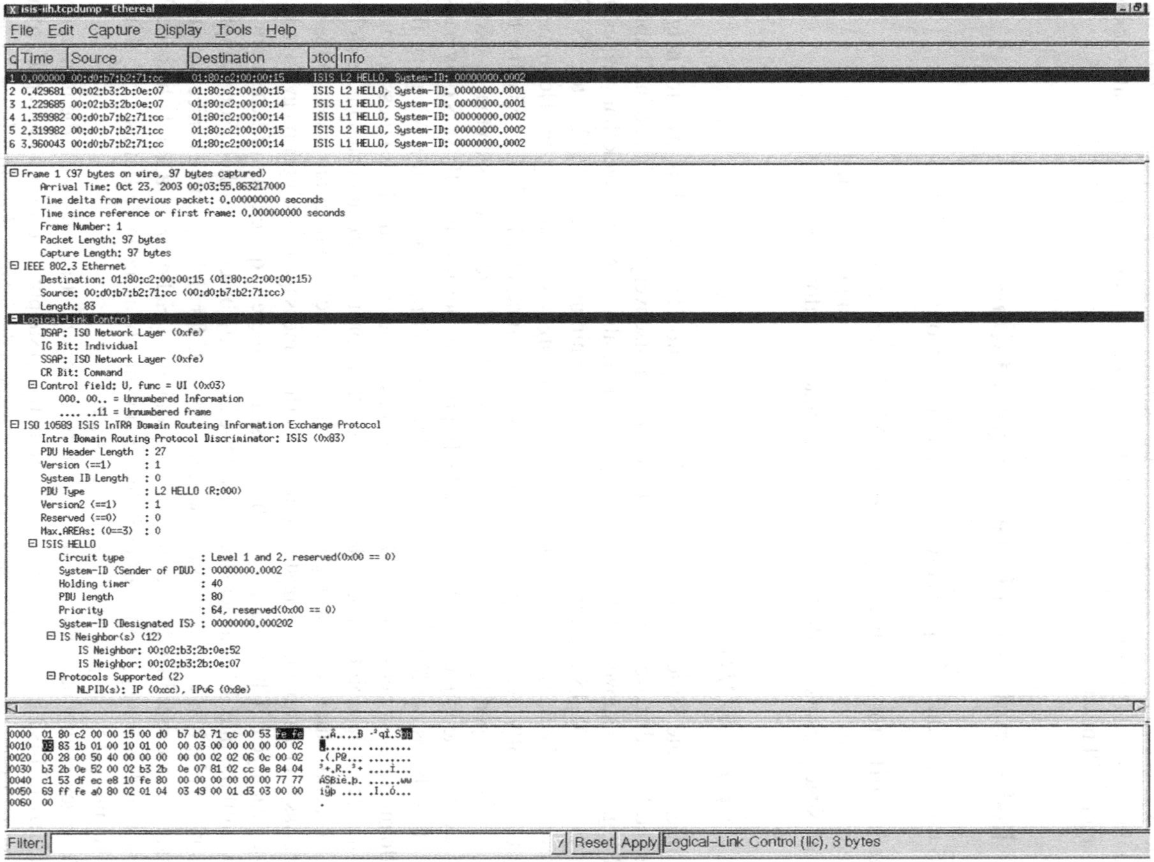

FIGURE 9.5. An IS-IS Frame recorded by Ethereal, a public domain Protocol Analyzer

It has already been mentioned that the official MTU that each circuit must support is 1492, as defined in the IS-IS base specification ISO 10589. However, as all vendors only implement LLC encapsulation, the *unofficial* MTU (don't quote us on that) that each IS-IS may use is *1497* bytes.

The next section takes a closer look to the term *application level fragmentation* and what it means. All the different IS-IS packets and how they are prepared for multi-packet messaging will be discussed.

9.4 IS-IS Application Level Fragmentation

IS-IS uses three different packet types for various purposes:

1. Hellos (IIHs) for neighbour discovery and MTU check
2. Sequence number packets (SNPs) for synchronization and reliable updates
3. Link-state packets (LSPs) for conveying reachability information

9.4.1 *Hellos (IIHs)*

The Intermediate System to Intermediate System Hello PDU, or IIH, is used for neighbour and MTU discovery. The purpose of neighbour discovery was explained in Chapter 5, "Neighbour Discovery and Handshaking". There is also an MTU check that verifies if both ends of an IS-IS adjacency comply with the minimum MTU of 1492 bytes. IS-IS achieves that check by using a technique called *padding*. Using padding, the Hello message is artificially pumped up to the MTU size of the link, or 1492 bytes. Whether the update gets pumped up to *just* 1492 bytes or the full MTU size is a decision that is solely dependent on the implementation of the IS-IS protocol. For instance, JUNOS only pads up to 1492 bytes but IOS always tries to pad to the maximum MTU size. A typical IIH (Hello message) is between 40–70 bytes these days. The size of the Hello message may vary as all new capabilities are added to the base IS-IS protocol are indicated in the Hello message, and it therefore gets bigger through the years as capabilities are added to IS-IS. There has been a trend in the past that the IS-IS Hello message gets bigger on average by 5 bytes each year. Ultimately, this is not an issue as there is quite a lot of headroom to grow until the max IIH packet size of (worst-case) 1497 bytes is reached. Some implementations like IOS can even utilize the full-link MTU for Hellos, which is nice because it postpones worries like these even more. Changing the Hello size is a purely link-local decision and as long as both parties do not complain about the large Hellos, everything will be fine and the adjacency goes into *Up* state.

However, even when an IS-IS Hello is 70 bytes in size, it is still far off the minimum MTU size of 1492 bytes that every IS-IS circuit has to support. How does IS-IS pad from 70 bytes of content to 1492 bytes? There is a special *Padding TLV* that helps to add nonsense data in a structured way just to make the frame bigger. In Figure 9.6 you can see the structure of the Padding TLV.

There is more about TLV encoding in Chapter 11 "TLVs and Sub-TLVs". The Padding TLV may contain an arbitrary set of data. The Padding TLV can also occur several times

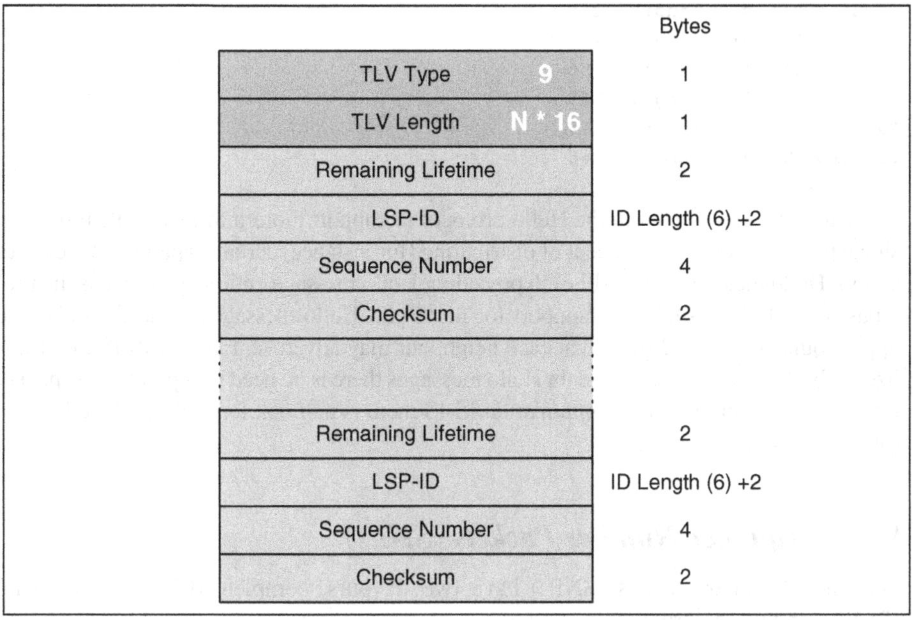

Field	Value	Bytes
TLV Type	9	1
TLV Length	N * 16	1
Remaining Lifetime		2
LSP-ID		ID Length (6) +2
Sequence Number		4
Checksum		2
⋮		
Remaining Lifetime		2
LSP-ID		ID Length (6) +2
Sequence Number		4
Checksum		2

FIGURE 9.6.

in the Hello message. Actually, it has to occur several times in the Hello because a single Padding TLV can only hold, and therefore pad, up to 255 bytes. So there may be up to five full-sized Padding TLVs necessary to make the frame big enough. The following tcpdump output shows several occurrences of the Padding TLV #8.

Tcpdump output

```
00:58:53.561521 OSI, IS-IS, length: 1497
        L1 Lan IIH, hlen: 27, v: 1, pdu-v: 1, sys-id-len: 6 (0), max-area: 3 (0)
            Point-to-point Adjacency State TLV #240, length: 1
              Adjacency State: Up
            Protocols supported TLV #129, length: 2
              NLPID(s): IPv4, IPv6
            IPv4 Interface address(es) TLV #132, length: 4
              IPv4 interface address: 193.83.223.237
            Area address(es) TLV #1, length: 4
              Area address (3): 49.0001
            Restart Signaling TLV #211, length: 3
              Restart Request bit clear, Restart Acknowledgement bit clear
              Remaining holding time: 0s
            Checksum TLV #12, length: 2
              checksum: 0xadbb (correct)
```

```
Padding TLV #8, length: 255
Padding TLV #8, length: 255
Padding TLV #8, length: 255
Padding TLV #8, length: 255
Padding TLV #8, length: 255
Padding TLV #8, length: 168
```

There is *no* mechanism in the Hello protocol to support more information than fits in a single packet. There is no concept of distributing (for instance) certain capability codes over several Hello messages. In IS-IS each preceding Hello message entirely supersedes the previous one. There is simply no support for multi-part Hello messages. That gives also the upper boundary of 1492 bytes that each neighbour may advertise. Luckily, IS-IS today utilizes only 5 per cent of that space. In Hello messages there is no need to support multi-packet messages and therefore in the *application* IS-IS there is no hook for multi-part Hello messages specified.

9.4.2 *Sequence Number Packets (SNPs)*

Sequence Number Packets (SNPs) have two flavours, complete (CSNP) and partial (PSNP), and three purposes:

1. Acknowledging receipt of a link-state packet (a job for PSNP)
2. Requesting a more recent version of LSPs due to detection of a mismatch of some LSPs in the link-state database (also PSNP)
3. Publishing all the headers of the link-state database (this is for CSNP)

There is more information about the details of synchronizing link-state databases and the use of CSNPs and PSNPs in Chapter 8. All you have to know is that IS-IS reports elements from the link-state database using a special envelope called the LSP Entry TLV #9. In Figure 9.7 you can see the structure of TLV #9. In the above-mentioned three uses of SNPs, all transport one, many or all LSP headers that the link-state database holds.

For an acknowledgement, typically only one occurrence of the LSP Entry TLV #9 is needed. The following tcpdump output shows you a PSNP that serves as an acknowledgement.

Tcpdump output

```
01:30:05.788280 OSI, IS-IS, length: 44
        L2 PSNP, hlen: 17, v: 1, pdu-v: 1, sys-id-len: 6 (0), max-area: 3 (0)
          source-id: 6b01.c219.07fa.00
          LSP entries TLV #9, length: 16
               lsp-id: 011c.9a4f.0d02.00-00, seq: 0x000014f4, lifetime:
                 65522s, chksum: 0xb1cf
            Authentication TLV #10, length: 8
              simple text password: Juniper
```

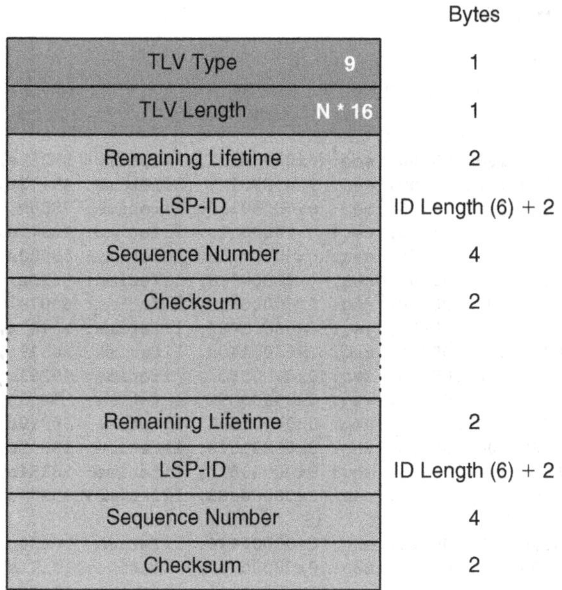

FIGURE 9.7. The LSP Entry TLV #9

This PSNP message was generated in response to an LSP with the LSP-ID of `011c.9a4f.0d02.00-00`. There is just one occurrence of TLV #9 and it holds just one entry. Finally, it is properly authenticated.

However, an implementation may decide to wait for a certain amount of time and then bundle a few acknowledgements together. There can be *more than one* LSP-ID in a PSNP frame mentioned using the LSP Entry TLV #9. What if all the acknowledged LSP-IDs in a PSNP frame do not fit into a single packet? No problem – as the atomic element in the PSNP is the *LSP Entry* field *itself*. In other words: All the LSP Entries are totally unrelated to each other. The particular order of an LSP-Entry TLV in a PSNP is totally meaningless. Unlike Hello messages where there are many different TLVs in a Hello message the entire Hello message is the atomic element – some TLVs are related to each other and therefore must occur in the same packet.

In the PSNP there is not much that may be related – there is only the LSP Entry TLVs (plus the authentication and checksum TLV) and it is not related to any other TLV. That is the reason why IS-IS may spread a large amount of acknowledgements over several packets – they are *not related to each other*.

The second application for PSNPs is requesting a more recent version of LSPs. During the adjacency formation phase an IS-IS router may detect that the other router holds newer versions of certain LSP Entries in the link-state database. By explicitly enumerating the LSP Entries that the router is interested in it is requesting a retransmission of the LSPs in question. The tcpdump shows a request of more recent LSPs.

Tcpdump output

```
01:29:48.567237 OSI, IS-IS, length: 44
  L2 PSNP, hlen: 17, v: 1, pdu-v: 1, sys-id-len: 6 (0), max-area: 3 (0)
    source-id: 6b01.c219.07fa.00, PDU length: 44
      LSP entries TLV #9, length: 240
 lsp-id: 1921.6800.1009.00-00, seq: 0x00000127, lifetime: 39281s, chksum: 0xbaee
 lsp-id: 1921.6800.1011.01-00, seq: 0x00000127, lifetime: 43412s, chksum: 0x4759
 lsp-id: 1921.6800.1017.00-00, seq: 0x00000122, lifetime: 7886s,  chksum: 0xf1c0
 lsp-id: 1921.6800.1018.01-00, seq: 0x0000012b, lifetime: 42379s, chksum: 0x2a17
 lsp-id: 1921.6800.1019.00-00, seq: 0x0000011b, lifetime: 59820s, chksum: 0x5644
 lsp-id: 1921.6800.1020.01-00, seq: 0x00000118, lifetime: 5239s,  chksum: 0x2b6b
 lsp-id: 1921.6800.1021.00-00, seq: 0x00000110, lifetime: 6007s,  chksum: 0x1862
 lsp-id: 1921.6800.1022.00-00, seq: 0x0000143f, lifetime: 50489s, chksum: 0x8489
 lsp-id: 1921.6800.1023.00-00, seq: 0x0000140d, lifetime: 26319s, chksum: 0xb590
 lsp-id: 1921.6800.1024.00-00, seq: 0x000026d1, lifetime: 49281s, chksum: 0x3464
 lsp-id: 1921.6800.1025.00-00, seq: 0x00002b52, lifetime: 19969s, chksum: 0x5f8d
 lsp-id: 1921.6800.1033.00-00, seq: 0x00001587, lifetime: 30940s, chksum: 0x13f3
 lsp-id: 1921.6800.1045.00-00, seq: 0x00001548, lifetime: 46855s, chksum: 0x9af1
 lsp-id: 1921.6800.1046.00-00, seq: 0x00000810, lifetime: 18354s, chksum: 0x6ced
 lsp-id: 1921.6800.1050.00-00, seq: 0x00000a88, lifetime: 15579s, chksum: 0x208b
      LSP entries TLV #9, length: 48
 lsp-id: 1921.6800.1078.00-00, seq: 0x00000424, lifetime: 18438s, chksum: 0xe15d
 lsp-id: 1921.6800.1089.00-00, seq: 0x000003e9, lifetime: 10171s, chksum: 0x0442
 lsp-id: 1921.6800.1099.00-00, seq: 0x00000167, lifetime: 18200s, chksum: 0x51ac
```

The PSNP header shows that PSNPs are not prepared for multi-packet transmission – the PSNP header does not carry sequence-number- or chain-number-like semantics. However, that is not a big issue: the integrity of the PSNP is under all circumstances maintained because the atomic element is the LSP-ID. So the bottom line of PSNPs is: the application IS-IS has put no hooks for multi-packet messages, as they are obsolete. Next, CSNPs are explored to see if *they* need multi-packet messages, and we will find out if IS-IS has reserved a few fields to convey these.

CSNPs are radically different to PSNPs. As the name implies, a router transmitting a *Complete* Sequence Number Packet (CSNP) transmits more than a router just transmitting a Partial Sequence Number Update (PSNP). Routers use CSNPs for initial synchronization once an adjacency comes up on point-to-point links and for periodical synchronization on LAN links. A discussion of the mechanics of what to do once a router receives a CSNP and how to react upon a mismatch comparing to the own link-state database is out of the scope of this chapter and was elaborated in more detail in Chapter 8 "Synchronizing Databases". The important thing to know is that these mechanisms fundamentally rely on the integrity of the CSNP message. This in turn means that a CSNP has to convey a *full* snapshot of the current link-state database. If there is something missing or, even worse, two CSNPs are accidentally mixed up on the same circuit, the receiver always assumes that the CSNP integrity is okay and may blast the link with a massive amount of LSP updates.

Link-state databases can be big (thousands of entries). And even if the CSNP has to report just the headers in a CSNP message by means of TLV #9, IS-IS may run the risk of exhausting the space that a single packet may transport. Just take a look at the CSNP recorded on an average backbone router and look at how all the content is filled up with fully sized LSP Entry TLVs #9 that show other routers all the contents of its link-state database.

Tcpdump output

```
01:29:48.567237 OSI, IS-IS, length: 1478
    L2 CSNP, hlen: 33, v: 1, pdu-v: 1, sys-id-len: 6 (0), max-area: 3 (0)
  source-id: 6b01.c219.07fa.00, PDU length: 1478
  start lsp-id: 1921.6800.1001.00-00
  end lsp-id: 1921.6802.0022.00-00
    LSP entries TLV #9, length: 240
      lsp-id: 1921.6800.1001.01-00, seq: 0x000003ac, lifetime: 15110s, chksum: 0xd551
      lsp-id: 1921.6800.1001.02-00, seq: 0x0000011c, lifetime: 17576s, chksum: 0x47a0
      lsp-id: 1921.6800.1001.03-00, seq: 0x00000166, lifetime: 21751s, chksum: 0x96c8
      lsp-id: 1921.6800.0011.00-00, seq: 0x000000b9, lifetime: 27108s, chksum: 0xb43d
      [ ... ]
      lsp-id: 1921.6801.0046.00-00, seq: 0x000006c7, lifetime: 47027s, chksum: 0x2c71
      lsp-id: 1921.6801.0057.00-00, seq: 0x000003cc, lifetime: 39228s, chksum: 0xa5c3
      lsp-id: 1921.6801.0063.00-00, seq: 0x000003ac, lifetime: 45114s, chksum: 0x4d09
      lsp-id: 1921.6801.0074.00-00, seq: 0x00000393, lifetime: 64927s, chksum: 0x048d
    LSP entries TLV #9, length: 240
      lsp-id: 1921.6801.0074.00-00, seq: 0x00000453, lifetime: 21053s, chksum: 0xcc1a
      lsp-id: 1921.6801.0074.02-00, seq: 0x000002fc, lifetime: 14740s, chksum: 0x67be
      lsp-id: 1921.6801.0074.03-00, seq: 0x000002d5, lifetime: 5065s, chksum: 0x97a2
      lsp-id: 1921.6801.0088.00-00, seq: 0x0000033e, lifetime: 59876s, chksum: 0xd3cc
      [ ... ]
      lsp-id: 1921.6802.0012.03-00, seq: 0x000000dc, lifetime: 43654s, chksum: 0xfc64
      lsp-id: 1921.6802.0018.00-00, seq: 0x00000530, lifetime: 56270s, chksum: 0x8b39
      lsp-id: 1921.6802.0018.00-00, seq: 0x00000494, lifetime: 14156s, chksum: 0xdd6a
    LSP entries TLV #9, length: 240
      lsp-id: 1921.6802.0019.00-00, seq: 0x0000041f, lifetime: 59421s, chksum: 0x985d
      lsp-id: 1921.6802.0019.02-00, seq: 0x000000d3, lifetime: 54186s, chksum: 0xde3a
      lsp-id: 1921.6802.0019.03-00, seq: 0x000000d4, lifetime: 44940s, chksum: 0xf814
      lsp-id: 1921.6802.0022.00-00, seq: 0x000019a1, lifetime: 12688s, chksum: 0x26f9
      [ ... ]
```

A single packet cannot hold up all the LSP headers of a fully blown link-state database of the sizes in the Internet today. However, if you take a look at the tcpdump above you may find, contrary to PSNPs, some mechanisms in the header that support multi-packet messages. Those are the Start-LSP and End-LSP fields in the CSNP header. CSNPs are prepared from day one to fully support multi-packet messages. Therefore it needs a marker to find out when the synchronization process is over and when the receiving router can start to compute the difference to its local link-state database and either flood or request more recent instances of a LSP. The Start-LSP-ID and End-LSP-ID fields help to indicate when a synchronization process is over. The Start-LSP-ID field of the first message in a multi-message CSNP is set to 0000.0000.0000.00-00 and the End-LSP-ID field is set to FFFF.FFFF.FFFF.FF-FF. If your environment is a very small one (like our sample topology) the full CSNP fits into a single packet and most probably looks like the following.

Tcpdump output

```
00:33:02.536076 OSI, IS-IS, length: 99
  L2 CSNP, hlen: 33, v: 1, pdu-v: 1, sys-id-len: 6 (0), max-area: 3 (0)
    source-id: 0000.0000.0002.00, PDU length: 99
    start lsp-id: 0000.0000.0000.00-00
    end lsp-id: ffff.ffff.ffff.ff-ff
```

```
LSP entries TLV #9, length: 64
  lsp-id: 1921.6800.1001.00-00, seq: 0x000022d8, lifetime: 1059s, chksum: 0xdd0b
  lsp-id: 1921.6800.1002.00-00, seq: 0x00000125, lifetime: 58193s, chksum: 0x7dc0
  lsp-id: 1921.6800.1002.02-00, seq: 0x0000011e, lifetime: 58164s, chksum: 0xb8e3
  lsp-id: 1921.6800.1003.00-00, seq: 0x0000011b, lifetime: 58191s, chksum: 0x5fb0
```

Recall that this packet-type is not the common case found in networks of even moderate size. So watch out and do not wonder if you receive in a small lab environment single-packet CSNPs with 0000.0000.0000.00-00 and FFFF.FFFF.FFFF.FF-FF as Start- and End LSP-IDs. One of us (Hannes) even thought that IS-IS implementers tried to avoid filling the CSNPs properly and only stumbled onto the reality during research into the graceful-restart (see Chapter 13 "IS-IS Extensions" for details). In IS-IS there is the notion of a Synchronization Start- and Stop event and it is important to fill these fields with proper values.

CSNPs encompass something that can be described as *application level fragmentation*. The *application* IS-IS knows that the underlying transport infrastructure cannot carry more than 1497 or 1492 bytes of *synchronization payload*. And therefore it spreads the database headers over different CSNP packets, which is a way of assuming a minimum MTU and fragmentation avoidance.

By discussing PSNPs and CSNPs it was assumed that the reader knows about the format and structure of LSP-IDs. Link-state packets are one of the places in IS-IS that was intended by the specification to span more than a single MTU.

9.4.3 *Link-state Packets (LSPs)*

In a link-state PDU a speaker originates a variety of information like capability codes, topological (IS) reachability and IP reachability information. For the latter two it can happen that an IS-IS speaker cannot squeeze all the IP prefixes or all the adjacencies it has to advertise into a single 1492/1497-byte packet. There are several occurrences in real networks for this situation, such as Frame Relay, ATM Hub routers or L1L2 routers, which leak Level-2 prefixes to Level-1.

For the IS-IS specification designers it was clear that in order to avoid fragmentation, the IS-IS protocol needed a few hooks that support multi-message LSP in a similar way that CSNPs do. Figure 9.8 shows that the LSP-ID has a special byte called the Fragment-ID that can indicate what fragment number the LSP is. Each LSP-ID is uniquely identified using the first seven bytes. The first six bytes are inherited from the System-ID that is part of the NET. The penultimate byte indicates if the issuing router is a real router (PSN-byte = 00) or a pseudo router (PSN-bytes = any non-zero value). More about pseudonodes and the use of the PSN bytes was detailed in Chapter 7, "Pseudonodes and Designated Routess". The last byte indicates the fragment of the original LSP message.

If an IS-IS router has to originate (for instance) a 4000 byte LSP, and it is a non-pseudonode (a real router) with a System-ID of 1921.6800.1077, and given that the common IS-IS MTU is 1492/1497 bytes, one needs to transmit three fragments. So the original LSP 1921.6800.1077.00 is split into three fragments: 1921.6800.1077.**00**, 1921.6800.1077.**01** and 1921.6800.1077.**02**, before transmission over the wire. The

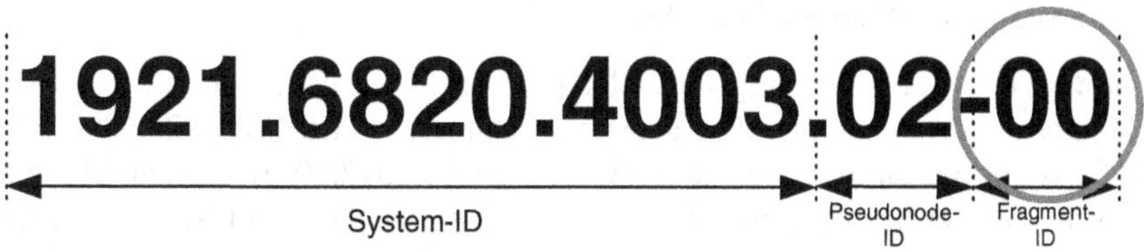

FIGURE 9.8. The application IS-IS has dedicated one byte in its LSP-ID format to include packet fragment numbers

receiving router simply installs all three fragments in the link-state database and IS-IS embedded synchronization mechanisms (CSNPs and PSNPs) make sure that all the fragments are known to all the routers in a network. Of course, everything that can go wrong with LSPs will go wrong in practice. IS-IS is very liberal in that respect. It does not care if all the fragments finally arrive at the receiver or delay an SPF calculation for route calculation because of a missing fragment. The embedded CSNP and PSNP mechanisms are considered to be robust enough to make sure that ultimately all LSPs get delivered. There is one exception to this rule: handling of Fragment zero has a few rules that every IS-IS speaker has to obey.

9.4.3.1 Fragment Zero

IS-IS does not care if any non-zero fragment is lost – nothing gets delayed or declared bogus because of that. Fragment zero, however, has some rules and restrictions.

First of all, if Fragment zero is not present, then the entire set of fragments will be declared invalid, as there is some mandatory information in Fragment zero that is vital, for example, to SPF computation. There are further restrictions such as: if it is not in Fragment zero, it must also not be contained anywhere else. And if Fragment zero is missing, then the SPF computation cannot start to process the link-state database. The most important information that needs to be present in SPF runs is:

1. The union of all L1 Areas encoded in the Area TLV #1
2. If Multi-Topologies extensions are enabled (see Chapter 13 “IS-IS Extensions”), the Multi-Topologies Supported TLV #229

Those two LSPs contain information that are vital to SPF processing (most important are the Overload and ATTach bits) if the state of information in Fragment zero is not known it becomes irrelevant to process an SPF operation. Fragment zero is the central dogma of IS-IS, everybody has to comply with the rules and properly advertise the Area TLV #1 and Multi-Topology Supported TLV #229, otherwise the entire LSP’s non-zero fragments will be disregarded and thereby purged off the forwarding topology. On the other hand, those two TLVs are considered to be illegal in any non-zero fragment and are at best ignored. This behaviour comes from Jon Postel’s famous rule about protocol interoperability: “Be tolerant what you receive and strict in what you send”. Both IOS and JUNOS follow this rule and only evaluate these two TLVs in Fragment zero.

9.4.3.2 Fragment "Wander" Problems

The atomic element for a trigger that leads to an SPF calculation is a change in an *LSP's fragment*. For example, if an adjacency is present in LSP-ID 1921.6800.1077.00-01 and it is not present in an updated LSP 1921.6800.1077.00-01, then an SPF calculation is scheduled as the trigger condition is met. However, an IS-IS LSP is a linear stream of data and a change in size of a stream element (TLV) may need to organize the entire stream, as all the fragments need to be rebuilt. This problem is described as fragment "wander" and today modern IS-IS implementations have come up with "clue" logic to prevent that.

Naive IS-IS implementations build up a stream of TLV-encoded information and break it apart afterwards for transmission on the circuits that have MTUs of 1492/1497 bytes. The word "naive" is used here because, although it does fulfil what is in the specification, it can create a lot amount of churn in the network by doing more than is mentioned in the specification.

Consider Figure 9.9 for a better illustration of fragmentation as a way of post-processing a TLV stream. An IS-IS router generates a set of TLV-encoded information including IS or IP Reachability TLVs. Now one adjacency goes down. A naive implementation builds the entire stream from scratch and chops everything into pieces afterwards. What happens is that even adjacencies that have been stable like Adjacency #27 are squeezed back into Fragment zero. That means that two fragments have to be rebuilt: Fragment zero and Fragment 1.

A "cluey" implementation builds the stream and fragments it first hand. When it has to re-originate one of its fragments, this approach tries to be as conservative as possible to save the network portions that do not necessarily involve a change of link-state updates. Remember,

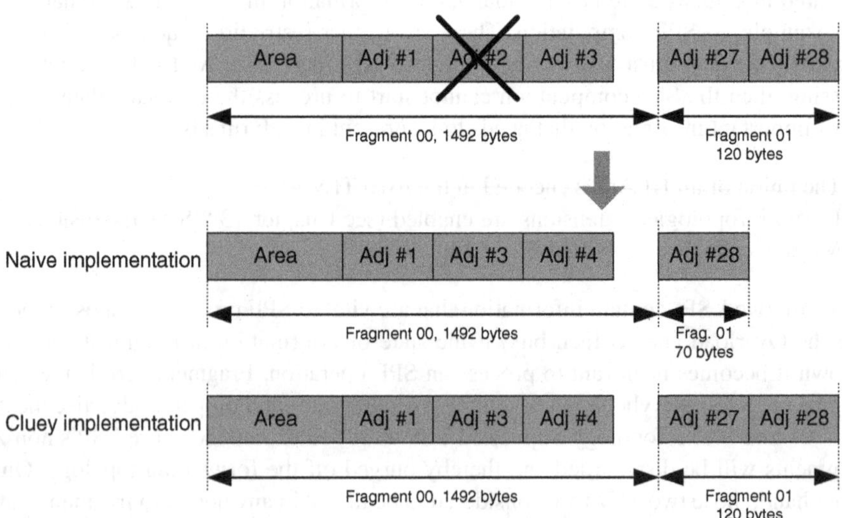

FIGURE 9.9. Naive implementation can generate a lot of churn in the network by blindly re-building every fragment on every change in adjacencies or IP reachability.

even if no SPF is triggered, flooding is still an expensive task. A "cluey" implementation tries to avoid fragment rebuilds as long as possible, as indicated below. If Adjacency #2 flaps the adjacencies in other fragments will not be affected. So the router has to rebuild and flood only *one* fragment throughout the network. Doing so also saves the network from churn when an adjacency comes back again. In the naive implementation, all fragments need to be rebuilt. The "cluey" implementation thinks in terms of fragments and only does a full rebuild of fragments when the LSP fragment space (currently 256) is reached. To avoid squeezing data into one of the not-100-per cent-full fragments, it does a full rebuild.

Good implementations of the IS-IS routing protocol like IOS and JUNOS of course are *fragment-aware* and try to be least disruptive by only rebuilding fragments that are affected by a change and are thereby friendly to their environment.

9.4.3.3 LSP Fragment Space and LSDB Size

How big is the LSP fragment space and is it big enough? This is a question that is often raised when talking about IS-IS, and distributed link-state databases. The Fragment byte is an 8-bit quantity and therefore it can store up to 256 fragments. Each fragment can hold up to 1492/1497 bytes; 256 fragments times 1497 – 27 (the LSP header) bytes equals to $1470 * 256$, which gives a storage space of 376,320 bytes that an individual System-ID can originate. Are 256 fragments enough? Look at the numbers of routes and adjacencies that can be stored in 376,320 bytes. In 376,320 bytes about 42.000 IPv4 routes or approximately 31,000 new-style (TLV #22) adjacencies can be stored. In our opinion, even for large hub routers injecting a vast amount of Level-2 routes into Level-1, typically not more than 15–20 fragments are used. For adjacencies, typically not more than 20 adjacencies are formed at the average core router. At Frame-Relay or ATM Hub Routers the number of adjacencies rises to a worst case of about 200. So the IS-IS architecture based on today's routers is not near its end.

However, the industry is changing, and multi-chassis routers (like the Juniper Networks TX Series or the Cisco Systems CRS-1 Series) can have up to ten times the number of interfaces than they had in the past. Assume for a moment that IS-IS is at the end of the fragment space.

In most IS-IS implementation you probably would see some entries in your log file such as:

JUNOS output

```
hannes@Frankfurt> show log messages
[ … ]
Aug 28 15:14:51 Frankfurt rpd[344]: RPD_ISIS_OVERLOAD: IS-IS database overload
Aug 28 15:24:52 Frankfurt rpd[344]: RPD_ISIS_OVERLOAD: IS-IS database overload
Aug 28 15:34:53 Frankfurt rpd[344]: RPD_ISIS_OVERLOAD: IS-IS database overload
```

Based on today's environment, somebody did something seriously wrong in the network, like trying to pump all Internet routes into IS-IS. There is a case study in Chapter 15

"Troubleshooting" that will help you troubleshoot these scenarios. When the router has reached its end of fragments space, then the only option it has left is to purge Fragment 01–255 and to re-originate fragment zero with the Overload Bit set in the LSP header. The Overload Bit tells other routers in the network that they should not calculate any transit paths through this router because it is overloaded and thus might black hole traffic. More about the Overload Bit and what can be done with it was covered in Chapter 6, "Generating, Flooding and Ageing LSPs". The good news is that a router setting the Overload Bit is very visible to the network, and the "bad guy" can quickly be spotted for further troubleshooting. The bad news is that some IS-IS implementations may not survive the first *killer-wave* of 42,000 routes piped into IS-IS.

Getting back to multi-chassis router architectures – what prevents a big, multi-chassis router from advertising its internal structure of chassis-to-chassis links to the outside world? Well, LAN adjacencies are scaled nicely using the idea of pseudonodes. The pseudonode concept can be used just as well to model a router that is surrounded by multiple shelves each having a dedicated System-ID and owning (perhaps) 376 KB each of distributed storage space. It worked with pseudonodes, why should it not work with real nodes? The answer is simple: Nothing! There is even an Internet-draft that describes this idea: draft-ietf-isis-ext-lsp-frags. Chapter 17, "Future of IS-IS", will explore these concepts in more detail. So far, no implementation has picked up on these ideas of modelling a *Real Router* as several *Virtual Routers,* as there has been no implementation pressure yet. However, that might change in the future.

Another option for scaling the distributed LSP storage space is extending the 1492/1497 MTU to something bigger. Today, virtually every interface in the core network of ISPs is based on SONET/SDH that have at least an MTU of 4474 at the link-layer. That means that IS-IS can transmit up to (4470 – 27)*256 = 1,137,408 bytes of distributed storage space. That's about tripling the size with moderate implementation effort. Changing the minimum MTU in a network is a daunting task and everybody knows that there may still be a hidden edge in the network that cannot change its MTUs. The protocol implementers wanted to have a last-resort warning that a node does not support larger MTUs by originating the so-called LSP Buffer Size TLV #14. This TLV was mentioned in the second version of ISO 10589 published in 1997. The TLVs contents simply represent a 16-bit value indicating the maximum MTU that the system can understand. You can see the structure of the TLV #14 in Figure 9.10.

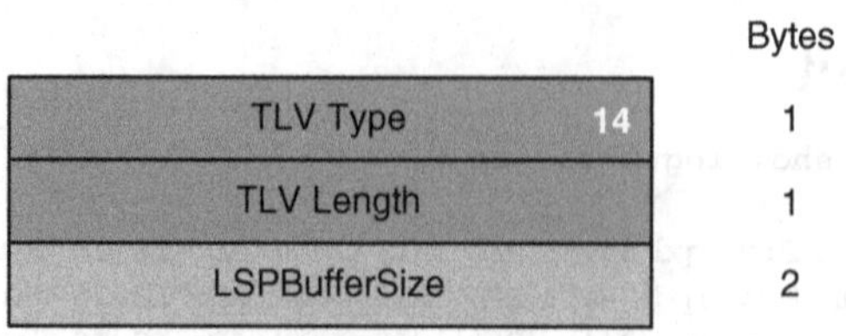

Field	Value	Bytes
TLV Type	14	1
TLV Length		1
LSPBufferSize		2

FIGURE 9.10. Any IS-IS router that wants to send bigger than 1492/1497 byte-sized LSPs must have the Buffer size TLV #14 present in Fragment zero

9.5 Summary

Contrary to IP routing protocols, IS-IS cannot rely on a network layer to do fragmentation for it. IS-IS runs directly on the link-layer, which has no possibility of fragmenting frames. IS-IS therefore needs to apply a few techniques to get around the too-small MTU problem if it has to transmit a message that is larger than the MTU. The two techniques IS-IS uses fall under the category of fragmentation avoidance and application level fragmentation. IS-IS assumes a minimum MTU that every link has to support. This limit today is theoretically 1492 and in practice 1497 bytes. Additionally in several packet types in IS-IS there is support for multi-packet messages like CSNPs and LSPs. There are also details of how the *application* IS-IS should fragment in order to avoid network-wide churn. "Cluey" implementations think in terms of fragments and try only to rebuild fragments that have been affected by an adjacency change. In current network architectures, the distributed LSP storage space is typically only utilized at 10 per cent, and even if the space *could* become exhausted, the IS-IS working group has come up with a solution that is similar to modelling adjacencies on a large LAN. There is also the possibility of raising the 1492 byte limit of LSP buffer size as all modern interface cards, especially in core environments, support MTUs up to 4474 bytes. Although not needed today, these developments are a good proof that the IS-IS infrastructure will exist for a long time to come in networks.

10

SPF and Route Calculation

In order for the hop-by-hop routing paradigm to work, link-state routers need a common algorithm to determine a loop-free path to all destinations in a network. In this chapter you will gain insight as to how the IS-IS related route-calculation and route-resolution algorithms work. There will be a step-by-step explanation of the main three elements in the route calculation process that is SPF calculation, route resolution and prefix insertion.

The SPF calculation process has been practically demonized in the past. There is no need to view this process negatively, in the authors' opinion. This chapter includes a performance assessment of each of the three elements needed for SPF calculation to correct this unfortunate perception. Also, common router OS implementation knobs for mitigating the CPU overload side-effects of the SPF calculation and route resolution will be discussed.

Finally there will be an implementation assessment of the most dominant performance-related element of the process, which is *prefix insertion*. The two common schemes for prefix insertion are presented and finally the cost of inserting a prefix and the metrics of current router hardware will be highlighted.

10.1 Route Calculation

From the time that a link-state PDU arrives to the time traffic is flowing through the changed path in a router, a lot of actions need to be taken. Figure 10.1 shows the three different steps that are applied for each route.

First, the SPF calculation needs to be run. Depending on the location in the network topology and which information has changed (topology, prefix), there are three choices of SPF runs:

- Full
- Partial
- Incremental

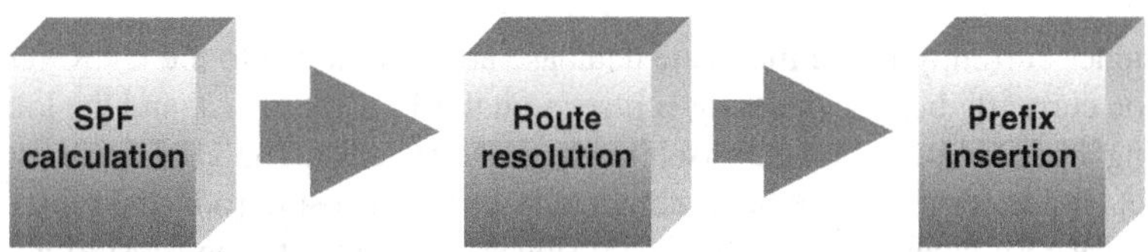

FIGURE 10.1. The three operations for calculating routes

Then, after executing the SPF calculation, the router needs to find out if there are *dependent* routes.

The route resolver determines if a change of the IS-IS-supplied topology and routes also results in a change of dependent routes. Routing protocols like BGP rely on a working IGP to map the *reachability* information to a *topology* in order to calculate the path cost properly. Finally, after the affected dependent routes have been determined, the router proceeds to the third stage, which is prefix insertion.

At the prefix insertion stage the router inserts, deletes or changes prefixes of all address families (IPv4, IPv6) and their corresponding Next-hops, then downloads the new forwarding tables to the line-cards and ASICs of the packet forwarding complex of the router.

The next sections explore all three elements both from a theoretical and practical perspective. At the end of each section performance considerations for the network designer are highlighted.

10.2 The SPF Algorithm

The Shortest Path First algorithm was invented and first documented by Edser Dijkstra, a Dutch mathematician who was researching the topic of graph theory and looking for an algorithm to determine the shortest spanning distance between two points on a graph. The SPF algorithm is perhaps one of the best-analyzed algorithms in computer science, and its scaling properties are well understood. There are many resources available on the Internet that explain and illustrate how the SPF algorithm works. A good tutorial to learn more about the algorithm, even running through an animated SPF calculation, can be found at http://www.tutor.ms.unimelb.edu.au/dijkstra/dijkstra.html

Briefly, SPF is based on a database of node-to-node costs and, using three lists, the SPF algorithm can determine the shortest path to all nodes in N steps, where N is the number of nodes in the network.

10.2.1 *Working Principle*

The SPF algorithm maintains three lists:

- UNKNOWN
- TENTative
- PATHs

All nodes currently in the link-state database are first moved to the UNKNOWN list. The node currently being evaluating is placed on the TENTative list, and the local router executing the SPF calculation puts itself on the TENTative list. The TENTative list consists of triplets in the form of neighbour, neighbours-cost and cost to root (the router running SPF). Once SPF determines the best path (lowest cost back to the root) to a node, the node is moved to the PATHs list. The PATHs list sometimes is called the *Known* list.

The list of explored PATHS starts at zero. Next, a loop of at most N steps starts, where N is the number of nodes in the link-state database. Each loop through the algorithm has these steps:

1. Find the node with the lowest cost and move it into PATHs
2. Find all neighbours reachable from that node and move the neighbours from UNKNOWN into TENTative, but ...
3. Before a node is moved from UNKNOWN into TENTative, apply a two-way check. If Node A claims that it can see Node B, re-verify that Node B also reports to see Node A. If not, ignore that adjacency.
4. For each node that moves onto the TENTative list, maintain the *cost* to get there and store the *first-hop* information. The first-hop is needed for populating the routing-table with routes when SPF is done. The forwarding-engine of a router thinks only in terms of *prefixes* and *directly connected next-hops* (the first-hop).

10.2.2 *Example*

The SPF algorithm can be very abstract. Consider the sample topology shown in Figure 10.2. For a better illustration of SPF calculation, we will do an SPF calculation

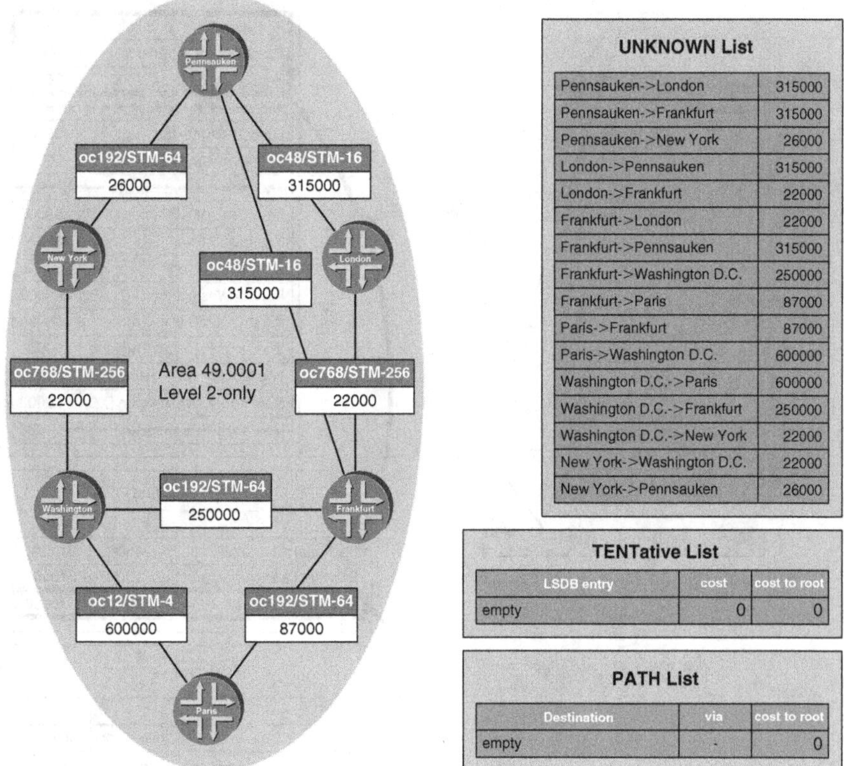

FIGURE 10.2. At initialization all information in the LSDB is moved on the UNKNOWN list

just as a router in this sample topology would, in this example, the Pennsauken router. The figure shows all the Level-2 routers and eight links to connect them. Those links have speeds varying from OC-12/STM-4 (622Mbit/s) up to OC-768/STM-256 (40Gbit/s). The link cost has been assigned on a composite bandwidth/cost scheme. (Those bandwidth-to-IGP cost values are taken from Figure 12.10 in Chapter 12 "IP Reachability Information.")

The full link-state database consists of six routers reporting eight links. Due to these eight links, the router holds $8 * 2 = 16$ unidirectional link-states in the link-state database (LSDB). At the beginning of the SPF calculation, all 16 links are moved, together with their respective cost field, into the UNKNOWN list, as shown in Figure 10.2.

Then the list of explored PATHs is cleared and each router performing the SPF calculation puts itself as the first entry into the TENTative list. In our example, we will execute the SPF calculation from Pennsauken's point of view as illustrated in Figure 10.3. All adjacencies that are reported via Pennsauken are moved into the TENTative list.

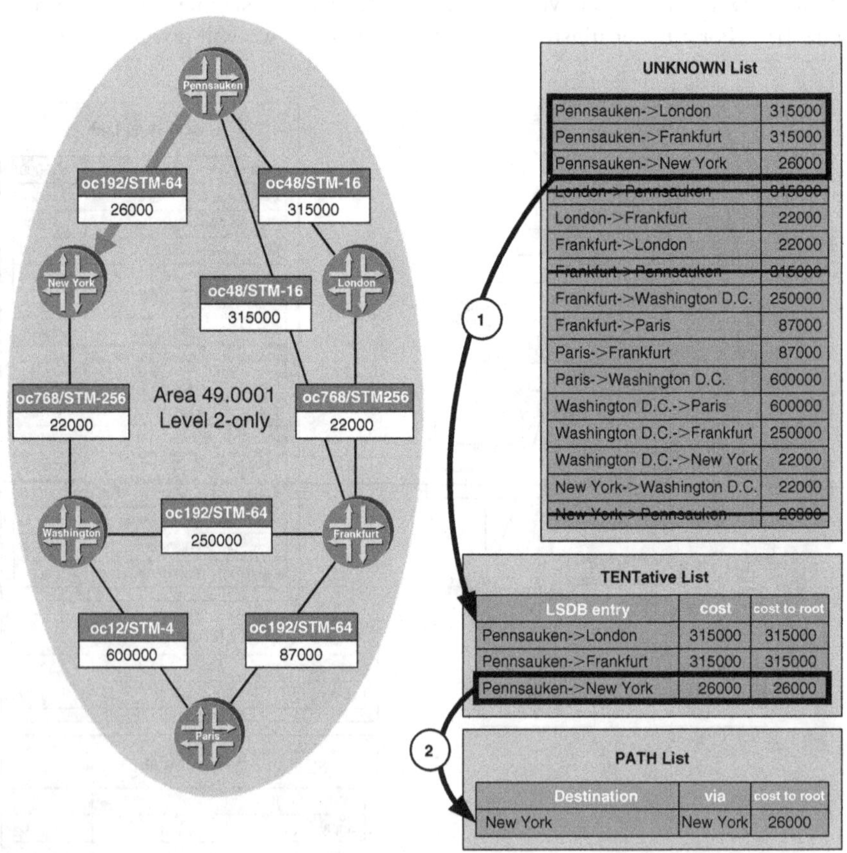

FIGURE 10.3. New York has the least-cost path to root and is moved onto the PATH list

Routers also execute a so-called *two-way* check. The two-way check verifies that neighbouring nodes are *mutually* connected on the graph. Routers are required only to announce two-way verified reachability information. However, there are cases where two neighbouring routers believe that they are connected when in fact they are not. Several broken two-way scenarios were presented and illustrated in Chapter 5, "Neighbour-Discovery and Handshaking".

Because of the two-way check requirement, Pennsauken takes a look in the LSDB to see if all its neighbours (New York, London, Frankfurt) have pointers pointing to Pennsauken as well. If all reported adjacencies pass this two-way check, they are purged from the UNKNOWN list.

The algorithm now tries to find the best path to the root node (Pennsauken). The least-cost path on the TENTative list is New York with a cost of 26000. Therefore, as indicated in Figure 10.3, New York's path cost is moved onto the PATH list. As a next step, the algorithm tries to further drill down the best path found so far and load all the *immediate successors* onto the TENTative list, since traffic obviously has to pass this way.

New York only has one immediate successor, which is Washington. In Figure 10.4, the Pensauken router loads all Washington-related LSDBs onto the TENTative list and verifies

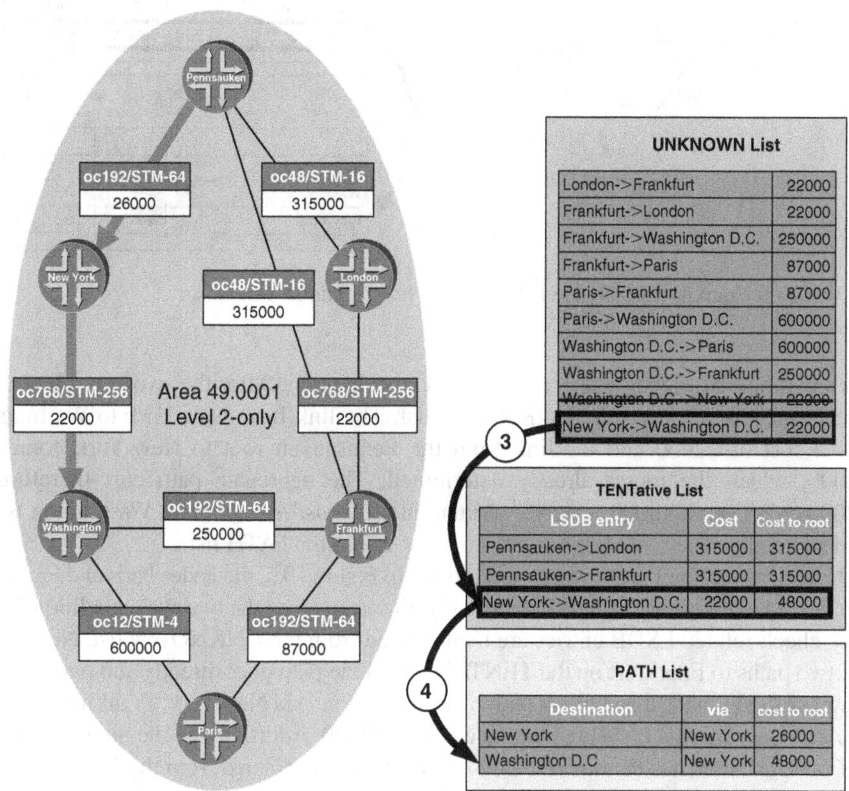

FIGURE 10.4. Washington has the least-cost path to root and is moved onto the PATH list

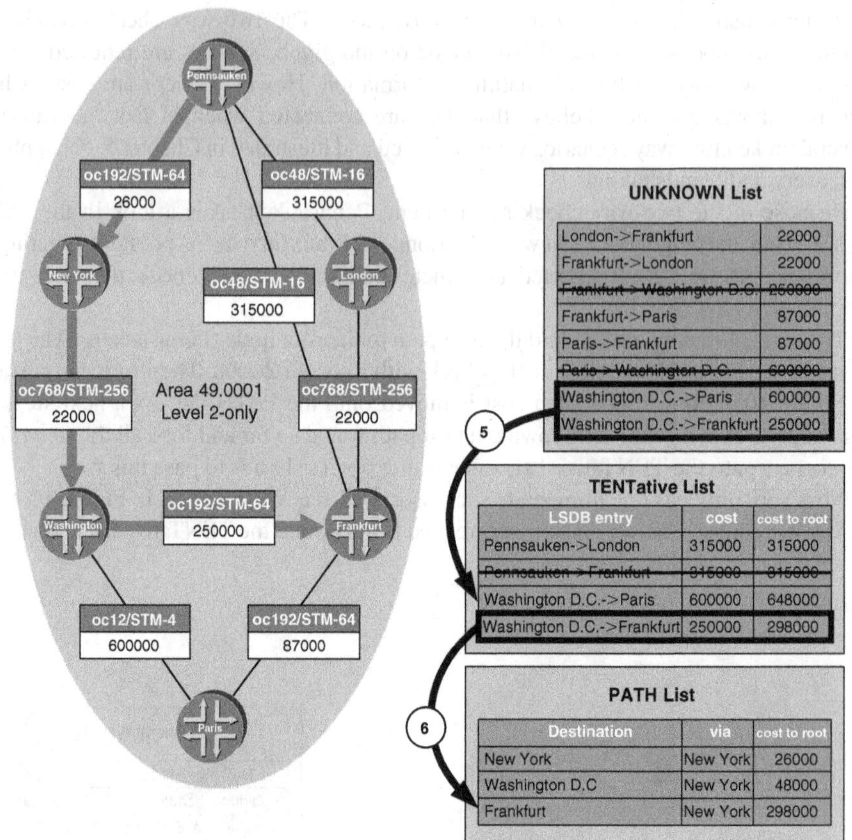

FIGURE 10.5. Frankfurt is routed via New York although a direct line exists

each claimed adjacency using the two-way check again. After the two-way check, the entries are deleted from the UNKNOWN list. The link from New York to Washington has a cost of 22000 and the link from the Pennsauken root to New York comes to 26000, which the router already determined. The aggregate path cost therefore is 22000 + 26000 = 48000 which is written into the *cost-to-root* field. Washington is the shortest path to the root and is therefore moved onto the PATH list.

Next, Washington's successors are explored. In Figure 10.5, the nodes Paris and Frankfurt are moved onto the TENTative list, but only after satisfying the two-way condition. Two-way-check-related LSDB entries are then deleted from the UNKNOWN list. Now, there are two paths to Frankfurt on the TENTative list. One path goes directly and one goes via New York. SPF adds the shortest path by cost, which is via New York. Frankfurt via New York moves onto the PATH list with a cost of 298000. Additionally, the higher cost path to Frankfurt, which is the direct OC-48/STM-16 link, is deleted from the TENTative list.

In Figure 10.6, the last step of the SPF calculation is described. The last node that has been put onto the PATH list is Frankfurt. Therefore, all nodes that are reported

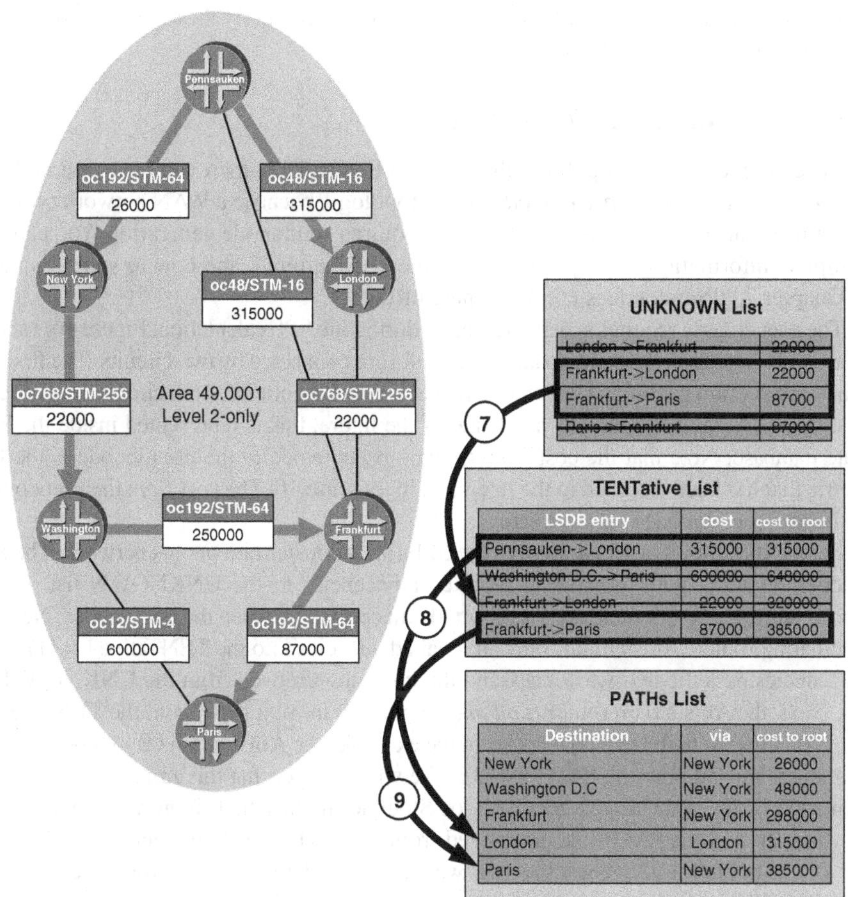

FIGURE 10.6. If the TENTative list is empty, the SPF calculation is terminated

via Frankfurt are further examined. The two remaining LSDB entries Frankfurt reports are the adjacencies to Paris and London. After passing the two-way check, the two links are moved onto the TENTative list. There are two ways to London: one direct link and one by way of New York to Washington and then to Frankfurt. The direct link has, in spite of the lower bandwidth, precedence in SPF over the indirect path. The direct link has a cost of 315000, which is better than the 320000 of the composite path. Finally, there are two paths to Paris, one by way of New York to Washington to Frankfurt at a cost of 385000, and one via New York to Washington at a cost of 648000. The path through Frankfurt is, due to the lower cost, moved into the PATH list.

Finally, there is no further information on the TENTative list, which is the condition that terminates the SPF calculation. Fortunately, the UNKNOWN list is also empty, but it does not necessarily have to be. There could be "stale" LSDB entries on it, which have not yet aged out, but also could list nodes that did not pass the two-way check. Anyway, those do no harm, as long as all nodes are reachable. Eventually these "extra" entries will age out of the link-state database.

10.2.3 *Pseudonode Processing*

In the example network topology illustrated in Figure 10.1, there are only *real* nodes in the network. There is no *pseudonode* on the topology, because a WAN network typically contains point-to-point links, which do not require pseudonode generation. You can find complete information about pseudonodes, their background, and how to suppress them, in Chapter 7, "Pseudonodes and Designated Routers".

The pseudonode requires special treatment during the SPF calculation. Figure 10.7 shows an example scenario. Amsterdam and Stockholm are connected by two circuits. The first one is a point-to-point circuit and the second one is a broadcast circuit. Both circuits have an IGP cost of 10 assigned. On the left-hand side of the figure, this is represented inside the link-state database. Note that the cost from the non-pseudonode *to* the pseudonode is the IGP metric that has been assigned to the interface, in this case 10. The cost *from* the pseudonode to the non-pseudonode is always zero.

Figure 10.8 shows an illustration of the SPF run at Amsterdam on this network. The SPF calculation starts with moving all reported adjacencies to the UNKNOWN list. In this small, sample network there are six reported adjacencies between the three nodes. Next the calculating router (Amsterdam) puts all local adjacencies into the TENTative list (1). Both adjacencies pass the two-way check and the links are removed from the UNKNOWN list (2). Next, the Amsterdam router *randomly* decides to move a node from the TENTative to the PATH list, as both have equal cost. In the example, the Amsterdam.00 to Stockholm.00 element is moved onto the PATH list (3). (We will see later that this *random* decision was a mistake.) The immediate successors of Stockholm.00, which is now the node under consideration in the PATH list, are moved from the UNKNOWN list onto the TENTative list (4). Stockholm.02 passes the two-way check and its links are removed from the UNKNOWN list (5). Now the Amsterdam router realizes it already has a path to Stockholm.00 with a cost of 10, so this link is discarded (6). As there are no further elements in the UNKNOWN list, the SPF calculation terminates and as a result just one path (the point-to-point link) is used between the two routers.

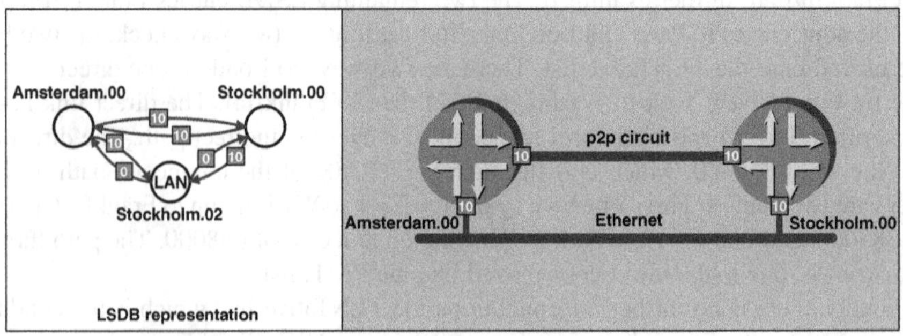

FIGURE 10.7. Two equal cost paths over a p2p and a broadcast circuit and its representation in the link-state database

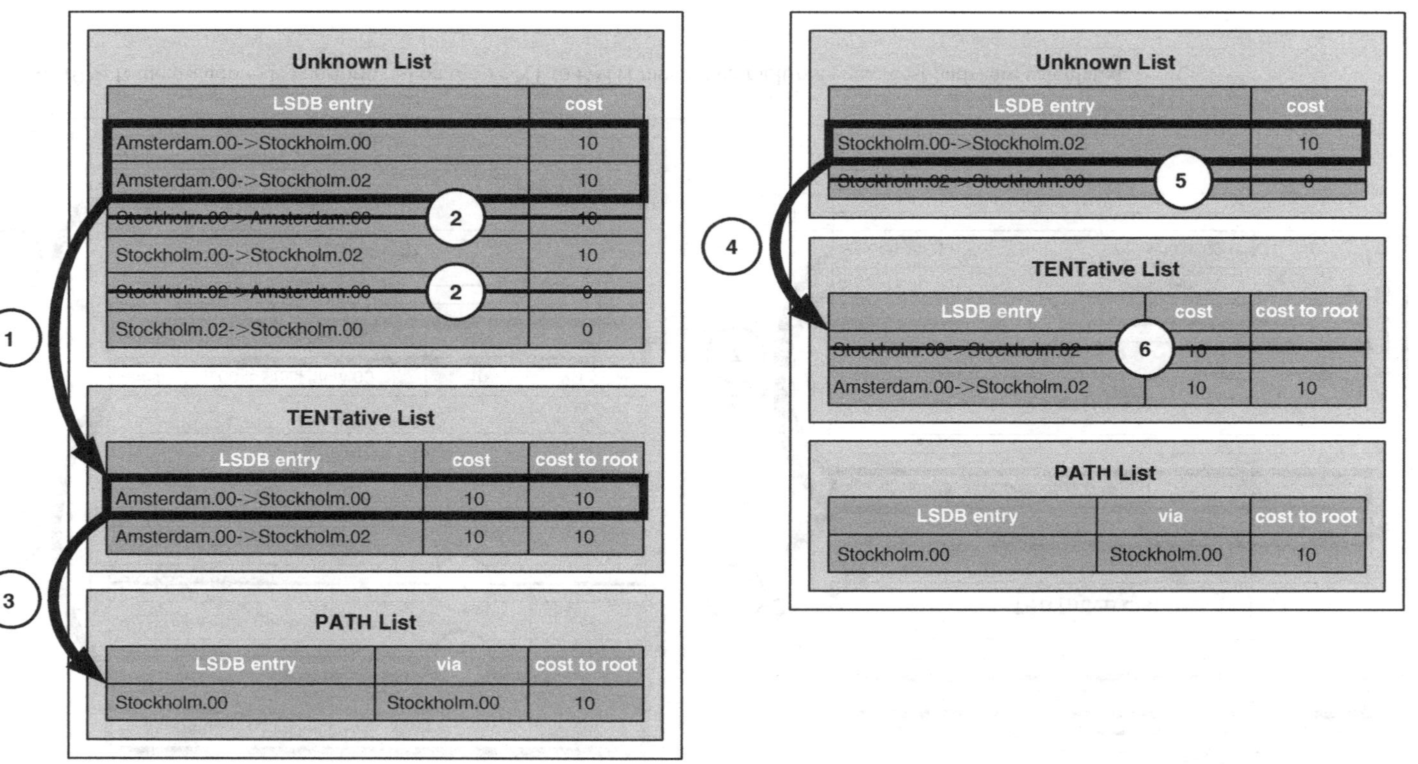

FIGURE 10.8. If the pseudonode is not prioritized on the TENT to PATH move then an equal cost path is lost

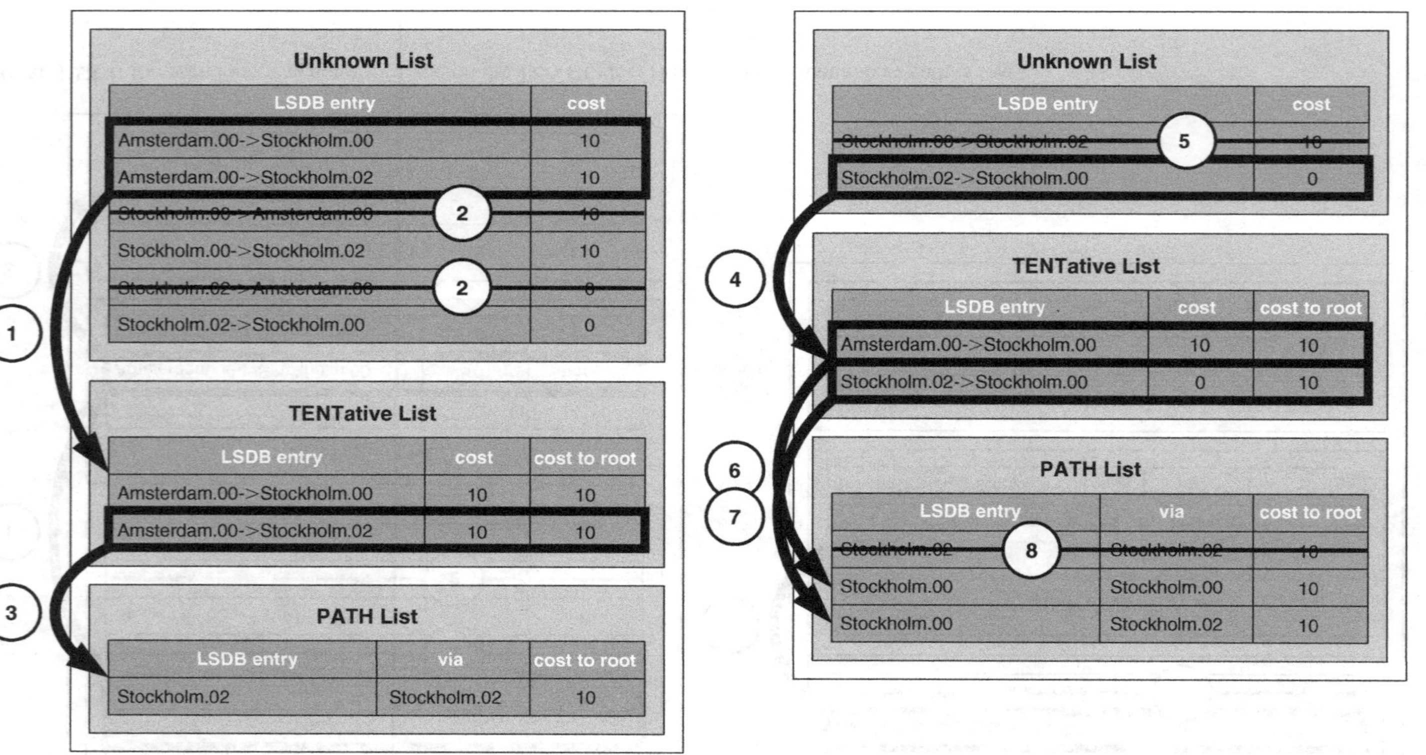

FIGURE 10.9. If the pseudonode is prioritized on the TENT to PATH move then multiple equal cost paths are calculated

Figure 10.9 illustrates another SPF run, but this time no *random* decision is made when moving a node from the TENTative list to the PATH list. Steps (1) and (2) are processed exactly as in the previous example. The difference now is that the system *prefers* the pseudonode (3) when moving an equal cost node from the TENTative to the PATH list. The router knows that the pseudonode will connect to a real node with a cost of zero, and so is a path of interest. Next, the router evaluates immediate successors from Stockholm.02 and puts them onto the TENTative list (4). After passing the two-way check, the links are removed (5). Next, the router evaluates the TENTative list and moves Stockholm.00 onto the PATH list (6). The remaining node in the TENTative list has a cost of 0 to a node (Stockholm.02) that is already on the PATH list. After summing up 0 plus the cost to reach Stockholm.02, it turns out that there is another path at cost 10 to Amsterdam.00 available, and this one moved into the PATH list (7). The TENTative and UNKNOWN lists are empty, which is the terminating condition for the SPF calculation. The result this time is that *both* paths are available, which is the desired result.

The above example has shown that any sane SPF implementation must prioritize the pseudonode when moving it from the TENTative to PATH list. Otherwise, paths in an equal cost multi-path environment get lost. The interesting thing is that the pseudonode prioritization is never mentioned in ISO 10589. Many implementers therefore make this mistake, and years later it is discovered in the field. JUNOS, for example, contained this oversight for 3 years until it was addressed in JUNOS 5.7.

The SPF calculation itself has been optimized during the course of networking history. So there are three different kinds of SPF calculations around. The next sections explore them and their particular performance and resource consumption properties.

10.3 SPF Calculation Diversity

There are two passes in the SPF calculation. The purpose of the first pass is to calculate the topological grid in an area. This tries to determine which routers are connected to each other. In the first pass, any prefix information is considered to be irrelevant for the structure of the grid and hence is disregarded. The router does its calculation of the topo logical grid purely on the information found in the IS Reachability and/or the Extended IS Reachability TLVs that are contained in each router's LSPs. In the previous section, this first pass was described in great detail.

In the second pass, all the leaf information is extracted. The router tries to find out if a given node speaks the correct Network Layer protocol. Each Network Layer protocol has to perform a leaf calculation. For instance, if a router does not speak IPv4, its IPv4-related TLVs (128,130,135), are completely disregarded during the second pass leaf calculation. At worst, an IS-IS router needs to calculate prefixes for three distinct address families (IPv4, IPv6 and CLNS). However, it is uncommon to run *all* three address protocols in an area. The most typical deployments are two protocols (IPv4 and IPv6 or IPv4 and CLNS) together in an area. In most SPF implementations of the IS-IS protocol the terms *full SPF run* and *partial SPF run* are used, which are different names for the first pass and the second pass, or leaf extraction.

10.3.1 *Full SPF Run*

The full SPF run is the heavyweight of SPF flavours. It both re-computes the topological grid in an area as well as re-computes the reachable IP prefixes. Full SPF runs are typically triggered by the following events:

- Local configuration change
- Update to a known LSP, which contains an adjacency change
- Local aged adjacency
- Receipt of a new/unknown LSP
- New Area-ID in the Level-1 network
- Link metric change
- Purging an LSP
- Periodically for additional robustness (every 15 minutes)

The full SPF run is not scheduled *immediately* after the above trigger events. Instead it is *delayed* for a configurable minimum amount of time. The most typical event from the above list is a *new* or *updated LSP*. In IS-IS networks, as in any other network running link-state routing protocols, there is a general observation that single LSP updates are very rare. They are almost always accompanied by other LSPs, which follow shortly after the first LSP shows up. The reason behind this is very clear: if a link fails there are always *two* routers that need to re-originate their LSPs. So it is better to wait a couple of milliseconds before starting an SPF calculation, which may tie the router down on the order of 100s of milliseconds.

So routers delay the SPF calculation. The typical pre-SPF delay value is 100 or 200 ms (depending on IOS or JUNOS). After the pre-SPF delay, the router *freezes* the link-state database and does the SPF calculation. Freezing means that during this time, no LSP additions or changes can be made.

10.3.1.1 Link-state Database Locking

It is absolutely mandatory for an IS-IS implementation to freeze the database during an SPF calculation run. An LSP change inserted during a run of the SPF calculation may result in bogus routes. Consider Figure 10.10 to get an idea what will happen if the link-state database is not locked. We are in the middle of an SPF calculation. The early stages of the SPF calculation considered the path through Washington the *best* path in the network. Now it is exploring the network downstream from Washington. Suddenly, the link between Washington and New York goes down. Unfortunately, the New York–Washington path is our best-path candidate. The SPF calculation does *not* backtrack through path candidates to see if the path properties have changed. If the router does not lock the link-state database then the result will be most likely bogus routes. Of course, IOS and JUNOS both lock the database (as any serious IS-IS implementation has to) and queue any incoming LSPs for insertion once the database is unlocked.

After the SPF calculation has completed, the router starts an *SPF hold-down timer* which blocks further SPF runs for self-protection reasons.

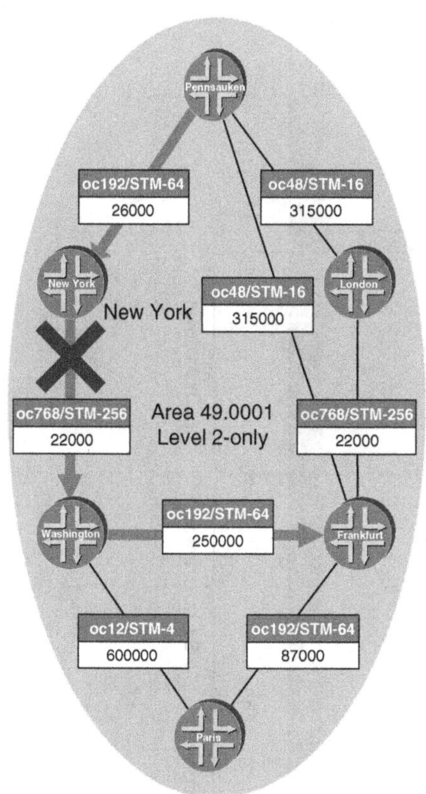

UNKNOWN List

London->Frankfurt	22000
Frankfurt->London	22000
Frankfurt->Paris	87000
Paris->Frankfurt	87000

TENTative List

LSDB entry	cost	cost to root
Pennsauken->London	315000	315000
Washington D.C.->Paris	600000	648000

PATH List

Destination	via	cost to root
New York	New York	26000
Washington D.C	New York	48000
Frankfurt	New York	298000

FIGURE 10.10. If the contents of the LSDB are not locked during the SPF computation, bogus routes will result

10.3.1.2 Self-protection

The purpose of hold-downs is to allow the IS-IS router to work less. Consider Figure 10.11 to see why SPF hold downs make sense. If there were no hold-down for SPF calculation, then the average utilization of the control plane CPU would be very high. During an SPF calculation (100–200 ms) the CPU utilization jumps to 100 per cent. But shortly thereafter it drops down to 0 per cent. If a network is shaky, then additional LSPs triggering new SPF calculations will follow, raising the CPU utilization to 100 per cent once again for a short period of time. By applying SPF hold-down timers, IS-IS keeps the *intervals* between the SPF calculations large and so lowers the *average* CPU utilization spent for SPF calculations. In other words, SPF hold-down is a self-protection mechanism to avoid meltdown of the router's control plane. SPF hold downs trade *responsiveness* for *stability*. What is gained is a router control plane that is stable in every situation and does not go down the "CPU churning spiral" when the network starts to get shaky. However, on the other hand, a router loses responsiveness. Consider a router that is in the middle of an

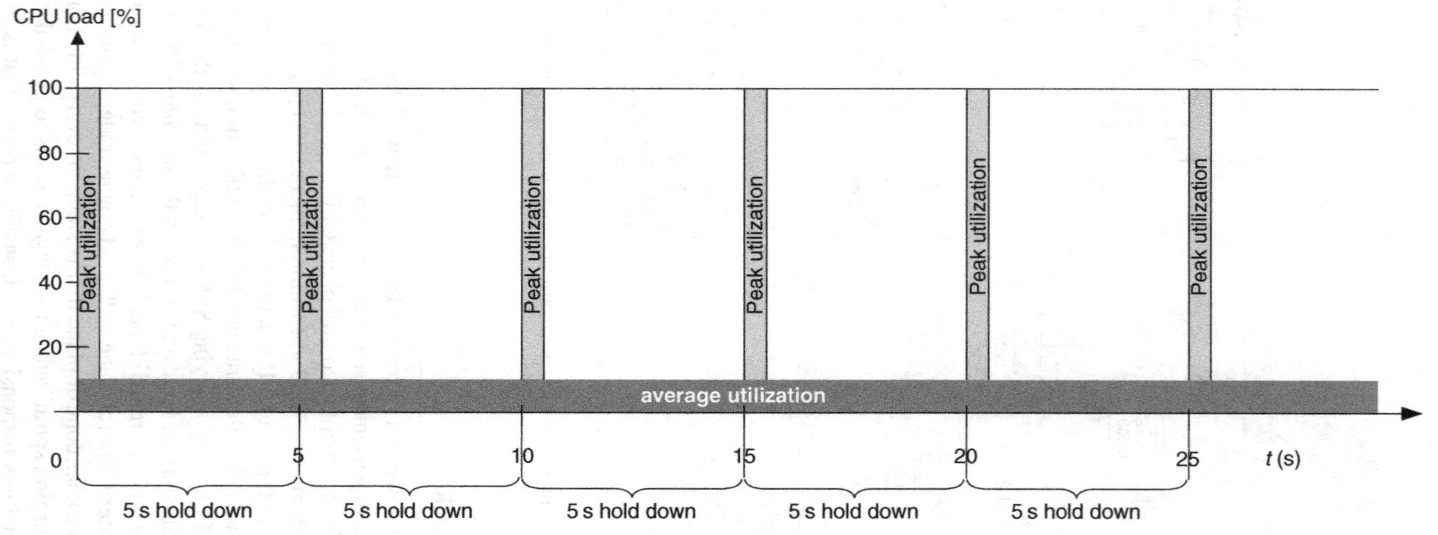

FIGURE 10.11. SPF hold-downs smooth the CPU utilization

SPF hold-down period: even if plenty of LSPs do rush in, the router has to wait until the hold down period is over before scheduling the SPF calculation again. Then there are considerations like "How short should the hold-down time be to still be responsive?" and "How long should the hold-timer be to be stable enough?" and even "What is the optimal hold-down timer value?"

Unfortunately there is no universal hold-down timer value that applies to all networking scenarios. Hold-down timers are always a compromise between *stability* and *responsiveness*. Look at stability to start with: this mostly depends on network size and link stability. Network engineers used to say "In a quiet environment, OSPF and IS-IS are quiet protocols".

In the infancy of link-state routing protocols there was usually a static SPF hold-down timer of 5 seconds between SPF runs. This was a conservative timer, the better to scale for large networks. Today, adaptive timers, which take into account the churn in the network, are more common. The basic idea behind the new schemes is that the first couple of SPF calculations are scheduled immediately without any notable delay and only subsequent, persistent SPF runs are delayed. The more SPF runs need to be scheduled, the longer the hold-down timer gets. Such schemes are a much better compromise between responsiveness and stability than static timers can ever be.

The typical adaptive timer algorithm implementation reacts very fast, and is very responsive at first. This covers 99 per cent of the typical network-changing events, which are link failures. That means that two LSPs arrive within a very short window. For the remaining 1 per cent of failure scenarios, the algorithm falls back to the older SPF hold-down static intervals for self-protection reasons.

JUNOS and IOS have different ways of implementing hold-down timers. IOS implements a technique called *exponential back off*. Here the hold-down interval gets doubled each time an SPF calculation is executed. The initial delay, the max-delay and the minimum hold-down interval can be configured using the using the spf-interval <max-holddown> [<initial-wait> <minimum-holddown>] configuration command. The following shows a custom configuration of the SPF hold down behaviour in IOS. This works as follows:

IOS configuration

In IOS there are three timers to control SPF hold-down. The first timer specifies the SPF hold-down in the slower phase expressed in units of seconds. The second timer specifies how many milliseconds to wait before scheduling the very first SPF calculation. The third timer specifies the minimum SPF hold-down in the fast phase. The last two timers are expressed in units of milliseconds.

```
London# show running-config
[ ... ]
router isis
 spf-interval 5 200 1000
[ ... ]
```

Figure 10.12 shows the timing behaviour of the exponential back-off algorithm compared to the JUNOS style, called a "3 × fast back-off" method. In IOS, the first SPF run is delayed for 200 ms. Next, the minimum-hold-down timer kicks in, so scheduling of the second SPF run will take at least 1000 ms as specified in the third argument of the `spf-interval` configuration command. All subsequent SPF runs will get delayed for double the previous hold-down time, 2 seconds for the third SPF run, 4 seconds for the fourth SPF run, and so on. Similarly, the LSP origination interval, which was explained in Chapter 6, "Generating, Flooding and Ageing LSPs", also has a precaution that the hold-down does not grow to infinite value. Clipping of the hold-down timer is done with the first argument (5 seconds) of the `spf-interval` command. During every fast-build, the SPF interval gets bigger until it hits the ceiling of 5 seconds. After a particular router has not scheduled an SPF run for 20 seconds, the SPF hold-down state will be reset. This means that from here on, any further SPF calculations will be scheduled "fast", like the first couple of SPF runs.

JUNOS takes a different approach. Instead of *gradually* getting slower, there is a fixed number of *fast* runs, and after that the router falls back into *slow* scheduling mode. The engineers at Juniper Networks argue that this linear form of back off has worked fine for the past 10 years, and more sophisticated methods are not needed. In most implementations, the static SPF hold-down period is set to 5 seconds and by straight switching between the two modes, fast and slow, no harm is done.

JUNOS has an initial pre-SPF timer that defaults to 200 ms. It can be changed using the `spf-delay` configuration command, which is available under the `protocols isis` stanza. This command affects both the partial and the full SPF calculation and can be changed in the range from 50 ms to 1000 ms.

JUNOS configuration

In JUNOS there is only *one* timer that controls SPF scheduling. The `spf-interval` configuration command determines in units of milliseconds the initial-wait and inter-SPF wait period when scheduling SPF calculations.

```
hannes@Vienna> show configuration
[ … ]
protocols {
  isis {
    spf-delay 100;
      interface lo0.0;
      interface so-0/0/0;
    }
}
```

All other values are hard coded into JUNOS. The number of fast runs is 3 and the minimum pre-SPF timer can go as low as 50 ms. In the above configuration example, the router has to wait 100 ms before an SPF calculation is scheduled, and 100 ms between SPF calculations.

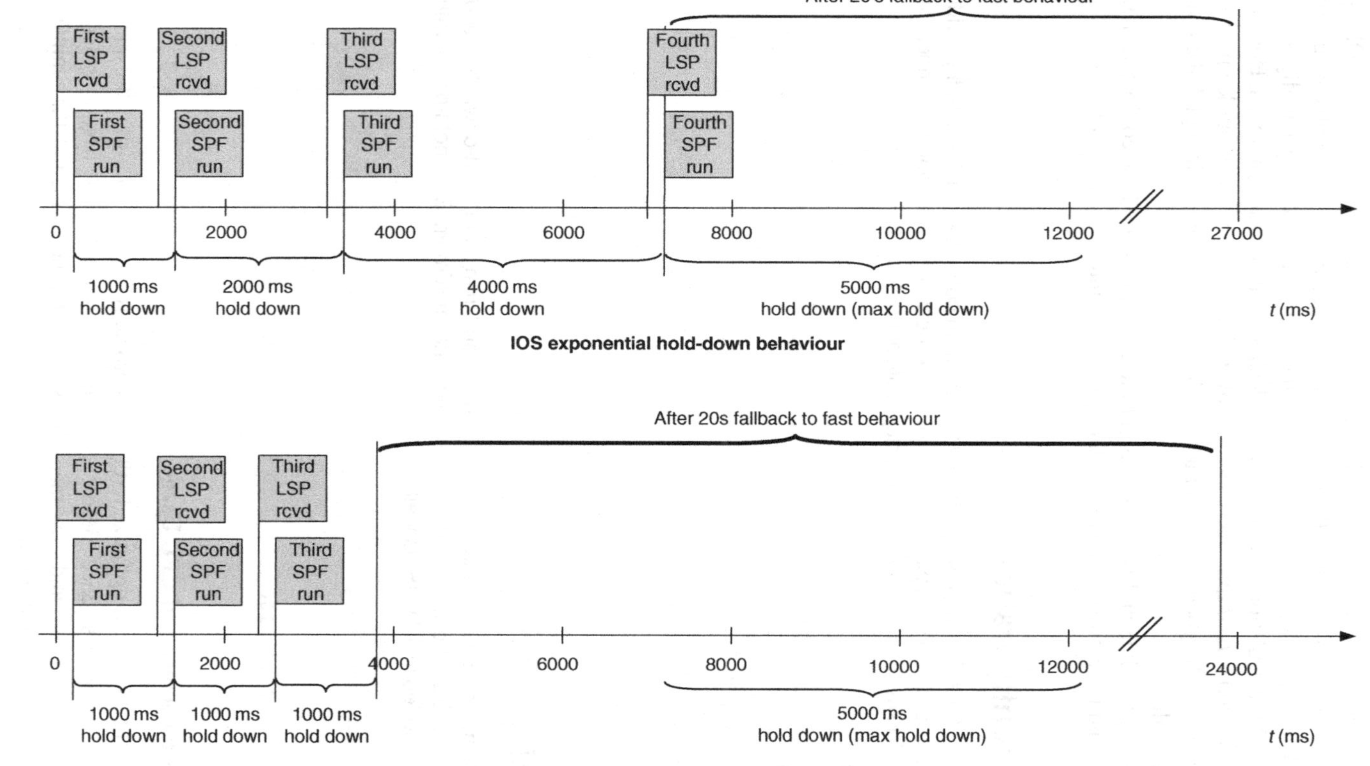

FIGURE 10.12. IOS makes the hold-down interval exponentially longer – JUNOS starts with three short and after that uses long hold-down intervals

10.3.1.3 Timer Compatibility Issues

It is recommended to keep at least the initial-wait timer the same across the IOS and JUNOS routers in a network. Once they are the same it is certain that the SPF calculations start and finish almost simultaneously. Due to the hop-by-hop routing paradigm, near simultaneous SPF calculations and re-routing is desired to avoid transient loops. However, it can never be *guaranteed* that two routers converge at the same time, but keeping the timers current is usually good enough, or at least does not break the desired global convergence intentionally.

The following two IOS and JUNOS configuration files are a good tradeoff between the two schemes and have proven to work well even in large multi-vendor networks.

JUNOS configuration

An SPF delay of 100 ms means that the SPF algorithm converges fast and still provides reasonable protection. The typical SPF run in large networks does not last longer than 100 ms. This 100 ms of quiet takes the average utilization down to 50 per cent.

```
hannes@Vienna> show configuration
[...]
protocols {
    isis {
      spf-delay 100;
      interface lo0.0;
      interface so-0/0/0;
    }
}
```

IOS configuration

The two 100 ms arguments make the initial-wait and minimum hold-down behaviour exactly like JUNOS. The first argument specifies the maximum SPF hold-down value, which is hard-coded in JUNOS as well.

```
London# show running-config
[ ... ]
router isis
  spf-interval 5 100 100
[ ... ]
```

10.3.1.4 Performance and CPU Usage

The CPU cost of a plain, un-optimized SPF run is probably one of the most well-examined algorithms in computer science. Before assessing worst-case figures, first consider two factors: how many routers and how many links are in the network. Let the number of routers be N and the number of links be L.

It is actually very hard to predict the SPF runtime, as it is highly dependent on the topology, that is, how the routers are meshed to each other. It has been shown above that the tracking of nodes on the PATH list consumes the most cycles. So what is done is to present a worst-case and an average-case scenario, considering the number of routers (N) or the number of links (L). To find out what the real SPF runtime will be, and it will be somewhere between the two figures, how densely meshed the network is has to be taken into account.

For a router-based, worst case estimate, simply take a look at the number of routers and the number of search operations, assuming that every router is in the worst case connected to every other router (a full mesh). Therefore, for a total of N nodes, at maximum N–1 iterations steps are needed for the search operation to find out if the actual path is better than the *TENTative* path. This is quite intuitive. Mathematically speaking, the runtime requirements of the SPF run equals $N * N–1$ or $O(N\^2)$. Squared growth is really, really the worst case.

Exploring all the feasible path scales directly, along with the absolute number of links it can be shown that the SPF computation time is proportional to the number of links in the network. Mathematically speaking, $O(L * \log(L))$.

For example, let the number of routers be 100 and the numbers of links be 400. Then the worst-case estimate would be that $O(N\^2)$ CPU-time-units ($100 * 100 = 10000$) are spent. The abstract unit "CPU-time units" is used because such observations only make sense in a comparative way. If there is a given number of nodes and a given number of links in a network, and the current SPF run time, a good estimate of the CPU runtime in the future, when the number of routers and the number of links is higher, can be made. The pure link-based observation results in a computational complexity of $L * \log(L)$, which is $400 * (\log(400)) = 1040$ of CPU time-units.

So there is a factor of 10 deviation between the two estimates. In reality both the number of links *and* the number of routers need to be considered. Both figures are needed for the *meshing factor*, that is, how densely a given set of routers is meshed. It will be shown shortly that the link-based model is a much better approximation than the worst-case estimate.

The model where the total SPF runtime equals $N\ (\log(N)*2*\log(L))$ turns out to work best in practice. In this formula, both the number of links and the number of nodes *plus* a factor of two go into the formula. The factor of two is needed because the two-way check is part of the path selection algorithm. Based on that formula, the resulting calculations come very close to reality. See Table 10.1 for the best model of route-processor CPU prediction around today.

The theoretical model was verified using a lab test based on two common route processors: the Juniper Networks RE 3.0 taken from the M & T-Series of Routers, and the GRP Routing Engine taking from the Cisco GSR 12000 series. The two route processors were exercised using the Agilent QA Robot Router Control-Plane Stress Testing Software. The Router Tester produces a grid, as shown in Figure 10.13.

Every 25 seconds, one link of the virtual topology was changed and the SPF runtimes have been recorded using the `show isis spf-log` operational level CLI command on IOS and `show isis spf log` on JUNOS.

TABLE 10.1. A prediction of real-world SPF runtime on common control plane CPUs.

Routers	Links	SPF runtime (ms) Juniper Networks Routing Engine 3.0	SPF runtime (ms) Cisco Systems GRP 12000
100	250	1,92	4,80
200	500	4,97	12,42
400	1000	12,49	31,22
600	1500	21,18	52,94
800	2000	30,67	76,67
1000	2500	40,78	101,94
1500	3750	68,11	170,27
2000	5000	97,68	244,21
2500	6250	128,98	322,45
3000	7500	161,69	404,22
4000	10000	230,53	576,33
5000	12500	303,09	757,72
6000	15000	378,67	946,67
7000	17500	456,82	1142,04
8000	20000	537,19	1342,98
9000	22500	619,55	1548,86
10000	25000	703,67	1759,18

IOS command output

```
London#show isis spf-log
   Level 1 SPF log
  When      Duration     Nodes    Count    Last trigger LSP        Triggers
04:17:46    0.021189     408      1        virtual-5-3.00-00       DELADJ
                                                                   TLVCODE
04:15:46    0.021224     408      1                                PERIODIC
04:00:46    0.021712     408      1                                PERIODIC
03:45:46    0.021323     408      1                                PERIODIC
[ … ]
```

JUNOS command output

```
hannes@Frankfurt> show isis spf log
  IS-IS level 1 SPF log:
Start time                       Elapsed  (secs)   Count  Reason
Sat  Nov  1   15:04:34           0.017179            1 Periodic    SPF
Sat  Nov  1   15:19:03           0.017067            1 Periodic    PF
Sat  Nov  1   15:31:47           0.017081            1 Periodic    SPF
Sat  Nov  1   15:44:19           0.017334            1 Periodic    SPF
[ … ]
Sat  Nov  1   15:45:07           0.017365            1 Updated LSP
[ … ]                                                  virtual-5-3.00-00
```

Both outputs show the reason (trigger) and the duration of the SPF calculation.

The disparity between the theoretical prediction model and the simulation on the virtual topology has been less than 3 per cent. Therefore, the model gives a good prediction of how long the full SPF run will last in practice. The result of the simulation and the prediction

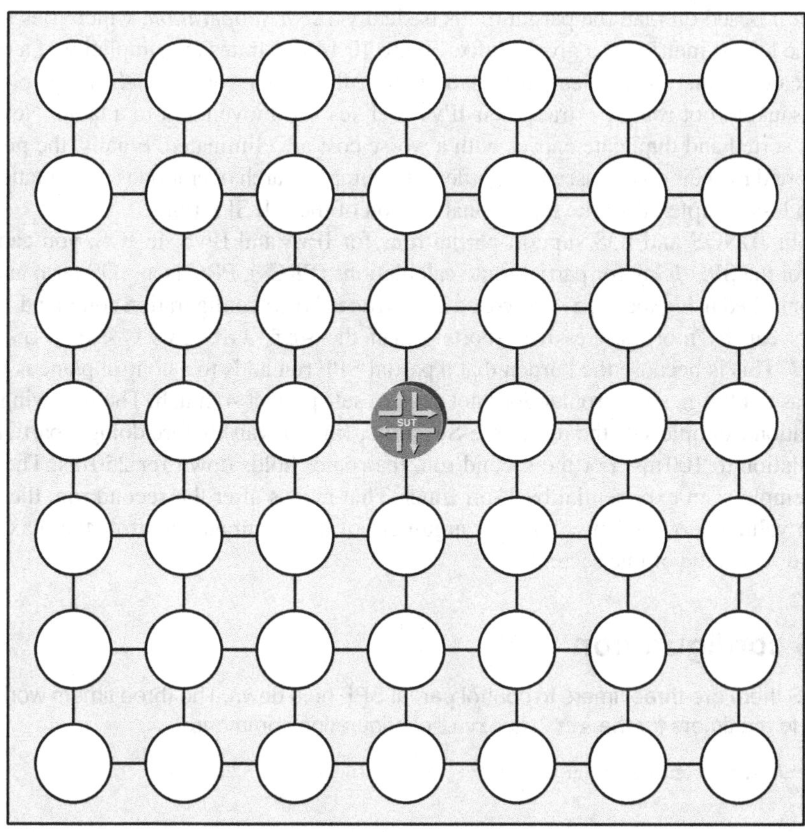

FIGURE 10.13. The SUT is exposed to a 7 × 7 virtual grid to test SPF calculation time

model are quite surprising. For even moderate to large topologies, the SPF calculation is quickly finished after several tens of milliseconds. There are barely 30 IS-IS networks in the world that have more than 400 routers and an SPF runtime greater than 50 ms for their Level-2 routers. So for the majority of networks, SPF-runtime is an *absolute non-issue*. It is certainly *not* the SPF runtime for the full SPF run that consumes a lot of CPU resources.

10.3.2 *Partial SPF Run*

A partial SPF run only does recalculation *leaf-related* information. Partial runs are typically triggered by the following events:

- Metric of prefixes change
- New prefixes
- Deletion of prefixes

The partial SPF run is basically an extraction of all the prefixes in the link-state database plus some information about the *proximity* of the prefixes (in simple words, a *metric*). Based on that, the partial run is basically a *search operation*, which tries to find out the lowest metric for a given prefix. Figure 10.14 illustrates the simplicity of a partial SPF calculation. All the leaf information from the routers on the PATH list, plus the Pennsauken root router, extract their IPv4 prefixes and move them to a table. Next, the list is sorted and duplicate entries with a worse cost are eliminated. Finally, the prefixes are sorted by their cost in ascending order. This simple search operation is computationally much less complex than the topological section of the full SPF run.

Both JUNOS and IOS support partial runs for IPv4 and IPv6. In IOS, you can also control the SPF delay for partial route calculations (PRCs). PRC is an IOS term and can be controlled using the `prc-interval router isis` configuration command. These timers can be more aggressive (shorter) than the `spf-interval <a> <b> <c>` timers. This is because the burden that a partial SPF run adds to a control plane is not as high as a full run, so the router does not need to self-protect so much. The following configuration example sets the router pre-SPF timer (initial wait) before doing a partial SPF calculation to 100 ms. For the second run, the router holds down for 250 ms. The PRC also employs an exponential back-off timer. That means after the second run, the hold-down value is now 500 ms. The first argument of the command controls the maximum hold-down value of one second.

IOS configuration

In IOS there are three timers to control partial SPF hold down. The three timers work similarly to the timers for the `spf-interval` configuration command.

```
London# show running-config
[ ... ]
router isis
  prc-interval 1 100 250
[ ... ]
```

JUNOS does not have a dedicated control knob to control the PRC behaviour. In JUNOS, there is just one hold-down logic path. For partial SPF runs, therefore, the same hold-down logic applies as for full SPF runs. it is recommended setting the three IOS parameters 5, 200 and 200 for compatiblity to the JUNOS default behaviour.

10.3.2.1 Performance and CPU Usage

Partial SPF runs are pretty cheap from the calculation point of view. A router has to scan through all the routers in its link-state database, extract the prefix information, add the prefix cost of the distance to the originating router, and sort the prefixes to find out which is closest. This exhibits absolutely linear behaviour, meaning the CPU processing time is directly proportional to the number of routes in the network. Mathematically speaking, this would be $O(R)$ with R being the number of prefixes of an address family. In practical implementations, the cost of the partial SPF run nears zero cost. Typically, the partial run is less than 10 ms execution time, even if R is unreasonably high (like 10,000) routes. So partial runs are even less of an issue than full SPF runs.

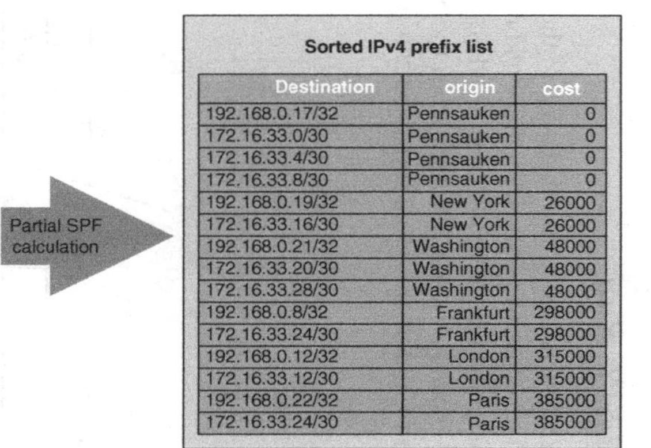

SPF Result list

Destination	via	cost
Pennsauken	-	0
New York	New York	26000
Washington	New York	48000
Frankfurt	New York	298000
London	London	315000
Paris	New York	385000

Extracted IPv4 Prefix list

Destination	origin	cost
192.168.0.21/32	Washington	48000
~~172.16.33.16/30~~	~~Washington~~	~~48000~~
172.16.33.20/30	Washington	48000
172.16.33.28/30	Washington	48000
192.168.0.19/32	New York	26000
~~172.16.33.0/30~~	~~New York~~	~~26000~~
172.16.33.16/30	New York	26000
192.168.0.22/32	Paris	385000
~~172.16.33.24/30~~	~~Paris~~	~~385000~~
~~172.16.33.28/30~~	~~Paris~~	~~385000~~
192.168.0.17/32	Pennsauken	0
172.16.33.0/30	Pennsauken	0
172.16.33.4/30	Pennsauken	0
172.16.33.8/30	Pennsauken	0
192.168.0.8/32	Frankfurt	298000
~~172.16.33.8/30~~	~~Frankfurt~~	~~298000~~
~~172.16.33.12/30~~	~~Frankfurt~~	~~298000~~
~~172.16.33.20/30~~	~~Frankfurt~~	~~298000~~
172.16.33.24/30	Frankfurt	298000
192.168.0.12/32	London	315000
~~172.16.33.4/30~~	~~London~~	~~315000~~
172.16.33.12/30	London	315000

Sorted IPv4 prefix list

Destination	origin	cost
192.168.0.17/32	Pennsauken	0
172.16.33.0/30	Pennsauken	0
172.16.33.4/30	Pennsauken	0
172.16.33.8/30	Pennsauken	0
192.168.0.19/32	New York	26000
172.16.33.16/30	New York	26000
192.168.0.21/32	Washington	48000
172.16.33.20/30	Washington	48000
172.16.33.28/30	Washington	48000
192.168.0.8/32	Frankfurt	298000
172.16.33.24/30	Frankfurt	298000
192.168.0.12/32	London	315000
172.16.33.12/30	London	315000
192.168.0.22/32	Paris	385000
172.16.33.24/30	Paris	385000

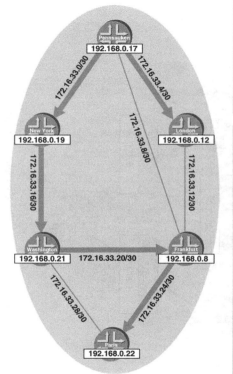

FIGURE 10.14. A partial route calculation (PRC) is basically a simple, computational cheap sort operation

10.3.3 *Incremental SPF Run*

The incremental SPF (iSPF) run is an optimized version of the full SPF run. What it does is maintain additional data structures, so-called *Neighbor* and *Parent* lists, during previous full SPF calculations. The paths that have *not* been used so far are of special interest. Consider Figure 10.15, which shows the SPF tree from the SPF calculation example. Note that the link between London and Frankfurt is not on the shortest path tree from

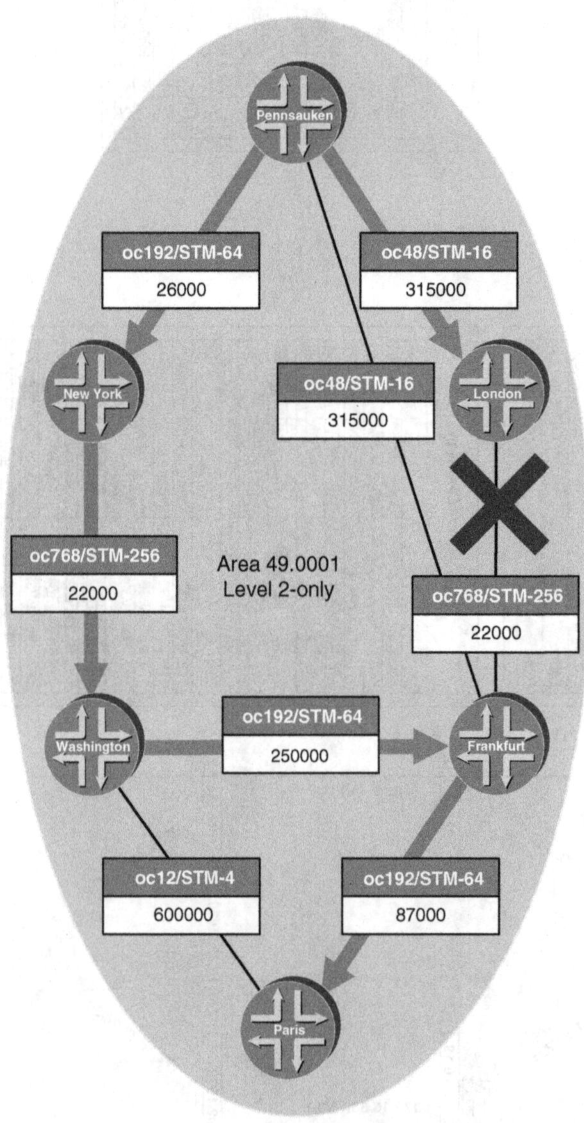

FIGURE 10.15. Incremental SPF does not need to re-compute a SPF calculation if a link is not on the shortest path tree

Pennsauken's perspective. If the Pennsauken router receives a new LSP reporting that this particular link is down, then Pennsauken does not need to schedule a full SPF run. The reason is that because the router doing the SPF calculation has not used the link *before* (when it was *up*), then it does not have to consider it when it is *down*.

Keep in mind that such considerations, whether to do a full SPF or an incremental SPF run, is a purely local decision that applies only to the *local* router. For other routers in the network, for example Frankfurt, the link between London and Frankfurt may be meaningful, and therefore on Frankfurt's shortest path tree. The iSPF advantage on the Pennsauken router is meaningless to the Frankfurt router. The incremental SPF run only spares the full SPF run on *some* of the routers in a given area but not to *all* of them. Which routers benefit from incremental SPF is heavily dependent on topology.

Another optimization of the incremental SPF run is to track network *dependencies*. Consider Figure 10.16, which shows a new router (Munich) attached as a leaf to the sample

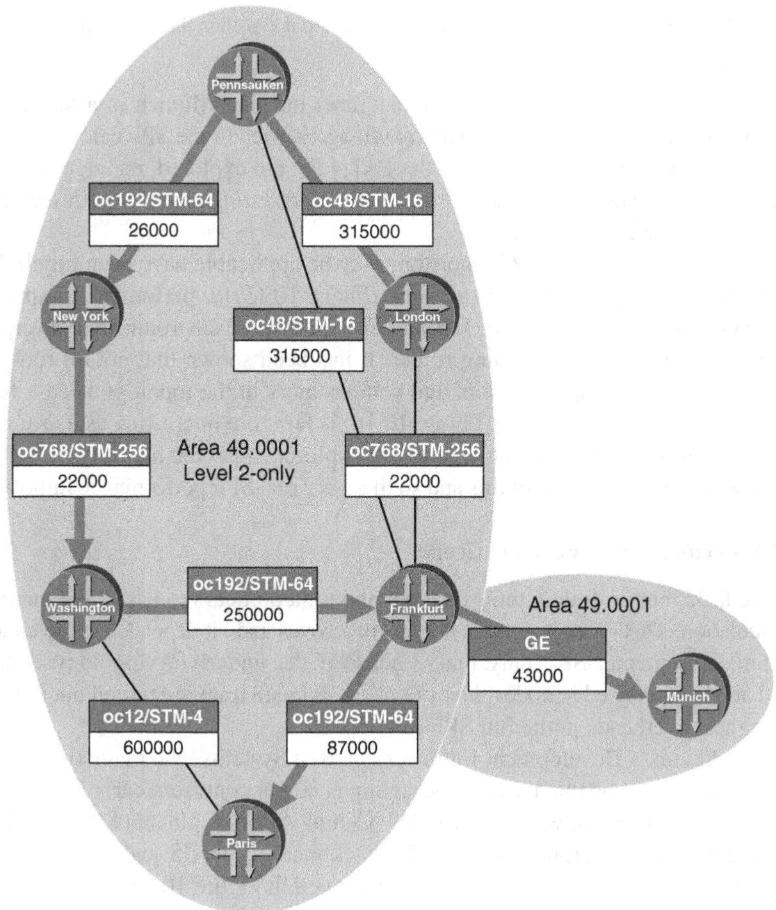

FIGURE 10.16. Leaf routers also do not need to re-run SPF on all event that would trigger a full SPF run

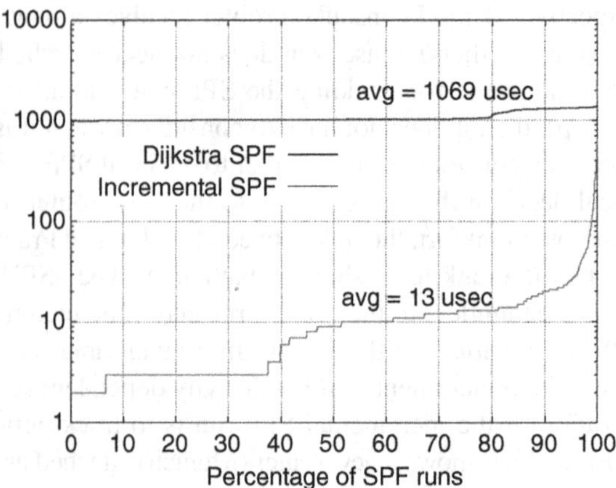

FIGURE 10.17. Incremental SPF performs by a factor of 80 better than the full (Dijkstra) SPF based on the QWEST topology

topology. The incremental SPF algorithm figures out that Munich is a leaf node and dependent on the Frankfurt router. That knowledge is used in the SPF calculation. Recall that once the immediate successors on the PATH list are explored, the algorithm knows that Munich is (because of its edge position) an *uninteresting* node for path searches and hence does not need to get explored.

Two scenarios where the iSPF algorithm may be applicable have been highlighted. It is the authors' opinion that in the first scenario (Figure 10.15) the performance improvement is next to nothing. This is due to the fact that, in a distributed environment, convergence is bound to the worst-case performing router. It has been shown that not all routers take equal advantage of the optimization, and some routers in the topology need a full SPF run anyway. The second example (Figure 10.16) is far more interesting as it dramatically reduces the number of nodes that need to get explored. Also the majority of the routers in the network take advantage of this and so there is a real SPF performance improvement.

10.3.3.1 Performance and CPU Usage

There are little, but profound, things known about theoretical models of the incremental SPF calculation. This is because there are lots of caveats and "it depends" in the underlying algorithm. Incremental SPF only makes sense if the underlying topology is sparsely meshed and has many edge nodes. Identification and path tracking turned out to have one of the highest overheads in the full SPF run.

Stefano Previdi, a Development Engineer at Cisco Systems who maintains their IS-IS routing protocol, claims that the average saving is 80 per cent from early field trials. The first practical examination was conducted by Cengiz Alaettinoglu and Stephen Casner of Packetdesign, who monitored the QWEST backbone in the US and analyzed full and incremental SPF runtimes. The results are illustrated in Figure 10.17.

It will be shown shortly that this is the misguided reason that people are afraid of frequent SPF runs. It is the post-processing of route resolving and prefix insertion, and not the SPF calculation itself, which makes the control planes of the core routers in the Internet busy.

The result of the SPF calculation is fed into the route resolution process. The route resolver checks to see if routes from other routing protocols have been affected by the result of the SPF calculation.

10.4 Route Resolution

Pure reachability protocols like BGP rely on a working IGP like IS-IS to map the *Reachability* information, such as customer and Internet routes, to a topology in order to properly calculate the path cost. After every SPF recalculation, the route resolver needs to track *dependent* routes and update their forwarding next-hops accordingly. Finally, the changed prefixes are downloaded to the line cards and ASICs. In the past there has been little attention to the nature and performance implications of tracking the *dependent* routes.

However, in an Internet environment with full routing tables, it turns out to be that finding out who is dependent and who is not is one of the most dominating factors in the total route-recalculation period.

10.4.1 *BGP Recursion and Route Dependency*

Routing protocols like BGP are somehow *agnostic* to the underlying topology and need an IGP that provides two services:

1. Connectivity between the internal loopback IP addresses of all the routers in an AS so that the BGP speakers can bootstrap their iBGP mesh
2. Topology awareness to calculate the IGP distance to a BGP speaker

Internal BGP neighbours are typically not directly connected, so a router *cannot* simply inherit the neighbour address from the routing update sender as other distance vector protocols (RIP and EIGRP) would do. Even if the neighbour is directly connected, the router still cannot inherit that information because it does not know if the neighbour is a BGP Route Reflector or not. The good news is that there is information contained in the BGP message that points to the IP address where the route originated. This field is called the next-hop and is a mandatory BGP attribute that points to the correct forwarding router. In the tcpdump output below, a BGP Update message containing a next-hop attribute is shown.

Tcpdump Output

The BGP Next-hop attribute carries an IP address that the IGP needs to resolve.

```
08:28:27.945234 IP 192.168.0.19.179 > 192.168.0.21.28161: BGP, length: 77
  Update Message (2), length: 77
    Origin (1), length: 1, Flags [T]: IGP
    AS Path (2), length: 14, Flags [T]: 3320 4711 12788 24896
    Next-hop (3), length: 4, Flags [T]: 192.168.0.8
    Local Preference (5), length: 4, Flags [T]: 100
    Community (8), length: 12, Flags [OT]: 5511:500, 5511:516, 5511:999
    Updated routes:
      81.21.0.0/20
```

After receiving the BGP update the router needs to look up 192.168.0.8 in the SPF result database and find the local forwarding next-hop. The BGP route 81.21/20 is now *dependent* on the IS-IS route pointing to 192.168.0.8. Whenever the IS-IS topology is recalculated, the router needs to check all dependent routes and find out if there is a better way to reach the BGP speaker.

A given route may arrive at a BGP router via many diverse paths. Certain rules in the BGP route selection process depend on the IGP calculated route.

10.4.2 *BGP Route Selection*

BGP performs tie-breaking to find the best path according to the following list:

1. *Is the BGP next-hop reachable?*
2. Prefer the highest Local Preference value
3. Prefer the shortest AS Path length
4. Prefer the lowest Origin value
5. Prefer the lowest MED value
6. Prefer routes learned via EBGP over routes learned via iBGP
7. *Prefer routes with the lowest IGP metric*
8. Prefer routes from the peer with the lowest RID
9. Prefer routes from the peer with the lowest peer ID

At the very top of the tie-breaking list, BGP is heavily dependent on IS-IS. BGP needs to validate its BGP next-hop and check if it is reachable before further comparing the route. The BGP next-hop is a mandatory BGP attribute that points to the correct forwarding router. In Rule #7, the BGP route again is dependent on IS-IS. This time the lower IGP metric provides BGP with some insight on how close a BGP speaker is. Consider Figure 10.18 for an example. Router Pennsauken has learned the prefix 81.21/20 from London, New York and Paris. After applying the BGP tie-breaking process, it turns out that the route from New York is best, due to a lower (better) IGP metric.

There are different ways of implementing route-recursion inside the router – the most common ones are to store *backtracking* pointers. Whenever a BGP route is resolved through an IS-IS route, the router stores a pointer from the IS-IS routes to the dependent BGP routes. If a change is needed to an IS-IS route, simply revisit the stored prefixes and look to see if the old IS-IS route is still the best route. The router does that by checking if the BGP next-hop is still on the shortest path. If it is – fine, then simply stop there (do not attempt to change forwarding state). If it is not, and there has been a path change (which could be a path becoming better or a path getting worse), then re-run the recursion for the prefixes stored in the backtrack-list. The router has to re-check to see if there are better paths pointing to the BGP next-hop. In a worst case, this means that 100 K prefixes need to re-run through the entire BGP tie-breaking process, which can be quite expensive in terms of computational cost (CPU load).

10.4.2.1 Performance and CPU Usage

Both JUNOS and IOS do a proper BGP recursion check, but implemented differently. The difference is in the way the BGP code is written and its performance implications.

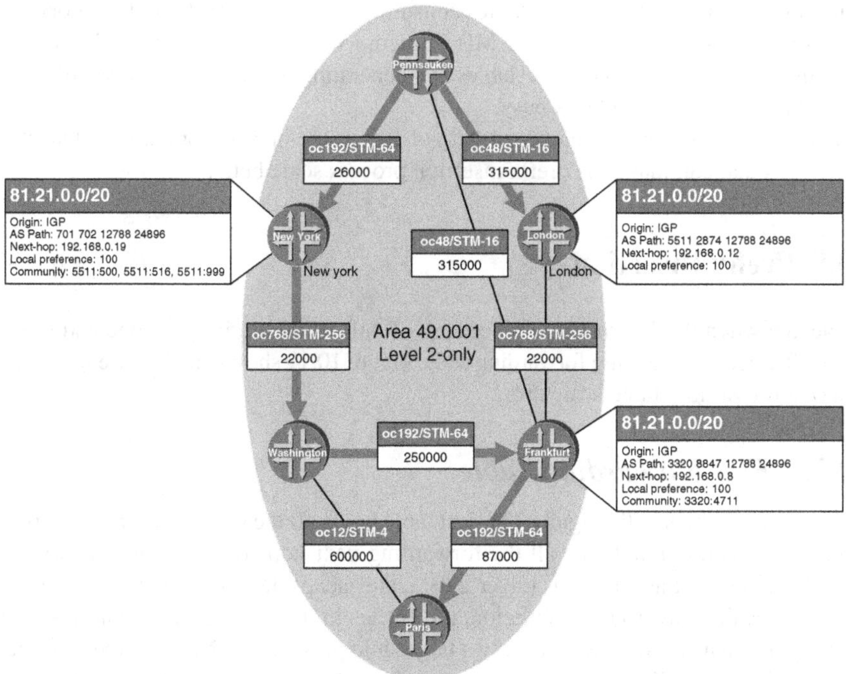

FIGURE 10.18. The transit route 81.21/20 via Pennsauken wins the BGP tie-breaking process

In IOS the BGP code is job-based. That means whenever there is a change to a BGP learned prefix only a flag in the data-structure of the prefix is set or cleared. Then there is a job that scans the BGP table for changed entries (called the BGP walker). Why is this information relevant for a book about IS-IS? It means that even if IS-IS has detected that a link has been broken, and must perform all the relevant actions (flooding, scheduling of an SPF full run etc.), it takes in the worst case the BGP walker duration in IOS (50 seconds) until the Cisco router starts to change prefixes, update forwarding states, and so on. So the implementation style of the BGP implementation dictates the convergence behaviour of the BGP routes. Perhaps this is not the best design choice. In all fairness, the first implementation of BGP in IOS was coded at a time when the Internet consisted of not even 1000 routes. So it is probably not bad design, but a legacy effect.

In contrast, JUNOS routing software is *event-driven*. That means that whenever a subsystem in the router notices that something has gone wrong, or is up again, that change is propagated throughout the system *immediately* and without any delay. Immediately after the SPF run, JUNOS does BGP recursion.

Both implementations result in a list of prefixes that need to change in the main routing table. After that, the router updates the forwarding state in the forwarding plane. Updating the forwarding plane is the most daunting task of all because it makes both the forwarding and control plane CPUs really busy. The reason this keeps both CPUs busy is the sheer amount of data and table sizes that has to be pumped through a router's chassis. Currently a full routing table of all Internet routes consumes about 120–200 MB of memory. A full forwarding table consumes about 2 MB of memory on each line-card in the router. So crunching at least 100 MB of BGP tables and generating N*2 MB sized forwarding tables is the main reason the router is busy.

The next section covers legacy and state-of-the-art methods of forwarding state change operations that can make the prefix insertion process scale better.

10.5 Prefix Insertion

In the age when the Internet was a network of only 1000 prefixes, no one had to worry about efficiency in changing forwarding state. Figure 10.19 shows an old-style implementation of a forwarding table structure.

10.5.1 *Flat Forwarding Table*

There are two tables in the figure. The first table holds all the prefixes of the main routing table. The second table holds all the forwarding next-hops of the router. A forwarding next-hop is a local interface plus Layer-2 data like encapsulation method, MAC addresses etc. As a result of the route calculation, the entries in the prefixes list are all pointing to the *forwarding* next-hops. To put the two tables into perspective: based on today's Internet routing tables, 100,000s of prefixes point to only 10s of forwarding next-hops.

It is exactly that *many-to-few mapping* that causes problems. Consider the sample topology shown in Figure 10.20 where each router is a public BGP speaker and injects BGP routes into the network. Each of the six routers carries a full BGP load, and after the BGP tie-breaking process the routers figure out which are the best routes. The figures in the box indicate how many active routes each router carries.

For simplicity, look at the Frankfurt routing and forwarding table only. The forwarding table looks very simple: all 120.000 prefixes map to one of three possible next-hops, which are the SONET/SDH links to London, Paris or Pennsauken. Now, assume the link between Washington and Frankfurt breaks. Both Washington and Frankfurt will quickly detect that one of their SONET/SDH interfaces is down. Next, both routers will originate

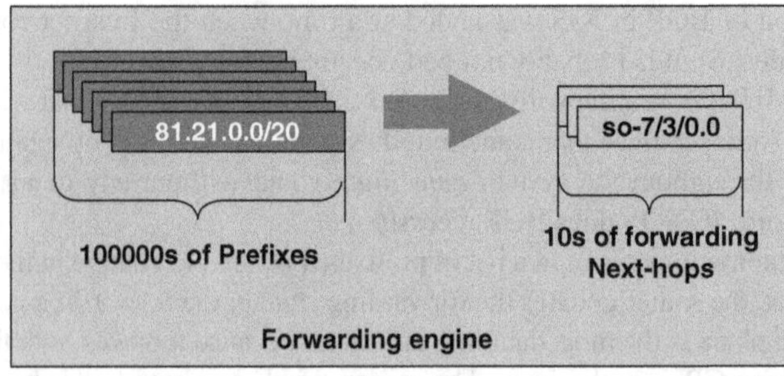

FIGURE 10.19. In a flat forwarding table a prefix points directly to a forwarding next-hop

a new LSP declaring the adjacency down. Because of the default values of the SPF hold-down timers in the network, the SPF run will be scheduled after 100 ms. As the number of nodes and links is low, in less than one millisecond the results will be available. Now the scary part begins: the recursion and change of forwarding state in the forwarding plane. The routing tables are traversed in 1–2 seconds and the control plane realizes that it has to change 40,000 prefixes. The route processor computes new forwarding tables and loads them down to the line-cards. Because of the fact that the router has to update

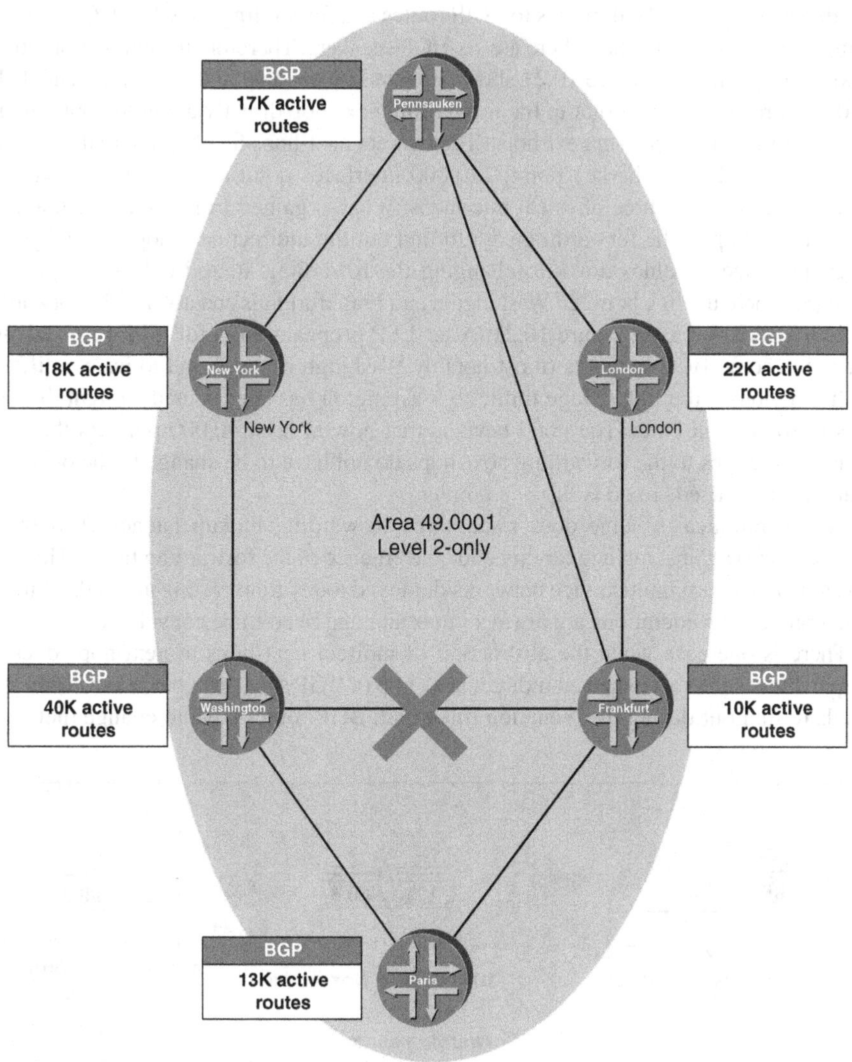

FIGURE 10.20. Each router in the sample topology is a BGP router and carries several thousand active paths

40 K prefixes, the total convergence time until the last prefix is updated takes about 40 seconds (if not minutes) depending on the router hardware. Updating forwarding tables under load is hard and quite expensive to achieve.

10.5.2 *Hierarchical Forwarding Table*

The alternate solution does not map the prefixes directly to the forwarding next-hops. There is instead the notion of an *indirect next-hop*. An indirect Next-hop is the originator of a prefix that is not directly connected to the router. It is a different way of modelling the dependency from BGP routes to IS-IS routes at a forwarding table level. Consider the sample network again, where there are six BGP speakers. Therefore the number of indirect next-hops equals six. Figure 10.21 shows how the forwarding table is implemented. The 120,000 prefixes do not point to the forwarding next-hop directly anymore, but rather to their corresponding *indirect* next-hops. The indirect next-hops finally point to the forwarding next-hop. This is the key point: 120.000 interfaces point to six indirect next-hops, which point to only three physical interfaces. What is gained from that, except another memory lookup in the forwarding path to find out the indirect next-hop? Actually, a *lot* is gained once it comes down to changing the fowarding state. Look at the previous example where the link between Washington and Frankfurt fails and assume the forwarding table is structured as in Figure 10.21. After LSP propagation, a full SPF run, and BGP recursion some BGP speakers (most notably Washington) are found to have a different path. Previously the link outage traffic to Washington has been routed straight, but now it is re-routed via Paris. The good news is that now at least 40.000 pointers that point from the prefixes to the forwarding next-hops do not have to be changed. The only thing that the router needs to do is flip *one* pointer!

The hierarchical scheme does trade some forwarding lookup latency (less than 1 microsecond) against maintainability and convergence of the forwarding tables. However, given that there are multiservice networks deployed today transporting all kinds of traffic, convergence considerations are always important and need to be considered.

There is one case when the abstraction of indirect next-hops to next-hops does not help, which is the case when an indirect next-hop (a BGP speaker) goes down. Then BGP needs to find out during the recursion run which BGP routes have to change their next-

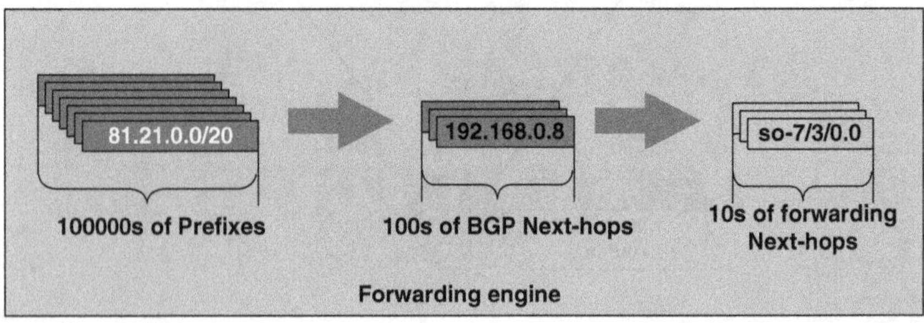

FIGURE 10.21. In a hierarchical forwarding table a prefix points first to an indirect next-hop, which maps finally to a forwarding next-hop

hop information and reassign these prefixes to other indirect next-hops. Ultimately this will result in a massive amount of forwarding state changes at the forwarding plane. The speed of the raw forwarding table changes at about 5000–6000 prefixes per second. A common design practice is (if possible) to balance the number of active BGP paths evenly across a network by incorporating a good and solid peering mesh with other ASs. Reducing the number of active routes per-AS makes sure that if an indirect next-hop (BGP speaker) goes down, the re-routing is done within several seconds.

10.6 Conclusion

The CPU impact of the SPF algorithm really has been "demonized" in the past. Fears that an SPF calculation may lock up a router entirely are not justified today. Modern control plane processors have sufficient CPU power to recalculate even large topologies in the sub-second range, so the bare SPF algorithm itself is not the problem anymore. The associated BGP recursion check can be completed in sub-second range as well. What persists as a challenge is the final stage of the post-processing cycle of the SPF results. Forwarding table maintenance in modern routers can fully engage the CPUs for several seconds, much more than SPF ever could do. This challenge can be tackled from two sides: on the vendor side, by applying clever implementation techniques like indirect Next-hops in the forwarding path and, on the service provider side, by doing a proper network design. With proper balancing of active BGP paths evenly across the network, a network carrying even 120,000 routes converges in a *both* fast and stable manner.

11

TLVs and Sub-TLVs

Charles Darwin's classic theory of evolution and its basic mechanism of natural selection through *mutation* can be re-applied to technology and the Internet. As the environment changes, entities within the environment must change as well or become extinct. Indeed, the relationship between the evolution of living creatures and the evolution of Internet technology is impressive. Each age of technology builds upon the discoveries of the previous age resulting in a constant change, which also helps humankind to adapt to or cope with their technological environment. Experience from the last decade of networking has shown that Darwin's Law is just as present and active in networking as anywhere else in life. When Darwin is translated to the routing protocols environment this means that not the strongest, most lightweight or most optimal routing protocol, algorithm and implementation at a fixed, given time will prevail in the end. The routing protocol that wins the technology prize for *survival of the fittest* will be the one that adapts best to its changing Internet environment and can add features mandated by passing time. Based on the historical development of the OSPF routing protocol, it will be shown why Darwin's Law is valid in the technology environment.

11.1 Taxonomy for Extensibility

First of all, the term *extensibility* as used in this chapter will be defined in more detail. In any discussion of extensibility, there are three things that need to be considered:

- How do current software maturation models work?
- What are the ramifications if a routing protocol is barely or not extensible at all?
- What does it mean when a routing protocol is called *extensible*?

Software quality assurance is still a young topic in computer science. This is especially true for the additional complexity of distributed systems, where one failing node may impact others, no really *clueful* model has been found. Best common practice to ensure software quality is *hardening by deploying*. This essentially means that if software is deployed frequently, all the inherent bugs will finally go away after a maturation cycle. In the next paragraph, a typical software maturation cycle is described.

11.1.1 *Current Software Maturation Models*

The most common software maturation model applicable in the last decade is briefly described in Figure 11.1 and explained as follows:

1. *Develop the base (alpha) code*. This is the first engineering cut at the program and will not be released publicly. This software is tested at the router vendor's internal test bed.

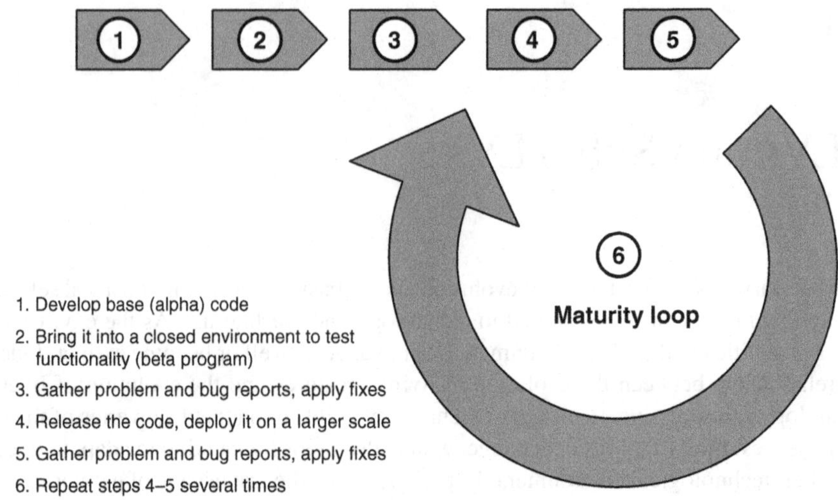
1
2
3
4
5
6
Maturity loop
1. Develop base (alpha) code
2. Bring it into a closed environment to test functionality (beta program)
3. Gather problem and bug reports, apply fixes
4. Release the code, deploy it on a larger scale
5. Gather problem and bug reports, apply fixes
6. Repeat steps 4–5 several times

FIGURE 11.1. The maturity cycle of IP routing protocol software

Once bugs are discovered they will be fixed. Typically the alpha code testing efforts are accomplished in a few days or at most a couple of weeks.

2. *Bring the code into a closed environment and test functionality.* This is often called the "beta" program. The beta code is usually released to friendly customers. The goal of the beta program is to get input from the various customers' testing labs. Each of these testing labs will focus their testing efforts of the feature or feature of most interest to the particular customer. The customer will test the beta to see if the features of interest are correctly supported, and working properly.
3. *Gather problem and bug reports, then apply fixes.* This is the feedback phase of the beta program. Typically lots of bugs are filed and fixed in this phase. Generally, the more bugs found at this stage, the more stable the release will be later. The customers will get the fixes to test against their respective network environment before the code is released.
4. *Release the code to deploy it on a larger scale.* Although closed environment testing is fine, and it is always a good idea to do some base-line testing, there is no better test than to expose the code to the real world. Here for the first time a routing protocol leaves the safety of the pool and is hit by the crashing waves of the Internet. Now there are things like constant BGP updates, flapping links causing IGPs to recalculate their SPF graph every couple of seconds, and many other events all putting stress on both router hardware and software. This is the phase where new, undocumented problems are found, and often actions that are nowhere mentioned in any specification. These new and unexpected issues sometimes lead to entire software projects being dismissed because of the problems that no one was aware of during the writing of the internal design specifications.
5. *Gather problem and bug reports, apply fixes.* Not all problems are discovered on Day One of an ongoing deployment – Murphy's Law is also, and *especially,* valid in the

networking environment. Typically, more problems are discovered when the last few routers in a customer's network are updated with the new software. If there is improperly functioning software in the customer's live network, then it is the router vendor's responsibility to provide fast, "hot" fixes for the problems being discovered. This is a scary phase for the ISP, because sometimes the hot fix has not been subjected to the full internal test bed, mostly because of urgency to bring the fix into the field. A full regression test of routing software can last from a few days to many weeks, depending on the complexity of the overall software architecture.

6. Repeat steps 4 and 5 (deploy and fix) several times. This is probably the most important phase of all. Because this software development activity concerns the Internet, an ever expanding and growing thing, there is no such thing as software that is working and complete at the same time. It might be that during the software life cycle the Internet as a whole or the ISP's network is hitting a new scaling barrier for the routing software. This is the development phase that one large router vendor refers to as the "Internet classroom" where both ISPs and router vendors have to learn every day about the changing environment. But this results in a feedback loop of constant improvement through extensibility.

The full deployment and fixing steps in the process and the repeated iteration of these key deploy and fix steps are increasingly important for the overall quality and maturity of the routing protocol software. Even if this software maturation model sounds expensive at first for the customers, who are asked to deploy software that is admittedly *incomplete*, there is really no other way to complete the process. Some customer agents buying software and hardware from the router vendors might ask if the software should or could be tested better and more rigorously before going into general release for customer use. This is a valid point. But experience has shown that even the most rigorous of testing environments cannot detect all bugs or lack of needed functions in a routing protocol. Now, for the first public release after the beta-program, enough experience and testing should have been done to avoid a large percentage of "severe" bugs, which are bugs that cause the failure of the routing protocol and/or router. But less severe bugs, or feature shortcomings in the routing protocol, often only reveal themselves during extensive and large-scale operations in the Internet environment.

What the deploy-and-fix steps really boil down to is the repeated application of the following related steps:

- Deploying routing software
- Getting further experience (sometimes based on a slightly changed environment), and
- Improving routing software

These steps are very important for the maturity – and continued survival – of the protocols. Ideally, routing protocols should be almost like good wine – *the older, the better.*

11.1.2 *Ramifications of Non-extensible Routing Protocols*

The allowance for constant improvement of the routing protocol through added features and bug fixes forms the essence of the extensible routing protocol. How do non-extensible routing protocols negatively impact the maturity cycle of routing protocol software? A routing protocol becomes stable after spending enough cycles in the maturity (deploy-and-fix) loop. So what happens if this maturity cycle is disrupted by (for example) the need to add new features to the protocol? It is clear that there will always be enhancements, new capabilities and features requested by customers dictating innovation by voting with their dollars. No router vendor (or any type of company, for that matter) can withstand customer-originated pressure and refuse to add needed and desirable functionality to an already stable protocol. Ironically, one of the toughest challenges for the router vendors is to strike a balance between the customers desiring rock-solid, stable routing protocols and the customers at the edge of the technology pushing for innovation. So the question turns into "How do I introduce new functionality without harming the existing code base?" It is important to realize what the last part of this question states – due to the prevailing software development model, vendors do not want to disrupt the maturity cycle by creating something radically different, and so incompatible, with the existing routing protocol. It turns out that this desired property (extensible, but not harmful) is solely dependent on the routing protocol's architecture. This architecture determines how easy it is (or is not) for the developer to incorporate new features into the routing protocol. First of all it is hard to extend a protocol whose architecture was never prepared for extension. The ramification of this uphill battle will be additional demand for time and resources for bringing the protocol to a mature state, which may delay new enhancements to your network. Competitively speaking, it may be that a competitor is already provisioning services while other vendors are still testing in the labs to verify the protocol and the accompanying new features are prime-time ready.

11.1.3 *What Does it Mean When a Routing Protocol Is Called Extensible?*

How can anyone tell if a routing protocol is *really* extensible or not? There are two places to look at in order to determine if a routing protocol is friendly to the developer (that is, ready for extensions). The two places are:

- Hellos and Capability Announcement messages
- NLRI (Network Layer Reachability Information) messages

11.1.3.1 Hellos and Capability Announcement Messages

Hellos are the packets that are regularly exchanged between routers to determine if there is basic connectivity between the routers. Since these types of packets are common and exchanged whenever adjacencies are established between routers, Hello packets are also a good place to indicate new capabilities in the routing protocol. These capabilities might include, but are not limited to, things such as:

- Support for additional networking protocols beside IPv4 (for example, IPv6, CNLP, IPX, and so on).
- Changes and modifications to the protocol interaction (for example, the basic handshake procedures for the protocol).
- Changes and modifications to the topological understanding of the routing protocol (for example, support for multiple topologies and link types, more than one area, and so on).

- Changes and modifications to the basic timers such as establishing a different baseline for the timers. Think of an extension to the routing protocol that allows for sub-second convergence and requires other routers to re-interpret their own timers, sometimes in violation of the original specification. For instance, a router wanting to indicate that the dead-timer value of 300 should not be interpreted in units of *seconds* (300 seconds), but should be now interpreted as a 300-millisecond dead-timer.
- Changes to the authentication scheme used on the link (for example, public-key authentication used instead of a simple password).
- Non-stop forwarding (also known as graceful restart) behaviour that allows neighbouring node to still forward traffic through a router with a failing control plane, as described in draft-ietf-isis-restart-05.

11.1.3.2 NLRIs

NLRI (Network Layer Reachability Information) is a term borrowed from BGP and used with IGPs like ISIS and OSPF. But the idea of an NLRI can be used for virtually any networking and routing protocol that has to pass on OSI-RM Layer 3 (L3) network prefixes (routes). The NLRI is basically a *per-Layer3 protocol envelope* for passing on *reachability information* ("if you have any packets for the IP addresses that follow, you can send them here. I know how to reach them."). Keeping the eventual need to transition to IPv6 in mind, any protocol should support multiprotocol extensions to a degree that one can convey both IPv4 and IPv6 NLRIs concurrently. The concept of a per-protocol container is needed because, virtually every network layer protocol has different L3 address formats and rules that routers follow to parse them. For instance, the bit string 192.168.1/24 could and does mean something totally different in IPv4 than in IPv6. So each prefix has to be packaged in a dedicated *envelope* telling the other routers what network layer protocol the prefix is targeted for.

It would be nice if Hellos and NLRIs formed two completely independent mechanisms of extensibility. Unfortunately, Hellos and NLRIs are related to each other. For example, if a node sends IPv6 reachability information inside an IPv6 NLRI to another router, the receiving router has to have a way of finding out ahead of time which of its neighbours can forward IPv6 in order to route the traffic closer to the destination. So a single look to see if a routing protocol supports a different NLRI type is only half the story. This makes it clear that a truly extensible routing protocol must easily accommodate both new capabilities in its Hello Messages *as well as* support for different NLRIs during route prefix update exchanges to facilitate extensions.

Two routing protocols often cited as models of extensibility and for their ease of adding new features while remaining stable are OSPF and IS-IS. The rest of this chapter is an analysis of how OSPF and then IS-IS achieve their extensibility.

11.2 Analysis of OSPF Extensibility

The analysis in this section is based on RFC 2328 "OSPF Version 2" Appendix A "OSPF Data Formats", and also RFC 2370 *The OSPF Opaque LSA Option.*

What this section basically does is try to pose some hypothetical questions of the routing protocol. For instance, we could ask, "in what parts or fields of the routing protocol could

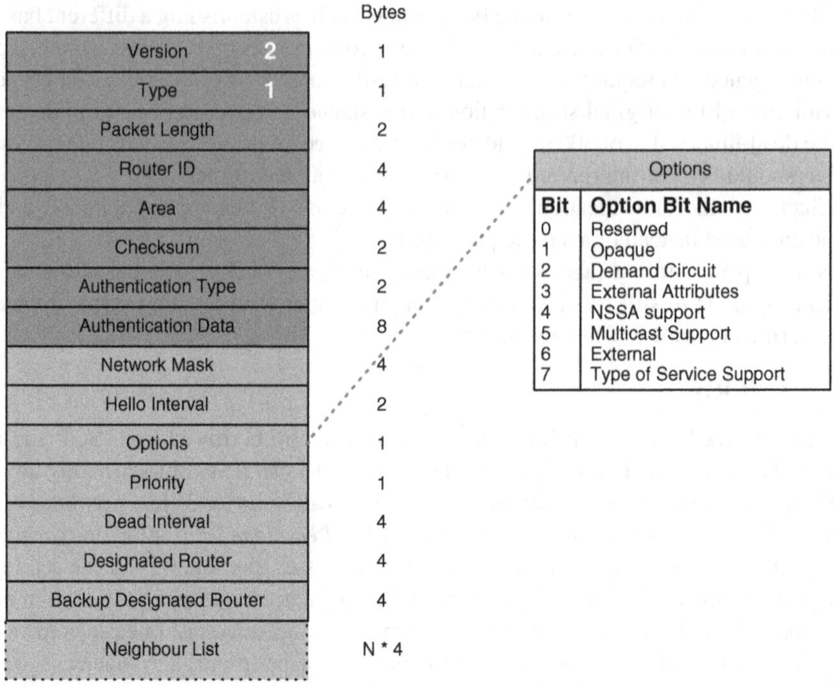

FIGURE 11.2. The OSPF Hello packet has no provisions for optional fields and the 8-bit options field is almost fully populated

OSPF extensions be placed?" Now, no one really would do this in real life. This procedure is just an exercise for the sake of finding out if a protocol is truly extensible or not. If there is no place to put extensions, then the routing protocol is just not extensible, no matter what the standard might say in this regard.

Figure 11.2 shows a generic OSPF header and an OSPF Hello in detail. One feature of the OSPF routing protocol is immediately obvious just by glancing at the figure. The OSPF routing protocol has a frame structure aligned to 32-bit (4 bytes) boundaries. Today, 32-bit alignment is merely a legacy from the times when CPU processing power was small and realigning a byte stream would have had a serious CPU impact. This optimization effort is considered to be a non-issue in modern networks. For CPU architectures that store 32-Bit integers in non-network order format (like for example the Intel x86 Architecture) this optimization is even more irrelevant because for network order to host order conversion the stream is read in 8-bit quantities anyway). The generic OSPF header as well as the OSPF Hello header has some occurrences of IPv4 addresses without explicit fields establishing that these addresses are in the IPv4 format. This is a bad thing, because it means that OSPF cannot send Hellos for any other address family such as IPv6. How would the parser in the receiving router know what's inside a field like the *Designated Router* field without implicitly expecting an IPv4 address? What if inside the address field is an IPv6 address, or even something else? Simply put, current OSPF extension mechanisms cannot be extended in that way to indicate multiple address families in the header.

But what about using fields *after* the Hello message? There is plenty of room in an IP packet (65,515 bytes for the IPMAX size field in the IP packet header. A good idea, but it won't work. The last field in the Hello message is the Neighbour List. The Neighbour List is an implementation of a 3-way handshake protocol. Consider when Router A and Router B first communicate. In the Hellos exchange, the Neighbour List basically lists routers, including Router A, by IP address in Router B's Hellos in order to indicate that there is bi-directional connectivity between Router A and Router B. However, the Neighbour List lacks a Length indicator field. How does the receiver then know where the "Neighbour List" ends? Recall that the software parsing the Hello knows the length of the entire OSPF packet. Knowing this, the router simply subtracts the OSPF generic header plus the OSPF Hello, which are in total 44 bytes. The result divided by four (each entry in the Neighbour-ID list is a 32-bit IPv4 address) and so reveals the number of neighbours that this specific router has "seen".

From a purely bit-field perspective the OSPF Hello is not extensible at all. This is because neither re-interpretation of existing fields nor attaching new fields at the end of the frame works to extend OSPF to other address families without breaking the base OSPF protocol. If such a multi-family feature were added to OSPF, the result would be incompatible with older versions of OSPF.

Right from it first version, OSPF included an 8-bit field called the "Options Field", which can be seen in Figure 11.2. Throughout the last decade, the Options field has been utilized for several extensions to OSPF. These extensions include:

- O – The router supports the Opaque LSA Types 9,10,11 which are mainly used for Traffic Engineering applications
- DC – Demand circuits (circuits that are not up all the time, such as dial-ups)
- EA – External LSA (deprecated, this option must no longer be used)
- N/P – NSSA support (allows external routes in a stub area)
- MC – Multicast OSPF (using OSPF to distribute multicast routing information)
- E – Indicating ASBRs (routers redistributing routes from another routing source such as RIP)
- T – TOS (type of service) routing support

As shown in Figure 11.2, the Options field has only three unused (Reserved) bits left. So there is not-much room to extend the protocol in a backward-compatible way. The option negotiating mechanism in OSPF is solved quite nicely because a router receiving Hellos and not having certain capabilities replies in its own Hellos with the Options field bits that are not supported cleared.

In the common OSPF frame there are fields indicating the Version and the Packet-Type. In Figure 11.2, the Packet-Type for the Hello is set to 1 (Hello Packet-Type) and the Version field is set to 2 indicating OSPF protocol version 2.

Mention has just been made of the OSPF Packet-Type field. A value of 1 indicates an OSPF Hello packet. In the base specification OSPF supports five different packet types:

1. Hello
2. Database description
3. Link-state request

4. Link-state update
5. Link-state acknowledgment

Database description, link-state update, and link-state acknowledgment are purely for synchronizing the link-state databases on demand. The element carrying network layer reachability information, the main source of detailed link state information, is the link-state update packet. If OSPF wants to announce IP prefixes and their related metrics, the vehicle to get this information across to other OSPF routers is the link-state update packets (LSAs).

The next step in exploring the extensibility of OSPF is to make sure the link-state update packet can be extended. Figure 11.3 shows that there is a field called Link-State Type. Simply adding new Link-State Types can extend OSPF. It is not necessary to go deeper into what link-state types exist today and what the various packet formats look like to understand that this is how OSPF can be extended for new features and functions. This information is available from a number of sources. After all, this is a book about IS-IS and not a book about OSPF.

Field		Bytes
Version	2	1
Type	4	1
Packet Length		2
Router ID		4
Area		4
Checksum		2
Authentication Type		2
Authentication Data		8
LSA Count		4
LSA age		2
Options		1
LSA Type		1
Link State ID		4
Advertising Router		4
Sequence Number		4
Checksum		2
Length		2

FIGURE 11.3. The LSA type field would be a possibility for extending OSPF

Consider extending OSPF by adding a new, hypothetical LSA type. The number could be anything not currently used or defined – LSA type 53, for example. Now, what if a router running older OSPF software does not recognize the new, hypothetical LSA type 53? Should the router flood the LSA further across the network or should the router simply discard the update? To explain what OSPF does with extensions that the router does not understand, it is necessary to borrow a term from BGP terminology. The term is called *transitivity*. Certain BGP attributes are *transitive* as the attributes flow from BGP router to BGP router. But the term can be applied to protocols other than BGP. Transitivity means that if a router cannot interpret a given message, the router will flood the message further across the network anyway. *Non-transitive* behaviour means that a router does *not* forward an LSA that the router cannot interpret in terms of the LSA payload.

OSPF is a strictly non-transitive protocol. OSPF routers will not flood LSA types that the routers themselves do not understand. The ramifications of that are a bit depressing. Non-transitive OSPF behaviour means that a new feature cannot be rolled out unless *all* OSPF routers in a given link-state domain are updated with the new software. Given the fact that the role of the IGP is changing from the narrow role of distributing NLRI information towards a wider role with regard to a topology discovery function, it might be necessary for new OSPF features of increasing interest to use the flooding sub-system of OSPF for distributing network-wide information. And this information must be spread all over the network, information that not each OSPF speaker must necessarily see. *I won't flood because I do not understand* behaviour is not migration-friendly, and therefore causes a lot of headache for preparing migrations.

Fortunately, the issue of OSPF transitivity has been addressed. RFC 2370, *The OSPF Opaque LSA Option*, describes an enhancement to base OSPF. A set of *opaque* LSAs is defined in this RFC that correct the problem with OSPF being non-transitive. Instead of using the BGP terminology of transitive, OSPF uses the concept of an LSA that is *visible* (and understandable) to some OSPF routes and yet not visible to all OSPF routers. The new LSAs are not transparent to all OSPF routers, but *opaque* to some routers, routers that must still pass on this LSA type through flooding nonetheless. With RFC 2370, type 9, 10 and 11 LSAs now become the universal transport vehicle for routing and topology-related data that need to get distributed by the flooding sub-system of OSPF. With those extensions in place, arbitrary data, including reachability information from other address families such as IPv6, could theoretically be distributed about an OSPF routing domain. A full discussion of opaque LSA types in OSPF is not needed in a book on IS-IS. It is enough to note the presence of opaque LSA types in OSPF for the purposes of extensibility.

11.3 Analysis of IS-IS Extensibility

IS-IS uses TLVs to encode Hellos, NLRIs, as well as miscellaneous other information needed for the IS-IS routing protocol to function properly. Virtually all these message elements use Type-Length-Value (TLV) encoding to get their data across to other IS-IS routers.

11.3.1 *TLV Format*

Figure 11.4 shows the basic elements for TLV encoding.

The first element of the TLV structure is the *Type* field. The size of the Type field is 8-bits wide, which gives room for 256 different codes. In fact, a lot of documents call this the *Code*-Length-Value (*C*LV) structure instead of TLV. But the TLV terminology is much more common and is therefore used here. Type number 0 is reserved for further expansion of the protocol. The Type field is a well-known field that should be understood by all routers in a given link-state domain (= IS-IS level). Next comes the *Length* field that indicates the length of the payload data, which is stored in the *Value* field. Why is the Length field needed if the Type code establishes the format of the information in the Value field? As long as all Type codes are well known, it would seem that the router has enough information to decipher the value that the Type contains. But it is not that simple.

Let's invent an example demonstrating the need for a Length field. Suppose we want to encode an IPv4 prefix. What we need is 8 bytes of space in the TLV. Four bytes are for the prefix itself and four bytes are for the Netmask. Next, let's give this Value field the hypothetical Type number, say 47. Because Type Code #47 is well known by all routers running the IS-IS protocol, one could suppose that there could be a rule in the IS-IS protocol that Code 47 always means an implicit length of 8 bytes for the Value field. However, what happens if a router running *older* software does not recognize our *new* hypothetical Type Code 47 Message? How is the Length made know to IS-IS routers that do not know what a Type Code 47 is? Even worse, the section of IS-IS code that parses all the incoming routing messages does not know when other messages-codes beyond the Type Code 47 begin, because the code has no indication when the unknown Type Code 47 message *ends*. Figure 11.5 illustrates the dilemma of the receiving router's message parser.

So an explicit Length field is always needed for TLVs. The Length field is again 8-bits wide, which leaves room for Values up to 255 bytes. Although this may sound like a small

Field	Range	Bytes
Type	1–255	1
Length	1–255	1
Value		1–255

FIGURE 11.4. Basic information encoding in (T)ype (L)ength (V)alue triplets

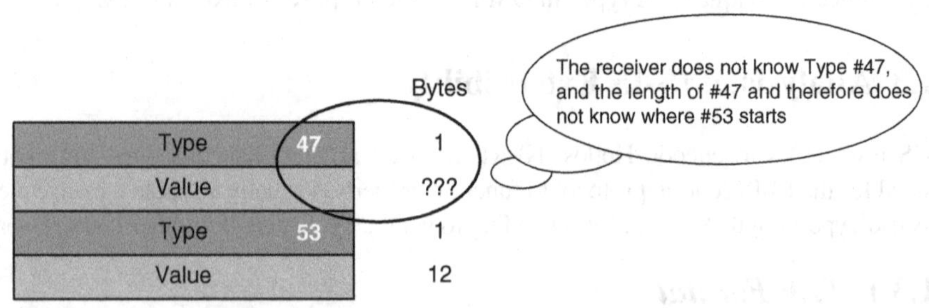

FIGURE 11.5. Implicit length fields do not work unless *all* routers know *all* the Type codes

number (just think of a router that has hundreds of adjacencies to advertise) it has turned out to be a sufficient size for most message types.

11.3.2 *TLV Encoding*

For the case of messages larger than 255 bytes, smaller message elements are scattered across multiple occurrences of a given Type Code. Figure 11.6 shows how a large chunk (30 in this case) of IPv4 prefixes are scattered over two occurrences of Type Code 128 messages. Type Code 128, which is *not* hypothetical, will be discussed in more detail in Chapter 12. The only thing a router needs to know is that the basic message format of TLV #128 is repeated occurrences of IPv4 prefixes, metrics and net masks having a fixed length of 12 bytes. So each IPv4 prefix consumes 12 bytes space in the message. What the TLV encoding engine needs to know is the maximum amount of IPv4 prefix data that can be stored in a 255 bytes sized message. As it turns out, the densest packaging is reached when 21 prefixes are squeezed into one TLV encoded message, filling up the message to 252 bytes. That still results in a TLV message space utilization of 98.4 per cent, which is fine for a routing protocol. The remaining nine prefixes get stored in a second occurrence of a Type #128 message.

Interestingly, IS-IS has a uniform Type Code space for both Hellos and NLRIs. This means that an arbitrary TLV can theoretically be present both in all three IS-IS packet types. The three packet types that IS-IS generates are:

- IIHs (Hellos)
- SNPs (sequence number PDUs)
- LSPs (link-state PDUs)

Although this uniform Type Code space makes it easier for humans to memorize the defined TLVs, not all TLVs are present in all three IS-IS PDU types. For instance, for authentication information it makes no sense to limit authentication only to IIH packets, because an attacker can do a lot of harm by forging any of the PDU types.

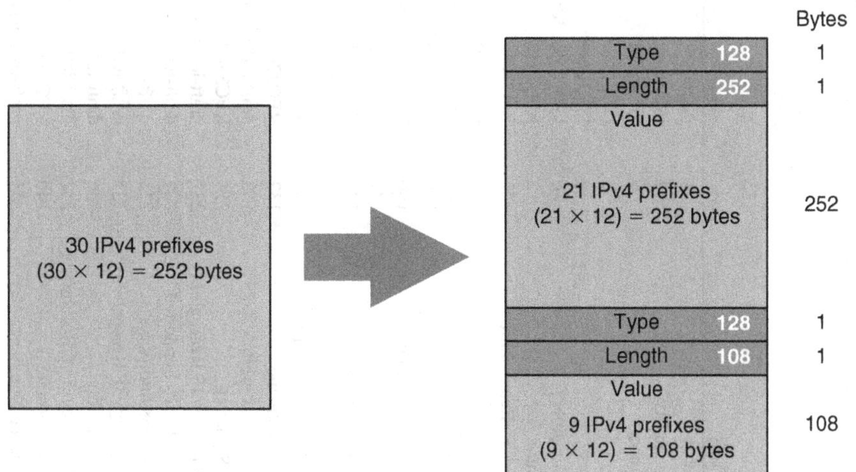

FIGURE 11.6. A large chunk of IPv4 prefixes, not fitting in a single TLV encoded message, is scattered across multiple occurrences of the same Type Code

TABLE 11.1. The list of TLVs that modern router OSs support.

			PDU type								
			15	16	17	18	20	24	25	26	27
	TLV		LAN Hello		p2p Hello	LSP		CSNP		PSNP	
IS-IS TLVs	#	Source	L1	L2		L1	L2	L1	L2	L1	L2
Area Address	1	ISO10589	X	X	X	X	X				
IS Reachability	2	ISO10589				X	X				
IS Neighbors	6	ISO10589	X	X							
Padding	8	ISO10589	X	X	X						
LSP Entry	9	ISO10589						X	X	X	X
Authentication	10	ISO10589, RFC3567	X	X	X	X	X	X	X	X	X
Checksum	12	RFC3358	X	X	X			X	X	X	X
Extended IS Reachability	22	RFC3784				X	X				
IS Alias	24	RFC3786				X	X				
IP internal Reachability	128	RFC1195, RFC2966				X	X				
Protocols Supported	129	RFC1195	X	X	X	X	X				
IP external Reachability	130	RFC1195, RFC2966 (*)					X(*)	X			
IDRP Information	131	RFC1195					X	X			
IP Interface Address	132	RFC1195	X	X	X	X	X				
TE Router ID	134	RFC3784					X	X			
Extended IP Reachability	135	RFC3784					X	X			
Dynamic hostname	137	RFC2763					X	X			
Shared link risk group	138	draft-ietf-isis-gmpls-extensions-19					X	X			
Restart Signaling	211	RFC3847	X	X	X						
Multi Topology IS Reachability	222	draft-ietf-isis-wg-multi-topology-07					X	X			
Multi Topologies Supported	229	draft-ietf-isis-wg-multi-topology-07	X	X	X	X	X				
IPv6 Interface Address	232	draft-ietf-isis-ipv6-06	X	X	X	X	X				
Multi Topology IP Reachability	235	draft-ietf-isis-wg-multi-topology-07					X	X			
IPv6 Reachability	236	draft-ietf-isis-ipv6-05					X	X			
Multi Topology IPv6 Reachability	237	draft-ietf-isis-wg-multi-topology-07					X	X			
p2p adjacency state	240	RFC3373			X						
IIH Sequence Number	241	draft-shen-isis-iih-sequence-00	X	X	X						
Vendor Proprietary	250	draft-ietf-isis-experimental-tlv-01	X	X	X	X	X	X	X	X	X

However, the 3-way handshake TLV on point-to-point (p2p) links, for example, only makes sense in p2p IIHs. This is because the problem that this specific TLV #240 is trying to fix is purely related to p2p Hellos, during the startup procedure.

Table 11.1 shows a list of the most important TLVs in IS-IS, and in which packet type the TLV might occur.

The Type field is an 8-bit entity, which is a relatively small space, given the fact that routing protocols can live dozens of years. In order to not exhaust the 8-bit space throughout the years the protocol designers carried the TLV orientation further *inside* the TLVs. This concept is called sub-TLVs.

11.3.3 *Sub-TLVs*

Sub-TLVs are used inside a TLV to encapsulate further message elements. Theoretically a dedicated TLV could be used as well for new message elements. This would, however, quickly exhaust the TLV space. The Extended IS Reachability TLV is a good example for use of sub-TLVs. The Extended IS Reachability TLV describes an IS-IS Adjacency and all sorts of link properties like Maximum Link Bandwidth, Link colours, Neighbours, IP addresses, Traffic Engineering metrics and so on.

Tcpdump output

The Extended IS Reachability TLV #22 carries an additional 69 bytes of link property information.

```
11:36:45.587565 OSI, IS-IS, length: 405
 L2 LSP, hlen: 27, v: 1, pdu-v: 1, sys-id-len: 6 (0), max-area: 3 (0)
    lsp-id: 1921.6800.1019.00-00, seq: 0x000002fd, lifetime: 1198s
    chksum: 0xe984 (correct), PDU length: 405, L1L2 IS
     [ … ]
      Extended IS Reachability TLV #22, length: 75
      IS Neighbor: 1921.6800.1021.00, Metric: 22000, sub-TLVs present (69)
        IPv4 interface address subTLV #6, length: 4, 172.16.33.6
        IPv4 neighbor address subTLV #8, length: 4, 172.16.33.5
        Traffic Engineering Metric subTLV #18, length: 3, 22000
        Unreserved bandwidth subTLV #11, length: 32
        priority level 0: 9953.280 Mbps
        priority level 1: 9953.280 Mbps
        priority level 2: 9953.280 Mbps
        priority level 3: 9953.280 Mbps
        priority level 4: 9953.280 Mbps
        priority level 5: 9953.280 Mbps
        priority level 6: 9953.280 Mbps
        priority level 7: 9953.280 Mbps
        Reservable link bandwidth subTLV #10, length: 4, 9953.280 Mbps
        Maximum link bandwidth subTLV #9, length: 4, 9953.280 Mbps
        Administrative groups subTLV #3, length: 4, 0x00000000
      [ … ]
```

In Table 11.2 you can see all current defined sub-TLVs. Chapter 14, "Traffic Engineering and MPLS", gives a more thorough discussion of the extended IS Reachability TLV which is just discussed here for the aspect of sub-TLVs.

Figure 11.7 shows a real-world example of the *Extended IS Reachability TLV*. In our example TLV, two adjacencies are reported. The first link adjacency is describing link characteristics to Neighbour 1921.6800.1008.00. The cost of using this link during the SPF cycle is 250,000 as described in the *Metric* field. After the *Metric* field each TLV terminates with an optional sub-TLV length. If the length field is zero, then no further link characteristic are reported for this adjacency. In our example there is indication that there are 11 further bytes of link properties.

The next byte contains the first sub-TLV type. Code-point #8 is used to indicate a remote neighbour's IP address. The sub-TLV Code is followed by a sub-TLV Length which is set to 4. What finally follows is the value of 4 bytes describing the actual *Neighbor IP Address*.

The encoding of the first sub-TLV consumed 1 + 1 + 4 = 6 bytes. So there is still 5 bytes left of sub-TLV information to decode.

The next sub-TLV is code-type 18 and the sub-TLV length field indicates 3 bytes of Metric Information. This sub-TLV carries a kind of metric information that is purely related to constrained based routing (CSPF) which is further illustrated in Chapter 14, "Traffic Engineering and MPLS".

The encoding of the second sub-TLV consumed 1 + 1 + 3 = 5 bytes. The original sub-TLVs field of the IS reach adjacency indicated a total sub-TLV length of 11 bytes.

What the router tries to find out next is to determine the remaining size of subTLVs – it does so by subtracting the actual offset from the entire TLV length of 33 bytes. So far 22 bytes (the first TLV plus the two sub-TLVs) have been processed so there must be 11

TABLE 11.2. The list of sub-TLVs that modern router OSs support.

IS Reach Sub-TLVs	Sub-TLV #	Source
Administrative Group	3	RFC3784
Link Local/Remote Identifier	4	RFC3784, draft-ietf-isis-gmpls-extensions-19
Link Remote Identifier	5	RFC3784
IPv4 interface address	6	RFC3784
IPv4 neighbor address	8	RFC3784
Maximum link bandwidth	9	RFC3784
Reservable link bandwidth	10	RFC3784
Unreserved bandwidth	11	RFC3784
Traffic Engineering Metric	18	RFC3784
Link Protection Type	20	draft-ietf-isis-gmpls-extensions-19
Interface Switching Capability	21	draft-ietf-isis-gmpls-extensions-19

IP Reach Sub-TLVs	Sub-TLV #	Source
32-Bit Administrative Tag	1	draft-ietf-isis-admin-tags-01
64-Bit Administrative Tag	2	draft-ietf-isis-admin-tags-01
Management Prefix Color	117	draft-ietf-isis-wg-multi-topology-07

bytes left. The parser therefore *knows* that the next 10 bytes is another IS adjacency pointing to neighbour 1921.6800.1019.00 plus an SPF metric of 22000. This second link is not carrying any sub-TLVs hence the sub-TLV length field is being set to zero.

It has already been shown that there are several *levels* of information packaging inside TLVs. The Extended IS Reachability TLV #22 is a good example. It contains several IS neighbours which may contain further sub-TLVs. There is lots of room for all sort of things that can go wrong here. Just imagine what happens if the sub-TLV length is bigger than the TLV length. Of course this can be avoided by all sorts of clever boundary checking. However, no specification expresses a mandate for boundary checking. In the next section you will learn about IS-IS TLV sanity checking and how vendors have hardened their implementations to catch corrupted information.

11.3.4 *TLV Sanity Checking*

Jon Postel postulated a famous guidance about protocol interoperability:

> *"Be tolerant of what you receive and strict in what you send!"*

The background was that a protocol's implementations should never assume that the receiver will get it right and should encode its information as concisely as possible. On the receiving side the rule mandates that the protocol should support error detection and

Field	Value	Bytes
Type	22	1
Length	33	1
Neighbor ID	1921.6800.1008.00	ID Length (6) + 1
Metric	250000	3
subTLVs Length	11	1
subTLV Type	8	1
subTLV Length	4	1
sub LV Value	172.16.33.12	4
subTLV Type	18	1
subTLV Length	3	1
subTLV Value	12000	3
Neighbour ID	1921.6800.1019.00	ID Length (6) + 1
Metric	22000	3
subTLVs Length	0	1

FIGURE 11.7. The sub-TLV length field of the Extended IS Reachability TLV #22 determines if there are any sub-TLVs following the basic IS reachability information

be tolerant about slightly malformed information structures. Link-state routing protocols do not allow implementers to follow that guidance, because of their highly distributed nature.

Consider the following example: A router receives a malformed TLV and detects that TLV is malformed. What should the router do? – further flood it or silently discard it and log an error message? ISO 10589 mandates that flooding should be transparent throughout the area. If the flooding stops what might be the biggest harm? Worst case, a routing loop. What happens if the router floods the LSP containing the malicious LSP further? Worst case, it may crash other routers in the network who do not encompass proper TLV sanity checking. In the past 10 years of IS-IS deployment there have been at least 20 major network meltdowns because corrupted LSPs got flooded further across the network. The first occurrence was back in the NSFNet backbone. Dr Rekhter, now a Distinguished Engineer with Juniper Networks, relates the following story:

"One thing that happened in the NSFNET backbone concerns the way my code handled ISIS link state updates. When a router received an ISIS link state update, the router would do some processing on that update, then flood the update to its neighbors, and then complete the rest of the processing on this update. Due to some bug in the code the last part ("the rest of the processing") caused router crash. But since the router crashed after it flooded the link state update to its neighbors, the update also caused the neighbors to crash as well, resulting in the overall network meltdown."

Implementers of the IS-IS protocol decided, because of the high inherent risk, to take a closer look to known TLVs and tightly check their formatting. The most common found TLV format tests are discussed in the next three subsections.

11.3.4.1 Maximum Length Checking

Each TLV and sub-TLV reports a certain length. The length field is typically an 8-bit field that can express Value fields between 0 and 255 bytes. However, not all TLVs and sub-TLVs can actually consume the full range of 255 bytes.

For example, in March 2001 there was a big meltdown in a large US transit carrier's network. The root cause was that a failing piece of hardware generated a malformed Area TLV #1. Figure 11.8 illustrates the structure of the Area TLV #1. The TLV contains a set of Area Lengths and their corresponding Area-IDs. In the OSI world only Area-IDs between 1–13 bytes length are supported. If the Area-ID is outside that range, then the entire TLV, if not the entire LSP, is highly likely to be corrupted. After parsing the TLV the receiving router did not check for the maximum Area-ID length and overwrote data structures in the SPF algorithm implementation, which were expecting Area-IDs not larger then 13 bytes. The routing software crash did not manifest itself immediately – there was unfortunately enough time to flood the *killer LSP* further, enough time to crash the entire network.

Since that incident, maximum length checking is employed for the Area TLV #1.

Continuing that thought there would be other TLVs that could get checked for Minimum and Maximum Length Fields. Table 11.3 lists the minimum and maximum length values for all TLVs.

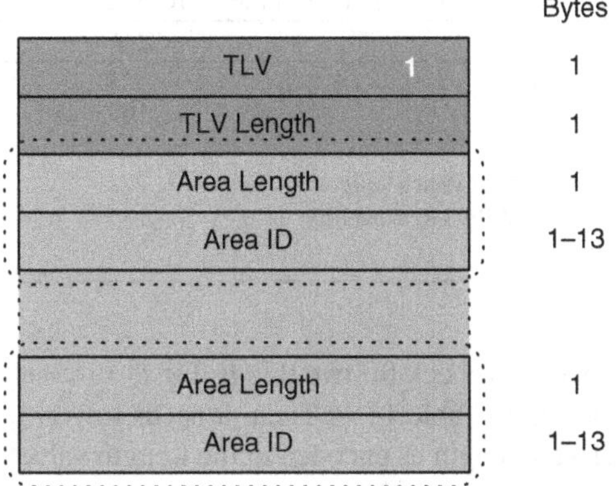

FIGURE 11.8. The Area TLV #1 lists all the variable length Area that a router participates

TABLE 11.3. Each TLV, due to its structure, has given minimum and maximum values.

TLV name	TLV #	Min. length	Max. length
Area Length field	1	1	13
IS Reachability	2	12	254
LSP Entry	9	16	240
Authentication (if Authentication Type = MD5 (54))	10	17	17
Checksum	12	2	2
Maximum LSP Buffer Size	14	2	2
Extended IS Reachability	22	11	–
IS Alias	24	8	–
IPv4 Internal Reachability	128	12	252
IPv4 External Reachability	130	12	252
IPv4 Interface Address	132	4	252
Traffic Engineering Router ID	134	4	4
Extended IPv4 Reachability	135	5	–
Restart Signaling	211	3	3
Multi Topology Extended IS Reachability	222	13	–
IPv6 Interface Address	232	16	240
Multi Topology Extended IPv4 Reachability	235	7	–
IPv6 Reachability	236	6	
p2p Adjacency State	240	1	15

All implementers are encouraged to check each received TLV against Table 11.1. Checking for the minimum TLEB Length Values reveals if there are broken TLVs around. Checking for the maximum value helps to avoid Buffer overruns.

11.3.4.2 Sub-TLV Overrun Checking

A sub-TLV parser should verify at any time that the sum of all parsed sub-TLVs does not get bigger than the original TLV minus the TLV specific overhead. Table 11.4 lists all the TLVs that support sub-TLVs and their maximum value they can grow.

TABLE 11.4. The sub-TLVs must not consume more space than the TLV offers.

TLV name	TLV #	Max. length
Extended IS Reachability	22	244
IS Alias	24	247
Extended IPv4 Reachability	135	250
Multi Topology Extended IS Reachability	222	242
Multi Topology Extended IPv4 Reachability	235	248
IPv6 Reachability	236	249

A receiving router needs to check for two things. First, is the sub-TLV shorter than the maximum value according to Table 11.4? Then, it needs to verify if the sub-TLV is not bigger than the actual TLV length as encoded in the Length value.

11.3.4.3 Discrete Length Checking

Some early ISO 10589 TLVs have a very structured layout. Some of the RFC 1195 IP Reach TLVs copied the ISO 10589 style and hence have a similar structured layout as well. That structured layout allows now to predict certain packet sizes. In the right-hand columns of Table 11.5 there is a small formula for each TLV. The factor N is typically the amount of information elements announced in that TLV. For example, a router with three IP addresses would advertise a $N * 4 = 3 * 4 = 12$ bytes Length Interface Address TLV #132 in is Hello.

The final check tries to verify certain patterns in the information elements.

TABLE 11.5. Certain TLVs because of their structure only have discrete sizes.

TLV name	TLV #	Formula
IS Reachability	2	$N * 11 + 1$
LSP Entry	9	$N * 16$
IPv4 Internal Reachability	128	$N * 12$
IPv4 External Reachability	130	$N * 12$
IPv4 Interface Address	132	$N * 4$
IPv6 Interface Address	232	$N * 16$
p2p Adjacency State	240	1, 5, 11, 15

11.3.4.4 TLV Content Pattern Checking

A good example for a pattern check is the Netmask field in the IPv4 Internal and External Reachability TLVs. Although the Netmask field is a 32-bit field, it only allows 33 certain values covering all permutations of prefix lengths. Another example would be the bandwidth values of some Extended IS-Reach #22 sub-TLVs like the Maximum Link Bandwidth sub-TLV #9 can only carry certain discrete bandwidth values. draft-ietf-isis-gmpls-extension-19 gives good guidance on which values are supported.

TLV sanity checking is a new discipline which is in contradiction to the fully transparent flooding model of ISO 10589. However, it turned out that service providers are happy to trade better stability against flooding transparency especially the one that experienced a full-scale network crash due to bogus TLVs that did not get detected.

11.4 Conclusion

Based upon this chapter's examination of the Hellos and the NLRI carrying packets, in both OSPF and IS-IS, OSPFv2 is not quite as extensible as IS-IS.

On the Hello side, OSPFv2 in general lacks extensibility. For the NLRI carrying packets, OSPF now contains a set of so-called "Opaque LSAs" that could be used to carry extensible information for additional address families. But to address the non-extensibility in OSPF in conjunction with the ongoing deployment of IPV6, the OSPF protocol designers had to develop a whole new version of OSPF. And unfortunately, OSPFv3 does not have much in common with OSPFv2, since the code was mostly a rewrite from scratch, so it doesn't use all the stable code of the OSPFv2 version. All routing software has to undergo a maturity process to become stable enough for productive use in the Internet backbones of the world and OSPFv3 maturity may take a little longer as it tries to be all things to all packets.

Compared to OSPF, IS-IS is almost like a case study on how to *do it right the first time*. From day one, IS-IS has been designed to stay neutral no matter which Network Layer protocol information it had to transport. IS-IS has always been effectively multi-protocol ready: in the 1980s it was used for routing CNLP traffic; in the 1990s IPv4 traffic was added; and, since 2001, IPv6 has been efficiently carried. It helps when the message elements and packet types of the base IS-IS routing protocol use the proper TLV encoding. In addition, special precautions have been made not to exhaust the small 8-bit code space through use of sub-TLVs, even in the newer TLVs. TLVs and sub-TLVs turn out to be a powerful vehicle to further extend the protocol. Due to the extra complexity of sub-TLV encoding and tight sanity checks based on known TLV structure, before loading TLV contents into the link-state database are recommended.

Finally, the code changes from the IPv4 to an IS-IS supporting IPv6 required only 400–600 lines of code, not an entire rewrite of the protocol. It is unlikely that active routing of IPv6 prefixes will do any harm to the base stability of the IS-IS code.

Adapting in a constantly changing environment is what Darwin's Law is all about. When it comes to routing protocols, extensibility is a prerequisite for routing protocol evolution. It is the authors opinion that IS-IS adapts better than OSPF, which is why it will continue to prevail in the largest routed networks in the world.

12

IP Reachability Information

IS-IS was ready from day one for extensibility. Originally intended to route CLNP prefixes, today IS-IS carries routing information about a variety of networking protocols including IPv4 and IPv6. In this chapter you will learn about the various places where IP prefixes or IP reachability information, which is the IS-IS term, is encoded. Support for IP prefixes came in three waves. The chapter covers both the old-style (first generation) and the new-style (second generation) TLVs. Additionally, the limitations of the first-generation IPv4-related TLVs defined in the *Integrated IS-IS Routing* specification (RFC 1195) will be highlighted. Finally, some of the reasoning surrounding the particular problems that the more recent traffic-engineering TLVs solve will be explained.

IS-IS has multiple places to convey IP reachability information. To understand why the IP-related TLVs have been re-engineered continually, it is necessary to take advantage of hindsight and consider the times when a specific protocol decision was made. Therefore, before exploring the style of the IP TLVs, a look at one of the original ISO 10589 TLVs is needed. Of course ISO 10589 is totally unrelated to IP; however, to acquire an understanding of how ISO 10589 *encodes* information, it is a good idea to also get a better understanding of why the first generation of IP TLVs are the way they are.

12.1 Old-style Topology (IS-Reach) Information

Figure 12.1 shows how IS-IS encodes neighbour reachability information in the IS Reachability TLV #2. The TLV conveys pure router-to-router connectivity information and is unrelated to IP. The first byte is the Virtual Flag, which is either set to zero or one. Typically this is set to zero. It is only set to 1 in Level 2 LSPs and indicates that this link is used to repair an area partition. However, partition repair isn't something that a protocol should address. Typically partitioning of Level 1 areas is avoided by putting enough links in the area. IOS supports area partitioning for CLNP. However, JUNOS lacks support for healing broken, partitioned areas. Therefore the least common denominator is the simplistic design rule: "Never let an area get partitioned", and try to avoid partitioning of an area by throwing enough links at the problem.

After the virtual flag there is a basic structure of 11 bytes that may be repeated throughout the TLV. That 11-byte structure holds 4 bytes of metric-related information and 6 bytes of System-ID appended with the one-byte Pseudonode-ID. Interestingly, the basic ISO 10589 specification supports *multidimensional* metrics. There are distinct metrics

Field			Value	Bytes
TLV Type			2	1
TLV Length			N*11 + 1	1
Virtual Flag			0	1
R 0	I/E 0	Default Metric		1
S 1	I/E 0	Delay Metric		1
S 1	I/E 0	Expense Metric		1
S 1	I/E 0	Error Metric		1
Neighbour ID				ID Length (6) +1
⋮				
R 0	I/E 0	Default Metric		1
S 1	I/E 0	Delay Metric		1
S 1	I/E 0	Expense Metric		1
S 1	I/E 0	Error Metric		1
Neighbour ID				ID Length (6) +1

FIGURE 12.1. The IS-Reachability TLV is the blueprint for all the old-style Reachability TLVs encompassing 6-bit metrics

for Delay, Error, Expense and a mandatory default metric. The basic idea behind this scheme is that each router computes four distinct "topologies" by running a dedicated SPF operation for each. However, at the time IS-IS was first deployed (end of the 1980s) people were cautious about using CPU cycles and therefore only computed the *mandatory* SPF topology, which is the default topology. If IS-IS would have been first deployed at the end of the 1990s, computing distinct SPF trees probably would have not been much of an issue due to the massive processing power available even in embedded router systems. For routing *IP*, the IS-IS implementation of IOS and JUNOS does not support computation of anything but the default topology. Both only propagate the default metric and ignore any other metrics during receipt and during the SPF run. IOS, however, does support multidimensional metrics for routing CLNP, as already mentioned.

Each of the four possible metrics is represented by a dedicated byte. The most significant bit (MSB) of the respective metric byte indicates what additional metrics an individual router supports. Typically the MSB is *set* in the Delay, Expense and Error metrics, which indicate that the metric is *not* supported. Next to the MSB there is the Internal/External bit, which expresses whether the Metric is *comparable* or not. Internal means it is *comparable*, while External means it is not. (Internal metrics are always based on the same routing protocol, while externals metrics are independent of IS-IS.) Typically the I/E bit is set to zero, indicating that the metric is *comparable*. Confused? Don't worry! Simply assume the I/E bit is always set to zero – in this TLV the I/E bit has no real *practical* meaning. Next, there are 6 bits that hold the metric information. Six bits can only express routing metrics ranging from 0 to 63, which is quite limited these days. Once again, the design choice of using 6 bits goes back to the anxiousness about the SPF calculation consuming too many CPU cycles.

In every step of the SPF calculation a *sorting* function needs to be executed. One can optimize that sorting function through the use of linear arrays. Consider Figure 12.2 where a router's *preliminary* metric during the SPF calculation is 456. Now the process needs to find out if there are any other routers offering a better path to a given destination (the System-ID) by applying a sorting function. Using index arrays, one can skip that sorting function. All that need be done is store a pointer to the System-ID at the 456th entry in the array. If the array gets traversed from zero to the end, the first non-null pointer must be the highest value. This implementation has the disadvantage that it consumes memory. By limiting the Link Metric to 63 and the Aggregated Metric to 1023, IS-IS makes sure that the indexing function does not consume too much memory. This is another place where CPU/memory constraints have made their way into the IS-IS protocol. In hindsight, almost always where protocol designers tried to address a particular CPU/memory/environment shortage issue of the time by protocol properties, those protocol properties finally got deprecated over time. It turned out that protocols live much longer than microprocessors or memory chip restrictions do.

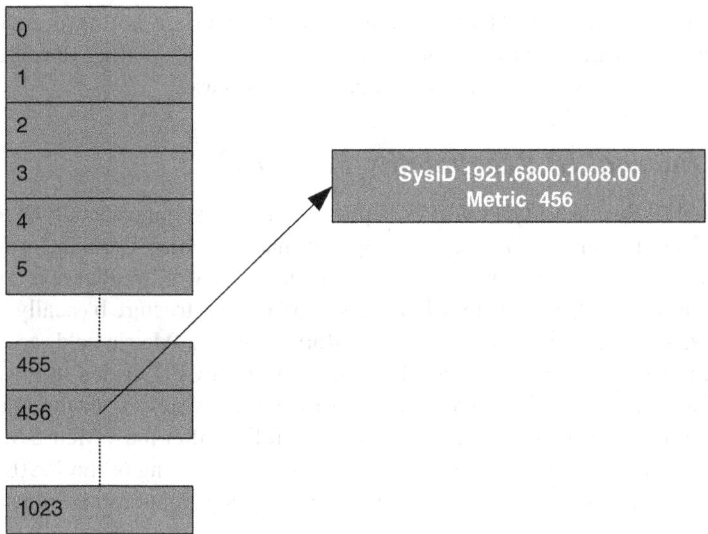

FIGURE 12.2. Index arrays helped to speed up search operations

For lower bandwidth links the limitation to just 63 distinct metric values was not much of an issue, because there was not much disparity between the smallest and the largest bandwidth links in a network. Consider (for instance) a DS0 (64 Kbps) circuit and a T1 (1.544 Mbps) circuit. The T1 has 24 times the bandwidth of the DS0. Inverse bandwidth metric schemes are commonly used (since the lower the metric, the more attractive the route), so setting the T1 line to a metric of 1 and the DSO to a metric of 24 provides good differentiation between the two bandwidths in the metric space. Now, consider that the highest bandwidth in the network becomes an OC-3/STM-1 circuit capable of carrying 155 Mbps. Assign the lowest-cost metric to the high-speed circuit, as before. About 100 times the capacity of a single T1 circuit fits into an OC-3/STM-1 circuit, so assign a metric of *100* to the T1. Stop! Assigning a metric of 100 doesn't work because there are only 6 bits available. The metric must be "clipped" to 63. Continuing with the 155 Mbps example, re-doing the calculation for the DS0 again exposes the limitations of a 6-bit metric space. About 2400 DS0s fit into an OC-3/STM-1 circuit. However, since there is no bigger metric, once again clip the metric to 63. The end result is that, from an IS-IS perspective, the DS0 link becomes now indistinguishable to the T1 line, as both metrics are now 63. That increasing disparity of IGP metrics became the motivation to introduce new TLVs that have a broader metric field than just 6 bits (called *wide-metrics* in IS-IS).

12.2 Old-style IP Reach (RFC 1195) Information

It is best to demonstrate the way of thinking embodied in the ISO 10589-defined TLVs first. Then it is easier to catch the spirit of the IP reachability information, which is very similar to the IS-Reach TLV #2.

RFC 1195 specifies six new IP-related TLVs that are used to convey IP reachability information. Two of the 6 TLVs became deprecated and are not used anymore. The remaining 4 TLVs are used for a variety of functions, like transporting IP routes, informing neighbours of new capabilities and troubleshooting ease.

12.2.1 *Internal IP Reachability TLV #128*

The Internal IP Reachability TLV #128 is probably the most important of the RFC 1195-defined TLVs. It conveys *internal* routing information, which is to say, directly connected routes. Figure 12.3 shows the basic structure of TLV #128. Please refer to Figure 12.1 for comparison. Correct – they look very similar. The structure basically starts, as in ISO 10589, with the same 4 bytes of metric information. The Metric fields are still 6 bits. Although broader metrics would not have an impact on CPU cycles (this is just leaf-information), the protocol designers decided to stay consistent with the spirit of ISO 10589. The IP Network Number and the Netmask follow after the 4 Metric bytes. These fields have these names because it was common at the beginning of the 1990s to specify IP reachability information not as prefixes and prefix lengths but rather as networks and network masks.

The internal IP Reachability TLV gets automatically advertised when IS-IS is run on an interface with a configured IP address, or through use of the `passive` option.

Whenever IS-IS is run on an interface, once an adjacency forms, all IPv4 addresses on that interface are encoded using TLV #128 in the router's LSP. Alternatively, if the router needs to be configured to advertise a sub-net but *not* form an adjacency (there are valid reasons to do this, as discussed in Chapter 16), use the `passive` option. The passive

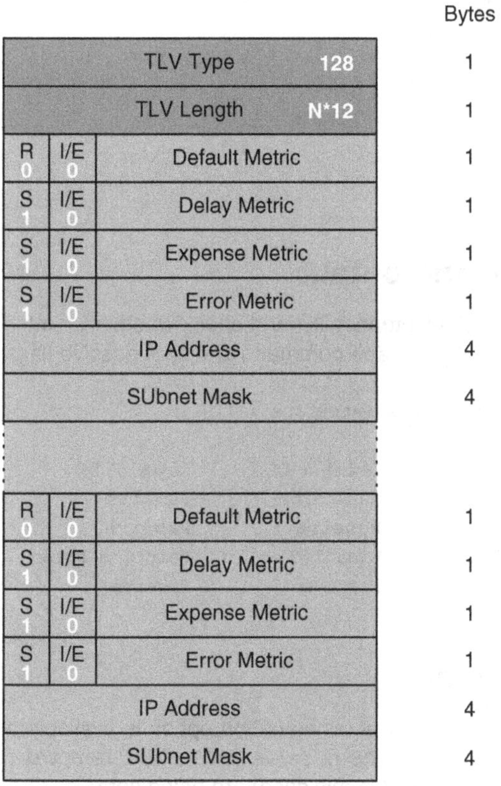

Field	Bytes
TLV Type 128	1
TLV Length N*12	1
R 0 | I/E 0 | Default Metric	1
S 1 | I/E 0 | Delay Metric	1
S 1 | I/E 0 | Expense Metric	1
S 1 | I/E 0 | Error Metric	1
IP Address	4
SUbnet Mask	4
...	
R 0 | I/E 0 | Default Metric	1
S 1 | I/E 0 | Delay Metric	1
S 1 | I/E 0 | Expense Metric	1
S 1 | I/E 0 | Error Metric	1
IP Address	4
SUbnet Mask	4

FIGURE 12.3. Structure of the IP Reachability TLV #128

option is a way to include an IP sub-net in the link-state announcement, however, there is no attempt to establish an adjacency over that link. This is achieved by suppressing all Intermediate Systems to Intermediate Systems Hellos (IIHs).

The `passive` option is available on both IOS and JUNOS. Consider the following two configuration examples.

JUNOS configuration

In JUNOS the `passive` option is a per-level or alternatively a per-interface property.

```
[edit]
hannes@Frankfurt# show
[ ... ]
protocols {
  isis {
    interface fe-4/2/0.0 {
      level 2 passive;
    }
```

```
    interface fe-1/3/1.0 {
      passive;
    }
    interface lo0.0;
  }
}
[ … ]
```

JUNOS command output

You can display the actual interface list and check whether an interface is passive or not using the `show isis interface` command and spot passive flags.

```
hannes@Frankfurt> show isis interface
IS-IS interface database:
Interface     L  CirID     Level 1 DR     Level 2 DR        L1/L2 Metric
fe-1/3/1.0    3  0x2       Munich.02      Passive           10/10
fe-4/2/0.0    3  0x1       Passive        Passive           10/10
so-0/0/0.0    1  0x1       Disabled       Point to Point    10/70
lo0.0         0  0x1       Passive        Passive           0/0
```

IOS configuration

In IOS the `passive-interface` configuration option is available across the entire routing-protocols including IS-IS. The `passive-interface` removes the interface from the list where CLNS PDU (= IS-IS in this case) are being sent.

```
New-York# show running-config
[ … ]
router isis
  passive-interface GigabitEthernet0/0
  net 49.0001.1921.6816.8007.00
  is-type level-2-only
[ … ]
```

IOS command output

The `show clns interface` command shows CLNS processing disabled for all passive interfaces.

```
New-York# show clns interface
GigabitEthernet0/0 is up, line protocol is up
  CLNS protocol processing disabled
```

Good network designs are not supposed to use the passive interface a lot. With the help of BGP, IS-IS is responsible for quick network discovery and re-routing and BGP is responsible for transporting the bulk amount of the discovered routing information.

In newer versions of IOS there is even a knob called *passive-only* which reduces the announcements of IP reachability information in IS-IS to a bare minimum, which is to announce the loopback interface only. In JUNOS similar behaviour can be created using routing policies. More about routing policy design philosophy and use of the `passive-only` knob appears in Chapter16.

12.2.2 *Protocols Supported TLV #129*

The Protocols Supported TLV makes IS-IS a true multiprotocol IGP. Using this TLV an IS-IS router can tell other routers what protocols it speaks. It is basically an envelope for Protocol Capability Codes. The Protocols Supported TLV is transmitted in Hellos and also in LSPs. It contains 1-byte Network Layer Protocol IDs (NLPIDs, one for each protocol that a router speaks on a per-interface (IIH), or on a per router basis (LSP)). The two most important NLPIDs are 0xCC, indicating IPv4 forwarding capability, and 0x8e indicating IPv6 forwarding capability. Table 12.1 shows a list of common NLPIDs.

For example, if an IS-IS v4-only router does not find this TLV or the NLPID containing IPv4 (0xCC) in the Hello from one of its neighbours, it keeps the adjacency down. Similarly, if a router speaks IPv4 on *any* interface, it will tell others that it globally speaks IPv4 and announce that capability in its LSP. If the NLPID is missing in the Protocol Supported TLV, then the router will be disregarded entirely during a SPF run. Chapter 13, "IS-IS Extensions", takes a closer look into this TLV and discusses the limitation specifically with regard to transport of new Network Layer Protocols like IPv6. It will be shown that, especially given the "router-global" nature of that TLV in LSPs, there is a problem when computing non-congruent Network Layer topologies. Furthermore, in Chapter 10 the exact steps and the role of TLV#129 during the SPF run was explored in great detail.

TABLE 12.1. In the OSI world every protocol has a one-byte Network Protocol ID, even for non-OSI protocols.

Code point	Code point name
0x00	NULL
0x01	T.70
0x02	X.29
0x03	X.633
0x08	Q.931, Q.932, Q.933, X.36, ISO 11572, ISO 11582
0x09	Q.2931
0x0c	Q.2119
0x81	CLNP
0x82	ES-IS
0x83	IS-IS
0x85	IDRP
0x8a	X25 ES-IS
0x8e	IPv6
0xcc	IPv4
0xcf	PPP

IOS and JUNOS work very differently with regard to when this TLV is sent in a Hello message and when it will be suppressed. IOS makes a general differentiation if an interface is used for *pure* CLNP routing or also for *integrated* IP routing. As soon as the `ip router isis` and a valid `ip address <address> <mask>` are configured on an IOS platform this TLV appears in the Hello PDUs. If one of the two statements is missing, generation of that TLV is suppressed.

Tcpdump output

As soon as the `ip router isis` configuration statement plus a valid `ip address <address> <mask>` is configured on an IOS platform you will see the Protocols Supported TLV in IIHs indicating that this router understands IPv4 on this circuit.

```
11:35:23.248504 OSI, IS-IS, length: 63
       p2p IIH, hlen: 20, v: 1, pdu-v: 1, sys-id-len: 6 (0), max-area: 3 (0)
         source-id: 1921.6800.0012, holding time: 30s, Flags: [Level 2 only]
         circuit-id: 0x01, PDU length: 63
           Point-to-point Adjacency State TLV #240, length: 1
             Adjacency State: Up (0)
           Protocols supported TLV #129, length: 1
           NLPID(s): IPv4 (0xcc)
           IPv4 Interface address(es) TLV #132, length: 4
             IPv4 interface address: 172.16.12.14
           Area address(es) TLV #1, length: 4
             Area address (length: 3): 49.0001
```

JUNOS had the advantage of being introduced to the market at a time when there was no need to support CLNP routing any longer. Therefore the pure-CLNP-routing case could easily be ignored. IS-IS in JUNOS is meant to transport IPv4 and IPv6 prefixes only. IS-IS is by definition multiprotocol, so JUNOS always generates the Protocols Supported TLV #129 irrespective of whether an IPv4 or IPv6 address is configured on that interface. The explanation why the NLPIDs are set unconditionally is deferred to Chapter 13, "IS-IS Extensions", which gives a better overview by example of the IPv6 transition.

Tcpdump output

Since Version 5.1 JUNOS unconditionally generates a Protocols Supported TLV with the NLPIDs of IPv4 (0xCC) and IPv6 (0x8e) in both Hello and LSP PDUs.

```
01:32:47.162118 OSI, IS-IS, length: 63
       p2p IIH, hlen: 20, v: 1, pdu-v: 1, sys-id-len: 6 (0), max-area: 3 (0)
         source-id: 1921.6800.0008, holding time: 27s, Flags: [Level 2 only]
         circuit-id: 0x01, PDU length: 63
           Point-to-point Adjacency State TLV #240, length: 15
             Adjacency State: Up (0)
```

```
  Extended Local circuit-ID: 0x0000001a
  Neighbor System-ID: 1921.6800.0012
  Neighbor Extended Local circuit-ID: 0x00000000
Protocols supported TLV #129, length: 2
  NLPID(s): IPv4 (0xcc), IPv6 (0x8e)
IPv4 Interface address(es) TLV #132, length: 4
  IPv4 interface address: 172.16.12.13
Area address(es) TLV #1, length: 4
  Area address (length: 3): 49.0001
```

RFC 1195 specifies *two* IP reachability-related TLVs. The first TLV has already been covered in this chapter. The next section shows why splitting IP reachability information over two TLVs makes sense, according to RFC 1195, and how the External IP reachability TLV is used today.

12.2.3 *External IP Reachability TLV #130*

At the end of the 1980s, there was the belief that there would be a *single* routing protocol for routing both *intra-domain* routes and *inter-domain* routes. So the routing protocols were prepared to mark routes Intra-Domain for internal routes from Inter-Domain for external routes. For that reason, everything had to be packaged in a dedicated TLV. Today, common sense is that IGPs like IS-IS, OSPF or Cisco Systems proprietary E-IGRP, do not transport large numbers of external routes very well, and so IGPs are not used according to the original purpose of conveying Inter-Domain routes. So if today no Inter-Domain routes are dumped into IS-IS, why does an *External* IP Reachability TLV still have a justification?

Remember there are always routes in a service provider's network which are sourced by another routing protocol, for example RIP or OSPF. If those routes are injected into the IS-IS "cloud" they are packaged in the External reachability TLV. Consider the setup shown in Figure 12.4. New York learns the RIP route 47.11/16 from the RIP router in the POP. New York exports the RIP routes via the following IOS configuration into the IS-IS cloud of the sample network.

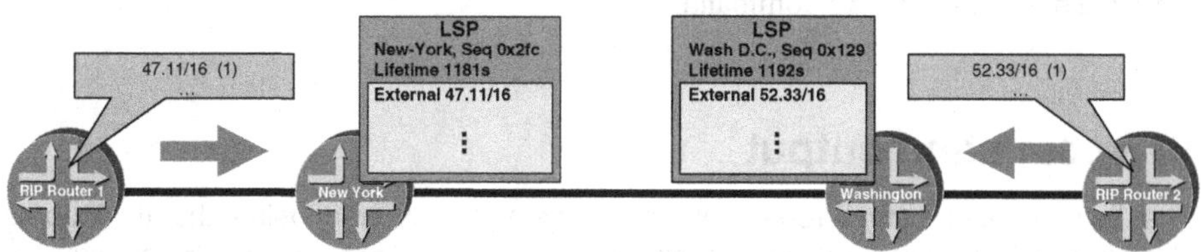

FIGURE 12.4. Two RIP routers injecting routes into IS-IS

IOS configuration

All the RIP routes, which are learned over FastEthernet0/0, get exported into IS-IS using the IP External Reachability TLV #130 with a metric of 8.

```
New-York# show running-config
[ … ]
! this is the interface to the RIP router
interface FastEthernet0/0
  ip address 172.16.67.133 255.255.255.252
router rip
  network 172.16.0.0
router isis
  net 49.0001.1921.6800.1189.00
  redistribute rip metric 8
[ … ]
```

New York's LSP looks in the tcpdump packet trace as follows:

Tcpdump output

A redistributed RIP route shows up in the LSP as an IP External Reachability TLV:

```
14:48:32.234806 OSI, IS-IS, length: 405
      L2 LSP, hlen: 27, v: 1, pdu-v: 1, sys-id-len: 6 (0), max-area: 3 (0)
        lsp-id: 1921.6800.1189.00-00, seq: 0x000002fd, lifetime: 1198s
        chksum: 0xe984 (correct), PDU length: 405, Flags: [ L1L2 IS ]
          [ … ]
          IP External reachability TLV #130, length: 12
                IPv4 prefix: 47.11/16
                Default Metric: 8, Internal, Distribution: up
          IS Reachability TLV #2, length: 67
                IsNotVirtual
                IS Neighbor: 0000.0000.0003.02, Default Metric: 10, Internal
                IS Neighbor: 0000.0000.0003.02, Default Metric: 10, Internal
[ … ]
```

You can also spot the IP External TLVs by looking into the isis database using the `show isis database` command.

IOS command output

The bold marked output represents the content transported using the IP External Reachability LSP, which can be displayed using the `show isis database` command.

```
Amsterdam# show isis database verbose
[ … ]
IS-IS Level-2 Link State Database
LSPID                LSP Seq Num    LSP Checksum    LSP Holdtime    ATT/P/OL
Amsterdam.00-00      0x00000762     0x6467          732             0/0/0
  NLPID:        0xCC 0x8E
```

```
  Area Address: 49.0001
  IP Address:   192.168.1.1
  Metric: 10                   IS London.02
  Metric: 10                   IP-External 172.16.33.2 255.255.255.252
[ ... ]
```

In JUNOS the external prefixes can be spotted at two places of the `show isis database` extensive command line output.

JUNOS command output

JUNOS yields information at two places of the `show isis database` command line output. First, at the LSP Overview Section next to LSP-Name, Sequence Number, Checksum and Lifetime Information and then in the detailed TLV Breakdown.

```
hannes@olive-2> show isis database extensive
[...]
IS-IS level 2 link-state database:
New-York.00-00  Sequence: 0x3a,  Checksum: 0x249e,       Lifetime: 64986 secs
   IS neighbor:         Wash-D.C..02     Metric:      24
   IP prefix:            47.11.0.0/16    Metric:       8  External
   IP prefix:          172.16.1.0/24     Metric:      24  Internal
   IP prefix:         192.168.1.2/32     Metric:       0  Internal
[ ... ]
  TLVs:
    Area address: 49.0001 (3)
    Speaks: IP
    Speaks: IPv6
    IP router id: 192.168.1.2
    IP address: 192.168.1.2
    Hostname: olive-2
    IS neighbor: Wash-D.C., Internal, Metric: default 24
    IP prefix: 192.168.1.2/32, Internal, Metric: default 0
    IP prefix: 172.16.1.0/24 Metric: default 63
    IP external prefix: 47.11.0.0/16, Internal, Metric: default 8
  No queued transmissions
```

Finally, look at a configuration example for JUNOS, which has the same effect as the above described IOS configuration.

In JUNOS all exchange of routes between routing protocols have to go through policies which are defined under the `policy-options` configuration branch. Each policy consists of one or more `from` and `then` parts. The `from` clause means more like "if", which is a bit counterintuitive, as one would understand `from` as something like "origin" at first. However the `from` statement always takes the inet.0 Routing Table as input and computes a subset of these routes. The `then` portion tells what to do with the prefixes that match the `from` part. In our example, the policy `rip-routes-to-isis` takes all routes in the main routing table inet.0 that match the `from` part. The `from` part matches all routes, all of which have been learned through RIP, and computes a list of prefixes plus relevant attributes like Metrics. Once the policy is called under the `protocols isis` section the previously computed list of routes will get inserted into an IS External Reachability TLV #130.

JUNOS configuration

In JUNOS a policy needs to scan the main routing table inet.0 for all routes that are learned via RIP. They get set to a metric of 8 and, through use of the `export` statement under the `protocols isis` section, are exported into IS-IS using the IP External Reachability TLV #130.

```
New-York# show configuration
[ ... ]
protocols {
  isis {
    export rip-routes-to-isis
    interface so-7/0/0.0;
    interface lo0.0;
  }
  rip {
    group washington-POP {
      neighbor fe-0/1/0.0;
    }
  }
}
policy-options {
  policy-statement rip-routes-to-isis {
    from protocol rip;
    then {
      metric 8;
      accept;
    }
  }
}
[ ... ]
```

Figure 12.5 shows that the External IP Reachability TLV #130 shares exactly the same format as the IP Internal Reachability TLV #128. The only difference is that certain combinations of the TLV Type and the Internal/External Bit of the Metric Bytes are not valid.

More about the valid and invalid combinations of the both TLVs, which finally led to the demise of the old-style IP-Reach TLVs, is covered in the section that discussed the extended IP Reachability TLV 135.

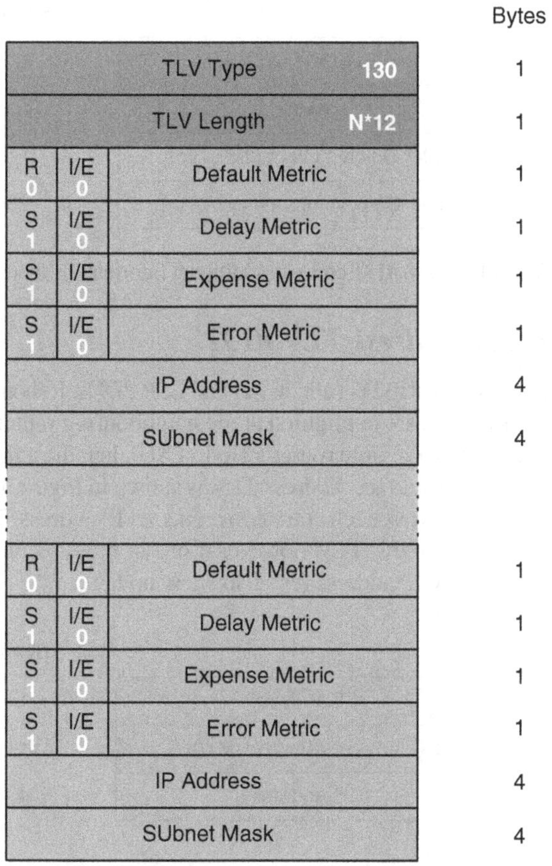

		Field	Bytes
		TLV Type 130	1
		TLV Length N*12	1
R 0	I/E 0	Default Metric	1
S 1	I/E 0	Delay Metric	1
S 1	I/E 0	Expense Metric	1
S 1	I/E 0	Error Metric	1
		IP Address	4
		SUbnet Mask	4
		⋮	
R 0	I/E 0	Default Metric	1
S 1	I/E 0	Delay Metric	1
S 1	I/E 0	Expense Metric	1
S 1	I/E 0	Error Metric	1
		IP Address	4
		SUbnet Mask	4

FIGURE 12.5. Structure of the External IP Reachability TLV #130

12.2.4 *Inter-Domain Information Type TLV #131*

The Inter-Domain Type TLV is related to the belief that Inter-Domain routes should be transported in the External IP Reachability TLV #130. It ought to give further evidence about the routing domain from where these routes have been obtained. This TLV has become obsolete, as Inter-Domain routes are not dumped into IS-IS anymore. Figure 12.6 shows the basic structure of that TLV.

The first byte contains information about the format of the Inter-Domain Information Value that follows. Three types are defined: Type 0 and 1 indicate reserved or local usage and Type 2 indicates that a two-byte AS number follows. Typically this Information TLV is inserted before an IP External Reachability TLV #130 and helps the receiving router to store AS-related information (where the route came from) with the external routes. Neither IOS nor JUNOS make use of this TLV, due to the harm to scaling that redistribution of Inter-Domain routes into IS-IS causes.

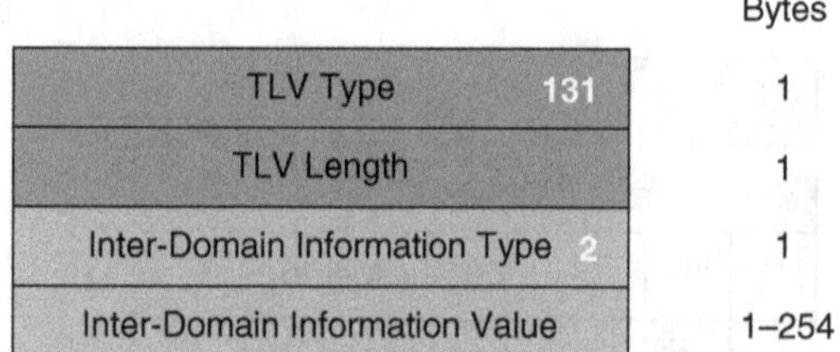

FIGURE 12.6. The obsolete TLV #131 conveys additional information about external routes

12.2.5 *Interface Address TLV #132*

The Interface Address TLV #132 is valid in IIH and LSP PDUs. It should tell a remote router about the IP addresses that are configured at the neighbouring router. If a router sees one of its own IP addresses in a remote router's Hello PSU, then the adjacency will not come up. The format of the IP Interface Address TLV is shown in Figure 12.7. The TLV length is always a multiple of 4 bytes, each entry conveying an IP address. Typically there is just one IP address contained in this TLV, however if one or more secondary address (es) are configured, the secondary IP address (es) also show up here.

Field	Bytes
TLV Type 132	1
TLV Length N*4	1
IP Address	4
IP Address	4

FIGURE 12.7. The IP Interface Address TLV #132 gets advertised in IIHs and LSPs

Watch the results of the following configuration.

IOS configuration

If you want to configure in IOS more than one IP address per interface, you have to use the keyword `secondary` after the IP address.

```
Amsterdam# show running-config
[ … ]
interface GigabitEthernet 3/0
  ip router isis
  ip address 172.16.33.1 255.255.255.0
  ip address 172.16.34.1 255.255.255.0 secondary
```

```
router isis
  net 49.0001.1921.6801.1001.00
  is-type level-1
[ … ]
```

Once we start tcpdump on a workstation, which is on the LAN, we will get a similar output. Note that the number in brackets behind the TLV is the length of that TLV.

Tcpdump output

All the configured IP addresses are listed in the IP Interface Address TLV.

```
16:19:27.486634 OSI, IS-IS, length: 84
  L1 Lan IIH, hlen: 27, v: 1, pdu-v: 1, sys-id-len: 6 (0), max-area: 3 (0)
    source-id: 0000.0000.0003, holding time: 40s, Flags: [Level 1, Level 2]
    lan-id: 0000.0000.0003.02, Priority: 70, PDU length: 84
      IS Neighbor(s) TLV #6, length: 6
        IS Neighbor: 0002.b32b.0e52
      Protocols supported TLV #129, length: 1
        NLPID(s): IPv4
      IP Interface address(es) TLV #132, length: 8
        IPv4 interface address: 172.16.33.1
        IPv4 interface address: 172.16.34.1
      Area address(es) TLV #1, length: 4
        Area address (3): 49.0001
```

You can also display the contents of the IP Interface Address TLV through use of a CLI command. In JUNOS the `show isis adjacency detail` command reveals information about the IP address that the neighbour holds.

JUNOS command output

In JUNOS you can explore the IP address of a neighbour using the `show isis adjacency` command.

```
hannes@New-York> show isis adjacency detail
NY-Access4
  Interface: ge-4/0/1.0, Level: 2, State: Up, Expires in 8 secs
  Priority: 70, Up/Down transitions: 1, Last transition: 2d
   21:54:18 ago
  Circuit type: 2, Speaks: IP, IPv6, MAC address:
  00:90:69:2b:0e:52
  Restart capable: Yes
  LAN id: NY-Access4.02, IP addresses: 172.16.33.1
  IPv6 addresses: fe80::7777:69ff:fea0:8001
[ … ]
```

In Cisco IOS you can display the IP addresses of your neighbour by issuing the `show clns neighbor detail` command.

IOS command output

In IOS you can display the contents of TLV #132, which are the IP address (es) of a neighbour, using the `show clns neighbor detail` command.

```
Amsterdam#show clns neighbors detail

System Id     Interface    SNPA      State   Holdtime    Type   Protocol
New-York      POS4/0       *HDLC*    Up      2           L2     IS-IS
  Area Address(es): 49.0001
  IP Address(es): 172.16.34.1*
  Uptime: 04:04:52
[ … ]
```

The IS-IS router will refuse to build an adjacency if the Hello message from any of the neighbouring routers contains an IP addresses that is local to the local router, assuming that there is something broken. IOS logs that event once you start turning on debug output for `isis adj-packets`.

IOS debug output

IOS logs if it receives a Hello PDU from a neighbour holding bogus IP addresses.

```
Amsterdam# debug isis adj-packets
IS-IS Adjacency related packets debugging is on
Amsterdam #
1d08h: ISIS-Adj: Rec L1 IIH from 0090.6994.a43e
 (GigabitEthernet3/0), cir type L1L2, cir id
1921.6800.1133.02, length 1492
1d08h: ISIS-Adj: No usable IP interface addresses in LAN IIH from
 GigabitEthernet3/0
1d08h: ISIS-Adj: Sending L2 LAN IIH on GigabitEthernet3/0, length 1497
[ … ]
```

In JUNOS you can log a sub-net mismatch by setting the `error` flag under the `protocols isis traceoptions` branch.

JUNOS debug output

JUNOS shows you in the `isis-log messagefile` that it could not find a matching IP subnet.

```
protocols {
  [ … ]
  isis {
    traceoptions {
      file isis-log size 1m microsecond-stamp;
```

```
      flag error;
      flag packets detail;
    }
  [ … ]
  }
}

Jun 16 10:24:18.154351 Received PTP IIH, source id Amsterdam on so-7/0/0.0
Jun 16 10:24:18.154430            intf index 2
Jun 16 10:24:18.154455            max area 0, circuit type l1l2, packet length 56
Jun 16 10:24:18.154476            hold time 27, circuit id 1
Jun 16 10:24:18.154500            ptp adjacency tlv length 5
Jun 16 10:24:18.154521            neighbor state down
Jun 16 10:24:18.154542            neighbor extended local circuit id 1
Jun 16 10:24:18.154563            speaks IP
Jun 16 10:24:18.154587            speaks IPV6
Jun 16 10:24:18.154615            IP address 10.0.0.6
Jun 16 10:24:18.154705            area address 49.0001 (3)
Jun 16 10:24:18.154730            restart RR reset RA reset holdtime 0
Jun 16 10:24:18.154772            ERROR: IIH from Amsterdam without matching
                                   addresses, interface so-7/0/0.0
```

From an IS-IS perspective, a multiprotocol IGP like IS-IS should not police adjacencies based on Layer 3 information such as IP sub-nets. Many developers argue that, particularly on broadcast interfaces, the forwarding next-hop resolver relies on a protocol to supply MAC addresses for correctly framing a routed packet. In the IP world this is typically the ARP protocol. The router OS kernel relies on ARP solely to resolve L3 next-hop to MAC address mapping, because such IP addresses belonging to the same sub-net need to be present in order for the next-hop resolution sub-system to work correctly. While this violates the multiprotocol nature of IS-IS a bit, it is common consensus among implementers of routing protocols to do it that way.

12.2.6 *IP Authentication TLV #133*

The IP Authentication TLV was meant to be a dedicated authentication method only applied for IP Reachability Information. The IOS and JUNOS implementers however never implemented that dedicated Authentication TLV. Instead they implemented the far more general Authentication TLV #10 that authenticates *all* TLVs in a given PDU. Because no vendor ever supported the IP Authentication TLV #133, it finally got deprecated. Now in the official TLV Code Point Allocation scheme (RFC 3359) it is marked as *illegal*.

Deployment experience in the mid 1990s has revealed the deficiencies of the RFC 1195 and ISO 10589 defined TLVs. Beside the obviously too small 6-bit Metrics, the mess surrounding Internal/External Routes and the limited functionality to add link-related information into the LSP caused the IS-IS community to define some new- and redefine some old TLVs. This set of TLVs is mostly referred to as *New-Style* Metrics, contrasting to the historical *Old-Style* Metrics.

12.3 New-style Topology (IS-Reach) Information

The IS Reachability TLV that was proposed in ISO 10589 actually has two major limitations. Besides the obvious limitation of the 6-bit metric space there is another limitation, which does not allow adding any link-related information to an adjacency. The old-style (ISO 10589 and RFC 1195) TLVs are quite strictly formatted: each neighbour adjacency consumes 11 bytes and so does not have any place where additional information could be attached to a particular adjacency. Given that, it was clear that a revision of both the IS-Reachability and IP-Reachability TLVs needed to have a bigger metric space and more importantly, it needed to be ready for further *extensions*.

The IETF revised the existing IS Reachability TLV #2 and IP Reachability TLVs #128 and #130 to correct these deficiencies and provide further extensibility mechanisms. RFC 3784 mentions two new TLVs:

- Extended IS Reachability TLV #22
- Extended IP Reachability TLV #135

These metrics are also known as *wide-metrics*.

Figure 12.8 show the basic structure of the extended IS Reachability TLV. The first seven bytes hold the System-ID plus pseudonode number. Next there is room for a 24-bit metric. Why 24-bits and not 32-bits? The basic idea behind that scheme was to be able to do all the calculations during an SPF run using 32-bit unsigned integers without exhausting the integer space. Therefore, the extended IS Reach TLV #22 theoretically supports up to 255 hops (1 byte), each at a maximum metric of 16.7 million, without wrapping the 32-bit integer space. Twenty-four bits are also enough for expressing a bandwidth range of 64 KBit/s to 1 Terabit/s in the inverse bandwidth metric scheme. The calculation for this is straightforward: just assume the lowest bandwidth (64 KBit/s) and assign it to the highest metric (2^24).

$$64\,\text{Kbit/s} * 2\text{\^{}}24 = 1073741824\,\text{Kbit/s}/1024 = 1048576\,\text{Mbit/s} = 1024\ \text{GBit/s} = 1\,\text{Tbit/s}$$

The next byte is probably the most powerful of this TLV. If this is non-zero then there is additional information included about this link/adjacency. In fact, the Extended IS Reach TLV #22 is the first TLV to have a variable length, including so-called sub-TLVs that carry additional information about the link. Please note that generally in IS-IS there is no notion of a *link*. All that IS-IS can express is *adjacencies*. In WAN environments the mapping of adjacencies to links is typically a one-to-one mapping. In LAN environments this can be a one-to-one relationship but does not have to be. Practically speaking, 95 per cent of all the circuits in a service provider core topology are pure point-to-point links, so in most environments the term link and adjacency can be used interchangeably. There is more detailed information about TLVs and sub-TLVs in Chapter 11, "TLVs and Sub-TLVs".

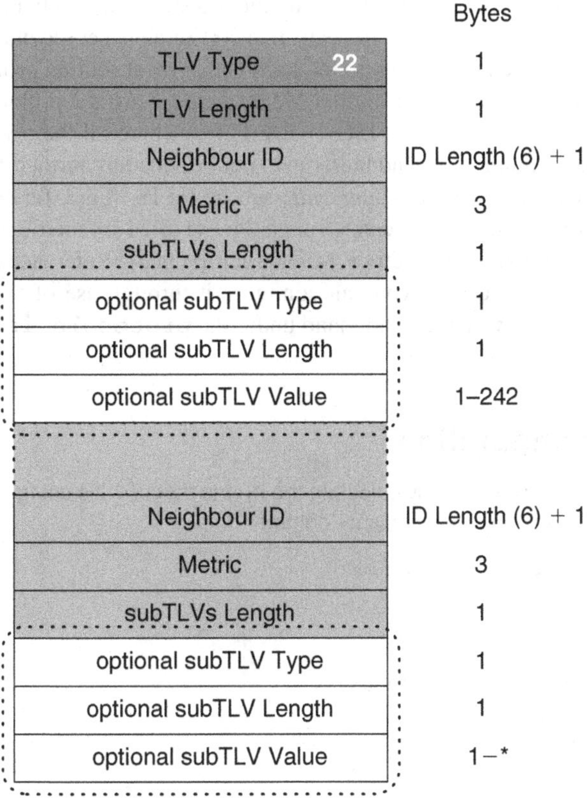

FIGURE 12.8. The most significant change of the Extended IS Reachability TLV #22 is the support for sub-TLVs and 24-bit metrics

12.3.1 *Automatic Metric Calculation*

The Metric field is typically a dimensionless scalar, which expresses the preference of using that link. Typically it is calculated according to the inverse bandwidth of that link. Each implementation allows to set an internal *Reference Bandwidth* parameter. The Reference Bandwidth is the base value which will be divided by the bandwidth of the interface to yield the metric. So, for instance, if the Reference Bandwidth is 1 Gbit/s, then a 10 Mbit/s circuit will be assigned a metric of 100. Similarly a Fast Ethernet circuit will be assigned a metric of 100.

The problem with Reference Bandwidth is that they are constantly changing, depending how fast the circuits in the network are being upgraded. Assume there are OC-192/STM-64 circuits deployed in the network, which are capable of transporting roughly 10 Gbit/s. As soon as the network turns on its first OC-768/STM-256 the metric scheme has to be revised. For instance, for a long time OSPF used to have the Reference-Bandwidth of 100 Mbps, because at the time when OSPF was specified the architects of the protocol thought that 100 Mbps would be sufficient forever. One could argue that what could be learned from that mistake was to simply define a Reference Bandwidth that will most likely not hit the ceiling in the next 10 years: like 100 Terabits per second. But the problem with setting the Reference Bandwidth too high is that most routing protocols (including IS-IS and OSPF) have finite and limited Metric fields. This is a problem similar to the 6-bit metric space of the original ISO 10589 TLVs, where all the low-speed links get clipped to the maximum value and thereby do not provide any further differentiation.

Today the most common *Auto-Bandwidth* setting for IS-IS is 1 Terabit per second (or 1000 Gigabit per second), which can, through the use of 24-bit metric fields, go down to 64 KBit/s without clipping the metrics. Manual setting of the Reference Bandwidth is not supported on IOS. In JUNOS you can configure it through use of the `reference-bandwidth <bandwidth>` command under the `protocols isis` configuration branch.

JUNOS configuration

In JUNOS you can automatically calculate the metric that IS-IS is using by configuring the `reference-bandwidth <bandwidth>` command.

```
hannes@New-York> show configuration
[ ... ]
protocols {
  isis {
      reference-bandwidth 1000g;
      interface so-0/0/0.0;
      interface lo0.0;
      }
}
[ ... ]
```

In very large IS-IS networks the policy to set the routing metric is not as simple as a division of the Reference Bandwidth. Typically the routing metrics should be controlled manually to have tighter control about the impact of all kinds of re-routing scenarios.

12.3.2 *Static Metric Setting*

Service providers do not always want IS-IS to calculate its own routing metrics with a simple formula such as inverse bandwidth. Typically for very expensive links like transatlantic links, there is an additional *de-preference* or negative bias expressed in an increased routing metric. Consider Figure 12.9 where one of the most important links in the European topology goes down. The SP does not want to heal the European core over the transatlantic links, as from a cost-per-bit perspective, it is not very economical to route traffic from Frankfurt to London via Pennsauken.

In order to avoid suboptimal rerouting there are tables similar to the one shown in Figure 12.10, which consider both *bandwidth* and *cost* of links. In the first column the different line speeds that are today typically deployed in service provider networks are listed. In the rows the routing metrics according to that line speed, depending on what kind of circuit type it is, are shown. If it is an intercontinental (expensive) link a very high

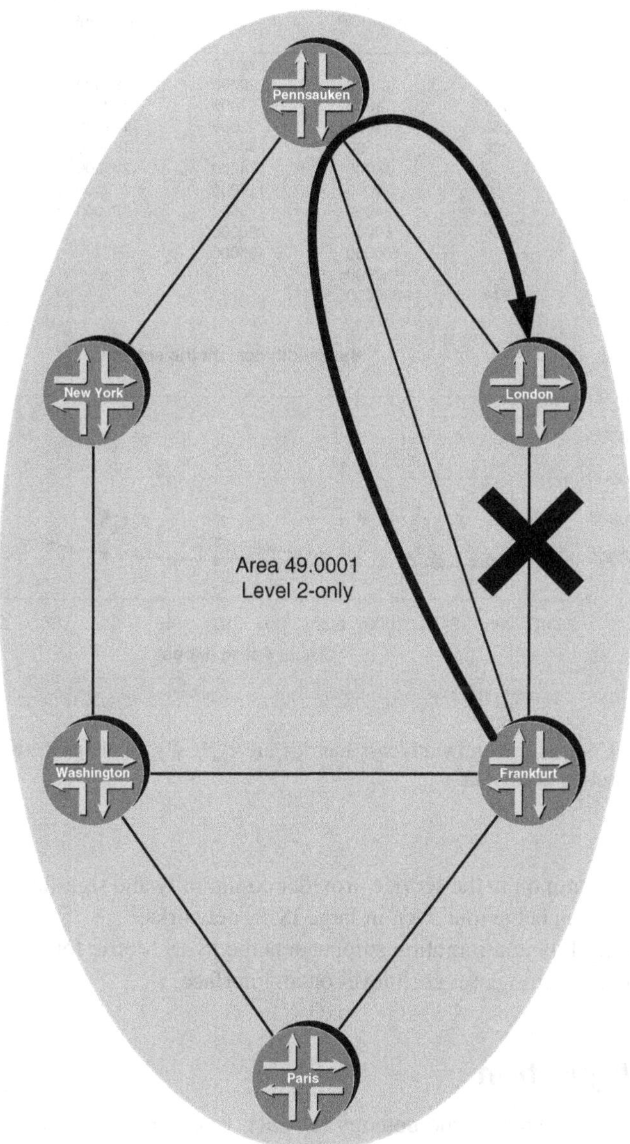

FIGURE 12.9. From a cost perspective not every possible path is a feasible path

routing metric is assigned, if it is a cheap circuit like a pair of fibres inside a POP, it gets a low routing metric. These per circuit-type metrics are not computed linearly. Typically there is an exponential function involved, which controls the offset and the gradient of the metric curve. The routing metrics shown in Figure 12.10 represent rounded-down values which follow an inverse logarithmic curve. Such logarithmic cost/bandwidth

Circuit Speed	Bandwidth (Mbps)	Intra-POP	In-country	Continental	Intercontinental
oc-768/STM-256	39808	125	22000	74000	220000
oc-192/STM-64	9952	400	26000	87000	250000
oc-48/STM-16	2488	1300	35000	112000	315000
Gigabit Ethernet	1000	3000	43000	141000	430000
oc-12/STM-4	622	4500	50000	185000	600000
oc-3/STM-1	155	14000	74000	275000	950000
Fast Ethernet	100	20000	117000	370000	
T3	45	34000	175000	580000	
E3	34	60000	250000		
Ethernet	10	100000	435000		
E1	2	150000			
T1	1,544	220000			

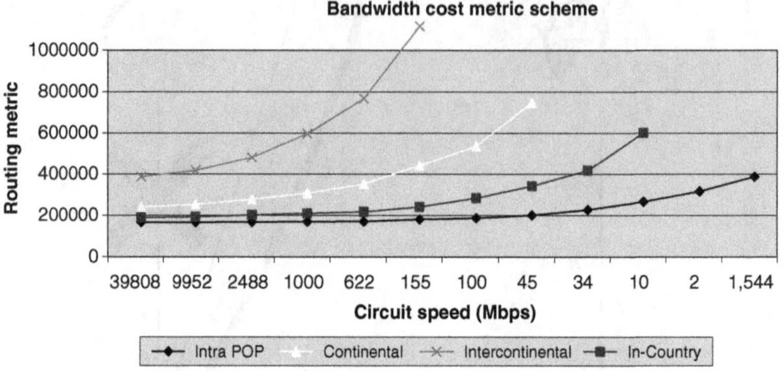

FIGURE 12.10. Composite bandwidth/cost metrics are typically for large networks in order to control the re-routing behaviour

tables are very common in the service provider community and significantly help to control the re-rerouting behaviour even in large IS-IS networks.

The following IOS configuration snippet sets the IS-IS Metric for an interface. There are distinct metric settings for each level on an interface.

IOS configuration

In IOS there are distinct metric settings for each level. The `isis metric <metric> level-<n>` command can be invoked in interface configur-ation mode. Values higher than 63, can only be set if the `metric-style` is set to `wide`.

```
Amsterdam# show running-config
[ ... ]
interface POS4/0
  ip address 172.16.7.21 255.255.255.252
  ip router isis
  isis metric 1700 level-1
  isis metric 2800 level-2
```

```
!
router isis
  net 49.0001.0010.0100.1004.00
  metric-style wide
!
[ … ]
```

The metric information can only be set if the metric style is set to "wide". If you (for example) unconfigure the metric style wide (metric-style narrow) and forget to change the metric down to below 63, the system will log the following message and fallback to automatic metric calculation:

IOS command output

Unconfiguring the `metric-style wide` back to `metric-style narrow` causes IOS to drop every static metrics at the interface level.

```
Amsterdam (config-router) #metric-style narrow
%Removing wide metrics also removes 'isis metric 1700 level-1'
 configured on POS4/0
%Removing wide metrics also removes 'isis metric 2800 level-2'
 configured on POS4/0
```

Below is a JUNOS configuration, which sets the IS-IS metrics on a given logical interface.

JUNOS configuration

In JUNOS all IS-IS related information is located under the `protocols isis` configuration branch. The routing metrics are properties of a given logical IS-IS interface.

```
hannes@New-York> show configuration
[ … ]
protocols {
  isis {
    interface so-7/0/0.0 {
      level 1 metric 1700;
      level 2 metric 2400;
    }
    interface lo0.0;
  }
}
[ … ]
```

The JUNOS configuration interface accepts all values ranging from 0 to 16777215. However, if an IS or IP reachability needs to get packaged in old-style TLVs, then

JUNOS simply clips those values to 63. The above configuration generates an LSP, which looks like the following using tcpdump:

Tcpdump output

JUNOS silently clips metrics bigger than 63 down to 63. In order to produce congruent topologies between ISs supporting old or new-style TLVs JUNOS even clips the new-style TLVs down to 63.

```
11:36:49.609255 OSI, IS-IS, length: 270
        L2 LSP, hlen: 27, v: 1, pdu-v: 1, sys-id-len: 6 (0), max-area: 3 (0)
          lsp-id: 2092.1113.4007.00-00, seq: 0x000006b2, lifetime: 1199s
          chksum: 0xb2a6 (correct), PDU length: 270, Flags: [ L1L2 IS ]
          [ ... ]
            IS Reachability TLV #2, length: 12
              IsNotVirtual
              IS Neighbor: 1921.6800.1004.00, Metric: 63, Internal
            Extended IS Reachability TLV #22, length: 10
              IS Neighbor: 1921.6800.1004.00, Metric: 63, no sub-TLVs present
            IP Internal reachability TLV #128, length: 12
              IPv4 prefix: 192.168.1.2/32, Distribution: up,
               Metric: 63, Internal
            Extended IPv4 Reachability TLV #135, length: 9
              IPv4 prefix: 10.254.47.8/30, Distribution: up, Metric: 63
          [ ... ]
```

The Extended IS Reach TLV #22 was just the first outcome of the Traffic Engineering Extensions. As the RFC 1195 Style IP reachability TLVs #128 and #130 also suffer from the same set of problems a new Extended IP Reachability TLV has been defined.

12.4 New-style Topology (IP-Reach) Information

The Extended IP Reachability TLV #135 collapses the two old-style IP reachability TLVs #128 and #130 together. Figure 12.11 shows the structure of the Extended IP Reachability TLV #135. The first four bytes is the Metric field which is 32 bits in size. The reason why it is 32 bits wide and not 24 bits wide is to stay compatible to other routing protocols like BGP and OSPF, which also have 32-bit metrics for their routing information. By picking a compatible metric size, the protocol designers made sure that the imported metric from these protocols does not get clipped. Next, there is the Header byte which consists of the Up/Down Bit, the Sub-TLV Indicator Bit, and 6 bits for storing the prefix length. The purpose of the Up/Down Bit will be explained in more detail in Section 12.6. The Sub-TLV Bit indicates if there are any further sub-TLVs stored after the prefix. As of writing this book, only three sub-TLVs have been defined. Most of them address a way to tag routes for administrative purposes. draft-martin-neal-policy-isis-admin-tags and draft-ietf-isis-wg-multi-topology specify the sub-TLVs 1, 2 and 117.

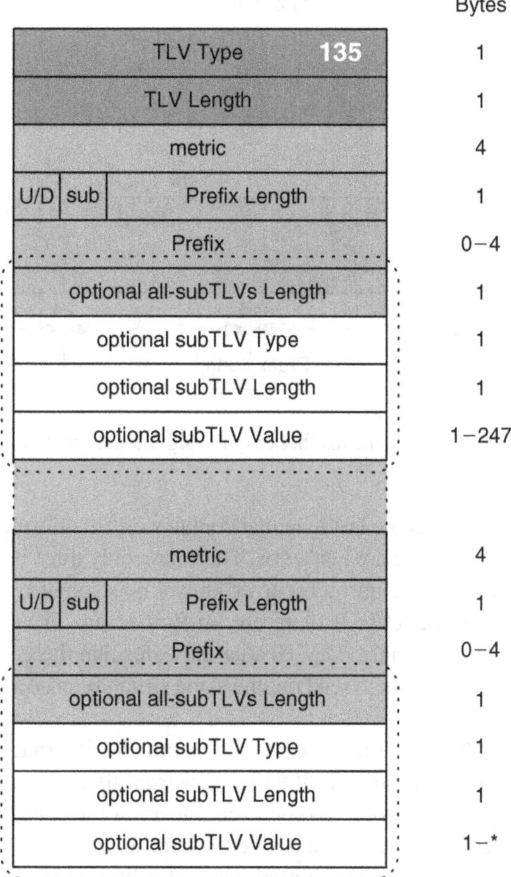

FIGURE 12.11. The Extended IP Reachability TLV #135 uses variable-length packaging of prefix information

Next follow 6 bits of prefix length. It would appear at first that since 2^6 = 64, 5 bits should be doing fine, but do not be misled. Although IP prefixes are 32 bits in size, there are still 33 distinct prefix lengths, keeping in mind that the default route (0/0) is a unique prefix as well. So only the values 0 to 32 are valid for encoding the prefix length. Next there are 0 to 4 bytes holding the prefix information. The extended IP Reachability TLV allowed variable packaging of IP prefixes for the first time. Recall that the old-style TLVs always consumed 12 bytes for the entire prefix, regardless of how many bits were redundant due to the network mask masking the bits out.

In the Extended IP Reachability TLV #135 the idea is to only encode the bytes that contain useful information. Consider Figure 12.12 where the example prefix 172.16.64/19 is encoded. The first question is: how many bits really contain information? To find that out, just map the prefix length to the grid shown in Figure 12.12. The /19 line goes through the

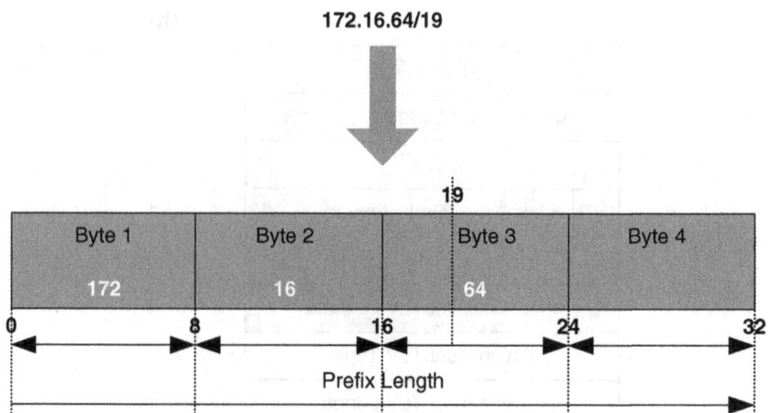

FIGURE 12.12. Variable packaging means that only the significant bits (byte chunks) are stored

3rd byte. So byte number 3 is the last byte that contains useful information. Byte 4 does not contain anything useful – there are just zeros. Therefore, only three bytes need to be stored. So by looking at the prefix length a receiver knows how many bytes to decode before the next prefix starts in the TLV. If there are no further sub-TLVs (as indicated by the sub-TLV bit) and the length in the TLV Header indicates that there are still some prefixes left, the receiving decoder starts to read out the same structure once again, starting with the 4-byte metric value.

The beginning of this section indicated that both the Internal and the External IP Reachability TLV got collapsed to TLV #135. However, there is no internal/external differentiation in the TLV anymore. Protocol engineers argue that prefixes are typically either internal or external, but not both. Quite the contrary: if the same prefix is known as both internal and external, there is something really broken in the network. Should a routing protocol support ugly corner cases? Probably not. However, there is another (non-obvious) reason why there is no further internal/external differentiation in the TLV. Henk Smit, one of the authors of RFC 3784, noted once on a posting to the ISIS-WG mailing list:

> *I have never really understood the need for both TLV128 and TLV130. This was also one of the reasons why we decided to not carry the I/E metric bit semantics forward into TLV135 (the new IP prefix TLV defined in the IS-IS TE extensions draft). The most important reason was of course the fact that we had no bits left, and did not want to spend another byte per prefix.*

Routing software is typically not upgraded frequently. Therefore it is clear that the old-style and new-style TLVs need to coexist for quite a while. Simply because it is practic-ally neither possible nor feasible to upgrade an IS-IS network with several thousand routers on a flag day. Unfortunately RFC 3784 gives no guidance about how the old- and new-style TLVs should interoperate, and therefore vendors have come up with schemes that are specified nowhere, which is bad, as it by definition prevents clean, interoperable solutions.

12.5 Old-, New-style Interworking Issues

Recent releases of IOS and JUNOS support both the old-style and the new-style behaviour. However, the implementations came up with different default behaviours as to how the old-style and the new-style TLVs are advertised.

IOS by default advertises only the old-style information. The old-, new-style generation can be controlled using the `metric-style <narrow|transition|wide> level <1|2|1-2>` router configuration command.

IOS configuration

In IOS you can control generation of old- and new-style TLVs using the `metric-style <narrow|transition|wide> [level-<1|2>]` router configuration knob. If the optional `level` statement is omitted then the metric-style applies to both levels.

```
Amsterdam# show running-config
[ ... ]
router isis
  metric-style wide level-2
  metric-style transition level-1
[ ... ]
```

The metric-style commands controls what information that IOS is advertising, but also implicitly what kind of information IS-IS *accepts*. If you set the metric style to wide, then IOS in turn also accepts wide TLVs from other routers. The behaviour is similar for the narrow metric style. If IOS only generates "narrow" style TLVs then it also just accepts narrow style TLVs from other routers. The metric-style transition sends both old- and new-style TLVs and accepts both. If you think that the plain narrow and wide modes are too restrictive for your network migration, then you can weaken the strictness by adding the keyword `transition` to the `metric-style` configuration command. The following IOS configuration sends new-style TLVs in the Level 2 but does accept both old- and new-style TLVs at receipt of LSPs.

IOS configuration

In IOS you can weaken the strict checking nature of non-matching TLVs (non-matching means receipt of old-style TLVs if wide metrics are configured, and receipt of new-style TLVs if narrow metrics are configured) through adding the transition statement after the `metric-style` configuration.

```
Amsterdam# show running-config
[ ... ]
router isis
  metric-style wide transition level-2
[ ... ]
```

JUNOS is more migration-friendly in that respect. First of all, JUNOS always accepts both old-style and new-style TLVs. If (for example) a prefix or IS reachability information is present in both old- and new-style TLVs, then the new-style TLVs take precedence over the old-style TLVs. This accept-everything behaviour can't be changed. What can be controlled is what JUNOS advertises. By default, both old and new-style metrics are advertised. Considering the previous example, one could best describe the JUNOS behaviour in (IOS words) as `metric-style transition`. In JUNOS, suppression of the old-style TLVs can be enabled using the `wide-metrics-only` configuration command which is located under the `protocols isis configuration` branch. Sorry for the awkward wording, "suppression can be enabled" – this wording tries to emphasize the default behaviour and how the behaviour can be changed.

JUNOS configuration

In JUNOS suppression of old-style TLVs can be enabled on a per-level basis through use of the `wide-metrics-only` keyword.

```
hannes@New-York> show configuration
[ ... ]
protocols {
  isis {
    level 1 wide-metrics-only;
    interface lo0.0;
    interface so-0/0/0;
  }
}
[ ... ]
```

JUNOS can also suppress generation of the new-style TLVs, although this is almost never used in practice. Everybody wants to leverage the broader metrics and additional functionality, which is encoded into the sub-TLVs that are found only in the new-style TLVs. Suppression of new-style TLVs is only available on an IS-IS global basis. It is not possible to turn the new-style TLVs off on a per level basis. The following JUNOS configuration shows how to turn off generation of new-style TLVs on a router-global basis.

JUNOS configuration

In JUNOS suppression of new-style TLVs can be enabled on a router-global basis through use of the `traffic-engineering disable` keywords. The newstyle TLVs have been defined in RFC 3784 as the first application of one of the new-style TLVs was conveying Traffic Engineering related information.

```
hannes@New-York> show configuration
[ ... ]
protocols {
  isis {
    traffic-engineering disable;
```

```
      interface lo0.0;
      interface so-0/0/0;
    }
  }
  [ ... ]
```

In today's networks there is a combination of the old- and new-style TLVs and both will co-exist for quite a while to come. Some of the original RFC 1195 old-style TLVs have been refined in order to support domain-wide prefix distribution, which is defined in RFC 2966. RFC 2966 re-defines the IP Reachability TLVs #128, #130 and also loosens a few restrictions of the original old-style TLVs. The following section clarifies why trading scalability versus optimal routing makes sense.

12.6 Domain-wide Prefix Distribution

The designers of IS-IS had scalability in mind during the drafting of the specification. There are several different places to look for scalability in IS-IS, and one is the way that prefixes get leaked between levels. Before explaining how IS-IS does this, it is best to first describe how OSPF, another link-state protocol, leaks routing information between OSPF areas. The assumption is a bit of familiarity with OSPF, enough to appreciate the differences between the two protocols. Consider Figure 12.13 to see how OSPF leaks prefixes between areas. The sample topology was introduced in Chapter 1, "Introduction", and is redesigned here as an OSPF network – the two networks almost look the same. The significant difference is that the borderline between the backbone and the non-backbone areas is in IS-IS on the link (for example, between Atlanta and New York) whereas in OSPF it is inside the Area Border Router (New York). There are three OSPF areas defined: the backbone Area 0, and two leak Areas 47 and 11. Now, explore how routes are leaked through the OSPF domain. First, the Area Border Routers (New York, Washington DC) between Area 47 and the backbone transfer (or leak) an internal route from Area 47 to the backbone. The two Area Border Routers re-package the internal route from a Type-1 LSA to a Type-3 LSA (Step 1). LSAs are information carriers in OSPF, similar to LSPs in IS-IS. A side effect of re-packaging New York and Washington is also to replace the Router-ID in the LSA field by the router's loopback IP address. Next, the route gets propagated through the backbone by means of the Type-3 LSA. Then the two Area Border Routers between Area 0 and Area 11 (London, Frankfurt) take the route that was packaged in the Type-3 LSA and translate them into the Area 11 (Step 2). Again, the two Area Border Routers replace the originating Router-ID by their own Router-ID which is typically the loopback address. Finally, all internal routes from Area 47 get propagated through area 0 and all attached non-zero areas like Area 11. A similar flow of routes goes in the reverse direction: internal routes from Area 11 get re-packaged into the backbone Area 0 as Type-3 LSAs by the Area Border Routers London and Frankfurt (Step 3). On the left-hand side of Area 0 the two Area Border Routers New York and Washington pick up the Type-3 LSA and inject it into Area 47 (Step 4). Finally, all the areas see all routes.

This behaviour is exactly the problem with scaling in a plain-vanilla OSPF setup: Smaller routers in the non-zero area get overwhelmed by a massive amount of routes.

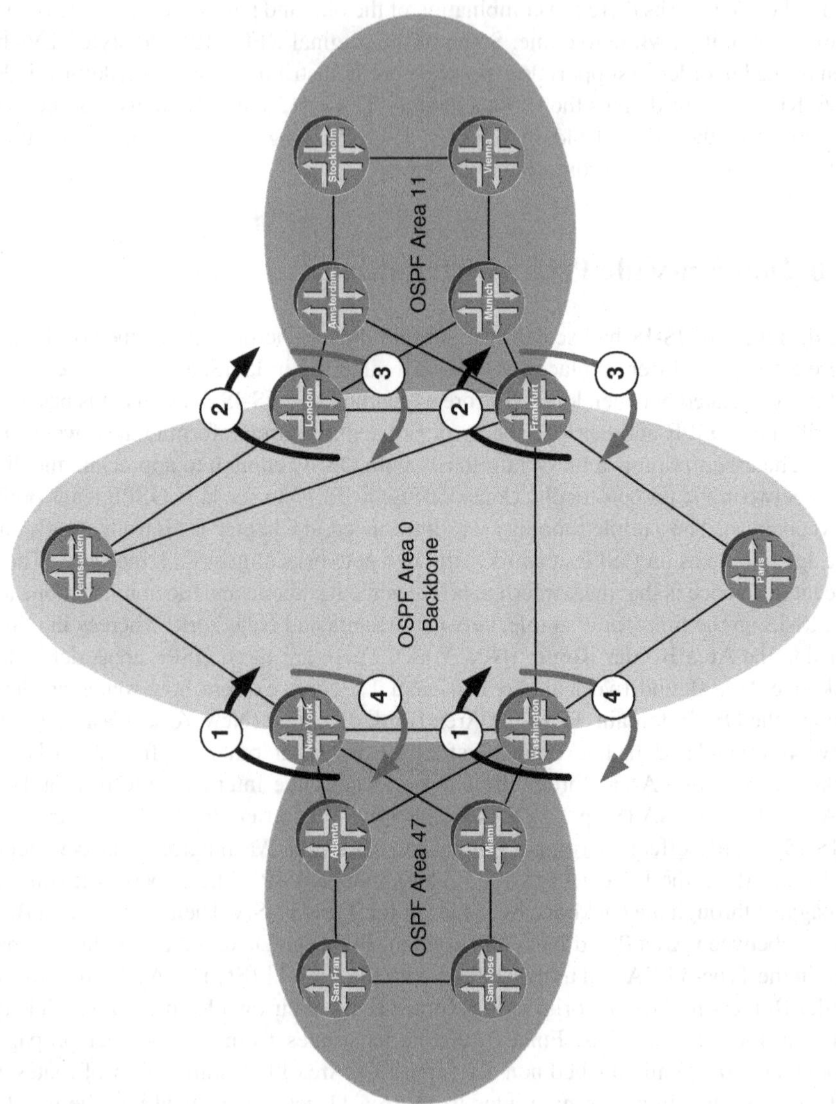

FIGURE 12.13. **OSPF leaks all prefixes into all areas, which is one of OSPFs scaling harms**

Typically, leakage of all routes into the non-zero areas is not necessary. All that the non-zero area needs to know is the area internal routes and a default route that points to the Area Border Routers.

IS-IS has much better scaling properties in that respect. Consider Figure 12.14. Very much like OSPF, IS-IS passes on Level 1 information to Level 2. However, the other direction is by default blocked: Level 1 routers have to rely on a *default route* generated by the L1L2 routers.

Flooding just a default route is clearly a very scalable approach; however, the use of the default route as the only routing information pointing towards the ATTached Level 2 router is very unspecific information. Sometimes it is necessary to trade protocol scalability for *optimality* of traffic flow. The side effect of unspecific information can be sub-optimal routing, as shown in Figure 12.15. Traffic towards 192.168.1.13/32 gets attracted to the closest L1L2 router, which is Router Barcelona, due to a lower metric of the default-route 0/0 of 2000, although from a total routing metric perspective, sending the traffic straight to the L1L2 Router Milan would be more optimal. The sub-optimal path-cost Madrid-Barcelona-Paris-Frankfurt is 22000. The more optimal path would be Madrid-Milan-Frankfurt with a composite path-cost of 11500. The use of unspecific routing-information makes IS-IS have a kind of "blind spot" and results in sub-optimal routing.

RFC 2966 lifts that strict requirement to pass just the default 0/0 route down to Level 1 and allows *leaking* of prefixes from Level 1 to Level 2. Additionally, RFC 2966 allows external routes to exist in Level 1, which was strictly forbidden according to RFC 1195. But allowing the routes to flow from Level 2 to Level 1 is still not enough, as shown in Figure 12.16.

Suppose some router, located beyond Paris in Level 2 originates (among others) its loopback IP address, either in the internal IP Reachability TLV #128 or the Extended IP Reachability TLV #135. Barcelona re-distributes the 192.168.1.1/32 prefix into Level 1. The Level-1 LSP travels through Level 1 finally arriving at Milan. Milan does what every L1L2 router has to do, and accepts unconditionally all Level-1 IP prefixes and injects them into Level 2. This creates a wonderful routing loop as from this point on nobody really knows where the route really did originate. Therefore a *Marker* Bit is needed to mark routes that have been marked as *Leaked* from Level 2 to Level 1. Additionally, all L1L2 routers need to suppress prefixes where the Marker Bit is set and not propagate them further. The Marker Bit is called, in RFC 2966 terminology, the *Up/Down* Bit. The Extended IP Reachability TLV #135 has had support for the Up/Down Bit from the beginning.

The old (RFC 1195) style TLVs do not have support for the Up/Down Bit in the original specification, because none of the original authors was aware that *too much scalability* could lead to a problem. RFC 2966 also redefines the MSB of the default-metric for the two old-style IP Reachability TLVs #128 and #130. Per RFC 1195, the MSB of the default-metric was specified as *Reserved* and should therefore be set to zero. See Figure 12.17 and Figure 12.18 for the revised version of the old-style TLVs.

12.6.1 *Leaking Level-2 Prefixes into Level 1*

In both IOS and JUNOS the default behaviour of IS-IS is RFC 1195 compliant and does not leak L2 prefixes from Level 2 to Level 1. When you want certain prefixes to leak through you have to explicitly configure that.

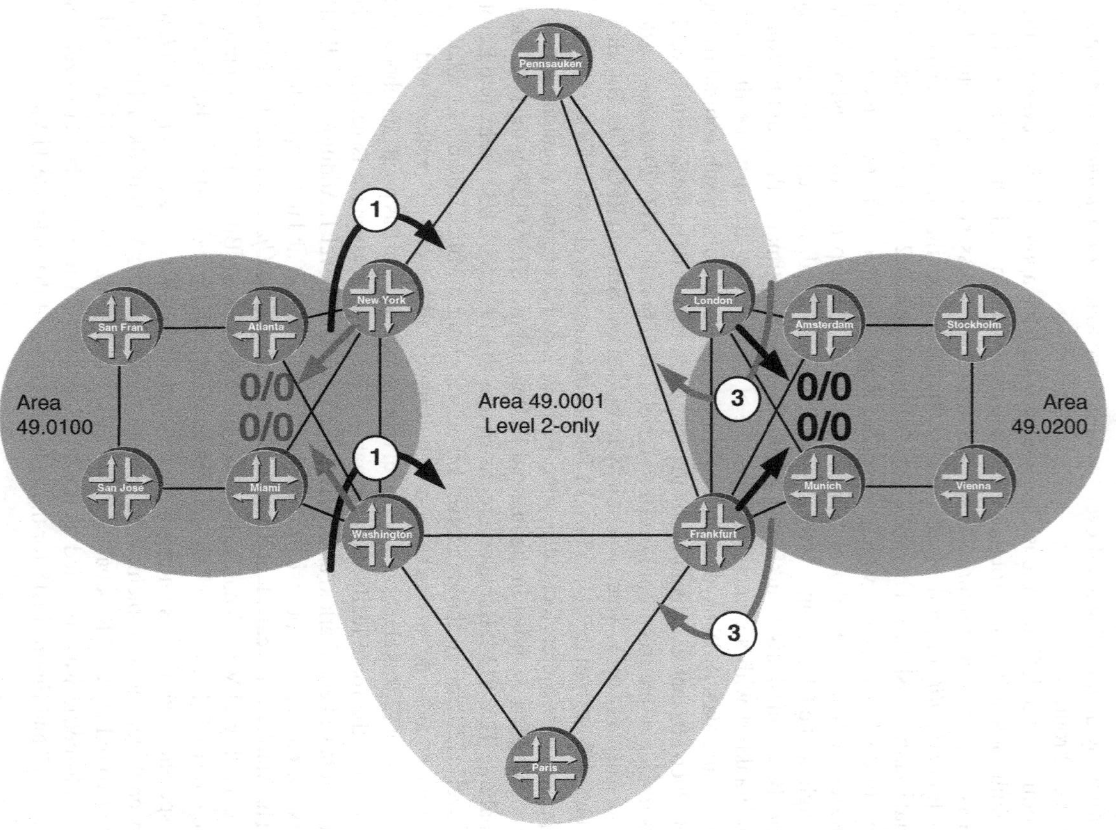

FIGURE 12.14. IS-IS suppresses per default Level 2 routing information to Level 1

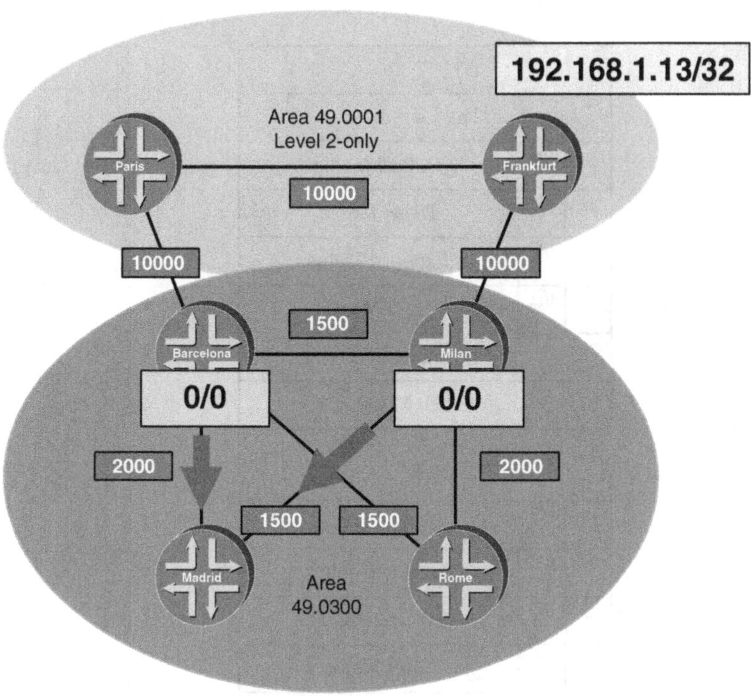

FIGURE 12.15. Injection of default routes often causes sub-optimal routings

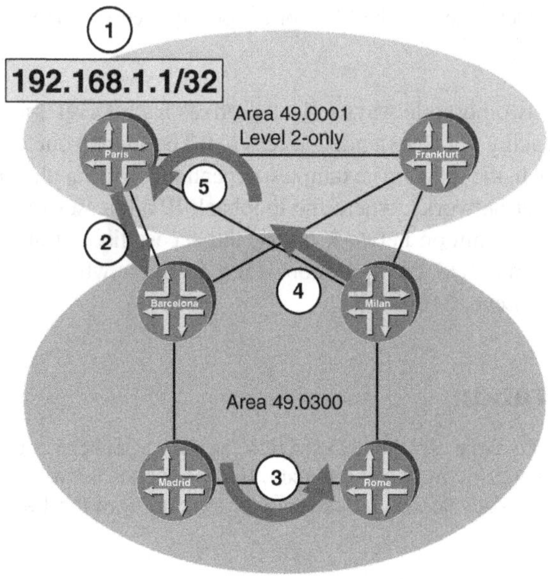

FIGURE 12.16. Leaked-down prefixes need to get marked, otherwise routing loops will form

Field	Bytes
TLV Type 128	1
TLV Length N*12	1
U/D | I/E 0 | Default Metric	1
S 1 | I/E 0 | Delay Metric	1
S 1 | I/E 0 | Expense Metric	1
S 1 | I/E 0 | Error Metric	1
IP Address	4
SUbnet Mask	4
⋮	
U/D | I/E 0 | Default Metric	1
S 1 | I/E 0 | Delay Metric	1
S 1 | I/E 0 | Expense Metric	1
S 1 | I/E 0 | Error Metric	1
IP Address	4
SUbnet Mask	4

FIGURE 12.17. RFC 2966 redefines the MSB of the default-metric of TLV #128 to support the Up/Down Bit

In IOS there are two possible ways to leak prefixes from Level 2 to Level 1. The first one controls the leaking via an extended access list. The second one controls route leaking via a route-map. In the following examples, depending on the application, both methods are used. For smaller networks, where the loopback IP addresses of all the routers in a network fall under a common network prefix, the access-list options is typically good enough. The following IOS configuration leaks prefixes, which match the extended access list 166 from Level 2 to Level 1.

IOS configuration

Using the redistribute `isis ip level-2 into level-1 distribute-list` command the network administrator can specify an extended IP access list which matches prefixes based on a simple prefix/wildcard bit scheme for leaking from the Level 2 database into the Level 1 database.

```
Amsterdam# show running-config
[ … ]
```

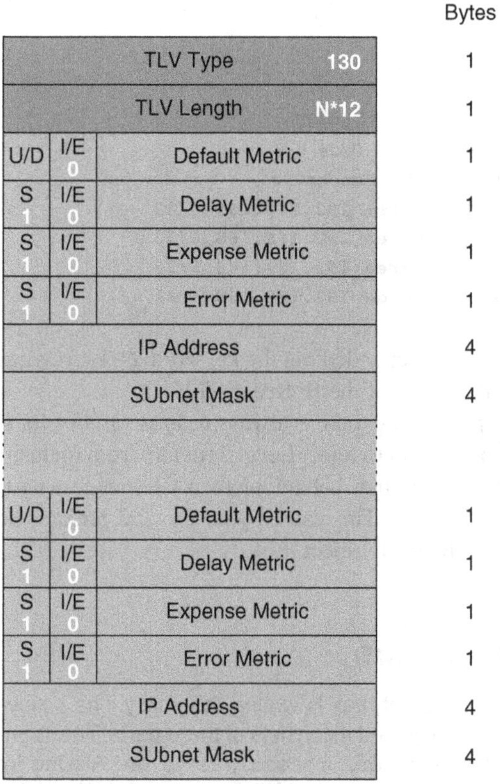

			Bytes
TLV Type 130			1
TLV Length N*12			1
U/D	I/E 0	Default Metric	1
S 1	I/E 0	Delay Metric	1
S 1	I/E 0	Expense Metric	1
S 1	I/E 0	Error Metric	1
IP Address			4
SUbnet Mask			4
U/D	I/E 0	Default Metric	1
S 1	I/E 0	Delay Metric	1
S 1	I/E 0	Expense Metric	1
S 1	I/E 0	Error Metric	1
IP Address			4
SUbnet Mask			4

FIGURE 12.18. RFC 2966 redefines the MSB of the default-metric of TLV #130 to support the Up/Down Bit

```
router isis
  redistribute isis ip level-2 into level-1 distribute-list 166
  passive-interface Loopback0
  net 49.0001.1921.6816.8007.00
  metric-style wide
!
access-list 166 permit ip 192.168.0.0 0.0.0.255 any
access-list 166 permit ip 192.168.168.0 0.0.0.255 any
[ … ]
```

IOS command output

Using the `show isis database` command you can spot the leaked prefixes.

```
Amsterdam# show isis database Amsterdam.00-00 detail
IS-IS Level-1 LSP Amsterdam.00-00
LSPID              LSP Seq Num     LSP Checksum    LSP Holdtime    ATT/P/OL
Amsterdam.00-00    * 0x00000003    0x94B7          1193            0/0/0
```

```
  Area Address: 49.0001
  NLPID: 0xCC
  Hostname: Amsterdam
  IP Address: 192.168.0.166
  Metric: 0     IP 192.168.0.166/32
  Metric: 10    IP 172.26.26.0/24
  Metric: 10    IS-Extended London.00
  Metric: 40    IP-Interarea 192.168.168.3/32
  Metric: 30    IP-Interarea 192.168.168.4/32
  Metric: 20    IP-Interarea 192.168.168.5/32
  Metric: 20    IP-Interarea 192.168.168.6/32
```

Leaked IP prefixes are prepended via the keyword `IP-Interarea` that is printed if the *Down* Bit is found in one of the IP Reach TLVs.

In JUNOS policy processing there is always a *default policy* for each routing protocol. The default policy for IS-IS is to reject Level 2 routers from inclusion in the Level 1 database. If you want to change that behaviour then you need to write a policy and call it using the `export` statement. This causes your Level 2 prefixes being evaluated *before* the default policy has chance to reject it.

JUNOS configuration

In JUNOS the most important task is writing the policy. The policy-statement `leak-L2-to-L1` is a single term policy and it consists of three parts. The `from` portion reads like "if" and the keywords `route-filter`, `protocol`, `level` are ANDed together. That is, if the prefix is originated within protocol isis AND it is Level 2 AND it falls under the route-filter 192.168.0/24 OR 192.168.168/24 THEN put it into the IS-IS Level 1 database.

```
[edit]
hannes@Frankfurt# show
[ … ]
protocols {
  isis {
    export leak-L2-to-L1;
  }
}
policy-options {
  policy-statement leak-L2-to-L1 {
    from {
      route-filter 192.168.0.0/24 orlonger;
      route-filter 192.168.168.0/24 orlonger;
      protocol isis;
      level 2;
    }
    to {
      protocol isis;
      level 1;
```

```
      }
      then accept;
    }
  }
[ ... ]
```

Using the `show isis database` detail command you can verify if your prefixes have been leaked correctly.

JUNOS command output

In JUNOS the leaked prefixes are marked with the Down Bit.

```
hannes@Frankfurt> show isis database detail
IS-IS level 1 link-state database:

Frankfurt.00-00 Sequence: 0x7, Checksum: 0x8cbb, Lifetime: 1187 secs
   IS neighbor:                   London.00 Metric:          10
   IP prefix:            172.26.26.0/24 Metric       :       10 Internal Up
   IP prefix:   192.168.0.167/32 Metric              :        0 Internal Up
   IP prefix:   192.168.168.3/32 Metric              :       40 Internal Down
   IP prefix:   192.168.168.4/32 Metric              :       30 Internal Down
   IP prefix:   192.168.168.5/32 Metric              :       20 Internal Down
   IP prefix:   192.168.168.6/32 Metric              :       20 Internal Down
[ ... ]
```

In the output you can identify leaked prefixes based on the down keyword, which is printed if the *Down* Bit is found in one of the IP Reachability TLVs.

12.6.2 *Leaking Level-1 External Prefixes into Level 2*

RFC 1195 explicitly forbids the use of External IP Reachability TLVs in Level 1. RFC 2966 loosens that restriction as well and allows injecting external information, such as from another routing protocol (RIP, OSPF, BGP, statics), into IS-IS as well. This is particular useful when networked-technology does not speak IS-IS or not even a routing protocol, and the network has to use static routes to inject reachability information. At this point, the authors do not want to encourage injection of reachability information (such as customer prefixes or dial-pools) into IS-IS. In modern network designs, all reachability information is typically carried into BGP, as BGP scales much better with respect to transporting massive amounts of routes. More consideration of these points will be covered in Chapter 16, which deals with IS-IS related network design issues and best current practices. If *wide metrics* are used in the network then that section can be skipped: the Extended IP Reachability TLV #135 has no notion of internal versus external prefixes and therefore all Level-1 prefixes get leaked to the Level-2 by default.

In IOS you can inject external information from Level 1 to Level 2 via a simple `redistribute isis ip level-2 into level-1` command. IOS transfers all routes that match the access list 155 from Level 1 to Level 2 irrespective of whether it is an external or an internal route.

IOS configuration

Like the Level 2 to Level 1 redistribution in IOS you can specify a Level 1 to Level 2 redistribution list which points either to a route-map or to an extented access list.

```
Amsterdam# show running-config
[ ... ]
router isis
  redistribute isis ip level-2 into level-1 distribute-list 155
  passive-interface Loopback0
  net 49.0001.1921.6816.8007.00
  metric-style wide
!
access-list 155 permit ip 10.0.0.0 0.0.255.255 any
[ ... ]
```

JUNOS makes distinction between internal or external prefixes. If you want to inject external prefixes into the Level 2 of your network you need to match against the `external` keyword in your routing-policy.

JUNOS configuration

The default policy for leaking external prefixes from Level 1 to Level 2 is `reject`. If you want to pre-empt the default policy you have to chain-in a policy called `leak-ext-L1-to-L2` which catches all external Level 1 routes which match the 10.0/16 prefix.

```
[edit]
hannes@Frankfurt# show
[ ... ]
protocols {
  isis {
    export leak-ext-L1-to-L2;
  }
}
policy-options {
  policy-statement leak-ext-L1-to-L2{
    from {
      route-filter 10.0.0.0/16 orlonger;
      protocol isis;
      external;
      level 1;
    }
    to {
      protocol isis;
      level 2;
    }
    then accept;
  }
}
[ ... ]
```

Notice the access lists and route filters that control the leakage between the two levels. It turned out that managing these access lists is a particular pain for large networks. Every time you deploy new routers whose loopback IP addresses need to be leaked then you need to touch all L1L2 routers in your network adjusting the access lists. Most ISPs mitigated the problem by assigning blocks of loopback addresses to different POPs. The access lists on the L1L2 routers therefore only need to be touched if a block in the POP is fully allocated. Another common practice is to filter based on a prefix length such as /32. Therefore only the loopback IP addresses get leaked – while this may seem as a modest approach for medium-sized networks it clearly does not scale for large networks. The largest networks in the world consist of about 7000–8000 IS-IS speaking routers. Leaking all 8000 prefixes at every L1L2 router may overwhelm the smaller routers in the POP. So what is needed is a more *selective* way of picking off the /32s from Level 2.

12.6.3 *Use of Admin Tags for Leaking Prefixes*

Most routing protocols support a *tagging* mechanism to enforce a route-redistribution policy. IS-IS has a similar extension formulated in draft-martin-neal-policy-isis-admin-tags.txt. The draft mentions two optional sub-TLVs to the Extended IP Reachability TLV #135 carrying 32-bit and 64-bit tags. Figure 12.19 shows how these administrative tags are being used in large-scale deployments. First, each interesting /32 prefix (in the figure it is Quebec's prefix 192.168.1.13/32) is tagged on the default leakage from Level 1 to Level 2. Interesting typically means all those routers that rely on a proper IGP metric like public Internet routing. In our example, the Tag #200 is used for all Internet routers that carry Internet routes. The L1L2 routers Boston and Chicago attach the Tag #200 along with the route. Next, those tagged prefixes travel through the Level-2. On the egress L1L2 routers (Frankfurt and Paris) the leaking policy now gets very simple as all we have to look for is Tag #200 to find out whether to leak the prefix or not. The policy needs to be configured only once and then all you have to do is properly tag the prefixes and your network will act accordingly.

In the following two configurations you will see two configurations for IOS and two configurations for JUNOS. The first of the two respective configurations does the tagging and the second one does the leakage based on the existence of a tag.

Applying admin tags is fairly simple in IOS. An admin tag is typically an interface property and can be set using the keyword `isis tag <tag>`.

IOS configuration

In IOS you set the Admin tag typically on the Loopback Interface. Using the `show isis database London.00-00 level-1 verbose` you can verify if the Admin tag has been successfully attached to your Loopback route.

```
London# show running-config
[ ... ]
interface Loopback0
  ip address 192.168.0.166 255.255.255.255
  isis tag 200
!
```

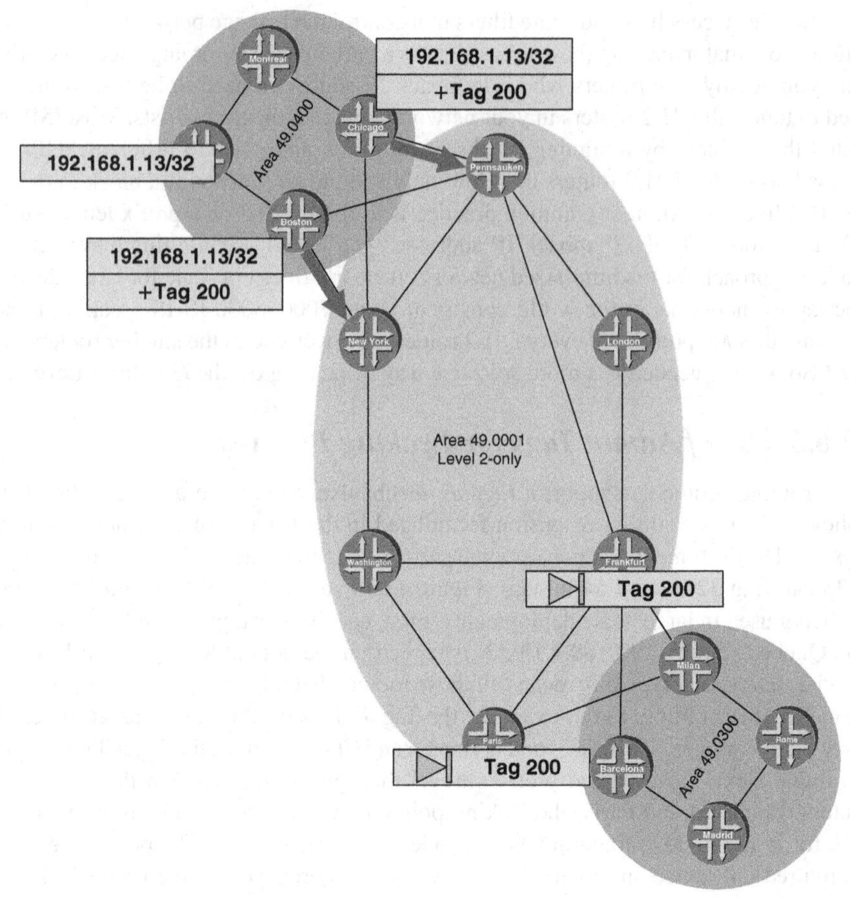

FIGURE 12.19. Admin tags are a convenient way of implementing an AS-wide policy for leaking /32s

IOS command output

```
London#show isis database London.00-00 level-1 verbose

IS-IS Level-1 LSP London.00-00
LSPID               LSP Seq Num    LSP Checksum    LSP Holdtime     ATT/P/OL
London.00-00      * 0x00000010     0x574C          819              0/0/0
  Area Address: 49.0001
  NLPID:            0xCC
  Hostname: London
  IP Address: 192.168.0.166
  Metric: 0  IP 192.168.0.166/32
    Route Admin Tag: 200
```

```
  Metric: 10 IP 172.26.26.0/24
  Metric: 10 IS-Extended London.00
[ … ]
```

The second IOS policy now needs to match against all previously tagged prefixes. See the example below, which uses a route-map for achieving that purpose.

IOS configuration

To match against the previously tagged prefixes you need to unconfigure the `redistribute isis ip level-2 into level-1 distribute-list 166` command and use the `redistribute isis ip level-2 into level-1 route-map` command instead. This commands points to a route-map, which has far more fine-grained control than an access list would offer.

```
London# show running-config
router isis
  redistribute isis ip level-2 into level-1 route-map
   leak-tagged-L2-to-L1
  passive-interface Loopback0
  net 49.0001.1921.6816.8007.00
  metric-style wide
!
route-map leak-tagged-L2-to-L1 permit 10
  match tag 200
!
[ … ]
```

The route-map `leak-tagged-L2-to-L1` is fairly simple. It permits all prefixes, which carry the tag 200 and report it back to the IS-IS redistribution process for inclusion in the Level-1 database.

You can verify the results of your policy by using the `show isis database <lsp-id> verbose` command. The `verbose` modifier also displays the Admin tags, which the `detail` modifier does not.

IOS command output

```
London#show isis database London.00-00 level-1 verbose

IS-IS Level-1 LSP London.00-00
LSPID            LSP Seq Num     LSP Checksum     LSP Holdtime     ATT/P/OL
London.00-00     * 0x0000000D    0x8140           797              0/0/0
  Area Address: 49.0001
  NLPID: 0xCC
  Hostname: London
  IP Address:  192.168.0.166
```

```
  Metric: 0              IP 192.168.0.166/32
  Metric: 10             IP 172.26.26.0/24
  Metric: 10             IS-Extended Frankfurt.00
  Metric: 20             IP-Interarea 192.168.168.5/32
      Route Admin Tag: 200
[ … ]
```

In JUNOS we need to perform the same two steps. First all the routers in the network need to tag all their loopback networks using the tag #200. This is achieved by applying the policy `tag-lo0`.

JUNOS configuration

In JUNOS the tagging is done once again via a policy. The policy `tag-lo0` reads as: take all IP addresses from your logical interface lo0.0 and apply an IS-IS tag #200 to it.

```
[edit]
hannes@Frankfurt# show
[ … ]
protocols {
  isis {
    export tag-lo0;
  }
}
policy-options {
  policy-statement tag-lo0 {
    from {
      interface lo0.0;
    }
    then {
      accept;
      tag 200;
    }
  }
}
[ … ]
```

You can verify if the tag has been correctly applied using the `show isis database extensive` output and spot the TLVs section of that output.

```
hannes@Frankfurt> show isis database Frankfurt extensive
IS-IS level 1 link-state database:
Frankfurt.00-00 Sequence: 0x5, Checksum: 0x47da, Lifetime: 1171 secs
[ … ]
  TLVs:
    Area address: 49.0001 (3)
    Speaks: IP
```

```
    Speaks: IPv6
    IP router id: 192.168.168.5
    IP address: 192.168.168.5
    Hostname: Frankfurt
    [ … ]
    IP extended prefix: 192.168.168.5/32 metric 0 up
      6 bytes of subtlvs
      Administrative tag 1: 200
    IP extended prefix: 172.16.33.5/30 metric 0 up
  No queued transmissions
```

If your policy is working correctly you should see the tag #200 applied to your loopback IP prefix. The tag is encoded using a sub-TLV to the Extended IP Reach TLV #135.

Now if everything is tagged correctly we change our leak-L2-to-L1 policy to match against the presence of Admin tags rather than specifying a list of cumbersome and error-prone route-filters.

JUNOS configuration

The old `leak-L2-to-L1` policy is renamed to `leak-tagged-L2-to-L1` – additionally the `from route-filter` statements are removed and the `tag` statement is inserted as primary identifier for routes that need to get leaked.

```
[edit]
hannes@Frankfurt# show
[ … ]
protocols {
  isis {
    export leak-tagged-L2-to-L1;
  }
}
policy-options {
  policy-statement leak-tagged-L2-to-L1 {
    from {
      tag 200;
      protocol isis;
      level 2;
    }
    to {
      protocol isis;
      level 1;
    }
    then accept;
  }
}
[ … ]
```

Using Admin tags for route leaking is a powerful tool that you will not like to miss in medium-to large-sized networks. Also interoperability between IOS and JUNOS is mature now and there are no reasons not to deploy it. As with the introduction of communities for iBGP routing it takes some time to set up all the tagging policies but once done you will enjoy not needing to administer access lists any more.

12.7 Conclusion

The IP Reachability TLVs have been facing constant evolution and change. First introduced in RFC 1195, later redefined in RFC 2966 and today obsoleted by the traffic engineering drafts, a variety of TLVs conveying IP reachability information is found in today's IS-IS networks. There is no indication that this evolution will stop and when looking at all these changes one thing remains certain: the process of change itself. The open nature of the Extended IP Reachability TLVs make sure that the protocols can and will be further extended. The Admin tag and multitopology drafts continue to further evolve the IP Reachability TLVs.

13

IS-IS Extensions

Comparing IS-IS based on the root specification ISO 10589 to how IS-IS is deployed today shows that almost none of the original TLVs are in use anymore. What still is almost unchanged are the original frame formats and PDU headers, another proof that IS-IS is an easily extended routing protocol.

In recent years many extensions for a variety of diverse applications have been specified and then deployed. Those enhancements are sometimes of a very different nature, ranging from name resolution functions, which are aimed to ease operations and management, to supporting new network address families like IPv6. There are even extensions that put "band-aids" on general protocol weaknesses like missing checksums in certain PDU types. Some go as far as to question the suitability of a single SPF calculation operation for a joint IPv4 and IPv6 topology.

This chapter covers the major IS-IS protocol extensions that have not yet been covered. It highlights recent enhancements, for example for IPv6, additional checksum protection, stronger authentication, multitopology SPF and graceful restart capability.

13.1 Dynamic Hostnames

The *entity* to uniquely describe an IS-IS router in a given topology is the System-ID. The System-ID is a 48-bit (6 byte) field that really does not fit in anywhere in the IP universe. This reveals two operational problems regarding the System-ID once deployed:

- It is hard to memorize
- It is hard to translate (resolve) to a name

Consider the CLI output below. If a NOC engineer needs to verify if a certain adjacency is up, they need to check lists and manually map the System-IDs to a router name. Luckily in our example the routers' loopback addresses are mapped to the System-ID using a binary coded decimal (BCD) scheme.

JUNOS command output

```
hannes@Frankfurt> show isis adjacency
Interface           System              L       State       Hold (secs) SNPA
so-0/0/0.0          1921.6800.1017      2       Up                   25
so-0/2/0.0          1921.6800.1012      2       Up                   26
```

```
so-1/0/0.0          1921.6800.1019          2       Up                22
so-1/1/0.0          1921.6800.1018          1       Up                20
so-1/2/0.0          1921.6800.1021          2       Up                22
so-2/0/0.0          1921.6800.1022          2       Up                24
so-2/1/0.0          1921.6800.1023          1       Up                26
[ ... ]
```

It is often possible to make the router translate Network Layer addresses to names using the Domain Name System (DNS). While utilizing the DNS for IPv4 and IPv6 addresses may be a viable solution, it is not for System-IDs. No DNS software today, nor any client resolver at the router, supports translation for these 48-bit entities.

To get a name translation service up and running, network service providers started to maintain mapping tables for name resolution.

In IOS you can manually configure those mapping tables using the `clns host` configuration command.

IOS configuration

The `clns host` configuration option translates names to a NSAP prefix. If you want to use it just for System-ID translation then enter the minimal NSAP (8-bytes) and set the Area-ID (first byte) and Selector Byte (last byte) to zero.

```
London#show running-config
[ ... ]
clns host Pennsauken 00.1921.6800.1021.00
clns host New-York 00.1921.6800.1021.00
clns host Washington 00.1921.6800.1021.00
clns host Frankfurt 00.1921.6800.1021.00
clns host Paris 00.1921.6800.1021.00
[ ... ]
```

In JUNOS you can manually configure static name to System-ID mappings using the `static-host-mapping` keyword under the `system` { } stanza:

JUNOS configuration

```
hannes@Frankfurt> show configuration
system {
[ ... ]
  static-host-mapping {
    Pennsauken sysid 1921.6800.1017;
    London sysid 1921.6800.1012;
    New-York sysid 1921.6800.1019;
    Washington sysid 1921.6800.1021;
    Paris sysid 1921.6800.1022;
  }
}
[ ... ]
```

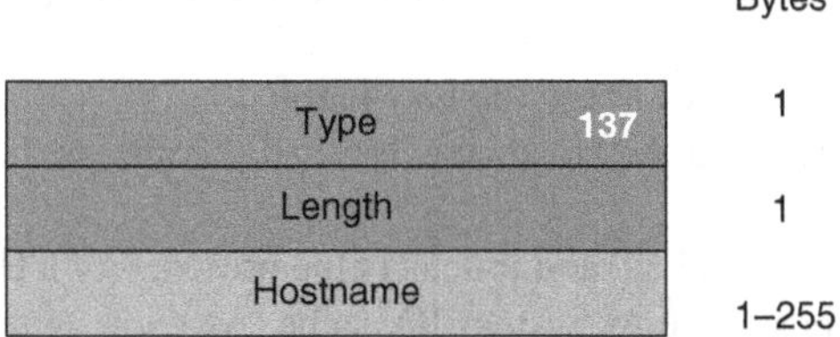

FIGURE 13.1. The dynamic Hostname TLV #137 is an envelope for transporting a simple ASCII string

Maintaining a mapping table on all of the routers is an easy thing if the network consists just of six routers like the example network does. However, over time it is very awkward to distribute mapping information each time a router is added, changed or removed. Relying on an external server like the DNS is not a viable choice either. If you troubleshoot your IS-IS network because there is a problem, then there may be a situation where connectivity to the name resolution server is disrupted and you have to fall back to manual translation. The best troubleshooting tool can be a problem if it does not work as expected when you need it most.

The ISIS-WG of the IETF found that the best place for a System-ID to name translation service is actually the routing protocol itself. RFC 2763 describes a TLV to advertise hostnames along with a router's LSP to distribute name to System-ID mapping information throughout a given level. The dynamic Hostname TLV is illustrated in Figure 13.1. The TLV is nothing but a freeform string that conveys the router's hostname. Usually the hostname is one of the very first things initially configured on a router.

IOS configuration

Setting of the `hostname` causes not only the prompt to change. Additionally the hostname is advertised using TLV #137.

```
London#show running-config
[ ... ]
hostname London
!
```

JUNOS configuration

In JUNOS the hostname is set inside the `system` { } stanza using the hostname keyword.

```
hannes@Frankfurt> show configuration
system {
  host-name Frankfurt;
  [ ... ]
}
```

As soon as you change the router's hostname two things happen:

- The router prompt changes to use the new name
- A new LSP is issued, and the Hostname TLV #137 contains the new name

Once a router receives an LSP and it detects the presence of a Hostname TLV #137, it starts to maintain a hostname to System-ID cache. As soon as the router synchronizes with one of its adjacent routers it learns all LSPs and, as a side benefit, all the known System-ID to name mapping information is learned.

The tcpdump output shows the Washington LSP.

Tcpdump output

```
11:36:45.587565 OSI, IS-IS, length: 405
  L2 LSP, hlen: 27, v: 1, pdu-v: 1, sys-id-len: 6 (0), max-area: 3 (0)
    lsp-id: 1921.8900.1021.00-00, seq: 0x000002fd, lifetime: 1198s
    chksum: 0xe984 (correct), PDU length: 405, Flags: [ L1L2 IS ]
      Area address(es) TLV #1, length: 4
        Area address (length: 3): 49.0001
      Protocols supported TLV #129, length: 2
        NLPID(s): IPv4 (0xcc), IPv6 (0x8e)
      Traffic Engineering Router ID TLV #134, length: 4
        Traffic Engineering Router ID: 192.168.1.21
      IPv4 Interface address(es) TLV #132, length: 4
        IPv4 interface address: 192.168.1.21
      Hostname TLV #137, length: 10
        Hostname: Washington
      Extended IS Reachability TLV #22, length: 75
        IS Neighbor: 2092.1113.4007.00, Metric: 5, sub-TLVs present (64)
          IPv4 interface address subTLV #6, length: 4, 172.16.33.6
          IPv4 neighbor address subTLV #8, length: 4, 172.16.33.5
      [ … ]
```

All receiving routers extract the first six bytes of the LSP-ID (System-ID) plus the content of the Hostname TLV #137 to populate the hostname cache.

You can display the hostname to System-ID mapping cache using the `show isis hostname` command which is available both on IOS and JUNOS.

JUNOS command output

In JUNOS you can display the System-ID to name cache using the `show isis hostname` command. The output shows if the mapping has been learnt by receipt of a Hostname TLV #137 (Type = Dynamic) or a static mapping defined under the `system { }` stanza (Type = Static). The local router always has its type set to Static.

```
hannes@Frankfurt> show isis hostname
IS-IS hostname database:
System ID              Hostname           Type
1921.6800.1017         Pennsauken         Dynamic
1921.6800.1012         London             Dynamic
1921.6800.1019         New-York           Dynamic
1921.6800.1021         Washington         Dynamic
1921.6800.1008         Frankfurt          Static
1921.6800.1022         Paris              Dynamic
1921.6800.1018         Stockholm          Dynamic
1921.6800.1023         Munich             Dynamic
1921.6800.1024         Vienna             Dynamic
[ … ]
```

IOS command output

IOS lists additionally from which level it learned the hostname mappings. The asterisk indicates that the information originated locally.

```
London# show isis hostname
Level        System ID              Dynamic Hostname (notag)
        *    1921.6800.1012         London
2            1921.6800.1017         Pennsauken
2            1921.6800.1019         New-York
2            1921.6800.1021         Washington
2            1921.6800.1008         Frankfurt
2            1921.6800.1022         Paris
1            1921.6800.1018         Stockholm
1            1921.6800.1023         Munich
1            1921.6800.1024         Vienna
```

If there is no hostname in the hostname cache, then most likely the router in question does not originate the Hostname TLV as part of its link-state PDU.

TABLE 13.1. The IS-IS Name Resolver replaces the System-ID by the cached Hostname string.

	Hexadecimal representation	Name representation
System-ID	1921.6800.1017	Pennsauken
Node-ID	1921.6800.1017.00	Pennsauken.00
LSP-ID	1921.6800.1017.00-00	Pennsauken.00-00

You can verify that the dynamic Hostname TLV is present by looking into the link-state database:

JUNOS command output

The presence of a Hostname line in the `show isis database extensive` output shows that the originating system did add the Hostname TLV.

```
hannes@Frankfurt> show isis database extensive
[ … ]
  TLVs:
    Area address: 49.0001 (3)
    Speaks: IP, IPv6


    IP router id: 192.168.1.18
    IP address: 192.168.1.18
    Hostname: Stockholm
    IS neighbor: Frankfurt.00, Metric: 1
      IP address: 172.16.33.45
[ … ]
```

IOS command output

```
London#show isis database verbose 1921.6800.1047.00-00

IS-IS Level-2 Link State Database:
LSPID           LSP Seq Num         LSP Checksum        LSP Holdtime        ATT/P/OL
1921.6800.      * 0x00000040        0xD323              491                 0/0/0
 1047.00-00
  Area Address:          49.0001
  NLPID:                 0x81
    IS neighbor: Vienna.02, Metric: 63
[ … ]
```

The LSP shown in the IOS command output does not contain the Hostname TLV. As it does not list any IP-related TLVs it may be that this is a CLNS-only router that is probably running older software that does not support the Hostname TLV.

If the hostnames made their way into the hostname cache, then all IS-IS occurrences of the System-ID are replaced using their respective name. See Table 13.1 for how Pennsauken's System, Node and LSP-IDs are represented using the new name resolution service.

Today IS-IS is one of the most convenient routing protocols. It aids the network engineer and troubleshooter by offering a kind of distributed name service. All of the IS-IS-related display functions like displaying adjacencies, examining the link-state database or logging functions make use of a System-ID to hostname translation cache and display System-IDs, Node-IDs and LSP-IDs with their name rather than their hexadecimal representation.

The next extension to IS-IS will cover the authentication scheme of LSPs and their implementation.

13.2 Authenticating Routing Information

Authenticating routing protocol messages is a basic building block for every network security strategy. Some people argue that authentication is pushing the envelope for IS-IS since all the messages run natively on Layer 2, which means that the protocol cannot be exposed to a remote attack from the Internet because there is simply no possibility for transporting a Layer-2 frame over the Layer-3 infrastructure. This is just another way to say "you can't route a frame".

An attacker needs to have local, physical access to inject malicious information. Others argue that an additional barrier like authentication helps to keep out the errors introduced by, for example, unskilled NOC personnel. One application is that new IS-IS adjacencies cannot be created on an interface without knowing the password beforehand (this is just one example).

Both attacks and errors are cases where the use of authenticating PDUs makes sense. ISO 10589 defines a dedicated Authentication TLV for confirming the authenticity of the PDU. Figure 13.2 shows the structure of this TLV.

The Authentication TLV uses a field called Authentication Type to further indicate how the password is encoded. Currently there are two encoding methods defined:

- Simple Text Authentication
- HMAC-MD5

The left-hand side of Figure 13.2 shows the formatting of the TLV if Simple Text Authentication is used. The password is a free-form string that can be between 1 and 254 bytes in size. On the right-hand side there is the formatting of TLV #10 if HMAC-MD5 Authentication is used. The size is fixed to 16 bytes and contains a MD5 sum of the entire packet.

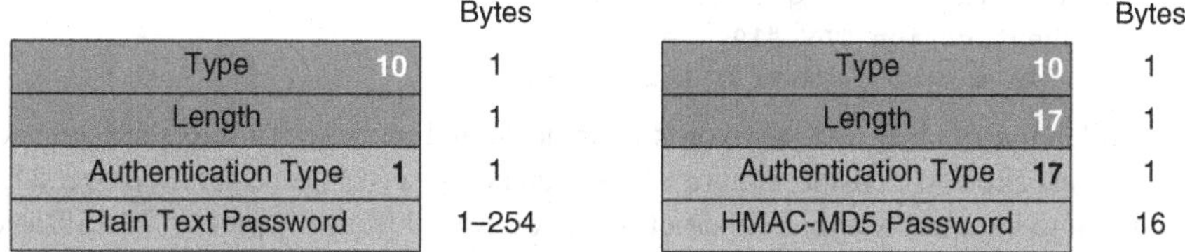

FIGURE 13.2. The Authentication TLV #10 supports two different authentication types

13.2.1 *Simple Text Authentication*

Code point 1 indicates simple text encoding of the password. *Simple* text encoding means that the password is encoded *clear* text. The following tcpdump output shows that the password contained in the IIH is transported clear text over the circuit.

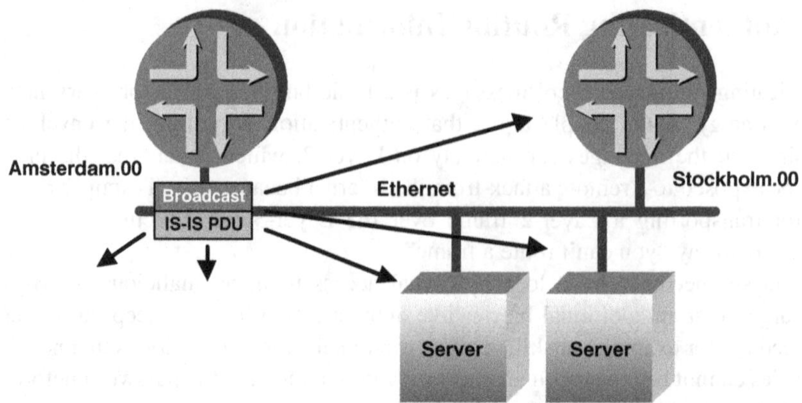

FIGURE 13.3. Each device connected to the LAN infrastructure receives IS-IS-related messages because the Destination MAC address has the Broadcast Bit set

Tcpdump output

```
11:35:23.248504 OSI, IS-IS, length: 52
  p2p IIH, hlen: 20, v: 1, pdu-v: 1, sys-id-len: 6 (0), max-area: 3 (0)
    source-id: 1921.6800.1009, holding time: 27s, Flags: [Level 2 only]
    circuit-id: 0x01, PDU length: 52
      Point-to-point Adjacency State TLV #240, length: 1
        Adjacency State: Up (0)
      Protocols supported TLV #129, length: 2
        NLPID(s): IPv4 (0xcc), IPv6 (0x8e)
      IPv4 Interface address(es) TLV #132, length: 4
        IPv4 interface address: 172.16.33.6
      Area address(es) TLV #1, length: 4
        Area address (length: 3): 49.0001
      Authentication TLV #10, length: 11
        simple text password: LeiaOrgana
```

The dilemma of clear text passwords is obvious, and more so if routers are connected via broadcast circuits. Consider Figure 13.3 – routers and servers are connected over a LAN infrastructure like, for example, Ethernet Switches. Recall from Chapter 4, "IS-IS Basics", that all the IS-IS messages on LANs are sent using functional MAC addresses *AllL1ISs* (0180:c200:0014) for Level 1 PDUs and *AllL2ISs* (0180:c200:0015) for PDUs aimed at Level 2. Note that these functional MAC addresses have the lowest bit of their most significant byte (MSB) set. The lowest bit of the MSB of the Destination MAC Address is also the "Broadcast Bit" which makes LAN switches treat it like a broadcast, that is, to flood it out on all ports. Ultimately all ports on the LAN switch see the Hello with the clear text password, which makes it far too easy for eavesdroppers to get hold of the password.

If a hacker gets access to a server, all they have to do is run a network analyzer such as tcpdump to sniff the IS-IS passwords and then the hacker has all they need: direct network access and the password used for authenticating network updates. Now it is easy to inject malicious routing updates and to take down the entire network. Therefore simple text authentication provides just a *marginal* additional protection.

13.2.2 *HMAC-MD5 Authentication*

The second encoding scheme is to use HMAC-MD5 hashes for securing the routing updates. By using MD5 hashes the password does not travel clear text over the circuit. The HMAC-MD5 algorithm is documented in RFC 2104. It describes a one-way operation to get a hash based on a bit field and a shared secret password. One-way function means that, based on the hash and the bit field, the password cannot be reconstructed.

The authentication type for HMAC-MD5 is 54 and it is always using a fixed length of 16 bytes. The following tcpdump output shows the 16-byte output of the hash. Note the TLV length is 17 bytes because the first byte is reserved for the Authentication Type field.

Tcpdump output

```
11:35:27.216425 OSI, IS-IS, length: 58
  p2p IIH, hlen: 20, v: 1, pdu-v: 1, sys-id-len: 6 (0), max-area: 3 (0)
    source-id: 1921.6800.1008, holding time: 27s, Flags: [Level 2 only]
    circuit-id: 0x01, PDU length: 58
      Point-to-point Adjacency State TLV #240, length: 1
        Adjacency State: Up (0)
      Protocols supported TLV #129, length: 2
        NLPID(s): IPv4 (0xcc), IPv6 (0x8e)
      IPv4 Interface address(es) TLV #132, length: 4
        IPv4 interface address: 172.16.33.6
      Area address(es) TLV #1, length: 4
        Area address (length: 3): 49.0001
      Authentication TLV #10, length: 17
        HMAC-MD5 password: a933242e676df1275e323b648ab5e387
```

13.2.3 *Weaknesses*

In contrast to OSPF, IS-IS lacks cryptographic sequence numbers. This means IS-IS is not prone to so-called "replay attacks". A replay attack means that an attacker is recording messages and replaying them at a later time in order to do something harmful. Using replay attacks it is quite easy to tear down an existing adjacency. Consider Figure 13.4. The hacker is constantly eavesdropping on a LAN and trying to record IS-IS IIH (Hello) messages in order to launch a replay attack. The first set of packets for adjacency establishment are of particular interest. Consider the adjacency finite state machine mentioned in Figure 5.16 in Chapter 5, "Neighbour Discovery and Handshaking". The idea is to catch the message when the router is transitioning from the *New* to the *Init* state and to replay that message at a later time.

Replaying a pre-recorded Hello that reports an *Init* state when the adjacency is already established immediately moves it to the *Down* state. The receiver has no chance of detecting that this is an attack, as the IIH is properly authenticated.

Of course, a few packet exchanges after the attack, the adjacency would move again to the *Up* state as the periodic Hellos from both Amsterdam and Stockholm declare the adjacency *Up* again. However, flapping adjacencies have a severe impact on the rest of the network because new LSPs need to be generated; they need to get flooded throughout the network, SPF calculations need to be scheduled and finally the new FIB state needs to get propagated

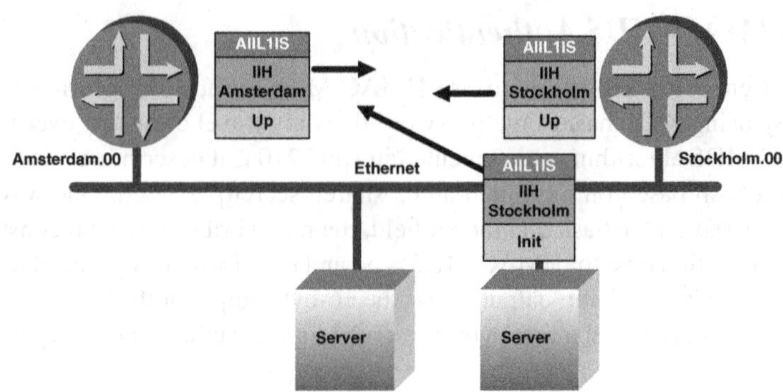

FIGURE 13.4. An attacker replays a previously recorded message where the adjacency was in Init state to tear it down

Field	Value	Bytes
Type	241	1
Length	4	1
Sequence Number		4

FIGURE 13.5. A monotonically increasing Sequence Number makes sure that the MD5-hash varies for each transmitted Hello

to the forwarding planes. Even if the router OS supports protection techniques like adjacency hold down, the attack disrupts adjacencies for a period of time.

The way to prevent replay attacks is to add an element that is changed for every Hello that is transmitted. By including a counter or *Sequence Number* (not to be confused with the Sequence Number of the LSP) in the hashing, a replay attacker needs to wait 2^{32} IS-IS packets in order to repeat an attack. Depending on the implementation-specific protection timers, an attacker needs to wait more than a hundred years before he can successfully repeat a pre-recorded message. The assumption here is that a router does not generate more than one IS-IS PDU per second in order not to cycle too fast through the sequence space. This assumption is absolutely valid, as most of the IS-IS PDU types are rate-limited by the specification, like the LSP-min-generation-, CSNP- or Hello-Interval.

Up until now, no such sequencing mechanism has been deployed. Naiming Shen, a development engineer with Redback, came up with a proposal for a new TLV on the IS-IS-WG list in the IETF. Figure 13.5 illustrates the proposed Sequence Number TLV. The basis structure of the TLV is to wrap a 32-bit number that is monotonically increasing.

Even if IS-IS is lacking in robustness against replay attacks, it is recommended to use MD5 authentication when deploying an IS-IS network. Most of the harm that can be done based on replay attacks can be avoided by network design techniques, such as not using broadcast circuits in the core. Using replay attacks, an attacker can create some moderate stress in other parts of the network. After all, modern routers have enough processing power to withstand such *moderate* attacks. So the most impacted place in the network will be where the hacker is trying to cycle adjacencies through the *Down* state, which puts the hacker on the spot because he needs to have a direct link to that network.

However, not using authentication may put a hacker in the position to attack any system he wants to in the network and cause network-global stress that is not easily detected in the first place. A nightmare for any NOC team.

13.2.4 *Point-to-point Interfaces*

Running authentication on point-to-point interfaces requires some explanation and caveats. First, point-to-point interfaces are different from LAN interfaces regarding their PDU types. Hello PDUs from the two levels need to share the point-to-point PDU type rather than having their own, like LAN IIHs do. Those constraints were further explained in Chapter 5, "Neighbour Discovery and Handshaking". The fact that both levels need to share a PDU type also has implications for authentication. Authentication in IS-IS always applies to the entire PDU. If the PDU type is shared between levels, then a single password needs to be shared for both levels as well. There is a potential for conflict in the configuration too, as (for example) if two passwords (one for each level) are configured, then the router needs to make a decision. In IS-IS the rule set is simple: for Hello authentication, the Level-1 password is used. If there is no Level-1 password configured, then no Hello authentication is performed.

In the configuration example authentication for Hellos is turned on for both levels using different passwords.

JUNOS configuration

The `authentication-key` HanSolo is configured for Level 2 and LeiaOrgana for Level 1 interface authentication. Because JUNOS scrambles all passwords, in the example we have written down the password as commentary.

```
hannes@Frankfurt> show configuration
[ … ]
protocols {
  isis {
    [ … ]
    interface so-0/1/2.0 {
      level 2 {
        hello-authentication-key "$9$dyVgJiHmTF/.P"; # HanSolo
        hello-authentication-type simple; # SECRET-DATA
      }
      level 1 {
        hello-authentication-key "$9$c-PSvLdVYoZjs25Q"; # LeiaOrgana
        hello-authentication-type simple; # SECRET-DATA
      }
    }
    interface lo0.0;
  }
}
```

The tcpdump output reveals that only the Level-1 authentication key is used.

Tcpdump output

For point-to-point IIH authentication the Level-1 password is used.

```
20:10:22.699068 OSI, IS-IS, length: 61
  point-to-point IIH, hlen: 20, v: 1, pdu-v: 1, sys-id-len: 6 (0),
   max-area: 3 (0)
    source-id: 1921.6800.1008, holding time: 27s, Flags: [Level 1, Level 2]
    circuit-id: 0x01, PDU length: 61
      [ … ]
      Restart Signaling TLV #211, length: 3
        Flags [none], Remaining holding time 0s
      Authentication TLV #10, length: 11
        simple text password: LeiaOrgana
```

Authentication is today imperative for securing routing protocols. Most authentication migrations have network-wide impact and require a strategy for gradually transitioning the network.

13.2.5 *Migration Strategy*

There are three main authentication-related migration scenarios. All three migration scenarios have one assumption in common: it is not possible to change the entire network in one "flag day" and there must not be any outage longer than (to cite a common example) a single adjacency reset.

13.2.5.1 General Decisions and Routing Software Selection

Before starting to implement authentication in an IS-IS, two questions need to be answered:

- What IS-IS PDU types need to be authenticated?
- What authentication type should be used?

The most likely answer is that HMAC-MD5 should be used as the authentication method for all PDU types. Unfortunately, there are some restrictions in older routing software. Particularly in IOS, IS-IS authentication has been neglected in the past. There are many caveats as to what PDUs are authenticated and which authentication types are supported in older releases of the IOS software. That has recently changed – as of 2004 there is full authentication support for all PDU types and both authentication methods. Full support has been available in versions equal or higher than IOS:

- 12.0(21)ST
- 12.2(11)S
- 12.0(22)S
- 12.2(13)T
- 12.2(14)S

If you do not have the choice, and are tied for some reason to a particularly IOS software release, then please proceed to Section 13.2.7, "Interoperability", which will discuss an approach for making authentication work using older IOS releases.

Here are three authentication migration scenarios for an IS-IS network. The first of the three migration scenarios is the "Greenfield" approach: transition from an entirely *un*authenticated IS-IS network to an authenticated one.

13.2.5.2 Greenfield Migration

The Greenfield migration strategy uses asymmetric authentication. The term "asymmetric" refers to the ways how and if authentication information is sent and verified. Asymmetric authentication sends authentication information, but does not verify it. That way routers can be configured *gradually* to send their PDUs augmented with authentication information. But they do not verify if the password is correct upon receipt. Once all the routers in the network send the correct authentication information, the routers can *gradually* switch to symmetric authentication that *does* check to see if the supplied authentication string is correct. If it is not, then the PDU is discarded.

The second migration scenario covers the case of *changing* an authentication key in a live network.

13.2.5.3 Key Migration

Any good security policy can change passwords over time. A core network – which is admittedly a cumbersome environment for any change – should change the authentication on a periodic basis as well. For authentication key migration there are two possibilities:

- Asymmetrical authentication
- Multiple key verification

Asymmetrical key verification is the panacea that works for all migration scenarios. This may even be a viable solution for the Greenfield scenario; however, for the key migration method, the drawback is that a door is opened during the migration phase.

An implementation can decide to store *many* authentication keys on the router. *One* of those keys is used for *sending* authenticated PDUs. The remaining keys represent older versions of the authentication string and each one is used against an incoming PDU. That way, network operators do not need to open the security gates for migrating keys.

Multiple key verification is clearly the preferred option to keep the security level of the network intact. IOS supports keychains with their initial support for HMAC-MD5. JUNOS 6.2 has no multiple keys available which means that as soon as JUNOS is introduced into the network, the network must fall back to asymmetrical authentication schemes and hope that during password migration there is no attack on the infrastructure (as slight as this vulnerability might be, it is nonetheless real).

The last migration scenario is presented for completeness. It is not even discussed in the IETF, but is still relevant.

13.2.5.4 Authentication Type Migration

Older IOS software only supports simple text authentication. For the time being this lowest common denominator (simple text authentication) is what both IOS and JUNOS has deployed. Network operators feel increasingly concerned about the non-existent security that simple text authentication provides and desperately want to switch to HMAC-MD5.

From a protocol perspective, nothing would prohibit the encoding of two versions of the Authentication TLV #10. The first one would carry the authentication key using MD5 authentication and the second would carry the same authentication key using simple text authentication. The biggest problem is that the deployed code only expects one Authentication TLV and there is little research into how the installed base of software would react to multiple occurrences of Authentication TLVs. The IETF has so far not coped with the problem, and typically refers inquiring parties to asymmetrical authentication for solving problems of that kind.

In the next two sections there are practical examples of how to turn on IS-IS authentication on IOS and JUNOS.

13.2.6 *Running Authentication Using IOS*

In Cisco IOS there are two general forms of authentication for IS-IS: interface authentication and per-level authentication. Interface configuration applies to a specific interface only, and authenticates IIH PDUs. Per-level authentication authenticates LSP and SNP PDUs. A pair of routers only needs to share the same password to successfully run interface authentication. Per-level authentication makes it necessary for all routers in a given level to share the same password.

13.2.6.1 Per-interface Authentication

We use a simple networking scenario such as that illustrated in Figure 13.6 for the authentication examples. Two routers are connected via a Gigabit Ethernet interface. Pseudonode suppression is turned on. The following configures an interface authentication between Madrid and Rome. All IIHs between the two routers on their Gigabit Ethernet interface are authenticated using MD5 authentication. Note that because the `isis network point-to-point` keyword has been configured, only Level-1 passwords are sent.

In IOS you first need to define a `key chain`. Key chains are generic IOS functions used for holding several authentication keys that can be configured for key rollover. Next, you need to configure the `isis authentication mode` and point to a `key chain` using the isis authentication `key-chain` command. Optionally, you can configure a `level` after the two commands. If you omit the `level` keyword then IOS takes the key chain for authenticating both IS-IS levels.

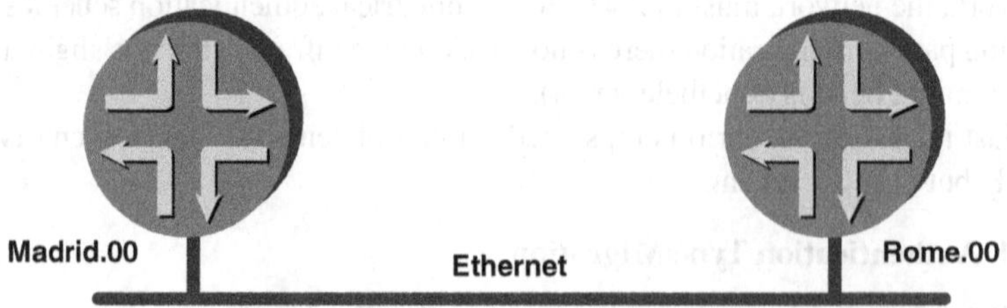

FIGURE 13.6. The simple setup will be used throughout the configuration examples

IOS configuration

```
Madrid#show running-config
[ … ]
key chain MY-INTF-PASSWD
  key 100
    key-string 0 ManInTheM0On
[ … ]
interface GigabitEthernet4/0
  ip address 172.16.34.5 255.255.255.252
  ip router isis
  isis authentication mode md5
  isis authentication key-chain MY-INTF-PASSWD
  isis network point-to-point
!
!
router isis
  net 49.0300.1921.6800.3003.00
[ … ]
```

Now, you need to verify that your IIHs are properly authenticated. If you see debug messages like

```
IIH no change, use the same hmac value
```

then an Authentication TLV #10 containing a HMAC-MD5 value is applied to your outgoing IIHs.

IOS debug output

If the router emits periodical messages like this after turning `debug authentication information` on, then authenticated Hellos are sent.

```
Madrid#debug isis authentication information
IS-IS authentication information debugging is on
Madrid#
Nov 5 00:48:07.233: ISIS-AuthInfo: IIH no change, use the same hmac value
Nov 5 00:48:16.781: ISIS-AuthInfo: IIH no change, use the same hmac value
Nov 5 00:48:24.609: ISIS-AuthInfo: IIH no change, use the same hmac value
```

If your adjacency does not come up due to bogus authentication information then the output of the `debug isis authentication information` reveals what the problem is.

IOS debug output

The output of the `debug isis authentication information command` reveals if there is a password mismatch.

```
Madrid#debug isis authentication information
IS-IS authentication information debugging is on
snail#
Nov 5 00:48:01.011: ISIS-AuthInfo: Packet failed the md5 check, 77 bytes, type 17
```

```
Nov 5 00:48:09.095: ISIS-AuthInfo: Packet failed the md5 check, 77 bytes, type 17
Nov 5 00:48:17.059: ISIS-AuthInfo: Packet failed the md5 check, 77 bytes, type 17
```

From a configuration keyword point of view, the per-level authentication is very similar to the per-interface configuration. The only difference is in what PDU types are authenticated.

13.2.6.2 Per-level Authentication

Applying per-level authentication authenticates all SNP and LSP PDUs on a per-level basis. The keywords are similar to the per-interface configuration.

The configuration example shows a simple text authentication for Level-1 SNP and LSP PDUs and a HMAC-MD5 authentication for Level-2 SNP and LSP PDUs.

IOS configuration

```
Madrid#show running-config
[ … ]
key chain MY-LEVEL1-PASSWD
  key 100
    key-string 0 ObiWanhelpMEyouAREmyLastHope
!
key chain MY-LEVEL2-PASSWD
  key 100
    key-string 0 DoITorDONTdoitThereisnoTry
!
router isis
  net 49.0300.1921.6800.3003.00
  authentication mode text level-1
  authentication mode md5 level-2
  authentication key-chain MY-LEVEL1-PASSWD
  authentication key-chain MY-LEVEL2-PASSWD
  metric-style wide
  passive-interface Loopback0
!
[ … ]
```

If an incoming LSP does not contain proper authentication then the output of the `debug isis authentication information` command will report a `Packet failed the md5 check` message. If you receive PDUs containing no authentication TLV at all then the debug output looks as follows:

IOS debug output

The `No auth TLV found` debug message indicates that no Authentication TLV #10 is present in the PDU.

```
Madrid#debug isis authentication information
IS-IS authentication information debugging is on
```

```
Nov 5 01:50:25.776: ISIS-AuthInfo: No auth TLV found in received packet
Nov 5 01:50:25.848: ISIS-AuthInfo: No auth TLV found in received packet
Nov 5 01:50:25.900: ISIS-AuthInfo: No auth TLV found in received packet
```

13.2.6.3 Suppressing Authentication Checks

In the previous migration strategies there was a need to suppress authentication checking. In IOS suppression can be configured using the `isis authentication send-only` configuration keyword under the interface stanza to suppress IIH checking. For suppressing SNP and LSP checking the `authentication send-only` command is applicable in the `router isis` stanza. Note that the command also suppresses generation of errors in the log file. So you may run the risk that you mask a security hole.

The configuration of authentication on JUNOS is very similar to IOS.

13.2.7 *Running Authentication Using JUNOS*

JUNOS also has two ways of authenticating IS-IS messages: per-interface and per-level configuration. The basic difference is the set of PDU types authenticated. Per-interface authentication authenticates interface Hellos.

13.2.7.1 Per-interface Authentication

Per-interface authentication is applied using the `hello-authentication-key` and `hello-authentication-type` configuration keyword in the `protocols isis interface level <*>` stanza.

JUNOS configuration

The `hello-authentication-key` and `hello-authentication-type` configuration keyword control authentication password and type for IIHs.

```
hannes@Stockholm> show configuration
[ … ]
protocols {
  isis {
    interface ge-4/0/0.0 {
      point-to-point;
      level 1 {
        hello-authentication-key "$9$/tjmCu1SyK7NbApRSeW-dk.PQz6pu1"; #
        ManInTheM0On
        hello-authentication-type md5; # SECRET-DATA
      }
    }
    interface lo0.0;
  }
}
```

13.2.7.2 Per-level Authentication

Unlike Cisco IOS, JUNOS authenticates all three PDU types by default. (Recall Cisco IOS only authenticates LSPs and SNPs). Because JUNOS per-level authentication also authenticates IIHs, this is also a convenient way to do per-interface authentication on a router with many interfaces. (Why only authenticate Hellos?)

JUNOS configuration

The `authentication-key` and `authentication-type` configuration keyword control Authentication-Key and Type for SNPs and LSPs.

```
hannes@Stockholm> show configuration
[ … ]
protocols {
  isis {
    level 1 {
      authentication-key "$9$3qTB/CuRhrKWxvW"; #
       ObiWanhelpMEyouAREmyLastHope
      authentication-type md5; # SECRET-DATA
    }
    level 2 {
      authentication-key "$9$fT390OReK8QFA0IcvMaZUHkPF39"; #
       DoITorDONTdoitThereisnoTry
      authentication-type md5; # SECRET-DATA
    }
    interface lo0.0;
  }
}
```

If the adjacency does not come up, and you suspect an authentication problem, then you need to set up JUNOS `traceoptions`. Bogus authentications are logged with an `error` flag.

JUNOS configuration

If you want to gather evidence that the authentication is broken you need to configure the `traceptions {}` stanza

```
hannes@Stockholm> show configuration
[ … ]
protocols {
  isis {
    traceoptions {
      file isis.log;
      flag error;
    }
  }
}
```

Next you need to check the log file or set up a monitor job that displays any recent additions to the file on the console.

JUNOS debug output

```
hannes@Stockholm> show log isis.log
Nov 5 04:16:02 trace_on: Tracing to "/var/log/isis.log" started
Nov 5 04:16:05 ERROR: LSP authentication failure
Nov 5 04:16:10 ERROR: LSP authentication failure
Nov 5 04:16:15 ERROR: LSP authentication failure
Nov 5 04:16:20 ERROR: LSP authentication failure
```

As you have seen in the migration examples, sometimes suppressing authentication checks is the only transition strategy you have got.

13.2.7.3 Suppressing Authentication Checks

JUNOS offers a single knob for suppressing all IS-IS-related authentication checks per routing instance. So in JUNOS the provisions for asymmetric authentication are much more coarse than in IOS, which allows suppression of authentication on a per-interface and per-level basis.

JUNOS configuration

The `no-authentication-check` reverts the entire IS-IS process so as to not verify any authentication information.

```
hannes@Stockholm> show configuration
[ … ]
protocols {
  isis {
    no-authentication-check;
    level 1 {
      authentication-key "$9$3qTB/CuRhrKWxvW"; #
       ObiWanhelpMEyouAREmyLastHope
      authentication-type md5; # SECRET-DATA
    }
    level 2 {
      authentication-key "$9$fT390OReK8QFA0IcvMaZUHkPF39"; #
       DoITorDONTdoitThereisnoTry
      authentication-type md5; # SECRET-DATA
    }
    interface lo0.0;
  }
}
```

Unfortunately JUNOS does not feature chaining of several authentication keys. In order to transition between authentication keys you need to utilize the `no-authentication-check` knob to turn authentication on and off during a single key transition.

IS-IS was often the routing protocol of choice because of its high multivendor interoperability, which is no surprise, since the specification was lean and well written. However, in the field of authentication, IOS and JUNOS were once not interoperable at all when it came to authentication. That has changed recently, and the next section explores the remaining interoperability caveats.

13.2.8 *Interoperability*

JUNOS supports MD5 and simple text authentication from the start, when the software shipped as JUNOS 3.0. Back in 1998, there was the conviction that authentication always had to apply for all three PDU types (IIHs, SNPs, LSPs). That behaviour did not match the IOS behaviour at that time, which only authenticated LSPs. Optionally IOS also allowed configuration of interface authentication, but that bought authentication of only two out of the three PDU types involved. JUNOS authenticated symmetrically and *expected* authentication also on those PDU types that it *sends* as Authenticated PDUs. This led to a problem, as IOS had no provision to authenticate SNPs – The only workaround was to configure `no-authentication-check` on JUNOS. Juniper Network's engineers were thinking of changing the behaviour, but that was not an option, because changing a default behaviour is always a dangerous thing, and service provider customers are not very happy if their vendor does change defaults very often. So with JUNOS 5.4, new knobs were introduced that suppress the all-PDU authentication styles. The three knobs are:

- `no-hello-authentication`
- `no-csnp-authentication`
- `no-psnp-authentication`

Originally, just a `no-hello-authentication` and `no-snp-authentication` knob was planned, but it turned out that there is IOS software deployed in the field that supports authentication of CSNPs. In order to adapt to any environment, three knobs were released. An older-IOS compatible configuration turns on all three knobs which finally *sends* just authenticated LSPs and also just *expects* LSPs to be authenticated.

JUNOS configuration

The `no-<*>-authentication` knobs are used for adapting any sort of IOS behaviour from past releases.

```
hannes@Stockholm> show configuration
[ ... ]
protocols {
  isis {
    level 1 {
      authentication-key "$9$3qTB/CuRhrKWxvW"; #
       ObiWanhelpMEyouAREmyLastHope
      authentication-type md5; # SECRET-DATA
      no-hello-authentication;
      no-csnp-authentication;
```

```
        no-psnp-authentication;
      }
      level 2 {
        authentication-key "$9$fT390OReK8QFA0IcvMaZUHkPF39"; #
         DoITorDONTdoitThereisnoTry
        authentication-type md5; # SECRET-DATA
        no-hello-authentication;
        no-csnp-authentication;
        no-psnp-authentication;
      }
      interface lo0.0;
    }
}
```

Networking engineers often believe that because IS-IS is still a somewhat "secret" protocol and that this "security by obscurity" works well. Also, no known hacking tools are able to handcraft IS-IS packets. But do not be misled! There *are* packet injection programs around that can handcraft any IS-IS packet (it's just that so far hackers have not used them to attack IS-IS). For example, the Nemesis Project is a toolset suite for crafting routing protocols of all kinds including IS-IS, RIP and OSPF. To learn more about Nemesis check out the Nemesis homepage at http://sourceforge.net/projects/nemesis/. While tools like this may be a threat to networks, it is the authors' opinion that they are useful tools to harden and secure existing networks. Deploying MD5 authentication is imperative when running IS-IS. What still needs to be done on the IETF is adding cryptographic sequence numbers to be robust against *all* sort of attacks.

- A corrupted CSNP may trigger excessive PSNPs and LSPs because the receiver of the broken CSNP thinks there are lots of unknown LSPs that it has to learn about. See Chapter 8, "Synchronizing Databases" for the dynamics of SNPs requesting LSPs.
- About the worst thing that can happen is that the corrupt frame does *not* get detected for the time being. If routing control traffic gets corrupted, then it is also highly likely that user payload traffic may be corrupted too. Most likely customer complaints about bad throughput will hit your desk.

In order to overcome this limitation of the base IS-IS protocol, the IETF has come up with an optional Checksumming TLV which is defined in RFC 3358. The idea of the Checksum TLV is to protect IIHs and SNPs. Figure 13.7 shows the basic structure of the

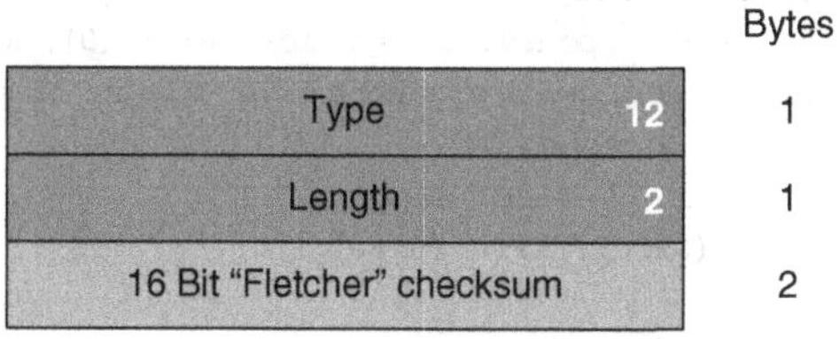

Field	Value	Bytes
Type	12	1
Length	2	1
16 Bit "Fletcher" checksum		2

FIGURE 13.7. The optional Checksum TLV #12 conveys an additional Fletcher Checksum that protects IIHs and SNPs

Checksum TLV. The length of the TLV is always two bytes. The payload is a standard "Fletcher" checksum described in ISO 8473 Annex C, which is calculated over the entire PDU.

As at December 2003 there is no support of the checksumming TLV in IOS. It is only available on JUNOS. Using the `checksum` keyword checksum protection can be activated on a per-interface basis.

JUNOS configuration

The `checksum` keyword in the `protocols isis interface configuration` stanza causes to send and verify the contents of TLV #12 on IIHs and SNPs.

```
hannes@Frankfurt# show configuration
[ … ]
  isis {
    interface so-1/2/0.0 {
      checksum;
      level 1 {
        hello-interval 10;
        hold-time 40;
      }
    }
    [ … ]
    interface lo0.0;
  }
}
```

After configuring and committing your configuration, you should see the additional checksum TLVs in the tcpdump output.

Tcpdump output

The Checksum TLV #12 augments the missing Checksum field in the IIH and SNP headers.

```
21:06:57.889875 OSI, IS-IS, length: 78
  L2 Lan IIH, hlen: 27, v: 1, pdu-v: 1, sys-id-len: 6 (0), max-area: 3 (0)
    source-id: 1921.6800.1008, holding time: 120s, Flags: [Level 1, Level 2]
    circuit-id: 0x01, PDU length: 78
      Protocols supported TLV #129, length: 2
        NLPID(s): IPv4 (0xcc), IPv6 (0x8e)
      [ … ]
      Checksum TLV #12, length: 2
        checksum: 0xbfb0 (correct)
```

```
21:17:30.950224 OSI, IS-IS, length: 135
  L2 CSNP, hlen: 33, v: 1, pdu-v: 1, sys-id-len: 6 (0), max-area: 3 (0)
    source-id:       0000.0000.0002.00, PDU length: 135
    start lsp-id:    0000.0000.0000.00-00
    end lsp-id: ffff.ffff.ffff.ff-ff
      Checksum TLV #12, length: 2
        checksum: 0x2d8f (correct)
      LSP entries TLV #9, length: 96
        lsp-id: 1921.6800.1017.00-00, seq: 0x000001a8, lifetime:
         63177s, chksum: 0xebb1
```

13.3 Checksums for Non-LSP PDUs

Almost all kinds of networking protocols protect their message content with *checksums*. Protecting messages through a checksum follows a simple recipe. Both the sender and the receiver of a message have to rely on a common way to build the checksum, the checksum *algorithm*. Popular checksum algorithms are CRC16, CRC32 and, for IS-IS, the ISO X.233/ISO 8473-1 "Fletcher" checksum. Each of these checksum algorithms has different properties. What they have in common is that all of them can detect at least one *bit error*. While the primary purpose of checksums is to detect bit errors, some algorithms, for example, try additionally to balance the proportion of zeros and ones in a message to *help* the transmission devices not to lose clock synchronization. Note that all modern communication infrastructure devices have extra payload scramblers before putting the bit-stream on the wire, so higher layers do not need to care if the frame contains a healthy proportion of zeros and ones any longer.

This section focuses just on the error-detecting properties of checksum algorithms and will not further discuss *other* applications like zero and one balancing. The checksum procedure works very simply.

First, the field in the message where the checksum is stored needs to be initialized to a common value, typically zero. Next, the sender and the receiver need to agree what *part* of the message needs to be protected. Typically, it is the entire frame excluding Layer-2 encapsulation like MAC addresses or PPP headers. In IS-IS the *LSP checksum* does not encompass the entire PDU. The checksumming starts at an offset of 12 bytes relative to the beginning of the IS-IS common header. This was done to exclude fields like the LSP Age, which may be subject to local time drift.

Finally, the checksum is calculated and inserted at the previously zeroed position.

The receiver needs to perform the checksum operation in a similar way: First, save the received checksum for later comparison. Set the original checksum position to zero. Next, calculate the checksum based on the agreed parts of the frame with the same algorithms that is typically defined in the protocol's specification. Finally, compare the *self-calculated* checksum to the previously saved *original* checksum that was received with the frame. If the two checksums match, then pass the frame on for further processing. If they do not match, discard the frame and increment a counter telling the operator that there must be something wrong. *Not* protecting routing protocol messages via checksums is a bad idea because it does not give the receiver a chance to differentiate between good and corrupted messages.

13.3.1 *PDUs Missing Checksum?*

IS-IS uses a total of five different PDU types (actually, there are nine, but some share the format like dedicated Level 1 and Level 2 PDUs). Take a look at those five PDU headers illustrated in Figure 13.8. Only one PDU type, the LSP, contains a Checksum field. All the other PDU types are not *protected* by a Checksum field.

Serious harm can result if a corrupt message is not recognized as such. Consider (for example) an adjacency between two routers. Now suppose a few bits in the arriving frame got flipped by (for example) a transmission problem. Depending on what TLVs are corrupted, the adjacency could be at best torn down or, worst, corrupted information is conveyed, as these examples show:

An adjacency that is reportedly in the *Up* state could be perceived to be in the *Down* state due to corruption of the Adjacency State TLV #240. The result is a broken adjacency which will trigger a new LSP which is flooded network-wide.

```
lsp-id: 1921.6800.1012.00-00, seq: 0x0000003c, lifetime: 64166s, chksum: 0x0e2b
lsp-id: 1921.6800.1019.00-00, seq: 0x000001a2, lifetime: 62579s, chksum: 0xba03
lsp-id: 1921.6800.1021.00-00, seq: 0x00000d31, lifetime: 63277s, chksum: 0x1dc4
lsp-id: 1921.6800.1008.00-00, seq: 0x00000124, lifetime: 61291s, chksum: 0xb30f
lsp-id: 1921.6800.1022.00-00, seq: 0x00000117, lifetime: 63277s, chksum: 0x5acf
```

The use of the Checksum TLV is optional. The only place where the specification is firm is that as soon as a receiver supports the Checksum TLV and the checksum is corrupt, it must discard the frame. RFC 3358 also discusses the case of a "checksumming collision". The collision of checksum occurs if both HMAC-MD5 authentication *and* checksumming is configured on an interface. HMAC-MD5 is nothing more than a very wide checksum under the inclusion of a shared secret. Which checksumming function should be prioritized? One of the rules of TLV encoding is that each TLV is independent of any other. In the authentication/checksumming case, the order does matter and would be a violation to that requirement. Final consensus was either to suppress or set the value of the Checksum TLV #12 to zero once the router knows that HMAC-MD5 authentication needs to be added to PDU. This is an acceptable behaviour, and is the mindset of many network engineers that HMAC-MD5 is nothing but a big *checksum* that makes sure that multiple bit flips get detected, which conventional checksumming methods are not capable of, so there is no problem there. A 128-bit *checksum* is simply stronger than a 16-bit one. The tcpdump output shows occurrence of both an Authentication TLV #10 and a Checksumming TLV #12 in an IIH message. Note that the contents of the Checksum TLV are set to zero, which is an indication that the receiver does not need to attempt to verify it. Also, one interesting side effect of the Fletcher sum is that it can never be zero. Zero is therefore a clear indication of an exception.

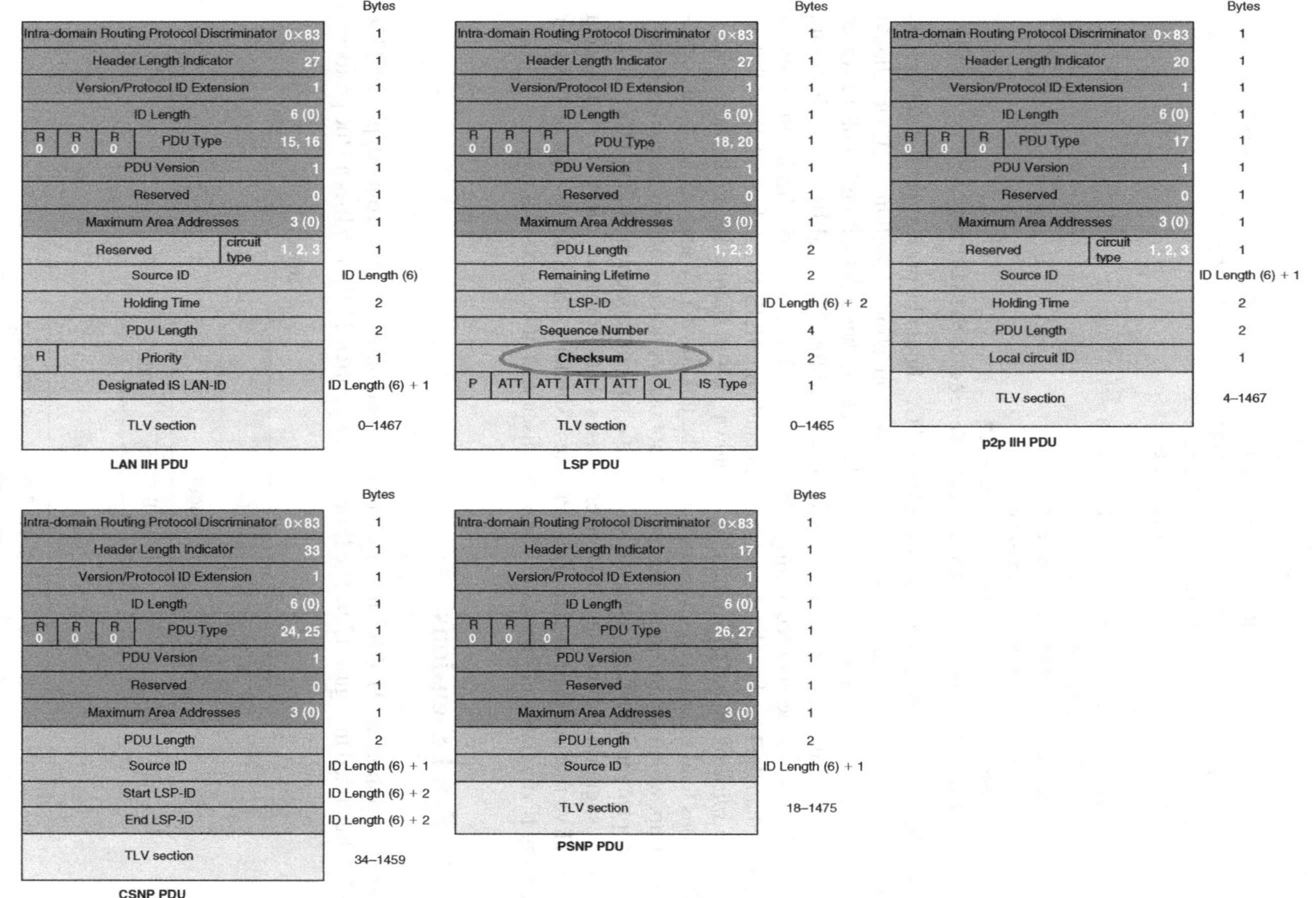

FIGURE 13.8. Only the LSP PDU is protected by a 16-bit Checksum field

Tcpdump output

```
23:55:58.367717 OSI, IS-IS, length: 97
  L1 Lan IIH, hlen: 27, v: 1, pdu-v: 1, sys-id-len: 6 (0), max-area: 3 (0)
    source-id: 0000.0000.0003, holding time: 40s, Flags: [Level 1, Level 2]
    lan-id:      0000.0000.0003.02, Priority: 64, PDU length: 97
      Protocols supported TLV #129, length: 2
        NLPID(s): IPv4 (0xcc), IPv6 (0x8e)
      [ … ]
      Restart Signaling TLV #211, length: 3
        Flags [none], Remaining holding time 0s
      Checksum TLV #12, length: 2
        checksum: 0x0000 (unverified)
      Authentication TLV #10, length: 17
        HMAC-MD5 password: 887d36216cc6b0c842b1b25a1b11880d
```

It is the authors' opinion that the Checksum TLV should be present per default in IIHs and SNPs if no authentication or simple text authentication is configured. Users should not need to configure it as they do now. It should be rather a default option of the router OS. Once HMAC-MD5 authentication is configured for SNPs and IIHs, the Checksum TLV #12 should be omitted entirely because the 128-bit MD5 checksum is much stronger than the Fletcher checksum. Unfortunately not all IS-IS implementations follow the *open spirit* of ISO 10589 where an unknown TLV is silently ignored. Those implementations tend to log error messages about the unknown TLV and refuse to take adjacencies up, which left the implementers with not many choices and causes contemporary IS-IS implementation to be as gentle as possible with introduction of new TLVs.

IS-IS is ignorant of the Network Layer prefixes that it transports. RFC 1195 defined a set of TLVs that are used to carry IPv4 Prefixes. Similarly, IS-IS needs a set of TLVs for carrying IPv6 related information. These are discussed in the next section.

13.4 IPv6 Extensions

The most important TLV for multi-protocol operation is the Protocols Supported TLV #129, illustrated in Figure 13.9. The Protocols Supported TLV #129 lists all the protocols

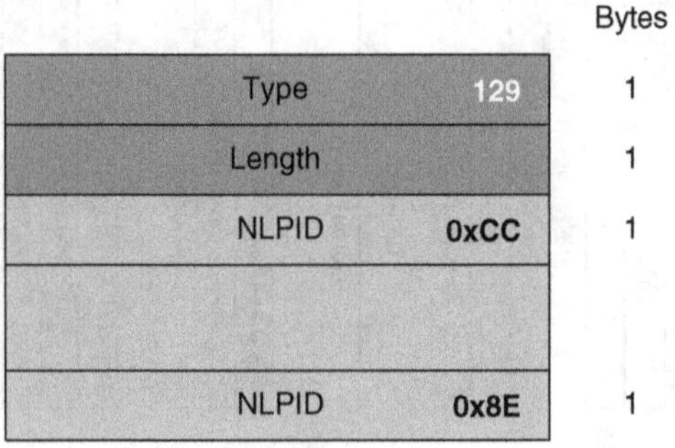

Field	Value	Bytes
Type	129	1
Length		1
NLPID	**0xCC**	1
NLPID	**0x8E**	1

FIGURE 13.9. The Protocols Supported TLV #129 lists all protocols that the router supports

that an individual router supports. This TLV is found both in IIHs and LSPs. However, it will be shown later that the inclusion of this TLV in the router's LSP is a next to useless exercise. The TLV contains a list of one-byte Network Layer Protocol ID (NLPID). Each major Network Protocol has an NLPID assigned. In modern networks, you will most likely see the NLPID for IPv4 (= 0xCC), CLNS (= 0x81) or IPv6 (= 0x8E).

The IPv6 extensions are specified in draft-ietf-isis-ipv6-06. This Internet draft mentions two TLVs which are aligned to their IPv4 counterparts, but just bigger in size. A nice touch of the IS-IS WG was to emphasize this similarity by picking a similar number for this TLV. Figure 13.10 illustrates the IPv6 Interface TLV #232. The TLV shares the semantics of its little sibling, the IPv4 Address TLV #132 that is described in Chapter 5, "Neighbour Discovery and Handshaking", in Figure 5.14.

The TLV holds one or several IPv6 addresses that are assigned on the sending interface. Hence the TLV is in multiples of 16 bytes. Typically only a single address, the IPv6 link-local address, is conveyed.

Surprisingly, there is not much to configure in order to run IPv6 over IS-IS. Configuring an IPv6 Address and activating the IS-IS on that interface is enough. The router starts to send IIHs that contain the IPv6 address on that interface, plus the IPv6 NLPID in the Protocol Supported TLV #129. The tcpdump output highlights the IPv6 additions.

Tcpdump output

```
23:55:58.367717 OSI, IS-IS, length: 72
  L1 Lan IIH, hlen: 27, v: 1, pdu-v: 1, sys-id-len: 6 (0), max-area: 3 (0)
    source-id: 1921.6800.1008, holding time: 40s, Flags: [ L1L2 IS]
    lan-id:      1921.6800.1008.02, Priority: 64, PDU length: 72
      Protocols supported TLV #129, length: 2
        NLPID(s): IPv4 (0xcc), IPv6 (0x8e)
      [ ... ]
      IPv4 Interface address(es) TLV #132, length: 4
        IPv4 interface address: 172.16.33.237
      IPv6 Interface address(es) TLV #232, length: 16
        IPv6 interface address: fe80::7777:69ff:fea0:8001
      Area address(es) TLV #1, length: 4
        Area address (length: 3): 49.0001
```

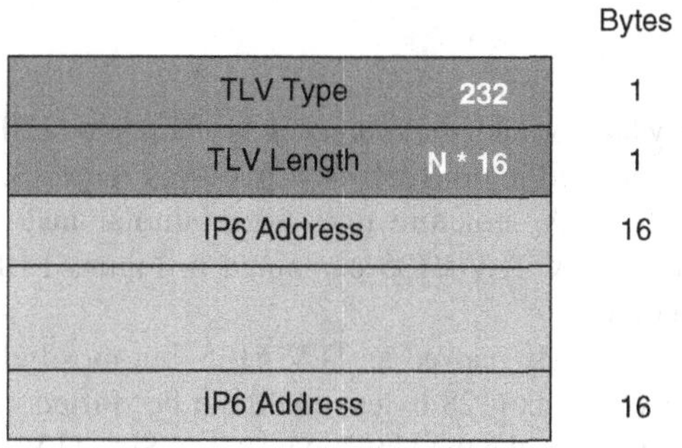

	Bytes
TLV Type 232	1
TLV Length N * 16	1
IP6 Address	16
IP6 Address	16

FIGURE 13.10. The IPv6 Interface Address #232 shares similar semantics to the IPv4 Interface Address TLV #132

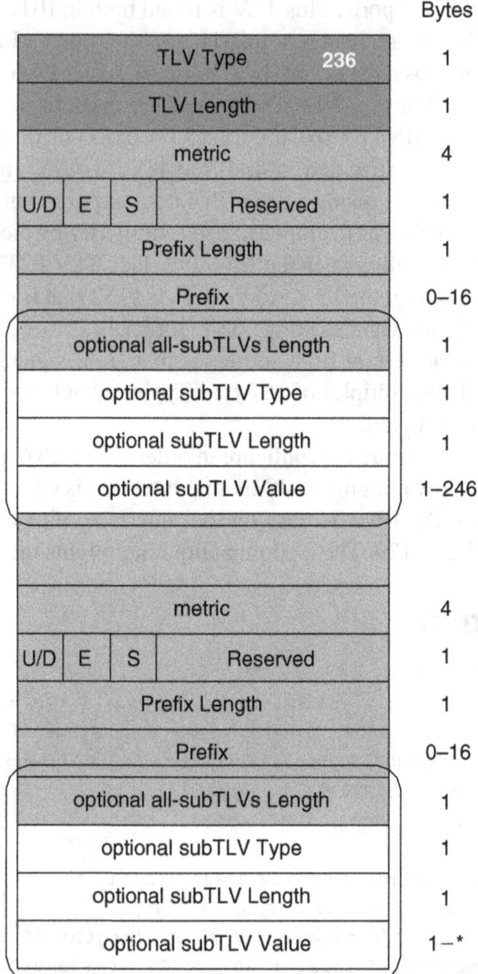

FIGURE 13.11. The IPv6 Reachability TLV #236 took the Extended IPv4 Reachability TLV #135 as its blueprint

After the adjacency has formed, the router sends an updated LSP that contains the second IPv6 TLV that is defined in draft-ietf-isis-ipv6-06. Figure 13.11 illustrates the IPv6 Reachability TLV. The TLV structure does seem similar and is borrowed from the Extended IPv4 Reachability TLV #135 explained in Figure 12.11 of Chapter 12, "IP Reachability Information".

TLV #236 is not as densely packed as TLV #135, but mostly because the maximum prefix length of an IPv6 prefix (128 bytes) could not be stuffed into a single byte along with the Flag bit information like the Up/Down bit and Sub-TLV Indicator bit. Tcpdump output is shown below for the IPv6 Reachability TLV.

Tcpdump output

```
01:15:43.232457 OSI, IS-IS, length: 182
  L2 LSP, hlen: 27, v: 1, pdu-v: 1, sys-id-len: 6 (0), max-area: 3 (0)
    lsp-id: 1921.6800.1008.00-00, seq: 0x00000033, lifetime: 65530s
    chksum: 0xdde3 (correct), PDU length: 182, Flags: [ L1L2 IS ]
      Area address(es) TLV #1, length: 4
        Area address (length: 3): 49.0001
      Protocols supported TLV #129, length: 2
        NLPID(s): IPv4 (0xcc), IPv6 (0x8e)
      [ … ]
      IPv6 Reachability TLV #236, length: 22
        IPv6 prefix: 2001:600::3/128, Distribution: up, Metric: 0, Internal,
         no sub-TLVs
      Extended IS Reachability TLV #22, length: 17
        IS Neighbor: 1921.6800.1021.00, Metric: 250000, sub-TLVs present (6)
          IPv4 interface address subTLV #6, length: 4, 172.16.33.237
```

In the following two sections there will be IPv6 configuration examples for both IOS and JUNOS.

13.4.1 *IOS Configuration*

In IOS the configuration is aligned to the IPv4 style: configuring an IP address and activating IS-IS on the router is enough. For IPv6, the `ipv6 address` and the `ipv6 router isis` configuration command include the IPv6 prefix in the router's link-state database and rebuilds the router's LSP.

IOS configuration

For including an IPv6 Address in IS-IS all you need to do is configure the `ipv6 router isis` keyword in the interface stanza.

```
London# show running-config
[ … ]
interface FastEthernet0/0
  [ … ]
  ipv6 address 2001:708:0:FF19::1/64
  ipv6 router isis
!
```

Next you may want to verify that the prefix gets installed in the link-state database.

IOS command output

You need to spot on IPv6 prefixes in the `show isis database` detail output.

```
London#show isis database detail

IS-IS Level-2 LSP
LSPID                LSP            LSP          LSP Holdtime      ATT/P/OL
                      Seq Num        Checksum
Frankfurt.00-00      0x00000023     0xBA64       3555              0/0/0
  Area Address:        49.0001
  NLPID:               0xCC 0x8E
  Router ID:           192.168.1.8
  IP Address:          192.168.1.8
  Hostname:      Frankfurt
  Metric: 250000         IS-Extended Washington.00
  [ ... ]
  Metric: 250000 IPv6 2001:708:0:FF19::2/64
  [ ... ]
```

Finally you need to check if the route made its way in the IPv6 routing table.

IOS command output

The show ipv6 route isis command limits the output to the isis installed routes.

```
London# show ipv6 route isis
IPv6 Routing Table - 9 entries
Codes: C - Connected, L - Local, S - Static, R - RIP, B - BGP
        U - Per-user Static route
        I1 - ISIS L1, I2 - ISIS L2, IA - ISIS interarea
        O - OSPF intra, OI - OSPF inter, OE1 - OSPF ext 1, OE2 - OSPF ext 2
I2 2001:708:0:FF19::2/64 [115/13]
  via FE80::2A0:A5FF:FE12:3398, GigabitEthernet2/0
  [ ... ]
```

The JUNOS configuration is similar, but simpler than the IOS configuration.

13.4.2 *JUNOS Configuration*

In JUNOS you need to configure two different stanzas. First, you need to configure the IPv6 address on a logical interface. Next, you add "family ISO" in order to be able to exchange IS-IS PDUs over that link. Finally, that interface is added to the interface list that the IS-IS router builds when IS-IS is enabled.

JUNOS configuration

As soon as family inet6 is configured on a referenced iso interface JUNOS starts to announce IPv6 Reachability Information.

```
hannes@Frankfurt> show configuration
[ … ]
interfaces {
  so-1/2/0.0 {
    unit 0 {
      [ … ]
      family iso;
      family inet6 {
        address 2001:708:0:FF19::2/64;
      }
    }
  }
}
protocols {
  isis {
    interface so-0/1/2.0;
  }
}
```

JUNOS command output

IP6 Reachability Information are indicated by the `V6 prefix` string of the `show isis database detail` operational command output.

```
hannes@Frankfurt> show isis database detail
[ ... ]
Frankfurt.00-00 Sequence: 0x23, Checksum: 0xba64, Lifetime: 3433 secs
  IS neighbor:                              Washington.00 Metric:      250000
  [ … ]
  V6 prefix: 2001:708:0:FF19::2/64 Metric:    0 Internal Up
```

Finally you can verify if the route was installed in the main routing table. You can display the route using the show route table inet6.0 operational level command.

JUNOS command output

The `show route table inet6.0 protocol isis` limits the output to isis installed routes.

```
hannes@Frankfurt> show route table inet6.0 protocol isis

inet6.0: 5 destinations, 5 routes (5 active, 0 holddown, 0 hidden)
+ = Active Route, - = Last Active, * = Both

2001:708:0:FF19::2 *[IS-IS/18] 00:24:29, metric 15 > to
                    fe80::203:fdff:fec8:3c00 via so-1/2/0.0
```

So far it was assumed that the router is running IPv4 and IPv6 in *dual* mode. Dual mode is a term borrowed from RFC 1195 which means that two protocols share a single SPF topology calculation and there is an assumption that the topology is *congruent*. That assumption may not be always correct, and there are scenarios where the dual assumption breaks even simple things like adjacency formation.

13.4.3 *Deployment Scenarios*

RFC 1195 introduced the Protocol Supported TLV #129. The TLV is used for two purposes:

- Convey the supported protocols during adjacency formation in IIHs
- Convey the supported protocols for SPF pruning in IIHs

During adjacency formation, both routers verify that they have a common set of protocols on a link. The reason is simple: if one side supports IPv6 only and the other side supports IPv4 only then there is no reason to let the adjacency go Up. That behaviour violates ISO 10589, which mandates that adjacency formation should be decoupled from any Network Layer reachability protocol. However, the deployed reality moves things into a different perspective. If there is no common Network Layer protocol then the system does not let the adjacency come Up. Figure 13.12 illustrates why there are good reasons to do so.

On almost all links in the network in the figure, both IPv4 and IPv6 are supported. But the link between London and Frankfurt is misconfigured. London only runs IPv6 and Frankfurt only runs IPv4. Assume for a moment that the routers comply with the spirit of ISO 10589 and then the adjacency between London and Frankfurt goes Up. From Washington's perspective, the shortest path to London is now via Frankfurt (1). However, if traffic is relayed via Frankfurt then it gets sent back because from Frankfurt's perspective the way back to Washington is the shortest path. A routing loop is created.

The JUNOS and IOS implementation of IS-IS both offer protection from such faults. However, they cannot protect from every fault. Consider what happens if London additionally activates IPv4 on its link to Frankfurt. Because the adjacency does find a common protocol, which is IPv4, it takes the adjacency Up. Unfortunately the problem still persists. There is a routing loop for traffic from Washington to London. More restrictive adjacency management (for example) could mandate that all NLPIDs inside the Protocols Supported TLV #129 need to match – however, that might be highly disruptive when, for example, another Network Layer protocol is added.

The problem is that there is no way for the IS-IS router to tell remote routers that the underlying link does not support IPv6. That implies that all links need to carry both IPv4 and IPv6. That raises the question if it is necessary to upgrade a network from IPv4 to IPv6 all at once on a *flag day*. We want to discourage any flag day transitions – in our professional careers, the authors have *never*, ever seen a flag-day migration that worked well. Typically what has happened, even in the best-planned migrations, is that one hour before that maintenance window closes, all the changes have to be undone because of persistent problems in the network. Even if a decision to go forward was made, then there were creeping errors in the entire network for the next few days. We still are not sure if these experiences are related to flaky routing software, or if it is just a fact that Murphy's Law always bites on flag days.

There are two approaches to IPv6 and the *flag day* problem:

- change the protocols and make the SPF calculation aware of a link that supports IPv6
- deploy IPv6 based on a "convex" topology

Changing the underlying protocols to support several SPF calculations is an approach that is described in the "Multi Topology Extensions" after this section. We focus here on

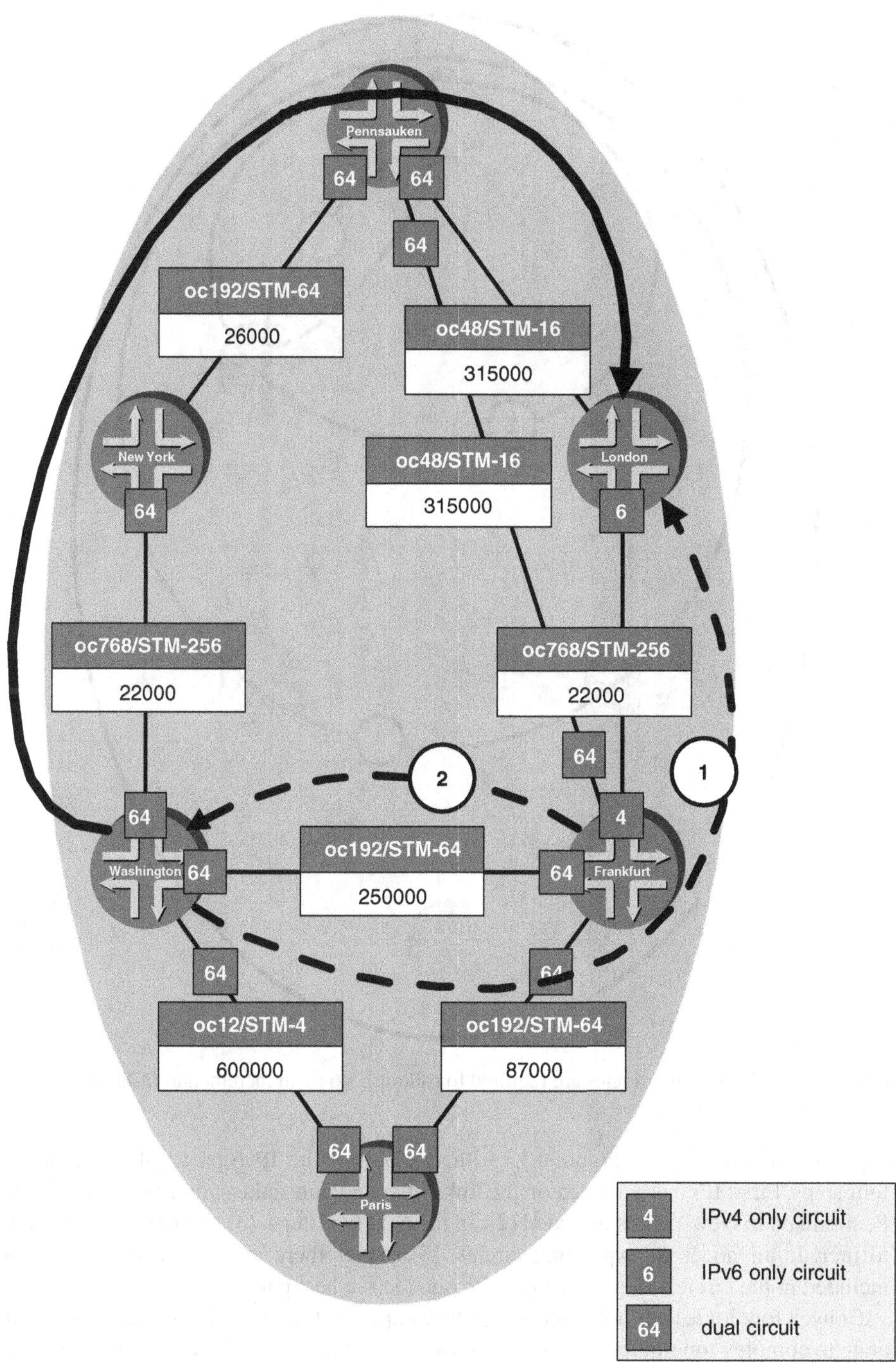

FIGURE 13.12. Protocol dependent adjacency management is imperative to avoid routing loops

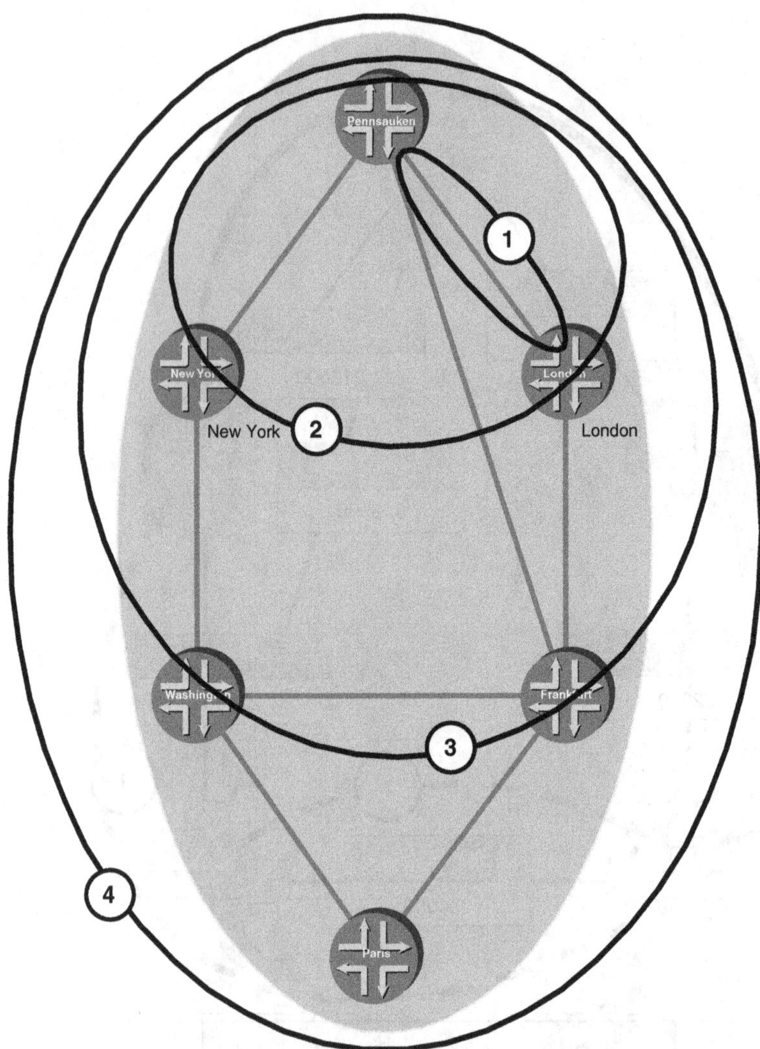

FIGURE 13.13. Convex topologies are required to rollout IPv6 in an incremental fashion

deploying a *convex style*. Figure 13.13 illustrates how the IPv6 protocol is enabled in four steps. First, IPv6 is activated on the link between Pennsauken and London (1). Next, Pennsauken to New York is included (2). In the next two steps, (3) and (4), it is important to include all nodes in expanding circles. Whenever there is a mesh, it needs to be included in the circle, otherwise it may be outside the best path.

Convex topologies are not always easy to compute (at least not for humans). In moderate to complex topologies it is recommended to let the router figure out where the link topology can carry IPv6 and where it can not. A similar problem exists for IPv4 unicast topologies. There are links and nodes that do support multicast processing and others that do not. For learning about the per-protocol processing capabilities of an IS-IS network the IETF has defined the multi topology extensions.

13.5 Multi Topology Extensions

The IGP evaluates all the paths in a *single* topology per level and selects by means of the SPF algorithm the *best* path among all the feasible paths. Topology discovery and SPF calculation is carried out in a *protocol neutral* fashion because it is done at the OSI-RM Layer 2. If we load the topology with a certain protocol (for example IP) reachability information then the assumption is that the circuits that are supposed to provide reachability between routers can also carry the respective protocol. Since the first IP migrations, it was clear to the ISP community that a new paradigm was needed in order to avoid flag-day style migrations. What is necessary to get around the assumptions of RFC 1195 is a proper per-address family orientation rather than a pure per-link orientation. As a result of that, a per-protocol SPF calculation is required also, which means additional CPU load. Today multiple SPF runs are easy to do because plenty of processing power is available on router control plane CPUs.

The multi topology extensions remodel existing TLVs and augment them with a so-called Topology ID. Each router in a given topology maintains its adjacencies and runs a per-topology SPF calculation. A topology is the set of joined nodes. The specification mentions a list of well-known topologies, which are:

- IPv4 Unicast (#0)
- In-Band Management (#1)
- IPv6 Unicast (#2)
- Multicast (#3)
- IETF Consensus (#4-#3995)
- Experimental (#3996-#4095)

We will focus here on the IPv4 and IPv6 Unicast topology. Consider Figure 13.14. The black lines indicate link membership in the IPv6 topology. And the gray line indicates membership to the IPv4 topology. Note that the two topologies are neither congruent nor convex.

Using regular TLVs, it would not be possible to build multiple topologies and run an SPF calculation based on it. The multi topology extensions first describe an extension to carry the set of supported protocols in the Hello. Figure 13.15 shows the structure of the Topology Supported TLV #229, which is a vector of 12-bit wide Topology IDs. After activating multi topology support on a link, it should carry all the topologies that the underlying circuit is able to relay. The tcpdump output shows a IIH after multi topology activation.

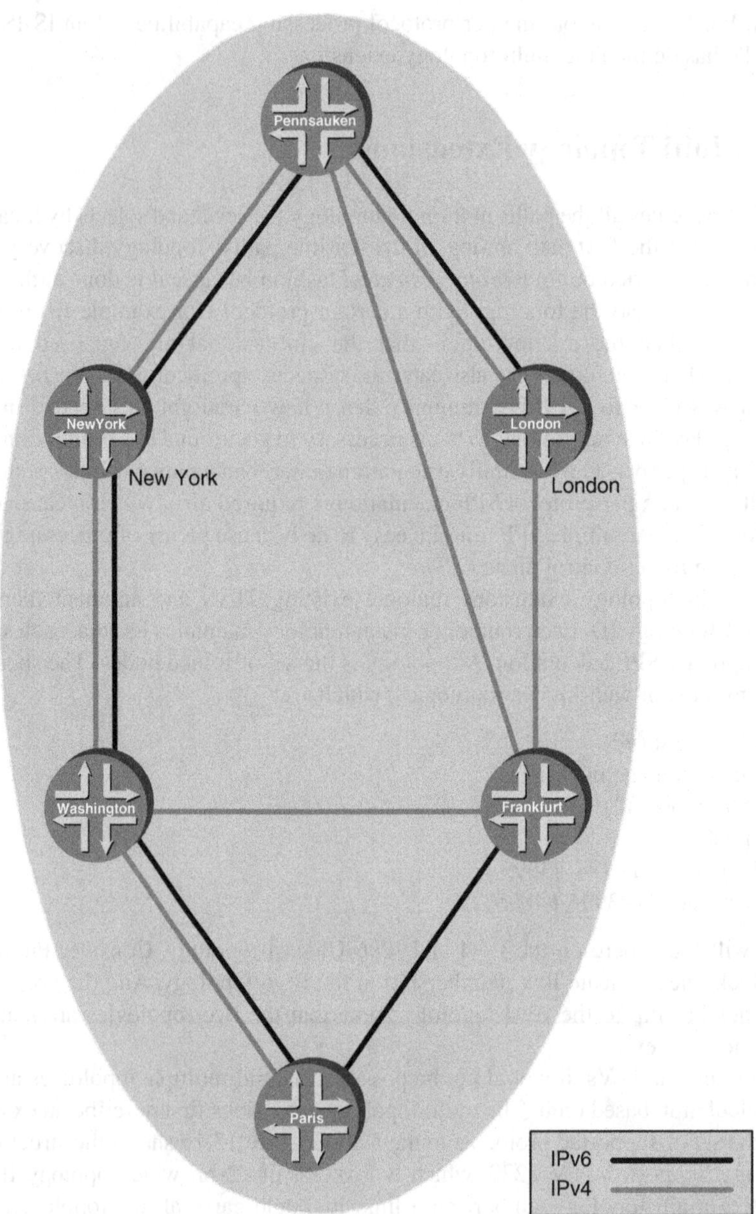

FIGURE 13.14. For each network topology a dedicated IS Reach is mesh processed

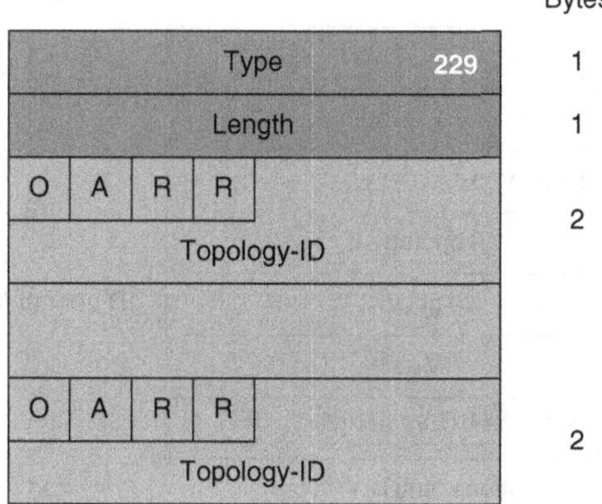

FIGURE 13.15. The Topologies Supported TLV #229 lists the topologies that the link carries

Tcpdump output

The Multi Topology Supported TLV reports that this link can be a member of both the IPv4 Unicast (0) and the IPv6 Unicast (2) Topology.

```
02:00:08.223369 Out OSI, IS-IS, length: 82
  p2p IIH, hlen: 20, v: 1, pdu-v: 1, sys-id-len: 6 (0), max-area: 3 (0)
    source-id: 1921.6800.1027, holding time: 27s, circuit-id: 0x01, Flags: [ L1L2 IS ]
    circuit-id: 0x01, PDU length: 82
      Point-to-point Adjacency State TLV #240, length: 15
        Adjacency State: Up
        Extended Local circuit ID: 0x00000001
        Neighbor SystemID: 1921.6800.1008
        Neighbor Extended Local circuit ID: 0x00000100
      Protocols supported TLV #129, length: 2
        NLPID(s): IPv4, IPv6
      IPv4 Interface address(es) TLV #132, length: 4
        IPv4 interface address: 172.16.33.213
      IPv6 Interface address(es) TLV #232, length: 16
        IPv6 interface address: fe80::2a0:a5ff:fe12:3398
      Area address(es) TLV #1, length: 4
        Area address (length: 3): 49.0001
      Restart Signaling TLV #211, length: 3
        Restart Request bit clear, Restart Acknowledgement bit clear
        Remaining holding time: 0s
      Multi Topology TLV #229, length: 4
        IPv4 unicast Topology (0x000), Flags: [none]
        IPv6 unicast Topology (0x002), Flags: [none]
```

The IIH reports that it can run IPv4 and IPv6. It lists valid IPv4 and IPv6 addresses and therefore the router can create valid next-hop entries. So the protocols are listed in the MT Topology TLV #229.

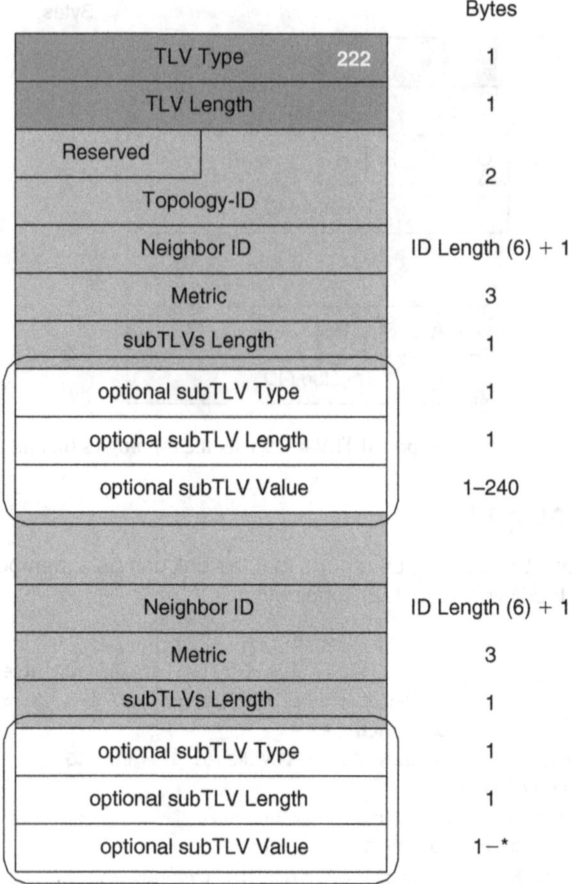

FIGURE 13.16. The Multi Topology IS Reachability TLV #222 is similar to the Extended IS Reachability TLV #22

Each router advertises an adjacency for a common topology adjacency using the Multi Topology IS-Reachability TLV #222 (see Figure 13.16).

Tcpdump output

```
02:10:39.192433 OSI, IS-IS, length: 151
  L1 LSP, hlen: 27, v: 1, pdu-v: 1, sys-id-len: 6 (0), max-area: 3 (0)
    lsp-id: 1921.6800.1027.00-00, seq: 0x00000050, lifetime: 1199s
    chksum: 0x1477 (correct), PDU length: 151, Flags: [ L1L2 IS ]
      [ ... ]
      Multi Topology TLV #229, length: 4
        IPv4 unicast Topology (0x000), Flags: [none]
        IPv6 unicast Topology (0x002), Flags: [none]
      Protocols supported TLV #129, length: 2
```

```
    NLPID(s): IPv4 (0xcc), IPv6 (0x8e)
  [ ... ]
  Multi-Topology IP6 Reachability TLV #237, length: 16
    IPv6 unicast Topology (0x002), Flags: [none]
    IPv6 prefix: 2001:708:0:ff19::/64, Distribution: up, Metric: 250000, Internal
  Multi Topology IS Reachability TLV #222, length: 13
    IPv6 unicast Topology (0x002), Flags: [none]
    IS Neighbor: 1921.6800.1008.00, Metric: 250000, no sub-TLVs present
```

The tcpdump output also shows that the link IPv6 prefix is not encapsulated in the IP6 Reachability TLV #236, but rather in the Multi Topology IP6 Reachability TLV #237. The structure of that TLV is illustrated in Figure 13.17.

TLV #237 almost looks identical and also shares the semantics of the IP6 Reach TLV. The only difference is that it gets prepended with the 12-bit Topology ID. A similar clone for the Extended IPv4 Reachability #135 exists, which is the MT IPv4 Reachability TLV #235, as illustrated in Figure 13.18.

For the default Topology #0 there is already an IPv4 Reachability TLV, which is #135 hence the usage of the TLV #235 is highly questionable in Topology #0. However, in other IPv4 related topologies such as the IPv4 multicast topology, usage of the MT IPv4 Reach TLV #235 does make sense.

13.5.1 *JUNOS Configuration*

Per JUNOS 6.2 the multi topology extensions are available. The configuration is a "one-liner" which turns on multi topology support on all interfaces that have `family iso` and `family inet6` configured and are listed in the `protocols isis interface {}` stanza. If you do not want to run multi topology support for a given Topology /Adress Family on a given interface, then you can disable multi topology generation by configuring `no-ipv6-unicast` or `no-ipv6-unicast` under the `protocols isis interface {}` stanza.

JUNOS configuration

The `topologies ipv6-unicast` configuration string turns on MT generation on all interfaces. The `no-ipv6-unicast` command under the `protocols isis interface` stanza disables MT generation for the IPv6 topology.

```
hannes@Frankfurt> show configuration
[ ... ]
protocols {
  isis {
    topologies ipv6-unicast;
    [ ... ]
    interface fe-0/3/3.0 {
      no-ipv6-unicast;
    }
    interface lo.0;
  }
}
```

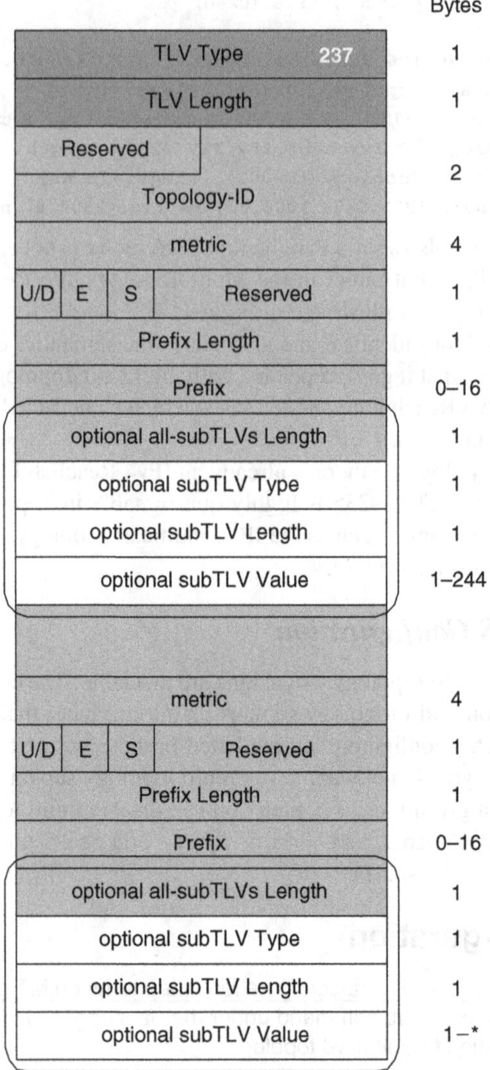

FIGURE 13.17. The Multi Topology IPv6 Reachability TLV #237 shares the semantics of the IP6 Reachability TLV #236

Next you need to verify if your neighbour also supports multi topology. This gets revealed in the `show isis adjacency` command output.

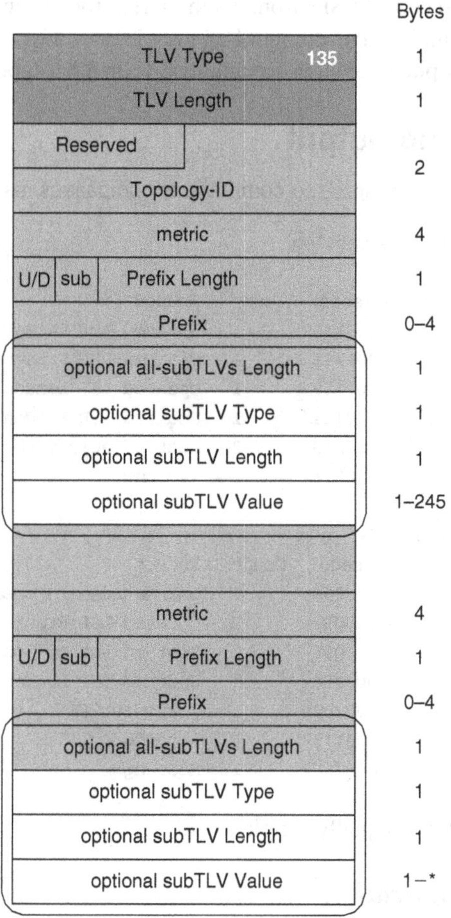

FIGURE 13.18. The Multi Topology IPv4 Reachability TLV #235 shares the semantics of the Extended IP Reachability TLV #135

JUNOS command output

The neighbour also supports multi topology for the IPv6 Unicast topology.

```
hannes@Frankfurt> show isis adjacency detail
[ … ]
London
  Interface: so-1/2/0.0, Level: 2, State: Up, Expires in 23 secs
  Priority: 0, Up/Down transitions: 11, Last transition: 00:24:12 ago
  Circuit type: 3, Speaks: IP, IPv6
  Topologies: Unicast, IPV6-Unicast
  Restart capable: Yes
  IP addresses: 172.16.33.29
  IPv6 addresses: fe80::203:fdff:fec8:3c00
  [ … ]
```

The router has now received LSPs from neighbouring routers and processed them in a per-protocol SPF calculation. The output of all the `show isis spf <*>` commands has changed. It now displays the statistics and results on a per-topology breakdown.

JUNOS command output

The output of the `show isis spf log` command encompasses results for each topology.

```
hannes@Frankfurt> show isis spf log
IS-IS level 2 SPF log:
Start time             Elapsed (secs)  Count   Reason
Fri Nov 7 01:58:29          0.000120       1   Updated LSP Paris.00-00
Fri Nov 7 01:58:33          0.000141       1   Updated LSP Frankfurt. 00-00
Fri Nov 7 01:58:38          0.000118       1   Updated LSP London.00-00
Fri Nov 7 01:59:54          0.000114       1   Updated LSP London.00-00
Fri Nov 7 01:59:59          0.000219       2   Lost adjacency London on so-1/2/0.0
Fri Nov 7 02:45:22          0.000084       1   Reconfig

IPV6 Unicast IS-IS level 2 SPF log:
Start time             Elapsed (secs)  Count   Reason
Fri Nov 7 01:58:15          0.000066       7   Lost adjacency Pennsauken on so-7/0/0.0
Fri Nov 7 01:58:16          0.000095       2   Updated LSP Frankfurt. 00-00
Fri Nov 7 01:58:19          0.000098       1   Lost adjacency London on so-1/2/0.0
Fri Nov 7 01:59:54          0.000084       1   Updated LSP London.00-00
Fri Nov 7 02:23:46          0.000202       1   Periodic SPF
Fri Nov 7 02:34:45          0.000113       1   Reconfig
Fri Nov 7 02:45:22          0.000267       1   Reconfig
```

The configuration in IOS is equally simple.

13.5.2 *IOS Configuration*

IOS now supports per-address family configuration. By configuring the `multi-topology` command under the `address-family ipv6` stanza, multi topology support is turned on all interfaces that have the `ipv6 router isis` command listed.

IOS configuration

```
London# show running-config
[ ... ]
router isis
  net 49.0001.1921.6800.1012.00
  metric-style wide
  passive-interface Loopback0
  !
  address-family ipv6
  multi-topology
  exit-address-family
!
```

Next you may want to verify that the peer supports multi topologies as well. Similar to the JUNOS example, in IOS the `show clns neighbors detail` command your neighbour states.

IOS command output

```
London# show clns neighbors detail
System Id      Interface      SNPA          State    Holdtime       Type      Protocol
Frankfurt      POS2/0         PPP           Up       25             L2        M-ISIS
  Area Address(es): 49.0001
  IP Address(es): 172.16.33.213*
  IPv6 Address(es): FE80::2A0:A5FF:FE12:3398
  Uptime: 00:13:42
  NSF capable
  Topology: IPv4, IPv6
```

Finally, you want to check how the processing of the IPv6 topology went. You can see the log for the IPv6 MT Topology using the `show isis ipv6 spf-log` command.

IOS command output

The `show isis ipv6 spf-log` command shows the SPF duration and reason for the last calculations based on the IPv6 Unicast Topology.

```
London#show isis ipv6 spf-log

    IPv6 level 2 SPF log
  When          Duration      Nodes    Count    First trigger LSP     Triggers
01:03:10        8            6        3       Frankfurt.00-00   NEWADJ DELADJ LVCONTENT
00:53:03        4            6        1                         PERIODIC
00:52:49        5            1        2       London.00-00      DELADJ TLVCODE
00:52:34        4            6        2       London.00-00      NEWADJ TLVCODE
00:38:01        4            6        1                         PERIODIC
00:28:24        4            6        1       Frankfurt.00-00   TLVCODE
00:22:57        4            6        1                         PERIODIC
00:17:46        4            2        2       London.00-00      DELADJ TLVCODE
00:07:54        4            1        1                         PERIODIC
```

13.5.3 *Summary and Conclusion*

Because of the stringent requirements of RFC 1195, which requires that all routers support all Network Layer protocols, it is hard to deploy IPv6 (for example) incrementally. Convex migration schemes help to avoid routing loops during a network rollout. However, if there is mis-configuration then it is relatively easy to break a multi protocol environment in IS-IS. For that purpose, the IS-IS WG defined four additional TLVs that make each router build distinct topologies and perform a per Network Layer protocol SPF calculation. Multi topologies are a viable solution for deploying IPv6 incrementally in the network, however, there is serious concern in the Service Provider community as to whether this complexity is necessary at all.

Most service providers have MPLS as the uniform transport vehicle, and MPLS is already deployed in their networks. The idea is that the inner core topology runs on IPv4 only and IPv6 Reachability Information is exchanged via BGP. BGP uses IPv4 to resolve the next-hops and then traffic is relayed between a pair of BGP speakers using the MPLS magic carpet. It is the authors' opinion that if there is a possibility to re-use that MPLS magic carpet, then there should be serious consideration whether an IPv6 control plane is required, necessary and worth the hassle.

13.6 Graceful Restart

The Internet is about to become the *new* public infrastructure. When the Internet will replace today's communication infrastructure is not as easy to predict. Common sense says that you can pull the plug when the new infrastructure is better, faster and more resilient than the *old* infrastructure. However, especially in terms of availability and software stability, IP switching platforms in the past lacked the resiliency and redundancy of the *old* infrastructure, like TDM multiplex networks and voice switches. Typically it is the *software* that makes systems fail (assuming that the hardware designers have done their job well). When it comes to software, TDM multiplexers do not expose any weaknesses due to their almost static configuration and so naturally avoiding any complex signalling software. On the other hand, voice switches have to rely on signalling protocols like SS7. Unfortunately, stability and "feature velocity" negatively impact each other. It is relatively easy to freeze code and do some bug fixing in order to get to stable signalling code and release the stable code in the hope that it does not break in the live network. In a fast progressing world like the IP world, that approach is not feasible because there will be always further enhancements/bug fixes to the base protocol. Modern software release models apply careful testing to the code base before it is released to the public. However, it turned out that there is a no more brutal reality-check to verify if the code works than exposing it to the live Internet. Furthermore, the support teams of the vendors had to be very responsive to fix any kind of problem really fast. Due to the 24×7 nature of the Internet (non-business hours traffic is just 70 per cent of the peak traffic during business hours) almost no maintenance window can be established. The necessary software upgrades are really painful for the users and operators, as a software upgrade always means about 60–180 seconds outage until the entire router complex (control plane and forwarding plane) is rebooted. A reboot of a routing node results in a changed topology. This topology change will have a negative impact on other routers, entailing AS-global SPF runs, BGP route flaps and subsequent route damping by external BGP peering partners.

Modern routers are based upon a clear separation between the control plane and forwarding planes. The two entities can work independently from each other for a short period of time. For example, the forwarding plane can easily keep forwarding state while the control plane (in Cisco, it is the Route-Processor; Juniper Networks calls it the Routing Engine) is rebooting. Keeping forwarding state means that the forwarding plane forwards packets based on the last good routing information, effectively freezing the forwarding table. The control plane can next reboot, while the forwarding engine is still passing traffic.

The trouble starts when the control processor is coming up again. Because it just rebooted, it does not have any state knowledge of its adjacencies nor does it have any topological insight (that is, the link-state database is empty). If a router is in that state and it generates an IIH and does not demonstrate that it has achieved 3-way state by listing its neighbour's adjacency state or SNPA (for more on adjacency management see Chapter 5, "Neighbour Discovery and Handshaking"), then the adjacency will be immediately disrupted and global SPF recalculation will occur.

Graceful restart attempts to fix the problem of missing state during reboot. It does not make a difference why the control plane processor has been rebooted. It could be because of a software crash or due to a controlled operation like a software upgrade. Figure 13.19 illustrates the timing after a reboot.

Router B requests Router A to stay quiet for 180 seconds. In that 180 seconds it needs to re-instate all adjacencies, bring up the BGP mesh and recalculate its routes. Finally it needs to compare the previously frozen forwarding plane information with the new calculated prefix list and apply, if necessary the required changes.

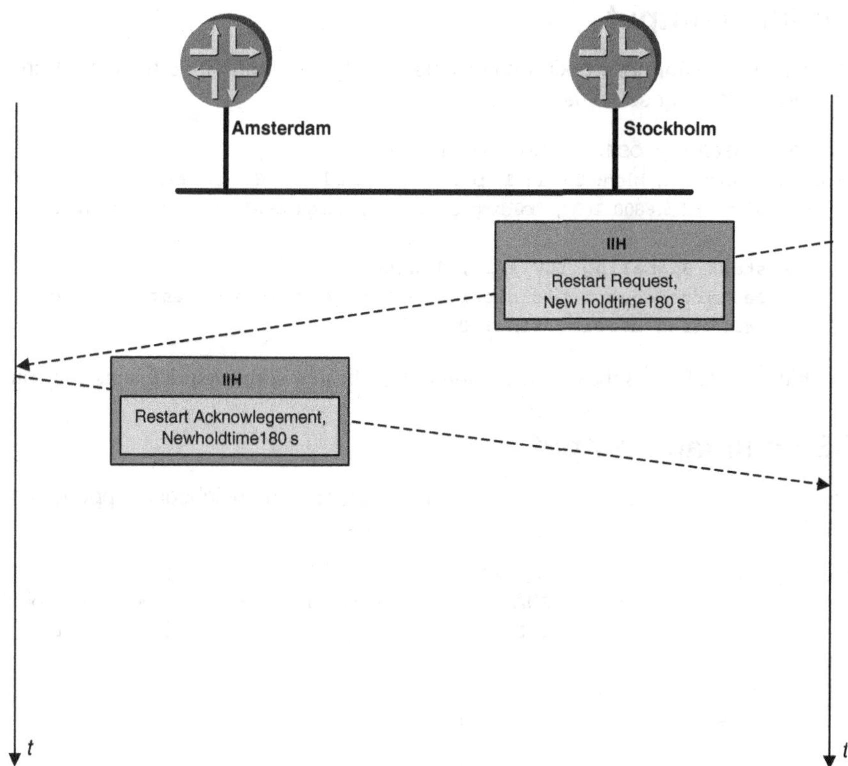

FIGURE 13.19. Router Stockholm requests a grace period of 180 seconds

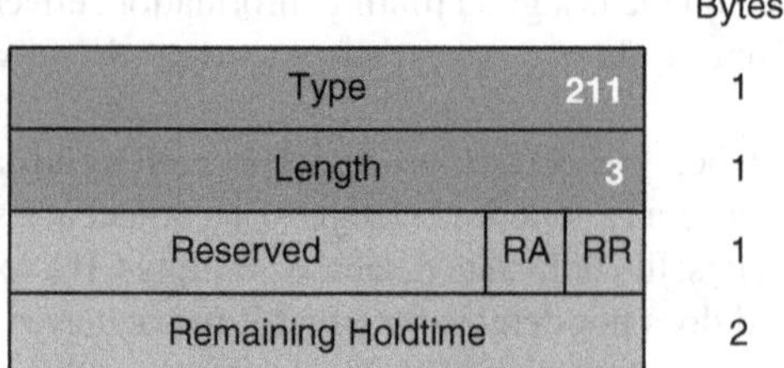

FIGURE 13.20. The Restart Signaling TLV is used for requesting an granting a new Hold timer

RFC 3847 describes the optional Restart Signaling TLV #211 that can be used to signal a grace period until adjacency formation is completed. Figure 13.20 illustrates the 3-byte fixed length TLV. The first byte contains the Restart Request and the Restart Acknowledge Flag. The remaining 16-bits contain the hold time that a node sets itself for performing the reboot.

Both IOS and JUNOS generate the Restart Signaling TLVs per default to indicate to remote neighbours that they support graceful restart in general.

Tcpdump output

TLV #211 under normal working conditions has the RR and RA Bits cleared and the remaining Hold timer set to 0s.

```
02:00:08.223369 Out OSI, IS-IS, length: 82
  point-to-point IIH, hlen: 20, v: 1, pdu-v: 1, sys-id-len: 6  (0), max-area: 3 (0)
    source-id: 1921.6800.1027, holding time: 27s, circuit-id: 0x01, Flags: [L1L2]
      [ … ]
      Restart Signaling TLV #211, length: 3
        Restart Request bit clear, Restart Acknowledgement bit clear
        Remaining holding time: 0s
```

In both IOS and JUNOS the restart capability is indicated in the detailed adjacency output.

IOS command output

The `show clns neighbors detail` command shows if the neighbour supports graceful restart.

```
London# show clns neighbors detail
System Id      Interface      SNPA         State    Holdtime    Type    Protocol
Frankfurt      POS2/0         PPP          Up       25          L2      M-ISIS
  Area Address(es): 49.0001
  IP Address(es): 172.16.33.213*
  IPv6 Address(es): FE80::2A0:A5FF:FE12:3398
  Uptime: 00:15:41
  NSF capable
  Topology: IPv4, IPv6
```

In the IOS terminology Non Stop Forwarding (NSF) is an alternative term for graceful restart.

JUNOS command output

```
hannes@Frankfurt> show isis adjacency detail
[ … ]
London
  Interface: so-1/2/0.0, Level: 2, State: Up, Expires in 23 secs
  Priority: 0, Up/Down transitions: 11, Last transition: 00:24:12 ago
  Circuit type: 3, Speaks: IP, IPv6
  Topologies: Unicast, IPV6-Unicast
  Restart capable: Yes
  IP addresses: 172.16.33.29
  IPv6 addresses: fe80::203:fdff:fec8:3c00
  [ … ]
```

Graceful restart will be the foundation for higher availability in core networks. It is not a single technology, but rather a concept that allows a node to still forward during control plane failure or intended downtime like router software upgrades. Because graceful restart is a cooperative technology (that means it needs to rely on the fact that all of its neighbours support it) it is recommended to deploy it on a broad scale on every network.

13.7 Summary

The last 10 years were filled with extensions to the IS-IS protocol. Deficits like missing checksums in certain PDU types got fixed. TLV #10, one of the original ISO 10589 TLVs, is used as an envelope to convey HMAC-MD5 strong authentication information. IPv6 routing has been introduced albeit with the same deployment restriction that RFC 1195 suffered from. Multi topology IS-IS attempts to solve that problem by defining extra TLVs and introduction per-protocol SPF runs. However, due to broad MPLS deployment, IPv6 for control plane purposes may become obsolete. BGP in conjunction with MPLS as a forwarding magic carpet may finally make MT-ISIS obselete. Finally, IS-IS got the ability for gracefully restarting a control plane processor without churning the network at all. Extensions like this are the prerequisite for the Internet becoming the dominant public infrastructure some day (soon).

14

Traffic Engineering and MPLS

At the end of the 1990s, the Internet was expanding at a breathtaking speed. Both capacity and geographic spread grew by factors of 2 to 4 per year. It appeared that capacity could not be provisioned in time and the network could suffer congestion anytime. Service providers needed to re-route traffic onto paths in the network that had been underutilized in order to take some of the load off the congested links. It quickly became evident that the IP world until this time lacked a sound load-balancing tool to adapt the traffic to the underlying topology in the most rational manner.

MPLS provided for the first time *source routing* intelligence to the Internet and, due to its path orientation, the necessary control to *guide* traffic. However, provisioning the label switched paths manually proved to be a daunting task and service providers and router vendors co-developed a kind of *distributed traffic control system* whereby MPLS paths can be brought up, loaded with traffic, and torn down based on constraints like bandwidth and hop count limits between POPs. The network service provider is now, for the first time, fully in control about the flow of transit traffic, based on high-level constraints likes hop-count, bandwidth utilization, and so on.

In this chapter the original motivations and problems for Internet traffic engineering, the limits of IGP metric balancing the rise of MPLS and the role that IS-IS plays in the distributed traffic control system will be highlighted. In addition, this chapter covers more advanced topics like DiffServ traffic engineering and forwarding adjacencies.

14.1 Traffic Engineering by IGP Metric Tweaking

In the IP world, routing protocols try to compute the *shortest* path between a pair of sub-nets. A common sense example from the real world says that the *shortest* path may not be the *best* path, as everybody getting stuck in the Monday morning and Friday evening traffic jams on the highways knows. The shortest path from a distance perspective means nothing if the load on that path is too high and therefore causes queuing delays. Consider Figure 14.1, where we have one "hot" link between Frankfurt and London suffering from 110 per cent loading and so dropping traffic. Historically network engineers tried to load balance traffic by modifying the IGP costs of the links to try and get some of the load off the "hot" link.

IGPs calculate their topology in a highly distributed fashion. If a single link cost is modified, this may have global impact in the IGP domain. This is not that much of a problem in small networks. On a small network, even a human brain can process the topology and estimate all the consequences resulting from an IGP link cost change manually.

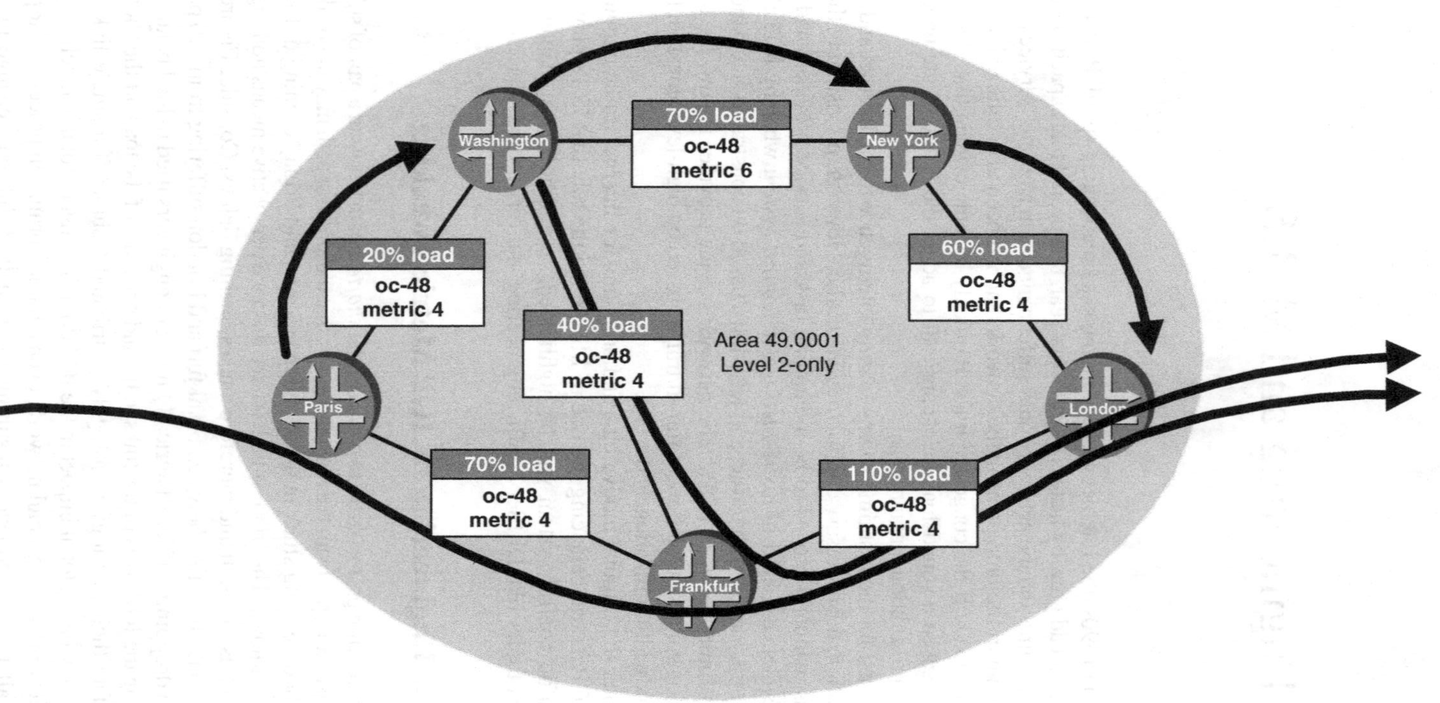

FIGURE 14.1. The segment between Frankfurt and London is congested

However, in moderately sized networks where the number of routers and links exceeds the processing capability of human operators, the IGP acts as a complex system and therefore produces undesired side effects during route calculations.

A change in the IGP cost may result in a too drastic change of load patterns across the network. It is almost like people jumping from one side of the bus to the other and almost tipping the bus over. Consider Figure 14.2, where the traffic engineer tries to offload some traffic on the Frankfurt to London link by changing the link-metric from 4 to 11. Now three links (Frankfurt–Paris, Frankfurt–London, Frankfurt–Washington) become unattractive for many routers in the network, and the traffic jumps onto the Washington–London path. In the end, nothing is gained, as there is still an imbalance, however, this time on a different link in the core network. In this example the change resulted in an even *worse* overall utilization because now *two* network segments are congested.

The main problem here is the *granularity* in controlling the traffic. Often the only granularity the IGP gives to the traffic engineers is loading or unloading an entire trunk line. Loading and unloading in smaller increments, for example, in 5 per cent incremental steps would be much better. Network operators need a tool where traffic engineering does not interfere with routing decisions. The first solution for decoupling routing and traffic engineering was achieved using so called *Layer-2 overlay network*, a popular technique during the mid-1990s.

14.2 Traffic Engineering by Layer-2 Overlay Networks

Figure 14.3 shows the basic structure of a Layer-2 overlay network. The core of the network is composed of a set of circuit-oriented Layer-2 switching devices (for example, ATM or Frame Relay switches). Routers sitting at the edge of the network surround the overlay network core. In the mid-1990s, when this type of network was popular, there was relatively little Layer-3 forwarding power. This was the heydays of the Cisco 7500 Series, which could forward at best 200 MBit/s of traffic. Therefore there was a lot of interest to keep the traffic as long as possible in the Layer-2 switching domain. Consequently, a full-mesh of VCs between the routers was built up. Now, traffic engineering is relatively easy: the traffic engineer simply needs to rearrange the VCs of the core network if a trunk is becoming *congested*, or in service provider speak, getting *hot*.

The bottom of Figure 14.3 shows the router's viewpoint from a logical perspective. Basically, each router sees each other router. This in turn severely stresses the flooding sub-system of link-state routing protocols enormously. Chapter 6, “Generating, Flooding and Ageing LSPs”, presented more details as to the catastrophic effects such full-mesh setups have during re-routing conditions. Ultimately, the flooding-explosion described in Chapter 6 were solved by a technique called *mesh-groups*.

What remained was not a technical but an *administrational* problem. In order to manage the router network, service providers needed to run two teams. The *ATM team* running the core network was responsible for traffic engineering, and the *IP team* was responsible for running the router infrastructure. Unfortunately, those two responsibilities cannot be strictly separated. Traffic engineering in the core is one thing, the other (and more important) aspect is *interdomain* traffic engineering, which controls the entrance point where traffic enters the

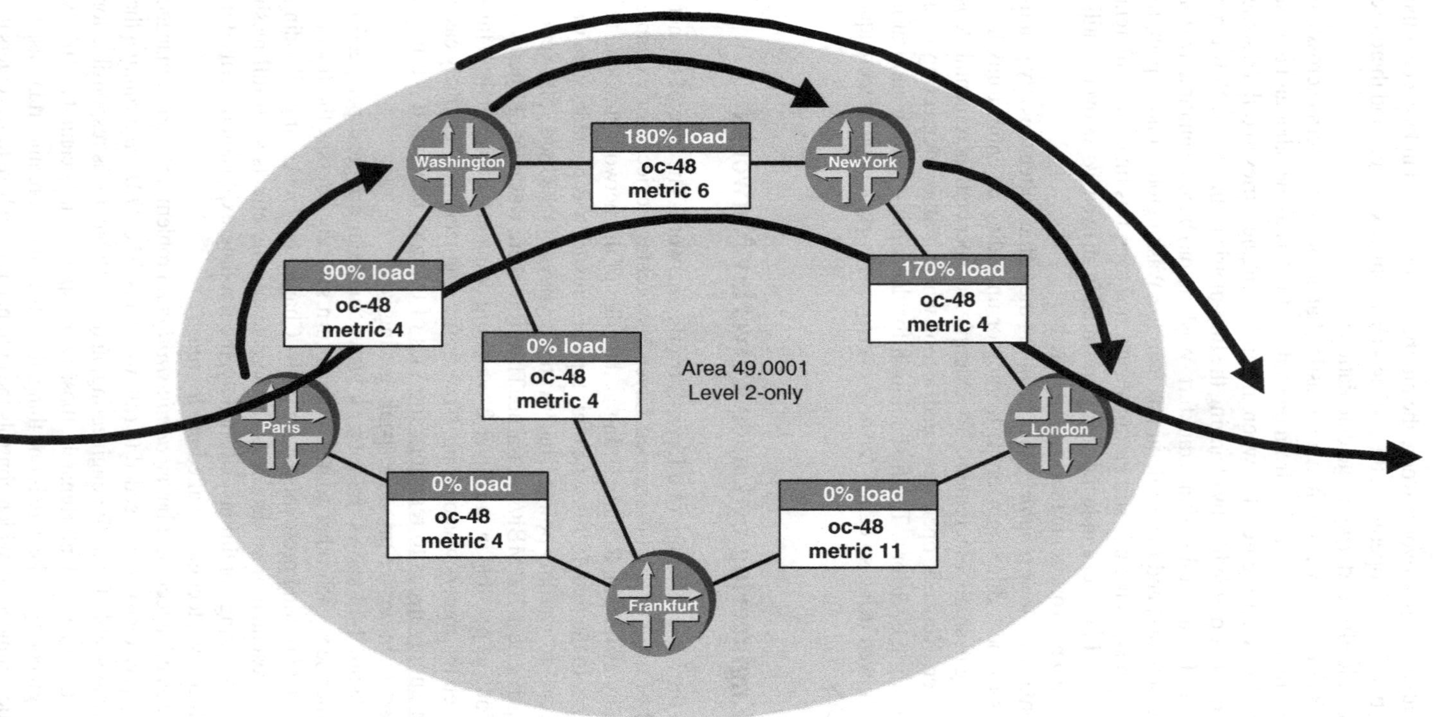

FIGURE 14.2. A change of a single IGP cost may have a global impact on the utilization of other trunks in the network

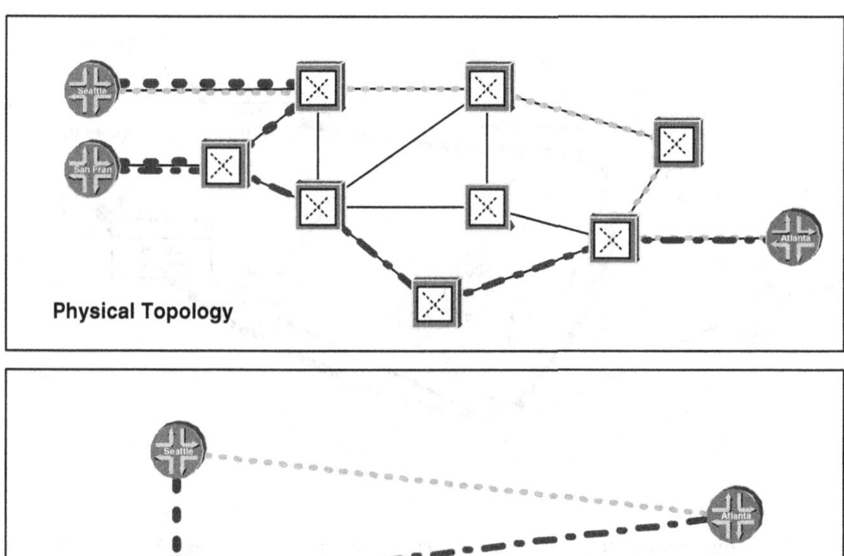

FIGURE 14.3. In overlay networks all routers are directly connected to each other from a network layer perspective

IP Network. Consider Figure 14.4, where router New York becomes very attractive by advertising a lower MED value than router London, and now large traffic volumes are relayed to router New York. As soon as the traffic arrives at New York, it may become a problem because the only thing left to do is balancing over the existing, internal VC infrastructure. In order to balance traffic efficiently, traffic engineers need to also control the *external* link with regard to how much traffic is flowing into the network. This is not an unsolvable problem; it is a matter of *coordination* between departments inside a service provider. But experience has shown that even this level of *minimal* coordination is often lacking or just did not work out very well. Aside from those coordination issues, service providers wanted to have an *integrated* solution so that they could perform both traffic engineering and routing on a *single* platform if for no other reason than cost.

The lack of router knowledge of the underlying topology also causes sometimes weird re-routing behaviour. Consider Figure 14.5, where the direct VC between Paris and Frankfurt fails. In the IGP topology every VC has a cost of 1. Because there is no direct alternate path (cost 1) available, the network takes the *next* best path which is at a cost of 2. Unfortunately, there are now a whole set of feasible paths available:

- Via Washington DC
- Via New York
- Via London

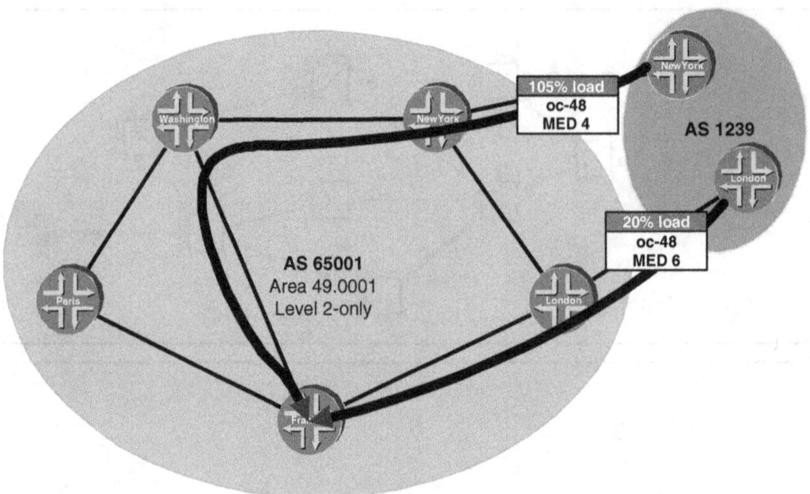

FIGURE 14.4. Interdomain traffic engineering cannot be done using local VC path changes and hence the IP group of a Network Service Provider still has traffic engineering responsibilities

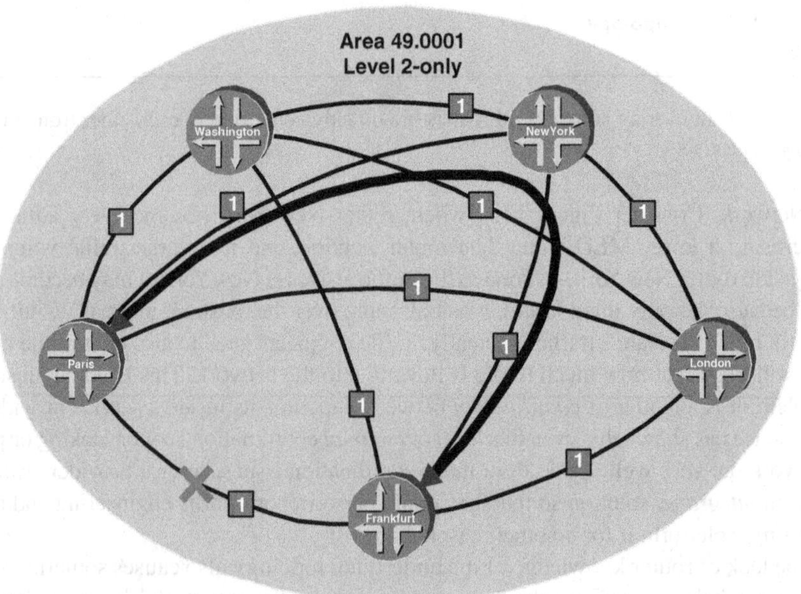

FIGURE 14.5. Because of lack of topological insight a single failing VC may impose additional delay

Depending on the Paris router configuration, either a random single path or limited set of paths will be picked. In the example, New York has been elected as the backup path, which causes an additional trans-Atlantic delay. The customers were used to having delays of about 5 ms between Paris and Frankfurt, and not the resulting 40 ms. And the trans-Atlantic routes are, by the way, very expensive because this capacity comes at a premium. The other constraint is that routers limit the number of equal cost paths that they use for path calculation. IOS used to limit this to six equal cost paths, and JUNOS limits it to 16 equal cost paths. Now, consider a full-mesh between 40 POPs and only the first 6 or 16 equal cost paths are being considered once a single VC fails. This results in completely unpredictable backup behaviour and is a capacity planner's nightmare.

In addition to those cost and delay problems, there is also the problem of the Layer-2 overhead in ATM networks. An ATM cell consists of a 5-byte header and a 48-byte payload. IP packets need to get chopped into pieces to fit in those ATM payload bytes. A sequencing scheme which numbers the fragments and detects the start and end of an IP packet is needed to reassemble the packet at the end of the cell-switching domain. In the ATM world those functions are performed by the ATM Adaptation Layer 5 (AAL-5). Before the IP packet is passed to the segmentation and reassembly (SAR) chip for generation of an ATM AAL-5 compliant cell-stream, a Layer-2 header has to be prepended for Layer-2 demultiplexing. Recall that at least two protocols are necessary in the network: IPv4 and OSI (for conveying the non-IP IS-IS packets). Typically, Layer-2 is implemented by prepending a *Sub Network Access Protocol* (SNAP) header for muxing/demuxing purposes. A SNAP header ensures that the receiver can differentiate between IPv4 and IS-IS packets on the wire. The SNAP, plus the AAL-5 information, represents a certain level of *static* overhead. However, there is also a *dynamic* overhead that results from inefficient packaging of IP packets into cells. Figure 14.6 shows a histogram of the packet size distribution on the Internet as measured by probes on public peering points. There is a peak of 35.5 per cent at the 40 bytes mark, which accounts for all the TCP Acknowledgements (ACKs). This is no big surprise as the majority of IP applications (and hence the majority of traffic) are based on TCP as the transport protocol. And that is where the problem begins.

Figure 14.7 shows a very good example of the inefficiencies resulting from the *dynamic* overhead contribution. Consider a TCP ACK of 40 bytes (20 bytes IP header plus 20 bytes of TCP header) that needs to have a SNAP header prepended, an AAL-5 trailer appended, and finally packaged in ATM cells. A single 40-byte packet with the entire static overhead contributed by the SNAP header and AAL-5 trailer *cannot* be squeezed into a single cell, and therefore has to use a second cell. However, in the second cell the majority of information is *padding* information. Clearly this is an extreme situation, in the sense that a single 40-byte packet consumes 106 bytes on the carrying media, which is an overhead of 63 per cent! However, there are dynamic overhead peaks resulting from "cell-ification" every 48 bytes across the entire packet size distribution histogram. Common experience is that the *nominal* overhead on an Internet traffic mix is about 20 per cent. In other words, only 115 MBit/s out of the potential channel capacity of an 148.5 MBit/s SONET/SDH pipe can only be used for transporting IP data. Extrapolating those numbers shows that on an OC-48/STM-16 trunk, roughly 500 MBits of capacity is burned due to cell-ification. That represents a lot of extra traffic, and also a lot of extra money that service providers could earn, if they could transport that traffic and not needing to purchase higher-speed transmission links, ATM and router equipment.

The third big problem resulting from ATM overlay cores is the reality that router vendors did not make ATM-interfaces with speeds higher than OC-12/STM-4 available.

Internet traffic mix

Packet size (Bytes)	Proportion of total	Bandwidth (Load)
28	1,20%	0,08%
40	35,50%	3,51%
44	2,00%	0,22%
48	2,00%	0,24%
52	3,50%	0,45%
552	0,80%	1,10%
576	11,50%	16,40%
628	1,00%	1,50%
1420	3,00%	10,50%
1500	10,00%	37,10%

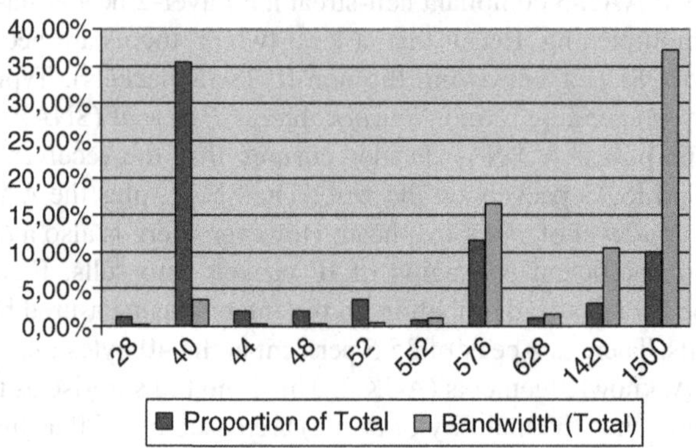

FIGURE 14.6. The majority of packets in the Internet are 40-byte sized

Although ATM engineers often claim that this is purely the result of a conspiracy from the router vendors (!); the reality is that on the semiconductor supplier market today there are still no SAR chips available that can segment and reassemble IP packets/cell-streams with a speed higher than OC-12/STM-4. The main reason for ATM SAR chips trailing behind the Internet growth curve is due to the technical complexity of generating AAL-5 frames at higher wire-speeds.

From an overhead and speed reality point of view, service providers quickly decided that the ATM road was a dead-end and provisioned their cores mainly using IP over SONET/SDH technology, thus making the ATM layer essentially obsolete. Somewhat ironically, Layer-2 overlay networks were not that bad from a control perspective. The nicest feature was the level of granularity available to control traffic flow in the core. The service provider could easily relay a single portion of City A to City B traffic, without having any impact on the AS-wide traffic distribution. This can be mainly accounted for by the path-orientation of ATM VC and Frame Relay DLCIs. It was now clear from this experience that any potential integrated traffic engineering solution for IP had to have a path orientation as well.

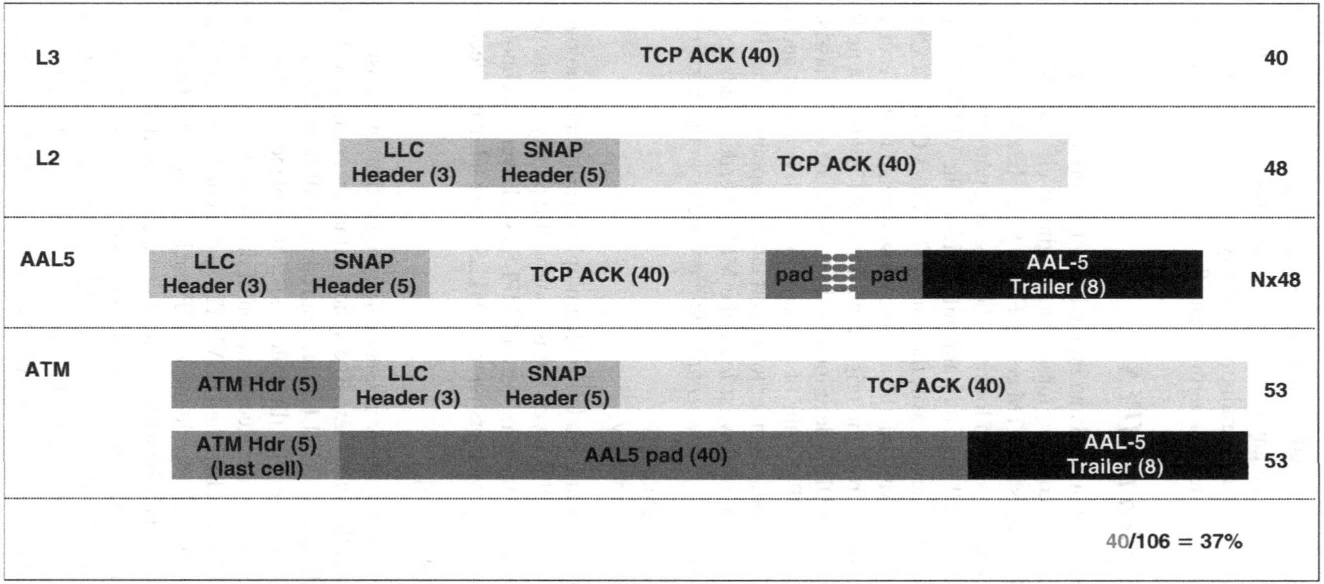

FIGURE 14.7. The worst case scenario is a 40-byte payload size, which requires two ATM cells

14.3 Traffic Engineering by MPLS

The first big application for MPLS is traffic engineering. Service providers should be able to guide traffic between any two points inside their network. To deviate from the prevailing hop-by-hop routing paradigm that always guides the traffic along the shortest path through a network, a new forwarding paradigm had to be introduced.

14.3.1 *Introduction to MPLS*

The forwarding decisions in ATM and Frame Relay networks are truly independent from the Network Layer protocol. The forwarding engine itself does not see the Network Layer protocol; all it sees is the ATM cell or Frame Relay header. Based on the VPI/VCI or DLCI field, the Layer-2 switch looks up the outgoing port and just as importantly, an outgoing VPI/VCI or DLCI. Based on this information, the VPI/VCI or DLCI is rewritten before the cell or the packet leaves the router. The VPI/VCI or DLCI field has purely local meaning and is only valid on the interface downstream to the receiver. The concept of label *swapping* comes from the original ability of ATM and Frame Relay Switches to change the VPI/VCI or DLCI descriptor as the traffic leaves the chassis. It was clear to the designers of the new MPLS suite of protocols that each IP packet and frame had to be preceded by an MPLS header in order to support label swapping in the IP protocol family.

The big question today is at what *layer* the MPLS header needs to exist. There are roughly two, unfortunately, *fundamentally different* views in the industry:

- MPLS is a Layer-2 technology
- MPLS is a Layer-3 technology

In order not to further confuse readers with multiple layering terminologies (ISO layers, ATM layers, IP layers, MPLS layers), this book will typically use the terms *cell-based MPLS* for the ATM switch vendors' view of MPLS as a Layer-2 technology, and *packet-based MPLS* for the router vendors' view of MPLS being a Layer-3 technology.

14.3.1.1 Cell-based MPLS

The proponents of MPLS as a Layer-2 technology argue that this transition path for existing ATM networks is the *smoothest*. The vision is that an existing ATM network which runs Q.2931 signalling and PNNI for internal routing will be replaced by an IP stack of signalling protocols. Figure 14.8 illustrates the control plane transformation of an ATM network to running IS-IS and the combination of one or both of the two major signalling protocols used with MPLS: LDP and RSVP-TE. As the combination of Q.2931 and PNNI established VCIs in the ATM world, now an IP stack sets up the *labels* in MPLS.

So the main question here is: what *is* a label in the cell-based MPLS world? In the control plane, much has been changed by radically replacing the prevailing ATM control plane with an IP one. However, on the forwarding plane, almost nothing has changed. Figure 14.8 shows that cell-based MPLS makes use of the VPI/VCI fields for MPLS as well. The label will be written into the VPI/VCI fields and the forwarding paradigm stays the same. The label look up determines the outgoing port and outgoing label, with which the cell will be rewritten upon transmission.

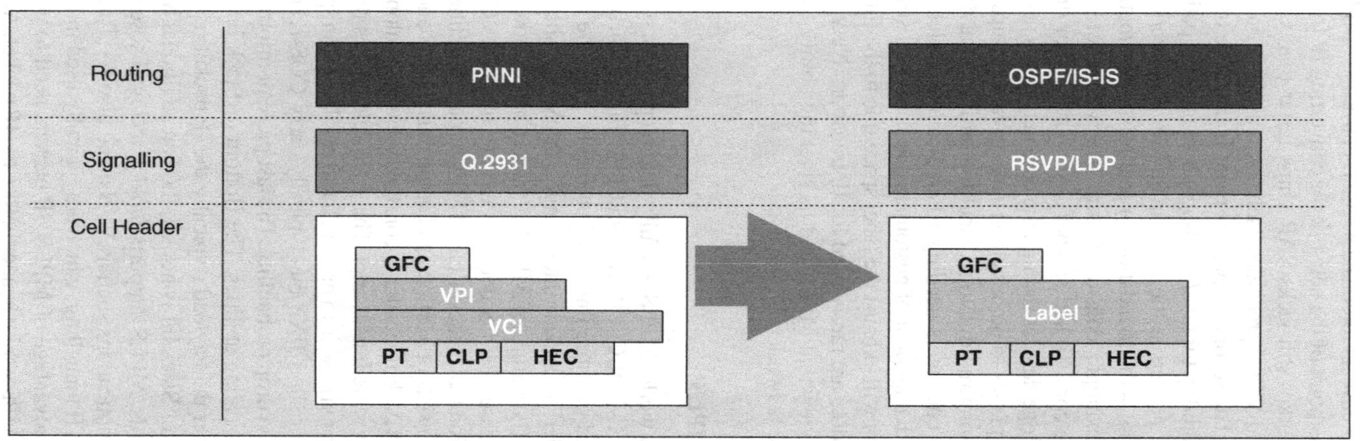

FIGURE 14.8. In the cell-based MPLS world, IP protocols do the label setup

Although cell-based MPLS may sound as being the panacea for smoothly rolling over to MPLS, there are important caveats to consider. First, cell-Based MPLS cores still need a SAR function at the ingress point of the network for converting IP frames to cells. And the semiconductor supplier market still lacks SAR chips faster than OC-12/STM-4. So the conclusion is that cell-based MPLS precludes itself for consideration as backbone technology for high-speed cores. The second important point is that, due to the finite size of the cell-header, there is no possibility for *label stacking* where multiple path labels are "pushed" and "popped" onto and off packets as they flow in an MPLS network. In large networks it turned out that label stacking is the foundation for scaling the distribution mesh for MPLS-based services. As a brief example, consider Figure 14.9, where for each customer VPN a set of LSPs is set up in the core. To add another customer, another distribution mesh that connects all the Provider Edge devices through the core network is needed. Although ATM vendors tune their control planes to process thousands of label setups per second, the system does not scale in the long run due to its label forwarding state explosion in the core. Consider, for example, 64 customers needing 10 applications which results in more than 20,000 connected paths – that amount of customers and paths will stress the control plane severely and in the long run will exhaust the label space due to the finite cell-header size.

Today, cell-based networks are rarely used for IP transport. Network operators mainly share the router vendors' view that MPLS and its stacking ability are the foundation for scaling services across the network.

14.3.1.2 Packet-based MPLS

In the packet-based MPLS world, MPLS is a fully fledged protocol type that runs on top of link-layers such as ATM, C-HDLC, Ethernet and PPP. Figure 14.10 shows examples of how MPLS is encapsulated on those link-layer protocols. After the Link-Layer Header, a 4-byte MPLS "shim header" is added. Interestingly, the MPLS shim header can also be present on ATM frames. The nature of MPLS is packet based, however the link-layer is MPLS. Note that packet-based MPLS does not modify the VPI/VCI labels of the ATM header. The only information that a packet-based MPLS router modifies is the shim header. The MPLS shim header consists of a 20-bit label value plus EXP, S and TTL bits. The label information inside the MPLS shim header is constantly rewritten along the switching path as in ATM or Frame Relay switch networks. The TTL field carries the same semantics as the IP TTL field. The main purpose is to prevent harm resulting from persistent forwarding loops. The Experimental or short EXP bits typically carry COS-related information like Forwarding Class Name and drop probability. The last piece of information is only a single bit, but it gives MPLS its scaling abilities. The Bottom of Stack bit, if set, indicates that after the MPLS shim header the Payload (typically the IP packet) is stored. Reverse logic implies that if the Bottom of Stack bit is not set, then an additional MPLS shim header is found inside. In other words, MPLS supports *label stacking*. Those stacking capabilities are used for a variety of applications such as VPNs, and also for Traffic Engineering tunnels for LDP over RSVP-TE tunnelling, which are typically used in large-scale networks.

In order for IP to take advantage of MPLS, IP packets need to get wrapped in MPLS packets by prepending an MPLS shim header before the IP packet. Adding an MPLS shim to the potential stack of MPLS shims is called a *push* operation. Consequently, taking off

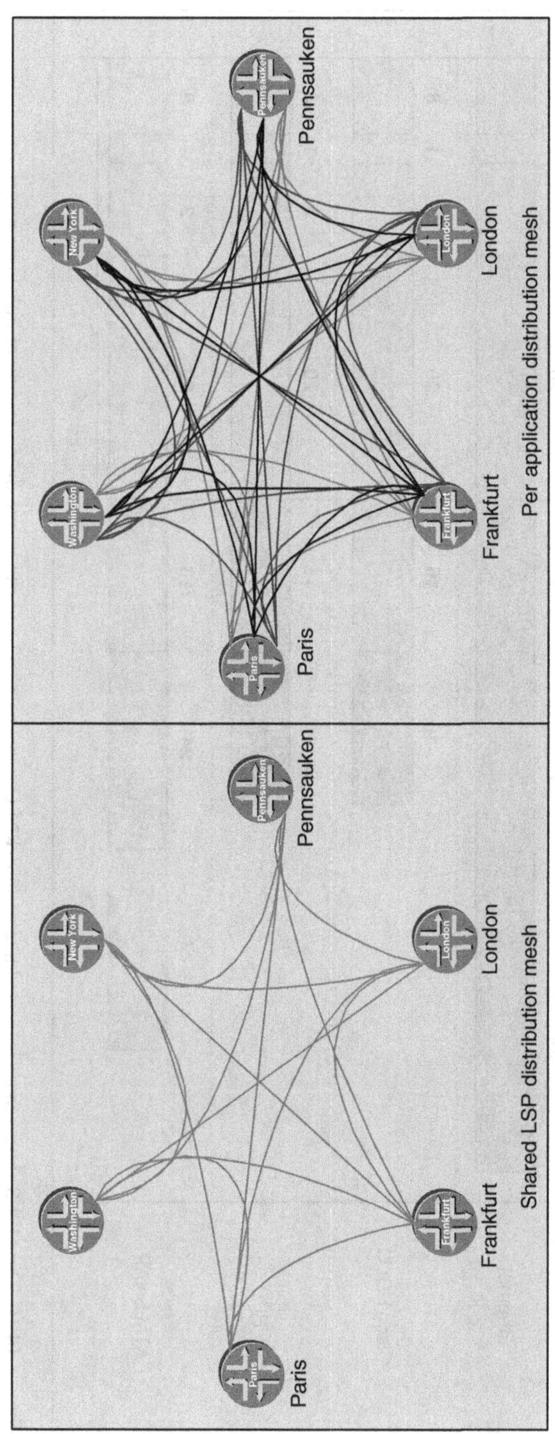

FIGURE 14.9. Cell-based MPLS requires for each service a dedicated label switched path mesh

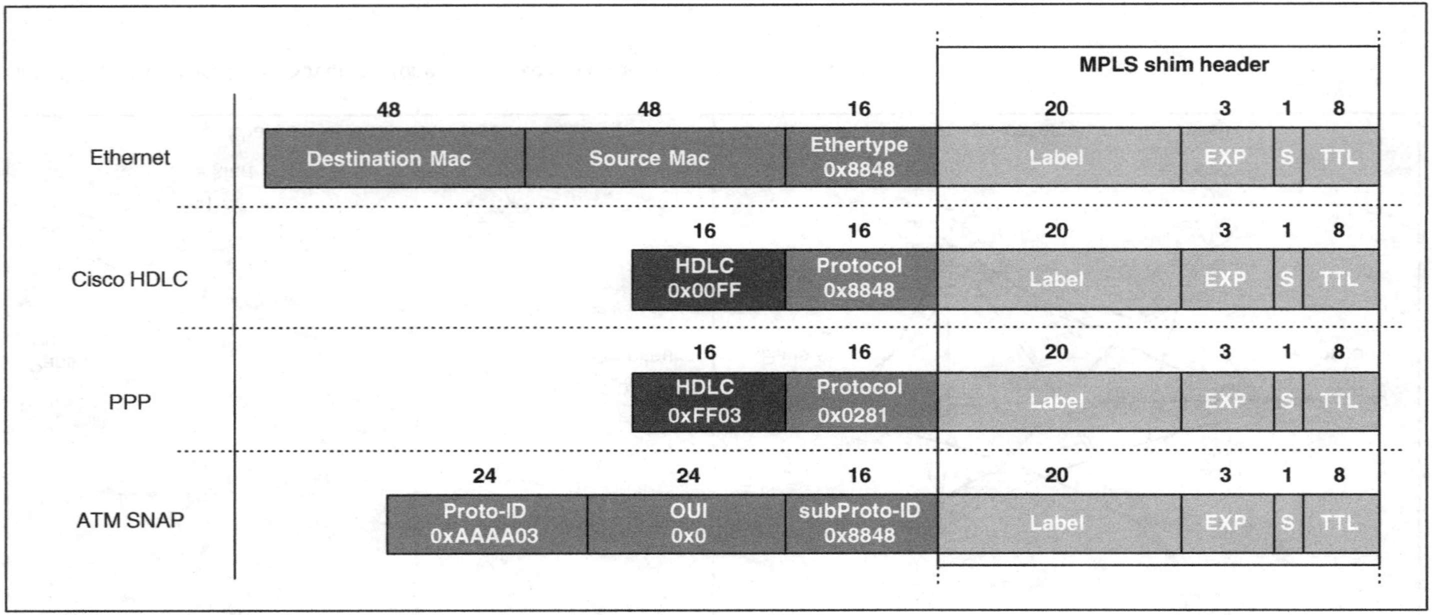

				MPLS shim header			
	48	48	16	20	3	1	8
Ethernet	Destination Mac	Source Mac	Ethertype 0x8848	Label	EXP	S	TTL
		16	16	20	3	1	8
Cisco HDLC		HDLC 0x00FF	Protocol 0x8848	Label	EXP	S	TTL
		16	16	20	3	1	8
PPP		HDLC 0xFF03	Protocol 0x0281	Label	EXP	S	TTL
	24	24	16	20	3	1	8
ATM SNAP	Proto-ID 0xAAAA03	OUI 0x0	subProto-ID 0x8848	Label	EXP	S	TTL

FIGURE 14.10. The MPLS shim header is treated like an OSI-RM Layer-3 protocol and can be run over a variety of link-layer protocols

a label from the MPLS shim stack is called a *pop* operation. Just changing a label value and not adding or removing a label off or on the stack is called a *swap* operation. Figure 14.11 shows where those three operations are applied to IP transit traffic.

Consider an MPLS label switched path from Frankfurt to Washington DC. Frankfurt is the *Ingress* or *Head End* of the label switched path. The Ingress router performs a push operation, which adds a label #397 to the IP payload and passes off the packet to the next downstream router, which is London. London's lookup table maps incoming labels #397 to the outgoing port facing Pennsauken and swaps label #397 to label #512. Pennsauken maps label #512 to its outgoing port facing New York and swaps the label to #438.

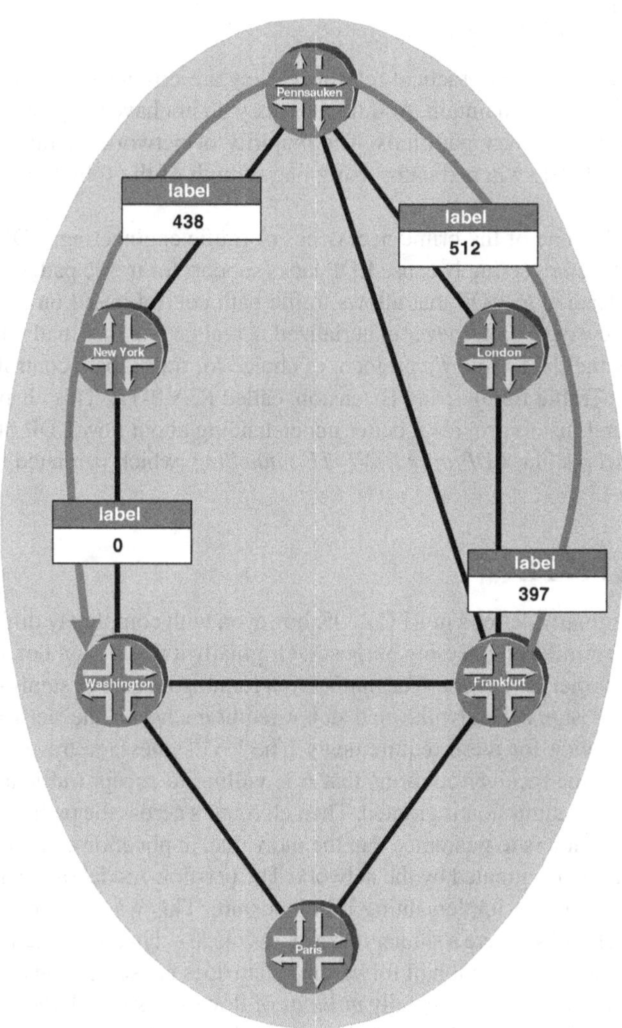

FIGURE 14.11. Each MPLS router along a label switched path changes, swaps the label

Pennsauken is the *penultimate router* on the forwarding path and therefore it has to tell the egress router to unwrap the packet. It does so by swapping the label to zero and forwarding it to Washington. The *Egress* or *tail end* router in Washington knows now to POP the top label off the stack and do a regular IP lookup on the packet inside.

14.4 MPLS Signalling Protocols

Now the next big question is: how are label switched paths established? As in the routing protocol world, there are generally two ways to bring up label switched paths:

- Static setup
- Dynamic (*signalled*) setup

Static setups have no real practical relevance: they are difficult to coordinate and to set up and cumbersome to maintain. Additionally they do not have the possibility to re-route traffic in case the primary path fails. The majority of network operators deployed *signalled* setup of label switched paths using one or both of the following protocols: LDP and RSVP-TE.

Path control is one of the prime necessities of traffic engineering. LDP is not directly related to traffic engineering because LDP lacks support for traffic path control. Although there is an extension to LDP that allows traffic path control based on *constraints* called *CR-LDP* the new extensions never materialized in real networks. Finally the CR-LDP got abandoned by the IETF. Today's protocol of choice for traffic-path control is RSVP, augmented with a Traffic Engineering Extension, called RSVP-TE. This chapter covers only LDP basics, and just to provide a better understanding about how LDP fits in with more advanced concepts like *LDP over RSVP-TE tunnelling*, which is related to traffic engineering and IS-IS.

14.4.1 *RSVP-TE*

RSVP was originally defined in RFC 2205, however, with completely different intentions than using it for traffic engineering purposes. Originally it was thought of as being the tool to make the Internet CoS aware. The *application* running on End Systems should be made CoS aware and signal bandwidth and delay requirements to the network, which was expected to provide for these requirements. The RSVP message travels throughout the network and, if the receiver confirms that it is willing to accept traffic according to the flow request, then admission is granted. Then all routers across the path are required to set up per-flow schedulers to guarantee that the individual application can transmit the traffic with the requirements granted by the network. The per-flow model failed due to the inherent scaling problems of implementing it in hardware. This was to some degree comparable to ATM networks, where a similar mistake was made – dynamic signalling of ATM VCs and the subsequent introduction of forwarding state does not scale. Consider that today on an OC-192c circuit there are typically *millions* of flows transported, then the limits of the design are immediately apparent. A hardware-scheduling engine that operates at such high speeds on so many flows cannot be built. RSVP was considered dead by the mid-1990s and there was no broader deployment of flow-aware networks. Finally, the vision of a flow-aware Internet was abandoned for the time being. However, there were three things about RSVP that still attracted interest within the developer community.

1. *Extensibility*. First of all, RSVP is a very extensible protocol. Like IS-IS, the RSVP header is quite generic and all the information is encoded using TLV containers called *Objects*. More about the advantages of TLV encoding were discussed in Chapter 13. Virtually all successful networking protocols have a TLV orientation. RSVP is actually a very good example of a protocol that, if it is just extensible enough, can be used for a totally different purpose many years later. All that is required is to define a different set of TLVs, and functionality is added as developers move forward with the protocol.
2. *Forwarding State Model*. RSVP uses two basic messages for requesting and granting forwarding state: the PATH and the RESV messages. The Path message describes what the sender wants to transmit to the receiver, and the RESV message describes what the receiver is willing to accept. The PATH message travels hop-by-hop downstream to the receiver and the RESV message travels upstream from the receiver to the sender along the path established. The receiver can set up forwarding state in a step-by-step fashion and, as soon the RESV message arrives at the requester, everything is ready and then the forwarding path can immediately be used. That property is a wide deviation from the usual "signalling" and routing paradigm found in IP networks. Routing typically does not get any feedback – at best a routing protocol tells its neighbour that it has received the routing update by sending back an Acknowledgement. However, the router cannot tell if the path will ever be used. RSVP is different. The router that requests a certain forwarding state from the network also gets immediate feedback that the network has set up the requesting state and now it is ready for use. For fast converging networks especially, fast feedback about whether a path can be used or not is imperative.
3. *Unidirectional Notion*. A flow was originally thought of as a *unidirectional* path between two nodes. Also, routed paths in the IP world are always unidirectional relationships. Therefore the IETF similarly defined a label switched path as a unidirectional relationship. As the RSVP flow-based model implied unidirectional operation as well, it was a natural choice for setting up label forwarding state between a pair of routers.

14.4.2 *Simple Traffic Engineering with RSVP-TE*

RSVP had a lot of interesting ingredients to serve as the protocol for setting up label switched paths across the Internet. However, a few changes and extra objects had to be defined before RSVP could be used to set up label switched paths. The most important change was that RSVP is not run between a pair of *End Systems*. Rather, RSVP-TE for MPLS is run between a pair of *routers*. The next evolutionary step was to get rid of some of the per-flow objects and to define a set of new objects that could be used for traffic engineering purposes. In RSVP, *Objects* is the term that is interchangeably used for *TLVs*.

Table 14.1 shows the additional RSVP-TE objects that are defined in RFC 3209 and used with MPLS.

TABLE 14.1. The major traffic engineering objects for RSVP-TE.

Code point	Object name
16	Label object
19	Label request object
20	Explicit route object
21	Record route object
22	Hello
207	Session attribute object

All the objects in Table 14.1 are used for Signalling Traffic Engineering LSPs. Most of them appear in RSVP RESV or PATH messages. The tcpdump output shows how these attributes look on the wire.

Tcpdump output

In the tcpdump output you see the contents of a PATH and RESV message of a RSVP call that requests and assigns a label. Many TE objects are embedded in the two messages.

```
12:35:47.351675 IP 209.211.134.9 > 209.211.134.8: RSVP
    v: 1, msg-type: Path, length: 216, ttl: 255, checksum: 0x4406
        Session Object (1) Flags: [reject if unknown], Class-Type: Tunnel IPv4 (7),
         length: 16
          IPv4 Tunnel EndPoint: 209.211.134.8, Tunnel ID: 0x0011,
           Extended Tunnel ID: 209.211.134.9
        RSVP Hop Object (3) Flags: [reject if unknown], Class-Type: IPv4 (1), length: 12
            Previous/Next Interface: 10.154.1.6, Logical Interface  Handle: 0x0853f4c8
        Time Values Object (5) Flags: [reject if unknown], Class- Type: 1 (1), length: 8
          Refresh Period: 120000ms
        Session Attribute Object (207) Flags: [ignore and forward if unknown],
         Class-Type: Tunnel IPv4 (7), length: 28
          Session Name: juncore02-juncore01
          Setup Priority: 7, Holding Priority: 0, Flags: [none]
        Sender Template Object (11) Flags: [reject if unknown], Class-Type:
         Tunnel IPv4 (7), length: 12
          IPv4 Tunnel Sender Address: 209.211.134.9, LSP-ID: 0x0007
        Sender TSpec Object (12) Flags: [reject if unknown], Class-Type: IntServ (2),
         length: 36
          Msg-Version: 0, length: 28
          Service Type: Default/Global Information (1), break bit not set,
           Service length: 24
             Parameter ID: Token Bucket TSpec (127), length: 20,  Flags: [0x00]
                 Token Bucket Rate: 0 Mbps
                 Token Bucket Size: 0 bytes
                 Peak Data Rate: inf Mbps
                 Minimum Policed Unit: 20 bytes
                 Maximum Packet Size: 1500 bytes
```

```
Adspec Object (13) Flags: [reject if unknown], Class-Type:  IntServ (2),
 length: 48
  Msg-Version: 0, length: 40
  Service Type: Default/Global Information (1), break bit not set,
   Service length: 32
    Parameter ID: IS hop cnt (4), length: 4, Flags: [0x00]
      IS hop cnt: 1
    Parameter ID: Path b/w estimate (6), length: 4, Flags: [0x00]
      Path b/w estimate: 0 Mbps
    Parameter ID: Minimum path latency (8), length: 4, Flags: [0x00]
      Minimum path latency: don't care
    Parameter ID: Composed MTU (10), length: 4, Flags: [0x00]
      Composed MTU: 1500 bytes
  Service Type: Controlled Load (5), break bit not set, Service length: 0
ERO Object (20) Flags: [reject if unknown], Class-Type: IPv4 (1), length: 28
  Subobject Type: IPv4 prefix, Strict, 10.154.1.5/32, Flags: [none]
  Subobject Type: IPv4 prefix, Strict, 10.154.6.1/32, Flags: [none]
  Subobject Type: IPv4 prefix, Strict, 10.254.1.45/32, Flags: [none]
Label Request Object (19) Flags: [reject if unknown], Class- Type: without
 label range (1), length: 8
  L3 Protocol ID IPv4
RRO Object (21) Flags: [reject if unknown], Class-Type: IPv4 (1), length: 12
  Subobject Type: IPv4 prefix, Strict, 10.154.1.6/32, Flags: [none]
```

This is the response to the previous Label Setup Message. Note that the Session object contents need to match in order for the router to match the RSVP message to a certain session.

```
12:35:51.199611 IP (tos 0xc0, ttl 255, id 6344, offset 0, flags [none], length: 164)
 10.154.1.5 > 10.154.1.6: RSVP
  v: 1, msg-type: Resv, length: 144, ttl: 255, checksum: 0x2efc
    Session Object (1) Flags: [reject if unknown], Class-Type: Tunnel IPv4 (7),
     length: 16
      IPv4 Tunnel EndPoint: 209.211.134.10, Tunnel ID: 0x0013, Extended
       Tunnel ID: 209.211.134.9
    RSVP Hop Object (3) Flags: [reject if unknown], Class-Type: IPv4 (1), length: 12
      Previous/Next Interface: 10.154.1.5, Logical Interface Handle: 0x0853f4c8
    Time Values Object (5) Flags: [reject if unknown], Class-Type: 1 (1), length: 8
      Refresh Period: 30000ms
    Style Object (8) Flags: [reject if unknown], Class-Type: 1 (1), length: 8
      Reservation Style: Fixed Filter, Flags: [0x00]
    Flowspec Object (9) Flags: [reject if unknown], Class-Type: IntServ (2),
     length: 36
      Msg-Version: 0, length: 28
      Service Type: Controlled Load (5), break bit not set, Service length: 24
        Parameter ID: Token Bucket TSpec (127), length: 20, Flags: [0x00]
          Token Bucket Rate: 0 Mbps
          Token Bucket Size: 0 bytes
          Peak Data Rate: inf Mbps
          Minimum Policed Unit: 20 bytes
          Maximum Packet Size: 1500 bytes
```

```
FilterSpec Object (10) Flags: [reject if unknown], Class-Type: Tunnel IPv4 (7),
 length: 12
   Source Address: 209.211.134.9, LSP-ID: 0x0005
Label Object (16) Flags: [reject if unknown], Class-Type: Label (1), length: 8
   Label 12324
RRO Object (21) Flags: [reject if unknown], Class-Type: IPv4 (1), length: 36
   Subobject Type: IPv4 prefix, Strict, 10.154.1.5/32, Flags: [none]
   Subobject Type: IPv4 prefix, Strict, 10.154.6.1/32, Flags: [none]
   Subobject Type: IPv4 prefix, Strict, 10.254.1.45/32, Flags: [none]
   Subobject Type: IPv4 prefix, Strict, 10.254.1.2/32, Flags: [none]
```

The *Label Request Object* is embedded in a RSVP-TE PATH message and gives RSVP-TE the ability to request a label and subsequently return a label using the *Label Object* in a RSVP-TE RESV message. The Explicit Route Object (ERO) allows RSVP-TE to specify a set of nodes that an RSVP-TE message has to traverse. Figure 14.12 shows sample EROs modelled using the Loose and Strict (L/S) path constraint. A *Strict* hop indicates that the next hop must be directly connected to the previous hop. The first example of Figure 14.12 shows a set of strict hops that specify a path. A sequence of strict hops is often used to nail down a path – that is, when the network administrator wants to enforce a certain path. A *Loose* hop means that the node has to be present in the path before the next hop, but does not have to *be* the next-hop. The second example of Figure 14.12 shows that only a subset of the nodes is listed in the ERO. With the Loose attribute, this means that there is some room for re-routing this path. The path could potentially run directly from Washington via Frankfurt to Pennsauken. In practice, the Loose option causes more problems than it solves. The network is not in full control of the traffic path anymore and in more complex topologies this may lead to strange results with long delay paths. The third example in Figure 14.12 shows a mix between loose and strict hops. The semantics of the ERO Objects allows for the combination of loose and strict hops in an arbitrary fashion.

There are two general ways to create an ERO. The first is a manual specification and the second, more sophisticated way, is automated computation. The manual configuration will be discussed first.

You can configure a label switched path using an ERO in similar ways on IOS and JUNOS. First you need to specify the ERO and next you need to link the ERO to a label switched path.

IOS configuration

In IOS you can specify an ERO manually using the `ip explicit-path` statement. The next-address specifies the `next-element` in the ERO. By default all hops in the ERO are strict except when you supply the `loose` keyword.

```
ip explicit-path identifier name via-Penssauken enable
  next-address 192.168.1.1
  next-address loose 192.168.2.1
  [...]
!
```

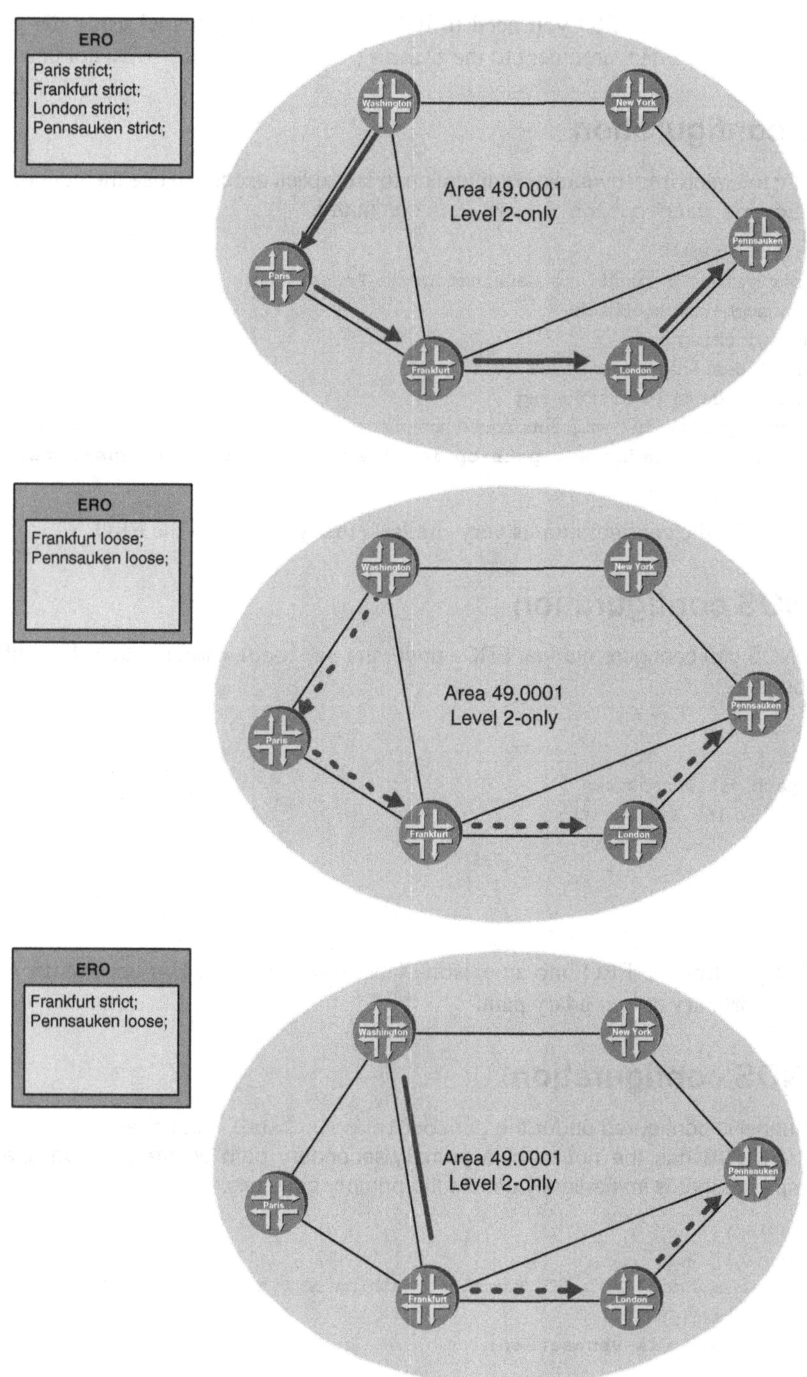

FIGURE 14.12. The ERO consists of a mix and match list of Strict and/or Loose Hops

After defining the ERO you need to link it to an existing tunnel using the `path-option explicit` argument to the `tunnel mpls traffic-eng` command.

IOS configuration

In order to switch from dynamic computation to an explicit execution use the `tunnel mpls traffic-eng path-option 5 explicit` command.

```
interface Tunnel0
  description TE Tunnel to Washington via Penssauken
  ip unnumbered Loopback0
  tag-switching ip
  tunnel destination 192.168.20.1
  tunnel mode mpls traffic-eng
  tunnel mpls traffic-eng autoroute announce
  tunnel mpls traffic-eng path-option 5 explicit name via-Penssauken
!
```

In JUNOS the configuration is very similar – first you specify the ERO.

JUNOS configuration

In JUNOS you configure manual EROs under the `protocols mpls path {}` configuration branch.

```
protocols {
  mpls {
    path via-Penssauken {
      192.168.1.1 strict;
      192.168.2.1 loose;
    }
  }
}
```

Next you link the ERO into an existing label switched path. You need to declare the path as a primary or secondary path.

JUNOS configuration

The tunnel is configured under the `protocols mpls label-switched-path {}` statement. JUNOS has the notion of a primary/secondary path where you can specify a backup path that is immediately used if the primary path fails.

```
protocols {
  mpls {
    label-switched-path "TE Tunnel to Washington via Pennsauken" {
      to 192.168.20.1;
      primary via-Pennsauken;
    }
  }
}
```

After you have configured your tunnels, you need to verify if the TE tunnel is up and if the tunnel is following the desired path. Because awkward combination of the Loose and Strict Hop option can cause unexpected results – the Record Route Object (RRO) provides better visibility for troubleshooting purposes. The Record Route Object is embedded in the RSVP-TE RESV messages. During its journey from the egress router to the ingress router all IP addresses are recorded and stored at the ingress router. On IOS, you have to explicitly turn on generation to the RRO object using a Tunnel Interface path option, in JUNOS it is automatic.

IOS configuration

In IOS the Record Route Object (RRO) is not automatically generated for a TE tunnel. It needs to get configured explicitly using the `tunnel mpls traffic-eng record-route` command.

```
interface Tunnel0
  [ ... ]
  tunnel mpls traffic-eng record-route
!
```

The contents of the RRO Object can be displayed using the `show mpls traffic-eng tunnels` command in IOS.

IOS output

The `show mpls traffic-eng tunnels` command contains all the information around a tunnel. The configured ERO, the tunnel's bandwidth, outgoing labels and more of interest is included in the Route Record Object (RRO).

```
London#show mpls traffic-eng tunnels
Name: TE Tunnel to Washington via Pennsauken (Tunnel0) Destination: 192.168.20.1
  Status:
    Admin: up    Oper: up    Path: valid    Signalling: connected

    path option 1, type explicit via-Pennsauken (Basis for Setup,path weight 10)

  Config Parameters:
    Bandwidth: 1 kbps (Global) Priority: 7 7 Affinity: 0x0/0xFFFF
    Metric Type: TE (default)
    AutoRoute: enabled LockDown: disabled Loadshare: 1 bw-based
    auto-bw: disabled

  InLabel  : -
  OutLabel : POS4/1, 100016
```

```
RSVP Signalling Info:
     Src 192.168.1.2, Dst 192.168.20.1, Tun_Id 0, Tun_Instance 511
   RSVP Path Info:
     My Address: 192.168.1.2
     Explicit Route: 192.168.1.1 192.168.168.3
     Record Route:
     Tspec: ave rate=1 kbits, burst=1000 bytes, peak rate=1 kbits
 RSVP Resv Info:
   Record Route: 172.16.33.1 172.16.38.1
   Fspec: ave rate=1 kbits, burst=1000 bytes, peak rate=1 kbits
 History:
   Tunnel:
     Time since created: 12 days, 17 hours, 39 minutes
     Time since path change: 1 minutes, 13 seconds
   Current LSP:
     Uptime: 1 minutes, 13 seconds
```

Most often you will notice a difference between the configured ERO and the recorded PATH. It is common practice to use a router's loopback ID as the address for a loose hop. However, the route recorder in the PATH message thinks entirely in terms of link addresses. So even if we used in our example the 192.168/16 addresses, the ones actually reported back in the RRO are from the link-address space 172.16/16.

In JUNOS you can also display the recorded path using the `show mpls lsp ingress detail` command.

JUNOS output

```
hannes@Frankfurt> show mpls lsp ingress detail
Ingress LSP: 1 sessions

192.168.1.1
  From: 192.168.1.2, State: Up, ActiveRoute: 0, LSPname: to-Washington
  ActivePath: (primary)
  LoadBalance: Random
  Encoding type: Packet, Switching type: Packet, GPID: IPv4
*Primary State: Up
    Computed ERO (S [L] denotes strict [loose] hops): (CSPF metric: 20)
      192.168.1.1 192.168.168.3 S
    Received RRO (ProtectionFlag 1=Available 2=InUse 4=B/W 8=Node):
      172.16.33.1 172.16.38.1
Total 1 displayed, Up 1, Down 0
```

JUNOS behaves similarly to IOS, where the Route Path Recording is done using link addresses.

If you want to achieve *any-to-any* MPLS connectivity between all routers in your network, then the consequence is to deploy a full-mesh of RSVP-TE tunnels. However, there are severe scaling implications with that approach. To overcome these scaling limitations a more lightweight MPLS label setup protocol called the *Label Distribution Protocol* (LDP) is used.

14.4.3 *LDP*

LDP is defined in RFC 3036 and it describes a lean, lightweight protocol that brings up a full-mesh of connectivity to all LDP speakers in the network. Generally, the term *full-mesh* raises warning flags in every network engineer's head due to the perceived scaling problems. However, LDP uses a technique called *label-merging* which is very conservative with label allocation. Consider the right-hand side of Figure 14.13. There are five drawings inside the figure, one for each possible egress router. The egress router is marked with an E, and the metric on each link is 4.

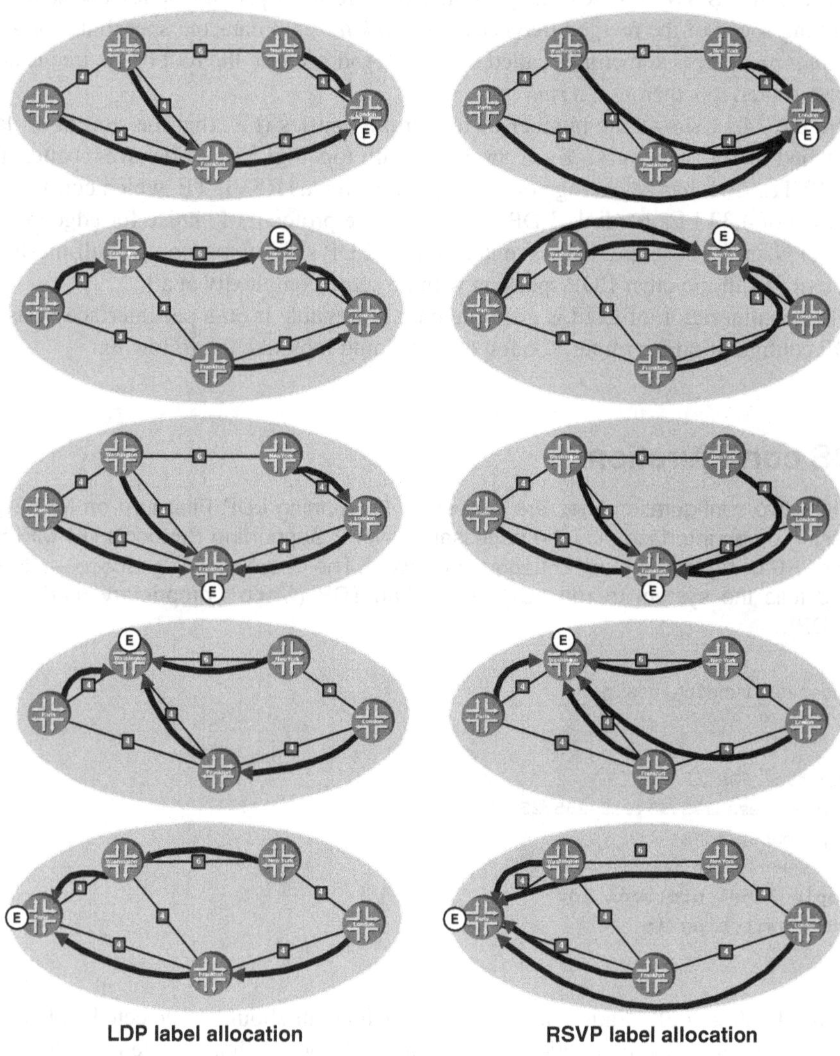

FIGURE 14.13. LDP consumes less forwarding state per link than RSVP does

The figure describes the LSPs and the necessary forwarding state to set up full-mesh connectivity between all five routers in the core network. Using RSVP-TE, we would need at least $N*(N-1)/2 = 10$ explicitly configured tunnels. Because LDP supports label merging, some labels can be re-used by other label switched paths. Unlike RSVP-TE, LDP signals its label using a mode called *downstream unsolicited,* which means that the labels are signalled from the egress router to the ingress router. Each LDP speaker advertises prefixes according to the *egress policy*. In JUNOS, the default egress policy is just to advertise the loopback IP address. The IOS default egress policy is to advertise *both* the loopback and all the directly connected interfaces. Upstream nodes create MPLS SWAP states and pass on the label-mapping message to their upstream nodes, which create again MPLS SWAP states, and pass them on to further upstream nodes, and so on. The resulting shape of the merged tree is called a *sink tree*. (In datacom speech the *egress* or *destination* point is sometimes called the *sink*.) And because the root of the tree is at the egress router, it is therefore a *sink tree*.

Figure 14.14 shows the number of forwarding entries (FE) that the sum of all label switched paths generates. Even in the small topology, LDP behaves better than RSVP-TE. LDP has an average of 3 FEs per link versus RSVP-TE, which consumes an average of 4.33 FEs per link. LDP is therefore the protocol of choice for edge systems like VPN and/or customer access routers, due to LDP's ability to supply a full-mesh connectivity to all the other LDP speakers with no setup complexity at all.

The configuration of LDP is a simple one: just enable it on a per-interface basis. An LDP configuration for router London on IOS could look like the following:

IOS configuration

In IOS two configuration lines are necessary for running LDP. First turn on MPLS processing on an interface plus the necessary Layer-2 Supporting Protocols like MPLSCP over PPP using the `tag-switching ip` keyword. The `mpls label protocol ldp` keyword tells the system to run LDP rather than TDP (Cisco's proprietary predecessor to LDP).

```
London#sh running-config
[ ... ]
!
interface POS4/1
  ip address 172.17.0.5 255.255.255.252
  ip router isis
  encapsulation ppp
  mpls label protocol ldp
  tag-switching ip
!
```

Shortly after configuration, a remote LDP neighbour should be detected and an LDP session is then set up automatically. You can verify the neighbour state using the `show mpls ldp neighbor` operational level command.

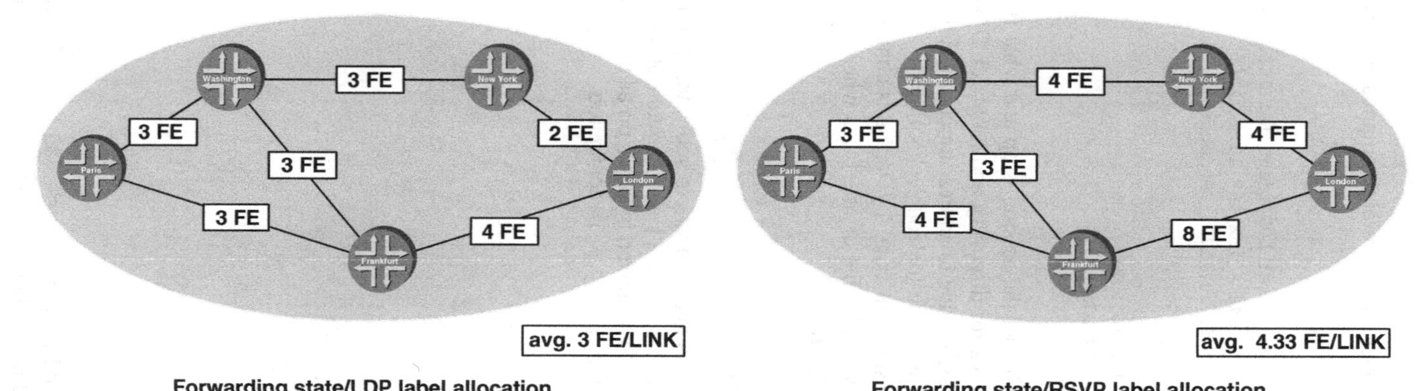

FIGURE 14.14. The sum of all forwarding states show that LDP is more frugal than RSVP

IOS output

Under the `show mpls ldp <*>` hierarchy several commands are available to verify neighbour state and timers.

```
London#show mpls ldp neighbor
  Peer LDP Ident: 192.168.0.1:0; Local LDP Ident 192.168.13.8:0
    TCP connection: 192.168.0.1.646 - 192.168.13.8.11000
    State: Oper; Msgs sent/rcvd: 207/179; Downstream
    Up time: 00:28:43
    LDP discovery sources:
      POS4/0, Src IP addr: 172.16.0.2
    Addresses bound to peer LDP Ident:
      172.16.0.2
```

The display output shows whether the session is up and what IP addresses are being used. LDP uses link IP addresses for discovery and loopback IP addresses for session setup. If a session does not come up due to addressing conflicts the output of this command is providing valuable information for troubleshooting.

In JUNOS we need to make sure that `family mpls` is configured under the logical interface branch. In addition we add a list of interfaces where we want to speak LDP under the `protocols ldp` stanza.

JUNOS configuration

In JUNOS you need to specify the interface where you want to run LDP both under the `protocols mpls {}` and `protocols ldp {}` stanza. Alternatively you can set the `mpls interface` list to `all` which allows allocation of labels on all interfaces. In addition every logical interface needs to have the `family mpls` configured.

```
hannes@Frankfurt# show
[ … ]
interface ge-0/0/0 {
  unit 0 {
    family mpls;
  }
}
protocols {
  mpls {
    interface all;
  }
  ldp {
    interface so-0/1/2.0;
  }
}
[ … ]
```

It remains unknown why `mpls interface all {}` is not the default option, since this does not break anything by being turned on. On the other hand, it *does* break proper label allocation if the interfaces are not listed under this command hierarchy. Not all default decisions are obvious.

The neighbour state is verified using the `show ldp neighbor` command.

JUNOS output

You can verify the neighbour state using the `show ldp neighbor detail` operational level command. The output displays the session IP addresses plus the neighbour's link IP address.

```
hannes@Frankfurt> show ldp neighbor detail
Address          Interface              Label space ID          Hold time
10.0.0.5 so-0/1/2.0                     62.154.13.8:0           11
  Transport address: 62.154.13.8, Configuration sequence: 0
  Up for 01:33:30
```

LDP is very much dependent on a working IGP. LDP itself cannot be run in stand-alone mode. Like BGP it is topology agnostic and cannot assert which label is better over another. LDP picks the label of the outgoing interface based on the best IGP distance. If the LDP topology is non-congruent than the IGP topology then LDP paths might get black holed.

One of the most frequent configuration mistakes is that the list of interfaces that run IS-IS and the list of interfaces which run LDP are not the same. Consider Figure 14.15. All links in the core network have IS-IS and LDP enabled, except the link between Washington and New York, which lacks LDP due to a configuration mistake. Paris learns the /32 FEC of the New York router via the London, Frankfurt, Washington path and selects the path via Washington because it is on the shortest path tree. The traffic gets labelled to Washington where it gets black holed because no valid MPLS labelled switched paths to the FEC of New York are available.

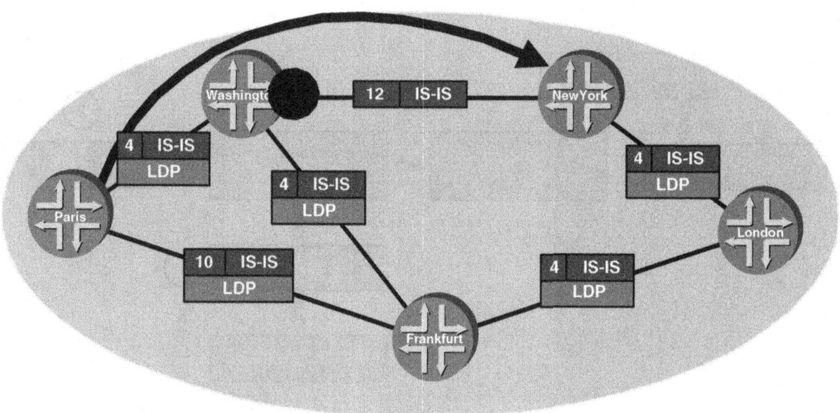

FIGURE 14.15. If the IS-IS and LDP topology is non-congruent Washington is black holing traffic

If you are troubleshooting an MPLS reachability problem, the first thing to check is if the IS-IS adjacencies match the LDP session. It remains problematic why router vendors do not change their default behaviour. LDP should be automatically brought up as soon as you enable IS-IS on an interface. If someone does not want to run LDP, they could then explicitly turn it off. That way you can prevent a network from black holing traffic.

14.4.4 *Conclusion*

Clients often ask what the "signalling protocol of choice" is. In 99 per cent of the cases, the answer is: both (LDP and RSVP-TE). Both protocols augment each other. LDP lacks path control, however. It is very frugal in its label usage and therefore inherently scalable. RSVP-TE is a heavyweight both from an administrative point of view as well as from a label allocation perspective; however, RSVP-TE has sound path control properties. So in general, networks use LDP, but once they need to offload some traffic from hot trunks, they use RSVP-TE in addition. There is no need to build full-mesh, explicitly configured RSVP-TE tunnels. First, pick a careful IGP metric scheme that provides *good-enough* routes, and then on top of that use RSVP-TE established TE-tunnels to take some heat off the hot trunks.

14.5 Complex Traffic Engineering by CSPF Computations

Traffic engineering is deployed in two general ways: the first option is when the network administrator wants to have the maximum level of control and explicitly configures all the label switched paths, plus the EROs. In moderately complex topologies, however, manually writing up tens to hundreds of EROs is a daunting task and almost certainly overwhelms the processing capabilities of humans. This is especially true if constraints like hop count and backup path diversity need to be considered; in these cases, automatic computation of EROs is the preferred choice. The computation of the EROs is done using a distributed traffic engineering database called the TED. The contents of this database are carried in IS-IS or OSPF. Figure 14.16 shows the differences between the two models.

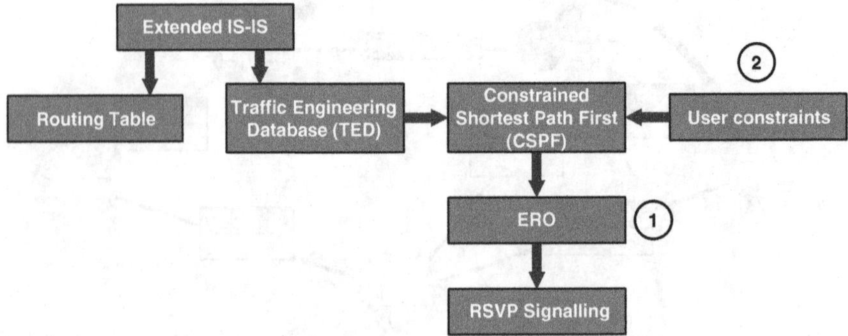

FIGURE 14.16. The RSVP Call Manager gets its input from the outcome of the CSPF calculation which is influenced by User Constraints and Topological Input

In the first method, the network administrator supplies the ERO data, and in the second the EROs are calculated using a Constrained Shortest Path First Calculation (CSPF) based on user constrained TED input from the routers. The final result is an ERO which gets passed to RSVP-TE for LSP setup.

You can display the contents of the TED database using the `show mpls traffic-eng topology` command in IOS and `show ted database extensive` command in JUNOS.

IOS command output

```
London#show mpls traffic-eng topology
My_System_id: 1921.6800.1008.00 (isis level-2)

Signalling error holddown: 10 sec Global Link Generation 5

IGP Id: 1921.6800.1012.00, MPLS TE Id:192.168.0.12 Router Node (isis level-2)
    link[0]: Point-to-Point, Nbr IGP Id: 1921.6800.1008.00, nbr_node_id:1, gen:2
          frag_id 0, Intf Address:172.16.0.2, Nbr Intf Address:172.16.0.1
          TE metric:10, IGP metric:10, attribute_flags:0x0
          physical_bw: 2488320 (kbps), max_reservable_bw_global: 2488320 (kbps)
          max_reservable_bw_sub: 0 (kbps)

                                        Global Pool           Sub Pool
             Total Allocated            Reservable            Reservable
             BW (kbps)                  BW (kbps)             BW (kbps)
             ---------------            -----------           ----------
  bw[0]:     0                          2488320               0
  bw[1]:     0                          2488320               0
  bw[2]:     0                          2488320               0
  bw[3]:     0                          2488320               0
  bw[4]:     0                          2488320               0
  bw[5]:     0                          2488320               0
  bw[6]:     0                          2488320               0
  bw[7]:     0                          2488320               0
```

The TED database contains all IP addresses, links and current bandwidth reservation states. The data found here is the foundation for the CSPF calculation which produces a path described by an ERO.

JUNOS command output

```
hannes@Frankfurt> show ted database extensive
TED database: 3 ISIS nodes 3 INET nodes
NodeID: Frankfurt.00(192.168.0.8)
  Type: Rtr, Age: 189 secs, LinkIn: 1, LinkOut: 1
  Protocol: IS-IS(2)
      To: London.00(192.168.0.8), Local: 172.16.0.1, Remote: 172.16.0.2
      Color: 0 <none>
      Metric: 10
      Static BW: 2488.32Mbps
      Reservable BW: 2488.32Mbps
```

```
    Available BW [priority] bps:
       [0] 2488.32Mbps [1] 2488.32Mbps [2] 2488.32Mbps [3] 2488.32Mbps
       [4] 2488.32Mbps [5] 2488.32Mbps [6] 2488.32Mbps [7] 2488.32Mbps
    Interface Switching Capability Descriptor(1):
      Switching type: Packet
      Encoding type: Packet
      Maximum LSP BW [priority] bps:
        [0] 2488.32Mbps [1] 2488.32Mbps [2] 2488.32Mbps [3] 2488.32Mbps
        [4] 2488.32Mbps [5] 2488.32Mbps [6] 2488.32Mbps [7] 2488.32Mbps
```

Why isn't the data for CSPF calculations taken straight from the link-state database of the routing protocol? Well, there still may be OSPF deployed in parts of the network. The TED is a *unified* view to the topology of the network, so no matter which IGP (OSPF, IS-IS, or even vendor-proprietary protocols) supplied the topology data. The TED is a *unified, abstracted view* and knows only about *nodes*, *links* and *link attributes*.

How does IS-IS generate and encode the data in the TED output? How does it know that a certain interface is an OC-48 interface? As soon as RSVP-TE is enabled on an interface, a lot of extra information is generated and conveyed using IS-IS.

Consider the following tcpdump output of a LSP before RSVP-TE has been turned on.

Tcpdump output

If RSVP-TE is not enabled on a core interface then no bandwidth relevant information is generated inside the Extended IS Reach TLV.

```
00:27:20.871975 OSI, IS-IS, length: 104
  L2 LSP, hlen: 27, v: 1, pdu-v: 1, sys-id-len: 6 (0), max-area: 3 (0)
    lsp-id: 0620.0000.0001.00-00, seq: 0x00000030, lifetime: 1196s
    chksum: 0x1d9d (correct), PDU length: 104, L1L2 IS
      Area address(es) TLV #1, length: 4
        Area address (length: 3): 49.0001
      Protocols supported TLV #129, length: 1
        NLPID(s): IPv4
      Traffic Engineering Router ID TLV #134, length: 4
        Traffic Engineering Router ID: 62.0.0.1
      IPv4 Interface address(es) TLV #132, length: 4
        IPv4 interface address: 62.0.0.1
      Hostname TLV #137, length: 9
        Hostname: Frankfurt
      Extended IS Reachability TLV #22, length: 23
        IS Neighbor: 0621.5401.3008.00, Metric: 10, sub-TLVs present (12)
          IPv4 interface address subTLV #6, length: 4, 10.0.0.2
          IPv4 neighbor address subTLV #8, length: 4, 10.0.0.1
      Extended IPv4 Reachability TLV #135, length: 18
        IPv4 prefix: 62.0.0.1/32, Distribution: up, Metric: 0
        IPv4 prefix: 10.0.0.0/30, Distribution: up, Metric: 10
```

Next, traffic engineering and RSVP-TE is configured on IOS and JUNOS and the resulting LSP structure is examined.

IOS configuration

In IOS you need to enable `traffic-eng` globally and under the `router isis` stanza. Additionally you need to enable it on each interface using the `mpls traffic-eng tunnels` command plus the `ip rsvp bandwidth` keyword specifies how much bandwidth can be reserved.

```
London#sh running-config
[ … ]
mpls traffic-eng tunnels
!
interface POS4/1
  [ … ]
  ip router isis
  mpls traffic-eng tunnels
  tag-switching ip
  ip rsvp bandwidth 2488320 2488320
!
router isis
  mpls traffic-eng router-id Loopback0
  mpls traffic-eng level-2
  metric-style wide level-2
  [ … ]
!
```

The `ip rsvp bandwidth` statement takes two parameters. The first is the maximum amount of bandwidth that is reservable on the interface, and the second is the maximum amount of bandwidth that is available for a *single* reservation. Typically those two values are the same, which means that a single reservation can eat up all the interface's bandwidth. Under the `router isis` stanza you need to specify the IS-IS level to which you want to send traffic engineering information. Unfortunately, you need to decide for Level-1 or Level-2. Both levels are not yet supported. Typically Level-2 is configured, and that is done here.

In JUNOS the sending of traffic engineering sub-TLV parameters is the default behaviour and there is no need to configure any further global options. All that needs to be configured is to add the interface under the `protocols rsvp` stanza.

JUNOS configuration

In JUNOS you need to specify the interface where you want to send bandwidth and reservation state both under the `protocols mpls {}` and `protocols rsvp {}` stanza. Alternatively you can set the `mpls interface` list to `all`. You can change the oversubscription of RSVP bandwidth by changing the default value of 100% using the `subscription` keyword.

```
hannes@Frankfurt# show
[ … ]
protocols {
  mpls {
    interface all;
  }
  rsvp {
    interface so-0/1/2.0 {
      subscription 120;
    }
  }
}
[ … ]
```

As soon as you enable RSVP-TE on an interface on which the router has established an adjacency, then the LSP gets updated with a lot of extra information, encoded by adding several sub-TLVs to the extended IS Reachability TLV #22.

Tcpdump output

An RSVP-TE enabled IS-IS adjacency shows the interface speed plus current reservation state using 8 pre-emption classes.

```
00:28:20.760649 OSI, IS-IS, length: 156
  hlen: 27, v: 1, pdu-v: 1, sys-id-len: 6 (0), max-area: 3 (0), pdu-type: L2 LSP
    lsp-id: 0620.0000.0001.00-00, seq: 0x00000031, lifetime: 1196s
    chksum: 0x2674 (correct), PDU length: 156, L1L2 IS
      Area address(es) TLV #1, length: 4
        Area address (length: 3): 49.0001
      Protocols supported TLV #129, length: 1
        NLPID(s): IPv4
      Traffic Engineering Router ID TLV #134, length: 4
        Traffic Engineering Router ID: 62.0.0.1
      IPv4 Interface address(es) TLV #132, length: 4
        IPv4 interface address: 62.0.0.1
      Hostname TLV #137, length: 9
        Hostname: Frankfurt
      Extended IS Reachability TLV #22, length: 75
        IS Neighbor: 0621.5401.3008.00, Metric: 10, sub-TLVs present (64)
          IPv4 interface address subTLV #6, length: 4, 10.0.0.2
          IPv4 neighbor address subTLV #8, length: 4, 10.0.0.1
          Unreserved bandwidth subTLV #11, length: 32
            priority level 0: 2488.320 Mbps
            priority level 1: 2488.320 Mbps
            priority level 2: 2488.320 Mbps
            priority level 3: 2488.320 Mbps
```

```
        priority level 4: 2488.320 Mbps
        priority level 5: 2488.320 Mbps
        priority level 6: 2488.320 Mbps
        priority level 7: 2488.320 Mbps
      Reservable link bandwidth subTLV #10, length: 4, 2488.320 Mbps
      Maximum link bandwidth subTLV #9, length: 4, 2488.320 Mbps
      Administrative groups subTLV #3, length: 4, 0x00000000
  Extended IPv4 Reachability TLV #135, length: 18
    IPv4 prefix: 62.0.0.1/32, Distribution: up, Metric: 0
    IPv4 prefix: 10.0.0.0/30, Distribution: up, Metric: 10
```

Figure 14.17 shows the contents of the Traffic Engineering Router ID TLV #134. It basically contains a single unique 32-bit ID in order to uniquely identify a router in the TED. The TE Router ID TLV #134 corresponds to the OSPF Router-ID and puts the topology gathered by the two protocols into a relationship in the TED. The underlying problem is that IS-IS identifies its nodes through System-IDs (48-bit) and OSPF does it using Router-IDs (32-bit). By issuing a TLV #134 the IS-IS speaker tells other routers what would be the corresponding OSPF router-ID in case one router is running both OSPF and IS-IS for transition purposes.

In Table 14.2 there is a list of sub-TLVs to the extended Reachability TLV #22. These are used for conveying various pieces of link information like Admin (Affinity) Groups, bandwidth parameters and IPv4 endpoint addresses. Chapter 11 "TLVs and Sub-TLVs" explores more about TLVs and sub-TLV nesting.

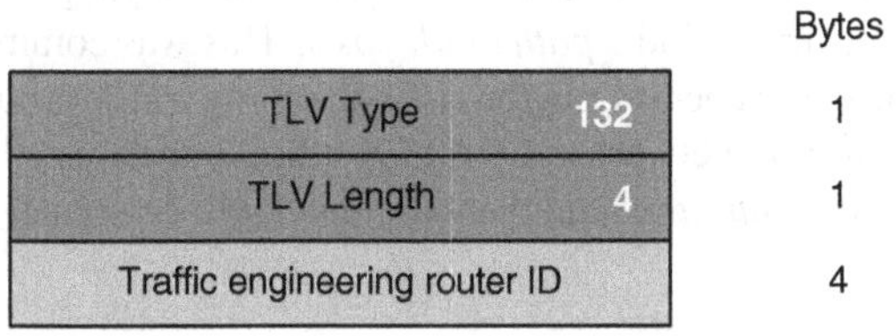

		Bytes
TLV Type	132	1
TLV Length	4	1
Traffic engineering router ID		4

FIGURE 14.17. The Traffic Engineering TLV #134 contains a unique ID which identifies a TE speaker throughout disjoint TE domains

TABLE 14.2. Sub-TLV code points.

Sub-TLV	Sub-TLV name
3	Administrative (Affinity) Group
4	Link Local ID
5	Link Remote ID
6	IPV4 Interface Address
8	IPV4 Remote Interface Address
9	Maximum Link Bandwidth
10	Reserve Able Bandwidth
11	Unreserved Bandwidth
18	TE-Metric
20	Link Protection Type (GMPLS)
21	Switching Capability (GMPLS)
Not yet assigned by IANA	Bandwidth Constraints

After the TED has been populated with the above link-related information, the routers engage in a CSPF calculation based on the network operator's constraints. The CSPF is a two-pass calculation where in the first pass all the links that do not fit a certain constraint are removed, and the second pass is a vanilla SPF calculation as was described in Chapter 10, "SPF and Route Calculation".

See Figure 14.18 for an example of CSPF. The network needs to compute a label switched path between Washington and New York which can only run on links carrying the "Internet" Link Colour (Affinity Group) and must not run on links carrying the "Maintenance" Link Colour (Affinity Group). The amount of reserved bandwidth is 600 MBit/s. In the first pass of the CSPF calculation all the links that do not belong to the required "Internet" administrative group are removed. The direct link between Washington and New York does not fit the constraint because it carries the "Maintenance" Link Colour. Next, all the links that do not have sufficient bandwidth are removed. The reservation of additional 600 MBit/s would oversubscribe the link between Washington and Frankfurt and is removed as well.

Based on the resulting "skeleton", the routers run an SPF calculation and try to find the shortest path node between the source and the destination point. In our example, the path via Paris, Frankfurt and London fits all the constraints and therefore the tunnel comes up. The result of the SPF calculation does not really matter because in this case there is only a single path left which fulfils all constraints.

If there are too many constraints during the first pass and there are no feasible paths at all, then the result of the SPF calculation will be that there is *no* shortest path between a pair of nodes. Note that in CSPF calculations, there is not any type of *crank-back* procedure where the systems try to find a *path at all costs.* This was common practice for voice networks, but crank-back schemes run the risk of sending traffic around the continent several times, like the overlay networks of the 1990s did. Sometimes the result of the CSPF calculation is even *no result at all* and then no tunnel will be signalled.

14.6 LDP over RSVP-TE Tunnelling

Which signalling protocol (LDP or RSVP-TE) to use is one of the first questions that network operators raise when deploying MPLS. Many people like the "call-oriented" notion of RSVP-TE and the amount of control the network operator has over traffic. On the other hand, LDP works like a charm – you turn it on and seconds later you have got label switched paths to every corner of your network at almost no cost and with nice scaling properties. To achieve the same connectivity matrix that LDP creates, one would have to deploy RSVP-TE in a full-mesh fashion with a dedicated tunnel between all the MPLS edge routers. In moderate size networks full-mesh RSVP-TE may be a design choice, however, in medium-to large-sized networks, this may be a scaling nightmare. Recall that in a full-mesh network with 1000 edge routers, one would need $1000 * (1000 - 1)/2 = 499{,}500$ label switched paths! The refresh noise alone from repeating each reservation every 30 seconds, which will be processed twice (PATH and RESV messages from all the core routers along the label switched path), would result in approximately 30,000 messages per second being processed by each core router. Although there are extensions to aggregate refreshes

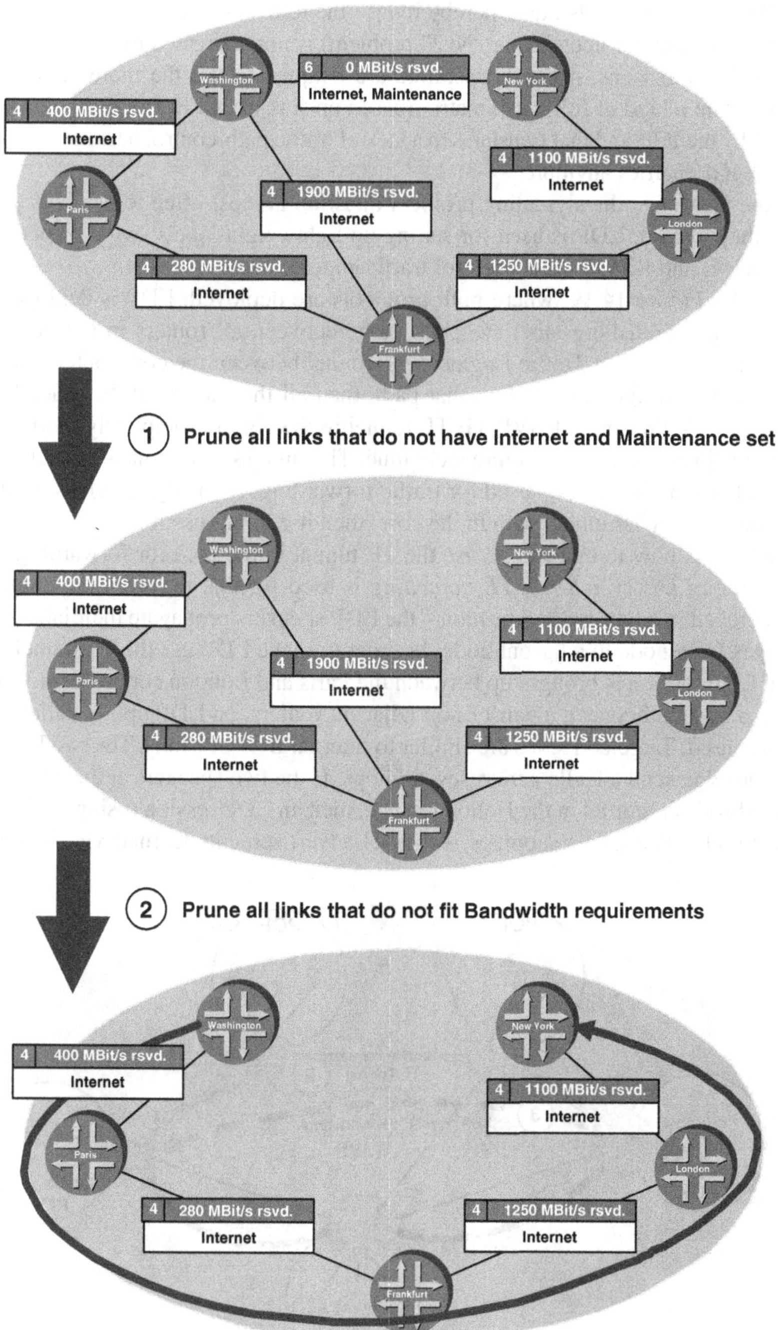

FIGURE 14.18. In the CSPF calculation all paths that do not meet any of the constraints are pruned off the final topology

(see RFC 2961 for details), and thereby reduce the refresh noise, the underlying problem (which is the familiar networking "N^2" problem) is not addressed by aggregation alone. For scalability reasons, network operators are tempted to use the more scaleable LDP, which sets up a kind of full-mesh matrix (based on sink trees). But LDP label selection is dictated by the IGP, and that translates to a lack of traffic path-control because no one wants to tweak IGP metrics anymore.

So the answer to the signalling protocol question is most often to use *both* protocols where they fit best. LDP is used for setting up lightweight labels switched paths across the network, and RSVP-TE is used for traffic engineering.

Consider Figure 14.19, where both protocols are deployed. LDP is deployed across the core for establishing label switched paths between all routers in the network (1). Additionally, there is a Traffic Engineering Tunnel between the core router in Paris and London (2). If traffic is loaded on that path, then all the traffic will be guided through LDP paths and the single RSVP-TE TE tunnel in the core is completely ignored. Why? Because MPLS is a *source routing* technique. The ingress router makes the choice as to which label switched path is used for traffic forwarding. If an edge (ingress) router does not know about a TE tunnel path in the core, then it will not use it.

The trick is now to make LDP *use* the TE tunnel in the core for forwarding. A technique called *LDP over RSVP-TE tunnelling* is used for that purpose. Previously, LDP was deployed in a hop-by-hop fashion – the LDP speakers propagate their label mapping messages from node to adjacent node. In order to make LDP use the TE tunnel, an additional LDP session is brought up between the Paris and London core router (3). For setting up a session between a pair of non-adjacent routers, an LDP option called *targeted Hellos* is used. Targeted Hellos are similar to internal BGP sessions. The two LDP speakers at the edge send a Hello across several hops. If the two speakers at the edge agree on the capabilities reported in the Hello message, then an LDP session (using TCP) is established to advertise label mappings. All label advertisements learned via the multi-hop

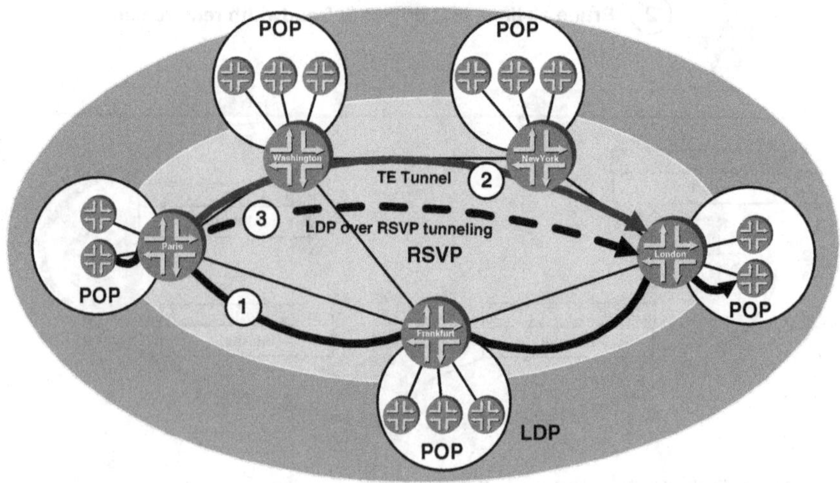

FIGURE 14.19. Traffic from Paris to London does not take the TE tunnel path

LDP session are now associated with the TE tunnel and then used for traffic forwarding. When Paris advertises a label back to its local POP routers, then a SWAP/PUSH state on the forwarding plane is generated. The label of the TE tunnel is PUSHed as top level label and the label learned via the multi-hop LDP session is the SWAPed label. The edge routers send their traffic down the LDP established paths and do not even know that their traffic is being engineered in the core topology. As soon as the traffic arrives at the ingress of the TE tunnel (Paris), an additional label is PUSHed on top of the label stack and the traffic is sent down the TE tunnel. The penultimate TE tunnel router (New York) removes the top label and the LDP label underneath becomes visible and is used for further relaying traffic towards the LDP egress router.

Configuration of LDP over RSVP-TE tunnelling is done using the `mpls ldp neighbor <address> targeted ldp` keyword in IOS and the `ldp-tunneling` keyword in JUNOS.

IOS configuration

In IOS LDP tunnelling is a global option which can be configured using the `mpls ldp neighbor <address> targeted` statement.

```
London# show running-config
[ ... ]
mpls ldp neighbor 192.168.1.1 targeted ldp
[ ... ]
!
```

If the multi-hop LDP session comes up and there is an RSVP-TE tunnel to this destination, then the resolver will automatically set up the SWAP/PUSH state. In JUNOS LDP over RSVP-TE tunnelling is a property of the TE tunnel and is configured under the `protocols mpls label-switched-path <name> {}` stanza.

JUNOS configuration

In JUNOS the `ldp-tunneling` keyword automatically sets up a session between two ends of a TE tunnel.

```
[edit]
hannes@Frankfurt# show
[ ... ]
protocols {
  mpls {
    label-switched-path to-London {
      to 192.168.0.8;
      ldp-tunneling;
    }
    interface so-1/2/0;
    interface lo0.0;
  }
[ ... ]
```

It is imperative that the loopback interface lo0.0 or *interface all* is listed when configuring LDP tunnelling. LDP multi-hop sessions are sourced using the IP address of the lo0.0 interface. If it is not listed, then the tunnelled LDP session stays down.

LDP over RSVP-TE tunnelling is a good example of how label stacking contributes to better scalability of the network. The LDP over RSVP-TE tunnelling example just needed to set up one additional forwarding state at the TE tunnel ingress router. The rest of the core topology was unaffected by the LDP tunnelling change. An additional advantage of the clear layering is that once the tunnel goes down, immediately alternate paths (that is, the LDP-only paths that are available) are available. Also, the churn for changing the label state is almost zero, because only the TE ingress routers need to change forwarding state to use the IGP guided paths.

Unfortunately LDP over RSVP-TE tunnelling does not solve the label selection issue for all topologies. Typically, it only attracts traffic being sourced from directly attached routers in the POP. For any edge router that is at least 2 hops upstream, it is not possible to force traffic onto a certain path. Figure 14.20 illustrates the problem.

The links from Paris to Washington, Washington to New York, and Paris to Frankfurt are congested. Frankfurt and Paris are major traffic sources. There is a TE tunnel between Frankfurt and New York (1) – LDP tunneling is turned on. Now, all the Frankfurt POP traffic is using the tunnel. What would be best is to also attract the traffic from Paris. But this is *not* possible in this topology because Paris selects the label switched path to New York via Washington, which is the shortest path.

In this simple topology the easiest fix would be to install another TE tunnel from Paris to New York. However, in complex topologies, often the administrative overhead of managing *several* local tunnels outweighs the convenience of having *fewer* tunnels to manage. It would be nice if there was a tool where networks could gradually suck traffic to the

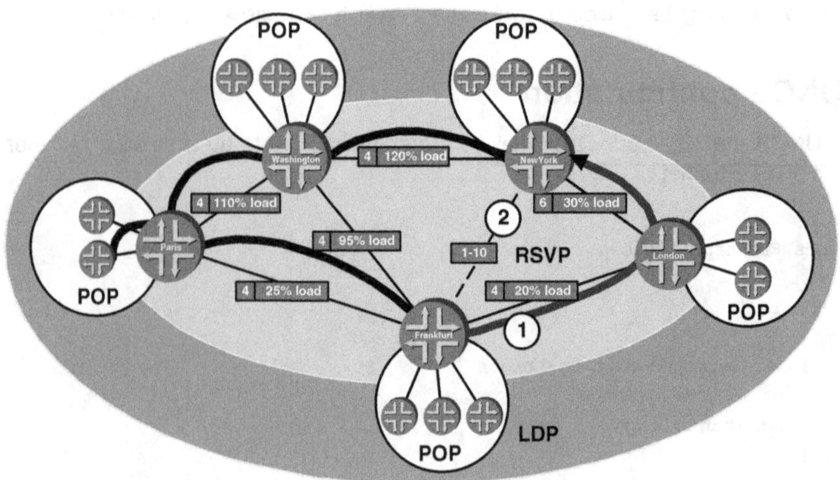

FIGURE 14.20. For traffic engineering of upstream routers forwarding adjacencies need to be configured

head-end of a TE tunnel. But to affect non-local forwarding decisions, the network needs to find a way to modify the route computation. And there is one. *Forwarding adjacencies* are a way of re-advertising a label switched path in the IS-IS database.

14.7 Forwarding Adjacencies

The Edge MPLS routers, which speak LDP, have to rely on the IGP (IS-IS) to find the shortest path to the destination. Recall that the general problem of traffic engineering is that the shortest path is not always the best path. The tunnel must be made somewhat attractive to the edge systems' traffic. One way of doing this is to model the core TE tunnel as a direct link and make the tunnels cost a little better than the resulting IGP cost. Because of that slight difference, the edge systems will prefer to load traffic onto the tunnel.

A decade ago it was common to run IGPs over a tunnel. But running dynamic routing protocols over a tunnel is almost always a recipe for disaster. Things behave *really* badly if the total IGP cost over the tunnel undermines the total topologies' cost. What happens next is that the tunnel "wraps" around itself, ultimately causing a meltdown of the entire network. Having those glorious meltdowns in mind, designers put a few restrictions on re-advertising a TE tunnel as part of the IS-IS topology. First of all, no IS-IS Hellos are sent down a tunnel. The router considers this forwarding adjacency to be up when the tunnel is up. If there is a change in topology and the tunnel goes down, then the forwarding adjacency will go down as well. Because no Hellos are sent down the tunnel there is *no infinite recursion* problem as there was when tunnelling IGPs in the 1990s. Still, there are some things to watch out for. If the cost of the forwarding adjacency becomes too low (that is, more attractive to the rest of the topology) then too much traffic is sucked towards that tunnel. This could even totally mess up the IGP routing.

Reconsider Figure 14.20. If the TE tunnel is advertised with IS reach information in the IS-IS database, then it seems as if there is now a direct, additional link between Frankfurt and New York (2). The nice thing is that the metric of this "virtual" adjacency can be configured arbitrarily. It can be set to a metric of 10, which makes the link totally unattractive because there are shorter paths available. However, if the forwarding adjacency metric is set (for instance) to 1, then even non-local traffic is sucked into the tunnel, including all the POP traffic from (for example) Paris. Depending on the IGP metric design, the power of forwarding adjacencies can do severe damage to the network. Consider the IGP metric proposal in Figure 12.10. A metric of 1 is not used today, mainly to leave some headroom for high speed links like OC768/STM-256 pipes. But if the advertised metric of the tunnel is 1, even regional traffic between cities can be sucked across the Atlantic. A common design rule is to keep the IGP cost slightly above the cost of the real topology, and it should not exceed the typical link-metric inside the POP. The idea is to suck the entire POP destinations across the tunnel, but keep the *sucking-distance* low enough not to affect other region's traffic.

In IOS forwarding adjacencies are a property of a TE tunnel and can be configured using the `tunnel mpls traffic-eng forwarding-adjacency` parameter in the tunnel interface configuration.

IOS configuration

In IOS you need to tell the tunnel interface that it has to re-advertise the TE tunnel into IS-IS using the `tunnel mpls traffic-eng forwarding-adjacency` statement. Additionally the resulting IS-IS metric needs to be specified using the regular `isis metric <*>` statement.

```
London# show running-config
[ ... ]
interface Tunnel0
  mpls traffic-eng tunnels
  tag-switching ip
  tunnel mode mpls traffic-eng
  tunnel mpls traffic-eng forwarding-adjacency
  isis metric 200 level-2
!
```

In JUNOS, a forwarding adjacency is an IS-IS property and is configured under the `protocols isis label-switched-path {}` stanza.

JUNOS configuration

In JUNOS you need to reference a valid label switched path which needs to exist under the `protocols mpls {}` stanza plus the IS-IS level and metric.

```
hannes@Frankfurt> show configuration
[ ... ]
protocols {
  isis {
    [ ... ]
    label-switched-path Paris-to-London {
      level 2 metric 200;
    }
  }
}
[ ... ]
```

How do the other routers know that an IS-IS adjacency is *real* (over physical links) or the result of a forwarding adjacency (over a TE tunnel)? In order not to run into recursive tunnel loop problems, there is a differentiation. If you consider the tcpdump output, then you can easily see the difference between a physical link adjacency and a forwarding adjacency.

Tcpdump output

A forwarding adjacency enabled IS reachability information does not carry any traffic engineering sub-TLVs.

```
   00:28:20.760649 OSI, IS-IS, length: 156
     hlen: 27, v: 1, pdu-v: 1, sys-id-len: 6 (0), max-area: 3 (0), pdu-type: L2 LSP
         lsp-id: 1921.6800.1014.00-00, seq: 0x0000df31, lifetime: 1196s
         chksum: 0x2674 (correct), PDU length: 156, L1L2 IS
           [ … ]
           Hostname TLV #137, length: 5
             Hostname: Paris
           Extended IS Reachability TLV #22, length: 86
physical link →IS Neighbor: 1921.6800.1008.00, Metric: 10, sub-TLVs present (64)
               IPv4 interface address subTLV #6, length: 4, 172.16.0.2
               IPv4 neighbor address subTLV #8, length: 4, 172.16.0.1
               Unreserved bandwidth subTLV #11, length: 32
                 priority level 0: 2488.320 Mbps
                 priority level 1: 2488.320 Mbps
                 priority level 2: 2488.320 Mbps
                 priority level 3: 2488.320 Mbps
                 priority level 4: 2488.320 Mbps
                 priority level 5: 2488.320 Mbps
                 priority level 6: 2488.320 Mbps
                 priority level 7: 2488.320 Mbps
               Reservable link bandwidth subTLV #10, length: 4, 2488.320 Mbps
               Maximum link bandwidth subTLV #9, length: 4, 2488.320 Mbps
               Administrative groups subTLV #3, length: 4, 0x00000000
Forw. Adjacency →IS Neighbor: 1921.6800.1012.00, Metric: 200, no sub-TLVs present
           Extended IPv4 Reachability TLV #135, length: 18
             IPv4 prefix: 62.0.0.1/32, Distribution: up, Metric: 0
             IPv4 prefix: 172.16.0.0/30, Distribution: up, Metric: 10
```

The forwarding adjacency gets advertised as simply Extended IS Reach Adjacency with no sub-TLVs at all attached to it. Therefore, the adjacency does not get moved to the TED. It is almost as if this virtual "link" does not exist for the TED. If a link does not exist in the TED, then no adjacency can be established over it, and the tunnel recursion problem is fixed. One of the key concepts of forwarding adjacencies is that the resulting virtual link should always be worse than a real link. Chapter 17, "Future of IS-IS", will extend the forwarding adjacency concept to several switching layers and examine how forwarding adjacencies can be utilized for G-MPLS applications.

Forwarding adjacencies are a nice tool to offload traffic from the shortest path with minimal configuration and maximum impact. However, one problem remains: if the path's physical characteristics change, the delay characteristics of that path may also change. In order to modify traffic paths for only some classes of traffic, DiffServ Traffic Engineering needs to be deployed.

14.8 DiffServ Aware Traffic Engineering

Originally, traffic engineering was used to offload just best-effort traffic. This was fine, because at that time, only best-effort traffic was routed. In recent years, however, there has

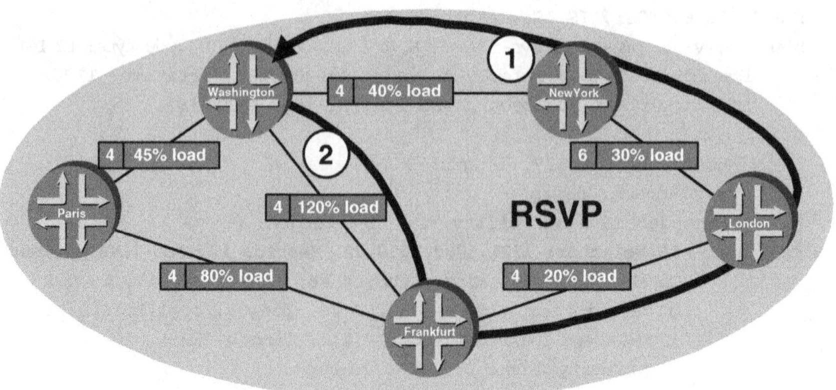

FIGURE 14.21. Bandwidth utilization optimization often makes delay characteristics of a path worse

been a shift from routing pure best-effort traffic toward *multi-service networks*, which could route voice, video and data. It turned out that the granularity of traffic engineering may be a bit too coarse, because it affects *all* the traffic between a pair of locations and does not offer a per-class granularity that would take voice traffic over a different path than for best-effort traffic. Consider Figure 14.21 for an illustration of the dilemma. There is a capacity problem between Frankfurt and Washington, so a TE tunnel between via London is applied. However, now the throughput was optimized at the expense of delay. Now voice traffic from London to Washington has an extra delay of 20 ms due to the traffic-engineering imposed delay. The good news is that typically voice applications do not consume much bandwidth. What is needed is to keep the London to Washington voice traffic untouched, and only route best-effort traffic across the alternate path.

DiffServ TE allows the network operator to engineer class-specific LSPs. In the above example, the traffic engineer could leave voice traffic on the direct link between Frankfurt and Washington and make sure that, as long the traffic does not violate the traffic contract, it gets through even if the interface is 120 per cent congested in the best-effort class (this means bandwidth guarantees get enforced).

DiffServ TE-capable software has not yet been released by the two major router vendors. Meanwhile, there are pre-standard implementations available, but given that the IETF has not yet agreed on a single TE standard and the necessary code-points, it will probably take another year until interoperable software is available.

14.9 Changed IS-IS Flooding Dynamics

IS-IS is the driver behind the TED. It carries dynamic information about the current network reservation state. In order to make good routing decisions one needs to make sure that a change in bandwidth reservation is propagated as quickly as possible. On the other hand, frequent LSP updates stress the flooding sub-system. Vendors need to make sure that in the event of many LSPs flapping (down/up), the update in reservation does not churn the network. JUNOS and IOS support throttling mechanisms in order to hold down quick reservation changes. In IOS, those throttling timers are configurable on a per interface basis.

JUNOS Configuration Snippet

In JUNOS the update-threshold parameter to control IGP updates based on reservation is a function of the rsvp interface {} stanza.

```
hannes@Frankfurt# show configuration

[ ... ]
protocols {
  rsvp {
    interface so-7/0/0.0 {
      update-threshold 10;
    }
  }
}
```

You can verify your setting by issuing the show rsvp interface <if-name> detail command.

14.10 Conclusion

IS-IS has become far more than just an IP routing protocol. It is now being used for traffic engineering purposes by sending a lot of extra topology-related information like bandwidth, link colours and additional TE metrics. All this information is conveyed using sub-TLVs to the Extended IS Reach TLV #22 and stored in a unified form in the TED. Based on the TED contents, Explicit Route Objects (ERO) are pre-determined, which will then be embedded in RSVP-TE path messages. The calculations are done using a CSPF calculation, which is a modified version of the SPF algorithm. The constrained SPF algorithm first prunes off links that do not follow certain constraints before doing a regular SPF. Setting up just the tunnel is not enough; one needs to care also about loading traffic on the tunnel. Re-advertising TE tunnels back into IS-IS is the way to attract enough traffic from other hops further downstream from the head of the TE tunnel. Optimizing for the best network utilization may not be desirable, especially for voice traffic, which requires low and stable delays. DiffServ TE allows the calculation and setup of per-traffic-class tunnels for optimizing the different goals of each class: best-effort traffic is optimized for bandwidth utilization and voice traffic is optimized for the shortest delay. Changes in bandwidth reservations also cause an extra amount of LSP updates, which need to be taken into account for assessing the overall scalability of large networks. Meanwhile, code supporting traffic engineering has been in the field now for 3–4 years and is in a mature state now. DiffServ Traffic Engineering Code has not been deployed yet in production networks, but is expected to be the "Swiss Army knife" of traffic engineering, fulfilling the purpose for all traffic types.

15

Troubleshooting

Now you know almost everything there is to know about IS-IS and you can go and configure it in your network. Seriously, IS-IS is quite easy to configure on router OSs. Most likely, a pair of routers will immediately start exchanging PDUs and then do an SPF calculation on the common set of entries in the IS-IS link-state database. If they don't, well, just continue reading. This chapter is all about IS-IS *troubleshooting*. First, this chapter will develop a common flowchart-like methodology that allows us to hunt down almost any IS-IS related problem. Next, the chapter explores the troubleshooting tools that are available on the router OS for gathering the information required by the troubleshooting methodology. Finally, the chapter will end by exploring real-world case studies of IS-IS-related problems in the areas of adjacency management, database overloading, and SPF calculations.

15.1 Methodology

Any good troubleshooting process starts with a step-by-step plan and an iterative comparison between the desired state of the network and the actual state. For example, it does not make sense to examine the contents of the link-state database if no adjacency is up to supply the LSDB with data. The starting assumption for this troubleshooting plan of attack is that the router has a working physical circuit, free of bit errors and other transmission-related faults.

Figure 15.1 illustrates a generic troubleshooting plan for IS-IS problems. The heart of the plan is an iterative comparison between results from the router's observed operation to the intended behaviour, typically the behaviour defined in the configuration file. In the illustrations in this chapter, configuration-related information (what the router *should* be doing) is indicated by *light* bubbles. Facts gathered from command outputs confirms what the router is *actually* doing, which is indicated by *dark* bubbles.

You start a troubleshooting session by verifying that adjacencies to other routers are up. If they are not, then there are three main sources of trouble. First, the problem could be related to the interface configuration (1). For example, an interface might not be included in the router's IS-IS interface list or it carries wrong IS-IS level information. The problem could even be buried at lower layers in the OSI reference stack: too small a protocol MTU or lack of OSI-CP support on point-to-point interfaces prevent IS-IS control planes from exchanging any information. Next, a good place to look is the addressing information like IPv4, IPv6 and OSI NLRIs. Most importantly, you first need to look

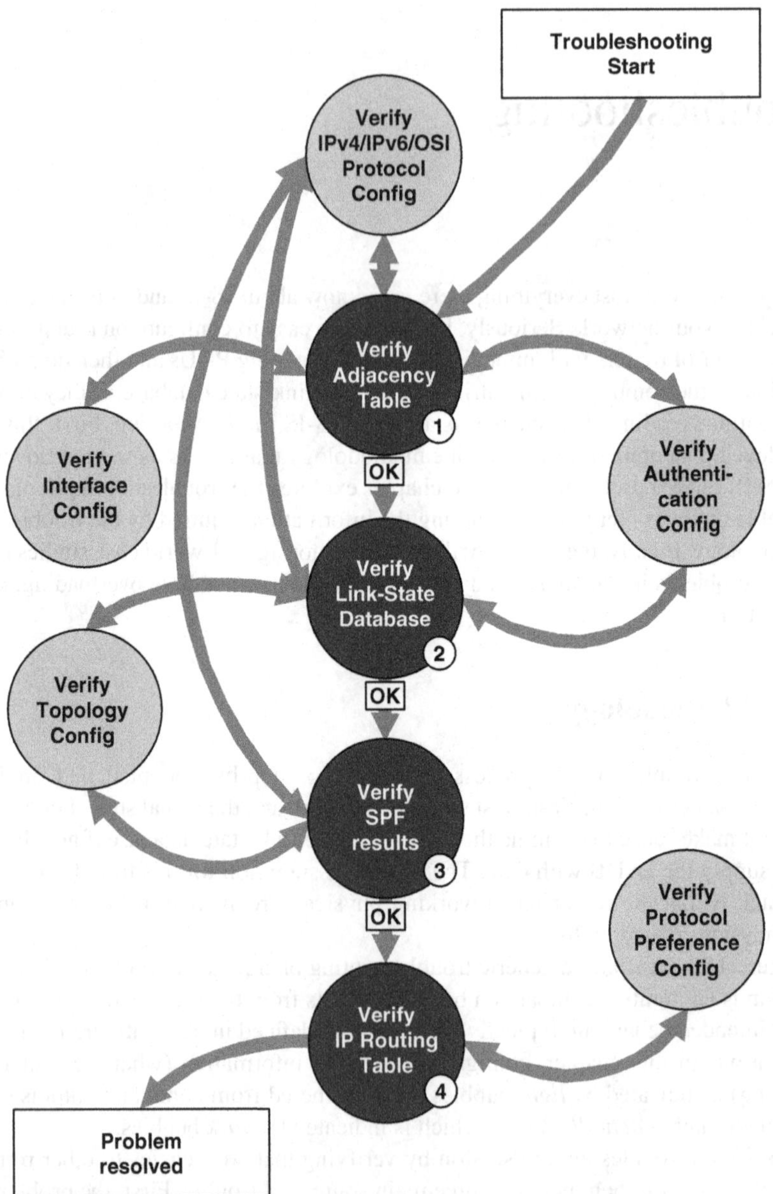

FIGURE 15.1. At the heart of the troubleshooting process are iterations between comparisons of configuration information and the actual state of the network

at the OSI router configuration, because that encompasses IS-IS Area- and System-ID configuration. If the System-ID and or Area-IDs are not configured, or wrongly defined, then any IS-IS network is condemned to failure. Unfortunately, adjacency management is no longer a protocol-neutral function in IS-IS. Many IS-IS implementations require a match for the IPv4 or IPv6 sub-nets in order to complete the IS-IS adjacency handshake. Also, a broken authentication configuration is a frequent reason why an adjacency does not come up.

The next major step is to check to see if the link-state database is filled with information (2). The major stumbling blocks here are duplicate System-IDs and mismatched authentication strings. After the router executes the SPF calculation, it shows you the calculated topology and the attached prefixes. If a node is missing in the SPF result list (3), we examine the link-state database to check for node isolation or unidirectional links and may even spot a problem on a remote router in the network. In the age of multi-topology IS-IS, it may be necessary to revisit the topology information and check to see if a given interface is in the required topology. A double check in the link-state database helps to spot missing IS Reachability Announcements and the like. If a node finally shows up in the SPF result list, and it has attached prefixes, those prefixes need to compete with prefixes from other routing protocols to become active routes. Because of its role as a topology discovery tool, IS-IS does not carry customer routes, but rather infrastructure routes. So IS-IS routes are typically preferred to routes from other routing protocols like BGP. However, in IOS, for example, external BGP paths have an *administrative distance,* which has a route preference of 20 versus an IS-IS route that ranks only at distance 115 of the route selection process. Particularly during routing protocol migrations (for example from EIGRP to IS-IS) it may be the case that the other routing protocol is still masking the routes from the new routing protocol. A modification of the protocol preference configuration helps to unveil the IS-IS routes. If the IP routes finally show up in the main IP routing table, the troubleshooting process may end.

In our explanation of the troubleshooting process, we already mentioned two *tools* for information gathering: Examining the router configuration and looking at the output of show commands are important tools during the troubleshooting process. In the next section we will explore those tools and more, tools that help operators examine, understand and resolve IS-IS problems.

15.2 Tools

IS-IS troubleshooting quality and the accuracy of problem assessments is based on one main factor: the tools that supply the network engineer with information. Based on the information derived from good tools, the network engineer makes a decision regarding the parts of the configuration and the environment that are broken.

The first and most important troubleshooting tools are the *show commands* that the router OS offers. Show command outputs are used on a daily basis and therefore it is imperative that each network engineer knows the meaning of each output field of these commands.

15.2.1 *Show Commands*

Following our troubleshooting plan illustrated in Figure 15.1, we need show commands to supply the current state of the network. The five main commands that we will use shortly to examine JUNOS and IOS are in the areas of:

- Displaying the IS-IS related interface properties
- Displaying the adjacency table
- Displaying the link-state database
- Displaying the results of the SPF calculation
- Displaying the routing table

First, the show commands for IOS will be discussed. In IOS, all five commands are not in the same command hierarchy. Some commands are tucked beneath the `show clns`, some in the `show isis` and others in the `show ip` command keyword hierarchy.

15.2.1.1 IOS Show Commands

In the IOS command line hierarchy all commands that deal with adjacency management and interface-related configuration are under the `show clns` branch. The two main commands to display IS-IS interface properties and adjacency tables are the `show clns interface` and `show clns neighbor` command.

IOS command output

The output of the `show clns` command contains many OSI-related fields which reveals that the initial purpose for IS-IS was to route OSI traffic. Below the routing protocol stanza the output shows level, metric and number of active adjacencies information.

```
London#show clns interface
POS4/0 is up, line protocol is up
  Checksums enabled, MTU 4470, Encapsulation PPP
  ERPDUs enabled, min. interval 10msec.
  RDPDUs enabled, min. interval 100msec., Addr Mask enabled
  Congestion Experienced bit set at 4 packets
  CLNS fast switching enabled
  CLNS SSE switching disabled
  DEC compatibility mode OFF for this interface
  Next ESH/ISH in 38 seconds
  Routing Protocol: IS-IS
    Circuit Type: level-1-2
    Interface number 0x0, local circuit ID 0x100
    Neighbor Extended Local Circuit ID: 0x1
    Neighbor System-ID: Frankfurt
    Level-1 IPv6 Metric: 10
    Number of active level-1 adjacencies: 1
    Level-2 IPv6 Metric: 10
```

```
    Number of active level-2 adjacencies: 1
    Next IS-IS Hello in 4 seconds
    if state UP
[ … ]
```

IOS command output

The show clns neighbors commands may be qualified using the detail option, which lists IP and Area addresses. Comparing addressing information against your neighbour's is an important step in troubleshooting adjacencies.

```
London#show clns neighbors detail
System Id     Interface     SNPA               State    Holdtime     Type Protocol
Frankfurt     Fa0/0         00a0.a512.339      Up       22           L1L2 IS-IS
  Area Address(es): 49.0002
  IP Address(es): 172.26.26.213*
  Uptime: 04:30:54
  NSF capable
[ … ]
```

After initial adjacency establishment, the link-state database needs to get filled with LSPs. The output of the show isis database lists the contents of the link-state database. Each line of the output represents a TLV. The keyword Extended indicates that this is a wide-metric style TLV.

IOS command output

The show isis database plus the optional detail or verbose command displays the LSP header and TLV contents of the LSPs in the link-state database.

```
London#show isis database verbose
IS-IS Level-1 Link State Database:
LSPID               LSP Seq Num     LSP Checksum     LSP Holdtime     ATT/P/OL
Frankfurt.00-00     0x000000BB      0x34F5           2503             1/0/0
   Area Address:      49.0002
   NLPID:             0xCC 0x8E
   Router ID:         192.168.0.8
   IP Address:        192.168.0.8
   Hostname: Frankfurt
   Metric: 250000        IS-Extended Washington.00
     Interface IP Address: 172.16.4.13
   Metric: 250000        IP 172.16.4.12/30
   [ … ]
```

After so-called "trigger" events like an LSP content (TLV) change, an SPF run is triggered. It is recommended that you keep an eye on the frequency of those SPF runs using the show isis spf-log command for IPv4 and the show isis ipv6 spf-log command for IPv6. If there are no topology changes like metrics changes or link flaps then you should only see the periodical SPF runs executed every 900 seconds (15 minutes).

IOS command output

In a quiet environment without link flaps a periodic SPF run is triggered every 15 minutes.

```
London#show isis spf-log

  IP level 1 SPF log

   When        Duration    Nodes   Count    First trigger LSP  Triggers
04:34:52            12        8       2     Frankfurt.00-00    ATTACHFLAG LSPHEADER
04:29:33             8        8       1                        PERIODIC
04:14:30             0        8       1                        PERIODIC
03:59:26             4        8       1                        PERIODIC
03:44:25             4        8       1                        PERIODIC
03:29:25            12        8       1                        PERIODIC
03:14:24            12        8       1                        PERIODIC
[ … ]
```

After the SPF calculation is finished a sorted list of nodes plus their associated neighbours (next-hops) is generated. The show isis topology command displays each node in the network plus the calculated cost to get there.

IOS command output

The show isis topology output displays the result of the IPv4 calculation. The show isis ipv6 topology provides the results of the IPv6 calculation in case that multi topology has been deployed.

```
London#show isis topology
[ … ]
IS-IS IP paths to level-2 routers
System Id        Metric       Next-Hop         Interface       SNPA
Frankfurt        22000        Frankfurt        POS4/0
Washington       272000       Frankfurt        POS4/0
New York         294000       Frankfurt        POS4/0
Pennsauken       315000       Pennsauken       POS5/0
London           –
[ … ]
```

The last step is to verify if the route in question has been inserted in the IP routing table. The output of the show ip route command shows if the IS-IS supplied route is the best in the system. If it is not, then we need to adjust protocol preferences.

IOS command output

The `show ip route` command displays all the contents of the IPv4 Unicast Routing Table. Alternatively, you can append the `isis` qualifier to the commands, which displays only the IS-IS supplied routes.

```
London#show ip route
[ … ]
       171.16.0.0/16 is variably subnetted, 2 subnets, 2 masks
i L2   171.16.33.0/29 [115/34] via 172.16.33.213, POS4/0
i L2   171.16.33.16/30 [115/18] via 172.16.33.213, POS4/0
       172.16.33.0/24 is subnetted, 1 subnets
C        172.16.33.0 is directly connected, POS5/0
       172.16.34.0/24 is variably subnetted, 16 subnets, 4 masks
i L2   172.16.34.8/30 [115/24] via 172.16.33.213, FastEthernet0/0
i L2   172.16.34.0/22 [115/34] via 172.16.33.213, FastEthernet0/0
i L1   172.16.34.12/30 [115/25] via 172.16.33.213, FastEthernet0/0
i L1   172.16.34.8/30 [115/15] via 172.16.33.213, FastEthernet0/0
```

JUNOS supplies similar command output to IOS.

15.2.1.2 JUNOS Show Commands

JUNOS does not carry any OSI forwarding legacy. As visible property of that "clean-sheet" design all the relevant IS-IS commands are under the `show isis` command hierarchy. The two most important commands are again to display the current adjacency state and the interface list with parameters.

JUNOS command output

The `show isis interface detail` command displays all parameters of an IS-IS circuit. Optional qualifiers are the `detail` and `extensive` keyword. On a broadcast circuit the command additionally lists the designated router plus a hint if it's us.

```
hannes@stockholm> show isis interface detail
IS-IS interface database:
e3-0/0/0.0
  Index: 64, State: 0x46, Circuit id: 0x1, Circuit type: 2
  LSP interval: 100ms, CSNP interval: 15s
  Level   Adjacencies   Priority   Metric   Hello (s)   Hold (s)
   Designated Router
     2            1         64        14      9.000         27
fe-0/3/3.0
  Index: 69, State: 0x6, Circuit id: 0x2, Circuit type: 1
  LSP interval: 100 ms, CSNP interval: 10 s
  Level   Adjacencies    Priority   Metric   Hello (s)   Hold (s)
    Designated Router
     1             1  64         5         3.000   9
    Stockholm.02 (us)
```

The show isis adjacency command provides you with a list of the active adjacencies on a given router. The optional command qualifiers detail and extensive provide more insight, such as a detailed property and timer breakdown plus an adjacency transition table.

JUNOS command output

The show isis adjacency command plus the optional detail and extensive qualifiers provide detailed addressing, topology and state machine output based on the current Adjacency Table.

```
hannes@Frankfurt> show isis adjacency extensive
London
  Interface: so-0/0/0.0, Level: 2, State: Up, Expires in 22secs
  Priority: 0, Up/Down transitions: 3, Last transition: 3d 04:43:07 ago
  Circuit type: 2, Speaks: IP, IPv6
  Topologies: Unicast, IPV6-Unicast
  IP addresses: 172.16.33.29
  IPv6 addresses: fe80::203:fdff:fec8:3c00
  Transition log:
  When                       State      Reason
  Tue Nov 11 16:45:17        Up         Seenself
  Thu Nov 13 17:12:26        Down       Interface Down
  Thu Nov 13 17:13:04        Up         Seenself
```

The output of the show isis database command lists the contents of the LSP header and payload entries including a list of all the encoded TLVs.

JUNOS command output

The output of the show isis database extensive gives a detailed breakdown on the LSP plus all associated internal timers like garbage collection and refresh.

```
hannes@Frankfurt> show isis database extensive
IS-IS level 2 link-state database:

Stockholm.02-00 Sequence: 0x13, Checksum: 0, Lifetime: 0 secs

  Header: LSP ID: Stockholm.02-00, Length: 37 bytes
    Allocated length: 1492 bytes, Router ID: 192.168.0.17
    Remaining lifetime: 0 secs, Level: 2,Interface: 0
    Estimated free bytes: 1416, Actual free bytes: 1455
    Garbage collection timer expires in: 1116 secs
  Packet: LSP ID: Stockholm.02-00, Length: 37 bytes, Lifetime : 0 secs
    Checksum: 0, Sequence: 0x13, Attributes: 0x3 <L1 L2>
    NLPID: 0x83, Fixed length: 27 bytes, Version: 1, Sysid length: 0 bytes
    Packet type: 20, Packet version: 1, Max area: 0

  TLVs:
    Authentication data: 8 bytes
  No queued transmissions
```

```
London.00-00 Sequence: 0xb8, Checksum: 0x10a, Lifetime: 546 secs
   IS neighbor:       Pennsauken.00      Metric:     315000
   IS neighbor:        Frankfurt.00      Metric:      22000
   IP prefix:       192.168.0.12/32      Metric:          0     Internal Up
   IP prefix:        172.16.33.0/30      Metric:      22000     Internal Up
   IP prefix:        172.16.33.4/30      Metric:     315000     Internal Up

  Header: LSP ID: London.00-00, Length: 119 bytes
    Allocated length: 1492 bytes, Router ID: 192.168.0.12
    Remaining lifetime: 546 secs, Level: 2,Interface: 0
    Estimated free bytes: 1373, Actual free bytes: 1373
    Aging timer expires in: 546 secs
    Protocols: IP, IPv6

  Packet: LSP ID: London.00-00, Length: 119 bytes, Lifetime : 3598 secs
    Checksum: 0x10a, Sequence: 0xb8, Attributes: 0xb <L1 L2 Attached>
    NLPID: 0x83, Fixed length: 27 bytes, Version: 1, Sysid length: 0 bytes
    Packet type: 18, Packet version: 1, Max area: 0

  TLVs:
    Area address: 49.0002 (3)
    Speaks: IP
    Speaks: IPv6
    IP router id: 192.168.0.12
    IP address: 192.168.0.12
    Hostname: London
    IS extended neighbor: Frankfurt.00, Metric: default 22000
      IP address: 172.16.33.2
    IS extended neighbor: Pennsauken.00, Metric: default 315000
      IP address: 172.16.33.5
      Neighbor's IP address: 172.16.33.6
    IP extended prefix: 172.16.33.0/30 metric 22000 up
    IP extended prefix: 172.16.33.4/24 metric 315000 up
  No queued transmissions
```

To check the frequency, trigger and duration of the SPF calculation, use the `show isis spf log` command. The optional keyword `topology` displays the SPF calculation for the IPv6 Unicast or IPv4 Multicast Topology. Note that for Multi Topology IS-IS, all the other configured topologies (such as IPv4 Multicast and IPv6 Unicast) are displayed as well.

JUNOS command output

```
hannes@Frankfurt> show isis spf log
  IS-IS level 2 SPF log:
Start time               Elapsed (secs) Count   Reason
Mon Nov 17 22:17:42      0.000170       1       Updated LSP Frankfurt.00-00
Mon Nov 17 22:17:44      0.000043       1       Updated LSP Frankfurt.00-00
Mon Nov 17 22:17:52      0.000246       1       Reconfig
Mon Nov 17 22:18:01      0.000166       3       New adjacency London on so- 7/0/0.0
Mon Nov 17 22:31:50      0.000180       1       Periodic SPF
```

The output of the `show isis spf results` displays both the nodal as well as the per-prefix result of the SPF calculation.

JUNOS command output

In contrast to IOS, JUNOS also includes the per-prefix metrics in the output of the topological results shown by the `show isis spf results` command. If Multi Topology is turned on, several SPF results are displayed.

```
hannes@Frankfurt> show isis spf results
  IS-IS level 2 SPF results:
Node              Metric      Interface           Via          SNPA
London.00          22000      so-7/0/0.0          London
                   22000      192.168.0.12/32
                   22000      172.16.33.4/30
                  337000      172.16.33.12/30
Pennsauken.00     315000      so-7/1/0.100        Pennsauken
                  315000      192.168.0.17/32
                  341000      172.16.33.16/30
                  630000      172.16.33.24/30
[ … ]
  14 nodes
```

The command for verifying if a route is present in the main routing tables is the `show route` command. It displays both the IPv4 Unicast Routing Table (inet.0) as well as the IPv6 Unicast Routing Table (inet6.0).

JUNOS command output

```
hannes@Frankfurt> show route
inet.0: 48 destinations, 58 routes (48 active, 0 holddown, 0 hidden)
+ = Active Route, - = Last Active, * = Both
[ … ]
192.168.0.12/32          *[IS-IS/15] 04:51:45, metric 22000
                           > to 172.26.26.29 via so-7/0/0.0
172.16.33.0/30           *[IS-IS/18] 5d 10:42:00, metric 315000
                           > to 10.0.2.5 via so-7/1/0.0
192.168.0.19/32          *[IS-IS/18] 5d 10:44:05, metric 22200
                           > to 10.0.2.5 via so-7/1/0.0
172.16.33.16/30          *[IS-IS/18] 3d 04:52:56, metric 395000
                           > to 10.0.2.9 via so-7/1/0.0
172.16.33.20/30          *[IS-IS/15] 5d 11:25:08, metric 22000
                           > to 10.0.4.10 via so-7/1/0.0
[ … ]
```

Based on the output of the show commands, network engineers often develop a theory as to what may be wrong. In order to harden the suspicion, more evidence is collected. Debug outputs often provide more detailed insight why a given configuration is not working as expected. An understanding of debug outputs is important to better understand what the router does not like about a given adjacency or configuration.

15.2.2 *Debug Logs*

IOS and JUNOS provide debugging functionalities for every IS-IS relevant function ranging from parsing PDUs to internal timing and scheduling. Figure 3.6 and Figure 3.13 in Chapter 3 "Introduction to the IOS and JUNOS Command Line Interface" shows the debug options that you have in IOS and JUNOS. The most notable differences between IOS and JUNOS is that in JUNOS, debugging functionality needs to be configured under the `protocols isis traceoptions {}` stanza. In IOS, debugging output is turned on using the operations level `debug isis` command that requires additional qualifiers as shown in Figure 3.6.

15.2.2.1 IOS Debugging

In IOS the most important `debug isis` command is the `adj-packets` qualifier. The command displays a line each time it sends and receives a Hello. You see additional lines that contain parsing results if, for example, the router does not like a certain parameter in the Hello message.

IOS debug output

The output of the `debug isis adj-packet` command points to a Level and Area ID mismatch.

```
London#debug isis adj-packets
IS-IS Adjacency related packets debugging is on
*Nov 18 19:54:25: ISIS-Adj: Rec serial IIH from *PPP* (POS4/1), cir type L1,
  cir id 01, length 48
*Nov 18 19:49:03: ISIS-Adj: rcvd state DOWN, old state INIT, new state INIT
*Nov 18 19:49:03: ISIS-Adj: No matching areas
*Nov 18 19:49:03: ISIS-Adj: Action = GOING DOWN
```

For additional authentication information debugging output you may add the authentication information qualifier to the `debug isis` command. The command provides you with more specific information about what it did not like during processing authentication information. In the example below, the router complains that there is no Authentication TLV present in the incoming Hello.

IOS debug output

```
London#debug isis adj-packets
IS-IS Adjacency related packets debugging is on
London#debug isis authentication information
IS-IS authentication information debugging is on
*Nov 19 22:56:48: ISIS-Adj: Rec serial IIH from *PPP* (POS4/1), cir type L1,
  cir id 01, length 58
*Nov 19 22:56:48: ISIS-AuthInfo: No auth TLV found in received packet
*Nov 19 22:56:48: ISIS-Adj: Authentication failed
```

Once the adjacency has been established it is also interesting to check if the LSP data exchange works and find out if Acknowledgements (PSNPs) are properly sent. The debug isis update-packets provides information about the parsing of LSP and building of PSNP packets.

IOS debug output

```
London#debug isis update-packets
IS-IS Update related packet debugging is on
*Nov 20 12:52:06: ISIS-Update: Rec L1 LSP 1921.6800.0021.00-00, seq 46, ht 65533,
*Nov 20 12:52:06: ISIS-Update: from SNPA *PPP* (POS4/1)
*Nov 20 12:52:06: ISIS-Update: LSP newer than database copy
*Nov 20 12:52:06: ISIS-Update: TLV code mismatch (2, 80)
*Nov 20 12:52:06: ISIS-Update: TLV code mismatch (2, 80)
*Nov 20 12:52:06: ISIS-Update: TLV contents different, code 0x2
*Nov 20 12:52:06: ISIS-Update: TLV code mismatch (16, 87)
*Nov 20 12:52:06: ISIS-Update: TLV contents different, code 0x16
*Nov 20 12:52:06: ISIS-Update: TLV code mismatch (80, 2)
*Nov 20 12:52:06: ISIS-Update: TLV contents different, code 0x80
*Nov 20 12:52:06: ISIS-Update: TLV code mismatch (87, 16)
*Nov 20 12:52:06: ISIS-Update: TLV contents different, code 0x87
*Nov 20 12:52:06: ISIS-Update: full SPF required
*Nov 20 12:52:06: ISIS-Update: IPv6 no change
*Nov 20 12:52:07: ISIS-Update: Build L1 PSNP entry for 1921.6800.0021-00, seq 46
*Nov 20 12:52:07: ISIS-Update: Sending L1 PSNP on POS4/1
```

15.2.2.2 JUNOS Debugging

JUNOS reveals its debugging output indirectly. You first need to configure the events you are interested in using the flag keyword underneath the protocols isis traceoptions { } stanza. The output is then written to a file which can be specified using the file qualifier.

JUNOS configuration

In JUNOS the flag keyword determines the amount of information that is written into the isis-trace.log file.

```
hannes@Frankfurt> show configuration
[ … ]
protocols {
    isis {
            file isis-trace.log size 1m microsecond-stamp;
            flag lsp receive detail;
            flag lsp-generation detail;
            flag error;
            flag hello detail;
            flag csn detail;
            flag psn detail;
        }
    }
}
```

You can specify a further qualifier after each flag. The `receive` or `send` qualifier lets you control the output of the debug log depending on the packets direction. The optional detail qualifier makes the output very verbose by giving you TLV and sub-TLV details. JUNOS offers you a nice tool when, for example, debugging LSP specific properties – you can differentiate between self-originated LSPs and LSPs that you flood further. The above combination of the `lsp receive detail` and `lsp-generation detail` knob does the trick. It displays all incoming LSPs and suppresses unnecessary output once it floods it out on every core-facing interface (which can involve massive output). On the other hand, outgoing self-originated LSPs are indeed interesting. If JUNOS would just trace down LSPs and not make the differentiation between self-originated and flooded, then your debug file would get overwhelmed after a LSP storm. If you want to see a detailed breakdown of all the packets, then just setting the flag `packets detail` can replace the `lsp, hello, csn, psn` flags.

JUNOS debug output

The `detail` qualifier after each flag in the JUNOS `traceoptions` generates a wealth of information. You can see the TLV contents of an outgoing Hello message plus the TLV Length of a Level 1 LSP build.

```
hannes@Frankfurt> monitor start isis-trace.log
*** isis-trace.log ***
Nov 20 18:47:03.340358    Sending P2P IIH on so-0/0/0.0
Nov 20 18:47:03.340431        max area 0, circuit type l1l2
Nov 20 18:47:03.340463        hold time 27, circuit id 0x01
Nov 20 18:47:03.340490        neighbor 0:2:b3:2b:e:7
Nov 20 18:47:03.340513        neighbor 0:2:b3:2b:e:52
Nov 20 18:47:03.340537        speaks IP
Nov 20 18:47:03.340557        speaks IPv6
Nov 20 18:47:03.340583        IP address 172.16.33.236
Nov 20 18:47:03.340617        IPv6 address fe80::7777:69ff: fea0:8002
Nov 20 18:47:03.340650        area address 49.0001 (3)
```

```
Nov 20 18:47:03.340680          restart RR reset RA reset holdtime 0
Nov 20 18:47:03.340711          1386 bytes of total padding
Nov 20 18:47:03.340752          checksum 0x6b7f
Nov 20 18:47:03.360591      Rebuilding L1 fragment Frankfurt.00-00, sequence 0x69
Nov 20 18:47:03.361195      Rebuilding LSP Frankfurt.00-00, free bytes 1320
Nov 20 18:47:03.361310          Next type: 1, estimated free bytes 1455,
                                 free bytes 1455
Nov 20 18:47:03.361463          Next type: 129, estimated free bytes 1449,
                                 free bytes 1449
Nov 20 18:47:03.361795          Next type: 134, estimated free bytes 1445,
                                 free bytes 1445
Nov 20 18:47:03.361880          Next type: 137, estimated free bytes 1433,
                                 free bytes 1433
Nov 20 18:47:03.362003          Next type: 22, estimated free bytes 1424,
                                 free bytes 1424
Nov 20 18:47:03.362100          Next type: 128, estimated free bytes 1353,
                                 free bytes 1353
Nov 20 18:47:03.362149          IP TLVs generated, used 29 bytes
Nov 20 18:47:03.362195      Rebuilt L1 fragment Frankfurt.00-00, size 168
```

After acquiring an understanding of what the network is doing wrong, perhaps the prerequisite for further troubleshooting is to know what the network is supposed to do. As such, you need to know where the router keeps IS-IS-related configurations and how to modify them.

15.2.3 *Configuration File*

The IS-IS-related configuration is scattered across many places in a router configuration. There is interface related configuration, router process related configuration, authentication information and finally routing-policies, route-maps and access-lists that deal with prefix exchange with other protocols.

In IOS most of the relevant IS-IS configuration is accommodated in the `router isis` and `interface` section. Authentication information (key chains) is present in the top level context and policies are defined as `route-maps`. In the configuration output below you can see an example of a full-blown IOS IS-IS configuration.

IOS configuration

In the IOS configuration most command parameters are set in the interface and `router isis` command hierarchy. Policies are defined inside `route-maps` and `access-lists`. The Authentication strings are stored within a `key chain`. Static host-name mapping is stored at the end of the configuration file underneath the `clns host` prefix.

```
London#show running-config
[ … ]
key chain MY-SECRET-KEYSTRING
  key 100
    key-string 7 0702244B4F0F16171417
```

```
!
interface FastEthernet0/0
  ip address 172.16.33.29 255.255.255.252
  ip router isis
  ipv6 router isis
  [ … ]
  isis authentication mode md5
  isis authentication key-chain MY-SECRET-KEYSTRING
  isis network point-to-point
  isis three-way-handshake ietf
!
router isis
  net 49.0002.1720.2602.6029.00
  authentication mode md5 level-2
  authentication key-chain MY-SECRET-KEYSTRING level-2
  metric-style wide
  passive-interface Loopback0
  redistribute level-2 route-map isis_leak
  !
  address-family ipv6
  multi-topology
  exit-address-family
!
access-list 1 permit 192.168.0.0 0.0.0.255
access-list 1 deny any
!
route-map isis_leak permit 1
  match ip route-source 1
!
clns host London 00.1921.6800.1019.00
[ … ]
```

The JUNOS configuration file follows a slightly different logic. Most notably routing protocol specific parameters are not in the `interfaces {}` hierarchy. There is an additional protocols `isis interface {}` stanza that holds IS-IS exclusive parameters. Almost all IS-IS behaviour is configured in the `protocols isis {}` stanza. The only IS-IS relevant configuration is the `family iso {}` stanza underneath a logical interface which tells the Packet Forwarding Engine (PFE) that we would like to receive IS-IS PDUs on this interface. One interface, preferably the `lo0` interface, also holds one or more `family iso address` statements that control the Area and System-ID settings of the router. IS-IS specific authentication strings are configured under the `protocols isis level` or `protocols isis interface level` stanza, depending on which PDU type you want to configure. In JUNOS, policy processing is a protocol-independent thing and so all policy relevant configuration is done in the `policy-options {}` stanza. Finally `static-host-mappings` for System-ID to Host Name translation services are configured in the `system stanza {}`.

JUNOS configuration

The most notable difference between JUNOS and IOS is that the majority of IS-IS parameters are configured under the `protocols isis {}` stanza. For IS-IS interface related configurations JUNOS features a `protocol isis interface {}` hierarchy that exclusively carries IS-IS per-circuit configuration.

```
hannes@Frankfurt> show configuration
[ … ]
system {
    static-host-mapping {
         London sysid 1921.6800.1019;
    }
}
interfaces {
    ge-0/5/0 {
        unit 0 {
      family inet {
        address 172.16.33.10/30;
      }
      family iso;
    }
}
lo0 {
    unit 0 {
        family inet {
            address 192.168.0.8/32;
        }
        family iso {
            address 49.0001.1921.6800.1008.00;
        }
    }
  }
}
protocols {
    isis {
        traceoptions {
            file isis-trace size 10m;
            flag error;
            flag lsp;
            flag state;
        }
        export lo0-only;
        level 1 {
            authentication-key "$9$I7ShyKX7V4aUM8aUjH5TRhS"; #
               SECRET-DATA
            authentication-type simple; # SECRET-DATA
            wide-metrics-only;
        }
        level 2 wide-metrics-only;
```

```
        interface all;
        interface ge-0/5/0.0 {
            point-to-point;
        }
    }
}
policy-options {
    policy-statement lo0-only {
        term 1 {
            from {
                interface lo0.0;
            }
            then accept;
        }
        term final {
            then reject;
        }
    }
}
```

Seeing the configuration and debug logs provides good insight for the majority of troubleshooting scenarios. Sometimes even the debug output, which often shows just an interpretation of the data, does not provide sufficient insight into what the router does not like about a given packet. Network analyzers can display every bit of a given packet and provide additional intelligence during the troubleshooting process.

15.2.4 *Network Analyzers*

Network analyzers are an excellent tool for the experienced network troubleshooter because they unveil what is *really* transported over the wire. The main disadvantage of evaluating debug logs is that they show only an *interpretation* of the protocol and not the actual content. If you need to deal with (for example) a malformed TLV, then the information that the debug log provides is probably not more than a line saying “bogus TLV”. The network analyzer in contrast *does* provide you with the exact data, and your vendor support organization can look for evidence as to what went wrong and *how* the data is corrupted.

When capturing data using commercial network analyzers, the authors found that all too often the network analyzer incorrectly interprets some of the newer TLVs, such as the Extended IS Reach, Multi-Topology IS Reach and their nested sub-TLVs. Surprisingly, the two *open-source* network analyzers, tcpdump and Ethereal, have sound support for IS-IS. Because the software is free and maintained on an ongoing basis, the authors warmly recommend use of tcpdump and/or Ethereal to troubleshoot your network and learn about IS-IS at the same time. Another reason to learn about tcpdump is that JUNOS embeds tcpdump as part of its router software.

Tcpdump in JUNOS is wrapped inside the `monitor traffic interface` command. If you enter that command, then tcpdump (with its default settings) will start producing single line output. If the output does not immediately start, then you should probably turn off DNS resolution, as the screen output may need to wait for a DNS response. The `no-resolve` knob turns off name resolution and makes the analyzer report one packet per line. Tcpdump also features a multi-line output if the `detail` flag is provided as a command option. Note that tcpdump by default only captures the first 96 bytes of an IP packet. While this short capture of the IP packet is sufficient to interpret the TCP headers (which are the origin of the name "tcpdump"), it is not enough to display the content of a control plane packet. For example, just recall that a link-state PDU may be up to hundreds of bytes in size. The `size` parameter controls the capture length of the data. For IS-IS, the highest possible packet size is 1492 bytes. However, specifying a capture size of 1492 is not enough because tcpdump does its capturing on the data-link layer and this implies that this 1492-byte frame length is the total length of the packet. For Ethernet, you need to add 17 bytes (Destination MAC Address, Source MAC Address, Length, DSAP, SSAP, Control – see Figure 4.2 for details) which results in a capture size of 1509. Many people just use the "default" Ethernet MTU of 1514 instead, as it also catches all IP control plane packets that can fit on an Ethernet. Tcpdump also allows you to filter the output using the `matching` keyword. Unfortunately, the filter string support for IS-IS is not very rich in the packet-capture library that Juniper is using. It only allows specifying the keyword `isis` for filtering just IS-IS frames. The public version of tcpdump has much broader support for IS-IS: it can filter based on level, PDU type and combinations of those.

Analyzing the traffic on a Gigabit Ethernet interface (for example) would require the following command string.

JUNOS command output

```
hannes@Frankfurt> monitor traffic interface ge-0/1/0.0 size 1514 no-resolve
 matching isis
08:04:12.675185 In OSI, IS-IS, L2 Lan IIH, src-id 1921.6800.0008, lan-id
                1921.6800.0024.02, prio 64, length 1492
08:04:12.972945 Out OSI, IS-IS, L1 Lan IIH, src-id 1921.6800.0024, lan-id
                1921.6800.0008.02, prio 64, length 1492
08:04:14.262970 Out OSI, IS-IS, L2 Lan IIH, src-id 1921.6800.0024, lan-id
                1921.6800.0024.02, prio 64, length 1492
08:04:14.295254 In OSI, IS-IS, L1 Lan IIH, src-id 1921.6800.0008, lan-id
                1921.6800.0008.02, prio 120, length 1492
08:04:16.783397 In OSI, IS-IS, L1 Lan IIH, src-id 1921.6800.0008, lan-id
                1921.6800.0008.02, prio 120, length 1492
08:04:16.933018 Out OSI, IS-IS, L2 Lan IIH, src-id 1921.6800.0024, lan-id
                1921.6800.0024.02, prio 64, length 1492
08:04:17.734220 In OSI, IS-IS, L1 CSNP, src-id 1921.6800.0008, length 96
08:04:19.525291 In OSI, IS-IS, L1 Lan IIH, src-id 1921.6800.0008, lan-id
                1921.6800.0008.02, prio 120, length 1492
08:04:19.732283 Out OSI, IS-IS, L2 CSNP, src-id 1921.6800.0024, length 113
08:04:19.943063 Out OSI, IS-IS, L2 Lan IIH, src-id 1921.6800.0024, lan-id
                1921.6800.0024.02, prio 64, length 1492
08:04:20.015298 In OSI, IS-IS, L2 Lan IIH, src-id 1921.6800.0008, lan-id
                1921.6800.0024.02, prio 64, length 1492
```

You can write the captured data to a file which can later be examined using third party analyzers like Ethereal.

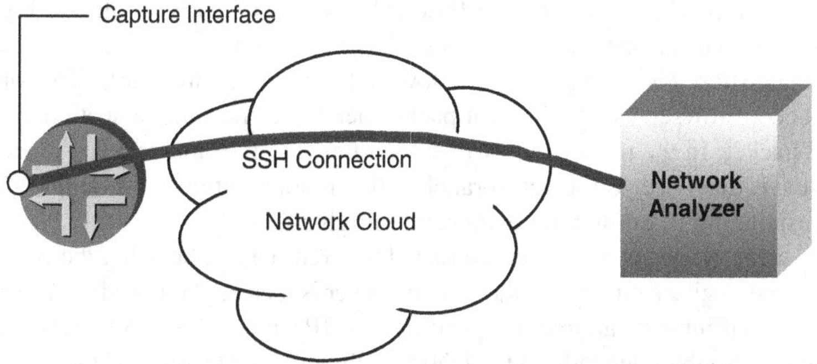

FIGURE 15.2. The JUNOS router captures data from one of its control plane interfaces and pipes it through the Secure Shell (SSH) Protocol to a workstation running the analyzer software

JUNOS command output

```
hannes@Frankfurt> monitor traffic interface ge-0/1/0.0 size 1514
 write-file hello-problem.pcap
Listening on ge-0/1/0.0, capture size 1514 bytes
```

You can now transfer the file to your workstation where you run your network analyzer and examine it closer there. Alternatively, you can pipe your captured data over an SSH session to a UNIX host and make the router a remote probe performing a live capture as illustrated in Figure 15.2. The captured stream is conveyed using the SSH protocol and fed into a network analyzer like Ethereal.

Unfortunately, real-time capturing and decoding cannot be done using the command line interface. You need to start a shell and become a super-user in order to do that. This practice is not encouraged by Juniper Networks, because of the potential for great harm to the router, but under the guidance of very experienced operators or with Juniper Networks technical assistance, this can be a valuable tool.

JUNOS/tcpdump output

The JUNOS embedded tcpdump command in combination with the SSH protocol can be a powerful remote capturing "device" for Ethereal. The command assumes that your UNIX machine is also your X11 display server for your Ethereal session. You have to replace the USER and REMOTEHOST fields with your username and IP address or name of the machine where you run Ethereal.

```
hannes@Frankfurt> start shell
% su
Password:
root@Frankfurt% tcpdump -i ge-0/1/0 -s1514 -w - "isis" | ssh
 USER@REMOTEHOST "( ethereal -knSli - )"
Listening on ge-0/1/0, capture size 1514 bytes

USER@REMOTEHOST's password: <PASSWORD>
```

After 1–2 seconds you should see Ethereal starting up, as illustrated in Figure 15.3. Two windows will be opened. On the foreground capture window you can see brief per-protocol statistics. The background window is divided into three parts. The top window is the packet browser which shows a packet per line. The middle section decodes the selected packet. In the third window there is a hex dump of the packet. A nice function of Ethereal is that once you select a branch in the middle section, for example a TLV, then the corresponding hex dump digits do get highlighted.

If the screen output needs to get redirected to a remote station using the X11 protocol, you first need to give a hint where the display server is located. You need to properly set the DISPLAY environment variable for specifying the IP address of the X11 server. Changing environment variables depends on the UNIX shell type. The example shows a remote X11 server and assumes that the shell for changing the DISPLAY variable is the Bourne Again Shell (bash) that is today the preferred shell on many UNIX-based systems.

JUNOS/tcpdump output

If your display server is not the machine where Ethereal is running, you need to specify the IP address of the X11 server. Replace the XSERVERHOST string with the name or IP address of your X11 server.

```
hannes@Frankfurt> start shell
% su
Password:
root@Frankfurt% tcpdump -i ge-0/1/0 -s1514 -w - "isis" | ssh USER@REMOTEHOST
"( export DISPLAY = XSERVERHOST:0; ethereal -knSli - )"
Listening on ge-0/1/0, capture size 1514 bytes

USER@REMOTEHOST's password: <PASSWORD>
```

Ethereal comes in two flavours: the first one features a graphical user interface (GUI). The GUI version has been utilized in the previous examples. The second one renders the entire packet as a text-only output that may be used for users that just have terminal access to a UNIX station. The text version of Ethereal is called *Tethereal* and displays the full networking stack, including Layer 2 information of a given packet.

JUNOS/Ethereal output

T-Ethereal provides a very nice text-only output variant displaying the full Networking Stack and all of its details.

```
hannes@Frankfurt> start shell
% su
Password:
root@Frankfurt% tcpdump -i ge-0/1/0 -s1514 -w - "isis" | ssh
 USER@REMOTEHOST "( tethereal -nVli - )"
Listening on ge-0/1/0, capture size 1514 bytes

USER@REMOTEHOST's password: <PASSWORD>
```

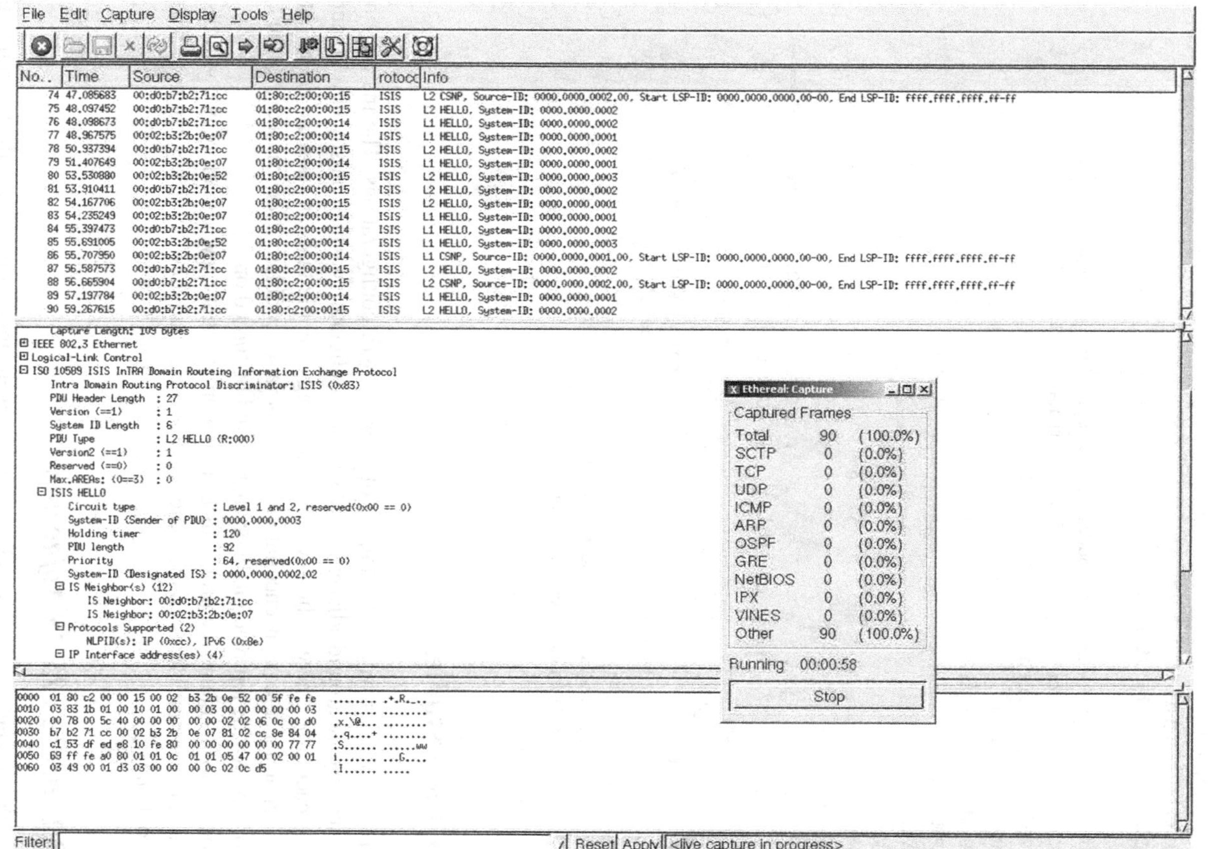

FIGURE 15.3. Ethereal starts with a capture window giving brief per-protocol statistics and a verbose decoder window in the background

```
Capturing on -
Frame 1 (1509 bytes on wire, 1509 bytes captured)
    Arrival Time: Nov 20, 2003 11:39:56.002525000
    Time delta from previous packet: 0.000000000 seconds
    Time since reference or first frame: 0.000000000 seconds
    Frame Number: 1
    Packet Length: 1509 bytes
    Capture Length: 1509 bytes
[ ... ]
ISO 10589 ISIS InTRA Domain Routeing Information Exchange Protocol
    Intra Domain Routing Protocol Discriminator: ISIS (0x83)
    PDU Header Length              :   27
    Version (==1)                  :   1
    System ID Length               :   6
    PDU Type   :                  L2 HELLO (R:000)
    Version2 (==1)                 :   1
    Reserved (==0)                 :   0
    Max.AREAs: (0==3)              :   0
    ISIS HELLO
        Circuit type                    :  Level 1 and 2, reserved(0x00 == 0)
        System-ID {Sender of PDU}       :  0000.0000.0001
        Holding timer                   :  27
        PDU length                      :  1492
        Priority                        :  64, reserved(0x00 == 0)
        System-ID {Designated IS}       :  0000.0000.0002.02
        IS Neighbor(s) (12)
            IS Neighbor: 00:d0:b7:b2:71:cc
            IS Neighbor: 00:02:b3:2b:0e:52
    [ ... ]
```

15.3 Case Studies

In this section you will see examples of broken IS-IS configurations. The majority of problems revolve around adjacency and sub-net configuration which mostly have router-local impact only. There is, however, a devastating example that can cause an entire network meltdown. Frequent encounters with this latter problem even caused the router vendors to provide a protection knob that should be turned on.

Most IS-IS problems are problems bringing up an adjacency. Therefore, we will discuss the main six problems on the topic of adjacencies and how to quickly diagnose what the problem is.

15.3.1 *Broken IS-IS Adjacency*

Rather than comparing individual configurations against another, we will start out with two configurations that encompass in total five mistakes and incrementally troubleshoot the two configurations.

JUNOS configuration

The complete IS-IS configuration of Frankfurt. We want to run an authenticated IS-IS Level 1 Adjacency over a SONET Link and route IPv4, IPv6 traffic over the circuit.

```
hannes@Frankfurt> show configuration
[ … ]
interfaces {
  so-0/2/0 {
    description "to London POS4/1";
    unit 0 {
        family inet {
            address 172.16.33.14/30;
        }
    }
  }
  lo0 {
        unit 0 {
        family inet {
            address 192.168.0.8/32;
            }
            family iso {
              address 49.0001.1921.6800.0008.00;
            }
        }
  }
  [ … ]
}
protocols {
  isis {
      level 1 {
          authentication-key "$9$LkT7dskqf5F/"; # SECRET-DATA
          authentication-type md5; # SECRET-DATA
          wide-metrics-only;
      }
      interface so-0/2/0.0 {
          level 1 disable;
      }
      lo0.0;
  }
  [ … ]
}
```

IOS configuration

The IOS configuration of London should match that of Frankfurt.

```
London#show running-config
[ … ]
key chain MY-ISIS-PASSWORD
```

```
  key 1
    key-string 0 secret789
!
interface POS4/1
  description "to Frankfurt so-0/2/0"
  ip address 172.16.33.17 255.255.255.252
  ip router isis
  encapsulation ppp
  crc 16
  clock source internal
  pos scramble-atm
  isis circuit-type level-1
!
router isis
  net 49.0010.1921.6800.0012.00
  authentication mode md5
  authentication key-chain MY-ISIS-PASSWORD
  metric-style wide
  is-type level-1
  passive-interface Loopback0
!
```

Let's see if the two configurations are working. Nope, neither router sees the other. What could be wrong?

```
London#sh clns neighbors
System Id       Interface       SNPA          State Holdtime Type Protocol

hannes@Frankfurt> show isis adjacency
hannes@Frankfurt> show isis interface
IS-IS interface database:
Interface      L     CirID     Level 1 DR        Level 2 DR        L1/L2 Metric
lo0.0          0       0x1     Disabled          Passive           0/0
```

15.3.1.1 Missing PPP-OSICP Configuration

In our phased troubleshooting approach, first we'll check the underlying physical and logical interface:

IOS command output

Only IPCP is up – The OSICP state is listening.

```
London#show interfaces pos4/1
POS4/1 is up, line protocol is up
  Hardware is Packet over SONET
  Description: "to Frankfurt so-0/2/0"
  Internet address is 172.16.33.13/30
  MTU 4470 bytes, BW 155000 Kbit, DLY 100 usec, rely 255/255,
  load 1/255
```

```
  Encapsulation PPP, crc 16, loopback not set
  Keepalive set (10 sec)
  Scramble enabled
  LCP Open
  Listen: CDPCP, OSICP
  Open: IPCP
  [ … ]
```

JUNOS command output

On the JUNOS side we do not even attempt to open up the OSICP because the router is not configured to do so!

```
hannes@Frankfurt> show interfaces so-0/2/0
Physical interface: so-0/2/0, Enabled, Physical link is Up
  Interface index: 148, SNMP ifIndex: 66
  Description: to London POS4/1
  Link-level type: PPP, MTU: 4474, Clocking: Internal, FCS: 16,
   Payload scrambler: Enabled
  Device flags : Present Running
  Interface flags: Point-To-Point SNMP-Traps
  Link flags : Keepalives
  Keepalive settings: Interval 10 seconds, Up-count 1, Down-count 3
  Keepalive: Input: 291 (00:00:04 ago), Output: 296 (00:00:03 ago)
  LCP state: Opened
  NCP state: inet: Opened, inet6: Not-configured, iso: Not-
   configured, mpls: Not-configured
  CHAP state: Not-configured
  [ … ]
```

On the IOS side, we encounter a circuit that is eager to speak OSICP, but does not receive any OSI frame from the other side. We can also rule out physical problems at this point as the Line Control Protocol (LCP) and IP Control Protocol (IPCP) are both up and running. On the JUNOS side, the output tells us that OSI support is not even configured. Checking the configuration reveals that we forgot to set the `family iso` keyword at the logical interface level (you'd be surprised how often this happens).

JUNOS configuration change

We forgot the family `iso` on the SONET interface on the JUNOS side. So the PPP-OSICP did not get started.

```
hannes@Frankfurt# show | compare
[edit interfaces so-0/2/0 unit 0]
+      family iso;
```

After adding the `family iso` statement at the logical interface Level, OSICP comes up, but our adjacency is still down. What else could be wrong?

15.3.1.2 Non-matching Level

Next, we check to see if there is a mismatch in our Level configuration by checking the debug logfiles.

JUNOS configuration/debug output

The JUNOS trace log reveals that there is a Level mismatch.

```
hannes@Frankfurt> show configuration protocols isis
traceoptions {
    file isis-trace.log;
    flag hello detail;
    flag error;
}
[ … ]
*** isis-trace.log ***
Nov 21 23:53:11      Received PTP IIH, source id 1921.6800.0012 on so-0/2/0.0
Nov 21 23:53:11          intf index 69
Nov 21 23:53:11          max area 0, circuit type 11, packet length 4469
Nov 21 23:53:11          hold time 30, circuit id 1
Nov 21 23:53:11      ERROR: IIH from 1921.6800.0012 with no matching
                      level, interface so-0/2/0.0, circuit type 1
```

The Frankfurt router complains that it got a Hello from London and there is a circuit mismatch reported.

IOS debug output

IOS does not detect any Level mismatches.

```
London#debug isis adj-packets
IS-IS Adjacency related packets debugging is on
*Nov 22 00:49:12: ISIS-Adj: Rec serial IIH from *PPP* (POS4/1),  cir type L2,
  cir id 01, length 67
*Nov 22 00:49:12: ISIS-Adj: rcvd state DOWN, old state INIT, new state INIT
*Nov 22 00:49:12: ISIS-Adj: Action = GOING DOWN
```

Note that in the IOS debug file there is no indication for a Level mismatch. But checking the JUNOS configuration, we find out that somebody must have set the Level 1 disable knob on the interface, which prevents a common Level to be found between the routers during the adjacency establishment process.

JUNOS configuration diff

Clearing the Level 1 `disable` flag makes the circuit a L1L2 circuit so that both peers have a common circuit type.

```
hannes@Frankfurt# show | compare
[edit protocols isis interface so-0/2/0.0]
-      level 1 disable;
```

Changing the pure L2 circuit into a L1L2 or L1 lets the routers have a common Level; however, there are still other caveats to overcome before out adjacency will go up. For example, on a Level 1 adjacency, the Areas have to match.

15.3.1.3 Non-matching Area-ID

Depending on the IS-IS circuit type, the Area-IDs need or need not match. For L1 adjacencies there needs to be a match of one of the Areas-IDs, but for L2 Adjacencies the Area-ID is not relevant.

JUNOS debug output

```
hannes@Frankfurt> show configuration protocols isis
traceoptions {
    file isis-trace.log;
    flag hello detail;
    flag error;
}
[ ... ]
*** isis-trace.log ***
Nov 22 00:09:25  Received PTP IIH, source id 1921.6800.0012 on so-0/2/0.0
Nov 22 00:09:25    intf index 69
Nov 22 00:09:25    max area 0, circuit type l1, packet length 4469
Nov 22 00:09:25    hold time 30, circuit id 1
Nov 22 00:09:25    17 bytes of authentication data
Nov 22 00:09:25    restart RR reset RA reset holdtime 0
Nov 22 00:09:25    ptp adjacency tlv length 1
Nov 22 00:09:25    neighbor state initializing
Nov 22 00:09:25    speaks IP
Nov 22 00:09:25    area address 49.0001 (3)
Nov 22 00:09:25    IP address 172.16.33.13
Nov 22 00:09:25    4371 bytes of total padding
Nov 22 00:09:25  ERROR: IIH from London with no matching areas, interface
                  so-0/2/0.0, our area 49.0100
```

JUNOS notes that there is no common Area-ID. It checks the Area-ID because the `circuit-type` is set to L1.

IOS debug output

The last change moves the circuit type from L1 to L1L2, however there are still no matching areas.

```
London#debug isis adj-packets
IS-IS Adjacency related packets debugging is on
*Nov 22 01:05:34: ISIS-Adj: Rec serial IIH from *PPP* (POS4/1),  cir type L1L2,
 cir id 01, length 48
*Nov 22 01:05:34: ISIS-Adj: rcvd state DOWN, old state INIT, new state INIT
*Nov 22 01:05:34: ISIS-Adj: No matching areas
*Nov 22 01:05:34: ISIS-Adj: Action = GOING DOWN
```

IOS makes a similar log entry in the debug output. As we have no matching areas, we have two options. Either we can change the circuit-type to be Level-2, or we can change the Area-ID. In our case, we discover that circuit-type cannot be changed on the London router and we have to change the Area-ID accordingly.

IOS configuration change

```
London#configure terminal
Enter configuration commands, one per line. End with CNTL/Z.
London(config)#router isis
London(config-router)# no net 49.0001.1921.6800.0012.00
London(config-router)# net 49.0100.1921.6800.0012.00
```

As the adjacency is still not up (take our word for it), we next check for an authentication match.

15.3.1.4 Non-matching Authentication

Before troubleshooting authentication information, we need to first find out which PDU types are authenticated.

JUNOS debug output

JUNOS reports an IIH Authentication failure because per-level configuration authenticates all PDUs including IIHs. Because authentication is always symmetric, the JUNOS router also expects that all IIHs are authenticated, but that is not the case.

```
hannes@Frankfurt> show configuration protocols isis
traceoptions {
    file isis-trace.log;
    flag hello detail;
    flag error;
}
[ ... ]
*** isis-trace.log ***
Nov 22 00:23:01    Received PTP IIH, source id 1921.6800.0012 on so-0/2/0.0
Nov 22 00:23:01        intf index 69
Nov 22 00:23:01        max area 0, circuit type 11, packet length 4469
Nov 22 00:23:01        hold time 30, circuit id 1
Nov 22 00:23:01        17 bytes of authentication data
Nov 22 00:23:01        ERROR: IIH authentication failure
```

The JUNOS router reports an authentication error for IIHs, quite the contrary to the IOS router, which does not report an authentication error. However, the IS-IS adjacency gets stuck on the *Initialize* state.

IOS debug output

On the IOS side, no authentication error is logged because IOS does not expect its Hellos to be authenticated.

```
London#debug isis authentication information
IS-IS authentication information debugging is on
London#debug isis adj-packets
IS-IS Adjacency related packets debugging is on
*Nov 22 01:19:34: ISIS-Adj:        Rec serial IIH from *PPP* (POS4/1),
  cir type L1L2, cir id 01, length 67
*Nov 22 01:19:34: ISIS-Adj:        rcvd state DOWN, old state INIT, new state INIT
*Nov 22 01:19:34: ISIS-Adj:        Action = GOING UP, new type = L1
```

Although IOS has enabled MD5 authentication, it authenticates only LSPs and SNPs and not IIHs. But JUNOS *does* authenticate all PDU types and also expects authentication from others, which breaks the adjacency in this case. There are two strategies to over come this.

IOS configuration change

```
London#conf t
Enter configuration commands, one per line. End with CNTL/Z.
London(config)#int pos4/1
London(config-if)# isis authentication key-chain MY-ISIS-PASSWORD
London(config-if)# isis authentication mode md5
```

The first is to configure an additional IIH authentication on the interface.

JUNOS configuration change

```
hannes@Frankfurt# show | compare
[edit protocols isis level 1]
+      no-hello-authentication;
```

Most network administrators are too lazy to maintain an additional IS-IS configuration statement, and it is decided decide to suppress the authentication of IIH PDUs through use of the `no-hello-authentication` on the JUNOS router.

15.3.1.5 Non-matching IP Sub-net

As our adjacency is *still* not up, we check the IP sub-net information using show commands. Additionally we keep an eye on the debug outputs.

JUNOS debug output

```
hannes@Frankfurt> show configuration protocols isis
traceoptions {
```

```
    file isis-trace.log;
    flag hello detail;
    flag error;
}
[ … ]
*** isis-trace.log ***
Nov 22 00:52:45     Received PTP IIH, source id London on so-0/2/0.0
Nov 22 00:52:45          intf index 69
Nov 22 00:52:45          max area 0, circuit type l1, packet length 4469
Nov 22 00:52:45          hold time 30, circuit id 1
Nov 22 00:52:45          17 bytes of authentication data
Nov 22 00:52:45          restart RR reset RA reset holdtime 0
Nov 22 00:52:45          ptp adjacency tlv length 1
Nov 22 00:52:45          neighbor state down
Nov 22 00:52:45          speaks IP
Nov 22 00:52:45          area address 49.0100 (3)
Nov 22 00:52:45          IP address 172.16.33.13
Nov 22 00:52:45          4371 bytes of total padding
Nov 22 00:52:45     ERROR: IIH from 1921.6800.2001 without matching
                     addresses, interface so-0/2/0.0
```

JUNOS refuses an adjacency if there is no common IP sub-net.

IOS debug output

```
London#debug isis adj-packets
IS-IS Adjacency related packets debugging is on
*Nov 22 01:40:52: ISIS-Adj: Rec serial IIH from *PPP* (POS4/1),
    cir type L1L2, cir id 01, length 1492
*Nov 22 01:40:52: ISIS-Adj: No usable IP interface addresses in
    serial IIH from POS4/1
```

IOS also checks to see if the Interface Address TLV is within the range of the own sub-net.

JUNOS configuration change

```
hannes@Frankfurt# show | compare
[edit interfaces so-0/2/0 unit 0 family inet]
+         address 172.16.33.14/30;
-         address 172.16.33.17/30;
```

In our example, there were two different IP sub-nets configured. Changing one side back to what was originally allocated should do the trick and at last bring the adjacency Up. (Don't worry: it's not usually this hard in the real world to get adjacencies up, even in multi-vendor environments.)

IOS debug output

```
*Nov 22 01:54:50: ISIS-Adj:        Rec serial IIH from *PPP* (POS4/1),cir type
  L1L2, cir id 01,length 1492
*Nov 22 01:54:50: ISIS-Adj:        rcvd state INIT, old state DOWN, new state INIT
*Nov 22 01:54:50: ISIS-Adj:        Action = GOING UP, new type = L1
*Nov 22 01:54:50: ISIS-Adj:        New serial adjacency
*Nov 22 01:54:50: ISIS-Adj:        Sending serial IIH on POS4/1, length 4469
*Nov 22 01:54:50: ISIS-Adj:        Rec serial IIH from *PPP* (POS4/1), cir type
  L1L2, cir id 01, length 58
*Nov 22 01:54:50: ISIS-Adj:        rcvd state UP, old state INIT, new state UP
*Nov 22 01:54:50: ISIS-Adj:        Action = GOING UP, new type = L1
*Nov 22 01:54:50: ISIS-Adj:        L1 adj count 1
```

The debug output shows the state transition from the Down to the Up state. Once we are there, our routers can talk to their neighbours and exchange LSPs. Sometimes routers exchange a bit too many LSPs, which is undesirable, too – there is a closer description of this problem in the following case study.

15.3.2 *Injecting Full Internet Routes into IS-IS*

It is the nightmare of every network operation engineer: getting paged in the middle of the night and all routers are unreachable. The iBGP mesh is collapsing and the network is literally falling to pieces. Particularly on JUNOS routers, there was a dangerous trap that many service providers ran into. In 2002, the Juniper Technical Assistance Center (JTAC) noticed several incidents of the type we describe here: through human error, a router attempts to inject the full set of Internet routes into IS-IS Level 2. The generated flooding and processing load eventually melts down the entire network.

During a network-wide failure, it is hard at first to determine where to look initially for traces and clues. A good place is the central syslog server. Often a few syslog messages that are logged just before the network go haywire and these provide a good starting point.

Syslog server logfile

The Munich router is logging every second that its IS-IS database is overloaded.

```
[ ... ]
Nov 21 18:22:22 Munich rpd[2235]: RPD_ISIS_OVERLOAD: IS-IS database overload
Nov 21 18:22:23 Munich rpd[2235]: RPD_ISIS_OVERLOAD: IS-IS database overload
Nov 21 18:22:24 Munich rpd[2235]: RPD_ISIS_OVERLOAD: IS-IS database overload
Nov 21 18:22:25 Munich rpd[2235]: RPD_ISIS_OVERLOAD: IS-IS database overload
Nov 21 18:22:26 Munich rpd[2235]: RPD_ISIS_OVERLOAD: IS-IS database overload
[ ... ]
```

By inspecting the syslog server, a set of log entries is spotted that indicates a database overload by a router running JUNOS. By consulting the documentation (System Log Messages Reference) we find out that the RPD_ISIS_OVERLOAD message is logged when the router has no memory (!) or is running out of LSP fragments.

Next, we inspect the link-state database on any router and try to verify if the Munich router has run out of fragments.

JUNOS command output

The `show isis database` output reveals that the Munich router is generating 256 LSP fragments that are purged already.

```
hannes@Munich> show isis database
[ … ]
IS-IS level 2 link-state database:
LSP ID                    Sequence   Checksum  Lifetime  Attributes
Munich.00-00                  0x11     0x6dac       982  L1 Overload
Munich.00-01                  0xca          0         0  L1
Munich.00-02                  0xca          0         0  L1
Munich.00-03                  0xca          0         0  L1
Munich.00-04                  0xca          0         0  L1
Munich.00-05                  0xca          0         0  L1
Munich.00-06                  0xca          0         0  L1
Munich.00-07                  0xca          0         0  L1
Munich.00-08                  0xca          0         0  L1
Munich.00-09                  0xca          0         0  L1
Munich.00-0a                  0xca          0         0  L1
Munich.00-0b                  0xca          0         0  L1
Munich.00-0c                  0xca          0         0  L1
Munich.00-0d                  0xc9          0         0  L1
Munich.00-0e                  0xc9          0         0  L1
Munich.00-0f                  0xc9          0         0  L1
[ … ]
Munich.00-f8                   0x1          0         0  L1
Munich.00-f9                   0x1          0         0  L1
Munich.00-fa                   0x1          0         0  L1
Munich.00-fb                   0x1          0         0  L1
Munich.00-fc                   0x1          0         0  L1
Munich.00-fd                   0x1          0         0  L1
Munich.00-fe                   0x1          0         0  L1
Munich.00-ff                   0x1          0         0  L1
Pennsauken.00-00              0x33     0xed52      1193  L1
London.00-00                 0x3af     0x865e       744  L1
Frankfurt.00-00               0x19     0x8612       980  L1
  268  LSPs
[ … ]
```

The output looks odd – the Munich router is generating in total 256 fragments, and the router is overloaded. Why? Inspecting the non-zero fragments shows another interesting trace:

JUNOS command output

All the Munich non-zero LSP fragments have the garbage collection timer set.

```
hannes@Frankfurt> show isis database Munich.00-01 extensive
IS-IS level 2 link-state database:
[ … ]
Munich.00-01 Sequence: 0xca, Checksum: 0, Lifetime: 0 secs

  Header: LSP ID: Munich.00-01, Length: 40 bytes
    Allocated length: 284 bytes, Router ID: 0.0.0.0
    Remaining lifetime: 0 secs, Level: 1,Interface: 64
    Estimated free bytes: 209, Actual free bytes: 244
    Garbage collection timer expires in: 1134 secs
[ … ]
```

The LSP fragments do not contain any data anymore. All of them are still in the database for their maximum LSP lifetime to avoid re-learning them in case the network gets partitioned. For our further troubleshooting, this means that somebody has purged the Munich LSP fragments. In IS-IS the only router that purges LSPs is the *originating* router. So we next inspect the Munich router and check out its router configuration file.

JUNOS configuration

The IS-IS configuration looks alright, but there is also an export policy configured which should be further inspected.

```
hannes@Munich> show configuration
[ … ]
protocols {
    isis {
        export static-to-isis;
        level 2 {
            wide-metric-only;
        }
        interfaces {
            [ … ]
            lo0.0;
        }
    [ … ]
  }
}
```

The IS-IS configuration looks alright – all interfaces are referenced. At the top there is a pointer to an export policy which we will examine closer.

JUNOS configuration

On first sight the `static-to-isis` policy looks good, however once you check the indentation of the terms and accept statements you will find out that the policy does not do what the network operator wanted it to do.

```
hannes@Munich> show configuration policy-options
[ … ]
policy-statement static-to-isis {
    term reject_management {
        from {
            route-filter 10.0.0.0/8 orlonger;
        }
        then reject;
    }
  term static {
        from protocol static;
  }
  then accept;
}
```

At first sight this policy looks good. However, once we start to compare the indentation of the `then` part we realize that the term `static` does not have a valid `then` statement. Due to a misconfiguration, it got inserted at the wrong level in the policy. What the standalone `then` accept term does is accept *every* unicast route in the inet.0 routing tables and mark it for export into the IS-IS link-state database. Because there is no `from` statement at the same indentation level as the final `then accept` statement, we have an unconditional export of the entire Internet routing table into IS-IS. (The final "then" logic is executed when no terms match the routes. The logic is here "Is the route 10/8 or longer?" No, that's a private address. "Is the route static?" No, it's an Internet route. "Okay, then unconditionally accept the route into IS-IS.")

The distributed storage space that each node may allocate is 1492(–27) * 256 = 375 Kbytes. How many IPv4 prefixes do fit in those 375 Kbytes? Figure 12.11 in Chapter 12 "IP Reachability Information" illustrates the structure and storage requirements of the Extended IP Reachability TLV #135. Worst case, the TLV consumes 9 bytes and best case 5 bytes due to variable prefix length packing. For the average Internet route we can assume a prefix length between /16 and /24 and safely assume a total storage requirement of 8 bytes per prefix. In a single TLV, on average, 31 TLVs fit, which requires 31 * 8 + 2 (TLV Overhead) = 250 bytes to store. An LSP fragment is at maximum 1492 bytes in size. For TLV information there is 1492 – Header size (=27) = 1465 space. That means in total we can store 31 * 5 + 26 = 181 routes per fragment. Inside 256 fragments we can store around 46 K routes, *which is too little to hold the entire Internet routing table*. As soon as the routers hit that limit, it pulls the "emergency brake" and sets the overload bit.

Finally, it cleans up the mess by purging the previously generated LSPs off the distributed link-state database. And that's what the router was showing us.

In order to fix the problem, the `then accept` statement is moved into the term `static`.

JUNOS configuration

```
hannes@Munich> show configuration
[ ... ]
policy-statement static-to-isis {
     term reject_management {
          from {
               route-filter 10.0.0.0/8 orlonger;
          }
          then reject;
     }
     term static {
          from protocol static;
          then accept;
     }
}
```

After committing the change, you will still see all those stale fragments in the database. They will be kept in the database until the garbage collection timer times out. Using default values, after a period of 20 minutes they are removed automatically.

JUNOS command output

After the router has changed, the broken routing policy the Overload Bit is automatically cleared.

```
hannes@Munich> show isis database
IS-IS level 2 link-state database:
LSP ID                   Sequence      Checksum       Lifetime       Attributes
Munich.00-00                0x1c2         0x2d3b           1192      L1 L2
Pennsauken.00-00            0xc77         0xec5e           711       L1 L2
Frankfurt.00-00             0x198         0xdd86           933       L1 L2
  14 LSPs
[ ... ]
```

The database looks normal again, and the Overload Bit has automatically been cleared.

Because that problem was encountered many times in the field, Juniper Networks finally introduced a prefix-export limiter that optionally controls the export behaviour and suspends route export if a predefined threshold is reached.

JUNOS configuration

The `prefix-export-limit` knob protects the rest of the network from a malicious policy by applying a threshold filter for exported routed.

```
hannes@Munich> show configuration
[ ... ]
protocols {
    isis {
        export static-to-isis;
        level 2 {
          wide-metrics-only;
          prefix-export-limit 2500;
        }
    }
}
```

The amount of prefixes heavily depends on the size of your network. Good design advice is to set it to double the total number of IS-IS Level 1 and Level-2 routers in your network – The minimum number of routes should be 1000 and the maximum number of routes about 10,000. Then you have some growth for even larger numbers of routes that need to get leaked from Level 1 to Level 2.

15.4 Summary

Most IS-IS problems can be resolved quickly if you stick to a troubleshooting plan and check from Layer-1 of the OSI Reference Model right up to the Application Layer. In IS-IS, the Application Layer represents the link-state database that holds the network's link state PDUs. The network engineer needs to develop an understanding of what functions each layer is performing and what tools he has available to gather information. After information gathering, the collected data needs to be analyzed and interpreted, which requires knowledge of the show commands and debug outputs. For detecting misconfiguration on a router, the network engineer needs to understand where the IS-IS relevant data in the configuration are stored.

The majority of IS-IS problems are related to adjacency formation. The network engineer needs to get familiar with all sorts of debug output for IOS and JUNOS. Just looking at the IS-IS specific configuration is often not enough to resolve a problem. We have demonstrated in the Internet route export case study that understanding of route export and policy processing is paramount for resolving complex problems.

16

Network Design

For a long time, link-state protocols were believed not to scale. However, today there are operational networks with more than 1200 routers in a single level. Still, networks that run link-state protocols need to be carefully designed and a lot of factors need to be considered to get to such a scale. By ignoring certain reasonable constraints, you can easily break a network in certain scenarios. In this chapter you will learn about the critical IS-IS network design factors, all forms of router stress, including flooding stress, SPF stress and forwarding state change stress, as well as what things to consider to build robust, fast-converging networks.

16.1 Topology and Reachability Information

In service provider networks there are always at least two protocols in use. The first is an IGP (which could be OSPF or IS-IS), and the other is BGP. One of the first questions asked by networking novices is why do we need *both*? It turns out that all IGPs (IS-IS, OSPF, EIGRP) lack one fundamental thing, which is *flow-control*. For IGPs, there is no way to tell an adjacent router that their updates have overwhelmed the receiver and the sender should throttle down. The only way to deal with the situation is to throw away the updates and wait for re-transmission. However, that is still a dangerous game, as it may offload stress at the expense of the sending router, which needs to queue retransmissions and therefore consumes CPU and memory. Careful protocol heuristics need to be implemented to make sure that both the sending and receiving router do not take themselves out of service. Dave Katz, a software engineer with Juniper Networks, *who can be blamed for writing the majority of IGP implementations on the Internet* (his own self-definition) puts the complexity around finding the right heuristics in a single quote:

Link State Protocols are hard! (Dave Katz)

What network engineers at service providers have been doing is to apply a *divide and conquer* strategy and separating topology from reachability information. Topology information contains the skeleton of the network – it is a graph that describes how the routing-nodes are connected to each other. It does not contain any information about customer networks and server networks, or so on. Ideally, it does not even contain information about the directly connected sub-nets. Figure 16.1 shows that the only information that the routers advertise is their loopback IP address, which is necessary to bring up an iBGP full-mesh distribution network which handles bulk transport of the routing information.

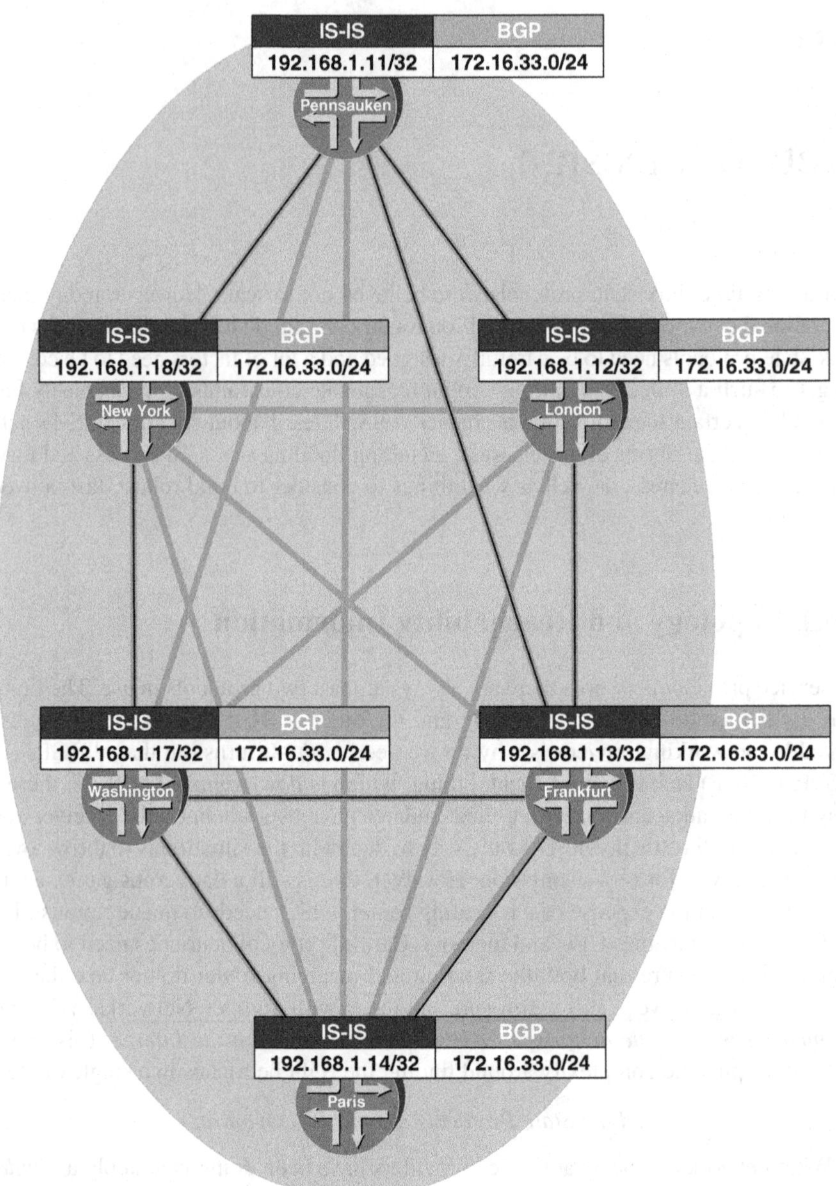

FIGURE 16.1. The minimal routing information that IS-IS needs to provide is the /32 of the Loopback IP address for bringing up the iBGP mesh. All customer routes are packed on BGP

When you run IS-IS over a link you typically advertise your local IP sub-net in your IS-IS LSPs. There is even the notion that local IP sub-nets should *not* be announced by IS-IS, but rather by BGP. Historically there has not been an option to preclude certain IP sub-nets from being announced. However, recent routing software allows you to change that behaviour. In IOS, there is a single knob that changes the advertising behaviour of directly connects sub-nets. Once you configure the `passive-only` knob, the routing software walks down the list of configured interfaces and looks for interfaces that are marked as `passive`. Recall that `passive` means that you include that interface's sub-net in your routing update, but you do not try to establish a neighbour relationship or an adjacency over that interface. The loopback interface is by default `passive` and so if you configure the `passive-only` option, only the loopback IP address of the router is advertised in its LSP.

IOS configuration

In IOS controlling whether directly connected route get advertised is provided using the `passive-only` knob.

```
New-York# show running-config
[ ... ]
router isis
  advertise passive-only
!
[ ... ]
```

In JUNOS there is no specific knob to control advertising behaviour. In JUNOS you write a policy for achieving that task. Later you call that policy as export policy in the `protocols isis {}` branch.

JUNOS configuration

In JUNOS you need to write an explicit policy that rejects all routes beside sub-nets on the lo0.0 interface.

```
hannes@Frankfurt# show
[ ... ]
protocols {
  isis {
    export lo0-only;
  [ ... ]
  }
}
policy-options {
  policy-statement lo0-only {
    term lo0 {
      from interface lo0.0;
      then accept;
    }
    term final {
      then reject;
    }
[ ... ]
```

The nice thing about the JUNOS policy is that you may explicitly control the level to suppress direct routes by introduction of a `to {}` statement. The following example shows how to restrict to the loopback0 interface related routes inside Level 2 LSPs only.

```
policy-options {
  policy-statement lo0-only {
    term lo0 {
      from interface lo0.0;
      to {
        protocol isis;
        level 2;
      }
      then accept;
    }
    term final {
      then reject }
    }
  }
[ ... ]
}
```

BGP has perfected flow-control capabilities because it runs on top of the Transmission Control Protocol (TCP). Flow control at the TCP level is built into the protocol: as soon as a receiver cannot keep up processing inbound routing updates, it can easily slow down transmission of acknowledgements or even drop the inbound update and indirectly indicate that the sender should back off and send information at a lower speed. Originally BGP was intended to process a certain maximum of routes. Yakov Rekhter, an Internet architect with Juniper Networks relates:

Kirk Lougheed (Cisco Systems) and myself's goal was to build a routing protocol able to convey 1000 routes and not fall into pieces – If you consider the total routes being today in the Internet we pushed the envelope a bit (Yakov Rekhter)

Based on BGP's superb scaling capabilities, the idea here is to "borrow" the existing BGP distribution mesh being used for transport of Internet routes for internal routes as well.

The conclusion as to why you always need *two* protocols is therefore: IS-IS scales too poorly for conveying a bulk amount of routes, however, it can quickly discover a topology and provide routing connectivity between router loopback IP addresses. BGP heavily depends on these IGP-supplied routes to bring up the iBGP. Second, BGP is really in the dark when it comes to ascertaining the distance between a pair of routers. Internal BGP sessions are not "targeted" and therefore need an IGP to resolve routes and to give BGP speakers directions.

In order to come up with a design recommendation, let's first evaluate the forms of *stress* that routers are exposed to and develop a set of critical design factors based on those insights. From there we will set up some rules to follow when designing an IS-IS network.

16.2 Router Stress

Generally routing software can exhaust resources in three possible areas:

1. Bandwidth
2. CPU
3. Memory

The next three sections investigate IS-IS implementations to see if they suffer from any limitations in those three areas. The first area is bandwidth – in IS-IS, the main bandwidth consumer is related to the flooding of LSPs.

16.2.1 *Flooding*

Unlike link-local packets like Hellos (IIH) or Synchronization packets (SNP), transmitting link-state PDUs (LSPs) has a network-wide bandwidth usage impact. Once a router floods LSPs, it is using bandwidth equal to the number of links in a given topology times the size of the LSP. Worst case, it can be that network-wide transmission of an LSP comes at a cost of using the number of all links times the size of a LSP squared. The big gap between the best and the worst case (recall the best case is linear behaviour and the worst case is N^2 behaviour) is solely explainable by the way the topology is meshed. Consider Figure 16.2, where in a strict ring topology of six routers there is no duplicate

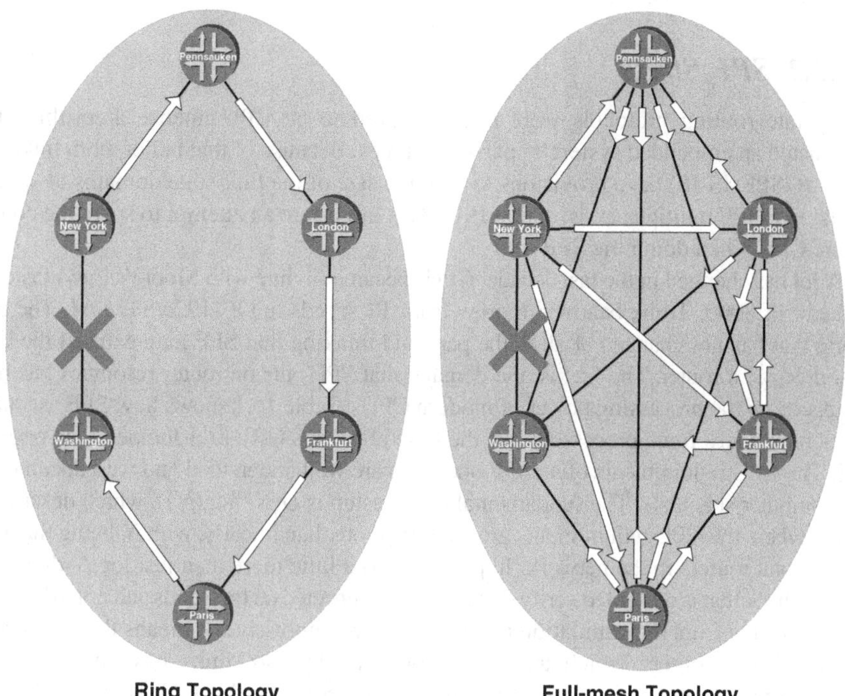

FIGURE 16.2. In a dense-meshed environment there are lots of duplicate LSPs to process

transmission of an LSP. As soon as a link breaks, the LSP travels round until every node gets a copy. Note that for greater visibility the propagation of only one LSP is shown. Of course, in real networks both ends of the link that breaks would originate a new LSP. As soon as you add links to the topology, the more redundant the transmission of LSPs gets. In the ring-topology each router sees the LSP one time.

The worst case is a full-mesh of all routers, where a single router failure triggers $(N-1)$ LSPs being flooded over $(N-2)$ links $(= O(N^2))$ through the network. The big problem in a dense- or full-mesh environment is that nodes that already got a copy of LSPs receive many redundant duplicates with the same information.

An additional source of flooding stress comes from turning on the TE extensions. Once you turn on features like Traffic Engineering, DiffServ Traffic Engineering or Auto Bandwidth, then the TEDs throughout the network topology need to be updated through the use of the IS-IS flooding sub-system. That means that every router in the network sees (and needs to see) accurate TE information. However, if the TE implementation permits changes to flooding timers, then let having very conservative timers guide your design. TE extensions are a major source of LSP updates and there should be an effort to reduce these to the minimum possible.

It is recommended that you consider the topology to evaluate the stress resulting from receipt of duplicate LSPs. Densely meshed environments scale poorly in flooding environments. Try to avoid full-mesh or near-full mesh topologies. Sometimes a lot of extra redundancy does not turn into more resiliency.

16.2.2 *SPF Stress*

Link-state routing protocols were once believed to be CPU intense algorithms that exhausted an embedded system's sparse resources. Because of that belief, both link-state IGPs (OSPF, IS-IS) have provisions to split the size of the link-state domains to smaller units. In OSPF multiple areas, and in IS-IS two levels, are an attempt to spare the control plane CPU when doing the SPF run.

A lot has changed in the last decade. CPUs became (in line with Moore's Law) faster by a factor of 8000; Trunk bandwidth grew from T1 speeds to OC-192c/STM-64. The only thing that has not changed at all is the paranoid thinking that SPF may exhaust the CPU resources of a router. The fact is, the demand that SPF puts on router resources has been outpaced by the processing power of modern CPUs. Table 16.1 shows how SPF execution fares on modern route processors like the Cisco Systems GRP or a Juniper Networks RE 3.0. The CPU requirements of an SPF operation are well understood and well documented by computer scientists. The fundamental relationship is $O(N * \log(N))$, which describes a curve where the CPU requirements grow a little more than linearly, with N being the number of total routers in the network. In practice it is a little more than just $\log N$ due to the 2-way check that is needed to verify that a node is connected on both ends and not a dead end.

The results from the simulation in Table 16.1 are impressive. It means that processing a grid of 2000 routers, which are in total connected by 5000 links, has a typical execution runtime of only 100–245 milliseconds. If you consider this table then it is obvious that raw SPF execution time is *not* a problem for large IS-IS networks. So what is it then?

TABLE 16.1. Modern route processors can calculate topologies for thousands of nodes and links sub second.

		SPF runtime (ms)	
Routers	Links	Juniper Networks Routing Engine 3.0	Cisco Systems GRP 12000
100	250	1,92	4,80
200	500	4,97	12,42
400	1000	12,49	31,22
600	1500	21,18	52,94
800	2000	30,67	76,67
1000	2500	40,78	101,94
1500	3750	68,11	170,27
2000	5000	97,68	244,21
2500	6250	128,98	322,45
3000	7500	161,69	404,22
4000	10000	230,53	576,33
5000	12500	303,09	757,72
6000	15000	378,67	946,67
7000	17500	456,82	1142,04
8000	20000	537,19	1342,98
9000	22500	619,55	1548,86
10000	25000	703,67	1759,18

Why are we all so scared of routers running excessive number of SPF runs back to back? What is it besides the SPF calculation itself that scares network operators so much?

16.2.3 *Forwarding State Change Stress*

The purpose of the SPF calculation is to find out the shortest path to every edge of the network. However, just the *insight* that there are better paths available is not *enough*.

There are no good things, unless you do them! (Erich Kästner)

The router has to pass on the new proximity results to a subsystem called the *resolver*, which is used to map third party next-hops to forwarding next-hops. Consider Figure 16.3, if the link between Washington and New York breaks, the SPF calculation will be finished in a matter of microseconds. Each IS-IS speaker is also a BGP speaker and carries several thousand active BGP routes. If the IS-IS topology changes, then the BGP routes that depend on IS-IS need to get changed as well. The resolver needs now to backtrack through all the BGP routes and verify that the BGP next-hop is affected by a change in the core topology. As you can imagine, walking down a table of several hundreds of thousands of BGP route-entries is a resource intensive task. In our example, there are tons of forwarding state changes to do: all Washington and New York routes need to be changed in a very short time.

After the BGP dependencies have been worked out, this may generate changes in the BGP topology as well: recall that the IGP distance is part of the BGP route selection process. But that is only half of the story, as those things still occur on the control plane.

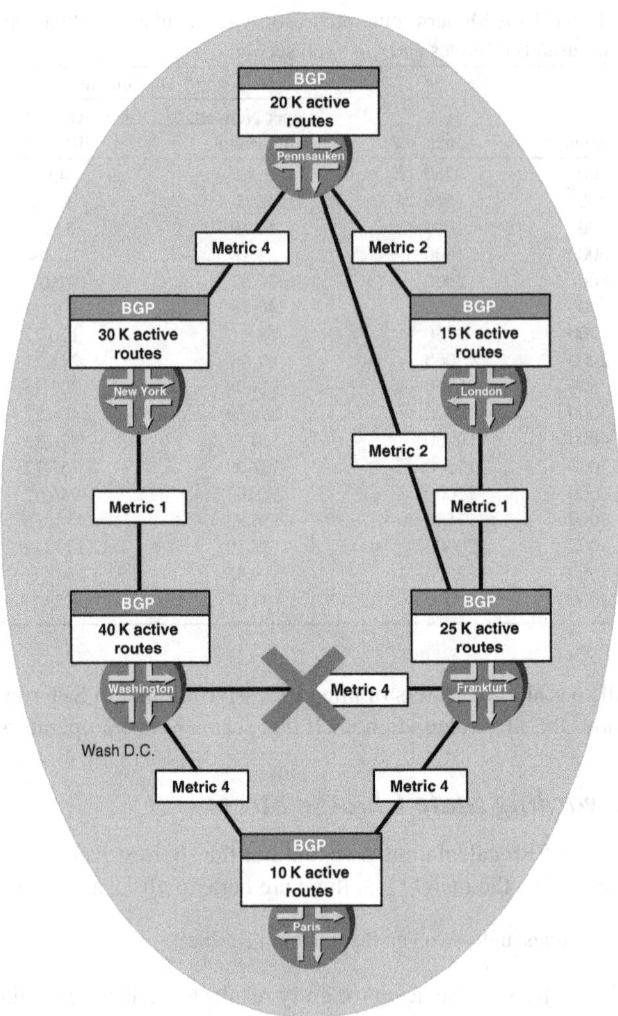

FIGURE 16.3. The resolver needs to track and map BGP next-hops to the shortest path resulting from the SPF calculation

The forwarding state change of tens of thousands of routes may stress several sub-systems of an Internet core router. It turns out that changing a forwarding state is one of the most expensive operations in a router. Meanwhile, both Juniper and Cisco have found a way to pass on third party next-hop information to the line-cards and retain the dependency of BGP routes to IS-IS speakers to forwarding interfaces. More on passing on third party next-hop information, and why it is not always a good idea to attempt to fully resolve a route to its forwarding next-hop, can be found in Chapter 10, “SPF and Route Calculation”.

16.2.4 *CPU and Memory Usage*

The two main things that utilize the CPU most in an IS-IS router are the SPF calculation and the resolver. SPF calculation puts a short burden on the system but even in large topologies that burden does not last more than 200 ms using modern route processors. As discussed in the previous section, the far bigger CPU hog is the resolver, which maps BGP routes to forwarding next-hops. SPF execution runtime is ultimately a non-issue; however, the burden that the resolver can put on the system needs to be carefully examined.

In the 1990s, during the explosive growth of the Internet, routers were constantly short of memory. Since then network service providers are cautious about the memory usage of their routing protocols. There is almost no IS-IS-related documentation regarding memory consumption. The majority of IS-IS implementations use memory in three areas:

1. Link-state database
2. SPF result table
3. Storing neighbour information

The link-state database size is the easiest to predict. It contains mostly raw data that was extracted from the TLVs in an IS-IS PDU. There are also overhead and index structures so the IS-IS software can quickly traverse the database when it is looking for a certain LSP. As a rough guideline, one can state that the size of the link-state database is about double the size that individual LSPs consume on the wire. For example, if the network knows about 100 LSPs with an average length of 400 bytes each, then the size to store this information in the router software is $100 * 400 * 2 = 80$ KB.

The size of the SPF result table depends largely on how many IP prefixes are known to IS-IS inside the network. A good estimation here is that each prefix consumes about 70 bytes. For example, if you have 1600 IS-IS prefixes in your network, then the memory consumption on the control plane is 112 KB.

The neighbouring table is the most complex one to calculate as all the flooding state and retransmission list needs to be kept on a per adjacency basis. That structure is also dependent on the size of the link-state database, because all the flooding states are tied to both the LSP and the adjacency. There is a lot of clever pointer work involved here, and the overhead to do efficient flooding is enormous. A good approximate figure is that this table is about 50 times the average LSP size multiplied by the number of active adjacencies. For example, if the average LSP is about 400 bytes and the number of adjacencies is eight, then the memory consumption is $400 * 50 * 8 = 160$ K.

If you sum the three memory areas up, then the result for a large network is unlikely to exceed 4–5 MB in total. In IS-IS, the memory consumption is minimal given that there are mainly route processors with 256 MB–2 GB memory deployed in the field. Interestingly, there are large overhead structures in the LSP databases to increase LSP lookup speed and to keep flooding state even for large numbers of adjacencies. This is just more evidence that memory consumption for IS-IS networks with big core routers is a non-issue.

16.3 Design Recommendations

Through the years of designing large IS-IS networks, and based on the experience of NOC engineers and software engineers at the big router vendors, the authors have come up with the following design tips to design truly scalable networks. Those recommendations are not rigid, that is, you do not need to follow them all to the letter. To be a good network designer, you have to find a healthy balance between what the products can do and what you want to achieve.

The rest of this chapter draws on many of the topics and ideas discussed throughout this book. There is no need to repeat more than the basics of the discussions, however, so we don't present all of the gory details all over again.

16.3.1 *Separate Topology and IP Reachability Data*

Perhaps the most important rule is keeping topology and IP reachability data separate. You saw that IGPs are not very good at transporting large numbers of routes, so just avoid it and pass the job to BGP. In large (more than 1000 routers per level) you may even decide to advertise directly connected routes in BGP as well. Given that an average IS-IS core router has about five or six directly attached sub-nets, then you clearly want to avoid that extra 2500–3000 prefixes at the IS-IS level in order to keep convergence times within an upper bound. An ideal IS-IS LSP contains just a single IP prefix, which is the router's loopback IP address, plus Extended IS Reach TLVs that point to neighbouring routers.

Tcpdump output

An *ideal* LSP just conveys a *single* IP prefix per router and passes all other routing information via BGP.

```
12:36:45.587565 OSI, IS-IS, length: 405
  hlen: 27, v: 1, pdu-v: 1, sys-id-len: 6 (0), max-area: 3 (0)
    L2 LSP, lsp-id: 2092.1113.4009-00, seq: 0x000002fd, lifetime: 1198s
    chksum: 0xe984 (correct), PDU length: 185, Flags: [ L1L2 IS ]
      Area address(es) TLV #1, length: 4
        Area address (length: 3): 49.0001
      Protocols supported TLV #129, length: 1
        NLPID(s): IPv4
      IPv4 Interface address(es) TLV #132, length: 4
        IPv4 interface address: 192.168.1.1
      Hostname TLV #137, length: 10
        Hostname: Washington
      Extended IS Reachability TLV #22, length: 99
        IS Neighbor: 1921.6800.1077.00, Metric: 4, sub-TLVs present (12)
          IPv4 interface address (subTLV #6), length: 4, 172.17.1.6
          IPv4 neighbor address (subTLV #8), length: 4, 172.16.1.5
```

```
  IS Neighbor: 1921.6800.1043.00, Metric: 4, sub-TLVs present (12)
    IPv4 interface address (subTLV #6), length: 4, 172.16.33.38
    IPv4 neighbor address (subTLV #8), length: 4, 172.16.33.37
  IS Neighbor: 1921.6800.1018.00, Metric: 4, sub-TLVs present (12)
    IPv4 interface address (subTLV #6), length: 4, 172.16.33.25
    IPv4 neighbor address (subTLV #8), length: 4, 172.16.33.26
Extended IPv4 reachability TLV #135, length: 9
  IPv4 prefix: 192.168.1.1/32, Distribution: up, Metric: 0
Authentication TLV #10, length: 17
  HMAC-MD5 password: 68e18feb2e29257113e4bb6580169310
```

16.3.2 *Keep the Number of Active BGP Routes per Node Low*

Vendors have come up with smart representations of BGP routes and how those routes depend on IS-IS routes. However, there is one fault condition where even smart route representations inside a router do not gain us much. If an entire BGP speaker disappears, then when the BGP speaker goes down the BGP control plane needs to re-route all those prefixes, which of course takes time. If an IS-IS router is carrying a large number of active routes, then it takes proportionally longer if that BGP router goes down. Figure 16.4 shows that, on the left-hand side, Washington is a "hotspot" BGP speaker that carries the majority of BGP routes. If this speaker goes down, then you need to re-route all 120 K routes, which can cause a network wide outage of up to 3 minutes. The logical step is to spread those 120 K routes among several routers as shown on the right-hand side of Figure 16.4.

In well-developed peering meshes, the average number of routes per border router is not more than 10 K. In our example, because of a lack of routers, we still did not put more than 30 K routes per node. In practice, if you receive more than 10 K routes per peer, then you may need to consider a redundant router and spread the incoming prefixes over the two redundant routers. Re-routing 10 K prefixes if the active router breaks down can be done in a matter of 5–10 seconds.

16.3.3 *Avoid LSP Fragmentation*

IS-IS has plenty of space (precisely 375,040 bytes per LSP) in the distributed database. Despite this vast amount of information that an individual IS-IS speaker can originate, you typically do not *want* to use that storage size – ever. You should try to accommodate all the information that you need in maxLSPsize (1492) – LSP header (27) = 1465 bytes. There may be a number of additional LSP updates if you cross an LSP boundary and have to break things up into another segment. Consider Figure 16.5 to see what happens if you are at the edge of Fragment 0 and an additional adjacency comes up. Router 1921.6800.1018 decides that it needs to break up another segment. Router 1921.6800.1018 generates the fragment and floods it. The troubles start if any of the router's other sub-nets or adjacencies become unavailable. Assume that Adjacency #4 falls down, and then the entire TLVs that follow this particular adjacency gets shifted, and also may fall into another fragment. Considering the example in Figure 16.5, there is no need to

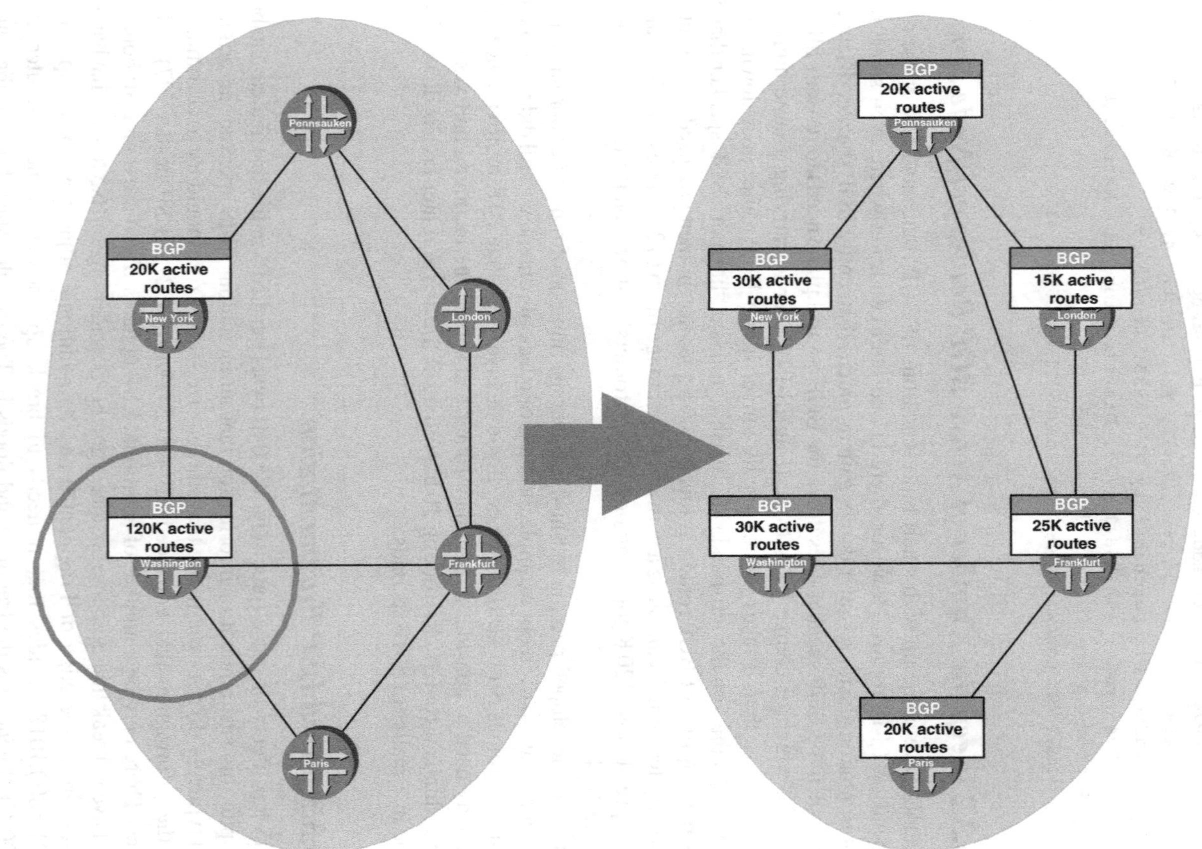

FIGURE 16.4. In a well-developed peering mesh the BGP routes are almost evenly distributed over the entire network

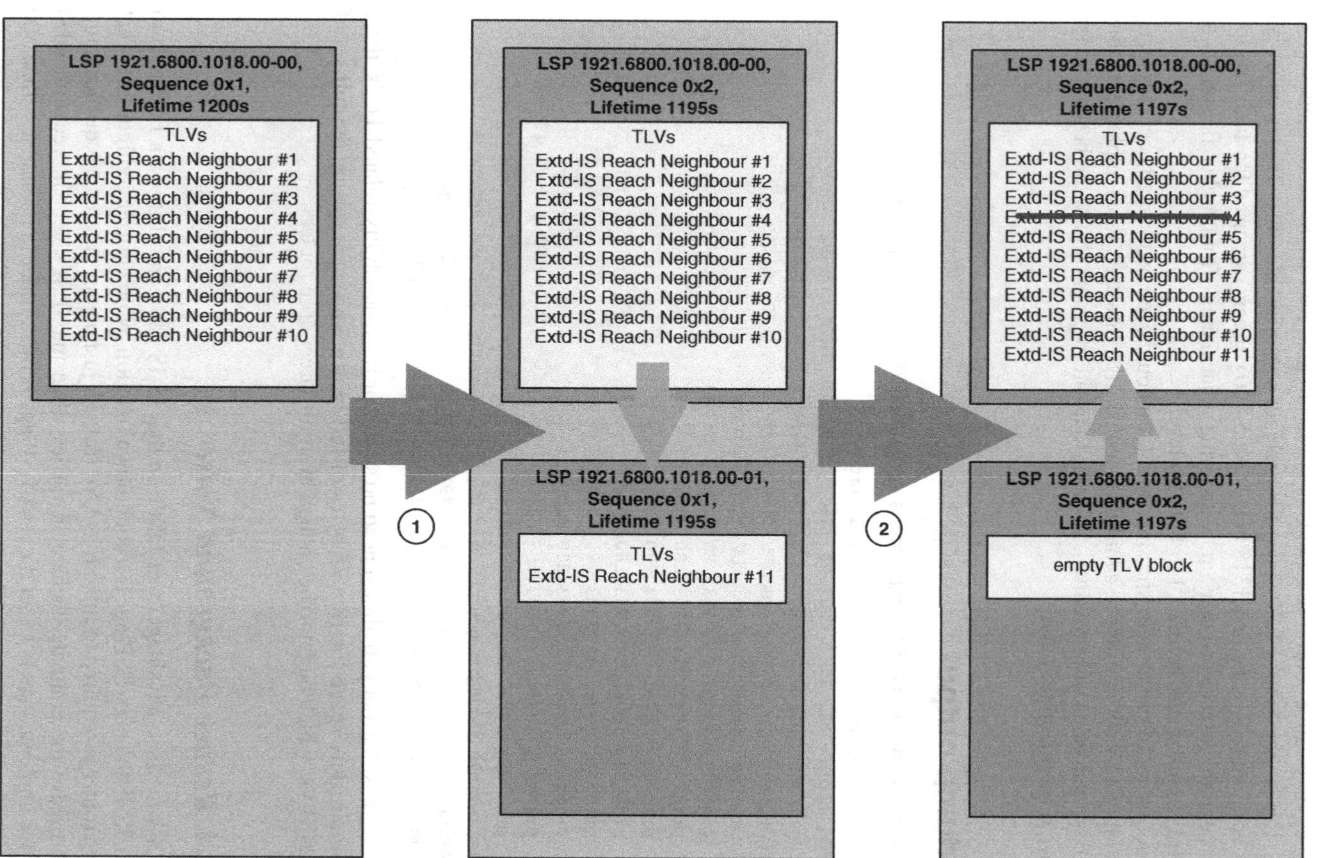

FIGURE 16.5. IS-IS fragmentation may cause excess LSP updates if adjacencies wander across several fragments

use Fragment #1 now, as everything would easily fit into Fragment #0. Fragment #1 is tossed using a network-wide purge. The trouble here is that a single change in a router's adjacency may cause several fragments to get re-aligned. ISO 10589 recommends sparing the top 10 per cent of LSP space for problem scenarios like this. That is, when an LSP is built, then only the first 1318 bytes (1465 – 10 per cent) are used for data. The top 10 per cent are reserved to take up "wandering adjacencies" from higher fragments as those fragments shrink below a 146-byte fill level.

There is a lot of clever heuristics involved (you could even pad lost adjacencies using the Padding TLV #8 in order to avoid fragment shifts); however, most implementations keep those heuristics to a minimum. In order to avoid fragment shifts, the best approach is to avoid fragmentation at all.

Tcpdump output

An adjacency carrying full TE extensions consumes 75 bytes on the wire.

```
Extended IS Reachability TLV #22, length: 75
  IS Neighbor: 2092.1113.4007.00, Metric: 5, sub-TLVs present (64)
    IPv4 interface address (subTLV #6), length: 4, 172.16.1.6
    IPv4 neighbor address (subTLV #8), length: 4, 172.16.1.5
    Unreserved bandwidth (subTLV #11), length: 32
      priority level 0: 9953.280 Mbps
      priority level 1: 9953.280 Mbps
      priority level 2: 9953.280 Mbps
      priority level 3: 9953.280 Mbps
      priority level 4: 9953.280 Mbps
      priority level 5: 9953.280 Mbps
      priority level 6: 9953.280 Mbps
      priority level 7: 9953.280 Mbps
    Reservable link bandwidth (subTLV #10), length: 4, 9953.280 Mbps
    Maximum link bandwidth (subTLV #9), length: 4, 9953.280 Mbps
    Administrative groups (subTLV #3), length: 4, 0x00000000
```

If you consider that you almost need no space for IP Reachability-related TLVs, there is approximately space for $18 * 75$ bytes of full-blown adjacencies using the full-set of TE sub-TLVs, which ought to be enough even for larger core routers.

16.3.4 *Reduce Background Noise*

IS-IS has the nice advantage over OSPF in that IS-IS can control its own LSP refresh rate. In IS-IS the max-LSP-age is a countdown function, which is user configurable. That is, each router is required to refresh its LSP (refresh just means bump the sequence number and leave the contents unchanged) in less than max-LSP-age. The recommended value for implementers is to set the max-LSP-age refresh timer to a value less than 300 seconds, but this is very low. The default value of the max-LSP-age is set to 1200 seconds, which is also the recommended value mentioned in ISO 10589. If you keep the default value, or use the 300 value, you end up tolerating a lot of "refresh noise" based on the relatively small interval of 1200 seconds (20 minutes). For example, in a network consisting of 400 routers, this means on average every 3 seconds a network-wide flood of an LSP from some router even when the network is quiet (there are no link flaps, and no topology changes, and so on).

Both IOS and JUNOS allow you to change that default value of 1200 seconds to get to a lower amount of refresh noise in your network. The recommended value is to set the max-LSP-age timer to 65,535 seconds, which extends the refresh period to 18.2 hours and therefore reduces the refresh noise by a factor of 50. There are no side-effects of changing the default value, and it remains an open question for router vendors as to why this higher value is not made the default value, because every service provider changes it to this value anyway. Keep in mind that in IOS you need to set both the `lsp-age` timer as well as the `lsp-refresh` timer and subtract the 300 seconds to get a proper refreshing. JUNOS internally calculates a "sane" timer based on the configured `lsp-age`.

16.3.5 *Rely on the Link-layer for Fault Detection*

Many service providers believe that the key for getting to sub-second convergence is to tweak all the timers in a router, particularly the Hello and Hold timers. Unfortunately today some implementations of routing protocols are not real-time capable. If you make your non-real-time capable IS-IS implementation generate a Hello every 333 ms on hundreds of adjacencies, this may cause some side-effects. Consider the processing of a big BGP batch run, where the router may not be able to revisit the code that submits the Hellos, which in turn may cause network-wide churn due to missed Hellos.

Considering that not all vendors support real-time control planes for IS-IS, we have to go down the road of the lowest common denominator. In many router implementations, generation of link-layer messages like keep-alives are handled by the forwarding complex, which typically *does* run a real-time OS (or at least a tweaked OS that is close enough). In order to get real-time detection, we offload this task to the forwarding complex. Fault detection works reasonably well on certain interface technologies like SONET/SDH. No surprise here! SONET/SDH have the best liveness protocol you can think of. Among the SONET/SDH overhead are bytes (K1/K2, K3, K4) that carry Remote Defect Indicator (RDI) bits which are immediately set if there is a problem along the SONET/SDH link. Due to SONET/SDH requirements, that message will be sent, worst case, within 50 ms of a failure and travel through every node along the path.

In the ATM world, end-to-end fault detection is performed by operation and management (OAM) cells that are inserted by routers at both ends of a Virtual Connection (VC). The OAM cells are a nice liveness protocol that can perform fault-detection for IS-IS as well.

The only remaining problem is Ethernet. Because of its inherent simplicity, there is no link-layer protocol where you could embed Ethernet keep-alive messages. Historically there was never any possibility to get quick fault detection on Ethernet except through tuning IS-IS Hold timers. But now there is a solution called bi-directional fault detection (BFD) for this purpose. BFD is described in draft-katz-ward-bfd-00.txt and the protocol and its mechanisms are simple: The idea is to set up a high frequency (<100 ms) exchange of UDP packets. If that exchange is disrupted there must be a problem with the underlying media and the link can be declared down. As soon as there are interoperable BFD implementations it will become the method of choice as a liveness protocol for Ethernet.

Table 16.2 shows a short summary of the preferred interface media type fault-detection protocols over IS-IS.

As for every major interface type there is a high-frequency fault detection protocol available and so there is no need to abuse IS-IS to provide that function. It is our recommendation to use the per-interface media type-dependent fault-detection protocols and leave IS-IS with its default Hello timers.

16.3.6 *Simple Loopback IP Address to System-ID Conversion Schemes*

The 6-byte System-ID field has an inherent drawback. For *administering* System-IDs there are almost no address management tools available that can cope with 6-byte address entities. For the network service operator there are two choices:

1. Develop a custom address management tool for 6-byte System-IDs
2. Do not manage System-IDs – rather auto-derive it from IPv4 loopback addresses

Typically, network service providers do not want to maintain yet *another* list of addresses, and therefore there are very simple mapping concepts for converting IPv4 loopback addresses to System-IDs. It is recommended to keep these schemes as simple as possible. The simplest form is the binary coded decimal (BCD) conversion where the IP address is represented in decimal notation and the resulting digits make up the System-ID. See Figure 16.6 for a few conversion examples.

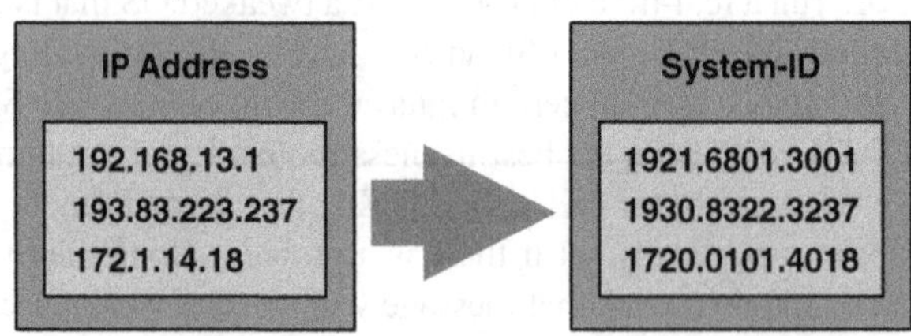

FIGURE 16.6. The best conversion tool is a simple binary coded decimal (BCD) conversion

TABLE 16.2. For every interface media type there is a high-frequency fault-detection protocol available.

Interface media type	Liveness protocol
SONET/SDH	SONET/SDH RDI
ATM	OAM cells
Ethernet	Bi-directional fault detection

Simple System-ID schemes also have the advantage that once you need to troubleshoot complex synchronization and flooding problems, it is convenient to have simple schemes to spot on certain routers.

Tcpdump output

When you are (for example) troubleshooting a synchronization problem, then it is handy if you can easily derive the IPv4 address of routers by use of a simple mapping scheme.

```
21:14:07.712478 OSI, IS-IS, length: 1478
  L2 CSNP, hlen: 33, v: 1, pdu-v: 1, sys-id-len: 6 (0), max-area: 3 (0)
    source-id: 6b01.c219.07fa.00, PDU length: 275
    start lsp-id: 1921.6800.1001.00-00
    end lsp-id: 1921.6800.1039.00-00
      LSP entries TLV #9, length: 240
        lsp-id: 1921.6800.1001.00-00, seq: 0x00000562, lifetime: 5014s,
         chksum: 0x03dc
        lsp-id: 1921.6800.1003.00-00, seq: 0x0000073a, lifetime: 31107s,
         chksum: 0xdb8b
        lsp-id: 1921.6800.1005.00-00, seq: 0x0000050c, lifetime: 5205s,
         chksum: 0xa8bf
        lsp-id: 1921.6800.1006.00-00, seq: 0x00000d20, lifetime: 30639s,
         chksum: 0x2699
        lsp-id: 1921.6800.1007.00-00, seq: 0x0000089f, lifetime: 52194s,
         chksum: 0x74ad
        lsp-id: 1921.6800.1011.00-00, seq: 0x00000319, lifetime: 61707s,
         chksum: 0xc69e
        lsp-id: 1921.6800.1011.00-01, seq: 0x0000008e, lifetime: 44126s,
         chksum: 0x6e4d
        lsp-id: 1921.6800.1013.00-00, seq: 0x000002c0, lifetime: 36610s,
         chksum: 0xb05d
        lsp-id: 1921.6800.1013.00-01, seq: 0x000000b0, lifetime: 5052s,
         chksum: 0x0e21
        lsp-id: 1921.6800.1013.00-03, seq: 0x0000029f, lifetime: 11790s,
         chksum: 0x5bfa
        lsp-id: 1921.6800.1033.00-00, seq: 0x00000318, lifetime: 11255s,
         chksum: 0xbb6e
        lsp-id: 1921.6800.1034.00-00, seq: 0x000006f4, lifetime: 48962s,
         chksum: 0x634f
        lsp-id: 1921.6800.1037.00-00, seq: 0x000005bf, lifetime: 44818s,
         chksum: 0x4701
        lsp-id: 1921.6800.1038.00-00, seq: 0x000013fc, lifetime: 8664s,
         chksum: 0x93d4
        lsp-id: 1921.6800.1039.00-00, seq: 0x000014b9, lifetime: 17862s,
         chksum: 0x2894
```

Particularly when you need to parse packet dumps like the above using network analyzers, and you do not have the name cache ready, then simple conversion logic makes troubleshooting much easier. You are doing operations and support people a big favour if you avoid fancy and complicated System-ID schemes.

16.3.7 *Align Throttling Timers Based on Global Network Delay*

In most IS-IS implementations there are many timers that the network operator can adjust. In order to build a network that converges in the sub-second range, you often need to tweak those timers. The first thought may be the faster the better, however, that's not always the case. The typical throttles that are on by default are LSP origination and SPF delay timers. Both JUNOS and IOS have a similar strategy to apply these throttles. Both implementations in common behave fast (almost no delay) for the first events in a series. However, the more quickly changes come, the more restrictive, and hence slower, the system behaves. This is achieved as a step function in JUNOS (the first three events are handled the fast way, and then the system immediately backs off to slow behaviour) and in IOS the router gets slower using an exponential curve. However, after three or four events, the system fully backs off to the slower behaviour. The art of good network design is to find a healthy compromise so that the majority (95 per cent) of network events falls under the fast window and you can take full advantage of the open throttles. Consider Figure 16.7. When parts of a network fail, then there is always more than one LSP in flight. Once the link between Washington and New York breaks, both routers have to update their LSPs. Ideally both LSPs arrive at all the routers at the same point in time.

Now you need to find a compromise between reasonably fast behaviour and waiting long enough that you can catch and process an SPF run for all the LSPs belonging to a particular network fault condition. How long is long enough? If you take a closer look at how an incident is processed, then the dominating element after mutual detection of a link-break is the propagation of the LSP. LSP propagation with reasonably fast circuits (greater then OC-3/STM-1 speeds) is mostly a function of the light-speed in a fibre plus the LSP processing delay of routers. A good estimation for the average global flooding delay is the worst case delay for network control traffic, plus the average hop count, multiplied by 10 ms (average LSP processing delay).

Speed of light in fibres is about 200.000 km/s = 200 km/ms

Example 1: Continental network (diameter 4.000 km) spanning over average 6 routers.

$$4.000\,\text{km}/200\,\text{km/ms} + 6 * 10\,\text{ms} = 20\,\text{ms} + 6 * 10\,\text{ms} = \mathbf{80\,ms}$$

Example 2: Intercontinental network (diameter 30.000 km) spanning over an average of 8 routers.

$$30.000\,\text{km}/200\,\text{km/ms} + 8 * 10\,\text{ms} = 150\,\text{ms} + 8 * 10\,\text{ms} = \mathbf{230\,ms}$$

It is recommended to change the LSP origination timer to a value that safely catches most link flaps. It should not be set too aggressively. A good recommendation here is 150 ms, which gives the router enough time to fully build an LSP no matter how large it may be.

It is recommended that you change the SPF delay timer based on the calculation for the average processing and LSP propagation delay. A recommendation for delaying the SPF calculation is between 50 ms and 250 ms depending on network size.

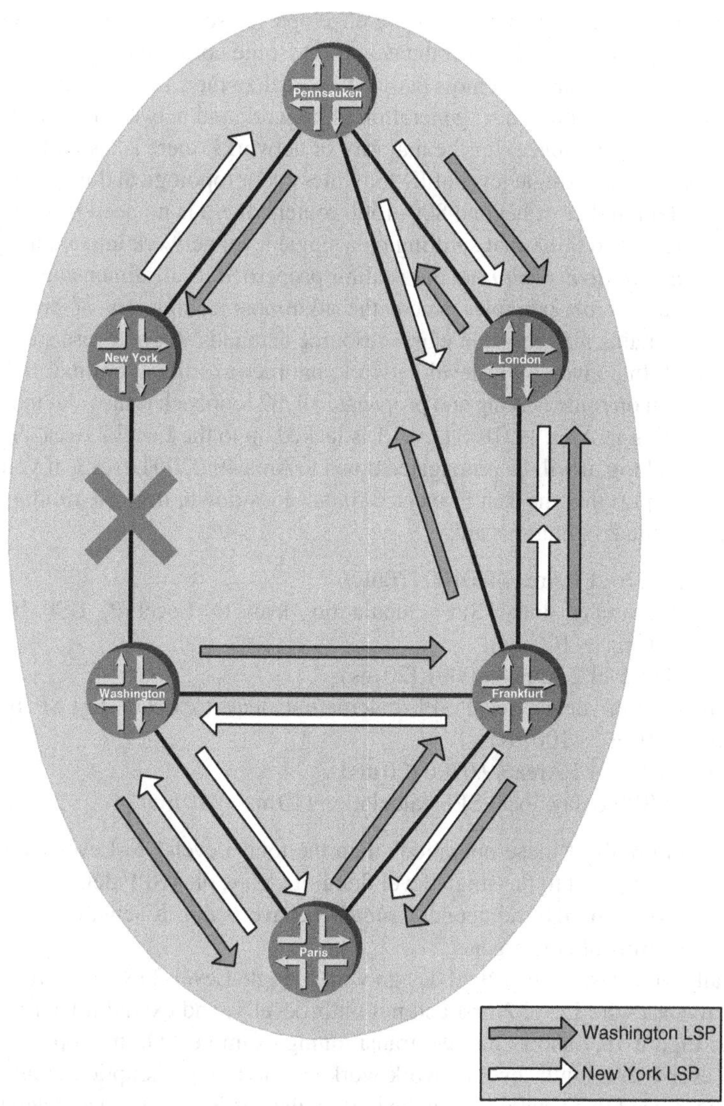

FIGURE 16.7. For true fast-convergence routing the throttling behaviour should match the LSP propagation properties of the network

16.3.8 *Single Level Where You Can – Multi-level Where You Must*

IS-IS has many useful scaling tools built in. One of them is the multi-level orientation that allows having hundreds of routing domains composed of hundreds of routers and routes between them. An important question to ask yourself is *how much scalability do you really need?* A couple of years ago, everybody in the communication industry was crazy over scaling, and even pushing the envelope for scalability was not enough for some network service providers. Fortunately today some normality (some say *sanity*) has come back to the industry, and most people now realize their true scaling needs and the associated time-span until a next generation of network and network routers are needed. According to our experience, for the majority of networks, there is a simple design rule, which is to start with a single level of IS-IS. Unless your topological domain (IS-IS level) grows to a total number of beyond 800–1500 routers, there is no need to split things up. Do not be misled and think that splitting up a single level network into a multi-level network must *automatically improve* the scaling properties in all dimensions of that network. There are some examples where the additional complexity of processing two topological domains may result in *worse* resource demands. A good case study is shown in Figure 16.8. In a given multi-level network, in order to still get optimal BGP routing, you need to turn on route leaking and propagate all /32 loopback routes. An individual /32 prefix originating in Area 49.0100 Level 1 is leaked up to the Level 2 Area 49.0001 and, due to route leaking, it will be propagated down to Area 49.0200 Level 1. If you now suppose (for example) that the San Francisco router goes down, then the timing properties of all the individual operations are:

1. Flood inside Level 1 Area 49.0100 (20ms)
2. Atlanta: SPF delay, local SPF calculation, leak to Level 2, LSP build delay (100 ms + 10 ms + 100 ms)
3. Flood inside Level 2 Area 49.0001 (20 ms)
4. Amsterdam: SPF delay, local SPF calculation, leak to Level 1, LSP build delay (100 ms + 10 ms + 100 ms)
5. Flood inside Level 1 Area 49.0200 (20 ms)
6. Stockholm: SPF delay, local SPF calculation (10 ms + 10 ms)

If you sum up all of these operations then the total Level-1-to-Level-1 convergence takes 500 ms compared to the single level flooding delay, plus SPF delay and SPF calculation (130 ms). Although the network *should* behave *better,* it actually got *worse* by a factor of 4 in terms of convergence.

Typically, you start a green-field design with a single Level-2 IS-IS network. You may ask why to start with Level 2 first and not with Level 1, and extend it later to a Level-2 network? Figure 16.9 shows the two transitioning examples. On the top, the migration from a Level-2 to a multi-level network works without any disruption at all. Only two level settings need to be changed. On the bottom the conversion from a Level-1 to Level-2 is troublesome, because Level-1 adjacencies require that the Area address matches on both ends, and in order to create several Level-1 areas you need to renumber the areas and touch every router. This means that for a short time you must disrupt your service. In the top example we assume that the network administrator has allocated the appropriate distinct Area-IDs so that they can change the level anytime. In Level 2 routing, different Area-IDs are tolerated – the Area-ID does not need to match. A little piece of *tolerance* is generally a good recipe for easy transitioning, and here it helps to be able to renumber the Area-IDs without any disruption. That is good news, as you do not need to worry about addressing from the start. You can at a later stage change the entire IS-IS Area addressing and add anything at any time.

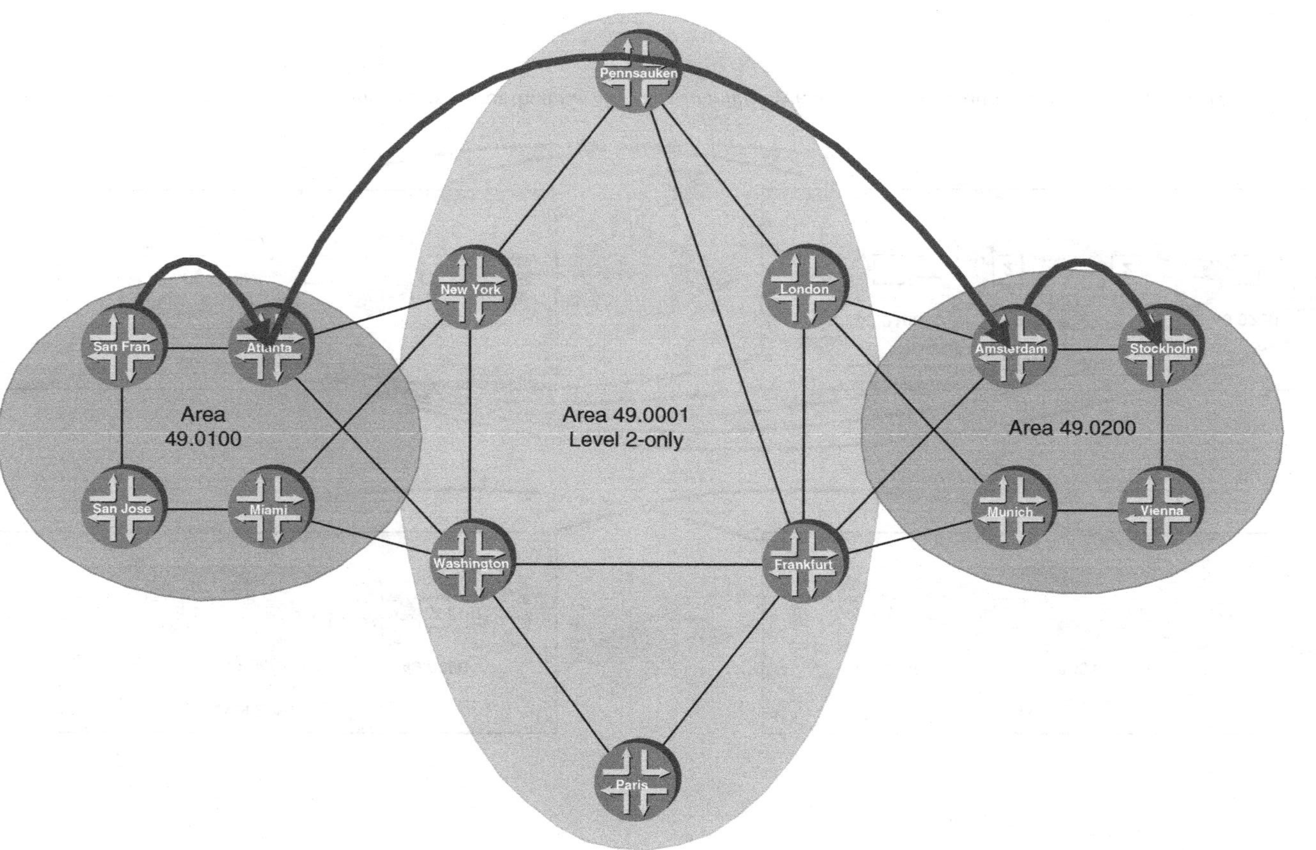

FIGURE 16.8. In a two level IS-IS network propagation through all levels does slow down convergence

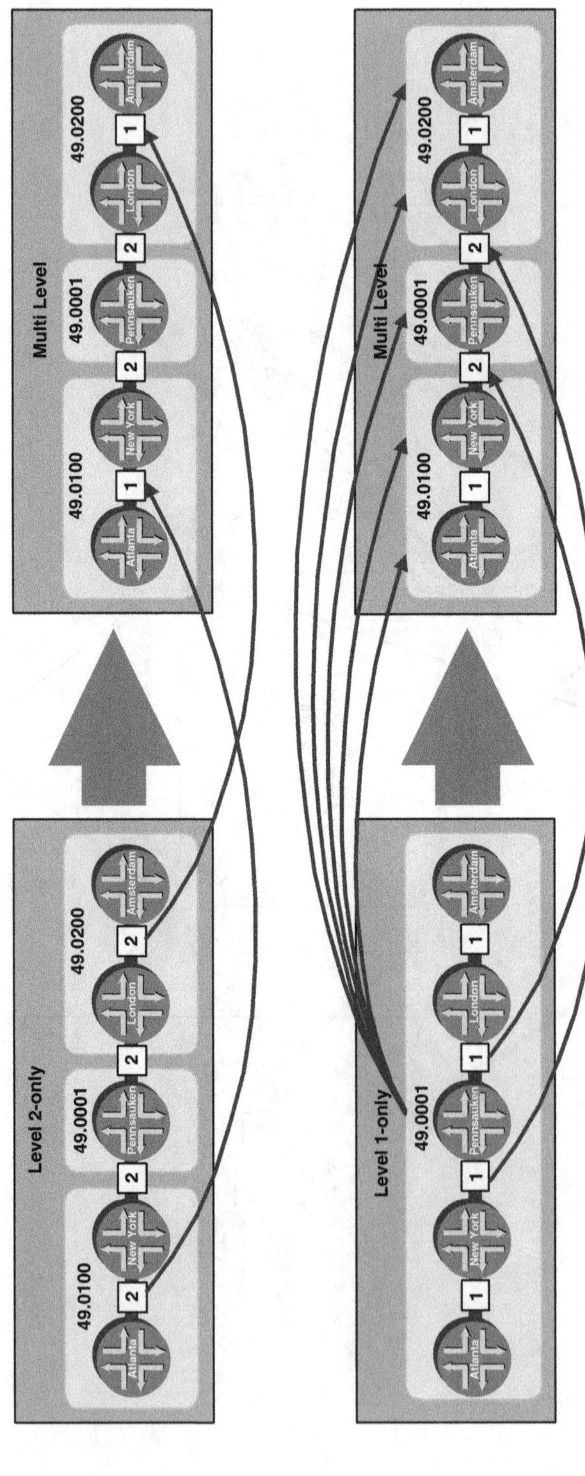

FIGURE 16.9. *Level 2-only to multi-level* transition is easier than *Level 1-only to multilevel*, as it does not require renumbering Area-IDs

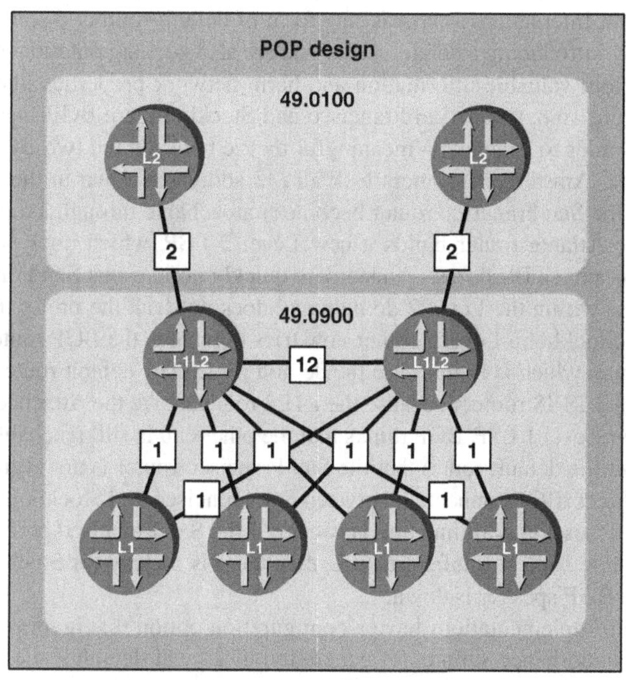

FIGURE 16.10. Common multi-level designs have two L1L2 routers and intra-POP routing is provided using L1 routing

In the case where you have a massive number of routers, or certain smaller routers with limited CPU and memory resources, you may decide to run a multi-level network. Best current practice is to have a point of presence (POP) where all the internal routers, reflectors, access servers and servers are routed using Level-1 routing. One or two L1L2 routers provide core access as illustrated in Figure 16.10.

Note the link between the two core routers – both a Level 1 and a Level 2 adjacency is established between the core routers. This is an example where one physical link can be shared between two IS-IS topologies. The purpose of the link is for backup in case there is a topology break either in the core or in the edge.

A POP-centric design has the nice advantage that there is a clean separation between core and edge, which is also typically run by different teams at a service provider. So there are almost no incidents where the edge-router department at a service provider modifies core-router related configuration and vice versa (some call this the *missing cross talk* problem). At large service providers it often turns out that technology has to follow organizational requirements. The POP centric design perfectly reflects that idea.

16.3.9 *Do Not Rely on Default Routes*

Default routes are a nice tool for scaling the network, particularly for routers that do not have the CPU and memory resources to load and hold full BGP Internet routing tables.

However, in an Internet environment, any form of default routing disturbs more than it does good. By introducing a default route, you are also keeping out more specific entries that may contain valuable information and harm network properties like convergence. Consider Figure 16.8, where San Francisco and Stockholm are BGP speakers in different areas. In order to calculate a meaningful metric between the two BGP speakers the L1L2 (Atlanta, Amsterdam) routers leak all /32 addresses down in the Level 1. Next, suppose that the San Francisco router becomes unreachable through a topology break in the core. The Atlanta router builds a new Level 2 LSP, which does not contain San Francisco's loopback IP address. Amsterdam quickly notices that San Francisco speaker is unreachable within the Level 2 domain and does not leak the prefix further down in Level 1. The Stockholm Level 1 router now tries to resolve the BGP routes through any other IGP route, which is in this case the default route. The default route is locally generated by all L1 IS-IS routers because the L1L2 routers have the Attached (ATT) Bit set as part of their Level 1 LSP. BGP thinks that the other end is still reachable and does not realize (due to the default route) that the San Francisco router is not available anymore. If there is a direct iBGP connection between San Francisco and Stockholm, then as a last resort the BGP session will time out. However, if the San Francisco prefixes are learned via a BGP Route Reflector infrastructure, then there is no way for Stockholm to realize that a remote BGP speaker is down.

Most router implementations have a configuration option that ignores the ATT Bit in Level 1 LSPs and hence suppresses generation of a local default route. Going back to Figure 16.8, that means that all Level 1 BGP speakers are configured *not* to listen to ATT Bits. Then the resolver immediately knows that there are no alternate paths available, and the BGP routes are immediately withdrawn and alternate paths become active.

Try to design your core network so that it does not rely on a default route in any single place. Try to avoid any form of explicit 0/0 route embedded in IP Reachability TLVs and actively filter those routes on any L1L2 choke point. Also try to control all implicit default routes that may be locally generated through the ATT Bit. If there are no default routes in the core network, then your end-customers will greatly benefit from the improved network convergence.

16.3.10 *Use Wide-metrics Only*

Both IS-IS implementations discussed in this book ship with a *compatibility mode* where both old-style and wide-style metrics are advertised in a router's LSP. That dual support for both old-style TLV #2, #128, #130 and new-style TLV #22, #135 comes at some cost. The drawback is that the metrics of the old-style topology and the new-style topology have to stay congruent in order to produce non-divergent topologies. The clipping of metrics makes the new-style metrics, although they have a broader metric width, behave like the old-style 6-bit metrics and does not carry any advantage despite being compatible at all costs. The default settings of JUNOS and IOS are either small-metrics and compatibility mode. It is recommended to turn off generation of any form of old-style TLV. All recent routing software has support for wide metrics, and there are no disadvantages to suppressing any *old-style* TLVs. Most real-world IS-IS router configurations turn off small metric generation and it is just a matter of time before router vendors pick

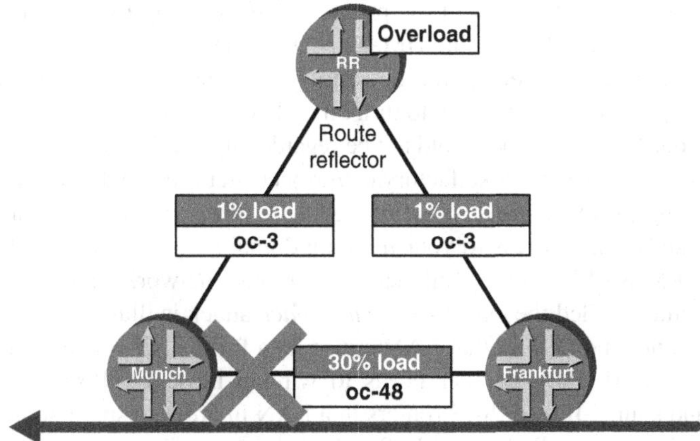

FIGURE 16.11. Static setting of the Overload Bit saves the route reflector from forwarding transit traffic

up the deployed reality and it becomes the default behaviour in JUNOS and IOS. Often downwards compatibility is preferred when changing defaults, and generally software engineers are reluctant to change behaviour. However, downward compatibility at all costs is not always the smartest way to evolve a protocol.

16.3.11 *Make Use of the Overload Bit*

The Overload (OL) Bit was intended to be an indicator that a router ran out of resources. Today it is used for administration purposes in order to avoid persistent transit traffic or to avoid the delay of transit traffic until the BGP mesh has been brought up. It is a convenient tool to avoid traffic flowing over certain nodes. The SPF calculation tries to find the shortest path between a pair of nodes in the IS-IS topology, however, sometimes the shortest path through a node may not be desired at all, particularly when it has to be routed over small-bandwidth routers serving (for example) as a route reflector. Consider Figure 16.11, where the core link between Router Munich and Router Frankfurt fail and the traffic can be re-routed over the dual homed route reflector. However, the route reflector is just attached with OC-3/STM-1 link speed, and if inadvertently abused as a transit router, may fully congest those links. Good connectivity of route reflectors is a desired property and multi-homing is often a way of achieving this.

If you statically set the Overload Bit, then all routers consider your route reflectors as non-viable transit paths for passing traffic. Any Edge Node, such as data centre access routers, may be candidates for setting the Overload Bit statically.

16.3.12 *Turn on HMAC-MD5 Authentication*

IS-IS is believed to be an inherently secure protocol because it natively runs on OSI Reference Model Layer 2 and hence an attacker cannot inject any malicious packets from remote locations, as can be done with the IP routing protocols. But there is no such thing as *too much* security. Part of the problem with securing IS-IS well was that until recently Cisco Systems did not ship HMAC-MD5 authentication support with their software, and simple text authentication does not yield true protection. Despite that lack, many service providers decided not to turn on authentication. But do not be misled – the security of your IS-IS network should not be regarded lightly. There are dedicated toolkits like Nemesis http://www.packetfactory.net/projects/nemesis/, which can generate all sorts of routing protocol packets, including IS-IS. There are forms of attacks known where a hacker having access to your flooding domain via some Ethernet segment can easily inject bogus LSPs and take all the routers in your network out of service. A dreadful form of attack called the *end-of-sequence-space* attack is illustrated in Figure 16.12. Every 10 seconds the DIS on that LAN transmits a full CSNP which contains all LSP-IDs of the network. The attacker needs to wiretap those CSNPs and extract MAC addresses and source IDs of IS-IS routers in a LAN in order to spoof some LSPs. Next, the attacker forges so-called *purge LSPs* which are typically used to revoke an issued LSP before it expires (this is sometimes called *premature ageing*).

Tcpdump output

```
06:56:44.928898 OSI, IS-IS, length: 54
  L2 LSP, hlen: 27, v: 1, pdu-v: 1, sys-id-len: 6 (0), max-area: 3 (0)
    lsp-id: 1921.6800.1018.00-00, seq: 0xffffffff, lifetime: 0s
    chksum: 0x0000, PDU length: 27, Flags: [ L1L2 IS ]
```

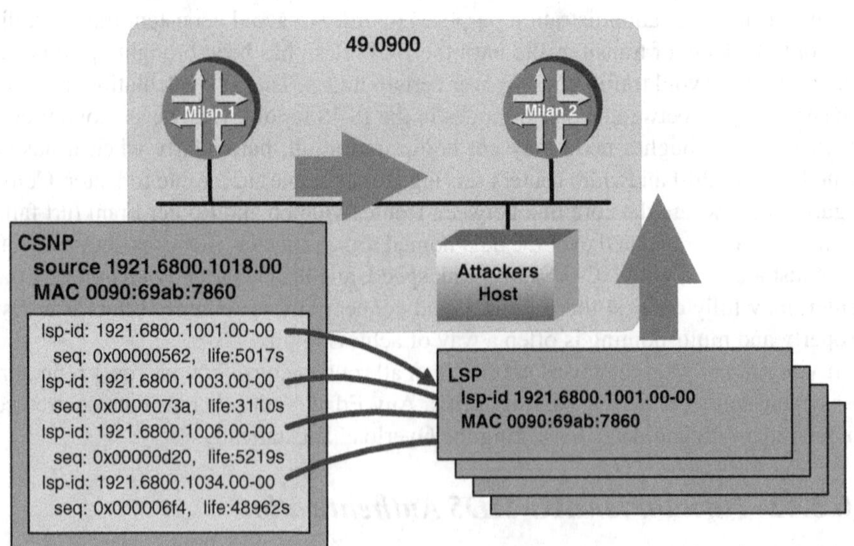

FIGURE 16.12. In an unauthenticated IS-IS environment it is very easy to take down an entire network using an end-of-sequence-space attack

The LSP in question does not contain any TLV at all. Note the sequence number 0xffffffff – this is the highest sequence number possible. When the packet is flooded through the Level 2 domain, it is ultimately received by the router with System-ID 1921.6800.1018. This router realizes that it was not the originator of that packet. Whenever a router sees non-self originated LSP carrying their very own System-ID number, they try to increment the sequence number and re-issue an accurate version of their LSP. However, that is not possible any more because the sequence space is exhausted. ISO 10589 requires that a router that reaches end-of-sequence space goes dormant for a max-LSP-age period. Most routers are configured with a max-LSP-age of 65,535 seconds, which is 18.2 hours.

Can you imagine the turmoil if all your routers go dormant for 18.2 hours and your iBGP distribution mesh falls to pieces? And it does not take much in the way of resources to achieve that – just an open Ethernet segment and a possibility to inject spoofed packets. Realize the small effort involved: no brute force Denial of Service attack is needed to take down an entire service provider's network, just a few hundred spoofed LSPs that can easily be generated with common security tools.

Security through obscurity does not generally work well. Running an IS-IS network without proper authentication using cryptographically strong algorithms like HMAC-MD5 is grossly negligent. Given the potential threat of an attack to the IGP, every networking architect should be concerned and it should be mandatory to turn on IS-IS strong authentication.

16.3.13 *Turn on Graceful Restart/Non-stop Forwarding*

Once the IGP fails, a network is literally breaking into pieces. If the IGP goes down, the BGP mesh will fail, and subsequently routing and forwarding is severely disrupted. Modern routing software is written where some components share a common fate. If, for instance, there is a bug in the resolver, then the entire routing process will crash. After a couple of seconds a watchdog component may find out that the process has been falling on its face and restart the faulty routing sub-system. The software will behave like on a cold start and send out IS-IS Hellos with no neighbour-related state mentioned in the adjacency-related TLVs (#6, #240), which will cause neighbouring routers to drop those adjacencies. Graceful restart/non-stop forwarding helps to protect the IGP subsystem in case of a failure. After being restarted, the router will request a graceful restart by setting the Restart Request Bit in TLV #211, which will cause neighbouring routers that support graceful restart/non-stop forwarding *not* to take down adjacencies for a grace-period (typically 180 seconds). Graceful restart/non-stop forwarding is all about tolerance of nodes that have failed previously. It is recommended to turn graceful restart/nonstop forwarding on wherever possible. You gain more availability of your network in case of local software failure and the problem does not spread network-wide anymore.

16.4 Conclusion

The biggest improvement for getting to a scalable IS-IS network is separating IP reachability information from IS reachability information and do not let IS-IS carry IP routes, except for the bare minimum needed to bring up the iBGP transport mesh. Once the iBGP transport mesh has been brought up BGP carries all IP information including link-local IP sub-net prefixes. That design choice is no real choice – it is paramount – all the other options depend on what you expect from the network and what is doable with the prevailing hardware/ software combination. Ultimately, one has to *listen* to what end-customers are expecting and what kind of services have to be modelled on top of that backbone. For good network designs there are two important insights. First, you always have to make a *compromise*. Networks are complex and changes of any kind have multi-dimensional impact. If you optimize on one direction then you deliberately have to jeopardize the other. So pick carefully which of the three areas you want to optimize on: *scalability*, *stability* or *convergence*. While it would be a highly desirable goal to maximize all three, in practice you can only optimize on *two*. The second insight is an old rule of systems design – keep it simple. Before exploring complex matters of route leaking and multi-level designs, first answer the question as to whether you really *need* all that complexity. Would the network work even if you go with a single level design, and what would be the overall scalability impact? Practical experience says that modern IS-IS implementations are more scalable than people think, and keep some sanity, sometimes network designers try to seek solutions for non-existent problems.

17

Future of IS-IS

Writing a book about IS-IS is a never-ending task. During the writing of this book a lot that was originally planned for this *future* chapter got implemented in routing software and is now available and deployed in the Internet. It became clear to the authors that whatever we put into this chapter would just be a snapshot of the thoughts and published Internet drafts at one particular time. You will find a lot of proposals here that may make their way into final products, and some ideas that will ultimately be tossed aside. This chapter is about a whole spectrum of IS-IS extensions, ranging from very ambitious projects like Generalized MPLS (G-MPLS) to very pragmatic ones like iBGP auto-discovery. However, this chapter is not limited to just a snapshot of the Internet drafts in mid 2004. The IS-IS universe is ever-expanding, and we will have to ask if it is a legitimate concern to enhance the IS-IS protocol at all costs, particularly for functions that it was not originally designed for.

17.1 Who Should Evolve IS-IS?

IS-IS is evolved by *different* standards bodies. The IETF is supposed to refine specification of IP-related extensions, and the ITU ought to take care of any modifications to the base specification. As part of the agreement between the IETF and ITU, there is a division of the assignable TLV space. The ITU is supposed to assign the lower 127 TLVs, and the IETF has been given the upper 127 TLVs. However, as shown in Chapter 13, "IS-IS Extensions", the IETF got away from their home turf and published specifications that are outside their assigned responsibilities – the Multi Topology Extensions and all generic IS-IS functions like Traffic Engineering, Authentication and Checksumming related TLVs (222, 22, 10, 12) violate this division. These TLVs have been specified and submitted in a time-to-market fashion, mostly to overcome the slow decision-making process within the ITU. There are voices in the IETF that would either force the two standards bodies to work together, or completely transfer responsibility for the IS-IS protocol from the ITU-T to the IETF. Dr Tony Li, once, IETF ISIS-WG chair, proposed just this merging once on the IETF ISIS-WG mailing list.

Let me offer a germ of an idea: As has been pointed out, there is a great deal of overlap between the actual folks doing the work in both organizations. No matter where we host it, it's the same folks, doing the same thing. Why then, does it really matter, where the group is hosted? Why not have just one joint, integrated working group, which reports to two bodies? This way, the group has the clear authority to issue definitive documents. These documents get published as BOTH ISO standards and RFCs.

The involvement of different standards bodies raises a plethora of issues. Because the IETF is not the "owner" of IS-IS, none of its documents go on the IETF standards track process. The standards track is a multi-year process that ensures protocol maturity and interoperability between different vendors. All the different stages of the maturity process is documented as RFCs and at the end of the standards track process there is promotion of the protocol to an Internet Standard, which not many documents achieve. As soon as the Internet Standard status is reached, the document becomes a *normative reference* in the ITU sense. Although the ITU's standards track process may take several years, one could argue that the ITU is much faster in this respect. The difference between the two standardization bodies is how they *approach* and handle standardization. In the IETF, things are pretty much evolution driven: the IETF defines a problem, Internet drafts get published and in many cases the equipment vendors ship software based on the Internet drafts, which are at this point not normative references at all. This process has the advantage of getting a new IS-IS feature deployed quickly, sometimes within six months (at the risk of changing the software several times unless the Internet draft has matured). In the ITU, there is much more emphasis on getting the first document flawless through rigid reviews and (of course) plenty of time. The ITU believes that specifications have to be finalized before they can be used in actual product shipments. While that approach is much more "clean slate", it runs the risk of missing the market during all these time-consuming review cycles. Meanwhile, the ITU has practically resigned from the task of evolving IS-IS. All of the work is done in the IETF. But because the ITU still formally owns the base protocol, the IETF must not publish any IS-IS-related RFCs as standards track RFCs, but rather as *informational* RFCs. Informational RFCs do not have the status of a normative specification – they are just supposed to make sure that things are documented. However, there is a paradox in that the ISIS-WG is the only valid source for further IS-IS development, and yet has to publish all IS-IS extensions as non-normative documents, the informational RFCs. Moreover, the ITU refers to the published IS-IS informational RFCs, and therefore is blessing the "informational" RFCs as normative references!

The double standardization, or lack of it, remains a real problem in the IS-IS community. And there are no signs that the situation will get better. Reunion of the IP and optical layer through G-MPLS will be the next severe challenge for the two IS-IS standardization bodies. Then there will be a full clash in terms of responsibility. Transmission networks are a true domain of the ITU, and recently all the IS-IS control plane-related extensions have been done at the ISIS-WG inside the IETF. It is the authors' opinion that the ITU should formalize what is the de facto status today and transfer responsibility for IS-IS to the ISIS-WG in the IETF and promote all IS-IS related extensions to IETF standards track documents.

17.2 G-MPLS

A networking stack in a service provider's network looks quite different today than it looked not long ago. Figure 17.1 shows a typical networking stack of the 1990s: there are several layers of networking protocols transporting the IP *application*. IP is wrapped on top of ATM, which performed traffic engineering functions. Next, there is a SONET/SDH

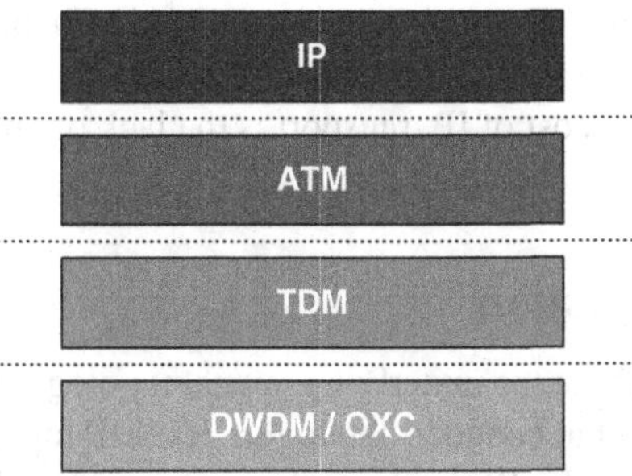

FIGURE 17.1. In the 1990s there were several layers of transport layers, most of them performing redundant functions

layer that is necessary for provisioning fixed pipes for the ATM trunks. Finally the SONET/SDH frame needs DWDM and Optical Cross Connect (OCX) technologies to get transported over the fibre.

Compare this relatively massive layering to today's networking layers. ATM got eliminated due to the rise of MPLS. SONET/SDH is no longer used for provisioning circuits. The only remnants of SONET/SDH technology is the frame format. Today, IP is transported almost natively over a DWDM infrastructure. There has been a massive *consolidation* of transport technologies. The rise of IP technology set a trend here: either a networking layer gets eliminated or its functions are ported into an IP routing or signalling protocol. MPLS is a good example here: a lot of ATM functions, such as the idea of source routing, CSPF and label swapping, made their way into a set of IP protocols. If you continue that trend, then IP will again likely control the next layer of networking beneath. This is the *optical* layer.

17.2.1 *Problems in the Optical Network Today*

The optical layer today is a closed network by itself. It consists of optical amplifiers and cross-connects which multiplex and de-multiplex wavelengths over optical fibres. All optical paths are provisioned *manually*. The manual nature of optical provisioning is quite counterintuitive – the strange thing about optical networks is that although almost everything is standardized, there is no open signalling protocol to set up optical channels and trails. As a result of this lack of a sound provisioning protocol, optical vendors have come up with their own proprietary software that does not interoperate with other vendors' methods. Service providers in general source equipment from several vendors, because they do not want to invest completely in proprietary technologies and get locked into a certain vendor's technology. As a result, the lowest common denominator is often picked and service providers set up their optical trails manually. The disadvantage of manual provisioning is obvious: too often it is tedious and error-prone. Much worse, it is time-consuming and it is not attractive to vendors if they keep losing customers because of too slow provisioning procedures.

The manual setup of optical channels creates the environment that the IP world has to live in. This is known as *overlay network*. Overlay networks and their impact and scaling damage to link-state routing protocols were explained in Chapter 14, "Traffic Engineering and MPLS". The cost of transporting IP data is today increasingly questioned, and the main problem of the high cost of IP transport is the lack of any real underlying topology that is tuned to IP.

17.2.2 *Cost of Transport*

Consider Figure 17.2, where the underlying optical topology consisting of optical amplifiers and cross-connects that connects the higher level IP topology is much more diverse and complex. Although to the IP topology, the trail from London to Frankfurt appears to be attractive, considering the full network stack reveals a different picture. It is quite expensive to relay IP traffic between London and Frankfurt as the traffic has to pass through several regeneration stages on its way between the two cities. The overall cost of transmission is dominated by the number of regenerator hops of the optical topology. If the IP world would have had the full picture of the underlying topology, it could produce more accurate IP costs that would reflect the real cost of transmission.

G-MPLS fixes the above two problems: it offers a unified routing and signalling layer for both the IP and the optical world. First, IP nodes can gather the structure of the optical topology and calculate the cost for IP transport accordingly. Next, optical components can signal optical channels using a standardized protocol (RSVP-TE).

Transitioning from the prevailing method of running the optical and IP network as disjoint networks to a full G-MPLS model requires three main migrations.

1. Transitioning from pure manual provisioning to a full signalled environment
2. Transitioning from the world of vendor proprietary protocols to the IP world of open protocols
3. Opening the optical layer to devices to the routing layer

Taking those three steps requires a lot of changes. Not every network service provider is willing to take all three steps at once. There is more demand for a constant *evolution* of networks than a rapid *revolution*, with the admirable goal of not destabilizing the network. Also, consolidation of networking elements has to pay off at the end of the day. Further reduction of operating expenses is the main driver for the G-MPLS ideas. However, many teams at service providers, especially optical groups, fear that their jobs may become obsolete if they pass on too much control to a consolidated, unified control plane. Today, full-scale G-MPLS causes much anxiety and so many service providers try to split up the migration into a two-step migration model. The first migration step is called the *overlay model* and the second step is called the *peer model*. The two models do not contradict each other, they can be seen more as complementary steps. Many optical vendors use the term *hybrid model* to reflect the fact that both models can be implemented at the same time.

17.2.3 *Overlay (UNI) G-MPLS Model*

The overlay model can best be characterized taking migration Step 1 and 2 (outlined above) towards G-MPLS, but not taking Step 3. So the optical topology is beefed up and now encompasses dynamic signalling using IP routing and signalling protocols; however,

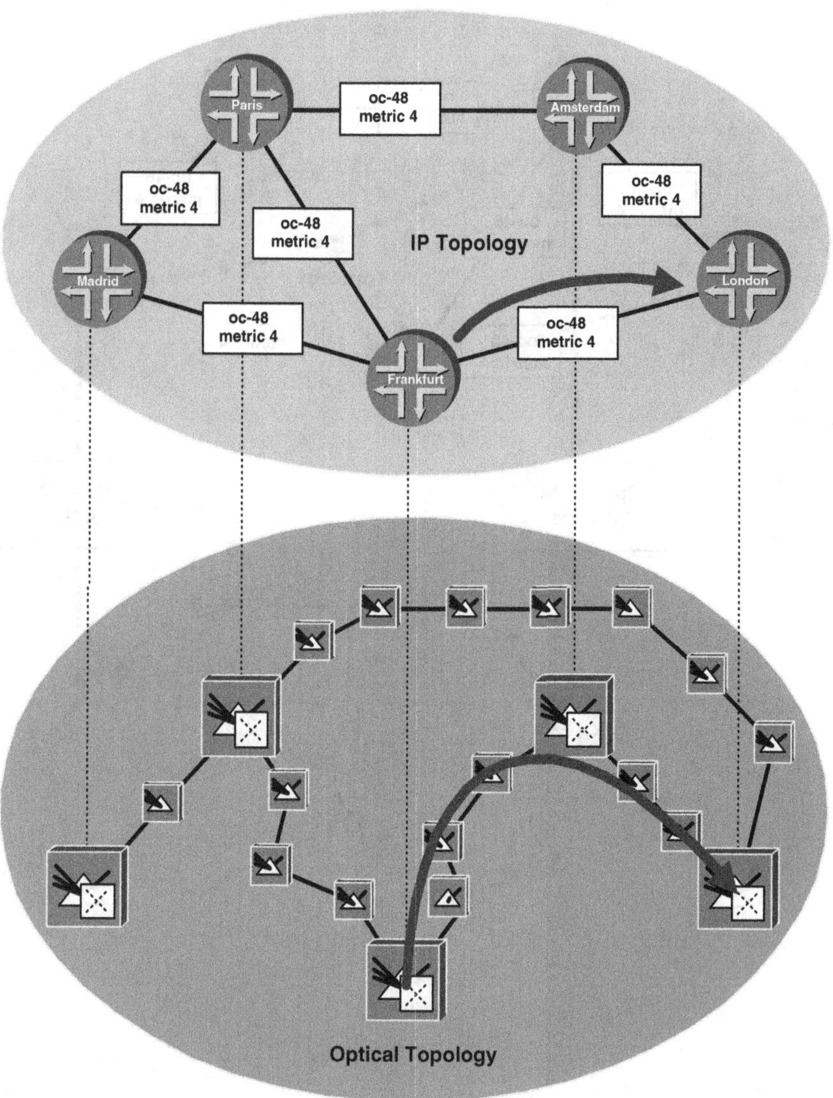

FIGURE 17.2. The cost of transmission may vary from the IP cost due to the lack of visibility between the networking layers

it does not yet reveal the topology of the optical domain to the IP routing layer. The router is typically treated as a client and the interface to the routers is termed a User to Network Interface (UNI). Consider Figure 17.3 where the router is requesting a direct link between Munich and Washington. The optical core now tries to find an optical trail with the lowest number of regeneration stages and sets up the path.

Once the path is up and running, the IP world treats that path just as if it were a *real physical interface* and includes it in the flooding topology of the IP world. Setting up

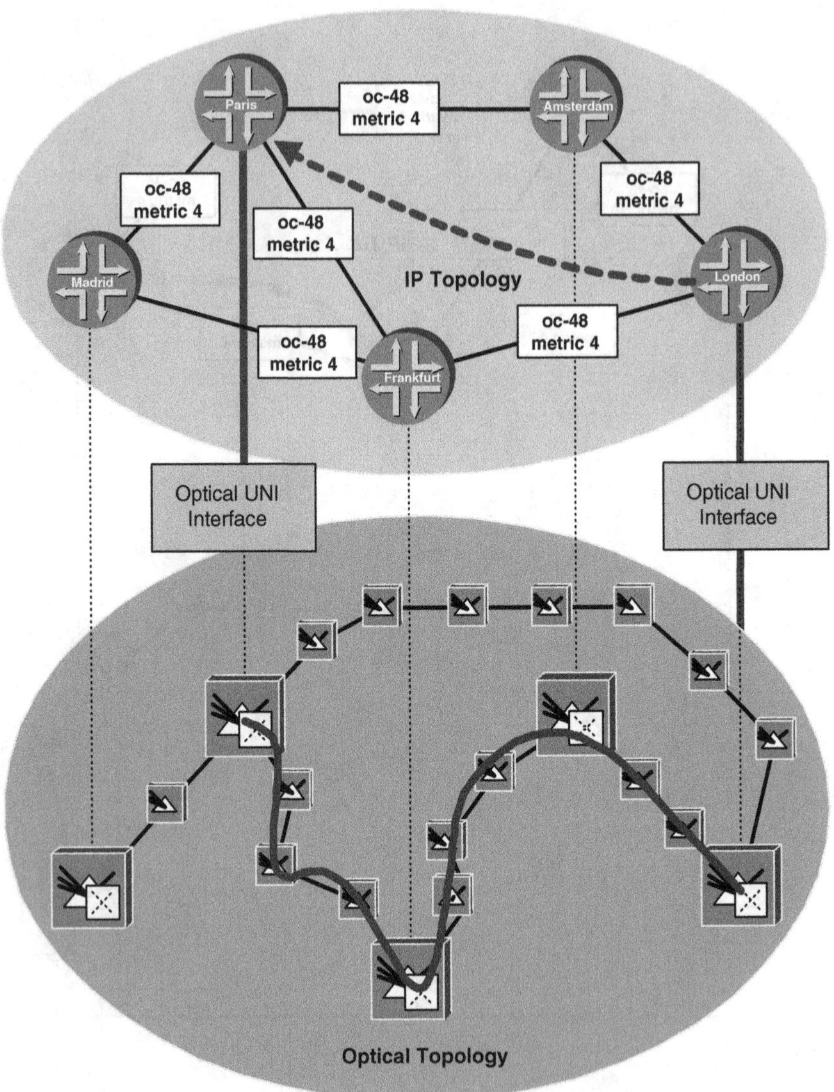

FIGURE 17.3. By connecting the router with a UNI interface the optical topology is not revealed to the IP routers

many optical trails using UNI-like signalling creates about the same problem ATM networks had, and is the reason most ATM networks have now been abandoned. As UNI interfaces, the optical trails make you create another overlay network, only this time on the *optical* layer. Chapter 14, "Traffic Engineering and MPLS", gives some reasons as to how overlay networks stress the IGPs and often produce strange routing decisions. Hiding the topology creates many support-related problems too. If the IP team does not know where their core trunks are routed, the Network Operations Center will have a hard time correlating local link faults to the global faults of the LSP mesh. Therefore it is essential to convey how *the real optical path* looks to the routers. Unfortunately, due to the UNI-like separation between optical network and client (router), there is little room for giving such feedback. A place where this kind of information could live is the Route Record Object (RRO) that should return the real path that a label switched path is taking. Research groups have identified the modifications to the RRO necessary to accommodate optical paths that have been computed and set up outside the IP domain. It remains questionable from a philosophical standpoint why at first hiding everything, and then eventually disclosing it, is a consistent and repeated model, but an odd one to base a networking architecture upon.

The overlay (UNI) model is a nice start for deploying the new G-MPLS routing and signalling protocols. It gives the optical engineers exposure to the IP world of addressing, signalling and routing, which is certainly a non-technical challenge. As soon as you want to roll it out on a larger scale, the inherent technical scaling limitations of optical networks are revealed. You clash completely with the restrictions of overlay networks and get a *déjà vu* of recent times when ATM overlay cores were pushing the limits of existing technology, a whole seven years ago.

In order to not repeat the mistakes from the past, the full-scale G-MPLS deployments need to have complete vision into the underlying optical topology, which is what the *peer G-MPLS model* describes.

17.2.4 *Peer G-MPLS Model*

The G-MPLS peer model represents the full conclusion of all three migration steps. The idea is that all components in a network, including

- Packet switches (routers)
- TDM switches (SONET/SDH cross-connects (TXC))
- Optical switches (lambda and fibre cross-connects (OXC))

all run an instance of a common routing and signalling protocol. The common routing protocol could be enhanced versions of IS-IS or OSPF. It is the authors' opinion that IS-IS finally will prevail as the routing protocol of choice in the unified routing cloud. IT will most likely be IS-IS mainly because IS-IS has been successfully deployed on a larger scale in IP networks, but also because the core IP routing teams do not want to run the risk of destabilizing the network by introduction of a *new* protocol. There is a belief in the market that IS-IS scales much better than anything else, but that belief is largely because of *implementation* issues. The fact is that the only *well-implemented, multivendor* IGP today is IS-IS. By continuing on its evolutionary path, IS-IS will remain, at least in the minds of network service operators, the IP IGP that *scales,* and therefore will likely be the candidate for a deployment of *thousands* of G-MPLS nodes in a given domain.

In G-MPLS each component in the network runs a control plane either in-band or out-of-band. That is a shift from pure IP routing, where routing protocols were always running on an in-band channel (*in-band* just means the signalling and traffic travel on the same channels). There is an Internet draft (draft-ietf-ccamp-lmp) which describes the

Link Management Protocol (LMP) that allows the control planes of G-MPLS devices to talk to each other without the need for an in-band control channel. Figure 17.4 illustrates the concept of an out-of-band control plane.

Suppose there are three interfaces between a pair of optical cross-connects that need to get advertised. As we cannot run IS-IS on those three links in-band, we must utilize the Link Management Protocol for discovering the bandwidth, the ID, and the state of each link and report it back to IS-IS. LMP goes through three stages:

1. Control Channel (CC) start up
2. Interface discovery and TE-ID mapping
3. Interface testing

First, a control channel is brought up. During that step, two-way connectivity is verified and the Control Channel IDs (CCiDs) are exchanged. The control channel

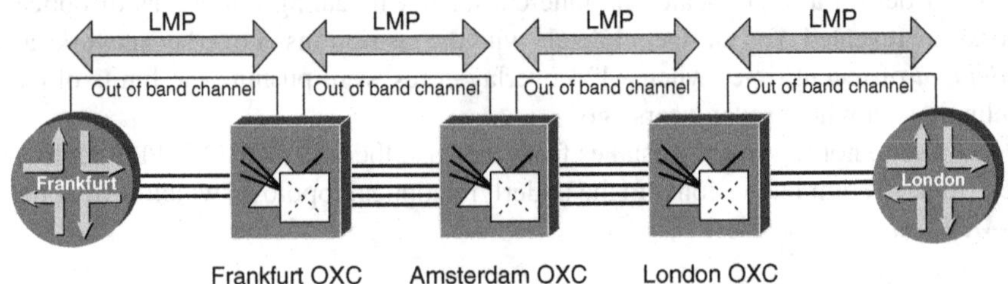

FIGURE 17.4. The Link Management Protocol features out-of-band control plane interaction

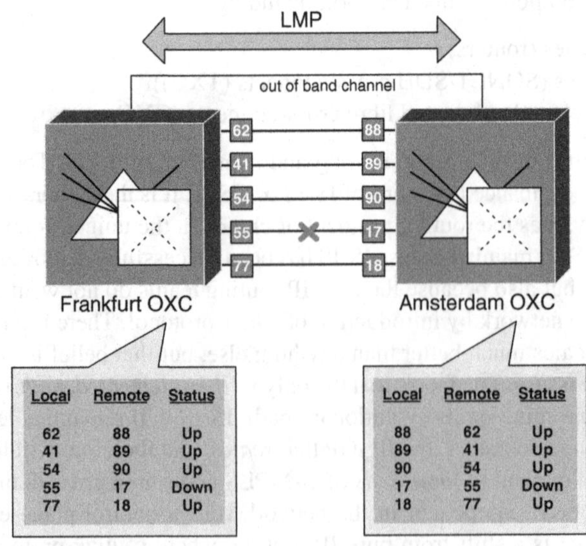

FIGURE 17.5. The Link Management Protocol allows control planes to discover interfaces and update interface state

additionally features high-speed detection of control plane failures and generates Hello messages typically at the pace of every 150 ms.

Figure 17.5 illustrates the next step, where both systems report and mutually discover the interfaces as well as the TE-IDs of those interfaces. Part of this discovery phase is also to find out about the interface switching type, which could be packet, TDM or lambda-based. Finally, all the interfaces are verified and reported either as up or down.

Once IS-IS learns about all the interfaces and interface properties such as bandwidth, TE-ID, and switching capability it has enough information to update its link-state PDU and advertise the link properties between the two switching nodes as sub-TLVs in the extended IS-Reach TLV #22. In the next section there is a list of these sub-TLVs and their contents.

IS-IS now has full visibility of all interfaces in the network and the interface switching capabilities. However, relaying of user traffic is not yet possible at this point. The higher switching layers like the packet or TDM switching devices still rely on the bringing up of the *optical* switching layers first. Consider Figure 17.6 for an example of how the optical switching layers are brought up.

1. The TDM cross-connect in Paris signals that it needs a lambda (wavelength) capable of transporting an OC-192c/STM-64 (10 Gbps) frame to Amsterdam via RSVP-TE. As the cross-connect in Paris now has complete knowledge of the optical topology, it could also predetermine the route or base it on constraints like hop count, delay, etc.
2. The lambda between Paris and Amsterdam can now be used for carrying higher layer traffic. In order to make it available to the higher switching layers, the routers use a technique called *forwarding adjacencies*. Chapter 14, "Traffic Engineering and MPLS", contained a short introduction to forwarding adjacencies and an example of how an existing TE tunnel is re-advertised in the IS-IS topology. In G-MPLS a similar technique is used. Whenever a lower switching layer sets up a tunnel, it re-advertises the TE-Tunnel in the higher switching layer. The forwarding adjacency needs to be marked so that the lambda switching layer does not "see" the adjacency anymore (for the reasons why this must happen, see Chapter 14). G-MPLS marks forwarding adjacencies by means of the Switching Capability field. In the example, the lambda tunnel between the TDM cross-connects gets advertised as an OC-192c/STM-64 pipe that has TDM switching capabilities. Each lambda cross-connect will ignore any adjacency of a lower switching layer for consideration of LSP setups at its own level in the networking hierarchy.
3. The router in Madrid signals via RSVP that it needs a TDM channel of SONET/SDH OC-48c/STM-16 speed (about 2.5 Gbps) to London and provides the desired path. After successful path establishment the TE tunnel is again re-advertised as a higher switching layer forwarding adjacency. This time the signalled OC-48c/STM-16 pipe gets re-advertised and marked as an interface with packet switching capabilities. This will "poison" it for any TDM switch and make it usable only by other routers.
4. The router now has a packet switching-capable tunnel between Madrid and London. The final step is to signal a packet Label Switched Path from a local POP router in the G-MPLS cloud (Madrid in this case) to any other (London) via RSVP and make use of the additional OC-48c/STM16 pipe by forwarding IP traffic down the packet switching Label Switched Path. Note that the IP routers in Paris, Amsterdam, Frankfurt are still

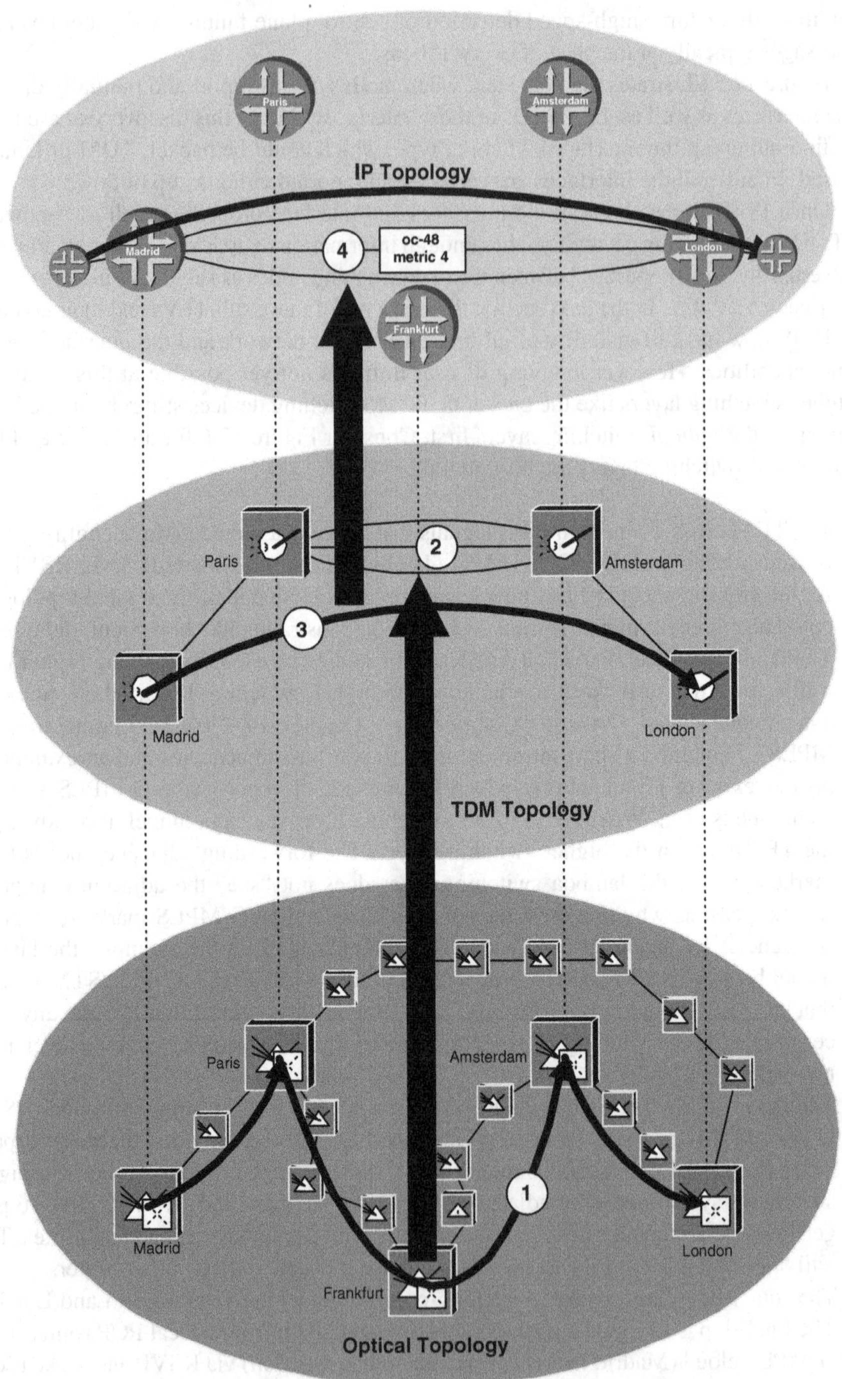

FIGURE 17.6. Each provisioned tunnel in the switching hierarchy N is represented as a forwarding adjacency of switching capability $N + 1$

isolated because there have been no paths established for them by the lower-layer switching layers.

Forwarding adjacencies are powerful tools for bringing up the network incrementally. Note that in the previous example a packet-over TDM-over lambda switching path has been used to illustrate the concept of multiple switching hierarchies. A network does not need to support all switching layers. If network service providers want to eliminate their SONET/SDH TDM network, one could also make (for example) the routers signal the lambdas directly.

17.2.5 *IS-IS G-MPLS Extensions*

The G-MPLS extensions to IS-IS are sub-TLVs to the extended IS Reach TLV #22. The sub-TLVs are listed in Table 17.1. The first (sub-TLV 4) is a redefinition. Originally defined in Internet Draft *draft-ietf-isis-traffic-05,* sub-TLV 4 was intended as a link-local identifier that should carry a unique number to identify unambiguously a link in the traffic engineering database. The sub-TLV is intended for unnumbered interfaces (those lacking IP addresses) and used to carry a 4-byte value. Most implementations used to fill that sub-TLV with their loopback address. There is one problem with using a loopback address as link-identifier: the loopback address does not uniquely identify a link between a pair of routers. The current G-MPLS Internet draft *draft-ietf-isis-gmpls-extensions-19* extends that sub-TLV to 8 bytes. Now, the combination of the loopback addresses between a given pair of routers can be used to uniquely identify the link between the two.

The Link Protection Type sub-TLV #20 tells other routers how risky it is to use a certain link. It does that by advertising the protection switching scheme of the underlying media. Values indicating that the underlying topology runs over a shared fibre, that other circuits run unprotected, as well as full blown 1:1 protection schemes, can be expressed. Table 17.2 lists the allocated protection scheme code points.

TABLE 17.1. Sub-TLVs that are used for conveying G-MPLS data inside IS-IS.

Sub-TLV	Length	Name
4	8	Link Local/Remote Identifier
20	2	Link Protection Type
21	36	Interface Switching Capability Descriptor

TABLE 17.2. Protection codes that may be announced for a G-MPLS link.

Code	Protection method
0x01	Extra Traffic
0x02	Unprotected
0x04	Shared
0x08	Dedicated 1:1
0x10	Dedicated 1 + 1
0x20	Enhanced
0x40	Reserved
0x80	Reserved

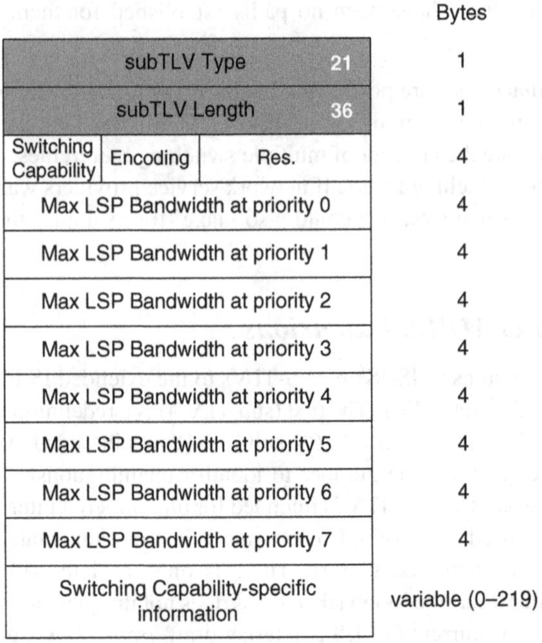

Field			Bytes
subTLV Type 21			1
subTLV Length 36			1
Switching Capability	Encoding	Res.	4
Max LSP Bandwidth at priority 0			4
Max LSP Bandwidth at priority 1			4
Max LSP Bandwidth at priority 2			4
Max LSP Bandwidth at priority 3			4
Max LSP Bandwidth at priority 4			4
Max LSP Bandwidth at priority 5			4
Max LSP Bandwidth at priority 6			4
Max LSP Bandwidth at priority 7			4
Switching Capability-specific information			variable (0–219)

FIGURE 17.7. The Interface Switching Capability Descriptor sub-TLV #21

TABLE 17.3. The Switching type indicates the multiplexing and de-multiplexing capabilities of the link.

Code	Switching type
1	Packet-Switch Capable-1
2	Packet-Switch Capable-2
3	Packet-Switch Capable-3
4	Packet-Switch Capable-4
51	Layer-2 Switch Capable
100	Time-Division-Multiplex Capable
150	Lambda-Switch Capable
200	Fiber-Switch Capable

The most important sub-TLV, as far as G-MPLS is concerned, is the Interface Capability Switching Descriptor sub-TLV #21. Figure 17.7 shows the structure of that sub-TLV. First, it has some information about the level of the underlying link in the optical hierarchy.

Table 17.3 shows the most common switching codes. There are values for virtually every switching technology defined. Ranging from packets to TDM, and from lambdas to even raw fibres, every interface in the optical hierarchy can be expressed.

17.2.6 *G-MPLS Summary*

Large parts of the standardization work for IS-IS G-MPLS have been finalized as of 2003. However, *neither* of the two big router vendors has yet shipped routing software that supports G-MPLS Extensions for IS-IS. Cisco has not shipped IOS routing software with G-MPLS extensions. Juniper Networks started (in JUNOS 5.6) G-MPLS support for OSPF, which seems to be the favourite IGP for the optical vendors for some reason. There seems to be sentiment in the optical community that IS-IS, because of its encoding style (Ethernet LLC, PPP-OSI) and the required operating systems infrastructure (most operating systems lack kernel support for OSI), was tied to OSI and therefore they stayed away from IS-IS. The router vendors, on the other hand, did not feel any pressure from the market to support G-MPLS extensions due to lack of implementation on the optical side. So one side was saying "Here's G-MPLS for OSPF to start" and the other was saying "Don't bother! We run IS-IS!" Neither side can figure out why the other doesn't get it.

G-MPLS is built around the idea of an integrated environment and common routing and signalling protocols for *all* equipment types. The ironic thing is that today, although G-MPLS extensions have been specified for all protocols, there is no common denominator yet. The majority of packet switching networks are based on IS-IS, but all that the optical infrastructure could support is OSPF. The authors believe that service providers are not willing to make a radical change in the core IGP, mostly because of the efforts and investments being made of maturing IS-IS to this point. So unless the optical vendors clean off their glasses and provide G-MPLS IS-IS implementations, there will not be any great progress in the G-MPLS idea. At best, we expect first production deployments in the 2005, 2006 timeframe.

There have always been concerns about the scalability and suitability of a 2-level routing hierarchy. The next section discusses a proposal on how to extend the 2-level to a multi-level (8-level) routing hierarchy.

17.3 Multi-level (8-level) IS-IS

ISO 10589 offers two distinct levels as a tool for splitting up a topological domain into a smaller one in order to scale the network. Today the two levels are sufficient for even large networks with thousands of routers. However, emerging technologies like the G-MPLS peer model, where the topology of transmission and SONET/SDH networks will be exposed to IS-IS, seriously pose the question if the two topology levels of IS-IS are enough.

Until now, no Internet drafts have been published for introducing a higher number of topological levels to IS-IS. There has been just some remarks on the ISIS-WG mailing list that this would be relatively easy to do. Figure 17.8 shows the structure of the IS-IS common header. A key to the easy extension of IS-IS is the 8-bit wide PDU-Type field, which may be used to indicate up to 256 distinct PDU types. Today, the three most significant bits (MSB) are reserved for future use and could be used for specifying further PDU types. Only the lower 5 bits are used today for encoding the existing PDU types. Figure 17.8 shows a list of the PDU types used by IS-IS today.

Table 17.4 has a listing of hypothetical code points that could be used for an 8-level IS-IS protocol. Note that there are four code points per level that need to be allocated for packaging Hellos, LSPs, CSNPs and PSNPs.

There is no need to make a differentiation between point-to-point (p2p) Hellos and LAN Hellos like 2-Level IS-IS does today. Proposals like running p2p PDUs over

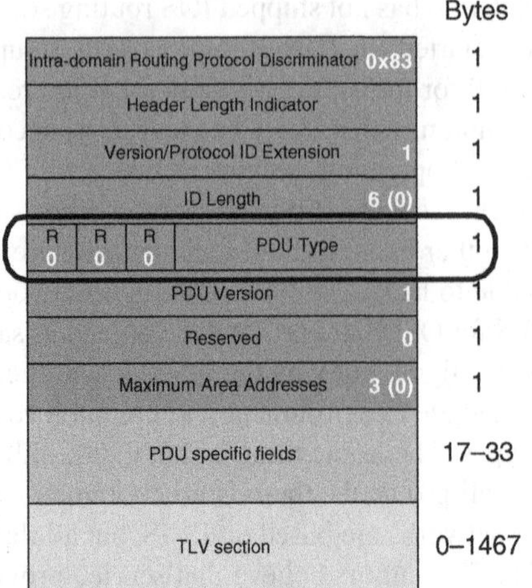

Type	Name
15	Level 1 LAN Hello
16	Level 2 LAN Hello
17	p2p Hello
18	Level 1 Link State PDU
20	Level 2 Link State PDU
24	Level 1 CSNP
25	Level 2 CSNP
26	Level 1 PSNP
27	Level 2 PSNP

FIGURE 17.8. The PDU-Type field in the IS-IS common header has room for 256 distinct PDU types

TABLE 17.4. A list of hypothetical code points that could be used for an 8-level enhancement of the IS-IS protocol.

PDU type	PDU name
32–39	Reserved
40	Level 3 Hello
41	Level 3 LSP
42	Level 3 CSNP
43	Level 3 PSNP
44	Level 4 Hello
45	Level 4 LSP
46	Level 4 CSNP
47	Level 4 PSNP
...	...
60	Level 8 Hello
61	Level 8 LSP
62	Level 8 CSNP
63	Level 8 PSNP

LAN circuits for pseudonode elimination, as described in draft-ietf-isis-igp-p2p-over-lan-02.txt, heavily dilutes the usefulness of separating the two different Hello types. So the draft proposes sending a p2p Hello inside an Ethernet frame. Even worse: the one-time optimization of running distinct p2p Hellos over a media turns out to be a legacy that now causes more problems than it solves. For example, because of this Hello separation, things like multi-level authentication are not possible today over p2p circuits. The lowest Level (Level 1) always contributes the authentication string for any occurrence of the Authentication TLV #10. So the best thing would be to avoid that problematic PDU type once and for all and create a *new* common Hello PDU type that can be used for all levels and for all circuit Figure 17.19 list such a hyptothetical PDU the LAN Hello format has

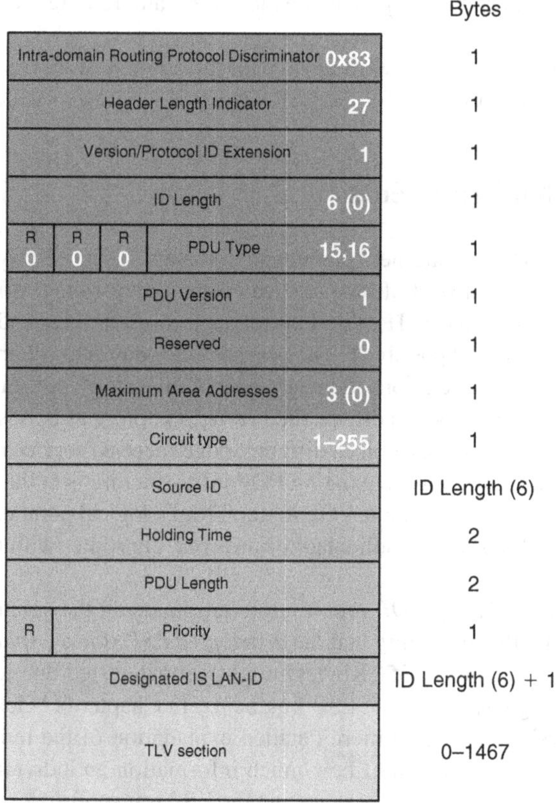

FIGURE 17.9. A common Hello PDU that can be used for all levels and all circuits types which shares the semantics of the LAN Hello PDU

all the necessary fields to run both over a LAN and a p2p infrastructure. Certain fields like the Priority and DIS LAN-ID do not make any sense on p2p circuits and hence should be set to zero, but they do no harm by just being there.

Today there is no draft even describing a multi-level IS-IS. Just the idea that it can be done in general exists, along with some excerpts taken from the IETF ISIS-WG Mailing List. There is not even any serious discussion about multi-level IS-IS. Offloading virtually all of the IP reachability information to BGP has made scaling efforts to reduce the amount of IP reachability information with the introduction of additional hierarchy levels a pointless exercise. The authors have discussed the 8-level IS-IS proposal for three reasons:

1. Showing that it can be done without any major protocol rework
2. Educational purposes (everybody was reminded that the PDU-type field is 8 bits wide)
3. Showing protocol engineers that it is *always* a good idea to leave some spare bits in the protocol headers (some actually object to this practice)

The first point is increasingly important, and once again OSPF is an example of how *not* to engineer a protocol. For the third time, OSPF ran out of bits again, because the architects failed to add enough spare bits which were later required to evolve and extend the protocol further.

The next future extension to IS-IS deals with the amount of information that an individual System-ID can originate for the LSP database, and how to scale it up further.

17.4 Extended Fragments

Now, at the end of the big Internet "gloom and doom age", service providers have begun exploring almost every aspect of how to save costs in their router infrastructure. A still open issue is the question of: "How do I eliminate intra-POP links and keep the cost per managed device the lowest possible?" The best answer today is to collapse different router functionalities into a bigger, consolidated router. Collapsing core transport and access functionality into a single box is often called *vertical pooling* as opposed to the *horizontal pooling* approach which combines different edge (access) services separate from the core. Figure 17.10 shows how an existing POP infrastructure is collapsed both horizontally and vertically to a single, large POP router. From a logical point of view, the smaller routers with a few links are consolidated towards one big router with many links, representing the entire POP.

Because the *consolidated POP router* has to terminate all the core circuits, there was some fear in the IS-IS community that the *distributed LSP storage space* that each router can originate (approximately 350 Kbytes) might get exhausted due to all the IS-Reach TLVs that need to get stored in the LSP fragments. In Chapter 6, "Generation, Flooding and Ageing LSPs", there was a more detailed explanation of the term *distributed LSP storage space* and a breakdown of how much information an individual router can originate. What can be done to avoid exhausting the LSP transport space is to make the single big router appear as *multiple* routers in the IS-IS topology by issuing smaller LSPs with *different* System-IDs. The different System-IDs are then connected using a simple star topology, and the IS Reach cost between those *aliased* systems is always zero.

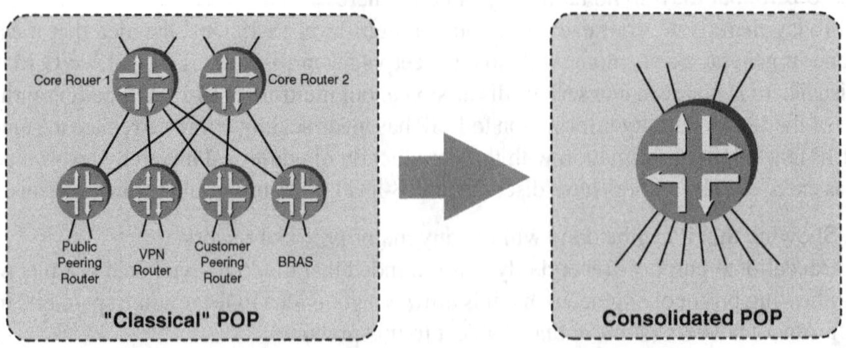

FIGURE 17.10. The traditional POP layout gets replaced by a big all-in-one router which terminates the whole set of edge services

Draft RFC 3786 increases the breadth of a single collapsed router by making the single router appear as a set of routers, as shown in Figure 17.11. Ironically, the result from a logical perspective looks a bit like the original topology before the consolidation took place. The draft describes a method for a collapsed router to express *zero cost adjacencies*. However, according to ISO 10589, zero cost adjacencies are illegal for non-pseudonode fragments and so must not be issued in IS Reach TLV #2 and the IS-Extended Reach TLV #22.

In order to stay backwards compatible, a new IS-Alias TLV #24 is defined which *can* issue zero cost adjacencies. The TLV format is illustrated in Figure 17.12. The format is almost identical to the IS-Reach TLV #22 (See Chapter 12, Figure 12.8) except the Metric field is missing, which is no big surprise because the Metric is implicitly zero. If the router needs to originate a *non-zero* adjacency, then the sender originates this adjacency using a regular Extended IS-Reach TLV #22.

Today there is no support in IOS and JUNOS for the IS Alias TLV #24, mainly because even in the largest core routers, the typical amount of IS adjacencies easily fits in 1 or 2 out of the 256 possible fragments. This may change when router vendors ship their multi-shelf systems like the HFR (Cisco) or TX (Juniper) for the first time. Given today's router hardware, there is no space-related problem at all for storing the adjacencies of large routers. However, there is another place where the limit of 255 fragments may become a problem, which is the L2L1 router in combination with route leaking. When route leaking is configured, the L2L1 router has to re-package all the /32 prefixes from the core into a Level 1 LSP. More about route leaking was covered in Chapter 123 "IP Reachability Information". In large networks today, 5000–6000 prefixes are advertised, and that takes 30–40 fragments in the Level 1 LSPs. If the 256 fragment limit is crossed some day (around 42,000 prefixes), which is unlikely, then an L2L1 speaker could issue the IS Alias TLV #24 for scaling the IP reachability information. Today, the extended fragments draft does not solve a *real* problem. However, it is nice to know that, due to the flexibility of IS-IS, even the 256 fragments limit is not a dead-end for the protocol.

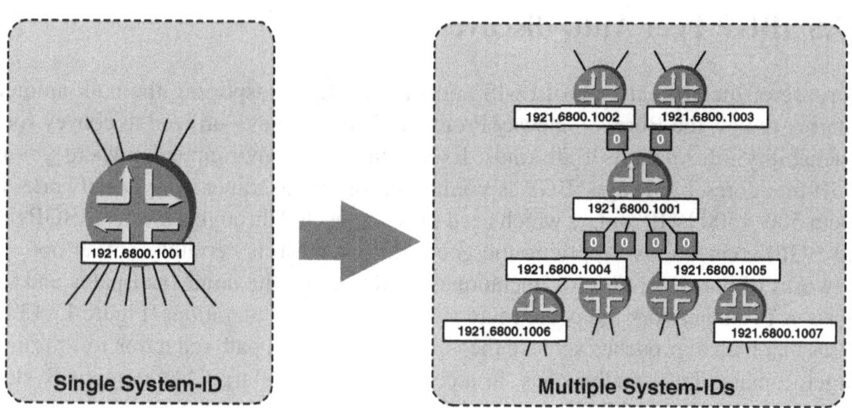

FIGURE 17.11. A single router generates several System-IDs and connects them through zero-cost adjacencies

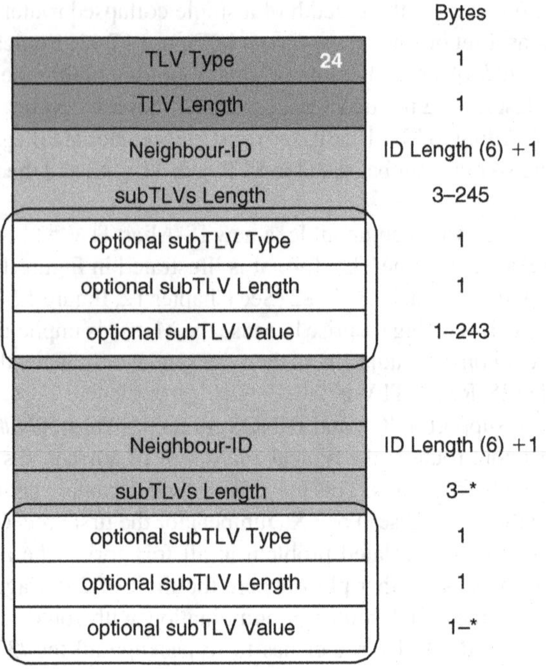

FIGURE 17.12. The IS-Alias TLV #24 looks almost identical to the IS-Reach TLV #22

In recent years IS-IS has become a *topology discovery* tool. There is now an extension under discussion which would add also *service discovery* capabilities to IS-IS, which allows setting up iBGP routing automatically.

17.5 iBGP Peer Auto-discovery

Because of the current lack of IS-IS applicability for transporting the bulk amount of Internet routes, the Border Gateway Protocol (BGP) is heavy utilized to convey routing reachability information of all kinds. Except in MPLS environments, where you have BGP-free cores by design, BGP is configured on every router. Larger networks have about 500–1500 BGP routers which need to be connected through a mesh of iBGP (internal BGP) connections. Applying the good-old full-mesh is certainly not an option for networks of that size. The two techniques used to scale the number of paths and iBGP sessions in the network today are route reflection and confederations. Figure 17.13 illustrates that both approaches achieve the goal of session and path reduction by splitting up larger domains into smaller ones. In a confederation, the large Autonomous System is split into smaller sub-ASs. In a route reflection environment, the flat iBGP mesh gets divided into *clusters*. The sub-domains in turn may or may not be full-meshed internally all over again. In a confederation environment one could further divide the sub-domain

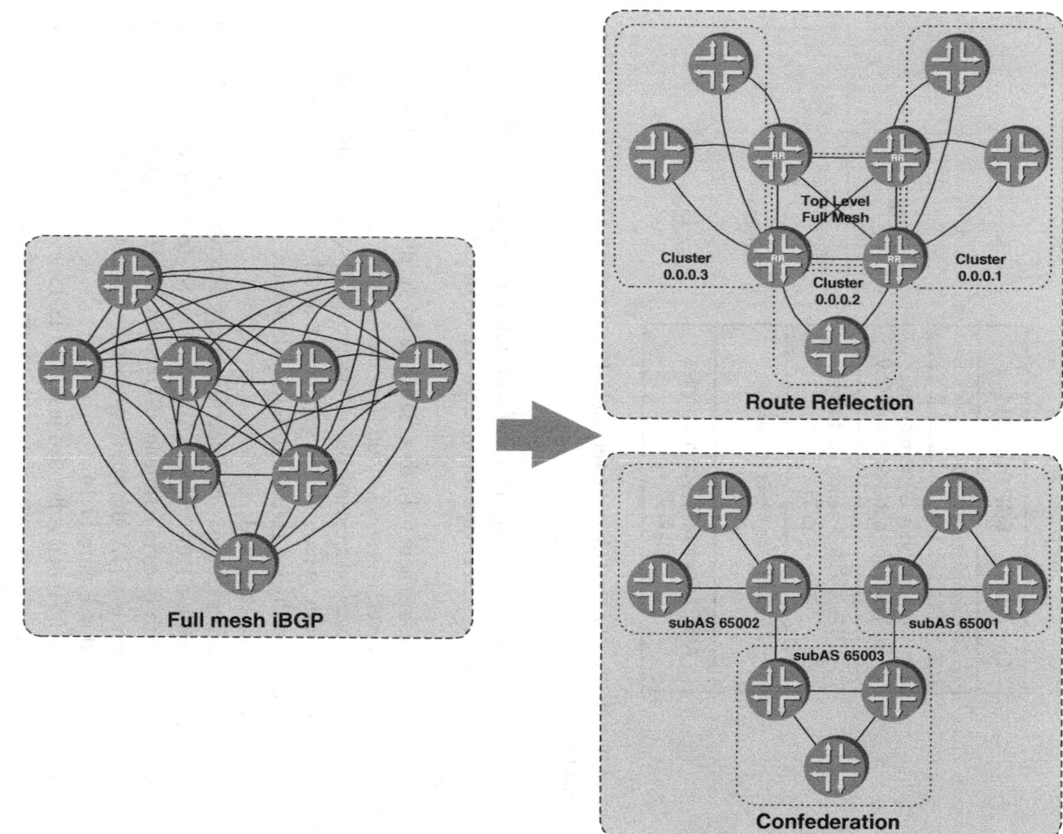

FIGURE 17.13. Both confederations and route reflectors reduce the overall number of paths in the network by splitting the big routing mesh into smaller domains

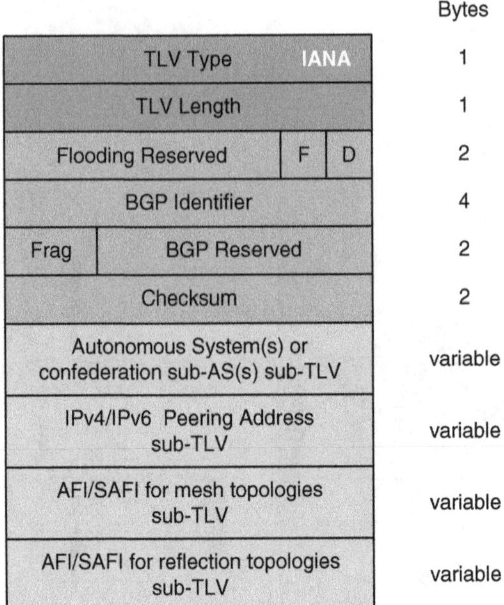

FIGURE 17.14. The BGP discovery TLV empowers an IS-IS speaker to automatically provision the iBGP distribution mesh

into "sub-sub-domains" by introducing a level of route reflection in the sub-AS. That would also work in a Route Reflection environment. A cluster of routers can serve another cluster of routers.

There is no need (or desire) here to further elaborate on the different methods of iBGP scaling techniques. However, it is now obvious that the resulting iBGP mesh is a lot more complicated to describe once you are using one of the two iBGP scaling tools. Furthermore, maintaining the iBGP mesh, which means verifying that all routers are homed to the right cluster and are all producing consistent routing decisions, is a daunting task for the operation teams at all service providers.

The Internet Draft draft-raszuk-isis-bgp-peer-discovery describes a method that Route Reflectors and Confederation sub-ASBRs (Autonomous System Border Routers) can use to advertise their capabilities to terminate iBGP sessions. The magic carpet to transport those announcements is a TLV, the number of which has not yet been determined by IANA. This is illustrated in Figure 17.14.

The TLV is part of the LSP that is flooded inside an IS-IS level. Upon receipt of such a TLV the receiving router checks to see if it wants to connect to that router. Figure 17.15 shows an example of how iBGP provisioning times can be radically reduced.

All Level 2 routers are part of the full mesh and advertise that they want to be full-mesh speakers in the IS-IS Level 2. Once that information is received by any Level 2 router, those routers try to connect to and bring up the BGP full mesh. In Level 1 the situation is a bit different. The L1L2 router advertises that it is a route reflector and so all the Level 1 routers connect to the proposed route reflectors.

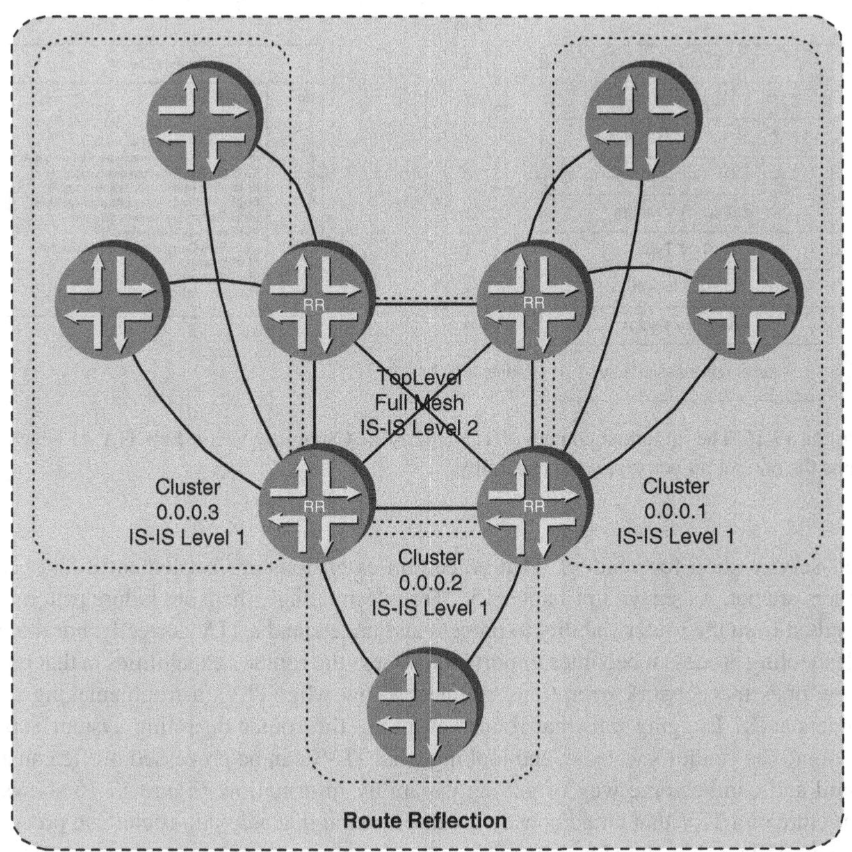

FIGURE 17.15. The Level 1 routers are looking for route reflector announcements, where the Level 2 routers are looking for full-mesh partner announcements

The authors of the draft keep emphasizing that this method should not replace the currently prevailing method of manual configuration, but rather should be taken in baby steps. *Auto iBGP Peer discovery* is seen as a complementary technique to foster a softer transition for fully automated peer discovery. Especially for larger networks, this seems to be a promising technique for migration from an overly cautious route reflection design to a full-mesh BGP setup producing good routes with diverse paths.

17.6 Capability Announcement

The IS-IS working group has been busy in the last 5 years producing a lot of extensions to the base protocol. All of the extensions are documented as Internet drafts which ultimately get published as informational RFCs, not normative references. There is now increasing concern that the extensions to IS-IS are getting to be a pick-and-choose

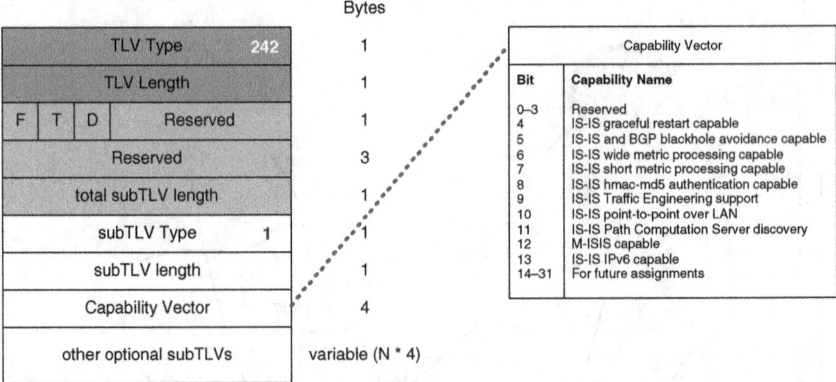

FIGURE 17.16. The important content of TLV 242 is the Capability Vector Sub-TLV #1 which contains the one set bit per supported capability

self-service shop for vendors. That is, certain extensions are implemented and certain others are not. As shown in Chapter 15, "Troubleshooting", there are failure patterns that resulted from the router's ability to process and understand a TLV correctly. For the troubleshooting process it becomes important to assess the router's capabilities in that regard. How does the network operations engineer know what TLVs a troublemaking router understands? Logging into that router, checking the router operating system version, going to the vendor's website, and looking what TLVs can be processed is often an awkward and cumbersome way of getting capability information. Figure 17.16 shows the structure of a TLV that could convey the information that a certain router can process.

This TLV is, like the Hostname TLV, a purely informational or convenience TLV that only addresses informational issues. There are no routing or traffic engineering decisions affected by the existence or non-existence of a bit in this TLV. It is purely a tool for giving the NOC engineer help supporting the network. The Capability TLV #242 triggered an interesting question: how much information should a routing protocol really carry? This a good question especially when there is non-routing and non-topology data involved.

17.7 Conclusion

The further extension of the IS-IS protocol is not going to stop anytime soon. Additional functionality is required by many service providers and will continue to force evolution of the protocol. However, there is some recent discomfort caused by this *functional* growth. Many network engineers share the view that virtually all routing protocols are being overloaded across the board. IS-IS is no exception to that concern. Functionalities like Hostname Resolution (TLV #137), iBGP router auto-discovery and Capability Announcement are utilizing the flooding sub-system of IS-IS to get non-IP routing-related data across the network. As discussed in Chapter 13, "IS-IS Extensions", there is always a tradeoff between new functionality and stability because software needs to go through a maturity cycle. IS-IS is a bit special in that respect because IS-IS represents a very critical part of the routing sub-system in a service provider network. If you overload BGP with a new functionality, then most likely bugs will stay within the given boundaries of that sub-system. For example, a bug in the MPLS-VPN code is unlikely to impact public BGP routing on the Internet. However, whenever you start to add new functionality to IS-IS, then you need to touch the LSP origination code, which is a much more dangerous place to play. The impact here may be much more catastrophic, as virtually all sub-systems in a network rely on a proper working IGP. If the IGP fails then everything else starts to fail: things like bogus TE databases, torn-down RSVP sessions, LDP sessions to a collapsing BGP mesh could easily result. So one needs to ask the question: How much "overloading" of the IGP is really useful? Perhaps the wise answer is to take a look at the risk versus the reward of certain functionality. In IS-IS, the risk of destabilizing things is very high and very real, so one needs to make a solid case for adding functionality to solve a real *engineering* problem.

While it makes perfect sense to add new functionality in order to solve *engineering* problems like producing new services for BGP, or consolidating infrastructure (as in the G-MPLS case), it is somewhat dangerous to jeopardize the stability of the current IS-IS code base for *convenience* or *administrative functions* like capability announcements. It is the authors' opinion that the IS-IS community should stay away from the temptation to enhance such fragile portions of the network with functionality that yields, at best, a questionable or intangible gain.

What is right or wrong, and what functionalities will finally be deployed in our networks, will always remain an open issue.

Walter would like to close this chapter with something called Walter's First Rule of Networking, formulated after more than 35 years of networking experience:

> When the new stuff is more risky to deploy, and more complex than the workaround – use the workaround!

Hannes would like to close this last chapter with an insight from Pedro Marquez, a well respected protocol engineer who was at Cisco Systems and now works for Juniper Networks. Pedro was concerned about the IP-only zealots – in response he used to say:

> No one is paying vendors for **not** doing things – however we need to still keep some common sense!

Index